CIVIL WAR SOLDIERS

of the

BIG SANDY VALLEY

of

KENTUCKY

John David Preston

HERITAGE BOOKS
2022

HERITAGE BOOKS
AN IMPRINT OF HERITAGE BOOKS, INC.

Books, CDs, and more—Worldwide

For our listing of thousands of titles see our website
at
www.HeritageBooks.com

Published 2022 by
HERITAGE BOOKS, INC.
Publishing Division
5810 Ruatan Street
Berwyn Heights, Md. 20740

Copyright © 2022 John David Preston

Heritage Books by the author:
Civil War Soldiers of the Big Sandy Valley of Kentucky
Civil War Soldiers of Boyd County, Kentucky
Civil War Soldiers of Letcher County, Kentucky
Civil War Soldiers of Magoffin County, Kentucky
Civil War Soldiers of Morgan County, Kentucky
History of the First United Methodist Church of Paintsville, Kentucky, 2nd Edition
Judges of the Twenty-fourth Circuit of Kentucky
The Civil War in the Big Sandy Valley of Kentucky, Second Edition

Library of Congress Control Number: 2021907153

All rights reserved. No part of this book may be reproduced or transmitted in any form or by any means, electronic or mechanical, including photocopying, recording or by any information storage and retrieval system without written permission from the author, except for the inclusion of brief quotations in a review.

International Standard Book Number
Paperbound: 978-0-7884-1708-5

CONTENTS

Introduction	2
Confederate Soldiers	
Boyd County	9
Floyd County	11
Johnson County	27
Lawrence County	36
Letcher County	43
Magoffin County	61
Morgan County	67
Pike County	90
Union Soldiers	
Boyd County	101
Floyd County	133
Johnson County	150
Lawrence County	185
Letcher County	241
Magoffin County	252
Morgan County	267
Pike County	278
Soldiers Who Served in Both Armies	309

INTRODUCTION TO LIST OF SOLDIERS

In 2008, I published *The Civil War in the Big Sandy Valley of Kentucky, Second Edition.* That book included a comprehensive list of Confederate and Union soldiers from the primary Big Sandy counties of Floyd, Johnson, Lawrence and Pike (present Martin County having been part of those four). That list contained more than 3,700 soldiers and included pertinent information relating to their Civil War service, including regiment, company, rank, date of enlistment, date of muster out, age at enlistment, eye and hair color, skin complexion, wounds, POW status, and such other information as was available. In 2015, I published *Civil War Soldiers of Boyd County, Kentucky; Civil War Soldiers of Letcher County, Kentucky; Civil War Soldiers of Magoffin County, Kentucky;* and *Civil War Soldiers of Morgan County, Kentucky.* Those counties are drained in part by the Big Sandy River. The lists for the four latter counties also contained information relating the residence of the soldiers, specifically census house numbers, and, where census house numbers were not available, other information which established residence in a county. A total of more than 2,200 soldiers were contained in those lists.

Since 2008, I have continually revised the original list of soldiers and have made numerous corrections and additions, based on additional information developed about individual soldiers and publication of additional source materials. In 2017, I began the process of completely revising the lists of soldiers in all eight counties, which took more than a year. That process included adding soldiers, deleting soldiers, and, most importantly, adding residence information for the four primary Big Sandy counties. Census house numbers were listed where available, and, when unavailable, information which established residence in a county was included.

The final result is what I believe to be the most nearly accurate listing of Civil War soldiers for the eight Big Sandy counties.

Finally, this book includes a list of 231 Big Sandy soldiers who served in both armies.

The lists of Big Sandy Civil War soldiers are separated by Union or Confederate service and by county. Inclusion in this list requires two elements: proof of residence in one of the Big Sandy counties, and proof of service in one of the Union or Confederate units. For the clear majority of individuals, residence is proved by inclusion in the 1860 Census. It has been suggested that the Census is not accurate, but it must remain the basis for proving residence. There is some other proof of residence. Descriptive muster rolls, which list a soldier's county of residence, exist for some of the soldiers of the Fourteenth, Thirty-ninth and Forty-fifth Kentucky Union regiments. Records for the Confederate Thirteenth Kentucky Cavalry show the county of residence for some soldiers. The Adjutant General's report contains a list of officers with their town of residence. Compiled Service Records occasionally contain information that points to a particular county of residence.

The second element is proof of service in a Union or Confederate military unit. In the great majority of cases, proof is found in the Adjutant General's Reports for Union and Confederate volunteers and in the Compiled Service Records. For men not listed on either source, but who may have served, consideration was given on a case by case basis. More weight was accorded to contemporaneous sources; little weight was given to pension applications, given the pecuniary motive of the applicant.

The list includes a number of Confederate soldiers who are not listed on either the Adjutant General's Report or the Compiled Service Records. Information has been gathered on these soldiers from a number of sources over the years, but the original sources of that information are unavailable to the author. Those Confederates are designated with the statement "Not on AG or CSR" in the remarks section of a soldier's record. The reader is advised to exercise due diligence and undertake additional research with respect to the service of these men.

Unless otherwise stated, place names are in Kentucky. Confederates taken prisoner were often kept prisoner at Camp Chase, Columbus, Ohio; Johnson's Island, Ohio; Rock Island, Illinois; Camp Douglas, Chicago, Illinois; Camp Morton, Indianapolis, Indiana; City Point, Virginia; Fort Delaware, Pea Patch Island, Delaware; or at Point Lookout, Maryland. Numerous Confederates were taken prisoner at Gladesville, Virginia.

The reader should be aware of the limitations of this methodology. For most soldiers, the available records do not state the residence of the soldier. Military records are often incomplete and sometimes inaccurate. When comparing a name found on a Census record with a name on a regiment list, there is ordinarily no clear indication whether the soldier and the person on the census are the same. The similarity and repetitiveness of names in the area makes the task more difficult. For example, the John Smith on the roster of the Thirty-ninth Kentucky Infantry may be the same John Smith as shown on the census for Pike County, or he might be John Smith from another place. The reader should be aware that inclusion in or exclusion from the list of soldiers of a particular man is often the result of subjective judgment on the part of the author.

For many of the soldiers, a descriptive muster roll exists, which lists a soldier's age, hair, eye and skin color, and height. Unless otherwise stated, the age given is as of time of enlistment. The reader should be aware that, for a number of reasons, the age stated may or may not be correct. Height is expressed in feet, then inches, separated by a dash.

Some question has been raised as to whether all the soldiers, primarily from Johnson and Lawrence Counties, who are listed on the Adjutant General's report as having served in the Sixty-fifth or Sixty-eighth Enrolled Militia, actually served. The theory has been advanced that many of those listed on the report were Confederate sympathizers who did not actually serve. In this regard, some facts need be stated. The Enrolled Militia list for Johnson County for 1861 included 765 men. The Adjutant General's Report lists 260 Johnson County men in the Sixty-fifth who served. The Lawrence County Enrolled Militia list for 1863 contained 1111 men. The Adjutant General's Report lists 466 Lawrence County men on the muster rolls. Obviously, many men are not included in the Adjutant General's report. Those who were on active military duty were not included. There is other information available concerning some of the men. On June 27, 1864, a letter was sent to the governor from the Sixty-fifth Enrolled Militia's camp at Louisa to the governor, demanding an election of officers. The men were apparently dissatisfied with their leadership. The letter was signed by 166 men. Their signatures constitute strong evidence that these men, at least, were in fact in government service at the time. In the list of soldiers, the soldiers who signed the letter are designated by the words "in camp" in the remarks section of a soldier's record.

Examination of the original muster rolls for the Sixty-fifth and Sixty-eighth reveals additional information. The names of some soldiers who did not report for duty were marked through on the muster rolls. Those individuals were not included on the Adjutant General's report. Other soldiers were listed as having deserted, having gone AWOL, or were simply not listed as having been mustered out. Likewise, those soldiers were not listed on the Adjutant General's report. From the information available, it appears that the soldiers listed on the Adjutant General's report did serve in those units.

Most of the Confederate soldiers from Letcher County joined the Thirteenth Kentucky Cavalry. Almost alone among Confederate units, the Compiled Service Records for the regiment includes residences for many of the soldiers. That information is most helpful but cannot always be taken at face value. For example, Company F of that regiment states that most of the men in that company were residents of Letcher County, but most were in fact Floyd County residents.

Several Magoffin County soldiers are listed as having been born in Floyd or Morgan Counties. Magoffin County was formed in 1860 from Floyd, Morgan and Johnson Counties. Those listed as having been born in Floyd or Morgan Counties may have been born in part of one of those counties which became Magoffin County.

The 1860 census for Boyd County was divided into three parts. One part was for the city of Ashland, the second for the city of Catlettsburg, and the third for the rest of the county. Designations for census house numbers in Ashland include the letter A before the number. Designations for census house numbers in Catlettsburg include the letter C before the number. Census house numbers with only a number are for areas of Boyd County outside Ashland or Catlettsburg. Several soldiers were stated to have been born in Greenup, Lawrence or Carter Counties. Since Boyd County was formed in 1860 from those counties, their places of birth may refer to a part of Boyd County that was part of one of those three counties. In addition, there was a demographic difference between Boyd County and other eastern Kentucky counties, in which most heads of household were born in Kentucky or Virginia. In Boyd County, sixty-three per cent of heads of household were born in either Kentucky or Virginia, while twenty per cent were born in states north of the Mason-Dixon line. Another thirteen per cent were born in foreign countries, mostly Germany or Ireland. The northern-born and foreign-born were less inclined to support the Confederacy.

Ceredo, Wayne County, and Wheeling refer to Virginia, later West Virginia. Those sites are listed without stating the city and state. Several Boyd County soldiers enlisted at Camp Pierpont, which was located at Ceredo. Others joined at Camp Jo Holt, which was in Indiana across from Louisville.

For the purposes of the 1860 census, Morgan County was divided into two districts, each with houses listed in numerical sequence. Houses in district one are designated with the number 1, followed by a dash and then followed by the house number in that district. Houses in district two are designated by the number 2, followed by a dash and then followed by the house number in that district.

The census for Floyd County was divided into two districts, Ford and Washam. In the list of soldiers, houses in the Ford district are designated by the letter F, followed by the census house number. Houses in the Washam district are designated by the letter W followed by the house number.

The census for Pike County was divided into two districts, District No. 1 and District No. 7. In the list of soldiers, houses in District No. 1 are designated by the number 1, followed by a dash, then followed by the census house number. Houses in District No. 7 are designated by the number 7, followed by a dash, then followed by the census house number.

For the war, a total of 4,046 Big Sandy Valley men served for the Union, and 2,031 served with the Confederates, a total of 6,077. Enlistments on each side by county are as follows:

County	Confederate	Union
Boyd	32	570
Floyd	390	324
Johnson	206	724
Lawrence	146	1,154
Letcher	373	231
Magoffin	91	232
Morgan	531	186
Pike	261	622
Total	2,030	4,043

Several abbreviations are used in the list of soldiers to preserve space. If no rank is given, the soldier's rank is that of private. The abbreviations and for what they stand are as follows:

age	age at enlistment
app	appointed
awol	absent without leave
b	born
cap	captured
capt	captain
co	company
col	colonel
com sgt	commissary sergeant
cpl	corporal
CSR	Compiled Service Record
des	deserted
dis	discharged
enr	enrolled
enl	enlisted
exch	exchanged
F&S	field and staff
house	house number on 1860 census
KIA	killed in action
lt	lieutenant

m/in	mustered in
m/out	mustered out
n/c	not listed on 1860 census
prom	promoted
pvt	private
r	rank
red	reduced
reg	regiment
s	sources
sgt	sergeant
surr	surrendered
trans	transferred

Abbreviations are also used for the regiments in which the men served as follows:

Union:
2Cav	Second Kentucky Cavalry
8	Eighth Kentucky Infantry
10Cav	Tenth Kentucky Cavalry
14	Fourteenth Kentucky Infantry
14Cav	Fourteenth Kentucky Cavalry
16	Sixteenth Kentucky Infantry
19	Nineteenth Kentucky Infantry
22	Twenty-second Kentucky Infantry
22EM	Twenty-second Enrolled Militia
24	Twenty-fourth Kentucky Infantry
39	Thirty-ninth Kentucky Infantry
40	Fortieth Kentucky Infantry
45	Forty-fifth Kentucky Infantry
47	Forty-seventh Kentucky Infantry
CG	Big Sandy Regiment, Capital Guards
65	Sixty-fifth Enrolled Militia
68	Sixty-eighth Enrolled Militia
5Va	Fifth Virginia Infantry
53	Fifty-third Kentucky Infantry
54	Fifty-fourth Kentucky Infantry
55	Fifty-fifth Kentucky Infantry
167WV	One-hundred Sixty-seventh West Virginia Militia
Har	Harlan County Battalion

Confederate:

5	Fifth Kentucky Infantry
10	Tenth Kentucky Cavalry
13	Thirteenth Kentucky Cavalry, aka Fourteenth Kentucky Cavalry
FR	Field's Rangers
VSL	Virginia State Line
1MR	First Battalion Mounted Rifles
2MR	Second Battalion Mounted Rifles
1BatCav	First Battalion Cavalry
6ConfCav	Sixth Confederate Cavalry
7ConfCav	Seventh Battalion Confederate Cavalry
8VaCav	Eighth Virginia Cavalry
16VaCav	Sixteenth Virginia Cavalry
34VaCav	Thirty-fourth Virginia Cavalry
21VaInf	Twenty-first Virginia Infantry
29VaIinf	Twenty-ninth Virginia Infantry
36VaInf	Thirty-sixth Virginia Infantry

The list of soldiers includes sources from which the information stated in the list was drawn, and which are listed numerically are as follows:

1	Compiled Service Records, National Archives, Washington, D. C.
2	*Report of the Adjutant General of the State of Kentucky*
3	*Report of the Adjutant General of the State of Kentucky: Confederate Kentucky Volunteers*
4	Regimental Files, Kentucky Military History Museum
5	Charles C. Wells, *1890 Special Veterans Census for Eastern Kentucky*
6	Pension applications, National Archives, Washington, D. C.
7	Stephen Douglas Lynn, *Confederate Pensioners of Kentucky*
8	Robert Baker, "Thirty-ninth Kentucky Infantry"
9	H. H. Hardesty, *Presidents, Soldiers, Statesmen*
10	John B. Wells III & James Prichard, *Tenth Kentucky Cavalry, C.S.A.*
11	John B. Wells III, "Johnson County Confederates"
12	Jeffrey C. Weaver & James Prichard, *"7th Battalion Confederate Cavalry"*
13	Jeffrey C. Weaver, *Nottoway Light Artillery and Barr's Battery Virginia Light Artillery*
14	Randall Osborne & Jeffrey C. Weaver, *The Virginia State Rangers and State Line*
15	Scott C. Cole, *34th Virginia Cavalry*
16	Jack L. Dickinson, *8th Virginia Cavalry*
17	Jack L. Dickinson, *16th Virginia Cavalry*
18	1863 Lawrence County militia list
19	1863 Johnson County militia list

20	West Virginia Adjutant General's Report
21	Faron Sparkman, "Big Sandy Confederates in Fifth Kentucky Infantry, Tenth Kentucky Cavalry & Thirteenth Kentucky Cavalry"
22	Stephen Douglas Lynn, *Confederate Soldiers of Kentucky*
23	Jack L. Dickinson, *Wayne County, West Virginia, in the Civil War*
24	J. L. Scott, *36th Virginia Infantry*
25	Broadfoot Publishing Co., *Roster of Union and Confederate Soldiers*
26	1860 Boyd County Census
27	Robert Baker & Brian Hall, "Alphabetical Roster for the 5th West Virginia Infantry"
28	Magoffin County Historical Society, *Legends in Blue and Gray*
29	Rhonda Robertson & Lillian Gobble, *Between Brothers: Civil War Soldiers of Wise & Dickenson County*
30	John B. Wells, "Eastern Kentuckians in the Georgia 13th Cavalry, CSA", *Highland Echo*, March 2004
31	Ben Caudill Camp No. 1629, *13th Kentucky Cavalry, C.S.A., Caudill's Army*
32	Adjutant General's Report, Union Soldiers, Alphabetical List of Officers
33	ancestry.com
34	John David Preston, "Congressional Election Contest Between Samuel McKee and John D. Young", *Highland Echo,* Spring 2015
35	Joe Nickell, *Raids and Skirmishes: The Civil War in Morgan*
36	Faron Sparkman, "Roster of Kentucky Partisan Rangers, Fields' Company, Confederate States Army", March 2019

CONFEDERATE SOLDIERS

BOYD COUNTY CONFEDERATE SOLDIERS

A

ALLEN, JAMES. reg 5, co C, enl 10/19/61 Prestonsburg, house A81, s 3.

B

BALDWIN, CREED F. reg 5, co C, enl 3/22/62 Moccasin VA, house 423, s 1,3.
BALDWIN, REESE M. reg 1MR, co B, enl 12/11/61 Boyd Co., trans to Capt. William Baldwin's company, house 423, s 1,3.
BALDWIN, WILLIAM M. reg 5, co C, enl 1/18/62 Camp Martin VA, house 423, s 1,3.
BALLARD, JAMES. reg 5, co I, enl 8/15/62 Richlands VA, dis 10/20/62 Hazel Green, house 381, s 1,3.
BARTEE, WILLIAM. reg 1MR, co E, enl 10/12/61 Cumberland Ford, dis 11/20/62 Abingdon VA, house 381, s 1,3.
BOTTS, JOSEPH. reg 1MR, co A, enl 10/18/61 Prestonsburg, dis 10/23/62, house A113, s 1,3.
BRADLEY, GEORGE W. reg 5, co H, enl 10/21/61 Prestonsburg, house 286, s 1,3.

C

COLBERT, ISAAC. reg 5, co C, enl 9/16/62 Montgomery Co., trans to 2nd Ky. Cav. 5/27/63, house 569, s 1,3.
CONDIT, MILTON BROWN. source 26 lists him as Confederate soldier, not on AG or CSR, s 26.
CONDIT, WILLIAM HENRY. source 26 lists him as Confederate soldier, not on AG or CSR, s 26.
COOK, ALGERNON SIDNEY. reg 7ConfCav, co D, reg Patton's Partisan Ranger Battalion, killed Castlewood, VA, house 263, s 3,12.

D

DEBOARD, JAMES. reg 5, co A, enl 10/27/61 Beaver, KY, dis 10/20/62 Hazel Green, reg 10, co B, r 3rd cpl, enl 12/31/62 West Liberty, house C39, s 1,3.

G

GRAY, JOHN H. reg 10, co D, enl 2/10/63 Piketon, clothing receipt 9/8/64, house A72, s 1,3.
GULLETT, FRANKLIN. reg 5, co C, enl 9/1/62 West Liberty, des 10/23/62 West Liberty, house 643, s 1,3.

H

HAMPTON, JOHN WESLEY. reg 5, co I, enl 9/10/63 Cynthiana, CSR: "left in Kentucky on retreat in October 1862 and may have been taken prisoner", house A65, s 1,26.
HENSLEY, JOHN. reg 5, co A, I, enl 12/28/61 Paintsville, dis 10/20/62 Hazel Green, rem cap Murfreesboro, TN 12/30/62, died 2/2/63 or 2/5/63 Camp Douglas, IL of measles, house 229, s 1,3.

J

JENKINS, JAMES F. reg 1BatCav, co A, enl 4/3/62, house A30, s 1,3.
JOHNSON, JOHN F. reg 5, co C, r 2nd lt., rem elected 2nd lt 9/22/62, house 340, s 1,22.

K

KOUNS, GEORGE WILLIAM. reg 5, co C, enl 8/27/62 Piketon, dis 10/20/62 Hazel Green, paroled Camp Dick Robinson 10/25/62, house 211, s 1,3.
KOUNS, WILSON S. reg 5, co C, r 1st lt, enl 10/29/61 Prestonsburg, house 376, s 1,3.

M

MILLER, WILLIAM E. reg 5, co D, enl 10/19/61 Carter Co. dis 10/20/62 Hazel Green, house 468, s 1, 3.
MYERS, WILLIAM J. reg 1MR, co D, enl l8/29/62 Piketon, house A87, s 1,3.

P

POLLARD, EDWARD YOUNG. source 26 lists him as Confederate soldier, not on AG or CSR, house 477, s 26.
POLLARD, JOHN CONDIT. source 26 lists him as Confederate soldier, not on AG or CSR, house 477, s 26.
POLLARD, THOMAS ORVILLE, source 26 lists him as Confederate soldier, house 477, s 26.
PORTER, LORENZO DOW. reg FR, enl 4/2/63 Boyd Co., b Grayson Co. VA, reg 10, co M, wounded in hip Saltville VA 10/2/64, house 347, s 3,10,36.

R

ROBERTSON, FRANCIS M. reg 1BatCav, co A, enl 10/22/61 Prestonsburg, house 491, s 3.

S

SANDS, WILLIAM JR. reg 8VaCav, co K, enl 8/20/62 Wayne Co., house A78, s 1,16,34.
SPARKS, JOHN L. reg 5, co D, enl 10/19/61 Carter Co. or Prestonsburg., house 379, s 1,3.

W

WHITE, ANDREW J. reg 5, co H, enl 10/26/61 Prestonsburg, not on CSR, house 370, s 3.
WILSON, WILLIAM. reg 5, co D, H, enl 10/19/61 or 10/21/61, Carter Co. or Prestonsburg, house A29, s 1,3.

FLOYD COUNTY CONFEDERATE SOLDIERS

A

AKERS, ANDREW. reg 10, co A, enl 9/14/62 Prestonsburg, house W285 or W291, s 3,10.
ALLEN, DAVID FARROW. reg 13, co F, r sgt, enl 10/14/62 mouth of Salt Lick, Floyd Co., residence stated on CSR, house F221 or F616, s 3,21,31.
ALLEN, GEORGE. reg 10, co A, enl Prestonsburg, house F192, s 3,10.
ALLEN, GEORGE WESLEY. reg 13, co F, enl 7/20/63 Floyd Co., house F246 or F286, s 21,31.
ALLEN, HEZEKIAH. reg 13, co F, enl 10/14/62 mouth of Salt Lick, Beaver Creek, house F321, s 3,21,31.
ALLEN, JOEL JR. reg 13, co F, enl 10/19/62 mouth of Salt Lick, Beaver Creek, reg 10, co A, house F246, s 3,10,21,31.
ALLEN, JOEL SR. reg 13, co F, enl 10/14/62 mouth of Salt Lick, Beaver Creek, house F247, s 3,21,31.
ALLEN, JOHN B. reg 13, co F, enl 10/14/62 mouth of Salt Lick, Floyd Co., house F616, s 3,21,31.
ALLEN, JOHN M. reg 13, co F, r 2nd lt, enl 10/10/62 mouth of Salt Lick, Floyd Co., resigned 8/11/63 for ulceration of bowels, Conf. pension application #1582, CSR lists Floyd Co. as residence, house F321, s 1,3,31.
ALLEN, JOSEPH. reg 13, co F, r sgt, enl 10/14/62 mouth of Salt Lick, Beaver Creek, rem cap Gladesville VA 7/7/63, exchanged Point Lookout MD 3/2/65, house F321, s 3,21,31.
ALLEN, REUBEN. reg 13, co F, r sgt, enl 10/10/62 mouth of Salt Lick, Floyd Co., house F616, s 3,21.
ALLEN, REUBEN M. reg 5, co E, enl 11/13/61 Prestonsburg, reg 13, co F, r sgt, enl 10/10/62 Floyd Co., reg 10, co A, enl Prestonsburg, house F248, s 3,10, 21,31.
ALLEN, SAMUEL DAVID. reg 10, co D, enl 7/20/63 Piketon, reg 13, co F, r sgt, house F221, s 3,10,21,31.
ALLEN, S. P. reg 5, co G, enl 11/1/61 Pound Gap, reg 13, co A, rem clothing receipt 3rd quarter 1864, house n/c, residence stated on s 31, s 1,31.
ALLEN, WILLIAM. reg 13, co F, enl 10/14/62 mouth of Salt Lick, Floyd Co., house F292, F616, or F634, s 3,21,31.
ALLEN, WILLIAM JAMES. reg 13, co F, enl 10/14/62 mouth of Salt Lick, Floyd Co., rem cap Gladesville VA 7/7/63, house F634, s 3,21.

B

BALDRIDGE, CHARLES. reg 10, co A, B, enl 12/31/62 Prestonsburg, rem not on AG or CSR, house F145, s 21.
BALDWIN, ALEXANDER. reg 5, co G, enl 11/11/61 Pound Gap VA, house W255, s 3.
BALDWIN, JAMES OR JARVY W. reg 5, co G, enl 11/11/61 Pound Gap VA, house W164, s 3.
BAYS, ANDREW J. reg 5, co E, enl 10/22/61 Prestonsburg, rem cap Fleming Co. 4/1/63, house W418, s 1,3.
BAYS, ASA B. reg 5, co E, enl 10/26/61 Prestonsburg, house F117, s 3.
BENTLEY, BABBETT. reg 10, co E, enl 1/1/63 Wolfe Co., reg 13, co H, enl 4/15/65 Brahsearville, house F80, s 1,3,10,31.
BENTLEY, HIRAM. reg 13, co D, enl 10/4/62 Whitesburg, house F504, s 3,21,31.
BENTLEY, WILLIAM. reg 13, co D, enl 10/4/62 Whitesburg, house F504, s 1,21,31.
BIGGS, WILLOUGHBY. reg 13, co F, enl 10/4/62 mouth of Salt Lick, Floyd Co., rem CSR lists Floyd Co. as residence, house n/c, s 1,3,21.

BLANKENSHIP, WILLIAM. reg 10, co A, enl 9/14/62 Prestonsburg, cap 11/1/63 Floyd Co., surrendered Mt. Sterling 4/30/65, house W267, s 3,10.

BOYD, JOHN. reg 5, co E, enl 10/26/61 Prestonsburg, rem not on AG or CSR, reg 10, co G, enl 3/23/63, Grundy VA, house F558, s 1, 21.

BRADLEY, JACOB. reg 13, co F, enl 10/14/62 mouth of Salt Lick, Floyd Co., rem residence stated on CSR, house n/c, s 1.

BRANHAM, JOHN. reg 5, co E, enl 10/26/61 Prestonsburg, house W170, s 3.

BRANHAM, WILLIAM. reg 10, co A, enl 6/26/63 Floyd Co., rem not on AG or CSR, house W147, s 21.

BROWN, JAMES A. reg 5, co E, enl 10/26/61 Prestonsburg, reg 10, co A, enl 4/21/64 Liberty VA, rem cap at Mt. Sterling 6/10/64 exch from Rock Island IL 2/1/65, surr Mt. Sterling 4/30/65, house F156, s 3,10.

BROWN, ROBERT. reg 5, co E, r cpl, enl 11/8/61, Prestonsburg, house F180, s 3.

BRYANT, JACOB. reg 13, co E, enl 10/5/62 Whitesburg, CSR lists Letcher Co. as residence, s 31 lists Floyd Co. as residence, house n/c, s 1,31.

BURCHETT, BENJAMIN. reg 5, co E, enl 10/26/61 Prestonsburg, house W120, s 3.

BURCHETT, SAMUEL. reg 10, co A, enl 2/17/63 Prestonsburg, rem KIA Cynthiana 6/13/64, house F31, s 3,10.

BURCHETT, THOMAS. reg 5, co E, enl 10/26/61 Prestonsburg, reg 10, co A, enl 6/13/63 Prestonsburg, rem cap Cynthiana 6/13/64, exch Point Lookout MD 2/19/65, took oath at Paintsville 5/65, house W48, W118, W121 or W128, s 1,3,10,21.

BURCHETT, WILLIAM. reg 5, co E, enl 10/26/61 Prestonsburg, house W29, s 3.

BURTON, JAMES L. reg 10, enl 9/10/62 Piketon, r 1st sgt, house W84, s 3,10.

C

CAMPBELL, ISAIAH. reg 10, co A, enl 9/14/62 Prestonsburg, rem paroled Mt. Sterling 4/30/65, house W134, s 3,10.

CAMPBELL, JEREMIAH. reg 10, co A, enl 9/14/62 Prestonsburg, house W134, s 3,10.

CAMPBELL, WILLIAM. reg 10, co A, enl 9/14/62 Prestonsburg, house W134, s 3,10.

CAUDILL, ABNER. reg 13, co B, E, r 2nd lt, enl 9/12/62 Whitesburg, rem trans to co E, 10/5/62, prom to 2nd lt 10/7/62, house F473, s 3,21,31.

CAUDILL, EPHRAIM H. reg 13, co B, r 3rd sgt, enl 9/12/62 Whitesburg, rem CSR lists residence as Floyd Co., house n/c, s 1,3,21,31.

CAUDILL, HARVEY. reg 13, co B, E, r 2nd lt, enl 8/21/62 Whitesburg, brown hair, blue eyes, 6-1, rem prom to 2nd lt 10/7/62 trans to co E 6/1/63, wounded in arm, cap Gladesville 7/7/63, cap in Floyd Co. 10/16/63, CSR lists Floyd Co. as residence, house n/c, s 1,3,21,31.

CAUDILL, ISAAC. reg 13, co B, E, enl 8/21/62 Whitesburg, trans to co E 10/7/62, residence stated on CSR, not listed on Floyd Co. census, house n/c, s 1,31.

CAUDILL, JACKSON. reg 13, co B, enl 8/21/62 Whitesburg. light hair, blue eyes, fair skin, 5-8, rem CSR lists Floyd Co. and Letcher Co. as residence, s 31 lists Floyd Co. as residence, house n/c, s 1,3,21,31.

CAUDILL, JARVEY. reg 13, co D, rem not on CSR, s 31 lists Floyd Co. as residence, house n/c, s 1,31.

CAUDILL, PRESTON. reg 13, co B, E, r 1st sgt, enl 8/21/64 Whitesburg, rem trans to co E 10/5/62, CSR lists Floyd Co. as residence, house n/c, s 1,3,21,31.

CAUDILL, WILLIAM B. reg 13, co B, enl 9/16/62 Whitesburg, cap Gladesville 7/7/63, sent to Camp Chase 7/20/63, to Camp Douglas 8/24/63, residence stated on CSR, not on Floyd Co. census, house n/c, s 1.

CECIL, ALEXANDER W. reg 5, co E, enl 3/22/62 Prestonsburg, reg 10, co A, r 1st lt, age 28, light hair, blue eyes, fair skin, 5-9, rem elected 1st 9/23/62, cap Cynthiana 6/12/64, house W150, s 1,3.

CHAFFIN, SAMUEL NELSON. reg 5, co E, enl 10/23/61 Prestonsburg, reg 13, co C, enl 10/1/62 Whitesburg, rem cap Floyd Co., 6/26/63 exch Point Lookout MD 2/24/65, took oath at Louisa 5/11/65, CSR lists Perry Co. as residence, house F357, s 3,21,31.
CLARK, ALEXANDER. reg 5, co E, enl 10/26/61 Prestonsburg, house W309, s 3.
CLARK, JOHN E. reg 5, co G, enl 11/11/61 Pound Gap VA, house W197, s 3.
CLARK, KENIS F. reg 5, co G, enl 11/1/61 near Pound Gap, rem not or AG or CSR, house W217, s 21.
COBURN, GEORGE. reg 13, co C, enl 10/14/62 mouth of Salt Lick, Floyd Co., house F295, s 1,21,31.
COBURN, JAMES POLK. reg 13, co F, enl 10/14/62 Floyd Co., house F324, s 3,21,31.
COBURN, JEREMIAH. reg 5, co B, enl 10/25/61 Prestonsburg, rem des, reg 13, co F, enl 10/14/62 Floyd Co., house F325, s 3,21,31.
COBURN, JOSEPH L. reg 13, co A, r 4th sgt, enl 11/1/62 Whitesburg, rem prom to 4th sgt 1/17/63, cap Morgan Co. 8/19/63, took oath 9/4/65, house F331, s 3,21.
COBURN, WILLIAM J. reg 10, co A, enl 4/24/64 Liberty Hill VA, rem not on AG or CSR, house F324, s 21.
COLLINS, ISAAC. reg 13, co F, r cpl, enl 10/14/62 mouth of Salt Lick, Floyd Co., house F371, s 3,21,31.
COLLINS, MARSHALL. reg 13, co F, enl 10/14/62 Floyd Co., rem cap Gladesville VA 7/7/63, d Camp Douglas, Chicago IL of lung inflammation, house F371, s 3,21,31.
COLLINS, WILLIAM. reg 13, co F, enl 10/14/62 Floyd Co., rem cap Gladesville VA 7/7/63, exch Pt. Lookout MD 2/24/65, house F371, s 3,21,31.
COMBS, JAMES. reg 5, co E, enl 10/23/61 Prestonsburg, house F360, s 3.
CONLEY, JOHN ASHFORD. reg 13, co F, enl 10/14/62 mouth of Salt Lick, rem cap Gladesville VA 7/7/63, sent to Camp Chase & Camp Douglas, exch Point Lookout MD 2/24/65, CSR lists Floyd Co. as residence, house n/c, s 1,21,31.
CONLEY, JACKSON. reg 5, co F, enl 9/24/62 Licking Station, house F94, s 3.
CONLEY, WILLIAM M. reg 5, co F, r 2nd sgt, enl 9/14/62 Licking Station, age 25, light hair, dark eyes & skin, 5-7, rem cap 5/4/63 Magoffin Co., taken to Camp Chase OH 5/3/63, trans to Johnson's Island OH, rel 1/10/64, house F163, s 1,3.
CONN, JESSE. reg 10, co A, enl 9/9/62 Prestonsburg, des 1/8/63, house F543 or F560, s 3,10.
COOLEY, JOSEPH D. reg 5, co E, enl 7/1/62, reg 10, co A, r capt, enl 12/30/62 Prestonsburg, rem prom to sgt major 3/11/63, to capt 6/30/64, house F20, s 3,10.
CRAGER, JAMES. reg 13, co F, enl 10/14/62 mouth of Salt Lick, Floyd Co., house F340, s 3,21,31.
CRIDER, JACKSON P. reg 5, co E, enl 10/23/61 Prestonsburg, house W78, s 3.
CRIDER, WESLEY. reg 5, co E, enl 10/23/61 Prestonsburg, house W78, s 1,3.
CRISP, BAILEY. reg 10, co A, enl 12/31/62 Prestonsburg, house F181, s 3,10.
CRUM, MARCUS LINDSEY. reg 10, co D, enl 8/20/63 Piketon, rem wounded at Big Creek 11/6/63, house W186, s 3,10.
CRUM, MICHAEL. reg 10, co A, r cpl, enl 9/9/62 Prestonsburg, rem cap at Cynthiana 6/13/64, exch Point Lookout MD 2/19/65, house F546, s 3,10.
CRUM, MICHAEL JR. reg 10, co A, enl 9/9/62 Prestonsburg, house F549, s 3,10.

D

DAVIDSON, GREENVILLE R. reg 5, co E, r 5th sgt, enl 3/21/62 Prestonsburg, reg 10, co A, r 2nd lt, enl 9/23/62 Prestonsburg, rem cap 12/20/62, house W151, s 3,10.
DAWSON, JOHN. reg 5, co E, enl 10/26/61 Prestonsburg, rem cap 5/26/63 Floyd Co., house F66, s 1,3.
DEROSSETT, SOLOMON. reg 5, co E, enl 10/26/61 Prestonsburg, dis 10/20/62 Hazel Green, rem not on AG or CSR, house F541, s 21.
DEROSSETT, TOLBERT. reg 5, co E, enl 10/26/61 Prestonsburg, rem not on AG or CSR, house F21, s 21.
DILES, MOSES. reg 5, co E, enl 10/26/61 Prestonsburg, house W334, s 3.

DILLON, HENRY. reg 5, co E, enl 10/26/61 Prestonsburg, house W163, s 3.
DILLON, JAMES. reg 5, co E, enl 10/24/61 Prestonsburg, house W163, s 3.
DINGUS, SAMUEL. reg 13, co F, enl 6/1/63 mouth of Salt Lick, Floyd Co., house F588, s 3,21.
DUNCAN, JAMES. reg 1MR, co A, enl 10/18/61 Prestonsburg, house F124 or F282, s 3.

E

ENGLE, RICHARD. reg 13, co F, enl 10/14/62 mouth of Salt Lick, Floyd Co., rem residence stated on CSR, house n/c, s 1,3.
ESTEP, JOEL. reg 5, co E, enl 10/26/61 Prestonsburg, house F38, s 3.

F

FITZPATRICK, STEPHEN. reg 10, co A, enl 5/20/63 Prestonsburg, rem cap 9/29/63, exch 10/15/63, house F635, s 3,10.
FLANERY, JAMES F. reg 5, co E, r 4th sgt, enl 10/19/61 Prestonsburg, reg 13, co F, reg 5 service not on AG, reg 13 service not on CSR or AG, s 31 states he is Floyd Co. resident, house n/c, s 1,31.
FLANNERY, WILLIAM J. reg 5, co D, enl 12/13/61 Camp Recovery, dis 10/20/62 Hazel Green, house F526, s 1,3,21.
FRALEY, GEORGE W. reg 5, co E, enl 10/26/61 Prestonsburg, dis 10/20/62 Hazel Green, house W92, s 1,3.
FRIEND, EDWIN J. reg 10, co A, enl 9/28/62 Prestonsburg, house F1, s 1.
FRIEND, ROBERT S. reg 10, co D, enl 1/24/63 Prestonsburg, black hair, gray eyes, dark skin, 6-0, took oath at Louisa 3/30/64, house F1, s 3,10.

G

GARRETT, JESSE. reg 5, co E, enl 10/23/61 Prestonsburg, house W162, s 3.
GARRETT, MIDDLETON. reg 5, co E, enl 10/23/61 Prestonsburg, house W156, s 3.
GARRETT, SAMUEL. reg 5, co E, enl 10/24/61 Prestonsburg, house F53, 3s 3.
GEARHEART, ADAM. reg 13, co A, r 1st lt, enl 10/10/62 mouth of Salt Lick, Floyd Co., rem resigned 6/18/63, house F309 or F337, s 3,21,31.
GEARHEART, ALEXANDER. reg 13, co D, r 2nd sgt, enl 10/10/62 mouth of Salt Lick, Floyd Co., rem cap Pike Co., 10/6/63, d of typhoid fever, Camp Morton, Indianapolis IN 8/10/64, house F489, s 1,3,21,31.
GEARHEART, ALLEN. reg 10, co A, enl 9/17/62, house F529, s 3,10.
GEARHEART, JOHN B. reg 13, co F, enl 10/14/62 Floyd Co., house F299, s 1,3,21.
GEARHEART, JONATHAN. reg 10, co D, enl 8/20/62 Piketon, rem cap 12/63 in Ky., house W204, s 1,3,10.
GEARHEART, REESE. reg 10, rem clothing receipt 10/25/64, house F309, s 1,21.
GEARHEART, RICHARD A. reg 10, co A, enl 9/14/62 Floyd Co., rem cap 9/14/63 Floyd Co., taken to Camp Morton IN, rel 5/20/65, not on AG or CSR, house F512, s 21.
GEARHEART, WILLIAM B. reg 13, co F, enl 10/14/62 Floyd Co., house F309, s 3,21.
GIBSON, HIRAM. reg 13, co D, enl 10/4/62 Whitesburg, house F401, s 3,31.
GIBSON, ISHAM. reg 13, co B, enl 9/9/62 Whitesburg, rem CSR lists Floyd Co. as residence, house F400, s 3,21.
GIBSON, JOHN D. reg 5, co F, enl 11/1/61 Whitesburg, reg 13, co D, enl 10/4/62 Whitesburg, house F400, s 3,31.
GIBSON, MILES. reg 5, co F, enl 11/1/61 Whitesburg, reg 13, co A, enl 10/4/62 Whitesburg, rem trans to co D fall 1863, house F400, s 1,3,21,31.
GIBSON, WINSTON. reg 13, co B, enl 9/11/62 Whitesburg, house F403, s 3,21.

GOBLE, ADAM. reg 10, co A, enl 9/18/62 Prestonsburg, rem cap 5/7/64 Jeffersonville VA, d of jaundice 1/29/65 Camp Chase OH, house W139, s 3,10.
GOBLE, ARMSTRONG. reg 5, co E, enl 10/23/61 Prestonsburg, house W73 or W111, s 3.
GOBLE, CHARLES. reg 5, co E, enl 10/23/61 Prestonsburg, house W112, s 3.
GOBLE, CHRISTOPHER. reg 5, co E, enl 10/26/61 Prestonsburg, house W111, s 3.
GOBLE, ELIJAH. reg 5, co E, r 2nd lt, enl 10/26/61 Prestonsburg, rem d Gladesville VA 2/28/62, house W139, s 3.
GOBLE, HUGH. reg 5, co E, rem age 20, brown hair, hazel eyes, light skin, 5-7, cap Floyd Co. 5/14/63, taken to Camp Chase OH 5/26/63, trans to Johnson's Island OH 6/14/63, d 11/2/63 typhoid fever, house W73, s 1,21.
GOBLE, JAMES. reg 5, co E, enl 10/26/61 Prestonsburg, dis 10/20/62 Hazel Green, reg 10, co A, enl 5/1/63 Prestonsburg, rem reg 5 service not on AG or CSR, wounded at Cynthiana 6/64, house W125, s 3,10,21.
GOBLE, WILLIAM A. reg 5, co D, enl 12/20/61 Paintsville, dis 10/20/62 Hazel Green, house W125, s 1,3.
GOODMAN, RICHARD. reg 10, co A, enl 9/21/62 Prestonsburg, house F272, s 3,10.
GRAY, JOSEPH. reg 5, co E, r 4th sgt, enl 10/26/61 Prestonsburg, house W142, s 3.
GUNNELL, AHIRA C. reg 10, co D, enl 9/10/62 Piketon, rem took oath Louisa 5/65, house W219, s 3,10.

H

HACKWORTH, GEORGE W. reg 5, co C, enl 10/19/61 Prestonsburg, dis 10/20/62 Hazel Green, house F153, s 1,3.
HAGER, RICHARD M. reg 5, co E, r 1st sgt, enl 10/19/61 Prestonsburg, rem cap Floyd Co. 1/11/62, house W27, s 1,3.
HALE, JAMES. reg 13, co F, enl 10/14/62 mouth of Salt Lick, Floyd Co., rem CSR lists Floyd Co. as residence, house n/c, s 1.
HALE, JOHN. reg 5, co E, enl 10/26/61 Prestonsburg, reg 10, co A, enl 9/11/62 Prestonsburg, rem des 9/9/63 near Liberty VA, admitted to Richmond VA hospital 3/22/65, house F150 or W137, s 1.
HALE, JOHN SR. reg 5, co A, enl 12/14/61 Middle Creek, dis 10/20/62 Hazel Green, reg 10, co A, enl 11/1/62 Prestonsburg, rem fair hair & skin, hazel eyes, 6-3, cap Cynthiana 6/13/64, took oath 6/26/65, house F534, s 1,3,10,21.
HALE, WILLIAM. reg 5, co A, enl 10/25/61 Prestonsburg, dis 10/20/62 Hazel Green, reg 10, co A, enl 3/1/63 Prestonsburg, rem cap 6/64, house F139 or F150, s 1,3,10,21.
HALE, WILLIAM W. reg 5, co E, enl 11/8/61 Prestonsburg, house F139 or F150, s 1.
HALL, ALFRED. reg 13, co E, r cpl, enl 10/5/62 Whitesburg, rem prom to cpl 4/30/63, cap Floyd Co. 11/7/63, d 1/31/64 of pneumonia at Camp Morton, Indianapolis IN, buried Crown Hill Cemetery, Indianapolis, s 31 states he is Floyd Co. resident, house F446, s 3,21, 31.
HALL, ALLEN. reg 13, co E, enl 10/5/62 Whitesburg, reg 7ConvCav, cap Piketon 4/15/63, taken to Camp Chase 4/19/63, exch City Point 5/13/63, CSR gives Letcher Co. as residence, s 31 states he is Floyd Co. resident, but he is not on Floyd Co. census, house n/c, s 3, 12, 31.
HALL, ANDREW JACKSON. reg 5, co B, enl 10/25/61 Prestonsburg, house W232, s 3.
HALL, CAMPBELL. reg 5, co B, rem dark hair, hazel eyes, sandy skin, 5-8, cap Floyd Co., reg 10, co D, on muster rolls 6/30/63 to 2/29/64, rem des 8/1/63, took oath 4/20/64, CSR lists residence as Floyd Co., house n/c, s 1,21.
HALL, HENRY. reg 5, co D, enl 10/19/61 Carter Co., reg 13, co F, enl 10/14/62 Floyd Co., house F464, s 1,3,21,31.
HALL, JAMES. reg 5, co B, enl 1/12/62 Camp Hager, reg 13, co F, enl 10/14/62 Floyd Co., house F83 or F451, s 3,21,31.
HALL, JARVEY. reg 10, co A, enl 9/21/62 Prestonsburg, house F110, s 3,10.

HALL, JOHN. reg 5, co G, enl 11/11/61 Pound Gap VA, reg 13, co F, house F463, s 3,21,31.
HALL, JOHN. reg 5, co E, enl 10/26/61 Prestonsburg, reg 13, co E, enl 10/5/62 dark hair, hazel eyes, 5-8, rem cap Letcher Co. 8/64, house F471, s 3,21,31.
HALL, JOHN H. reg 13, co E, enl 10/5/62 Whitesburg, dark hair, hazel eyes, 5-8, cap Letcher Co. 5/64, released on oath 7/1/64, CSR states Floyd Co. is residence, house F471, s 1, 3, 31.
HALL, JOHN LEYTON. reg 13, co E, r cpl, enl 10/5/62 Whitesburg, house F506, s 1,31.
HALL, LEE. reg 13, co E, r 2nd sgt, enl 10/5/62 Whitesburg, prom to sgt 4/30/63, cap Floyd Co. 11/7/63, taken to Louisville 11/18/63, to Camp Morton 11/21/63, died 11/21/63 or 8/10/64 of typhoid fever, buried grave #1047 Crown Hill cemetery, Indianapolis, CSR lists Letcher Co. as residence, house F450, s 1, 3, 31.
HALL, LEWIS. reg 5, co G, enl 11/11/61 Pound Gap VA, reg 10, co C, enl 5/63, rem des 2/20/62 cap 11/7/63 Floyd Co., d Camp Morton IN 5/28/65 diarrhea, reg 10 service not on AG or CSR, house F446, s 3,21.
HALL, LILBURN H. reg 5, co E, enl 10/26/61 Prestonsburg, house F112, s 3.
HALL, MARSHALL. reg 13, co E, enl 10/5/62 Whitesburg, CSR states he is Letcher Co. resident, but he is not on Letcher Co. census, s 31 says he is Floyd Co. resident, but he is not on Floyd Co. census, house n/c, s 3, 31.
HALL, MILES. reg 13, co E, enl 10/5/62 Whitesburg, rem res 6/8/63 from chronic rheumatism, house F449, s 3,21,31.
HALL, MORGAN. reg 5, co G, enl 11/8/61 Pike Co., house W257, s 3.
HALL, RILEY. reg 5, co E, age 18, dark hair & eyes, hazel eyes, 5-5 or 5-7, rem cap Floyd Co. 5/27/63, residence stated as Floyd Co., took oath 6/10/63 Camp Chase OH, house n/c, s 1,21.
HALL, RILEY. reg 13, co B, enl 9/12/62 Middle Creek, dark hair, blue eyes, fair skin, 5-8, rem cap 5/27/63 Floyd Co., took oath 5/64 at Louisa, CSR gives Floyd Co. as residence, house F447, s 1,3,21,31.
HALL, RILEY. reg 13, co E, enl 10/5/62 Whitesburg, house F485, s 1,3,21,31.
HALL, SAMUEL. reg 5, co G, enl 11/4/61 Pike Co., house W269, s 1,3.
HALL, WILLIAM C. reg 1BatCav, co A, r cpl, enl 10/20/61 Prestonsburg, house F451, F501 or W232, s 3.
HALL, WILLIAM J. reg 13, co E, r capt, enl 10/23/62 Whitesburg, rem prom to sgt 4/63, elected capt, house F444, s 1,3,21,31.
HALL, WILLIAM J. JR. reg 13, co E, enl 10/5/62 Whitesburg, house F451 or F501, s 3,21,31.
HALL, WILLIAM R. reg 10, co C, enl 3/21/63 Floyd Co., house F451, F501, or W232, s 3,10.
HALL, WILLIAM W. reg 5, co E, enl 11/8/61 Prestonsburg, house F451, F501 or W232, s 3.
HALL, WILSON. reg 10, co A, enl 9/13/62 Prestonsburg, house F110 or F501, s 3,10.
HAMILTON, JOHN. reg 5, co G, enl 11/11/61 Pound Gap VA, age 30, light hair & skin, blue eyes, 5-10, rem cap 5/1/63 Magoffin Co., house W262 or W292, s 3.
HAMILTON, SAMUEL JR. reg 5, co G, enl 11/11/61 Pound Gap VA, house W262, s 3.
HAMILTON, STEPHEN. reg 5, co E, enl 11/8/61 Prestonsburg, house F123, s 3.
HAMILTON, TANDY. reg 5, co E, enl 11/6/61 Prestonsburg, dark hair, gray eyes, fair skin, 6-0, rem cap Floyd Co. took oath 4/30/64 Louisa & released, house F123, s 1,3.
HAMILTON, WILLIAM. reg 5, co G, enl 11/8/61 Pike Co., house F200, F214 or W284, s 3.
HAMMOND, ARCHELOUS JACOB. reg 5, co E, enl 11/11/61 Pound Gap VA, reg 13, co E, r capt, enl 10/5/62 Whitesburg, rem resigned spring 1863, house F476, s 3,21,31.
HANDSHOE, ADAM. reg 5, co E, enl 10/26/61 Prestonsburg, reg 13, co F, enl 10/14/62 Floyd Co., rem des 11/18/62, house F314, s 3,21,31.
HANDSHOE, ANDREW. reg 13, co F, enl 10/14/62 Floyd Co., house F230, s 3,21,31.
HARMAN, AQUILLA C. reg 10, co A, r cpl, enl 9/13/62 Prestonsburg, house F622, s 3,10.
HARMAN, JAMES W. reg 5, co E, enl 10/26/61 Prestonsburg, house W21, s 3.
HARMAN, WILLIAM W. reg 10, co A, K, enl 4/12/63 or 8/27/63 Jeffersonville VA or Prestonsburg, house F622, s 3, 10.

HARRIS, E. G. HARMAN. reg 5, co E, r 2nd lt, enl 5/8/62 Prestonsburg, reg 10, co K, r 1st lt, enl 7/7/63 Liberty Hill VA, dark hair & skin, gray eyes, 6-0, rem capt Mt. Sterling 6/9/64, took oath 5/19/65 at Johnson's Island OH, age at oath 32, house W138, s 1,3,10.

HARRIS, JAMES F. reg 10, co K, r 1st sgt, enl 4/1/63 Floyd Co., rem app sgt 8/7/63, house W138, s 1,3,10.

HARRIS, JOHN. reg 13, co E, enl 10/25/62 Whitesburg, rem app sgt 4/3/63, took oath 3/15/64 at Louisville, house F424, s 3,21,31.

HARRIS, JOHN B. reg 10, co A, enl 11/7/62 Prestonsburg, house F44, s 3,10.

HARRIS, KELSEY T. reg 10, co K, enl 7/10/63 Jeffersonville VA, house W138, s 3,10.

HARRIS, SQUIRE. reg 13, co E, enl 10/5/62 Whitesburg, house F425, s 3,21,31.

HARRIS, THOMAS J. reg 10, co K, enl 7/1/63 Camp Bowen VA, house W138, s 1,21.

HARRIS, THOMAS M. reg 10, co A, r 5th sgt, enl 3/20/63 Prestonsburg, rem cap Mt. Sterling 6/10/64, d Camp Morton, Indianapolis IN 2/11/65 of typhoid fever, house W135, s 3,10.

HARRIS, WILLIAM J. reg 5, co E, enl 10/26/61 Prestonsburg, reg 10, co A, r 1st sgt, enl 9/20/62 Prestonsburg, rem wounded in face & left forearm, cap at Mt. Sterling 6/10/64 exch Point Lookout MD 3/24/65, d 3/29/65 Richmond VA of chronic diarrhea, house F424, or W135, s 1,3,10.

HARRIS, WILLIAM JEFFERSON. reg 10, co K, enl 4/1/63 Jeffersonville VA, rem mortally wounded at Mt. Sterling 6/8/64, house F424 or W135, s 3,10.

HATCHER, ANTHONY W. reg 5, co E, reg 10, co D, r AAQM, enl 10/8/62 Piketon, rem wounded 11/8/61 Battle of Ivy Mountain, reg 5 service not on AG or CSR, house W190, s 3,10,21.

HAYES, RICHARD A. (EPPERSON). reg 5, co E, enl 10/26/61 Prestonsburg, reg 13, co F, enl 10/14/62 mouth of Salt Lick, brown hair, blue eyes, 5-10, cap Floyd Co. 11/19/63, rel from Louisville Prison 12/19/63, house n/c, s 1,3,21,31.

HAYS, JOHN. reg 13, co D, surr Mt. Sterling 4/30/65, Ky Conf. Pension #4210, s 31 states he is Floyd Co. resident, but he is not on Floyd Co. census, house n/c, s 3, 31.

HAYS, NELSON. reg 5, co E, enl 10/23/61 Prestonsburg, rem cap 9/26/63 Floyd Co, rel 10/16/63, house F367, s 1,3.

HAYWOOD, HENRY. reg 5, co E, enl 11/8/61 Prestonsburg, house F133, s 3.

HAYWOOD, HIRAM. reg 5, co E, enl 11/8/61 Prestonsburg, house F143, s 3.

HAYWOOD, ROBERT. reg 5, co E, enl 11/8/61 Prestonsburg, house F133, s 3.

HENSON, WILLIAM. reg 13, co D, enl 10/4/62 Whitesburg, age 18, CSR states he is Letcher Co. resident, but he is not on Letcher Co. census, s 31 states that he is Floyd Co. resident, house F273, s 1,3, 31.

HERALD, JAMES H. reg 5, co E, enl 10/23/61 Prestonsburg, house W123, s 3.

HERALD, JOHN W. reg 5, co E, r 2nd lt, enl 10/26/61 Prestonsburg, house W122, s 3.

HERALD, WILLIAM O. reg 5, co E, enl 10/26/61 Prestonsburg, reg 10, co A, rem wounded & captured at Cynthiana 6/13/64, house W99 or W122, s 3,10.

HEREFORD, JAMES H. reg 13, co K, rem not on CSR, house F67, s 21,31.

HEREFORD, JAMES H. JR. reg 5, co E, r cpl, enl 10/26/61 Prestonsburg, reg 13, co K, rem reg 13 service not on CSR, house F67, s 3,21,31.

HERRON, WILLIAM. reg 5, co E, cpl, enl 10/26/61 Prestonsburg, house W184, s 3.

HICKS, HENRY G. reg 5, co G, enl 11/11/61 Pound Gap VA, house F183, s 3.

HICKS, HIRAM. reg 5, co E, enl 10/26/61 Prestonsburg, reg 10, co A, enl 12/8/62 Prestonsburg, rem cap after Battle of Ivy Mountain 11/8/61 & exch., cap Floyd or Pike Co., 9/20/63 or 10/6/63, d Camp Morton, Indianapolis IN 3/4/64 of brain inflammation, house F183, s 1,3,10,21.

HIGNITE, THOMAS JEFFERSON. reg 10, co A, enl 5/1/63 Prestonsburg, dark hair & skin, blue eyes, 5-9, rem cap Cynthiana 6/13/64, took oath 6/12/65, house W126, s 1,3,10.

HIGNITE, WILLIAM. reg 5, co E, enl 10/26/61 Prestonsburg, house W126, s 3.

HOLBROOK, KELSEY. reg 5, co K, enl 10/26/61 Prestonsburg, rem not on AG or CSR, house F162, s 21.

HOLDERFIELD, JACOB. reg 5, co E, r 3rd sgt, enl 10/13/61 Prestonsburg, reg 10, co A, r 3rd sgt, enl 12/1/62 Prestonsburg, house F598, s 1,3,10.
HOWARD, JAMES. reg 10, co A, enl 7/1/64 Liberty VA, rem wounded, house W332, s 1,3,10.
HOWARD, MARTIN. reg 13, co F, enl 10/14/62 mouth of Salt Lick, residence stated on CSR, house n/c, s 1.
HUBBARD, HENRY CLAY. reg 10, co A, r 4th sgt, enl 9/13/62 Prestonsburg, rem wounded, cap at Mt. Sterling 6/10/64, d Camp Morton, Indianapolis IN of spinal meningitis, 2/27/65, house F134, s 3,10.
HUBBARD, WILLIAM. reg 10, co A, r cpl, enl 9/13/62 Prestonsburg, rem cap Blue Springs TN 8/24/64, exch Rough & Ready GA, 9/22/64, house F134, s 3,10.
HUFF, JAMES A. reg 13, co B, enl 9/9/62 Whitesburg, rem d during the war, house F399, s 3,21.
HUGHES, WALTER. reg 13, co F, enl 10/14/62 mouth of Salt Lick, Floyd Co., house F194, s 3,4.
HUNTER, JOHN. reg 5, co E, enl 10/23/61 Prestonsburg, reg 10, co A, enl 11/10/62 Prestonsburg, age 26 (at oath), blue eyes, fair skin, 5-8, took oath at Charleston WV 6/24/65, house F604, s 1,3,10.
HUTTON, W. J. reg 5, co E, r 2nd sgt, enl 10/30/61 Prestonsburg, reg 10, co K, enl 7/10/63 Liberty Hill VA, rem cap Mt. Sterling 6/9/64, may have served as 1st lt, co B, French's Btn, joined U.S. Army 10/13/64, house W133, s 1,3,10.

I

ISAACS, GEORGE WASHINGTON. reg 13, co E, enl 7/20/62 or 10/5/62 Piketon, auburn hair, blue eyes, light skin, 5-10, cap Pike Co. 10/6/63, taken to Camp Morton 10/24/63, to Ft. Delaware 3/19/64, released on oath 6/9/65, Conf. Pension #2602, CSR & s 31 state he is Floyd Co. resident, but he is not on Floyd Co. census, house n/c, s 1,3,31.
ISAACS, GERMAN. reg 13, co E, enl 10/5/62 Whitesburg, rem took oath at Louisa, house F438, s 3,21,31.
ISAACS, JONATHAN. reg 13, co E, enl 10/5/62 Whitesburg, house F455, s 3,21,31.
ISAACS, TERMAN. reg 13, co E, enl 10/5/62 Whitesburg, rem trans to co F 10/14/62, surr Dublin Depot VA 1865, house F438, s 3,21,31.

J

JARRELL, ALEXANDER. reg 10, co A, enl 9/27/62 Prestonsburg, dis 4/10/63 Breathitt Co., rem cap 6/28/63 in Floyd Co., d smallpox at Camp Douglas, Chicago IL, 8/5/64, house F565, s 3,10.
JARVIS, JAMES L. reg 5, co E, enl 10/26/61 Prestonsburg, reg 13, co E, house W116, s 3,31.
JOHNS, JOHN GRAHAM. reg 5, co E, enl 10/25/61 Prestonsburg, rem not on AG or CSR, house W145, s 21.
JOHNSON, ABISHA J. (SR.) reg 13, co E, enl 10/5/62 Whitesburg, house F469, s 3,21,31.
JOHNSON, ABISHA J. (JR.). reg 13, co E, enl 10/5/62 Whitesburg, rem cap Gladesville 7/7/63, exch Point Lookout MD 3/2/65, house F480, s 3,21,31.
JOHNSON, ANDREW J. reg 13, co E, enl 10/5/62 Whitesburg, age 18, clothing receipts 9/1/64 9/15/64, took oath at Louisa, CSR states that he is Letcher Co. resident, s 31 states he is Floyd Co. resident, but he is not on Floyd Co. or Letcher Co. census, house n/c, s 1,3,31.
JOHNSON, CALEB C. reg 13, co E, r 4th sgt, enl 10/5/62 Whitesburg, house F467, s 3,21.
JOHNSON, ELI. reg 13, co E, enl 10/5/62 Whitesburg, rem paroled at Lexington, house F462, s 3,21,31.
JOHNSON, ELISHA. reg 13, co E, enl 10/5/62 Whitesburg, rem took oath 4/65, house F472, s 1,3,21,31.
JOHNSON, GABRIEL. reg 10, co A, enl 9/9/62 Prestonsburg, rem cap Mt. Sterling 6/10/64, exch Point Lookout MD 3/2/65, house W127, s 3,10.
JOHNSON, HARVEY. reg 13, co E, enl 10/5/62 Whitesburg, house F468, s 3,21,31.
JOHNSON, JAMES W. reg 5, co G, enl 11/1/61, house F144, F233, F563 or W16, s 3.

JOHNSON, JOAB. reg 13, co E, enl 10/5/62 Whitesburg, rem cap Gladesville 7/7/63, exch Point Lookout MD 3/2/65, paroled at Louisa 4/18/65, house F480, s 3,21,31.
JOHNSON, JOHN. reg 13, co E, enl 10/5/62 Whitesburg, rem cap Gladesville 7/7/63, discovered hanged at Camp Douglas, Chicago IL 7/6/65, house F238, F443 or F480, s 3,21,31.
JOHNSON, ZACHARIAH. reg 5, co C, reg 10, co B, rem cap Morgan Co. 9/12/63, d Camp Douglas IL 2/5/65 smallpox, not on AG or CSR, house F233, s 21.
JONES, JOEL. reg 13, co B, enl 9/15/62 Whitesburg, rem cap 11/7/63 in Floyd Co., trans for exch 3/15/65, house F411, s 1,3,21,31.
JONES, JOHN. reg 5, co D, r cpl, enl 10/9/62 Jackson, rem cap 6/22/64 Richmond, house F212 or W339, s 3.
JONES, LINDSEY. reg 5, co G, r cpl, enl 11/11/61 Pound Gap VA, house F279, s 3.
JONES, WILLIAM W. reg 5, co C, r 2nd sgt, enl 10/26/61 Prestonsburg, dis 10/20/62 Hazel Green, reg 13, co E, enl 10/5/62 Salt Lick Floyd Co., rem cap Greenville TN 9/27/63, rel from McLean Barracks, Cincinnati 10/16/63, house F411, s 1,3,21,31.
JORDAN, ROBERT. reg 13, co F, enl 10/14/62 Salt Lick Floyd Co., dis 4/22/65 Scott Co. VA, house F324, s 3,21,31.

K

KEATH, ENGLISH. reg 10, co A, enl 9/23/62 Prestonsburg, rem des 10/2/63, house F628, s 1,3.
KENDRICK. DAVID J. reg 5, co E, enl 10/26/61 Prestonsburg, house W124, s 3.
KILE, ROBERT. reg 13, co F, enl 10/14/62 mouth of Salt Lick, Floyd Co., rem residence stated on CSR & s 31, house n/c, s 1,3.
KING, JAMES. reg 13, co E, enl 10/5/62 Whitesburg, des 10/25/62, Ky.Conf. Pension #3920, CSR states he is Letcher Co. resident, s 31 states he is Floyd Co. resident, but he is not on Floyd Co. or Letcher Co. census, house n/c, s 3,31.
KING, TANDY LEWIS. reg 13, co E, enl 10/5/62 Whitesburg, des 10/25/62, CSR states he is Letcher Co., s 31 states he is Floyd Co. census, but he is not on Floyd or Letcher census, house n/c, s 3,31.

L

LAFERTY, JAMES. reg 10, co A, enl 9/20/62 Prestonsburg, age 23, dark hair & skin, hazel eyes, 5-8, rem took oath at Charleston WV 5/4/65, house F540, s 1,3,10.
LEWIS, WILLIAM W. reg 5, co C, r cpl, enl 9/2/62 West Liberty, house W302, s 3.
LITTLE, WILLIAM. reg 13, co B, enl 9/9/62 Whitesburg, rem cap Gladesville 7/7/63, house F478, s 3,21,31.
LITTON, JAMES H. reg 5, co E, enl 10/26/61 Prestonsburg, reg 10, co D, enl 10/1/62 Piketon, rem cap 5/20/63 Floyd Co., house W82, s 1,3,10.

M

MANUEL, MACK C. reg 13, co F, enl 10/14/62 Floyd Co., reg 10, co D, enl 12/5/62 Whitesburg, house F304, s 3,10,21,31.
MARSHALL, HENRY. reg 5, co E, enl 10/28/61 Prestonsburg, age 21, dark hair & skin, hazel eyes, 5-10, rem cap 5/27/63 in Floyd Co., house F625, s 1,3.
MARSHALL, THOMAS JEFFERSON. reg 13, co G, enl 1/8/63 Whitesburg, cap Gladesville 7/7/63, s 31 states he is Floyd Co. resident, house W19, s 1, 3, 31.

MARTIN, ADAM. reg 13, co F, r capt, enl 9/21/62 mouth of Salt Lick, Floyd Co., house F370, s 3,21,31.

MARTIN, ALEXANDER. reg 5, co E, enl 11/13/61 Prestonsburg, rem not on AG or CSR, cap 6/27/62 Carter Co. trans to Newport Barracks 2/10/64, house F9, s 21.

MARTIN, ALLEN. reg 13, co F, r 4th sgt, enl 10/14/62 Letcher Co., house F417, s 3,21,31.

MARTIN, GEORGE. reg 13, co F, enl 10/14/62 mouth of Salt Lick, Floyd Co., house F415, s 3,21,31.

MARTIN, JAMES. reg 5, co G, enl 11/11/61 Pound Gap VA, reg 13, co F, enl 10/14/62 mouth of Salt Lick, Floyd Co., house F519, s 3,21,31.

MARTIN, JOSEPH. reg 5, co G, enl 11/7/61 camp near Pound Gap VA, reg 10, co A, r cpl, enl 9/20/62 Prestonsburg, reg 13, co F, r 1st sgt, enl 10/14/62 Whitesburg, house F370, s 1,3,21,31.

MARTIN, RICHARD. reg 13, co F, enl 10/14/62 mouth of Salt Lick, Floyd Co., house F336, s 3,21,31.

MARTIN, TANDY. reg 13, co F, enl 10/14/62 Floyd Co., rem cap Gladesville 7/7/63, d of 8/24/63 of measles at Camp Douglas, Chicago IL, house F418, s 3,21,31.

MARTIN, WILLIAM J. reg 5, co G, r cpl, reg 13, co F, enl 10/14/62 Floyd Co., house F372, s 3,21,31.

MARTIN, WYATT. reg 13, co R, r cpl, enl 10/14/62 mouth of Salt Lick, Floyd Co., cap Gladesville VA 7/7/63, sent to Camp Chase & Camp Douglas and to Point Lookout, MD 2/29/65, house F409, s 1,3,21,31.

MAY, SAMUEL J. reg 5, co A, enl 10/25/61 Prestonsburg, dis 10/20/62 Hazel Green, house F94 or F259, s 1,3.

MAY, SAMUEL S. reg 5, co F, r cpl, enl 9/11/62 Licking Station, rem cap Johnson Co. 6/4/63, house F94 or F259, s 1,3.

MAY, SOLOMON. reg 10, co D, enl 6/1/63 Camp Bowen VA, rem KIA 6/9/64 at Mt. Sterling, house F69, s 21.

MCGUIRE, DAVID. reg 5 co E, enl 10/26/61 Prestonsburg, reg 10, co A, enl 6/17/63 Prestonsburg, house F620, s 1,3,10.

MCGUIRE, JAMES M. reg 5, co A, enl 10/21/61 West Liberty, house W70, s 3.

MCGUIRE, JOHN P. reg 5, co E, enl 10/26/61 Prestonsburg, house W68, s 3.

MCGUIRE, RICHARD. reg 10, co A, enl 6/17/63 Prestonsburg, house F540, s 3,10.

MCGUIRE, WILLIAM. reg 10, co A, enl 6/17/63 Prestonsburg, house F621, s 3,10.

MCKINNEY, JAMES. reg 5, co C, enl 6/6/62 Holston VA, house W247, s 3.

MCLEVISA, WILLIAM. reg 10, co A, enl 9/8/62 Prestonsburg, house F532, s 3,10.

MEADE, LEMUEL. reg 10, co A, enl 9/14/62 Prestonsburg, rem cap 7/25/63 Floyd Co., took oath at Cincinnati 9/17/63, house W298, s 3,10.

MEAD, MCDONALD. reg 10, co A, enl 9/6/62 Prestonsburg, house W298, s 3,10.

MEAD, RHODES W. reg 13, co E, enl 10/5/62 Whitesburg, cap Floyd Co. 7/7/63, taken to Camp Morton, released on oath 5/22/65, Ky Conf. Pension #859, CSR states he is Floyd Co. resident, house W294, s 3, 31.

MILAM, JAMES. reg FR, enl 5/24/63 Johnson Co., residence stated on s 36, house n/c, s 1,3,36.

MITCHELL, ANDREW JACKSON. reg 5, co E, enl 11/8/61 near Pound Gap, rem not on AG or CSR, house W278, s 21.

MOORE, CALVIN. reg 10, co A, enl 9/20/62 Prestonsburg, reg 13, co E, enl 10/5/62 Whitesburg, house F496, s 3,10,21,31.

MOORE, EDWARD. reg 13, co E, enl 10/5/62 Whitesburg, house F497, s 3,21.

MOORE, ISAAC. reg 10, co A, enl 9/20/62 Prestonsburg, reg 13, co E, enl 10/14/62 Whitesburg, rem cap 7/13/64, house F442, s 3,10,21.

MOORE, JEREMIAH. reg 13, co E, enl 10/5/62 Whitesburg, des 11/1/62, CSR states he is Letcher Co. resident, s 31 states he is Floyd Co. resident, but he is not Floyd or Letcher census, house n/c, s 3,31.

MOORE, JOEL. reg 10, co A, enl 9/23/62 Prestonsburg, reg 13, co E, enl 10/5/62 Whitesburg, house F492, s 3,10,21,31.

MOORE, WILLIAM HENDERSON. reg 5, co E, enl 10/26/61 Prestonsburg, reg 10 co A, enl 9/13/62 Prestonsburg, reg 13, co E, enl 10/5/62 Whitesburg, rem reg 5 service not on AG or CSR, cap Cynthiana 6/13/64, exch Pt. Lookout MD 2/19/65, took oath Lebanon VA 5/65, house F280, s 1,3,10,21,31.

MOORE, WILLIAM TANDY. reg 13, co E, enl 10/5/62 Whitesburg, rem cap 7/7/63 at Gladesville, house F496, s 3,21,31.

MORRIS, EZEKIEL. reg 13, co F, r cpl, enl 10/14/62 Floyd Co., light hair, blue eyes, fair skin, 6-0, rem cap Floyd Co., spring 1864, enlisted in U.S. forces to gain release, house F349, s 3,21,31.

MOSLEY, WILLIAM. reg 5, co E, enl 10/29/61 Prestonsburg, reg 10, co A, enl 12/14/62 Prestonsburg, rem cap 6/12/64, taken to Camp Chase OH 8/13/64, d of pneumonia 2/9/65, house F538, s 3,10.

MULLINS, ANDREW. reg 5, co E, enl 10/17/61 Prestonsburg, des 1/18/62, house F60, s 1,3,21.

MULLINS, ELISHA. reg 13, co E, enl 10/5/62 Whitesburg, CSR states he is Letcher Co. resident, s 31 states he is Floyd Co. resident, but he is not on Floyd or Letcher census, house n/c, s 3, 31.

MULLINS, ELLIOTT G. reg 13, co E, r 1st lt, enl 10/5/62 Whitesburg, rem prom to 1st lt 7/1/63, house F442, s 3,21,31.

MULLINS, HIRAM. reg 5, enl 11/5/61 Pound Gap, reg 13, co E, r 3rd sgt, enl 10/5/62 Whitesburg, CSR lists Letcher Co. as residence, s 31 lists Floyd Co. as residence, house n/c, s 1, 31.

MULLINS, OWEN. reg 13, co C, enl 10/1/62 Whitesburg, rem not on CSR, house F31, s 1,31.

MULLINS, ROBERT. reg 5, co E, enl 10/17/61 Prestonsburg, des 1/18/62, house F605, s 1,3,21.

MULLINS, WILLIAM. reg 5, co E, enl 10/17/61 Prestonsburg, house F584, s 1,3.

MUSICK, ABRAM. reg 5, co E, enl 10/30/61 Prestonsburg, reg 13, co K, age 47, gray hair, blue eyes, 5-9, rem reg 5 service not on AG or CSR, cap Floyd Co. 5/17/63, exch 4/16/64, surr Cumberland Gap, 4/30/65, house F51, s 21,31.

N

NOLIN, LEONARD. reg 13, co F, enl 10/14/62 mouth of Salt Lick, Floyd Co., rem residence stated on CSR, house n/c, s 1,3.

O

ODEL, JAMES. reg 5, co E, enl 10/26/61 Prestonsburg, rem d 3/28/63 camp hospital Scott Co. VA, house W363, s 1,3.

ONEY, DOUGLAS. reg 13, co F, r cpl, enl 10/14/62 mouth of Salt Lick, Floyd Co., dis 7/7/63, house F294, s 1,3,21,31.

ONEY, JOHN C. reg 13, co F, enl 10/14/62 Whitesburg, cap Wise Co. VA 6/25/63 or 7/7/63, taken to McLean Barracks 7/18/63, to Camp Chase 9/6/63, to Rock Island 1/14/64, joined Union army to fight Indians, s 31 states he is Floyd Co. resident, house F326, s 1, 3, 31.

ONEY, RUNYON. reg 13, co F, enl 10/14/62 Floyd Co., rem cap Magoffin Co., 9/16/63, house F301, s 3,21,31.

OSBOURNE, CHARLES C. reg 10, co E, enl 4/30/63 Piketon, brown hair, black eyes, dark skin, 5-7, rem took oath of allegiance 6/8/65 Chattanooga TN, house F76, s 1,3,10.

OSBORNE, DAVID EDWARD. reg 13, co F, enl 10/14/62 mouth of Salt Lick, Floyd Co., house F590, s 1,3,21,31.

OSBORNE, REPTS B. reg 13, co F, enl 10/14/62 Floyd Co., rem cap Floyd Co. 5/26/63, house F590, s 3,21,31.

OSBORNE, W. SALISBURY. reg 10, co C, enl 3/25/63 Floyd Co., rem not on AG or CSR, house F505, s 21.
OSBORNE, THOMAS. reg 13, co F, enl 10/14/62 mouth of Salt Lick, Floyd Co., rem cap Floyd Co. 5/26/63, house F590, s 3,21,31.
OSBORNE, WILLIAM. reg 10, co E, enl 1/1/63 Wolfe Co., dark hair & skin, gray eyes, 5-7, CSR states Floyd Co. as residence, house n/c, s 1, 3, 22.
OSBORN, WILLIAM J. M. reg 5, co E, enl 10/28/61 Prestonsburg, house F76, s 3.
OWENS HARVEY. reg 5, co D, F, enl 9/3/62 Licking Station, rem d 6/30/63 Nickelsville VA, house F324, s 1,3.

P

PATTON, ALLEN. reg 5, co G, enl 11/2/61 camp near Pound Gap, Pike Co., house F253, s 1,3.
PATTON, DAVID F. reg 5, co C, enl 10/19/61 Prestonsburg, dis 10/20/62 Hazel Green, house F36, s 1,3.
PATTON, HENRY CLAY. reg 5, co G, enl 11/2/61 Piketon, dis 10/20/62 Hazel Green, rem not on AG or CSR, house F259, F261 or F263, s 21.
PATTON, JAMES. reg 5, co E, enl 10/26/61 Prestonsburg, house F255 or W130, s 3.
PATTON, JOHN FRANKLIN. reg 5, co I, enl 10/25/61 Prestonsburg, reg 13, co F, enl 10/14/62 Floyd Co., house F244, s 3,31.
PATTON, SAMUEL. reg 5, co G, enl 11/2/61 camp near Pound Gap, Pike Co., house F244, s 1,3.
PATTON, STEPHEN. reg 13, co F, enl 10/14/62 Floyd Co., residence stated on CSR, house n/c, s 1,3,21,31.
PENDLETON, JAMES K. reg 10, co A, enl 9/8/62 Prestonsburg, house F597, s 1,3,10.
PRATER, JOHN. reg 5, co C, enl 10/31/61 Prestonsburg, reg 13, co F, enl 10/14/62 Floyd Co., house F298, s 3,21,31.
PRATER, NEWMAN. reg 13, co F, enl 6/1/63 Floyd Co., house F300, s 3,21,31.
PRATER, WILLIAM W. reg 5, co E, enl 10/26/61 Prestonsburg, reg 13, co F, enl 10/14/62 Floyd Co., house F296, s 3,21,31.
PREWITT, ELIJAH. reg 5, co B, enl 10/25/61 Prestonsburg, dis 10/20/62 Hazel Green, house W360, s 1,3.

R

RATLIFF, JOHN. reg 10, co D, blue eyes, sandy eyes & hair, 5-11, rem cap Floyd Co., 12/63, took oath 12/30/63, house F267, s 1.
RAY, REUBEN. reg 5, co G, enl 11/5/61 camp near Pound Gap, Pike Co., house W279, s 1,3.
REFFETT, JAMES. reg 10, co A, enl 9/21/62 Prestonsburg, rem cap Cynthiana 6/13/64, transported to Point Lookout MD for exch 2/19/65, house W10, s 3,10.
REYNOLDS, WILLIAM. reg 13, co E, enl 10/14/62 Whitesburg, rem dark hair & skin, black eyes, 5-9, cap Floyd Co., took oath Louisa 5/64; CSR states is a Letcher Co. resident; s 31 & oath state is resident of Floyd Co.; dual listing with Letcher Co., house F486, s 1,3,31.
ROBERTS, HENDERSON. reg 5, co E, enl 10/26/61 Prestonsburg, house F528, s 3.
ROBERTS, RILEY. reg 13, co B, enl 9/9/62 Whitesburg, house F457, s 3,21,31.
ROBINSON, HARRISON. reg 10, co A, enl 9/23/62 Prestonsburg, house F611, s 3,10.
ROBINSON, JAMES PATRICK. reg 10, co A, enl 9/8/62 Prestonsburg, house F614, s 3,10.

ROBINSON, JEFFERSON. reg 5, co E, enl 12/30/61 Prestonsburg, dis Hazel Green 10/20/62, house F576, s 3,21.
ROSE, THOMAS. reg 10, co H, enl 5/15/63 Buchanan Co. VA, house F14, s 1,3,10.
RUSSELL, WILLIAM HENRY. reg FR, enl 10/18/62 Johnson Co., rem des 10/25/62 house F86, s 1,3,36.

S

SALISBURY, GREENVILLE. reg 10, co A, enl 9/8/62 Prestonsburg, rem prom to co blacksmith 6/30/63, house F531, s 3,10.
SALYER, REUBEN. reg 5, co C, enl 9/18/62 Salyersville, dis 6/18/63 for disability, rem trans to co K, house F344, s 1,3.
SAMMONS, THOMAS. reg 2MR, co E, enl 1/20/62 Prestonsburg, reg 13, co F, enl 10/14/62 Whitesburg, house F577, s 1,3,21,31.
SCALF, ARCHIBALD. reg 5, co E, enl 10/26/61 Prestonsburg, rem dark hair, gray eyes, fair skin, 5-10, cap Floyd or Pike Co. 7/8/63, received Camp Chase OH 7/20/63, received Camp Douglas IL 8/63, dis 5/15/65, CSR lists Pike Co. as residence, house W109, s 1,21.
SELLARDS, DRURY. reg 5, co E, rem light hair, blue eyes, 5-9, age 30 at cap, cap Pike or Floyd Co. 4/15/63, trans to Camp Chase OH 4/22/63, trans to Johnson's Island 6/14/63, trans to Point Lookout MD, joined US Army for frontier service 1/29/64, records misfiled in 5th Ky. Cav., house W108, s 21.
SELLARDS, ELIAS. reg 5, co E, enl 10/30/61 Prestonsburg, house W108, s 3.
SHEPHERD, BRICE F. reg 5, co C, enl 10/26/61 Prestonsburg, reg 13, co F, enl 10/14/62 Floyd Co., rem cap Gladesville 7/7/63, exch Point Lookout MD 2/24/65, house F333, s 1,3,21,31.
SHEPHERD, DANIEL. reg 13, co F, enl 10/10/62 Floyd Co., residence stated on CSR, house n/c, s 1,3,21.
SHEPHERD, DAVID. reg 13, co F, house F323, s 1,3,21,31.
SHEPHERD, WILLIAM R. reg 13, F&S, enl 10/14/62 Floyd Co., rem cap Gladesville VA 7/7/63, rel Pt. Lookout MD 2/24/65, took oath at Louisa, CSR states he is Perry Co. resident, house F191, s 3,21,31.
SIMON, JOHN. reg 5, co E, enl 1/9/62 Prestonsburg, house F22, s 3.
SIZEMORE, JOHN. reg 10, co A, enl 9/21/63 Prestonsburg, house F290 or F517, s 3,10.
SIZEMORE, WILLIAM. reg 10, co A, enl 9/20/62 Prestonsburg, reg 13, co A, rem cap 1863 on Beaver Creek, Floyd Co., reg 13 service not on CSR, house F517, s 1,3,10,21.
SKEANS, THOMAS. reg 5, co C, enl 10/26/61 Prestonsburg, rem gray hair, light eyes, fair skin, 5-11, cap Floyd or Pike Co., 10/6/63, took oath, paroled & sent north 12/63, house F198, s 1,21.
SLONE, GEORGE W. reg 13, co B, enl 9/9/62 Whitesburg, house F377, s 1,3,21,31.
SLONE, HARDIN. reg 13, co E, enl 10/5/62 Whitesburg, cap & sent to Louisville 1863, took oath 1865, Ky. Conf. Pension #3098, CSR states he is Letcher Co. resident, s 31 states he is Floyd Co. resident, but he is not on Floyd or Letcher census, house n/c, s 1, 3, 31.
SLONE, HENRY F. reg 13, co D, E, enl 10/4/62 Whitesburg, rem trans to co E, 10/5/62, cap Pike Co. 10/6/63, d typhoid fever Camp Morton, Indianapolis IN 7/29/64, house F82, s 1,3,21.
SLONE, ISHAM. reg 13, co A, enl 1862, rem cap Gladesville 7/7/63, exch Point Lookout MD 2/24/65, house F406, s 1,3,21,31.
SLONE, ISOM. reg 5, co F, enl 11/1/61 Camp near Pound Gap, reg 13, co E, r cpl, enl 10/5/62 Whitesburg, rem cap Floyd or Pike Co. 6/29/63, trans to Camp Douglas, Chicago IL, house F392, s 1,3,21,31.
SLONE, JACOB. reg 13, co E, enl 10/5/62 Whitesburg, house F378, s 1,3,21,31.

SLONE, JAMES A. reg 5, co F, enl 11/1/61 camp near Pound Gap, reg 13, co A, enl 11/1/62 Whitesburg, dis Gladesville VA, house F391, s 1,3,21,31.
SLONE, JASPER. reg 13, co F, enl 10/10/62 Floyd Co., rem cap 11/7/63 Floyd Co., d Camp Morton, Indianapolis IN 7/30/64 of typhoid fever, house F379, s 1,3,21.
SLONE, JOHN. reg 13, co B, enl 9/9/62, house F380, s 1,3,21,31.
SLONE, JOHN C. reg 13, co E, enl 10/5/62 Whitesburg, house F428, s 3,21,31.
SLONE, JOHN P. reg 13, co E, enl 10/5/62 Whitesburg, house F379, s 1,3,21,31.
SLONE, MONROE. reg 13, co E, F, enl 10/5/62 Whitesburg, rem trans to co F 6/1/63, house F428, s 1,3,21,31.
SLONE, NATHANIEL. reg 13, co B, enl 9/9/62 Whitesburg, house F377, s 3,21,31.
SLONE, PLEASANT. reg 13, co E, enl 10/5/62 Whitesburg, rem served until 8/31/63, house F381, s 1,3,21,31.
SLONE, SHADRACK. reg 13, co E, enl 10/5/62 Whitesburg, F393, s 1,3,21,31.
SLONE, SPENCER. reg 13, co F, enl 10/10/62 Floyd Co., sandy hair, blue eyes, light skin, 6-1, rem cap Floyd Co., 11/7/63, rel from Camp Morton, Indianapolis IN 5/22/65, house F408, s 1,3,21,31.
SLONE, TANDY. reg 13, co F, enl 10/14/62 Floyd Co., dark hair, blue eyes, florid skin, 6-1, rem cap Floyd Co. 10/5/63, rel on oath from Camp Morton, Indianapolis IN 6/21/65, house F407, s 1,3,21,31.
SLUSHER, GARDNER. reg 13, co F, enl 10/14/62 mouth of Salt Lick, Floyd Co., rem residence stated on CSR, house n/c, s 1,3,31.
SLUSHER, JOHN. reg 13, co F, enl 10/14/62 mouth of Salt Lick, Floyd Co., rem residence stated on CSR, cap Gladesville, VA 7/7/63, trans to Camp Douglas 8/23/64, died at Camp Douglas 8/31/64, house n/c, s 1,3,31.
SMITH, BENJAMIN. reg 5, co E, enl 10/23/61 Prestonsburg, reg 13, co F, r 2nd sgt, enl 10/14/62 Whitesburg, house F368, s 1,3,21,31.
SMITH, GEORGE. reg 13, co E, enl 10/5/62 Whitesburg, reg 10, co A, enl 9/23/62 Prestonsburg, house F416, s 1,3,10,21,31.
SMITH, JAMES M. reg 10, co A, enl 9/23/62 Prestonsburg, house F3, s 3,10.
SMITH, NICHOLAS. reg 5, co F, enl 11/1/61 Whitesburg, house F387, s 3.
STEPHENS, DAVID. reg 5, co D, enl 11/13/61 Floyd Co. or Pound Gap, rem des 1/62, house F249, s 1, 21.
STEPHENS, GREENVIL. reg 13, co F, enl 10/10/62 Floyd Co., house F240, s 1,3,21,31.
STEPHENS, THOMAS. reg 5, co C, enl 10/19/61 Prestonsburg, house F228, s 3.
STEPHENS, WILLIAM D. reg 13, co B, enl 10/10/62 Floyd Co., house F242, s 1,3,21,31.
STINSON, JAMES H. reg 13, co F, enl 8/24/63 Floyd Co., house F127, s 3,21,31.
STURGILL, HIRAM. reg 10, co D, enl 10/20/62 Piketon, hazel hair, dark eyes, florid skin, 5-6, rem cap 8/20/63 or 10/6/63 Pike Co., took oath 6/12/65, house W155, s 1.
SUTTON, JEFFERSON. reg 5, co E, enl 10/23/61 Prestonsburg, house F354, s 3.

T

TACKETT, WILLIAM. reg 5, co E, enl 10/26/61 Prestonsburg, house F599, s 3.
TAYLOR, HENRY. reg 5, co E, enl 9/26/62 Pike Co., dis 10/20/62 Hazel Green, rem not on AG or CSR, house F624, s 21.
TEETERS, JOHN. reg 13, co F, enl 10/14/62 mouth of Salt Lick, Floyd Co., rem residence stated on CSR, cap Floyd Co. 10/15/63, taken to Camp Morton, Indianapolis, IN, house n/c, s 1,3.
TERRY, THOMAS. reg 13, co F, enl 10/14/62 mouth of Salt Lick, Floyd Co., residence stated on CSR, house F405, s 1,3.

THACKER, REUBEN. reg 5, co F, enl 11/1/61 Whitesburg, reg 13, co A, enl 11/1/62 Whitesburg, rem reg 5 service not on AG or CSR, house F320, s 3,21,31.

THORNSBERRY, ENOCH. reg 13, co E, enl 10/5/62 Whitesburg, house F352, s 1,3,21,31.

THORNSBERRY, JOHN B. reg 10, co A, enl 9/15/62 Prestonsburg, reg 13, co B, enl 9/14/62 Whitesburg, cap Floyd Co. 10/8/64, taken to Camp Chase OH 10/22/64 & Pt. Lookout MD 2/12/65, house F402 or W22, s 1,3,10,21,31.

THORNSBERRY, MARTIN V. reg 13, co E, enl 10/5/62 Whitesburg, house F412, s 1,3,21,31.

TRIMBLE, EDWIN. reg 5, co E, r 1st lt, enl 1/9/62 Prestonsburg, reg 10, co A, r lt colonel, enl 9/25/62, rem prom to lt col 8/3/64, KIA Saltville VA 10/2/64, house F16, s 3,10.

TRIPLETT, WILLIAM. reg 5, co E, enl 10/23/61 Prestonsburg, reg 13, co F, r cpl, enl 10/14/62 Floyd Co., rem cap Louisa 11/17/63, house F347, s 1,3,21,31.

TURNER, MORGAN. reg 13, co F, enl 10/10/62 Floyd Co., house F499, s 1,3,21,31.

TURNER, WILLIAM JEFFERSON. reg 10, co A, enl 9/23/62 Prestonsburg, house F515, s 3,10.

V

VAUGHN, JOHN, reg 10, co A, C, rem cap Floyd Co. 4/16/63, took oath at Point Lookout MD prison 1/10/64, house F90 or W307, s 1.

VAUGHN, THOMAS J. reg 5, co K, E, r 1st sgt, enl 8/23/61 Camp Moccasin VA, dis 10/20/62 Hazel Green, rem trans to co E 10/1/62, house F43, s 1,3,21.

W

WALKER, JAMES CALHOUN. reg 13, co F, r capt, enl 10/10/62 Floyd Co., rem prom to 2nd lt 11/2/62, cap Cynthiana 6/12/64, prom to capt while in prison, escaped McLean Barracks, Cincinnati OH 6/30/65 while awaiting trial, house F10, s 1,3,21,31.

WALLACE, RICHARD. reg 5, co E, enl 10/26/61 Prestonsburg, reg 13, co F, enl 10/10/62 Floyd Co., rem KIA Middle Creek summer 1863, CSR lists residence as Floyd Co., house n/c, s 1,3,21,31.

WALLEN, ELISHA B. reg 13, co K, paroled Cumberland Gap 4/30/65, s 31 states he is Floyd Co. resident, house F313, s 1,31.

WALLEN, HANSFORD. reg 5, co E, enl 10/13/61 Prestonsburg, reg 13, co C, F, enl 8/24/63 Floyd Co., rem trans to co C 10/1/62, house F355, s 1,3,21,31.

WALLEN, GEORGE W. reg 5, co E, enl 10/20/61 Prestonsburg, age 36, light hair, blue eyes, fair skin, 5-9, rem cap Floyd Co. 4/17/63, took oath 4/11/64, house W81, s 1,3.

WALLEN, SHELBY. reg 13, co C, rem cap Gladesville 7/7/63, exch Point Lookout MD 2/24/65, house F177, s 21, 31.

WATSON, LORENZO DOW. reg 10, co A, enr 9/9/62 Prestonsburg, rem des Liberty VA 9/9/63, house F571, s 3,10.

WATSON, WILLIAM J. reg 10, co A, enl 9/9/62 Prestonsburg, rem des Liberty VA 9/9/63, house F571, s 3,10.

WHITT, JAMES P. reg 3MR, co A, rem cap Floyd Co. 9/22/63, took oath 10/25/63, rel 10/16/63, House F277, s 1,3,22.

WHITT, JOHN B. reg 5, co E, r 2nd sgt, enl 10/23/61 Prestonsburg, reg 10, co A, rem cap Floyd Co. 12/16/63, took oath 12/30/63, house F277, s 1,3,10,21.

WICKER, JOHN. reg 13, co F, enl 8/24/63, unit disbanded at Whitesburg 4/65, took oath at Louisa 5/65, house F369, s 21,31.

WICKER, ROBERT. reg 5, co E, enl 10/23/61 Prestonsburg, reg 13, co F, enl 10/10/62 Floyd Co., house F369, s 1,21,31.
WORKMAN, NATHAN. reg 13, co C, F enl 9/11/62 Floyd Co. or Whitesburg, rem trans to co C 10/1/62, house F363, s 1,3,21,31.

Y

YATES, ALEXANDER. reg 5, co B, r cpl, enl 10/25/61 West Liberty, house F61, s 3.
YATES, BENJAMIN FRANKLIN. reg 5, co E, enl 10/28/61, rem cap Morgan Co. 5/18/63, house F65, s 1,3.
YATES, JACKSON. reg 5, co B, enl 10/25/61 Prestonsburg, house F61, s 3.

JOHNSON COUNTY CONFEDERATE SOLDIERS

A

ARROWOOD, GARRETT DEWEESE. reg 5, co E, enl 12/26/61 Camp Hager, dis 10/20/62 Hazel Green, rem not on AG or CSR, house 198, s 21.
AUXIER, JAMES K. POLK. reg 5, co E, enl 12/29/61 Camp Hager, rem not on AG or CSR, house 158, s 21.
AUXIER, SAMUEL. reg 5, co E, enl 12/29/61 Camp Hager, rem re-enlisted 6/62, not on AG or CSR, house 156 or 159, s 21.

B

BAILEY, DANIEL. reg 5, co K, enl 12/14/61 Camp Recovery, dis 10/20/62 Hazel Green, house 631, s 1,3.
BAILEY, JAMES. reg 5, co K, enl 12/14/61 Camp Recovery, house 615, s 3.
BAILEY, SAMUEL. reg 5, co C, enl 10/19/61 Prestonsburg, house 633, s 3.
BAILEY, WILLIAM WALLACE. reg 5, co F, enl 9/30/62 Licking Station, house 631, s 3.
BALDRIDGE, WILLIAM. reg 5, co F, enl 9/24/62 Licking Station, house 181, s 3.
BARNETT, JOHN W. reg 10, co B, rem cap 10/15/63 Magoffin Co., taken to Camp Morton IN, took oath 5/18/65, not on AG or CSR, house 437, s 21.
BAYS, WILLIAM. reg 5, co B, enl 3/28/62 Camp Moccasin, house 752, s 1.
BLEVINS, DANIEL. reg 5, co B, K, r capt, enl 10/25/61 Prestonsburg, reg FR, enl 1/1/62 Montgomery Co., rem elected capt co K 12/14/61, res 9/30/62 Mt. Sterling, house 717, s 1,3.
BLEVINS, LEWIS. reg 5, co B, K, enl 10/25/61 Prestonsburg, dis 10/20/62 Hazel Green, rem not on AG or CSR, house 441, s 21.
BROWN, DAVID. reg 13, co F, enl 10/14/62 mouth of Salt Lick, Floyd Co., house 495, s 3,21.
BROWN, WILLIAM W. reg 5, co C, enl 10/19/61 Prestonsburg, dis 10/20/62 Hazel Green, house 496, s, 1,3.
BURCHETT, LEONARD. reg 5, co K, enl 12/14/61 Camp Recovery, Middle Creek, reg FR, enl 10/6/62 Johnson Co., rem des 10/27/62, house 690, s 3,36.
BUTCHER, JOHN W. reg 10, co F, enl 3/28/63 Buchanan Co. VA, house 317, s 3.

C

CANTRELL, GEORGE. reg 5, co K, enl 12/14/61 Camp Recovery, Middle Creek, rem des 10/22/62, house 716, s 1,3.
CANTRELL, HENRY. reg 5, co K, enl 12/14/61 Middle Creek, dis 10/20/62 Hazel Green, reg FR, enl 10/6/62 Johnson Co., reg 10, co K, enl 5/15/64 Jeffersonville VA, cap 6/9/64 Mt. Sterling, rem not on AG or CSR, des 10/18/62, house 716, s 3,21,36.
CANTRELL, JOHN. reg 5, co K, enl 12/14/61 Camp Recovery near Prestonsburg, rem des 10/20/62, house 724, s 1,3.
CANTRELL, WILLIAM. reg 5, co K, enl 12/14/61 Middle Creek, dis 10/20/62 Hazel Green, reg 10, co K, enl 5/25/64 Jeffersonville VA, rem reg 5 service not on AG or CSR, may have served in C 13, co A or K, CSR lists Paintsville as residence, cap Mt. Sterling 6/9/64, took oath at Camp Morton IN 6/12/65, house 716, s 1,3,10,21.
CARTER, CHARLES W. reg 5, co K, enl 12/14/61 Camp Recovery, Middle Creek, rem des 1/9/62 Middle Creek, house 704, s 1,3.

CARTER, WILLIAM. reg 5, co K, enl 12/14/61 Camp Recovery near Prestonsburg, rem des 1/9/62 Middle Creek, house 704, s 1,3.
CASSIDY, HENRY. reg 5, co H, enl 10/21/62 Prestonsburg, dis 10/22/62 Salyersville, house 229, s 1,3.
CASSIDY, WILLIAM H. reg 5, co B, r cpl, enl 10/25/61 Prestonsburg, reg 13, co F, K, enl 6/1/63 Whitesburg, rem trans to co K 8/16/63 Lee Co. VA, took oath at Louisa 5/65, house 218, s 1,3,21,26.
CASTLE, JAMES C. reg 5, co E, enl 9/12/62 Salyersville, rem not on AG or CSR, house 48, s 21.
CASTLE, JOHN W. reg 5, co E, enl 9/12/62 Salyersville, dis 10/20/62 Hazel Green, reg 10, co D, r 1st lt, enl 6/20/63 Pike Co., rem reg 5 service not on AG or CSR, paroled 6/12/65 Charleston WV, house 48, s 3,10,21.
CHANDLER, THOMAS. reg 5, co Riffe's, enl 11/26/61 Lawrence Co., rem not on AG or CSR, cap 11/26/61 Emmanuel Brammer's farm, Lawrence Co., taken to Newport Barracks, house 535, s 21.
COLDIRON, HIRAM J. reg 5, co D, enl 9/14/62 Licking Station, rem des 3/1/63, trans from co F, served as 1st sgt in co F, house 841, s 3.
COLLINS, JOHN C. reg 5, co B, enl 9/11/62 Jackson, light hair & skin, gray eyes, 5-9, rem des 10/17/62 Salyersville, rejoined 4/25/63, des Hansonville VA 8/10/63, cap 10/10/63 or 10/13 or 10/22 Magoffin Co., recd Camp Morton 10/28/63, place of residence stated on CSR, house n/c, s 1,22.
COLVIN, ALLEN RILEY. reg 1MR, co B, enl 10/21/61 Johnson Co., reg 10, co B, r capt, enl 1/2/63 West Liberty, age 23, sandy hair, hazel eyes, light skin, 5-11, rem cap Cynthiana 6/12/64, taken to Johnson's Island OH, took oath 6/14/65, house 837, s 1,3,10,21.
COLVIN, HENRY G. reg 5, co A, enl 10/25/61 Prestonsburg, dis 10/20/62 Hazel Green, re-enlisted reg 5, co F, 9/24/62 Licking Station, r capt, rem cap 5/19/63 Morgan Co., taken to Johnson's Island OH, exch 3/3/64, house 837, s 1,3.
COLVIN, WILLIAM. reg 5, co F, enl 9/30/62 Licking Station, age 20, blue eyes, fair skin, 5-8, rem cap 5/27/63 Johnson Co., house 838, s 1,3.
CONLEY, LEVI. reg FR, enl 10/18/62 Magoffin Co., house 604, s 1,3,36.
CONLEY, THOMAS M. reg 5, co D, enl 9/24/62 Licking Station, rem trans from Co F, des 3/1/63, house 94, 133 or 620, s 3.
CONLEY, WILLIAM F. reg 5, co D, enl 9/30/62 Licking Station, rem trans from co F, house 647, s 3.
CRUM, ADAM. reg 5, co E, dis 2/4/62 Rockhouse KY, rem not on AG or CSR, dis for age, house 334, s 21.

D

DAVIS, JAMES H. reg 1BatCav, co A, rem discharged, house 305, s 3.
DAVIS, JOHN. reg 5, co C, enl 10/19/61 Prestonsburg, rem arrested Lawrence Co. 5/8/62, exch 8/25/62, house 60, 545 or 798, s 1,3.
DAVIS, JOSEPH. reg 5, co H, enl 8/13/62 Tazewell Co. VA, house 467, s 3.
DIALS, WILLIAM. reg 5, co K, enl 9/12/62 Salyersville, house 666, s 3.
DOBINS, JACKSON. reg 5, co K, enl 9/12/62 Salyersville, house 640, s 3.

E

ESTEP, HIRAM. reg 5, co K, r cpl, enl 12/14/61 Camp Recovery, near Prestonsburg, dis 10/20/62 Hazel Green, reg 10, co H, enl 5/15/63 Buchanan Co. VA, house 742, s 1,3,10.
ESTEP, LILBURN. reg 5, co K, enl 12/14/61 Camp Recovery, dis 10/20/62 Hazel Green, house 422, s 1,3.
ESTEP, WILLIAM. reg 5, co K, enl 12/14/61 Camp Recovery, dis 10/20/62 Hazel Green, house 55 or 710, s 1,3.

ESTEP, WILLIAM W. reg 5, co K, enl 9/22/62 Salyersville, dis 10/20/62 Hazel Green, 2MR, co D, enl 8/26/62 Logan Co. VA, reg 7ConfCav, co G, rem des 2MR 11/22/62, house 55 or 710, s 1,12,21.
EVANS, MEREDITH. reg 5, co F, enl 9/30/62 Licking Station, house 639, s 3.
EVANS, THOMAS. reg 5, co K, enl 12/14/61 Camp Recovery, near Prestonsburg, dis 10/20/62 Hazel Green, rem cap 6/23/63 Johnson Co., house 705, s 1,3.

F

FAIRCHILD, ABNER. reg FR, enl 10/6/62 Johnson Co., rem des 10/18/62, house 21, s 3.
FERGUSON, JOHN W. reg 5, co F, r 2nd lt, enl 1/62 Licking Station, age 32, light hair & skin, blue eyes, 5-11, rem elected 2nd lt 9/30/62, cap 5/27/63 Johnson Co. or 5/18/63 Floyd Co., released on oath 4/27/65, house 757, s 1,21.

G

GREEN, FRANCIS MARION. reg FR, enl 2/27/63 Floyd Co., house 99, s 3,36.
GREEN, WILLIAM MARTIN. reg FR, enl 2/27/63 Floyd Co., house 99 or 543, s 3,36.
GRIM, BENJAMIN HARRISON. reg 5, co K, dis 10/20/62 Hazel Green, rem not on AG or CSR, house 377, s 21.
GRIM, CHARLES JEFFERSON. reg 5, co K, enl 12/14/61 Middle Creek, dis 10/20/62 Hazel Green, rem not on AG or CSR, house 533, s 21.
GRIM, JOHN FRANKLIN. reg 5, co K, enl 12/14/61 Middle Creek, dis 10/20/62, rem not on AG or CSR, house 376, s 21.
GULLETT, IRA. reg 5, co C, enl 9/12/62 Paintsville, dis 10/20/62 Hazel Green, rem not on AG or CSR, surr 5/3/65 Paintsville, house 842, s 21.

H

HAGER, DANIEL. reg 5, co E, r 1st lt, A.Q.M., enl 10/21/61 Prestonsburg, rem not on AG or CSR, service confirmed on Amnesty Petition, house 443, s 21.
HALL, WILLIAM. reg 5, co A, enl 10/21/61 West Liberty or Prestonsburg, rem re-enlisted co B 10/20/62, house 456, s 1,21.
HAMILTON, ANDREW JACKSON. reg 5, co D, enl 10/15/62 Licking Station, house 809, s 1,3.
HAMILTON, BENJAMIN. reg 5, co D, enl 10/19/61 Carter Co., rem cap Middle Creek 1/13/62, d of wounds or disease, house 734, s 1,3.
HICKS, ISAAC. reg 5, co F, enl 11/1/61 near Pound Gap, reg 10, co F, K, enl 1/1/64 Virginia, rem not on AG or CSR, wounded in leg 6/12/64 Battle of Cynthiana, took oath 5/12/65 Louisa, house 339, s 21.
HILL, BARTON (BRETON). reg 5, co K, enl 12/14/61 Camp Recovery, Prestonsburg, rem des 7/4/62 Whitesburg, house 152, s 1,3.
HILL, HENRY D. OR H. reg 5, co E, enl 10/23/61 Prestonsburg, rem d Jeffersonville VA 6/30/62, house 558, s 3.
HILL, THOMAS C. reg 7ConfCav, co G, rem took part in 1864 Paintsville raid, house 152, s 12.
HOLBROOK, JAMES F. reg 5, co D, enl 9/11/62 Licking Station, house 643, s 3.
HURT, WILLIAM. reg 5, co I, enl 12/28/61 Paintsville, dis 10/20/62 Hazel Green, house 160, s 1,3.

J

JACKSON, JASPER. reg 5, co K, r cpl, enl 12/14/61 Camp Recovery, rem re-enlisted 10/20/62, house 440, s 3.
JAYNE, ANDREW J. reg 7ConfCav, co G, rem took part in 1864 Paintsville raid, house 702, s 12.

JAYNE, DANIEL J. V. reg 5, co K, r cpl, enl 12/14/61 Camp Recovery, dis 10/20/62 Hazel Green, reg FR, enl 10/22/62 Johnson Co., house 703 or 709, s 1,3,36.
JAYNE, HENRY. reg 5, co D, r 2nd sgt, enl 9/22/62 Licking Station, rem trans from co F, cap near Jonesboro GA 9/1/64, house 706, s 3.
JAYNE, HENRY T. reg 5, co K, r 1st lt, enl 10/26/61 Beaver Hill, dis 10/20/62 Hazel Green, reg FR, enl 10/22/62 Johnson Co., rem was 3rd sgt from 12/24/62 to 5/1/63, reg 7ConfCav, co G, rem took part in 1864 Paintsville raid, house 706, s 1,3,12,36.
JAYNE, WILLIAM. reg 5, co D, r sgt, enl 9/17/62 Licking Station, brown hair, hazel eyes, dark skin, 5-8, rem trans from co F, wounded & disabled at Intrenchment Creek 7/22/64, took oath 5/21/65 at Nashville, house 706 or 747, s 3.
JAYNE, WILLIAM W. reg 1MR, co B, enl 10/21/61 Johnson Co., age 29, dark hair & skin, black eyes, 5-5, rem cap 1/8/62 at Jennies Creek, Johnson Co., reg FR, enl 4/11/63 Johnson Co., house 706 or 747, s 1,3,36.
JOHNSON, JOHN. reg 5, co K, enl 12/14/61 Camp Recovery, dis 10/20/62 Hazel Green, house 266, s 1,3.
JOHNSON, MARTIN. reg 5, co K, enl 12/14/61 Camp Recovery, age 32, black hair, blue eyes, fair skin, 5-7, rem cap 9/5/6_, house 635, s 1,3.
JONES, TANDY. reg 5, co K, enl 12/14/61 Camp Recovery, house 575, s 3.
JUSTICE, SAMUEL. reg 10, co H, enl 5/15/63 Buchanan Co. VA, house 549 or 553, s 1,3,10.

L

LEMASTER, DANIEL P. reg 5, co F, enl 9/11/62 Licking Station, house 771, s 3.
LEMASTER, ELEAZER. reg 5, co K, enl 12/14/61 Camp Recovery, dis 10/20/62 Hazel Green, house 591, s 1,3.
LEMASTER, ELIJAH. reg 5, co F, r 3rd sgt, enl 9/11/62 Licking Station, house 755, s 3.
LEMASTER, JAMES. reg 5, co K, enl 12/14/61 Camp Recovery, Prestonsburg, dis 10/20/62 Hazel Green, house 423 or 743, s 1,3.
LEMASTER, JOHN J. reg 5, co F, enl 9/14/62 Licking Station, age 22, light hair, blue eyes, fair skin, 5-10, rem disabled from wound through left lung, house 750, s 1,3.
LEMASTER, JOHN R. reg 5, co K, enl 12/14/61 Middle Creek, dis 10/20/62 Hazel Green, rem not on AG or CSR, house 592, s 21.
LEMASTER, RICHARD. reg FR, enl 9/18/62 Johnson Co., rem des 10/18/62, house 423, s 3.
LEMASTER, THOMAS. reg 5, co K, enr 12/14/61 Camp Recovery, dis 10/20/62 Hazel Green, age 22, house 715, s 1,3.
LEMASTER, WILLIAM. reg FR, enl 9/18/62 Carter Co., rem des 1/63, house 593 or 688, s 3,36
LEMASTER, WILLIAM. reg 5, co F, enl 9/25/62 Licking Station, house 593 or 688, s 3.
LYON, JOHN. reg 5, co F, enl 9/20/62 Licking Station, house 640, s 3.
LYON, WILLIAM. reg 5, co K, enl 12/14/61 Camp Recovery, dis 1/6/62, house 273, s 3.
LYONS, JAMES. reg 5, co K, enl 12/14/61 Camp Recovery, dis 10/20/62 Hazel Green, dark hair & skin, gray eyes, 6-2, rem took oath of allegiance, 5/21/65 at Nashville TN, house 634, s 1,3.

M

MARSHALL, HUGH. reg 5, co E, enl 10/19/61 Prestonsburg, reg 10, co A, enl 4/23/63 Prestonsburg, rem cap & held at Cincinnati until paroled 11/63, house 27, s 3,10.
MARSHALL, JOHN. reg 5, co E, enl 10/18/61 Prestonsburg, house 417 or 760, s 3.
MCCARTY, DAVID J. reg 5, co D, enl 9/14/62 Licking Station, dis 12/4/63 rem trans from co F, cap 10/5/63 at Louisa, house 839, s 1,3.
MCCARTY, NELSON. reg 5, co F, enl 9/23/62 Licking Station, house 840, s 3.
MCINTYRE, JOHN. reg 5, co I, enl 12/28/61 Paintsville, house 35, s 3.

MCKENZIE, A. J. reg FR, enl 10/1/62 Johnson Co., rem des 10/28/62, house 727, s 3.
MCKENZIE, ELIAS H. reg 5, co F, enl 9/6/62 Licking Station, house 740, s 3.
MCKENZIE, HENRY. reg 5, co K, enl 12/14/61 Camp Recovery, reg 5, co F, r musician, enl 9/24/62 Licking Station, reg FR, enl 10/1/62 Johnson Co., rem des 10/28/62, house 679, s 3,36.
MCKENZIE, HIRAM E. reg 5, co F, r musician, enl 9/13/62 Licking Station, reg 10, co L, enl 6/20/64 Pike Co., house 678, s 3,10.
MCKENZIE, LAFAYETTE. reg 5, co F, enl 9/18/62 Licking Station, house 825, s 3.
MCKENZIE, OLIVER. reg 5, co F, enl 9/18/62 Licking Station, house 824, s 3.
MEADE, LEVI. reg 5, co K, enl 12/14/61 Middle Creek, rem not on AG or CSR, absent sick at muster out, house 524, s 21.
MEEK, DAVIS. reg 10, co D, enl 4/24/63 Piketon, rem paroled Louisa 5/11/65, house 326, s 3,10.
MEEK, ISAAC. reg 5, co K, enl 9/12/62 Salyersville, dis 10/20/62 Hazel Green, reg 10, co K, enl 1/1/64 Tazewell Co. VA, rem not on AG or CSR, paroled 5/65 Louisa, house 346, s 21.
MOLLETT, JAMES W. reg 5, co E, enl 10/19/61 Prestonsburg, house 258, s 3.
MOLLETT, LEVI. reg 10, co D, enl 12/1/63 Tazewell VA, rem not on AG or CSR, paroled 5/11/65, house 259, s 21.
MORGAN, JACKSON. reg 13, co F, r cpl, enl 10/14/62 mouth of Salt Lick, Floyd Co., rem may be Floyd Co. resident, house 486, s 3,21.
MURPHY, ROBERT. reg 10, co G, r cpl, enl 3/21/63 Buchanan Co. VA, reg 2VSL, co D, r cpl, house 314, s 3,10,14.
MUSIC, ARCHIBALD. reg 5, co E, enl 10/19/61 Prestonsburg, house 299, s 3.
MUSICK, C. MILTON. reg 5, co E, enl 10/19/61 Prestonsburg, house 299, s 3.

O

O'BRYAN, WILLIAM. reg 5, co K, enl 12/14/61 Middle Creek, dis 10/20/62 Hazel Green, rem not on AG or CSR, house 537, s 21.
OSBORNE, ANDREW J. reg 5, co K, enl 12/14/61 Camp Recovery, near Prestonsburg, dis 10/20/62 Hazel Green, house 625, s 1,3.

P

PELPHREY, DANIEL. reg 5, co H, enl 10/25/61 Prestonsburg, rem re-enlisted co D, 9/11/62 Licking Station, des 3/1/63, house 749 or 781, s 3.
PELPHREY, DAVID. reg 5, co F, enl 9/14/62 Licking Station, reg FR, enl 10/10/62 Morgan Co., rem des 5/16/63, house 851, s 3,36.
PELPHREY, ISAAC. reg 5, co F, enl 9/11/62 Licking Station, house 823, s 3.
PELPHREY, JAMES. reg 5, co C, enl 10/25/61 Prestonsburg, house 751, s 3.
PELPHREY, JOHN. reg 5, co H, enl 10/25/61 Prestonsburg, rem re-enlisted co F, r cpl, enl 9/17/62 Licking Station, house 823 or 853, s 3.
PELPHREY, JOHN W. reg 5, co F r 2nd cpl, enl 9/17/62 Licking Station, house 823 or 853, s 3.
PELPHREY, LEWIS. reg 5, co D, r cpl, enl 9/11/62 Licking Station, rem trans from co F, d 2/22/63 Jonesville VA of disease, house 749, s 3.
PENNINGTON, CLABORN. reg 5, co K, enl 12/14/61 Camp Recovery, house 811, s 3.
PENNINGTON, DAVID. reg 5, co K, enl 12/14/61 Camp Recovery, dis 10/20/62 Hazel Green, house 721, s 1,3.
PENNINGTON, JAMES. reg FR, enl 10/6/62 Johnson Co., reg 7ConfCav, co G, house 821, s 3,12,36.

PENNINGTON, JOSHUA. reg 5, co K, enl 12/14/61 Camp Recovery, dis 10/20/62 Hazel Green, sandy hair, gray eyes, florid skin, 5-11, rem cap 10/22/63 Magoffin Co., released on oath 6/12/65, residence may be Louisa, house 813, s 1,3.
PENNINGTON, MILTON. reg 5, co K enl 10/25/61 Prestonsburg, dis 10/20/62 Hazel Green, house 721, s 1,3.
PENNINGTON, WILLIAM. reg 13, co K, enl 8/18/63 Lee Co. VA, house 813, s 3,21,31.
PERRY, GEORGE WASHINGTON. reg 5, co E, dis 10/20/62 Hazel Green, rem not on AG or CSR, present 1/62 & 6/62, house 628, s 21.
PICKLESIMER, WILLIAM. reg 5, co F, 5th sgt, enl 9/18/62 Licking Station, house 827, s 3.
PRESTON, HENRY. reg FR, enl 10/8/62 Johnson Co., rem des 10/16/02, house 32, s 3.
PRESTON, MOSES COBY JR. reg 10, co B, enl 10/21/63, dis 12/24/64, rem not on AG or CSR, dis for illness, house 11, s 21.
PRINCE, ELIAS. reg 5, co K, enl 12/14/61 Camp Recovery, Prestonsburg, dis 10/20/62 Hazel Green, house 644, s 1,3.

R

RAMEY, SAMUEL. reg 5, co C, enl 9/15/62 West Liberty, rem des 10/23/62 Bath Co., house 434, s 3.
REED, JOHN. reg 5, co B, enl 10/25/61 Prestonsburg, dis 10/20/62 Hazel Green, reg FR, enl 3/26/63 Carter Co., rem cap 5/28/63 in Morgan Co. or Lawrence Co., received Camp Chase OH 6/14/63, exch 12/25/63 Point Lookout MD, age 17, light hair, dark skin, 5-9, house 799, s 1,3,21,36.
RICE, ANDREW J. reg 5, co F, enl 9/11/62 Licking Station, house 116, s 3.
RIGSBY, JOHN H. reg 5, co K, enl 12/14/61 Camp Recovery, dis 10/20/62 Hazel Green, rem leg severely burned night before Battle of Middle Creek, rejoined unit before 9/1/62, house 645, s 3,21.
RIGSBY, THOMAS T. reg 5, co K, enl 10/25/61 Prestonsburg, house 645, s 1,3,21.
ROBERTSON (ROBINSON), JAMES. reg 7ConfCav, co G, house 139, s 12.
ROSS, STEPHEN. reg 5, co D, enl 9/22/62 Licking Station, rem trans from co F, des Camp Noah VA 11/20/62, house 605, s 3.
ROWLAND, JOHN. reg 5, co E, enl 10/20/61 Prestonsburg, house 77, s 3.

S

SALYER, BENJAMIN. reg 5, co F, enl 9/20/62 Licking Station, house 587 or 648, s.3.
SALYER, DAVID J. reg 10, co B, enl 1/30/63 West Liberty, rem des 1/64, house 783, s 3.
SALYER, HENDERSON. reg FR, enl 10/8/62 Johnson Co., rem des 10/62, house 696, s 3,21.
SALYER, JOHN. reg 5, co C, enl 8/19/62 Hansonville VA, rem wounded 7/22/64, house 699, s 1,3.
SALYER, MARSHALL LANEY. reg FR, enl 10/8/62 Johnson Co., rem des 10/62, house 588, s 3,36.
SALYER, RILEY. reg 5, co F, enl 9/14/62 Licking Station, reg 10, co B, age 17, dark hair, blue eyes, light skin, 5-6, rem cap Floyd Co. 5/2/63, taken to Johnson's Island OH, joined U.S. service 2/5/64, house 587, s 1,3,21.
SEGRAVES, WALTER. reg 5, co K, enl 12/14/61 Camp Recovery, house 618, s 3.
SEGRAVES, WILLIAM. reg 5, co K, enl 12/14/61 Camp Recovery, house 622, s 3.
SEGRAVES, WILLIAM L. reg 5, co K, enl 12/14/61 Camp Recovery, age 34, black hair, blue eyes, dark skin, 5-3, house 621, s 3.
SELVAGE, ISAAC. reg 5, co K, enl 12/14/61 Camp Recovery, rem d 3/7/62 Moccasin VA, house 433, s 3.

SHERMAN, THOMAS J. reg 5, co E, enl 10/26/61 Prestonsburg, rem cap Floyd Co. 5/15/63, house 652, s 1,3.

SKAGGS, JOHN. reg 5, co F, enr 9/20/62 Licking Station, house 626, s 3.

SKAGGS, THOMAS. reg 5, co K, enl 12/14/61 Camp Recovery, reg FR, enl 10/8/62 Johnson Co., rem des 11/62, house 627, s 3,36.

SPARKS, DANIEL. reg FR, enl 5/14/63 Johnson Co., house 629, s 3.

SPARKS, JESSE. reg 5, co K, enl 12/14/61 Camp Recovery, rem cap 1/13/62 Johnson Co., house 630, s 1,3.

SPARKS, NATHAN. reg 5, co K, enl 12/14/61 Camp Recovery, house 605, s 3.

SPARKS, WILLIAM HENRY. reg 5, co K, enl 12/14/61 Camp Recovery, reg 7ConfCav, co G, rem took part in 1864 Paintsville raid, house 604, s 3,12,36.

SPEARS, GEORGE W. reg 5, co E, enl 10/28/61 Prestonsburg, dis 10/20/62 Hazel Green, reg 25VaCav, co K, enl 6/1/63 Scott Co. VA, black hair, gray eyes, 5-8, rem reg 5 service not on AG or CSR, taken prisoner in Johnson Co., took oath in Lawrence Co., 5/64, house 195, s 21, Lambert 25th Virginia Cavalry.

SPEARS, MOSES. reg 5 co E, enl 10/28/61 Prestonsburg, age 21, dark hair & skin, blue eyes, 5-9, rem cap Morgan Co. 5/18/63, took oath 4/29/65, house 195, s 1,3.

SPEARS, THOMAS J. or W. reg 10, co D, enl 9/1/62 Piketon, age 24, dark hair & skin, gray eyes, 5-9, rem cap Pike Co. 5/63, took oath 4/28/65 at Louisa, house 195, s 1,21.

SPEARS, WILEY. reg 10, co B, age 31, dark hair & skin, blue eyes, 5-7, rem cap Floyd Co. 4/15/63, house 197, s 1.

SPENCER, GEORGE W. reg 5, co H, enl 10/26/61 Prestonsburg, dis 10/20/62 Hazel Green, house 430, s 3.

SPRADLIN, JAMES H. reg 5, co E, enl 10/19/61 Prestonsburg, rem not on AG or CSR, house 49 or 95, s 21.

SPRIGGS, HIRAM S. reg 5, co E, enl 10/19/61 Prestonsburg, house 329, s 3.

STAFFORD, JAMES. reg 5, co D, rem wounded in arm at Middle Creek 1/10/62, house 35, s 1,3.

STAPLETON, ALLEN. reg 5, co D, enl 9/20/62 Licking Station, rem trans from co F, des Camp Nelson 11/20/63, house 707, s 3.

STAPLETON, JOSEPH. reg 5, co D, enl 9/16/62 Licking Station, rem trans from co F, des at Camp Nest VA, house 648, s 3.

STAPLETON, WILLIAM S. reg 5, co C, enl 9/18/62 Salyersville, rem des 12/23/62, house 698, s 3.

STRONG, HIRAM. reg 13, r surgeon, enl 11/2/62, house 47, s 3,21.

STRONG, JULIUS C. reg 13, co H, enl 4/15/63 Perry Co., house 47, s 21.

T

TACKETT, WILLIAM. reg 5, co K enl 12/14/61 Camp Recovery, dis 10/20/62 Hazel Green, house 722 or 852, s 1,3.

TACKETT, WILLIAM. reg 5, co F, enl 9/18/62 Licking Station, house 722 or 852, s 3.

TACKETT, WILLIAM. reg 5, co K, enl 12/14/61 Camp Recovery, dis 10/20/62 Hazel Green, house 722 or 852, s 1,3.

TRIMBLE, WILLIAM H. reg 5, co A, enl 10/21/61 West Liberty, house 776, s 3.

V

VANHOOSE, ELIPHUS P. reg 5, co K, enl 12/14/61 Middle Creek, reg 10, co B, enl 1/1/64 Jeffersonville VA, rem not on AG or CSR, cap 6/15/64 Johnson Co., paroled 4/25/64 Louisa, house 450, s 21.

W

WALTERS, JOHN CALVIN. reg 5, co E, enl 9/12/62 Salyersville, dis 10/20/62 Hazel Green, reg 13, co K, enl 8/18/63 Lee Co. VA, rem reg 5 service not on AG or CSR, surr Mt. Sterling 4/30/65, house 463, s 1,3,21,26,31.
WARD, DAVID B. reg 5, co I enl 12/28/61 Paintsville, dis 10/20/62 Hazel Green, house 257, s 1,3.
WARD, GREENVILLE. reg 5, co E, enl 9/12/62 Prestonsburg, dis 10/20/62 Hazel Green, reg 10, co B, enl 1/1/64 Jeffersonville VA, rem not on AG or CSR, cap 6/15/64 Johnson or Lawrence Co., house 318, s 21.
WARD, JAMES APPERSON. reg 5, co E, enl 9/12/62 Salyersville, dis 10/20/62 Hazel Green, rem not on AG or CSR, house 515, s 21.
WARD, WILLIAM JEFFERSON. reg 5, co E, enl 12/28/61 Paintsville, dis 10/20/62 Hazel Green, rem not on AG or CSR, cap Middle Creek 1/10/62, surr Charleston WV 6/9/65, house 64, 331, 465, 466, 490 or 515, s 21.
WEBB, AARON. reg FR, enl 11/6/62 Johnson Co. des 10/27/62, house 738, s 1,3,36.
WEBB, JONATHAN. reg 5, co K, enl 12/14/61 Camp Recovery, house 342, 469, or 513, s 3.
WELLS, CHARLES MORGAN. reg 5, co E, enl 9/29/62 Salyersville, rem not on AG or CSR, house 185, s 21.
WELLS, DAVID C. reg 5, co K, enl 12/14/61 Middle Creek, rem not on AG or CSR, house 191, s 21.
WELLS, JAMES W. reg 5, co E, enl 12/28/61 Paintsville, rem not on AG or CSR, house 191, s 21.
WELLS, JOHN PRESTON. reg 5, co E, enl 12/28/61 Paintsville, dis 10/20/62 Hazel Green, re-enlisted 9/12/62 Salyersville, reg 13, co D, enl 8/13/63 Lee Co. VA, dark hair, hazel eyes, 5-8, rem reg 5 service not on AG or CSR, trans to co F 9/1/63 Floyd Co., back to co D 4/7/64, surr Lawrence Co. OH 5/15/65, house 187, s 1,3,21,26,31.
WELLS, MARCUS L. K. reg 10, co D, enl 4/24/63 Piketon, house 325, s 3,10.
WELLS, MOSES. reg 5, co E, r fifer, enl 12/28/61 Paintsville, rem not on AG or CSR, house 325, s 21.
WELLS, WILLIAM. reg 5, co H, enl 12/28/61 Paintsville, rem d Gladesville VA 3/8/62, house 174 or 325, s 1,3.
WELLS, WILLIAM GREEN. reg 5, co E, r 5th sgt, enl 12/28/61 Paintsville, re-enlisted 9/12/62 Salyersville, dis 10/20/62 Hazel Green, reg 54VaInf, co E, enl 11/21/61 Cedar Bluff, VA, rem reg 5 service not on AG or CSR, des 12/28/61 Paintsville, cap Morgan Co. 11/7/62, surr 5/11/65 Louisa & 6/12/65 Charleston WV, house 325, s Sherwood & Weaver, 54th Virginia Infantry, 21.
WHEELER, HENRY D. reg 5, co A, enl 10/25/61 Prestonsburg, rem d Moccasin VA 3/24/62, house 389, s 3.
WILLIAMS, ANDREW J. reg 5, co K, r 4th sgt, enl 12/14/61 Camp Recovery, dis 10/20/62 Hazel Green, house 729, s 1,3.
WILLIAMS, DAVID. reg 5, co B, enl 10/25/61 Prestonsburg, gray hair & eyes, dark skin, 5-11, dis 4/20/62 for rheumatism disability, reg FR, enl 11/6/62 Johnson Co., rem des 10/27/62, house 817, s 1,3,36.
WILLIAMS, ELLIOTT. reg 5, co K, r cpl, enl 12/14/61 Camp Recovery, dis 10/20/62 Hazel Green, house 735, s 1,3.

WILLIAMS, ELIPHUS P. reg 5, co D, r 3rd sgt, enl 9/4/62 Salyersville, rem trans to co F, wounded Dallas GA 5/28/64, house 747, s 3.

WILLIAMS, HARDIN H. reg 5, co K, r 3rd sgt, enl 12/14/61 Camp Recovery, dis 10/20/62 Hazel Green, house 736, s 1,3.

WILLIAMS, JAMES. reg FR, enl 11/6/62 Johnson Co., rem des 10/27/62, house 803 or 822, s 3.

WILLIAMS, JAMES HADEN. reg 5, co A, r musician, enl 10/21/61 West Liberty, dis 12/19/61, brown hair, hazel eyes, dark skin, 5-7, house 803 or 822, s 1,3.

WILLIAMS, JOHN. reg 5, co G, cap Irvine 6/20/63, received Camp Chase OH 6/26/63, sent to Point Lookout MD 10/30/63, house 820, s 1,21.

WILLIAMS, JOHN B. reg 5, co K, r 1st lt, enl 12/14/61 Camp Recovery, dis 10/20/62 Hazel Green, house 735, s 1,3.

WILLIAMS, LUCAS P. reg 5, co K, r musician, enl 12/14/61 Camp Recovery, rem d 1/29/62 on Beaver Creek, KY, house 723, s 1,3.

WILLIAMS, MOSES. reg FR, enl 11/6/62 Johnson Co., rem des 10/27/62, house 739, s 3.

WILLIAMS, NOAH H. reg FR, enl 11/6/62 Johnson Co., rem des 10/27/62, house 718, s 3.

WILLIAMS, ROBERT. reg 5, co K, enl 12/14/61 Camp Recovery, rem des 1/7/62 Abbott Creek, reg FR, enl 11/6/62 Johnson Co., rem des 10/27/62, house 601 or 610, s 1,3,36.

WILLIAMS, ROBERT R. reg 5, co K, r 5th sgt, enl 12/14/61 Camp Recovery, Prestonsburg, dis 10/20/62 Hazel Green, rem prom to 5th sgt 10/1/62, house 601 or 610, s 1,3.

WILLIAMS, THOMAS A. reg 5, co K, enl 12/14/61 Camp Recovery, Prestonsburg, dis 10/20/62 Hazel Green, house 610, s 1,3.

WILLIAMS, THOMAS J. reg 5, co A, enl 10/20/61 Prestonsburg, dis 10/20/62 Hazel Green, rem drummer from 3/10/62, re-enlisted for the war, house 739, s 1,3.

WILLIAMS, WILLIAM R. reg 5, co K, r cpl, enl 12/14/61 Camp Recovery, dis 10/20/62 Hazel Green, house 735, s 1,3.

WRIGHT, BAYLESS. reg 5, co K, enl 12/14/61 Camp Recovery, dis 10/20/62 Hazel Green, house 730, s 1,3.

LAWRENCE COUNTY CONFEDERATE SOLDIERS

A

ADAMS, JAMES FRANKLIN. reg 5, co C, enl 12/11/61 Prestonsburg, dis 10/20/62 Hazel Green, house 115, 540 or 674, s 1,3.
ADAMS, WILLIAM F. reg 5, co F, enl 9/15/62 Licking Station, house 115, 541 or 674, s 3.
ADAMS, WILLIAM P. reg 5, co C, enl 12/11/61 Prestonsburg, dis 10/20/62 Hazel Green, house 115, 541 or 674, s 1,3.
AUXIER, JOHN M. reg 5, co C, enl 10/19/61 Prestonsburg, dis 10/20/62 Hazel Green, reg FR, enl 12/1/62 Lawrence Co., cap Buffalo Furnace 10/11/63, taken to Louisville prison, house 302, s 1,3,36.

B

BARKER, HARVEY. reg 5, co D, enl 10/26/61 Paintsville, dis 10/20/62 Hazel Green, house 476, s 1,3.
BATES, DAVID. reg 8VaCav, co K, r cpl, enl 8/20/62 Wayne Co. VA, house 1200, s 3,7,16.
BERRY, JOHN L. reg 5, co C, enl 12/16/61 West Liberty, rem wounded 6/23/64, house 683, s 3.
BLACKBURN, ALLEN. reg 10, enl 8/16/64 Johnson Co., rem not on AG or CSR, cap Lawrence Co. 2/6/65, house 874, s 21.
BLANKENSHIP, JOHN. reg 5, co Riffe's, enl 11/61 Lawrence Co., rem not on AG or CSR, cap 11/26/61 Emmanuel Brammer's farm, taken to Newport Barracks, house 298, s 21.
BOGGS, HUGH. reg 5, co D, enl 12/26/61 Paintsville, house 398, s 3.
BOGGS, JAMES. reg 5, co D, enl 12/26/61 Carter Co. or Prestonsburg, dis 10/20/62 Hazel Green, house 380, s 3.
BOGGS, JOHN R. reg FR, enl 10/3/62 Carter Co., rem des 10/22/62, house 661, s 3.
BOOTON, RALPH S. reg 1BatCav, co C, enl 10/21/61 Prestonsburg, reg 10, co D, r sgt major, enl 4/1/63 Pike Co., rem wounded & cap at Cynthiana 6/11/64, exch 3/11/65, surr at Louisa 4/65, house 351, s 2,3,10.
BRADLEY, SYLVESTER. reg 5, co C, enl 10/19/61 Prestonsburg, dis 10/20/62 Hazel Green, house 120, s 1,3.
BRAMMER, EMMANUEL. reg 5, co Riffe's, enl 11/61 Lawrence Co., rem not on AG or CSR, KIA 11/26/61 skirmish at Brammer's farm, Lawrence Co., house 304, s 21.
BROWN, GEORGE W. reg 5, co H, enl 10/21/61 Prestonsburg, rem d of disease camp hospital 3/25/62, house 303, s 1,3.
BURGESS, JOHN G. W. reg 5, co G, enl 11/5/61 Pike Co., rem in hospital 8/18/62, returned to duty 3/20/63, house 745, s 1,3.

C

CARTER, GEORGE W. reg 5, co G, enl 12/29/61 Camp Hager, house 118, s 3.
CARTER, JOHN A. reg 5, co K, enl 12/14/61 Camp Recovery, rem des 10/22/62, house 205, s 1,3.
CARTER, JOHN W. reg 5, co L, enl 12/14/61 Camp Recovery, rem des 10/22/62, house 134, s 1,3.
CHAFIN, JOHN M. reg FR, enl 9/24/62 Lawrence Co., house 333, s 3.
CHAPMAN, DAVID C. reg 5, co F, enl 11/1/61 Whitesburg, reg 13, co A, enl 11/1/62 Whitesburg, rem reg 5 service not on AG or CSR, house 718, s 3,21,31.
CHAPMAN, RYBURN. reg 7ConfCav, co G, rem killed 4/12/65, house 1094, s 12.

CLAY, GEORGE WILSON. reg FR, enl 5/27/63 Carter Co., house 53, s 3,36.

COMBS, DANIEL. reg 5, co G, enl 12/29/61 Camp Hager, dis 10/20/62, reg FR, reg 7ConfCav, age 19, brown hair, hazel eyes, sandy skin, 5-8, rem cap 4/28/63 Magoffin Co., sent to Camp Chase OH 4/30/63, house 471, s 1,3,36.

COMBS, MATTHEW. reg 5, co K, enl 10/29/61 Beaver Hill, dis 10/20/62, reg FR, enl 3/4/63 Breathitt Co., house 471, s 1,3,36.

CYRUS, WILLIAM J. reg FR, enl 11/18/62 Lawrence Co. age 28, dark hair, blue eyes, 5-8, dis 2/12/63, rem not of AG or CSR, residence stated in s 36, house n/c, s 1,36.

D

DIAMOND, GEORGE R. reg 5, co C, r capt, enl 10/19/61 Prestonsburg, rem prom from 2nd lt to capt 2/4/62, reg 10, co D, r col, rem prom from capt to major 10/9/63, to lt col 8/3/64, to col 10/2/64, cap Athens GA 5/8/65, house 160, s 1,3,10.

DIAMOND, JAMES W. reg 10, co G, r sgt, rem cap Mt. Sterling 6/9/64, house 160, s 1.

DIAMOND, JOHN G. reg 5, co C, cpl, enl 10/19/61 Prestonsburg, dis 10/20/62 Hazel Green, reg 10, co D, E, r 2nd lt, enl 10/26/62 Piketon, rem app 4th sgt 3/5/63, app 2nd lt 6/8/64, trans to co E 5/1/64, wounded in left lung & captured at Mt. Sterling 6/9/64, taken to Camp Chase OH, house 160, s 1,3,10.

DYER, JAMES. reg 5, co F, K, enl 12/14/61 or 9/30/62 Prestonsburg or Licking Station, des Camp Hager 1/6/62, house 345, s 1,3.

E

ENDICOTT, GABRIEL. reg 5, co E, enl 10/26/62 Prestonsburg, dark hair, eyes & skin, 5-10, rem took oath 3/30/64, house 902, s 1,3.

F

FIELDS, PRESTON. reg 5, co G, r 2nd sgt, enl 12/19/61 Camp Hager, dis 10/20/62 Hazel Green, reg FR, enl 2/1/63 Lawrence Co., reg 10, co M, rem clothing receipts 9/8/64 & 9/25/64, house 486, s 1,3,36.

FIFE, JOHN. reg 10, co D, enl 8/15/63 Piketon, rem des 10/1/63, house 423 or 424, s 3,10.

FRALEY, DANIEL B. reg 5, co E, enl 10/26/61 Prestonsburg, house 939, s 1,3.

FRALEY, WILLIAM B. reg 5, co D, enl 10/19/61 Piketon or Carter Co., dis 10/20/62 Hazel Green, reg FR, enl 11/28/62 Carter Co., house 939, s 1,3,36.

FRASHER, ANDREW J. reg 16VaCav, co E, enl 9/5/62 Wayne Co. VA, house 1178, s 3,17.

FRASHER, GEORGE W. reg 16VaCav, co E, enl Wayne Co. VA, rem cap 10/26/64 taken to Camp Douglas, Chicago IL, joined U.S. Army, house 1178, s 17.

FRASHER, GRANVILLE H. reg 8VaCav, co K, enl 8/13/61 Wayne Co. VA, dark skin & hair, blue eyes, 5-11, rem cap Lawrence Co. took oath at Louisville & sent north 11/20/63, house 1216, s 3,7,16.

FULLER, JOHN BENTON. reg 5, co C, enl 10/26/61 Prestonsburg, dis 10/20/62 Hazel Green, reg 10, co D, enl 6/16/61 Piketon, rem d 5/10/64 Saltville VA of sickness, house 200, s 1,3,10.

G

GAMBRELL, HENRY. reg 5, co C, enl 9/18/62 West Liberty, rem des 10/22/62 West Liberty, house 405, s 3.

GAMBRELL, JOHN. reg 5, co C, enl 9/1/62 West Liberty, rem des 10/23/62 West Liberty, house 404 or 405, s 3.
GILLUM, PETER H. reg 5, co F, enl 9/11/62 Licking Station, house 420, s 3.
GRIFFITH, DAVID. reg 5, co C, enl 10/19/61 Prestonsburg, dis 10/20/62 Hazel Green, reg 10, co M, rem clothing receipts 9/8/64, 9/14/64 & 9/25/64, house 320, s 1,3.
GRIFFITH, JOHN. reg 5, co C, enl 10/19/61 Prestonsburg, dis 10/20/62 Hazel Green, house 305, s 1,3.
GRIFFITH, JOHN. reg 5, co C, enl 12/29/61 Camp Hager VA, dis 10/20/62 Hazel Green, reg FR, enl 11/22/62 Lawrence Co., house 37 or 693, s 1,3,36.
GRIFFITH, ROBERT. reg 5, co C, enl 10/19/61 Prestonsburg, rem cap 1/9/62 Prestonsburg, exch 8/25/62, house 320, s 1,3.

H

HALL, ELISHA. reg 5, co D, enl 12/26/61 Paintsville, dis 10/20/62 Hazel Green, house 228, s 1,3.
HAY, JAMES. reg 5, co E, enl 1/2/62 Morgan Co., house 451, s 3.
HAY, JOHN. reg 5, co F, enl 9/14/62 Licking Station, house 455, s 3.
HAY, THOMAS A. reg 5, co F, enl 9/9/62 Licking Station, house 454, s 3.
HAY, WILLIAM. reg 5, co G, enl 1/2/62 Morgan Co., house 456, s 3.
HEWLETT, JOHN A. reg 5, co C, enl 10/19/61 Prestonsburg, rem d 1/31/62 Whitesburg, house 197, s 1,3.
HINKLE, JOHN. reg 5, r asst surgeon, rem not on AG or CSR, app before 3/1/62, res 12/2/62, house 897, s 21.
HOLBROOK, CALVIN. reg 5, co K, enl 12/14/61 Middle Creek, dis 10/20/62 Hazel Green, rem not on AG or CSR, house 96, s 21.
HOLBROOK, JOHN F. reg 5, co F, enl 9/20/62 Licking Station, house 413, s 3.
HOLBROOK, JOHN H. reg 5, co D, enl 12/26/61 Paintsville, dis 10/20/62 Hazel Green, house 406, s 1,3.
HOLBROOK, WILLIAM H. reg 5, co K, enl 12/14/61 Camp Recovery, house 417, s 3.

J

JACKSON, ELIJAH. reg 5, co G, enl 12/29/61 Camp Hager, reg FR, enl 9/16/62 Lawrence Co., rem des 4/16/63, house 487, s 3,36.
JACKSON, JAMES. reg 5, co G, enl 12/29/61 Camp Hager, house 1186, s 3.
JOHNSON, ALFRED. reg FR, rem des 10/20/62, house 479, s 3,36.
JOHNSON, HENRY. reg FR, enl 10/1/62 Carter Co., rem cap 5/11/63, house 503, s 3,36.
JOHNSON, HENRY. reg 5, co G, enl 1/4/62 Morgan Co., house 660, s 3.
JOHNSON, JAMES C. reg FR, enl 5/14/63 Carter Co., house 591, s 3.
JOHNSON, JAMES T. reg 5, co G, enl 1/1/62 Morgan Co., rem re-enlisted 10/20/62, house 1041, s 1,3.
JOHNSON, MASON. reg 5, co K, enl 12/14/61 Camp Recovery, near Prestonsburg, dis 10/20/62 Hazel Green, reg FR, enl 5/14/63 Carter Co., rem re-enlisted 10/20/62, cap 3/29/63 Johnson Co., paroled Camp Chase 5/13/63, house 452, s 1,3,36.
JORDAN, JOHN. reg 5, co C, enl 10/26/61 Prestonsburg, house 227, s 3.

K

KAZEE, HARVEY. reg 5, co D, enl 10/19/61 Lawrence Co., gray eyes, sandy hair, 6-4, rem dis for disability 12/28/61 Paintsville, house 613, s 3,21.

KAZEE, JOHN. reg 5, co D, enl 10/19/61 Prestonsburg, house 616, s 1,21.

KELLY, GEORGE W. reg 5, co D, enl 10/19/61 Lawrence Co., dis 10/20/62 Hazel Green, house 410, s 1,3.

KELLY, JOHN. reg 5, co K, enl 12/14/61 Camp Recovery, house 643, s 3.

KELLY, MATHIAS. reg 5, co K, enl 12/14/61, dis 10/20/62 Hazel Green, house 411, s 1,3.

KITCHEN, WILLIAM. reg FR, enl 10/29/62 Lawrence Co., rem des 2/63, house 240, s 3,36.

L

LEMMONS, WILLIAM H. reg 5, co D, enl 10/19/61 Piketon or Carter Co. or Harrison Co., dis 10/20/62 Hazel Green, house 656, s 1,3.

LIVINGSTON, JOHN H. reg 2MR, co A, enl 9/1/62 Morgan Co., house 557, s 3,21.

LYON, AMOS. reg 5, co D, enl 9/22/62 Licking Station, rem trans from co E, des 3/1/63, house 409, s 3.

LYON, AZEL. reg 5, co K, enl 12/14/61 Camp Recovery, dis 10/20/62 Hazel Green, reg FR, enl 2/1/63 Lawrence Co., house 480, s 1,3,36.

LYON, JESSE EPHRAIM. reg 5, co K, enl 12/14/61 Camp Recovery, Prestonsburg, dis 10/20/62 Hazel Green, reg FR, enl 12/14/62 Johnson Co., reg 10, co M, r 1st sgt, house 478, s 1,3,36.

LYON, JESSE. reg 5, co F, enl 9/20/62 Licking Station, reg FR, enl 10/22/62 Magoffin Co., house 447, s 3,36.

LYON, MARION. reg 5, co K, 3rd sgt, enl 12/14/61 Camp Recovery, dis 10/20/62 Hazel Green, reg FR, enl 10/23/62 Johnson Co., reg 7ConfCav, house 614, s 1,3,12,36.

LYON, REASON. reg 5, co K, r 2nd sgt, enl 12/14/61 Camp Recovery, dis 10/20/62 Hazel Green, reg FR, enl 10/20/62 Johnson Co., reg 7ConfCav, co G, house 614, s 1,3,12,36.

LYON, WESLEY. reg 5, co C, enl 10/19/61 Prestonsburg, dis 10/20/62 Hazel Green, reg FR, enl 10/20/62 Lawrence Co., reg 10 co M, rem reg 10 service not on AG, clothing receipt 9/14/64, 9/25/64, residence stated on s 36, house n/c, s 1,3,36.

LYON, WILLIAM. reg FR, enl 9/23/62 Carter Co., house 593, s 3,36.

M

MARCUM, ANDREW J. reg 5, co C, enl 12/27/61 Camp Hager VA, dis 6/13/62, house 685, s 3.

MARCUM, WATSON A. reg 1VSL, co A, B, enl 12/31/62 Smyth Co. VA, rem taken prisoner in Wayne Co. VA 2/28/64, received Louisville Military Prison 3/6/64, sent to Camp Chase 3/9/64, d 3/30/64 Camp Chase OH of pneumonia, buried grave no. 126, house 81, s 3,14.

MARCUM, WILLIAM. reg 5, co C, enl 12/27/61 Camp Hager VA, house 81, s 3.

MCCORMICK, GEORGE W. reg 5, co C, r cpl, enl 10/19/61 Prestonsburg, dis 10/20/62, Hazel Green, house 126, s 1,3.

MCCORMICK, MEREDITH. reg 5, co C, enl 10/19/61 Prestonsburg, dis 10/20/62 Hazel Green, house 126, s 1,3.

MCGUIRE, JOEL C. reg 5, co C, enl 9/12/62 Salyersville, age 29, dark hair, eyes & skin, 5-8, rem cap 5/21/63 Magoffin Co., house 91, s 1,3.

MOORE, JOHN W. reg 7ConfCav, dark hair & skin, yellow eyes, 5-5, rem took oath at Louisa 4/30/64, house 269 or 1020, s 12.

MURPHY, JOHN. reg 5, co Riffe's, enl 11/61 Lawrence Co., reg 7ConfCav, co G, rem reg 5 service not on AG or CSR, cap 11/26/61 Brammer's farm Lawrence Co., taken to Newport Barracks, killed in Lawrence Co. in 1865, house 301, s 12,21, Tree Shaker 7/86.

O

OSBORNE, JAMES. reg 5, co G, enl 11/5/62 Morgan Co., house 506, s 3.
OSBORNE, JAMES L. reg 5, co K, enl 1/5/62 Morgan Co., rem re-enlisted 10/22/62, house 512, s 1,3.

P

PENNINGTON, ANDREW. reg 2MR, co D, r sgt, enl 8/26/62 Logan Co. VA, house 512, s 1,3.
PENNINGTON, HENRY C. reg FR, enl 3/7/63 Lawrence Co., reg 10, gray hair & eyes, dark skin, 6-1, rem took oath 6/8/65, house 508, s 1,3,21,36.
PENNINGTON, HUSE L. reg FR, enl 1/5/63 Lawrence Co., house 658, s 3,36.
PENNINGTON, JAMES R. reg FR, enl 10/6/62 Johnson Co., rem des 10/16/62, house 509, s 3,36.
PENNINGTON, JOHN M. reg 5, co D, enl 12/31/61 Lawrence Co., rem des 1/62, reg 2MR, co D, enl 8/26/62 Logan Co. VA, house 515 or 520, s 3.
PENNINGTON, JOHN P. reg FR, enl 3/7/63 Lawrence Co., residence stated on s 36, house n/c, s 1,3,36.
PENNINGTON, JOHN W. reg 2MR, co D, enl 8/26/62 Logan Co. VA, rem des Lawrence Co. 11/16/62, house 667, s 1,3.
PENNINGTON, SOLOMON. reg FR, enl 9/12/62 Carter Co., house 659, s 3,36.
PENNINGTON, WILLIAM NELSON JR. reg 13, co K, enl Lee Co. VA, house 511, s 1,31.
PERKINS, ISAAC S. reg 5, co C, enl 10/25/61 Prestonsburg, dis 10/20/62 Hazel Green, house 649, s 1,3.
PETERS, GARRED or JARRET SEE. reg 8VaCav, co K, enl 9/15/63 Wayne Co. VA, age 26, fair skin, dark hair & eyes, 5-8, rem took oath 4/4/65 Charleston WV, house 944, s 2,7,16.
PETERS, WILLIAM D. reg 8VaCav, co K, enl 9/15/63 Wayne Co. WV, dark skin, brown hair, blue eyes, 5-7, cap 12/21/64 Lacey Springs, rem POW at Pt. Lookout MD 1/3/65, took oath & released 6/16/65, house 944, s 2,16.
PHILLIPS, MEREDITH. reg 5, co K, enl 12/14/61 Camp Recovery, dis 10/20/62 Hazel Green, rem re-enlisted 10/22/62, reg FR, enl 12/14/62 Johnson Co., house 597, s 1,3,36.
POWERS, JAMES. reg 5, co H, enl 10/21/61 Prestonsburg, house 338, s 1,3.
PRINCE, JOHN. reg 5, co K, enl 12/14/61 Camp Recovery, rem d 1/28/62 at Martin's, KY, house 443 or 534, s 3.

R

RIFE, JEREMIAH. reg 5, co Riffe's, r capt, enl 11/61 Lawrence Co., reg 2MR, co D, r 2nd lt, enl 8/26/62 Logan Co. VA, age 35, dark hair, blue eyes, light skin, 6-0, rem reg 5 service not on AG or CSR, prom from 1st sgt to 2nd lt 3/21/63, cap 5/23/63 or 6/8/63 Lawrence Co., received Camp Chase OH 7/7/63, paroled 2/24/65, house 90, s 1,3,21.
RIGSBY, LARKIN. reg 5, co K, enl 9/12/62 Salyersville, dis 10/20/62 Hazel Green, age 17, light hair, gray eyes, dark skin, 5-8, rem cap Lawrence Co. 5/15/63, taken to Johnson's Island OH 6/14/63, trans to Point Lookout MD 10/30/63, took oath and released 4/11/64, house 426, s 1,3,21.
RIGSBY, MILES. reg 5, co F, enl 9/20/62 Licking Station, house 601, s 3.

RIGSBY, THOMAS. reg 5, co K, enl 12/14/61 Camp Recovery, rem d 4/12/62 Moccasin VA, house 426, s 3.

RIGSBY, THOMAS T. reg 5, co K, enl 12/14/61 Camp Recovery, dis 10/20/62 Hazel Green, age 22, light hair, blue eyes, fair skin, 5-10, rem cap Lawrence Co. 4/26/63, released on oath 4/11/64, house 599, s 1,3.

ROSE, JOHN. reg 5, co K, enl 12/14/61 Camp Recovery, dis 10/20/62, house 416 or 648, s 3.

ROSE, WILLIAM W. reg 5, co D, enl 10/19/61 Carter Co., dis 10/20/62 Hazel Green, house 416, s 1,3.

S

SAMMONS, ROLAND. reg 34VaCav, co B, enl 4/13/62 Logan Co. VA, house 923, s 2,15.

SCAGGS, LEWIS. reg 5, co K, r cpl, enl 12/14/61 Camp Recovery, dis 10/20/62 Hazel Green, house 438, s 1,3.

SCAGGS, PETER. reg 5, co D, enl 9/22/62 Prestonsburg, dis 10/20/62 Hazel Green, house 441, s 1,3.

SCOTT, WILLIAM H. reg 5, co B, enl 10/25/61 Prestonsburg, house 189, s 3.

SEAGRAVES, WILLIAM L. reg FR, age 34, dark hair, blue eyes, 5-3, rem took oath at Louisa 10/11/63, house 590, s 1,36.

SKAGGS, ANDREW. reg 5, co F, enl 9/19/62 Licking Station, house 433, s 3.

SKAGGS, MARTIN. reg 5 co F, enl 9/20/62 Licking Station, house 430 or 432, s 3.

SPARKS, HENRY W. reg 5, co G, r cpl, enl 12/29/61 Camp Hager, house 583, s 3.

SPARKS, HUGH S. reg 5, co C enl 10/26/61 Prestonsburg, dis 10/20/62 Hazel Green, prom 1st sgt 2/4/62, reg FR, enl 3/26/63 Lawrence Co., age 35, dark hair, blue eyes, 5-10, capt 9/6/62 Lawrence Co., sent to Camp Chase OH, residence stated on s 35, house n/c, s 1,3,36.

SPARKS, ISAAC NEWTON. reg 5, co K, enl 12/29/61 Camp Hager, dis 10/20/62 Hazel Green, reg FR, enl 10/22/62 Carter Co., residence stated on s 36, house n/c, s 1,3,36.

SPARKS, JOHN L. reg 5, co B, enl 10/25/61 Prestonsburg, reg FR, enl 1/10/63 Lawrence Co., house 448, s 3,36.

SPARKS, JOHN WESLEY. reg 5, co G, r 1st lt, enl 10/28/61 Camp Recovery, dis 10/20/62 Hazel Green, reg FR, r 1st lt, enl 9/13/62 Lawrence Co., cap Magoffin Co. 10/18/63, dark hair & skin, gray eyes, 5-11, released on oath Johnson's Island 5/16/65, CSR lists Blaine, Ky. as residence, house 465, s 1,3,36.

SPARKS, MARTIN. reg 5, co G, enl 12/29/61 Camp Hager, dis 10/20/62 Hazel Green, house 461, s 1,3.

SPARKS, REUBEN R. reg FR, enl 9/23/62 Lawrence Co., rem des 10/63, house 393, s 1,3,36.

STEPHENS, ISAAC. reg 5, co B, enl 10/25/61 Prestonsburg, house 476, s 3.

STEPHENS, JOHN. reg 5, co G, enl 1/1/62 Morgan Co., house 482, s 3.

T

TAYLOR, WILLIAM. reg 5, co C, enl 9/13/62 Lewis Co., house 86, s 1,3.

THOMAS, WILLIAM. reg 5, co A, enl 10/27/61 Beaver Creek, rem dis 4/7/62 Moccasin VA, because of disease of the leg, house 1073, s 1,3.

THOMPSON, FLEMING. reg 2MR, reg FR enl 9/24/62 Morgan Co. elected 1st cpl, 10/23/62, rem cap Louisa 9/12/63, took oath, house 315, s 1,3,36.

THOMPSON, JOHN. reg 5, co Riffe's, rem not on AG or CSR, KIA 12/21/61 Lawrence Co., house 1010, s 21.

THOMPSON, LINDSEY. reg 2MR, enl 8/26/62 Logan Co. VA, house 317, s 1,3.

THOMPSON, WILLIAM ALEXANDER. reg 5, co D, r cpl, enl 10/19/61 Carter Co., dis 10/20/62 Hazel Green, rem prom to cpl 1/1/62, reg FR, enl 11/26/62 Carter Co., rem cap 5/11/63 in Kentucky, house 1011, s 1,3,36.

TRIPLETT, TROY. reg 5, co C, Riffe's, enl 11/61 Lawrence Co., rem not on AG or CSR, house 693, s 1,21.

TROY, WILLIAM. reg 5, co C, rem not on AG or CSR, cap 11/8/61 Battle of Ivy Mountain, house 1202, s 21.

V

VAUGHN, WILLIAM. reg 5, co B, enl 12/25/61 Camp Hager VA, house 783, s 3.

W

WADDLE (WEDDLE), ALFRED. reg 5, co K, enl 1/6/62 Carter Co., dis 10/20/62 Hazel Green, reg FR, enl 11/1/62 Carter Co., rem des 5/18/63, house 500, s 1,3,36.

WILLIAMS, NING. reg 5, co K, enl 12/14/61 camp on Middle Creek, rem des 1/7/62 Abbott's Creek, house 595, s 1.

WOODS, ANDREW J. reg 5, co F, enl 11/1/61 Whitesburg, house 332 or 335, s 3.

WORKMAN, ALFRED. reg 8VaCav, co K, fair skin, light hair, blue eyes, 5-7, rem cap & took oath Lawrence Co. 3/30/64, house 937, s 2,15.

WRIGHT, WILLIAM W. reg 5, co C, enl 12/11/61 Prestonsburg, dis 5/31/62 Camp Calfee, age 31, dark hair & skin, blue eyes, 5-8, house 218, s 1,3.

Y

YOUNG, JESSE. reg 2MR, co D, enl 8/16/62 Logan Co. VA, clothing receipt 9/15/64, house 307, s 3,7.

LETCHER COUNTY CONFEDERATE SOLDIERS

A

ADAMS, ANDREW ABSALOM. reg 13, co A, enl 12/23/61 Whitesburg, age 20, cap 12/2/62 Whitesburg, may have served in 5th Ky. Inf., co F, but no record on CSR, house 13, s 1,3,31.

ADAMS, BENJAMIN. reg 13, co H, enl 10/18/62 Whitesburg, CSR states Letcher Co. as residence, house 334, s 3,31.

ADAMS, BENJAMIN B. reg 13, co D, r 2nd lt, enl 10/4/62 Whitesburg, elected lt 11/2/62, cap Gladesville 7/7/63, CSR states Letcher Co. as residence, house 118, s 1,3,31.

ADAMS, GEORGE WASHINGTON. reg 13, co D, enl 10/4/62 Whitesburg, CSR states Letcher Co. as residence, house 249, s 1,3,31.

ADAMS, GILBERT. reg 13, co A, enl 9/29/62 Whitesburg, age 28, brown hair, blue eyes, sallow skin, 5-6, cap Gladesville 7/7/63, taken to Camp Chase 7/20/63, to Ft. Delaware 3/14/64, took oath and released 6/9/65, house 491, s 1,3,31.

ADAMS, JAMES W. reg 5, co F, enl 11/1/61 Whitesburg, house 80, s 3.

ADAMS, JAMES WEALTH. reg 13, co G, reg 10, co D, r sgt, reg 5, co F, took oath at Louisa 4/30/65, clothing receipts 6/29/64 & 9/7/64, house 80, s 1,31.

ADAMS, JESSE. reg 13, co H, enl 10/18/62 Whitesburg, CSR states Letcher Co. as residence, house 342 or 437, s 1,3,31.

ADAMS, JESSE B. reg 13, co D, enl 10/4/62 Whitesburg, CSR states Letcher Co. as residence, house 263, s 1,3,31.

ADAMS, JOHN. reg 13, co H, enl 10/18/62 Whitesburg, CSR states Letcher Co. as residence, house n/c, s 1,3,31.

ADAMS, JOHN D. reg 5, co F, enl 11/1/61 or 11/6/61 Whitesburg, house 263, s 1, 2.

ADAMS, JOHN W. reg 13, co E, enl 10/5/62 or 10/14/62 Whitesburg, CSR states Letcher Co. as residence, house 12, 47, 313, 334, 360 or 463, s 1,3,31.

ADAMS, MOSES. reg 13, co A, enl 9/27/61 Whitesburg, age 30, house 472, s 1,3,31.

ADAMS, RANDOLPH DIXON. reg 13, co A, enl 12/23/61 or 11/1/62 Whitesburg, age 24, originally joined 5th Ky., serving time in 13th Ky. Cav. for lost time in 5th Ky., 5th Ky. service not found on CSR, house 116, s 1,3,31.

ADAMS, SPENCER. reg 5, co F, enl 11/1/61 Whitesburg, house 359 or 500, s 1,3.

ADAMS, WATSON ETCHISON. reg 13, co H, enl 9/28/62 or 10/18/62 Whitesburg, CSR states Letcher Co. as residence, house 13, s 1,3.

ADAMS, WILLIAM. reg 13, co D, enl 10/4/62 Whitesburg, CSR states Letcher Co. as residence, house 263, 359, 310, 573, or 360, s 1,3,31.

AMBURGEY, ALFRED. reg 13, co A, enl 11/1/62 or 4/14/63 Whitesburg, cap Gladesville 7/7/63, taken to Camp Chase 7/20/63, to Camp Douglas 8/24/63, exch Point Lookout 2/24/65, residence stated in s 31, house n/c, s 1,3,31.

AMBURGEY, AMBROSE A. reg 5, co F, enl 11/1/61 or 11/5/61 Whitesburg, house 257 or 455, s 1,2.

AMBURGEY, ANDERSON. reg 5, enl 11/1/61 Whitesburg, reg 13, co A, age 21, dis 4/14/63 served time in 13th Ky. to make up for time in 5th Ky., house 454, s 1,3.

AMBURGEY, ELIJAH. reg 5, co F, enl 11/1/61 Whitesburg, house 519, s 1,3.

AMBURGEY, FRANCIS. reg 5, co F, enl 11/1/61 Whitesburg, house 256, s 1,3.

AMBURGEY, HUMPHREY. reg 13, co A, enl 9/29/62 Whitesburg, house 449 or 454, s 1,3,31.

AMBURGEY, JOHN JESS. reg 13, co B, enl 9/15/62 Whitesburg, cap Gladesville 7/7/63, taken to Camp Chase 7/20/63, to Camp Douglas 8/24/63, CSR states Letcher Co. as residence, house 455, 1,3,31.

AMBURGEY, JOHN WALKER. reg 5, co F, enl 11/1/61 Whitesburg, reg 13, co A, enl 11/1/62 Whitesburg, rem capt Booneville 8/19/63, sent to Camp Chase OH 9/2/63 to Rock Island IL 1/22/64, rel 10/6/64 in exchange for enlisting is US Army for frontier service, house 255, s 1,3,31.

AMBURGEY, THOMAS H. reg 13, co A, enl 9/21/62 or 9/27/62 or 10/20/62 Whitesburg, Confederate veteran pension #1196, clothing receipts 4/7/64, 6/29/64 & 9/7/64, residence stated on source 31, house n/c, s 1,3,31.

AMBURGEY, WILBURN. reg 13, co A, r 1st lt., enl 9/11/62 Whitesburg, age 26, light hair, blue eyes, dark skin, 5-10, cap Gladesville 7/7/63, taken to Camp Chase 7/20/63, to Johnson Island 11/10/63, to Baltimore, MD 2/9/64, took oath Ft. Delaware, released 6/12/65, CSR states Letcher Co. as residence, house n/c, s 1,3 31.

AMBURGEY, WILLIAM. reg 5, co F, enl 11/1/61 Whitesburg, reg 13, co A, enl 11/1/62 Whitesburg, dis 4/14/63, served out time lost in 5th Ky., age 25, house 330, s 1,3.

AMBURGEY, WILLIAM W. reg 5, co F, enl 11/1/61 Whitesburg, house 518, s 1,3.

ANDERSON, AARON. reg 13, co D, enl 10/4/62 Whitesburg, des 11/5/62 Whitesburg, CSR states residence as Letcher Co., house n/c, s 1,3,31.

ANDERSON, JOHN. reg 13, co D, enl 10/4/62 Whitesburg, cap 7/20/63 Lawrence Co., released on oath 9/17/63 by Special Order No. 240 by Lt. Col. Eastham, CSR states Letcher Co. as residence, house 191, s 1,3,31.

ASHLEY, FRANKLIN M. reg 13, co B, enl 9/15/62 Whitesburg, dis 9/29/62, CSR states Letcher Co. as residence, house 33, s 1,3,31.

ASHLEY, JORDAN TOLLIVER. reg 13, co I, enl fall 1862, reg 5, co I, Confederate pension #2916, 13th Ky. service not on CSR or AG, 5th Ky. service not on CSR or AG, took oath spring 1865 Louisa, house 33, s 31.

AUSTIN, ANDREW JACKSON. reg 13, co D, r 4th sgt, enl 10/4/62 Whitesburg, cap Gladesville 7/7/63, taken to Camp Douglas 8/24/63, died 1/28/64 of typhoid, buried grave #979, Chicago City cemetery, CSR states Letcher Co. as residence, house 154, s 1,3,31.

B

BACK, DAVID. reg 13, co H, A, enl 10/18/62 Whitesburg, reg 10, co A, cap Cynthiana 6/12/64, taken to Camp Douglas 6/30/64, received flesh wound in lower extremity at Cynthiana, died 12/6/64 of smallpox, buried near Camp Douglas, CSR states Letcher Co. as residence, house 276 or 282, s 1,3,31.

BACK, DAVID J. reg 5, co F, enl 11/5/61 Whitesburg, des 3/8/62, reg 13, co A, age 20, house 276 or 282, s 1,3,31.

BACK, HENRY. reg 5, co F, enl 11/1/61 Whitesburg, des 3/8/62, returned from desertion 3/4/63, reg 13, co A, enl 11/1/62 Whitesburg, house 276 or 471, s 1,3.

BACK, HENRY J. reg 13, co B, enl 8/29/62 Whitesburg, clothing receipts 6/27/64, 9/1/64 & 9/15/64, CSR states Letcher Co. as residence, house 481, s 1,3,31.

BACK, ISAAC. reg 13, co A, enl 11/1/62 Whitesburg, cap 1864, Confederate pension #1884, residence stated on source, house n/c, s 1,3,31.

BACK, JAMES C. reg 13, co B, enl 10/12/62 Whitesburg, CSR states Letcher Co. as residence., house 282, s 1,3,31.

BACK, LEWIS. reg 5, co F, enl 11/5/61 near Pound Gap, r 3rd cpl, des 3/8/62, enl 9/7/62 Jackson, app 3rd cpl 9/18/62, des 8/10/63 Harrison Mills VA, reg 13, co F, dis 4/14/63, served time in 13th Ky. to make up 5th Ky. time, age 27, house 274, s 1,3,31.

BACK, WILLIAM. reg 13, co B, enl 4/65, not on AG or CSR, house 481, s 5,31.

BACK, WILLIAM CODY. reg 13, co B, enl 1863, not on AG or CSR, widow received Confederate pension #28, house 276, s 31.

BAKER, HENRY C. reg 13, co D, enl 10/4/62 Whitesburg, house 155, s 1,31.

BAKER, IRA D. reg 13, co A, enl 11/1/61 Whitesburg, des 1/20/62 Whitesburg, reg 5, co F, B, enl 9/11/62 Jackson, des 11/4/62 Pike steam mill, house 603, s 1,3,31.

BANKS, ALFORD. reg 13, co B, enl 9/15/62 Whitesburg, paroled Lee Co. VA 5/2/65, CSR states Letcher Co. as residence, house 10, s 1,3,31.

BANKS, ELIJAH. reg 13, co H, enl 10/18/62 Whitesburg, dis 10/18/62, house 443, s 1,3,31.

BANKS, JAMES H. reg 13, co D, enl 10/4/62 Whitesburg, house 11, s 1,3,31.

BANKS, ZACHARIAH. reg 13, co B, enl 8/29/62 Whitesburg, clothing receipts 9/7/64 & 9/24/64, CSR states Letcher Co. as residence, house 10, s 1,3,31.

BARNES, WILLIAM. reg 13, co B, enl 9/12/62 Whitesburg, cap Gladesville 7/7/63, taken to Camp Chase 7/20/63, to Camp Douglas 8/24/63, CSR states Letcher Co. as residence, house 308, s 1,3,31.

BATES, HENRY C. reg 13, co D, enl 10/4/62 Whitesburg, clothing receipt 6/29/64, house 496, s 1,3,31.

BATES, JAMES. reg 5, co F, r sgt, enl 11/1/61 Whitesburg, was 5th sgt until 3/13/62, cap by enemy while on leave, house 496, s 1,3

BATES, MARTIN VAN BUREN. reg 7ConfCav, co A, house 143, s 3.

BATES, ROBERT. reg 7ConfCav, co A, age 38, brown hair, hazel eyes, sandy skin, 5-9, cap Piketon 4/15/63, taken to Camp Chase, exch City Point 5/13/63, French's Btn, co A, r capt, house 32, s 12.

BATES, URIAH. reg 5, co F, enl 11/1/61 camp near Pound Gap, died Scott Co. VA 5/1/62, house 502, s 1,3.

BENTLEY, AARON RICE. reg 13, co H, r 1st lt, enl 10/18/62 Whitesburg, age 26, dark hair & skin, gray eyes, 6-0, cap Gladesville 7/7/63, taken to Johnson's Island 10/10/63, released on oath 5/12/65, elected 2nd lt 11/2/62, prom to 1st lt 2/16/65, CSR states Letcher Co. as residence as do amnesty papers, house n/c, s 1,3.

BENTLEY, BENJAMIN. reg 13, co H, enl 10/18/62 Whitesburg, dis 4/1/63, CSR states Letcher Co. as residence, house 105, s 1,3.

BENTLEY, JOHN Q. reg 13, co D, enl 10/4/62 Whitesburg, CSR states Letcher Co. as residence, house 144, s 1,3.

BENTLEY, LAFAYETTE. reg 13, co D, enl 10/4/62 Whitesburg, CSR states Letcher Co. as residence, house n/c, s 1,3.

BENTLEY, MAY. reg 13, co D, enl 10/4/62 CSR states Letcher Co. as residence, house 150, s 1,3.

BENTLEY, SOLOMON D. reg 13, co D, enl 10/4/62 Whitesburg, CSR states Letcher Co. as residence, house n/c, s 1,3.

BLANKENSHIP, JOHN. reg 13, co D, enl 10/4/62 Whitesburg, CSR states Letcher Co. as residence, house 509, s 1,3.

BOGGS, ELIJAH. reg 13, co D, enl 10/4/62 Whitesburg, des 10/20/62, CSR states Letcher Co. as residence, house 233, s 1,3.

BOGGS, HENRY. reg 13, co D, enl 10/4/62 Whitesburg, des 10/20/62, CSR states Letcher Co. as residence, house 232, s 1,3.

BOGGS, LEVI. reg 13, co D, enl 10/4/62 Whitesburg, des 10/20/62, CSR states Letcher Co. as residence, house 230, s 1,3.

BOLLING, DANIEL BOONE. reg 13, co A, r 2nd sgt, enl 9/9/62 Whitesburg, age 25, prom to 2nd sgt 1/17/63, residence stated on source 31, house n/c, s 1,3,31.

BOWENS, WILLIAM. reg 13, co H, enl 10/18/62 Whitesburg, age 45, des 11/12/62, CSR states Letcher Co. as residence, age 19 on census, house 260, s 1,3.

BOWLING, CALEB. reg 5, co F, enl 11/1/61 Whitesburg, reg 13, co A, dis 4/30/63, age 18, 5th Ky. service not on CSR, house 264, s 1,3.

BOWLING, JOHN. reg 5, co F, enl 11/1/61 Whitesburg, reg 13, co A, r 3rd cpl, enl 11/2/62, age 21, 5th Ky. service not on CSR, house 264, s 1,3.

BRANSON, JAMES. reg 13, co H, enl 11/15/62 Whitesburg, CSR: "killed in Kentucky", house 266, s 1, 3.

BRANSON, LEONARD. reg 13, co H, rem not on AG or CSR, house 156, s 31.

BRANSON, R. A. or R. S. reg 13, co B, r 4th sgt, enl 8/29/62 Whitesburg, died 6/11/63 at home, CSR states Letcher Co. as residence, house n/c, s 1,3.

BRASHEAR, WILLIAM T. B. reg 13, co A, C, enl 9/21/62 Whitesburg, age 30, house 379, s 1,3.

BROOKS, FRANCIS. reg 13, co D, enl 10/4/62 Whitesburg, CSR states Letcher Co. as residence, house n/c, s 1,3.

BRYANT, JACOB. reg 13, co E, enl 10/5/62 Whitesburg, cap Perry Co. 6/6/63, taken to Camp Chase, Johnson's Island & Point Lookout, CSR states Letcher Co. as residence, not on Letcher census, source 31 lists Floyd Co. as residence, not on Floyd Co. census, house n/c, s 1,3,31.

C

CALHOUN, JOHN C. reg 13, co B, enl 8/29/62 Whitesburg, cap Mt. Sterling 6/10/64, sent to Rock Island 6/22/64, CSR states Letcher Co. as residence, house 300 or 301, s 1,3,31.

CALHOUN, ROBERT. reg 13, co H, enl 10/18/62 Whitesburg, des 11/20/62, not on CSR, house 505, s 3,31.

CALHOUN, S. C. reg 5, co F, enl 11/1/61 Whitesburg, reg 13, co A, des 10/25/62, house 301 or 320, s 1,3.

CALHOUN, SILAS C. reg 5, co F, enl 11/1/61 Whitesburg, reg 13, co A, r 5th sgt, enl 11/1/62 Whitesburg, prom to sgt 1/17/63, 5th Ky. Inf. service not on CSR, house 486, s 3.

CALHOUN, THOMAS. reg 5, co F, enl 11/1/61 Whitesburg, reg 13, co A, trans from 5th Ky., age 30, house 292, s 1,3.

CAMPBELL, JOHN C. reg 13, co B, enl 8/20/62 Whitesburg, CSR states Letcher Co. as residence, house 94, s 1,3,31.

CAUDILL, ABEL. reg 13, co A, enl 11/1/61 Whitesburg, des 11/10/62, house 299, s 3,31.

CAUDILL, ABNER. reg 13, co B, E, r 2nd lt, enl 9/12/62 Middle Creek, prom to 2nd lt 10/7/62, resigned 4/29/63, CSR states he is resident of both Floyd and Letcher Counties, house 299, s 1,3,31.

CAUDILL, BENJAMIN E. reg 13, r col., enl 11/2/62, cap Gladesville 7/7/63, sent to Camp Chase 7/20/63, to Johnson's Island 10/10/63, to Baltimore, MD 2/9/64, to Ft. Delaware 6/19/64, to Hilton Head, SC 6/25/64, exchanged 9/1/64, house 259, s 1,3,31.

CAUDILL, DAVID. reg 13, co B, Ky. Confederate Pension Application #1254, house 271, 277 or 482, s 31.

CAUDILL, DAVID D. reg 13, co B, Ky. Confederate Pension Application #1634, not on CSR, house 271, 277, or 482, s 31.

CAUDILL, DAVID JESSE. reg 13, co B, r lt col, enl 5/22/61 Rose Hill VA, age 23, wounded Perry Co. 10/14/62, elected capt 11/2/62 or 9/9/62, CSR states Letcher Co. as residence, house n/c, s 1,3,31.

CAUDILL, HENRY. reg 5, co F, enl 11/29/61 Whitesburg, died 3/18/62 Camp Moccasin, Scott Co. VA, not on AG or CSR, house 97, 277, 348, 423 or 482, s 31.

CAUDILL, HENRY C. reg 13, co B, enl 8/29/62 Whitesburg, dis 1/1/63, CSR states Letcher Co. as residence, source 31 states Rowan Co. as residence, house 348, 423 or 482, s 1,3,31.

CAUDILL, HENRY H. reg 13, co B, enl 8/29/62 Whitesburg, CSR states Letcher Co. as residence, house 97, 277, 348, 423, or 482, s 1,3,31.

CAUDILL, HENRY M. reg 13, co B, enl 9/3/62 Whitesburg, dis 9/29/62, CSR states Letcher Co. as residence, house 97, 277, 348, 423, or 482, s 1,3,31.

CAUDILL, HENRY R. S. reg 13, co H, r 2nd lt, enl 10/18/61 Whitesburg, elected 2nd lt 11/2/62, cap Gladesville 7/7/63, taken to Camp Chase 7/20/63, to Johnson's Island 10/10/63, to Fortress Monroe 9/16/64, CSR states Letcher Co. as residence, house 94, 277, 348, 413 or 482, s 1,3,31.

CAUDILL, ISAAC. reg 13, co B, E, enl 6/1/62, 8/21/62 or 10/14/62 Whitesburg, trans from co B to co E 10/7/62, cap Breathitt Co. 4/5/62, taken to Camp Morton 4/64, to Point Lookout 3/15/65, Ky. Confederate pension #3286, CSR states both Floyd and Letcher Counties as residence, not on Letcher Co. census, house n/c, s 1,3,31.

CAUDILL, ISHAM (ISOM). reg 13, co B, enl 8/29/62 or 9/9/62 Whitesburg, CSR states Letcher Co. as residence, may be Perry Co. resident, house n/c, s 1,3,31.

CAUDILL, ISHAM (ISOM) JR. reg 13, co B, enl 8/29/62 Whitesburg, CSR states Letcher Co. as residence, house 597, s 1,31.

CAUDILL, JAMES AARON. reg 13, co B, enl 8/29/62 Whitesburg, clothing receipts 6/29/64, 9/7/64 & 9/24/64, CSR states Letcher Co. as residence, house 29, 31 or 102, s 1,3.

CAUDILL, JAMES P. reg 5, co C, D, enl 9/20/62 Jackson or Licking Station, pardoned Charlotte NC 5/3/65, not on CSR, house n/c, s 3.

CAUDILL, JAMES W. reg 5, co F, enl 12/13/61 Whitesburg, reg 13, co A, 5th Ky. service not on AG or CSR, house 597, s 1,3.

CAUDILL, JESSE H. reg 5, co F, enl 11/3/61 camp near Pound Gap, reg 13, co A, B, r 5th sgt, enl 9/9/62, trans to co B 1/1/63, app sgt 6/24/63, house 350 or 389, s 1,3,31.

CAUDILL, JOHN. reg 13, co B, enl 8/21/62 or 10/10/62 Whitesburg, paroled at Cumberland Gap 5/3/65, CSR states Letcher Co. as residence, house 29, 259, 347, or 470, s 1,3,31.

CAUDILL, JOHN DIXON. reg 13, co B, r 1st sgt, enl 8/29/62 Whitesburg, clothing receipts 4/7/64, 6/29/64, 9/7/64 & 11/19/64, CSR states Letcher Co. as residence, house 29, 259, 347, or 470, s 1,3,31.

CAUDILL, JOHN M. reg 5, enl 11/1/61 Whitesburg, age 30, reg 13, co A, cap 7/7/63 Gladesville, taken to Camp Chase 7/20/63, to Camp Douglas 8/24/63, to Point Lookout 2/24/65, house 470, s 1,3,31.

CAUDILL, JOHN W. reg 5, co F, reg 13, co A, rem capt Gladesville 7/7/63, sent to Camp Douglas, neither regiment on AG or CSR, house 29, s 31.

CAUDILL, PRESTON. reg 13, co B, E, r 1st sgt, enl 6/1/62 or 8/21/62 Whitesburg, age 27, trans to co E 10/5/62, CSR lists both Floyd and Letcher Counties as residence, source 31 lists Floyd Co. as residence, but he is not on Floyd Co. census, house n/c, s 1,3,31.

CAUDILL, SAMUEL B. reg 13, co B, enl 8/29/62 or 10/10/62 Whitesburg, clothing receipts 6/29/64, 9/7/64 & 11/19/64, CSR states Letcher Co. as residence, house 277, 299 or 492, s 1,3,31.

CAUDILL, SAMUEL C. reg 13, co A, G, r 2nd lt, enl 11/1/61 Whitesburg, age 30, trans to co G, prom to 2nd lt 2/27/63, house 492, s 1,3,31.

CAUDILL, STEPHEN JACOB. reg 13, co B, enl 8/29/63 Whitesburg, paroled 5/8/65 Cumberland Gap, clothing receipt 9/7/64, CSR states Letcher Co. as residence, house 351, s 1,3,31.

CAUDILL, WILLIAM. reg 13, co E, enl 10/5/62 Whitesburg, not on CSR, house 16, 278, 472 or 597, s 3.

CAUDILL, WILLIAM A. reg 5, co F, enl 11/1/61 Whitesburg, reg 13, co A, enl 10/3/62 Whitesburg, age 35, discharged by surgeon spring 1863, house 308, s 1,3,31.

CAUDILL, WILLIAM B. reg 13, co B, r 2nd cpl, enl 9/9/62 Whitesburg, cap Gladesville 7/7/63, taken to Camp Chase 7/19/63, to Camp Douglas 8/24/63, to Point Lookout 2/24/65, CSR states he is Floyd Co. resident, source 31 states he is Letcher Co. resident, house 278, s 1,3,31.

CAUDILL, WILLIAM J. reg 13, co B, r 4th sgt, enl 8/29/62 Whitesburg, CSR states Letcher Co. as residence, house 16, 31, 278, 308, 422 or 597, s 1,3,31.

CAUDILL, WILLIAM W. reg 13, co B, enl 10/5/62 Whitesburg, Ky. Confederate pension #15, took oath 4/30/65 Louisa, not on CSR, not on Floyd Co. census, house 278, s 3,31.

CHILDERS, ABRAHAM D. reg 5, co F, enl 11/1/61 Whitesburg, des 3/8/62, reg 13, co A, H, r 4th sgt, enl 10/18/62, trans from 5th Ky. Inf., CSR states Letcher Co. as residence, house 204, s 1,3,31.

CHILDERS, GOULBY. reg 5, co F, enl 11/1/61 camp near Pound Gap, not on CSR, house 478, s 3.

CHILDERS, JAMES M. reg 13, co H, r 2nd cpl, enl 9/8/62 or 10/18/62 Whitesburg, clothing receipts 4/7/64 & 9/24/64, CSR states Letcher Co. as residence, house 478, s 1,3,31.

CHRISTIAN, WILLIAM. reg 5, co A, enl 11/1/61 Whitesburg, reg 13, co A, enl 11/2/62 Whitesburg, age 22, clothing receipts 4/7/64, 6/29/64, 9/1/64 & 9/15/64, CSR states Letcher Co. as residence, house 262, s 1,3,31.

COLLIER, ISOM W. reg 5, co F, r 1st sgt, enl 2/18/62 Whitesburg, app 1st sgt 6/1/62, house 556, s 1, 3.

COLLIER, JOHN B. reg 13, co A, enl 11/1/61 or 9/25/62 Whitesburg, age 30, cap Buffington Island, OH 7/19/63, sent to Camp Chase, died 10/22/63 of measles, buried in Grave No. 757, City Cemetery, Chicago IL, house 547, s 1,3,31.

COLLIER, JOHN HENDERSON. reg 13, co A, enl 11/1/61 Whitesburg, rem cap Gladesville VA 7/7/63, to Camp Douglas 8/24/63, house 556, s 3,31.

COLLIER, SAMUEL PETER. reg 13, co D, enl 10/4/62 Whitesburg, des 11/5/62, CSR states Letcher Co. as residence, house 332, s 1,3,31.

COLLIER, STEPHEN. reg 13, co H, enl 10/18/62 Whitesburg, des 10/18/62, CSR states Letcher Co. as residence, house 332, s 1,3,31.

COLLINS, CARTER. reg 13, co H, enl 9/28/62 or 10/18/62 Whitesburg, des 11/2/62 or 11/6/62, CSR states Letcher Co. as residence, house 340, s 1,3,31.

COMBS, ENOCH. reg 13, co I, enl 10/18/62 Whitesburg, rem des 11/1/62, CSR states he is Perry Co. resident, house 541, s 1,3,31.

COMBS, GEORGE A. reg 13, co H, enl 10/18/62 Whitesburg, des 10/27/62, CSR states Letcher Co. as residence, house 494 or 541, s 1,3,31.

COMBS, GRANVILLE. reg 13, co A, B, enl 9/23/62 Whitesburg, trans from co B to co A 1/1/63, CSR states he is Perry Co. resident, house 544, s 1,3,31.

COMBS, RUSSELL HACKER. reg 13, co C, rem not on AG or CSR, house 60, s 31.

COMBS, SHADERICK (SHADRACK). reg 13, co H, enl 10/18/62 Whitesburg, des 12/7/62, CSR states Letcher Co. as residence, house 7 or 494, s 1,3,31.

COOK, JACOB. reg 13, co H, enl 9/20/62 or 10/18/62 Whitesburg, des 11/12/62, CSR states Letcher Co. as residence, house 178, s 1,3,31.

CORNETT, JOHN BAXTER. reg 13, co H, r 5th sgt, enl 9/29/62 or 10/18/62 Whitesburg, CSR states Letcher Co. as residence, house 2, s 1,3,31.

CORNETT, JOSEPH. reg 5, co F, enl 11/1/61 Whitesburg, des 5/18/62 Camp Perry, Tazewell Co. VA, house 291, 298 or 398, s 1,3,31.

CORNETT, JOSEPH E. reg 5, co F, enl 11/1/61 Whitesburg, reg 13, co A, age 18, cap Gladesville 7/7/63, taken to Camp Chase 7/20/63, d Camp Chase 8/10/63 of diarrhea, house 398, s 1,3,31.

CORNETT, SAMUEL A. reg 13, co H, enl 9/17/62 or 10/18/62 Whitesburg, CSR states Letcher Co. as residence, house 2, 291, 413 or 415, s 1,3,31.

CORNETT, WILLIAM A. reg 13, co E, cap Jonesville, TN 12/17/63, taken to Rock Island 1/17/64, house 488, s 1,31.

CORNETT, WILLIAM E. reg 13, co B, r 2nd lt, enl 10/10/62 Whitesburg, prom to sgt major 2/20/63, prom to 2nd lt 6/24/63, cap 12/63 in Kentucky, CSR states Letcher Co. as residence, house 398, 411, 413 or 488, s 1,3,31.

CORNETT, WILLIAM G. reg 5, co F, enl 11/1/61 Whitesburg, cap Booneville 8/19/63, taken to Camp Chase 9/1/63, to Rock Island 1/22/64, released 10/28/64, house 398, 411, 413 or 488, s 1,3,31.

CRACE, JAMES. reg 13, co D, enl 10/4/62 Whitesburg, CSR states Letcher Co. as residence, on leave in 1862 with a wound, house 580, s 1,3,31.

CRAFT, ENOCH A. reg 13, co D, enl 10/4/62 Whitesburg, clothing receipts 4/7/64, 6/29/64 & 9/7/64, CSR states Letcher Co. as residence, house 114, s 1,3,31.

CRAFT, JASON L. reg 13, co D, r 2nd lt, enl 10/4/62 Whitesburg, CSR states Letcher Co. as residence, elected 2nd lt 11/2/62, wounded and in Kentucky since 10/20/64, house 501, s 1,3,31.

CRAFT, JOHN. reg 13, co D, enl 10/4/62 Whitesburg, CSR states Letcher Co. as residence, house 45, 154 or 592, s 1,3,31.

CRAFT, JOHN HENDERSON. reg 5, co F, enl 11/1/61 Whitesburg, reg 13, co A, C, r 1st lt, age 28, cap Gladesville 7/7/63, taken to Camp Chase 7/20/63, to Johnson's Island 10/16/63, to Point Lookout 2/16/65, house 154, s 1,3l.

CRAFT, JOSEPH P. reg 13, co D, paroled 5/2/65 Cumberland Gap, house 114, s 1,31.

CRAFT, NEHEMIAH. reg 13, co D, enl 10/4/62 Whitesburg, CSR states Letcher Co. as residence, house 45 or 591, s 1,3,31.

CRAFT, NELSON ROBERT. reg 13, co D, r 1st sgt, enl 10/4/62 Whitesburg, CSR states Letcher Co. as residence, house 357, s 1,3,31.

CRAFT, WILLIAM H. 1MR, co B, enl 11/27/62 Letcher Co. trans to W. T. Havens' co 11/18/62, house 147 or 441, s 3.

CRAFT, WILLIAM RICHARDSON. reg 13, co D, r 2nd sgt, enl 4/1/64 Whitesburg, not on CSR, house 147, s 3,31.

CREECH, FELIX GILBERT. reg 13, co D, r 1st sgt, enl 4/1/64 Whitesburg, CSR states Letcher Co. as residence, house 235, s 1,3,31.

D

DAY, DAVID. reg 13, co B, enl 8/21/62 Whitesburg, age 40, cap Gladesville 7/7/63, taken to Camp Chase 7/20/63, to Camp Douglas 8/24/63, to Point Lookout 2/24/65, CSR states Letcher Co. as residence, house 425, s 1,3,31.

DAY, WILLIAM. reg 5, co F, enl 12/18/61 Whitesburg, house 445, s 1, 3, 22.

DAY, WILLIAM H. reg 13, co H, enl 10/18/62 Whitesburg, CSR states Letcher Co. as residence, house 425, s 1,3,31.

DAY, WILLIAM L. reg 5, co F, enl 11/1/61 Whitesburg, reg 13, co A, source 31 states he is Perry Co. resident, but he is not on Perry Co. census, house 495, s 1,3,31.

DIALS, ROBERT. reg 13, co H, enl 10/8/62 or 10/18/62 Whitesburg, des 12/20/62, rejoined from desertion 8/27/63, CSR states Letcher Co. as residence, house n/c, s 1,3,31.

DIXON (DICKERSON), ISAAC D. reg 13, co H, r 3rd cpl, enl 10/18/62 Whitesburg, prom to cpl 3/18/63, CSR states Letcher Co. as residence, house 596, s 1,3,31.

DUKE, JAMES M. reg 13, co B, enl 8/21/62 or 9/9/62 Whitesburg, age 35, cap Letcher Co. 8/4/63 or Boonville TN 8/19/63, CSR states Letcher Co. as residence, enlisted US 3rd Ky. Battery, house 473, s 1,3,31.

DUKE, PAYTON MADISON. reg 13, co B, r 1st lt, enl 8/21/62 Whitesburg, age 35, dark hair, hazel eyes, fresh skin, 5-8, elected lt 11/2/62, prom to 1st lt, resigned on certificate of disability for nephritis

6/13/63, cap Cynthiana 6/14/64 or cap at home 6/10/64, taken to Rock Island 6/24/64, took oath 5/23/65, house 293, s 1,3,31.

E

ELDRIDGE, JOHN C. reg 5, co F, enl 11/5/61 camp near Pound Gap, des 3/19/62, reg 13, co A, enl 11/1/61 Whitesburg, age 28, house 275, s 1,31.

ELDRIDGE, LEVI. reg 5, co F, enl 1/5/61 Whitesburg, age 56, black hair, blue eyes, dark skin, 5-1, b Washington Co. VA, house 273, s 1,3.

ENGLAND, ENOCH. reg 13, co H, enl 10/18/62 Whitesburg, des 10/24/62, CSR states Letcher Co. as residence, house 362, s 1,3,31.

ESTEP, JONATHAN. reg 13, co E, r 2nd sgt, enl 10/14/62 Whitesburg, CSR states Letcher Co. as residence, house 184, s 1,3,31.

ESTEP, JOSEPH. reg 13, co E, enl 10/5/62, 10/14/62 or 10/23/62 Whitesburg, des 3/63, CSR states Letcher Co. as residence, house n/c, s 1,3.

EVERIDGE, BENJAMIN. reg 5, co F, enl 11/1/61 Whitesburg, house 511, s 1, 3,31.

EVERIDGE, WILLIAM. reg 13, co B, enl 8/21/62, 8/29/62 or 9/9/62 Whitesburg, des 7/9/63 Gladesville, CSR states Letcher Co. as residence, house 471, s 1,3,31.

F

FIELDS, DANIEL B. reg 13, co H, enl 10/18/62 Whitesburg, CSR states Letcher Co. as residence, house 268, s 1,3,31.

FIELDS, DAVIS. reg 5, co F, enl 4/11/62 Moccasin VA, house 479, s 1, 3.

FIELDS, STEPHEN H. reg 13, co H, enl 10/18/62 Whitesburg, CSR states Letcher Co. as residence, house 212, s 1,3,31.

FOUCH, ANDREW JACKSON. reg 13, co E, r 4th cpl, enl 10/5/62, 10/14/62 or 12/23/62 Whitesburg, CSR states Letcher Co. as residence, source 31 lists Harlan Co. as residence, but he is not on Harlan Co. census, house n/c, s 1,3,31.

FRANCIS, JOHN WESLEY. reg 13, co A, enl 9/29/61 Whitesburg, age 21, cap Gladesville 7/7/63, taken to Camp Chase 7/20/63, to Camp Douglas 8/24/63, d 8/19/64 of smallpox, buried near Camp Douglas, house 331, s 1,3,31.

FRANCIS, SAMUEL. reg 5, co F, enl 11/1/61 Whitesburg, house 446, s 1, 3.

FRANCIS, SIMEON. reg 5, co F, enl 11/1/61 Whitesburg, reg 13, co A, cap Buffington Island, 7/19/63, taken to Camp Douglas, d 2/24/64 of diarrhea, buried grave 992, Chicago city cemetery, house 451, s 1,3,31.

FRANCIS, SIMEON J. reg 5, co F, enl 11/1/61 Whitesburg, reg 13 co A, enl 11/2/62, cap Gladesville VA, taken to Camp Chase 7/20/63, to Camp Douglas 8/24/63, house 446, s 1,3,31.

FRANKLIN, JAMES BRANDLEY. reg 13, co D, enl 10/4/62 Whitesburg, des 11/5/62, CSR states Letcher Co. as residence, house n/c, s 1,3,31.

FRANKLIN, KELLY. reg 5, co F, enl 11/1/61 Whitesburg, des 1/15/62, reg 13, co A, age 26, age 14 on census, house 516, 1,3,31.

FRAZIER, JAMES R. reg 5, co D, I, enl 10/9/62, Licking Station, des Rock House VA, house 389, s 1, 3.

FUGATE, IRA CHARLEY. reg 13, co H, enl 9/16/62 or 10/18/62 Whitesburg, cap Booneville 8/15/63, taken to Camp Douglas 8/22/63, to Point Lookout 3/22/65, CSR states Letcher Co. as residence, house 377, s 1,3,31.

FULLER, JESSE ARCHIBALD OR ARCHELAUS. reg 13, co B, C, I, enl 9/6/62 Whitesburg, trans to co C 1/1/63, CSR lists Letcher Co. and Perry Co. as residence, source 31 lists Perry Co. as residence, but he is not on Perry Co. census, house n/c, s 1,3,31.

G

GIBSON, ELIJAH. reg 13, co H, r 3rd cpl, enl 9/12/62 or 10/18/62 Whitesburg, CSR states Letcher Co. as residence, house 100, s 1,3,31.
GIBSON, JESSE J. reg 13, co D, enl 10/4/62 Whitesburg, not on CSR, house 317, s 3,31.
GIPSON, WILLIAM. reg 13, co A, enl 10/14/62 Whitesburg, CSR states Letcher Co. as residence, house n/c, s 1.
GOINS, JOHN. reg 13, co D, enl 10/4/62 Whitesburg, des 10/8/62, CSR states Letcher Co. as residence, house n/c, s 1,3,31.
GRAY, GEORGE MARION. reg 13, co D, E, enl 10/4/62 or 10/14/62 Whitesburg, CSR states Letcher Co. as residence, house 146, s 1,3,31.
GRAY, OLIVER STEWART. reg 13, co A, enl 11/1/62 Whitesburg, age 22, house 146, s 1,3,31.

H

HAGANS, ALLEN CHRISTIAN. reg 13, co A, E, r 1st sgt, enl 10/14/62 Whitesburg, rem prom to 1st sgt 1/17/63, clothing receipt 4/7/64, CSR states he is Letcher Co. resident, not on Floyd or Letcher census, house n/c, s 1,3,31.
HAGANS, THOMAS C. reg 13, co A, enl 10/14/62 Whitesburg, CSR states Letcher Co. as residence, house 483, s 1,31.
HALL, ALVIN. reg 13, co E, enl 10/5/62 or 10/14/62 Whitesburg, des 11/1/62, CSR states Letcher Co. as residence, house 24, s 1,3,31.
HALL, ANTHONY. reg 13, co E, enl 10/5/62, 10/14/62 or 10/23/62 Whitesburg, CSR states Letcher Co. as residence, house 166, s 1,3,31.
HALL, BENJAMIN. reg 13, co D, r 4th sgt, enl 10/4/62 Whitesburg, CSR states Letcher Co. as residence, house 125, s 1,3,31.
HALL, DAVID. reg 13, co E, r 4th cpl, enl 10/5/62 10/14/62 or 10/23/62 Whitesburg, CSR states Letcher Co. as residence, house 171 or 395, s 1,3,31.
HALL, FIELDING. reg 5, co F, enl 11/1/61 Whitesburg reg 13, co E, enl 10/5/62, 10/14/62 or 10/23/62 Whitesburg, cap Floyd Co. 11/7/63 taken to Camp Morton 1/20/63, d 3/10/64 of smallpox, buried grave #833, Greenlawn Cemetery, house 24, s 1,3,31.
HALL, HENRY. reg 13, co E, F, enl 10/5/62 10/14/62 or 10/23/62 Whitesburg, CSR states Letcher Co. as residence, source 31 states he is Floyd Co. resident, house n/c, s 1,3,31.
HALL, HIRAM. reg 13, co D, enl 10/4/62 Whitesburg, CSR states Letcher Co. as residence, house 24 or 204, s 1,3,31.
HALL, JAMES P. reg 13, co E, enl 10/5/62 or 10/14/62 Whitesburg, CSR states Letcher Co. as residence, house 165, 169 or 171, s 1,3,31.
HALL, JOHN C. reg 13, co E, enl 10/5/62 10/14/62 or 10/23/62 Whitesburg, clothing receipt 9/7/64, CSR states Letcher Co. as residence, house 24, 187 or 395, s 1,3,31.
HALL, JOHN HIRAM. reg 13, co E, enl 8/8/63 Whitesburg, Confederate Pension #3976, cap Louisa, taken to Louisville, paroled on oath, CSR states Letcher Co. as residence, house 24, s 1,3,31.
HALL, JOHN L. reg 13, co E, r cpl, enl 10/5/62 or 10/23/62 Whitesburg, trans to May's regiment, CSR states Letcher Co. as residence, house 24, 187 or 395, s 1,3,31.

HALL, JOHN WASH. reg 13, co E, enl 10/14/62 Whitesburg, des 2/63, CSR states Letcher Co. as residence, house 24, 287 or 395, s 1,31.

HALL, JONATHAN J. reg 5, co F, enl 11/1/61 Whitesburg, reg 13, co A, Confederate Pension #675 and #3650, paroled 6/3/65, house 194, s 1,3,31.

HALL, REUBEN. reg 13, co E, r 1st cpl, enl 10/5/62, 10/14/62 or 10/23/62 Whitesburg, app cpl 4/30/63, CSR states Letcher Co. as residence, house 125 or 186, s 1,3,31.

HALL, RICHARD. reg 13, co E, enl 8/1/63 Whitesburg, house 190, s 1,31.

HALL, SAMUEL F. reg 5, co C, enl 8/27/62 Piketon, dis 10/20/62 Hazel Green, went to Davidson's Battery 10/20/62, house 201, s 1,3.

HALL, THOMAS. reg 13, co D, enl 10/4/62 Whitesburg, CSR states Letcher Co. as residence, house 137, s 1,3,31.

HALL, WILEY. reg 13, co H, enl 10/18/62 Whitesburg, dis 10/18/62, CSR states Letcher Co. as residence, house 170, s 1,3,31.

HAMILTON, ROBERT S. reg 5, co F, r 4th sgt, enl 11/1/61 Whitesburg, prom to 3rd sgt 3/13/62, d Scott Co. VA 3/25/62, house 517, s 1,3.

HAMMONDS, EPHRAIM F. reg 13, co D, enl 10/4/62 Whitesburg, des 10/21/62, CSR states Letcher Co. as residence, house n/c, s 1, 3.

HAMPTON, ABEL. reg 13, co D, enl 10/4/62 Whitesburg, CSR states Letcher Co. as residence, house 123, s 1,3,31.

HAMPTON, JOHN S. reg 5, co F, enl 11/1/61 Whitesburg, reg 13, co A, r 1st cpl, enl 11/1/62 Whitesburg, age 21, clothing receipts 6/29/64, 9/7/64 & 11/19/64, house 21, s 1,3,31.

HAMPTON, NELSON. reg 13, co D, enl 10/4/62 Whitesburg, CSR states Letcher Co. as residence, house 122, s 1,3,31.

HAMPTON, S. M. reg 13, co B, r 4th cpl, enl 8/29/62 or 9/9/62 Whitesburg, CSR states Letcher Co. as residence, clothing receipt 9/7/64, house 21, s 1,3,31.

HAMPTON, SOLOMON. reg 13, co H, enl 10/18/62 Whitesburg, captured, paroled 5/2/65 Cumberland Gap, CSR states Letcher Co. as residence, house 121, s 1,3,31.

HAMPTON, SOLOMON M. reg 13, co D, rem not on AG or CSR, house 121, s 1,31.

HART, JAMES H. reg 5, co F, enl 11/1/61 Whitesburg, reg 13, co A, age 35, cap Gladesville 7/7/63, taken to Camp Chase 7/20/63, to Camp Douglas 8/24/63, to Point Lookout 2/24/65, age 47 on census, house 294, s 1,3,31.

HOGG, GEORGE. reg 5 co F, enl 11/5/61 r sgt, prom to 5th sgt 3/13/62, reg 13, co B, r capt, elected capt 12/2/62, age 18, dark hair, hazel eyes, light skin, 5-10, cap Gladesville 7/7/63, taken to Camp Chase 7/24/63, to Johnson's Island 10/10/63, to Point Lookout 3/21/65, took oath and released 6/12/65, CSR states Letcher Co. as residence, house 76, s 1,3,31.

HOGG, HIRAM H. reg 13, co H, r sgt major, enl 9/18/62 or 10/18/62 Whitesburg, clothing receipt 9/7/64, CSR states Letcher Co. as residence, house 376 or 424, s 1,3,31.

HOGG, HIRAM WESLEY. reg 13, co H, r 2nd sgt, enl 9/2/62 or 10/18/62, Whitesburg, killed in battle at Blountville TN 9/22/63, house 424, s 1,3,31.

HOGG, JAMES. reg 5, co F, enl 11/5/61 Whitesburg, house 76, 367 or 390, s 1,3,22.

HOGG, SILAS. reg 5, co F, enl 11/5/61 Whitesburg, house 76, s 1,3.

HOGG, STEPHEN. reg 5, co A, B, enl 9/7/62 or 9/11/62 Jackson, des 8/10/63 Hansonville VA, house 76 or 414, s 1,3.

HOGG, STEPHEN. reg 13, co B, enl 8/29/62 or 9/9/62 Whitesburg, CSR states Letcher Co. as residence, house 76 or 424, s 1,3,31.

HOGG, WESLEY. reg 5, co F, enl 11/5/61 Whitesburg, house 344, s 1,3.

HOLBROOK, JESSE S. reg 13, co D, enl 10/4/62 Whitesburg, clothing receipt, 4/7/64, CSR states Letcher Co. as residence, house 70, s 1,3,31.

HOLBROOK, RANDOLPH H. reg 13, co D, enl 10/4/62 Whitesburg, CSR states Letcher Co. as residence, house 311 or 497, s 1,3,31.

HOLBROOK, RANSOM T. reg 13, co D, enl 10/4/62 Whitesburg, dark hair, hazel eyes, fair skin, 5-6, cap Letcher Co. and released on oath 4/20/64, CSR and oath papers state Letcher Co. as residence, house 497, s 1,3,31.

HOLCOMB, DAVID WESLEY. reg 13, co H, enl 10/18/62 Whitesburg, clothing receipt, 4/7/64, CSR states Letcher Co. as residence, house n/c, s 1,3,31.

HOLCOMB, WILLIAM. reg 13, co H, enl 10/18/62 Whitesburg, des 11/10/62, CSR states Letcher Co. as residence, house n/c, s 1,3,31.

HONEYCUTT, ALFRED. reg 5, co F, enl 11/1/61 Whitesburg, house 522, s 1, 3.

HUFF, CHARLES. reg 5, co F, enl 11/1/61 Whitesburg, des 5/14/62 Camp Moccasin, Scott Co. VA, house 237, s 1,3.

HUGHES, GABRIEL. reg 5, co F, enl 11/1/61 Whitesburg, reg 13, co A, age 20, house 464 or 499, s 1,3,22.

HUGHES, GABRIEL. reg 13, co D, enl 10/4/62 Whitesburg, house 464 or 499, s 3,31.

HUGHES, WILLIAM. reg 13, co B, enl 1/25/63 Whitesburg, CSR states he is Floyd Co. resident, but he is not on Floyd Co. census, house 499, s 1,31.

HYLTON, ELISHA ELMER. reg 5, co F, enl 11/1/61 Whitesburg, des 3/18/62, reg 13, co A, dis 4/30/63, house 526, s 1,3,31.

HYLTON, RHODES MARION. reg 13, co H, enl 10/18/62 Whitesburg, cap Gladesville 7/7/63, taken to Camp Douglas 8/22/63, to Point Lookout 2/24/65, CSR states Letcher Co. as residence, house n/c, s 1,3,31.

I

INGRAM, CLARK. reg 5, co F, enl 11/1/61 Whitesburg, reg 13, co A, age 30, trans from 5th Ky., house 420, s 1,3.

ISOM, ELIJAH JR. reg 13, co H, enl 9/12/62 Whitesburg, CSR states Letcher Co. as residence, house 392, s 1,3,31.

ISOM, ELIJAH SR. reg 13, co H, r 1st sgt, CSR states Letcher Co. as residence, des 11/3/62, house 393, s 1,3,31.

ISOM, ELISHA. reg 13, co H, r sgt, enl 9/2/62, reduced to ranks 3/18/63, killed by the enemy, CSR states Letcher Co. as residence, house 392, s 1,3,31.

ISOM, GEORGE. reg 13, co H, enl 10/18/62 Whitesburg, des 12/10/62, CSR states Letcher Co. as residence, house 388 or 392, s 1,3,31.

J

JOHNSON, ANDREW J. reg 5, co G, enl 3/20/62 Scott Co. VA, reg 13, co E, enl 10/5/62 or 10/14/62 Whitesburg, unit disbanded New River VA 5/65, took oath at Louisa, CSR states Letcher Co. as residence, house n/c, s 1,3,21,31.

JOHNSON, LESLIE. reg 13, co B, enl 8/21/62 or 9/22/62 Whitesburg, des 10/12/62, CSR states Letcher Co. as residence, house 323, s 1,3,31.

JONES, JONATHAN F or H. reg 5, co C, enl 10/19/61 Prestonsburg, m/out Hazel Green 10/20/62, reg 13, co H, r comm. sgt, enl 10/18/62 Whitesburg, age 26, light hair, hazel eyes, fair skin, 5-11, cap Morgan

Co. or Magoffin Co. 5/4/63, taken to Camp Chase 5/10/63, to Johnson's Island 6/20/63, to Point Lookout 10/30/63, released on oath 1/18/64, paroled at Cumberland Gap 5/10/65, CSR states Letcher Co. as residence, house 22, s 1,3,31.

K

KEITH, RILEY M. reg 13, co H, enl 10/18/62 Whitesburg, dis 10/18/62, CSR states Letcher Co. as residence, house 370, s 1,3,31.

KELLY, JOHN. reg 13, co H, enl 10/18/62 Whitesburg, CSR states Letcher Co. as residence, house 101, s 1,3,31.

KELLY, JOHN T. reg 13, co H, r 3rd sgt, enl 9/10/62 Whitesburg, clothing receipt 4/7/64, house 101, s 1,3,31.

KELLY, WILLIAM E. reg 5, co K, enl 12/14/61 Camp Recovery, m/out 10/20/62 Hazel Green, reg 13, co H, enl 10/18/62 Whitesburg, cap Cynthiana or at home 6/10/64, sent to Rock Island 6/24/64, CSR states Letcher Co. as residence, house 101, s 1,3,31.

KINSER, DAVID. reg 13, co D, r sgt, enl 10/4/62 Whitesburg, CSR states Letcher Co. as residence, house 358, s 1,3.

M

MADDEN, ANDREW JACKSON. reg 5, co F, enl 11/1/61 Whitesburg, reg 13, co A, cap Gladesville 7/7/63, taken to Camp Chase 7/20/63, to Camp Douglas 8/2/463, may have died 10/4/63 of typhoid, buried grave #708, City Cemetery, Chicago IL, house 533, s 1,3,31.

MADDEN, GEORGE WASHINGTON. reg 5, co F, enl 11/1/61 Whitesburg, reg 13, co A, cap Gladesville 7/7/63, taken to Camp Chase 7/20/63, to Camp Douglas 8/24/63, d 2/16/64 of chronic diarrhea, buried #1012, Chicago City Cemetery, house 533, s 1,3,31.

MADDEN, JOHN. reg 5, co A, enl 11/1/61 Whitesburg, reg 13, co A, enl 8/31/63 Whitesburg, clothing receipts, 6/29/64, 9/1/64 & 9/15/64, house 506, s 1.

MADDEN, WESLEY. reg 5, co F, enl 11/1/61 Whitesburg, cap Booneville 8/19/63, taken to Camp Chase 9/1/63, to Rock Island 1/22/64, house 533, s 1,3,31.

MADDEN, WILLIAM D. reg 5 co F, enl 11/1/61 Whitesburg, des 2/7/62, reg 13, co A, r 1st sgt, age 33, orderly sgt from 1/1/63 to 1/17/63, sgt major from 1/17/63 to 2/20/63, house 507, s 1,3,31.

MAGGARD, JOHN C. reg 13, co B, enl 8/31/62 Whitesburg, des 9/8/62, CSR states Letcher Co. as residence, house 532 or 561, s 1,3,31.

MARTIN, TANDY. reg 13, co E, enl 10/14/62 Floyd Co., cap Gladesville 7/7/63, taken to Camp Chase 7/20/63, to Camp Douglas 8/24/63, d 11/18/63, buried grave #848, Chicago City Cemetery, CSR states he was Letcher Co. resident, may have been Floyd Co. resident, house n/c, s 1,2,31.

MCDANIEL, JOHN. reg 5, co A, B, enl 9/11/62 Jackson, app 4th sgt 9/18/62, relieved of duty 5/30/63, des 8/10/63 Hansonville VA, house 38, s 1,3.

MCDANIEL, WILLIAM. reg 13, co H, enl l0/14/62 or 10/18/62 Whitesburg, des 1/6/62, CSR states Letcher Co. as residence, house 38, s 1,3,31.

MCRAE OR MCCRAE, BENJAMIN. reg 13, co D, enl 10/4/62 Whitesburg, dark hair & skin, gray eyes, 5-8, surrendered at Louisa 6/7/64, took oath 7/1/64, released 7/7/64, oath documents state he is Johnson Co. resident, but he is not on Johnson Co. census, CSR states Letcher Co. as residence, house n/c, s 1,3,31.

MEAD, JAMES MADISON. reg 13, co E, enl 10/5/62 or 10/14/62 Whitesburg, des 10/25/62, CSR states Letcher Co. as residence, house n/c, s 1,3,31.

MEAD, REUBEN. reg 13, co E, enl 10/5/62, 10/14/62 or 10/23/62 Whitesburg, r 4th cpl, app cpl 4/30/63, CSR states Letcher Co. as residence, house 185, s 1,3.

MEAD, RILEY. reg 13, co D, enl 10/4/62 Whitesburg, des 1/21/62, CSR states Letcher Co. as residence, house 182, s 1,3,31.

MILES, WILLIAM RILEY. reg 13, co H, enl 10/18/62 Whitesburg, des 12/20/62, CSR states Letcher Co. as residence, house n/c, s 1,3,31.

MOORE, ISAAC. reg 13, co H, enl 10/14/62 Whitesburg, clothing receipt 3rd quarter 1864, CSR states Letcher Co. as residence, house n/c, s 1,31.

MORGAN, JAMES. reg 13, co D, enl 10/4/62 Whitesburg, des 10/5/62, CSR and source 31 state he is Letcher Co. resident, may be Pike Co. resident, house 354, s 1,3,31.

MORGAN, JOHN. reg 13, co H, enl 10/18/62 Whitesburg, not on CSR, house 354, s 3,31.

MULLINS, FRANKLIN. reg 5, co F, enl 11/1/61 Whitesburg, house 538, s 1,3.

MULLINS, HIRAM. reg 5, co F, enl 11/5/61 Whitesburg, reg 13, co E, r 3rd sgt, enl 10/5/62 or 10/14/62 Whitesburg, clothing receipt 9/7/64, CSR states Letcher Co. as residence, house n/c, s 1,3,31.

MULLINS, J. A. reg 13, co A, enl 11/1/61 Whitesburg, died Letcher Co., house 238, 326, 245, 327 or 249, s 1,3.

MULLINS, JOHN. reg 13, co D, r 4th sgt, enl 10/4/62 Whitesburg, CSR states Letcher Co. as residence, house 248, 326, or 537, s 1,3,31.

MULLINS, JOHN A. reg 5, co F, enl 11/1/61 camp near Pound Gap, reg 13, co A, house 248 or 326, s 1,3,31.

MULLINS, JOSEPH. reg 13, co H, enl 10/10/62 or 10/18/62, Whitesburg, cap Gladesville 7/7/63, taken to Camp Chase 7/20/63, to Camp Douglas 8/24/63, CSR states Letcher Co. as residence, house 245 or 327, s 1,3,31.

MULLINS, SOLOMON. reg 13, co D, enl 10/4/62 Whitesburg, source 31 states he is a resident of Wise Co. VA, house 247, s 1,3,31.

MULLINS, VALENTINE. reg 5, co F, enl 11/1/61 Whitesburg, house 537, s 1, 3.

MULLINS, WILLIAM A. reg 13, co D, enl 10/4/62 Whitesburg, cap Cynthiana 6/14/64, taken to Camp Morton 6/25/64, CSR states Letcher Co. as residence, house 249 or 528, s 1,3,31.

MUSIC, WILLIAM R. reg 5, co F, r 2nd cpl, enl 11/1/61 Whitesburg, house 302, s 1,3.

N

NEACE, JACOB. reg 13, co G, enl 1862, cap Gladesville 7/7/63, paroled Camp Douglas, taken to Point Lookout for exchange 3/2/65, house 369, s 1,31.

NEWLAND, JOSPEH C. reg 5, co F, r 3rd sgt, enl 11/1/61 Whitesburg, not on CSR, house 290, s 3.

P

PIGMAN, CAMPBELL. reg 5, co F, enl 11/1/61 Whitesburg, reg 13, co A, r 2nd lt, enl, elected 2nd lt 11/2/62, resigned 2/22/64, age 32, house 288, s 1,3,31.

PIGMAN, JAMES MADISON. reg 13, co B, enl 9/7/62 Whitesburg, dis 1/1/63, CSR states Letcher Co. as residence, house 289, s 1,3,31.

PIGMAN, WILBURN. reg 5, co F, enl 11/1/61 Whitesburg, house 522, s 1,3.

PIGMAN, WILLIAM T. reg 13, co A, B, enl 9/7/62 or 11/1/61 Whitesburg, 1/1/63 trans to co A, des 4/10/63 from Whitesburg, CSR states Letcher Co. as residence, house 468, s 1,3,31.

POTTER, REUBEN. reg 13, co D, enl 10/4/62 Whitesburg, des 10/5/62 CSR states Letcher Co. as residence, house 129, s 1,3,31.

PRATT, JOHN M. reg 13, co B, enl 8/29/62 or 9/9/62 Whitesburg, CSR states Letcher Co. as residence, house 93, s 1,3,31.

PRATT, STEPHEN S. reg 5 co F, r 3rd cpl, enl 11/1/61 Whitesburg, prom to 3rd cpl 5/19/62, reg 13, co A, enl 9/12/63 Whitesburg, clothing receipt 6/29/64, house 476, s 1,3,31.

PRATT, WILLIAM H. reg 5, co F, enl 11/1/61 Whitesburg, reg 13, co A, trans from 5th Ky., house 476, s 1,3,31.

Q

QUILLIN, DREWRY. reg 13, co D, enl 10/4/62 Whitesburg, CSR states Letcher Co. as residence, house 189, s 1,3,31.

QUILLIN, MALON. reg 13, co D, E, enl 10/5/62 or 10/23/62 Whitesburg, CSR states Letcher Co. as residence, house 189, s 1,3,31.

QUILLIN, RICHARD. reg 13, co D, enl 10/4/62 Whitesburg, des 10/27/62, CSR states Letcher Co. as residence, house 199, s 1,3,31.

R

REYNOLDS, WILLIAM HENRY. reg 13, co D, enl 10/4/62 Whitesburg, des 10/15/62, CSR states Letcher Co. as residence, house n/c, s 1,3,31.

REYNOLDS, JOHN. reg 5, co F, enl 11/1/61 Whitesburg, reg 13, co A, dis 3/28/63, house 306, s 1,3,31.

REYNOLDS, STEPHEN N. reg 13, co D, r 3rd cpl, enl 10/4/62 Whitesburg, CSR states Letcher Co. as residence, house 141, s 1,3,31.

REYNOLDS, WESLEY. reg 5, co F, enl 11/1/61 Whitesburg, house 306, s 1,3.

ROBERTS, PRESTON. reg 13, co H, enl 9/22/62 or 10/18/62 Whitesburg, CSR states Letcher Co. as residence, house 270, s 1,3,31.

ROSS, JAMES PRESTON. reg 13, co B, enl 8/21/62 Whitesburg, des 9/15/62, CSR states Letcher Co. as residence, house 113, s 1,3,31.

S

SALLEY, GREEN BERRY aka BERIAH. reg 13, co D, enl 10/4/62 Whitesburg, des 10/21/62, CSR states Letcher Co. as residence, house 571, s 1,3,31.

SEXTON, ELLSBURY. reg 13, co B, r 2nd cpl, enl 9/9/62 Whitesburg, cap Gladesville 7/7/63, taken to Camp Chase 7/20/63, to Camp Douglas 8/24/63, trans to Point Lookout 2/24/65, CSR states Letcher Co. as residence, house 363, s 1,3,31.

SEXTON, HATLER HASCUE. reg 5, co F, enl 11/1/61 Whitesburg, prom to 3rd sgt 3/13/62, reg 13, co A, r 1st sgt, clothing receipts 4/7/64, 6/29/64, 9/7/64 & 9/15/64, house 512, s 1,3,31.

SEXTON, JOHN. reg 5, co H, enl 10/21/61 camp near Pound Gap or Prestonsburg, dis 10/27/62 Salyersville, house 363 or 440, s 1,3.

SEXTON, JOSEPH. reg 5, co F, enl 11/1/61 Whitesburg, reg 13, co A, r 2nd cpl, enl 11/1/62 Whitesburg, house 511, s 1, 3.

SEXTON, NATHANIEL D. reg 13, co H, r 1st cpl, enl 9/13/62 or 10/18/62 Whitesburg, clothing receipts 6/29/64, 9/7/64 & 9/24/64, CSR states Letcher Co. as residence, house n/c, s 1,3,31.

SEXTON, STEPHEN A. reg 5, co A, F, enl 11/1/61 Whitesburg, reg 13, co A, clothing receipts 6/29/64 & 9/7/64, house 205, s 1,3,31.

SEXTON, WILLIAM. reg 13, co H, enl 10/18/62 Whitesburg, rem CSR states Letcher Co. resident, house 513, s 1,3,31.

SEXTON, WILLIAM M. reg 5, co H, enl 10/21/61 Prestonsburg, r sgt, m/out 10/22/62 Salyersville, reg 13, co H, enl 9/22/62 or 10/18/62 Whitesburg, clothing receipts 9/1/64 & 9/15/64, CSR states Letcher Co. as residence, house 363, s 1,3,31.

SHORT, BOOKER. reg 13, co H, enl 10/4/62 or 10/18/62 Whitesburg, reg 7ConfCav, co G, r 4th cpl, reg 10, co H, b Russell Co. VA, paroled Charleston WV, house 508, s 1,3,12,31.

SHORT, WILSON ESLIN. reg 13, co H, enl Whitesburg or Gladesville, source 31 says he is Letcher Co. resident, house n/c, s 1,3,31.

SHULER, FRANKLIN. reg 13, co E, F, enl 10/5/62 or 10/14/62 Whitesburg, clothing receipt 9/7/64, CSR states Letcher Co. as residence, house 167, s 1,3,31.

SHULER, STEPHEN. reg 5, co F, enl 11/1/61 Whitesburg, reg 13, co E, F, enl 10/5/62 Whitesburg, clothing receipts 6/29/64 & 9/7/64, house 167, s, 1,3,31.

SINGLETON, JOSHUA B. reg 13, co D, enl 10/4/62 Whitesburg, CSR states Letcher Co. as residence, house 557, s 1,3,31.

SKEEN, HENRY A. reg 13, co I, enl 10/18/62 Whitesburg, des 5/10/63, CSR states he is Perry Co. resident, but he is not on Perry Co. census, source 31 says he is Letcher Co. resident, house 462, s 1,3,31.

SLONE, JAMES. reg 5, co F, enl 11/1/61 Whitesburg, house 469, s 1,3.

SLONE, LEVI TRUMBULL. reg 13, co E, enl 10/5/62 or 10/14/62 Whitesburg, des 11/15/62, CSR states Letcher Co. as residence, house n/c, s 1,3,31.

SMITH, ANDREW B. reg 5, co F, enl 11/1/61 Whitesburg, reg 13, co A, cap Letcher Co. 6/18/64, died Camp Douglas 2/21/65, buried Block 3, grave 819, Chicago City Cemetery, house 404, s 1 3.

SMITH, EMORY B. reg 5, co F, reg 13, co A, enl 11/1/61 Whitesburg, discharged by surgeon spring 1863, source 31 states he is Letcher Co. resident, house n/c, s 1 3 31.

SMITH, JACOB G. reg 10, co L, cap 3/22/63 Mason Co., not on AG, house 402, s 3.

SMITH, JEREMIAH M. reg 13, co H, enl 10/8/62 or 10/18/62 Whitesburg, des 11/23/62, CSR states he is Perry Co. resident, but he is not on Perry Co. census, source 31 says he is Letcher Co. resident, house 543, s 1,3,31.

SMITH, JOHN. reg 13, co I, enl 7/15/63 or 10/18/63 Whitesburg or Gladesville, des, house 307, 399 or 418, s 1,3,31.

SMITH, JOHN JR. reg 5, co F, r cpl, enl 2/8/62 Pound Gap, dis 2/62 for disability, age 30, dark hair & skin, blue eyes, not on AG, house 307, s 1.

SMITH, JOHN SR. reg 5, co F, enl 9/30/62 Licking Station, not on AG, house 307 or 309, s 1

SMITH, JOHN B. reg 5, co F, r 4th cpl, enl 11/1/61 Whitesburg, dis 2/26/62, house 307, 399 or 418, s 1,3.

SMITH, SAMUEL. reg 13, co I, enl 10/18/62 or 8/1/63 Whitesburg or Gladesville, house 418, s 1,3,31.

SMITH, SAMUEL P. reg 13, co B, r 2nd lt, enl 8/29/62 Whitesburg, elected 2nd lt 6/2/64, clothing receipt 4/7/64, CSR states Letcher Co. as residence, house 418, s 1,3.

SMITH, SAMPSON B. reg 13, co B, r 2nd lt, enl 8/29/62 Whitesburg, rem cap Cynthiana 6/12/64, house 95, s 1,3,31.

SMITH, WILLIAM BRANHAM. reg 5, co F, enl 11/1/61 Whitesburg, reg 13, co A, house 307, 402 or 544, s 1,3,31.

SMITH, WILLIAM B. reg 13, co B, enl 9/15/62 Whitesburg, clothing receipts 6/29/64, 9/7/64, & 11/19/64, CSR states Letcher Co. as residence, house 307, 402 or 544, s 1,3.

SPARKMAN, JOHN S. reg 5, co F, enl 11/1/61 Whitesburg, des 2/8/62, reg 13, co A, r 5th sgt, cap Gladesville 7/7/63, taken to Camp Chase 8/24/63, to Camp Douglas, to Point Lookout 2/24/65, house 285, s 1,3,31.

SPARKMAN, RICHARD. reg 13, co B, enl 9/9/62 or 9/29/62 Whitesburg, cap Johnson Co. 5/31/64, sent to Rock Island 6/14/64, enl in US Army for frontier service 10/6/64, CSR states Letcher Co. as residence, house n/c, s 1,3,31.

SPARKMAN, SAMUEL SAMPSON. reg 5, co F, enl 11/1/61 Whitesburg, des 2/8/62, reg 13, co A, house 303, s 1,3,31.

SPARKMAN, WILLIAM. reg 13, co H, enl 10/18/62 Whitesburg, dis 10/18/62, CSR states Letcher Co. as residence, house 401 or 460, s 1,3,31.

STAMPER, HIRAM H. reg 13, co A, r capt, enl 11/1/61 Whitesburg, age 28, dark hair & skin, blue eyes, 6-1, elected capt 11/2/62, cap Gladesville 7/7/63, taken to Camp Chase 7/20/63, to Johnson's Island 10/10/63, to Point Lookout 3/21/65, to Ft. Delaware 4/28/65, took oath 6/12/65 at Ft. Delaware and released, oath documents state Letcher Co. as residence, house 265, s 1,3,31.

STAMPER, HIRAM W. reg 5, co F, enl 11/1/61 Whitesburg, r 2nd lt, reg 13, co H, r 5th sgt, enl 10/5/62 or 10/18/62 Whitesburg, des 11/8/62, 5th Ky. service not on CSR, CSR states Letcher Co. as residence, house 442, s 1,3,31.

STAMPER, JOHN W. reg 13, co H, r 1st sgt, enl 10/18/62 Whitesburg, prom from cpl to 1st sgt 3/18/63, clothing receipts 6/29/64 & 11/19/64, CSR states Letcher Co. as residence, house 18, 87 or 265, s 1,3,31.

STAMPER, WILLIAM RILEY. reg 13, co H, enl 10/1/62 or 10/18/62 Whitesburg, des 4/15/63, CSR states Letcher Co. as residence, house 265 or 442, s 1,3,31.

STEWART, JACKSON, probably erroneously listed as STEWARD, JASPER. reg 13, co H, enl 10/18/62 Whitesburg, des 12/17/62, CSR states Letcher Co. as residence, house 296, s 1,3,31.

STIDHAM, CALVIN W. reg 13, co D, r 4th cpl, enl 10/4/62 or 4/1/64 Whitesburg, CSR states Letcher Co. as residence, house 564, s 1,3,31.

STURDIVANT, PLEASANT G. reg 5, co F, enl 11/1/61 Whitesburg, reg 13, co C, house 386, s 1,3,31.

STURDIVANT, THOMAS KENT. reg 13, co A, enl 9/14/61 Whitesburg, house 386, s 3,31.

STURGILL, ISAAC. reg 13, co D, enl 10/4/62 Whitesburg, CSR states Letcher Co. as residence, house 72, s 1,3,31.

STURGILL, JOHN A. reg 13, co D, r 2nd cpl, enl 10/4/62 Whitesburg, source 31 states he is Letcher Co. resident, house 238, s 1,3,31.

STRUGILL, JOHN G. reg 13, co D, r 3rd sgt, enl 10/4/62 Whitesburg, CSR states Letcher Co. as residence, house 567, s 1,3,31.

STURGILL, JORDAN. reg 5, co F, enl 11/1/61 Whitesburg, house 562, s 1,3.

STURGILL, MCGUIRE. reg 5, co F, enl 11/1/61 Whitesburg, house 525, s 1, 3.

SUMMER, JOHN WESLEY. reg 13, co B, enl 9/11/62 or 9/11/62 Whitesburg, des 11/1/62, CSR states Letcher Co. as residence, house 280, s 1,3,31.

SUMNER, WESLEY. reg 13, co B, enl 9/6/62 Whitesburg, cap Gladesville 7/7/63, taken to Camp Chase 7/20/63, to Camp Douglas 8/24/63, died 11/4/63 of typhoid, buried grave #792, Chicago City Cemetery, house 280, s 1,3,31.

T

TUCKER, OLIVER PERRY. reg 13, co D, enl 10/4/62 Whitesburg, des 11/6/62, house 152, s 1,3,31.

TYRA, JOSEPH. reg 13, co H, enl 10/29/62 Brasherville, cap Gladesville 7/7/63, taken to Camp Chase 7/20/63, to Camp Douglas 8/24/63, house 349, s 1,3.

TYRA, MATISON aka PATTERSON. reg 13, co H, enl 10/18/62 Brasherville, cap Gladesville 7/7/63, taken to Camp Chase 7/20/63, to Camp Douglas 8/24/63, d 1/10/65, house 349, s 1,3,31.

TYRA, WILLIAM. reg 13, co C, enl 10/1/62 Whitesburg, rem not on CSR, house 361, s 3,31.

W

WATTS, ENOCH. reg 5, co A, B, H, enl 12/26/61 or 9/11/62 Jackson or Paintsville, dis 10/20/62 Hazel Green, reg 10, co D, enl 10/29/62 Pike Co., clothing receipt 8/9/64, house 536, s 1,3.

WATTS, GEORGE. reg 5, co C, enl 11/1/61 Whitesburg, house 535, s 1,3.

WATTS, GEORGE WASHINGTON. reg 13, co A, B, enl 11/1/61 or 9/2/62 Whitesburg, trans to co A 1/1/63, CSR states Letcher Co. as residence, house 85 or 535, s 1,3,31.

WATTS, JOHN C. reg 13, co A, B, enl 11/1/61 or 9/2/62 Whitesburg, trans to co A 1/1/63, cap Gladesville 7/7/63, taken to Camp Chase, d 12/19/63 of pulmonary problems, house 539, s 1,3,31.

WEBB, ARCHELAUS or ARCHIBALD C. reg 13, co D, enl 10/4/62 Whitesburg, CSR states Letcher Co. as residence, house possibly 356, s 1,3,31.

WEBB, ENOCH A. reg 13, co D, r capt, enl 10/4/62 Whitesburg, elected capt 11/2/62, resigned 7/20/63, paroled 5/3/65 Letcher Co., CSR states Letcher Co. as residence, house 40, s 1,3,31.

WEBB, HENRY M. reg 13, co D, enl 1862, paroled 5/2/65 Cumberland Gap, received Confederate pension #1104, house 40, s 1,31.

WEBB, LEWIS A. reg 13, co D, r 3rd sgt, enl 10/4/62 or 4/1/64 Whitesburg, CSR states Letcher Co. as residence, house n/c, s 1,3.

WEBB, RILEY. reg 13, co D, r 1st cpl, enl 10/4/62 Whitesburg, paroled 5/2/65 Lee Co. VA, CSR states Letcher Co. as residence, house 40, s 1,3,31.

WELLS, SOLOMON. reg 5, co F, enl 11/1/61 Whitesburg, house 108, s 1,3.

WHITAKER, ISAAC J. reg 13, co B, enl 8/29/62 Whitesburg, cap Gladesville 7/7/63, taken to Camp Chase 7/20/63, to Camp Douglas 8/24/63, to Point Lookout 2/24/65, CSR states Letcher Co. as residence, house 83, s 1,3,31.

WHITAKER, JOHN. reg 13, co H, enl 3/28/63 Brasherville, deserted, house 91 or 490, s 1,3,31.

WHITAKER, JOHN W. reg 13, co B, enl 8/29/62 Whitesburg, app wagoner 12/17/62, clothing receipt 4/7/64, CSR states Letcher Co. as residence, house 91 or 490, s 1,3,31.

WHITAKER, MOSES E. reg 13, co B, enl 8/29/62 Whitesburg, CSR states Letcher Co. as residence, house 75, s 1,3,31.

WHITAKER, STEPHEN A. reg 13, co B, H, r 1st lt, enl 8/29/62 Whitesburg, prom to 1st lt 10/4/62 or 10/15/62, des 10/64, dropped from rolls by order of Secretary of War 2/16/65, house 484, s 1,3,31.

WHITE, WILLIAM. reg 13, co H, enl 10/18/62 Whitesburg, clothing receipts 4/7/64 & 6/29/64, CSR states Letcher Co. as residence, house 382, s 1,3,31.

WILLIAMS, HENRY. reg 13, co D, enl 10/4/62 or 12/1/62 Whitesburg, house 337, s 1,3,31.

WORRIC, JOHN FOUNT also spelled **WARRICK.** reg 13, co D, enl 10/4/62 Whitesburg, des 10/21/62, CSR states Letcher Co. as residence, may be Pike Co. resident, house n/c, s 1,3,31.

WRIGHT, ANDREW JEFFERSON JR. reg 13, co A, D, r cpl, enl 11/1/61 Whitesburg, trans from 5th Ky., but 5th Ky. service not on CSR, house 126, s 1, 3,31.

WRIGHT, ANDREW JACKSON SR. reg 5, co F, enl 11/1/61 Whitesburg, reg 13, co A, D, house 149, s 1,3,31.

WRIGHT, BENJAMIN. reg 13, co B, D, enl 9/2/62 Whitesburg, trans to co D 1/63, CSR states Letcher Co. as residence, house 127, s 1,3,31.

WRIGHT, HIRAM. reg 13, co D, enl 8/1/63 Whitesburg, house 126, s 1,3,31.

WRIGHT, JAMES HARRISON. reg 13, co D, r 1st cpl, enl 10/4/62 or 4/1/64 Whitesburg, prom to 1st cpl, CSR states Letcher Co. as residence, house 139, s 1, 3,31.

WRIGHT, JOEL. reg 5 co F, enl 11/1/61 Whitesburg, r 2nd cpl, reg 13, co D, enl 10/4/62 or 4/1/64 Whitesburg, r 2nd cpl, prom to 2nd cpl, CSR states Letcher Co. as residence, house 120 or 148, s 1,3.

WRIGHT, JOHN. reg 5, co F, enl 11/1/61 Whitesburg, reg 13, co D, G, enl 9/26/62 or 10/4/62 Whitesburg, CSR states Letcher Co. as residence, house 126 or 148, s 1, 3.

WRIGHT, JOHN VENT. reg 13, co G, enl 9/23/62 Whitesburg, house 128 or 149, s 3, 31.

WRIGHT, SOLOMON. reg 5, co F, r 1st lt, enl 11/1/61 Whitesburg, prom to 2nd lt 10/4/62, to 1st lt 11/2/62, CSR states Letcher Co. as residence, house 148, s 1,3.

WRIGHT, WILLIAM. reg 5, co F, enl 11/1/61 Camp near Pound Gap, des 1/11/62, not on AG, house 128 or 149, s 1.

WRIGHT, WILLIAM. reg 5, co F, enl 11/1/61 Whitesburg, reg 13, co A, house 128 or 149, s 1,3.

Y

YOUNTS, CHARLES. reg 13, co D, enl 10/4/62 Whitesburg, CSR states Letcher Co. as residence, house 198, s 1,3,31.

YOUNTS, ELIJAH. reg 13, co D, enl 10/4/62 Whitesburg, des 11/5/62, CSR states Letcher Co. as residence, house 157, s 1,3,31.

YOUNTS, JOHN. reg 5, co F, enl 11/1/61 Whitesburg, reg 13, co D, house 200, s 1,3.

YOUNTS, SOLOMON. reg 13, co D, enl 10/4/62 Whitesburg, des 11/5/62, CSR states Letcher Co. as residence, house 196, s 1,3,31.

MAGOFFIN COUNTY CONFEDERATE SOLDIERS

A

ALLEN, JOHN. reg 10, co D, enl 11/10/62 or 3/10/63 Wolfe Co. or Piketon, cap Wise Co. Va. 7/7/63, 2/65 wanting to take oath of allegiance, house 75 or 223, s 1,3,28.

ALLEN, JOSEPH SR. reg 13, co F, enl 10/14/62 mouth of Salt Lick, Floyd Co., CSR lists Floyd Co. as residence, but he is not on Floyd Co. census, house 76, s 1,3,31.

ALLEN, WOODSON. reg 13, co C, enl 10/1/62 Whitesburg, house 85, s 1,3,31.

ARNETT, FARRISH. reg 10, co A, house 278, not on AG or CSR, house 278, s 22,28.

ARNETT, HIRAM. reg 10, co A, not on CSR, house 544, s 22, 28.

ARNETT, REBUEN. reg 10, co B, captured 5/2/65 Magoffin Co. sent to Camp Chase 5/10/65, not on AG or CSR, house 572, s 28.

ARNETT, STEPHEN M. reg 5, co K, r 2nd lt, date of rank 10/11/62, d 10/21/62, house 4, s 1,28.

B

BAILEY, ANDREW. reg 5, co C, enl 10/26/61 Prestonsburg, reg 13, co F, K, enl 10/14/62 Floyd Co., mouth of Salt Lick, age 25, light hair, gray eyes, fair skin 6-0, cap Perry Co. 5/10/63, sent to Camp Chase OH, Johnson's Island and Point Lookout, rel on oath 1/10/64, house 70, s 1,3,28,31.

BAILEY, GARDNER F. reg 10, co B, enl 4/17/63 Jackson, des 5/23/63, d 1/23/64, house 179, s 1,3.

BAILEY, HENRY. reg 13, co C, F, enl 10/1/62 or 5/15/63 Whitesburg, cap Gladesville, 7/7/63, taken to Camp Chase 7/20/63, sent to Camp Douglas 8/24/63, enl 5th U.S. Volunteers 4/6/65, house 8 or 441, s 1,3,28,31.

BAILEY, HENRY C. reg 5, co C, enl 10/19/61 Prestonsburg, dis 10/20/62 Hazel Green, house 441, s 1,3,28.

BAILEY, JOHN. reg 13, co F, enl 10/14/62 Floyd Co., not on CSR, descriptive index lists Floyd Co. as residence, but he is not listed on Floyd Co. census, b 1843, house 33, s 3,28,31.

BAILEY, SAMUEL. reg 13, co C, F, enl 10/1/62 Whitesburg, cap Gladesville, 7/7/63 house 8 or 179, s 1,3,28,31.

BAILEY, SAMUEL. reg 5, co C, enl 10/19/61 Prestonsburg, dis 10/20/62 Hazel Green, house 8 or 179, s 1,3,28.

BAILEY, WILLIAM. reg 5, co C, enl 10/19/61 Prestonsburg, house 179 or 449, s 2.

BARNETT, WILLIAM. reg 5, co D, enr 9/20/62 Jackson, enl 11/18/62 Jackson or Licking Station, house 305 or 351, s 1,3,28.

BARNETT, WILLIAM A. reg 10, co K, enl 7/10/63 Liberty Hill VA, age 30, dark hair & skin, gray eyes, 5-5, took oath of allegiance 6/12/65 Charleston WV, house 351, s 1,3,28.

BAYS, WILLIAM. reg 5, co B, enl 3/28/62 Moccasin VA, may be Johnson Co. resident, house 330 or 340, s 1,3.

BLANTON, MADISON. reg 5, co K, reg 13 Ga. Cav., co K, disbanded Christiansburg VA 4/12/65, took oath Paintsville 5/3/65, reg 5 service not on CSR, no CSR on reg 13 Ga. Cav., house 353, s 30.

BROOKS, CAMPBELL C. reg 10, co E, r 3rd cpl, enl 5/10/64 Smyth Co. VA, cap Cynthiana 6/12/64, sent to Camp Morton, 6/25/64, house 114, s 1,3,28.

BROOKS, SAMUEL W. reg 5, co A, enl 10/25/61 Prestonsburg, dis 10/20/62 Hazel Green, age 41, dark hair, blue eyes, light skin, 5-11, house 114, s 1,3.

BROOKS, THOMAS B. reg 5, co A, r 2d lt., enl 10/25/61 Prestonsburg, dis 10/20/62 Hazel Green, age 18, dark hair, black eyes, fair skin, 5-9, b. Tazewell Co. VA, elected 2d lt. 10/6/62, house 114, s 3,28.

C

CAUDILL, ABEL. reg 5, co C, F, enl 11/1/61 Whitesburg, cap Booneville 8/9/63, received at Camp Chase 9/18/63, received at Rock Island, 1/22/64, house 423 or 569, may have served in Union reg 45, s 1,3,28.
CAUDILL, JESSE. reg 5, co F, enl 11/5/61 Whitesburg, house 569, s 1,3.
CAUDILL, JOHN M. reg 5, co F, enl 11/1/61 Whitesburg, house 568, s 1,3.
CAUDILL, SAMUEL C. reg 5, co F, r 2d sgt, enl 11/1/61 Whitesburg, house 423, s 1,3.
COCHRAN, ELIJAH D. reg 5, co C, enr 9/8/62 Salyersville, enl 9/10/62 Salyersville, age 28, black hair & eyes, 5-5, cap Maynardville TN 12/3/63, received at Camp Chase 12/16/63, d 12/21/63 affliction of the brain, house 239, s 1,3,28.
COLDIRON, JAMES. reg 5, co I, enl 10/25/61 Prestonsburg or Pound Gap, musician, house 434, s 1,3.
COLE, SHEPHERD. reg 13, co F, enl 10/18/62 Whitesburg, rem des 12/12/62, not on AG, CSR lists Letcher Co. as residence, source 31 lists Magoffin Co. as residence, house 26, s 1,31.
CONLEY, DAVID. reg FR, enl 10/18/62 Magoffin Co., house 410, s 3,36.
CONLEY, GEORGE WASHINGTON. reg FR, enl 8/1/63 Magoffin Co., house 98, s 1,3,36.
CONLEY, JOSEPH C. reg 5, co H, enl 10/21/61 Prestonsburg or Pound Gap, reg 13, co F, enl 5/15/63 Floyd Co., cap Gladesville 7/7/63, to Kemper Barracks 7/18/63, to Camp Chase 8/24/63, exch Point Lookout 3/2/65, house 346, s 1,3,28.
CRAGER, HENRY (HARVEY) M. reg 5, co B, C, enl 10/25/61 Prestonsburg, dis 10/20/62 Hazel Green, age 39, light hair, dark eyes & skin, 5-10, arrested Magoffin Co. 5/4/63, taken to Camp Chase, 5/13/63, taken to Johnson's Island 6/14/63, sent to Point Lookout 11/30/63, released on oath 1/10/64, house 61 s 1, 3,28.

D

DUNN, JEREMIAH M. reg 10, co E, enl 3/20/63 Wolfe Co., clothing receipt 9/14/64, house 172, s 1,3, 28.

E

ENGLAND, RICHARD. reg 5, co C, enl 10/26/61 Prestonsburg, reg 13, co F, enl 10/14/62 Floyd Co., reg 13 service not on CSR, house 64, s 1,3,28,31.

F

FRANKLIN, JOHN. reg 5, co C, r sgt, enl 10/20/61 or 9/20/62 West Liberty or Salyersville, prom from 4th cpl to 4th sgt 8/1/63, severely wounded 5/14/64, hospital card lists Bloomington as Post Office, house 403, s 1,3,28.

G

GARDNER, JOSEPH H. reg 5, r lt, assistant commissary, not on AG or CSR, records in Record Group 109, s 28.
GIBSON, SQUIRE. reg 10, co F, r capt, age 30, dark hair, blue eyes, fair skin, 6-0, elected captain 2/28/63, took oath of allegiance at Charleston WV 5/30/65, house 504, s 1,3,10.

GULLETT, ASA P. reg 5, co A, age 28, dark hair and skin, blue eyes, 5-10, cap Morgan Co. 5/15/63, taken to Camp Chase 6/9/63 to Sandusky OH 11/4/63, to Point Lookout 11/30/63, to Fortress Monroe VA 3/2/64, house 254, s 1,3,22,28.
GULLETT, WILLIAM W. reg 5, co C, enr & enl 9/8/62 Salyersville, trans to co G, wounded at Intrenchment Creek GA in left foot 7/22/64, house 427 or 584, s 1,3,28.

H

HALE, JAMES. reg 13, co F, enl 10/14/62 mouth of Salt Lick, Floyd Co., may be Floyd Co. resident, house 67, s 1,28,31.
HILL, WILLIAM F. reg 5, co A, enl 10/25/61 Prestonsburg, dis 10/20/62 Hazel Green, age 23, dark hair & skin, hazel eyes, b. Giles Co. VA, house 318, s 1,3,28.
HOWARD, LARK. reg 5, co B, not on AG or CSR, house 16, s 28.
HOWARD, MARTIN. reg 5, taken to Camp Chase 5/2/63, took oath 5/9/63, age 23 (at Camp Chase), auburn hair, blue eyes, dark skin, 5-8, CSR lists Magoffin Co. as residence, house 543, s 1.
HOWARD, SAMUEL. reg 5, co B, cap Magoffin Co. 10/13/63, taken to Camp Chase 10/24/63, not on AG, house 55 or 89, s 1,28.
HOWARD, STEPHEN B. reg 5, co B, enl 10/21/61 Prestonsburg or West Liberty, dis 10/20/62 Hazel Green, house 153, s 1,3,28.

I

INGLAND (ENGLAND), RICHARD. reg 5, co C, enl 10/26/61 Prestonsburg, house 64, s 3.

J

JACKSON, JAMES FRANKLIN. reg 5, co K, enl 12/29/61 Camp Hager, des 1/6/62, house 324, s 1,3,28.
JENKINS, WILLIAM. reg 2MR, co F, enl 9/62, not on CSR, house 418, s 3,28.
JONES, JOSEPH. reg 13, co F, enl 10/14/62 Floyd Co., not on CSR, house 12, s 3,31.
JONES, WILLIAM JASPER. reg 5, co C, enl 9/7/62 Salyersville, d of fever Hansonsville VA 8/23/63, house 490, s 1,3,28.

K

KEATON, RILEY M. reg 13, co H, enl 10/18/62 Whitesburg, rem cap Gladesville VA 7/7/63, taken to Kemper Barracks 7/18/63, to Camp Chase 7/20/63, to Camp Douglas 8/24/63, not on AG, CSR lists Letcher Co. as residence, house 452, s 1,31.

L

LEMASTER, MEREDITH. reg 5, co C, enl 9/6/62 Salyersville, age 29, light hair, blue eyes, 6-1, age 18 on census, arrested near Maynardsville TN 12/3/63, taken to Camp Chase 12/16/63, d 2/7/64 Camp Chase of smallpox, buried grave no. 106, house 244, s 1,3,28.
LEMASTER, WINSTON. reg 5, co C, r sgt, enl 9/8/62 Salyersville, age 20, dark hair, gray eyes, 5-8, reduced to ranks 8/1/63, captured Maynardsville TN 12/3/63, taken to Camp Chase 12/10/63, d 2/20/65 of pneumonia, buried grave no. 1359 Camp Chase, age 20 on census, house 266, s 1,3,28.

LYKINS, ELI S. reg 5, co A, r 3rd lt., enl 10/21/61 Prestonsburg or West Liberty, dis 10/20/62 Hazel Green, elected 3rd lt 9/24/62, house 496 or 564, s 1,3.

M

MCGUIRE, JAMES M. reg 1MR, co B, r 3rd sgt, enl 10/26/61 Prestonsburg or Magoffin Co., age 23, light hair, blue eyes, fair skin, 6-0, b Tazewell Co. VA, house 541, s 1,3,28.
MULLINS, AMBROSE. reg 13, co F, enl 10/14/62 mouth of Salt Lick, Floyd Co., CSR lists Floyd Co. as residence, house 78, s 1,3,28.

N

NICKELL, ROBERT F. reg 2MR, co E, r 5th sgt, enl 8/7/62 Morgan Co., house 583, s 1,3.

O

ONEY, DAVID. reg 13, co F, enl 10/14/62 or 8/21/63 Floyd Co., house 333, s 1,3,31.
ONEY, JAMES. reg 5, co A, enl 10/21/61 West Liberty or Prestonsburg, captured Morgan Co. 5/24/63, released 5/28/63 on taking oath, house 235, s 1,3,28.
ONEY, RICHARD. reg 5, co A, enl 10/21/61 Prestonsburg or West Liberty, cap Morgan Co. 5/24/63, released 5/28/63 on taking oath, house 235, s 1,3,28.
ONEY, WILLIAM. P. reg 5, co I, enl 10/25/61 Prestonsburg or Pound Gap, dis 10/20/62, reg 13, co F, enl 10/14/62 mouth of Salt Lick, Floyd Co., CSR lists Floyd Co. as residence, b 1838, probably Magoffin Co. resident, s 31 lists Magoffin Co. as residence, house 235, s 1,3,28,31.

P

PATRICK, ALEXANDER. reg 5, co B, enl 5/10/63 Camp Carr or Camp Cox, des, house 520, s 1,3.
PATRICK, CHARLES. reg 5, co B, enl 10/25/61 Prestonsburg, dark hair, blue eyes, florid skin, 5-6, cap Magoffin Co., 4/1/64, received Camp Morton 4/23/64, released on oath 5/22/65, may be Montgomery Co. resident, s 1,3,28.
PATRICK, LEVI. reg 3MR, co B, not on AG or CSR, house 5, s 28.
PATRICK, SAMUEL H. reg 5, co D, r 1st cpl, enr 10/9/62 Jackson or 10/9/62 Licking Station, house 450, s 1,3.
PATTON, ANDY J. reg 5, co B, not on AG or CSR, house 369, s 28.
PERKINS, ELIJAH. reg 3MR, co B, E, enl 3/5/62 Gladesville, cap in Kentucky and exchanged 5/63, house 407, s 1,3.
PRATER, WILLIAM RILEY. reg 13, co F, enl 10/14/62 Floyd Co., b 1837, CSR lists Floyd Co. as residence, age 40 on census, house 335, s 1,3,31.

R

REED, JOHN. reg 5, co C, enl 1/24/64 Dalton, GA, killed at Battle of Resaca GA 5/14/64, house 218 or 238, s 1,3.
REED, WILEY. reg 5, co B, enl 10/25/61 Prestonsburg, house 294, s 1,3,28.

RIGGS, WILLIAM C. reg 5, co C, enl 10/26/61 Prestonsburg, reg 13, co F, r sgt, enl 10/14/62 mouth of Salt Lick, Floyd Co., cap 5/8/63 Morgan or Magoffin Co., sent to Camp Chase 5/20/63, residence stated on CSR, house 180, s 1,3,28,31.

ROBINSON (ROBERTSON), HENRY JACKSON. reg 5, co A, K, r capt, enl 10/25/61 Prestonsburg, dis 10/20/62 Hazel Green, elected capt of new company K 10/10/62, house 214, s 1,3,28.

S

SALYER, CAMBRIDGE C. reg 5, co B, not or AG or CSR, house 6, s 28.

SALYER, DAVID J. reg 10, co B, enl 1/30/63 West Liberty, des 1/10/64 Johnson Co., may be Johnson Co. resident, house 10, s 1,3,28.

SALYER, ISAIAH. reg 5, co A, C, H, enl 4/6/62 Moccasin, Scott Co. VA, dis 10/20/62 Hazel Green, re-enlisted 6/6/63, lost arm at Resaca GA 5/14/64, age 44, house 6, s 1,3.

SALYER, MORGAN M. reg 10, co B, not on CSR, house 32, s 10,28.

SALYER, RUFUS G. reg 10, co B, enl 1/25/63 Bloomington or West Liberty, house 10, s 1,3,28.

SALYER, WILLIAM J. reg 5, co F, cap Magoffin Co. 4/28/63, taken to Camp Chase 5/19/63, accused of violating parole, not on AG, house 37, s 1,28.

SALYER, WILLIAM W. reg 10, co B, enl 1/29/63 West Liberty, cap 3/19/63, paroled and rejoined 6/20/63, house 41, s 1,3,28.

SHEPHERD, MARTIN. reg 13, co B, enl 9/12/62 Middle Creek or Whitesburg, CSR lists Floyd Co. as residence, but not on Floyd Co. census, s 31 lists Magoffin Co. as residence, house 69, s 1,28,31.

STAMPER, JOHN C. reg 5, co C, enr 4/62/62 Moccasin VA, enl 9/14/62 West Liberty, dis 10/20/62 Hazel Green, killed Chickamauga GA 9/20/63, s 1,3.

T

TACKETT, WILLIAM. reg 5, co C, age 30, dark hair & skin, blue eyes, 5-10, cap 5/3/63 Morgan Co. or Magoffin Co., charged with being a rebel officer, sent to Camp Chase 5/13/63, released 6/9/63, CSR states he is Magoffin Co. resident, house n/c, s 1.

TAULBEE, JAMES P. reg 5, co D, enr & enl 9/20/62 Jackson, des Rockhouse VA 5/12/63, house 271. s 1,3.

V

VANDERPOOL, HEZEKIAH. reg 5, co B, I, enl 10/25/61 Prestonsburg, des 1/10/62 Middle Creek, house 143, s 1,3,28.

W

WADKINS, AMBROSE. reg 10, co B, enl 2/10/63 Prestonsburg, age 17, light hair & eyes, dark skin, 5-5, cap 4/30/63 or 5/4/63 Salyersville, received Camp Chase 5/13/63, sent to Johnson's Island, 6/14/63, sent to Point Lookout 10/30/63, house 56, s 1,3,28.

WADKINS, JOHN. reg 5, co C, enl 10/26/61 Prestonsburg, des, house 58, s 1,3.

WADKINS, WILLIAM. reg 5, co C, enl 10/20/61 Prestonsburg, reg 10, co E, enl 6/5/63 Tazewell Co. VA, resident of Wolfe Co. in 1870, house 56 or 576, s 1,3,10.

WHITAKER, WILLIAM C. reg 10, co B, not on AG or CSR, house 15, s 10.

WILLIAMS, JOHN. reg 5, co G, cap Irvine 6/20/63, taken to Camp Chase 6/26/63, to Point Lookout 10/30/63, not on AG, house 194, s 1,22.

WIREMAN, MORGAN. reg 13, co F, enl 10/14/62 Floyd Co., cap Gladesville 7/7/63, taken to Camp Chase 7/20/63, to Camp Douglas 8/24/63, to Point Lookout 2/24/65, CSR lists Floyd Co. as residence, but not on Floyd Co. census, house 79, s 1,28.

MORGAN COUNTY CONFEDERATE SOLDIERS

A

ADAMS, CHARLES T. reg 5, co A, enl 10/21/61 West Liberty, dis 10/20/62 Hazel Green, grizzly hair, dark eyes & skin, 5-7, cap Morgan Co., took oath 3/30/64, CSR lists Morgan Co. as residence, house 1-111, s 1,3,34.

ADAMS, LOUIS CHAMBERS. reg 5, co A, enl 10/21/61 West Liberty, grizzly hair, dark eyes & skin, 5-7, reg 2MR, co A, enl 9/10/62 or 10/11/62 Morgan Co., dis 11/10/62, reg 13, co F, enl 5/15/63 Whitesburg, took oath of allegiance 5/30/64 Louisville, CSR lists Morgan Co. as residence, house 1-111, s 1,3,31,35.

ADAMS, SIMPSON. reg 5, co F, enl 11/1/61 Whitesburg, des 3/29/62 Moccasin Scott Co. VA, house 2-285, s 1,3,22.

ADAMS, WILLIAM H. reg 5, co C, 10/21/61 West Liberty, reg 10, co B, enl 1/25/63 Bloomington, house 2-459, s 1,3,22.

ADKINS, ELIJAH. reg 5, co A, B, enl 10/23/61 Prestonsburg, black hair, blue eyes, sallow skin, 6-2, cap Montgomery Co. 7/3/63, taken to Camp Chase 8/9/63, to Ft. Delaware 3/4/64, released 6/7/65, prison records list Morgan Co. as residence, house 1-233 or 1-533, s 1,2.

ADKINS, GILBERT. reg 5, co G, enl 11/11/61 camp near Pound Gap, house 1-555, s 1,3,22.

ADKINS, GREEN G. reg 5, co B, enl 10/26/61 Prestonsburg, cap 1/27/62 and sent to Newport Barracks, 5/62 left home sick at Morgan Co., house 1-209, s 1,3,22.

ADKINS, HARRISON. reg 5, co B, enl 10/21/61 West Liberty, reg 2MR, co A, enl 10/16/62 Morgan Co., took oath 12/21/63, oath papers list Morgan Co. as residence, house 1-279, s 1,3,22.

ADKINS, HAWKINS. reg FR, enl 10/13/62 Morgan Co., des 10/24/62, house 1-541, s 1,3,35.

ADKINS, HEZEKIAH. reg 5, co B, cap 10/1/63 Morgan Co., taken to military prison at Louisville 10/22/63, to Camp Morton 10/24/63, trans for exchange to Point Lookout 3/15/65, house, 1-555, s 1,22.

ADKINS, JAMES K. P. reg 5, co B, musician, house 1-567, s 3,22.

ADKINS, JOSEPH. reg 5, co B, r capt, enl 10/21/61 West Liberty, age 35, black hair, gray eyes, dark skin, 6-2, cap Morgan Co. 8/28/63, sent to McLean Barracks, Cincinnati, released on oath 10/16/63, house 1-155 or 1-541, s 1,3,35.

ADKINS, NATHANIEL. reg 5, co D, light hair & skin, hazel eyes, 5-10, arrested Lawrence Co. 3/25/63, taken to Camp Chase 4/8/63, sent to City Point for exchange 5/13/63, house 1-226, s 1,22.

ADKINS, NOTEN. reg 5, co B, enl 10/21/61 West Liberty, 5/62 left home sick in Morgan Co., house 1-179, s 1,3,22.

ADKINS, SAMUEL (PETER). reg 13, co C, enl 10/1/62 Whitesburg, cap Gladesville 7/7/63, rel from Camp Douglas 4/6/65 to enlist in U.S. Army, house 1-402, s 3,21,31

ADKINS, SAMUEL S. reg 5, co B, r 2nd lt, enl 10/26/62 Prestonsburg, age 26, black hair, gray eyes, dark skin, 5-10, cap Magoffin or Morgan Co., taken to Johnson Island's 10/16/63, to Ft. Delaware 6/25/64, to Hilton Head SC 8/20/64, house 1-569, s 1,3,22.

ADKINS, STANLEY. reg 5, co B, r sgt, enl 10/21/61 West Liberty, died 1/20/62 of fever, "a good soldier", house 1-568, s 1,3,22.

ADKINS, WILLIAM. reg 5, co B, enl 10/25/61 Prestonsburg, reg 7ConfCav, co G, b 11/10/1842 Morgan Co., house, 1-401, 1-402 or 1-576, s 1,3,34.

AMYX, JOHN W. reg 1MR, co B, enl 10/19/61 Morgan Co., missing 1/7/62 from action at Jennies Creek, refuses to rejoin, house 1-3, s 1,3,22.

ASBERRY, ALEXANDER J. reg 5, co I, musician, enl 10/25/61 Prestonsburg, dis 10/20/62 Hazel Green, house 2-258, s 1,3,22.

ASBERRY, GEORGE. reg 10, co E, killed in battle, house 2-257, s 3,22.
ASBERRY, HENRY R. R. reg 10, co E, r 2nd sgt, enl 10/20/62 Wolfe Co., prom to 2nd sgt, cap 6/8/64 Mt. Sterling, died 12/28/64 in prison of diarrhea, buried grave no. 677, Camp Chase, house 2-257, s 1,3,22.
ASBERRY, THOMAS G. reg 5, co I, r 1st sgt, enl 12/26/61 Prestonsburg, dis 10/20/62 Hazel Green, reg 10, co E, r 2nd lt, enl 10/20/62 Prestonsburg or Wolfe Co., dropped from rolls 3/1/64, house 2-257, s 1,3,22.
ASHFORD, JOHN D. reg 1MR, co B, enl 11/12/61 Morgan Co., reg 3MR, co E, enl 10/30/62 Abingdon VA, house 1-669, s 1,3,22.

B

BACK, ALFRED. reg 5, co A, enl 1/1/62 Paintsville, des 1/5/62 Moccasin VA, house 2-667, s 3,22.
BACK, JOHN W. reg 5, co A, B, r cpl, enl 10/21/61 West Liberty, enl co B 9/11/62 Jackson, r 4th cpl, prom to 1st cpl, wounded Dallas GA 5/28/64, house 2-660, s 1,3,22.
BACK, JOSEPH D. reg 1MR, co A, enl 4/6/62 Osborn's Ford, des 5/28/62 Camp Liberty Hill, reg 2MR, co A, E, cap Morgan Co. 1/28/64, sent to Camp Chase 8/11/64, d 12/21/64 of convulsions, buried grave 669, house 2-667, s 1,3,22.
BAILEY, JAMES (JR.). reg 5, co C, enl 10/20/61 Prestonsburg, house 2-46, s 1,2.
BAILEY, MASON C. reg 5, co I, enl 10/25/61 Prestonsburg, dis 10/20/62 Hazel Green, house 2-296, s 1,3,22.
BAILEY, WILLIAM. reg 5, co D, enl 10/9/62 Jackson or Licking Station, reg 10, co E, enl 5/1/63 Wolfe Co., killed Raytown TN, house 2-460 or 2-759, s 1,3,22.
BANKS, ALLEN. reg 5, co D, enl 9/20/62 Jackson, house 2-218, s 1,3,22.
BARKER, ALLEN M. reg 5, co C, enl 9/1/62 West Liberty, 11/62 absent home sick in Morgan Co., wounded at Chickamauga GA 9/20/63, at Jonesboro GA 9/1/64 and at Sandersville GA, house 1-544 or 2-27, s 3,22.
BARKER, GEORGE. reg 5, co A, D, r 2nd cpl, enl 10/21/61 West Liberty, dis 10/20/62 Hazel Green, enl reg 5, co D, 2/1/63 Rock House VA 2/1/63, wounded at Chickamauga GA, prom to 2nd cpl 12/1/63, house 1-252, s 1,3,22.
BARKER, HARDEN J. reg 5, co D, enl 10/19/61 Lawrence Co., dis 10/20/62 Hazel Green, house 2-356, s 1,3,22.
BARKER, HARVEY. reg 5, co D, enl 12/26/61 Paintsville or Carter Co., dis 10/20/62 Hazel Green, house 2-594, s 1,3,22.
BARKER, HENRY. reg 5, co A, enl 10/21/61 West Liberty, dis 10/20/62 Hazel Green, on list of prisoners shipped from Lexington to Louisville 12/18/6_, house 2-27, s 1,3,22.
BARKER, HENRY M. reg 5, co A, enl 10/21/61 West Liberty, dis 10/20/62 Hazel Green, wagon maker, house 2-176, s 1,3,22.
BARKER, JOHN. reg 5, co D, enl 10/19/61 Piketon, Prestonsburg or Lawrence Co., dis 10/20/62 Hazel Green, cap 2/17/64, sent to Camp Chase 3/24/64, released by order of the President 3/24/65 on taking oath of allegiance, house 1-545, 1-596, 1-659, 2-27, 2-124, or 2-304, s 1,3,22.
BARKER, JOHN. reg 5, co C, enl 9/1/62 West Liberty, 10/62 at home sick in Morgan Co., on list of prisoners shipped from Lexington to Louisville 12/18/6_, house 1-545, 1-596, 1-659, 2-27, 2-124, or 2-304, s 3,22.
BARKER, JOHN C. reg 5, co A, enl 10/21/61 West Liberty, dis 10/20/62 Hazel Green, wagon master, house 1-545, 1-596, 1-659, 2-27, 2-124, or 2-304, s 1,3,22.

BARKER, WILLIAM. reg 5, co A, enl 10/21/61 Prestonsburg, house 1-252, 1-277, 2-476 or 2-594, s 1,3,22.
BARKER, WILLIAM LYKIN. reg 5, co K, enl 12/29/61 Camp Hager, d 3/14/62 Moccasin VA, house 1-252, s 1,22.
BAUMGARDNER, WILLIAM. reg 5, co B, enl 10/21/61 West Liberty, reg 7ConfCav, co G, killed 5/6/65 in Carter Co., house 1-479, s 3,12,22.
BENTON, JAMES. reg 5, co A, enl 10/25/61 Prestonsburg, dis 10/20/62 Hazel Green, house 2-55, s 1,3,22.
BIRCHFIELD, ADAM. reg 5, co I, enl 10/9/62 Licking Station or Jackson, house 2-89, s 1,22.
BIRD, CHARLES L. reg 5, co A, enl 10/21/61 Prestonsburg or West Liberty, house 2-458, s 1,3,34.
BIRD, MICHAEL T. reg 5, co A, enl 12/11/61 West Liberty, dis 10/20/62 Hazel Green, house 2-129, s 3,34.
BIRD, SAMUEL C. or P. reg 5, co A, enl 10/21/61 Prestonsburg, house 2-111, s 1,3,34.
BIRD, WILLIAM A. reg 10, co B, K, enl 3/25/63 West Liberty, house 2-318 or 2-696, s 1,35.
BLEVINS, ELI. reg FR, enl 10/7/62 Floyd Co., des 10/27/62, house 347, s 1,3,22.
BLEVINS, JEFFERSON. reg FR, enl 10/7/62 Floyd Co., des 10/27/62 or 10/29/62, house 1-547, s 1,3,22.
BOWLING, HARVEY M. reg 5, co B, enl 10/21/61 West Liberty, house 1-289, s 1,3,22.
BOWLING, ISAAC. reg FR, enl 10/3/62 Morgan Co., des 10/27/62, house 1-289, s 1,3,22.
BOWLING, J. W. reg 10, co B, enl 1/22/63 Hazel Green, des 5/23/63, house 1-289, s 1,3,22.
BOWLING, R. M. reg FR, enl 10/23/62 Morgan Co., cap & paroled 10/62 Grayson, des 10/25/62, house 2-673, s 1,3,35.
BRADSHAW, JOHN H. reg 5, co I, enl 12/3/61 Whitesburg, dis 12/20/62 Hazel Green, reg 2MR, co E, m/in 9/14/62 Powell Co., r capt, house 1-432, s 1,3, 22.
BREWER, BRECKINRIDGE. reg 5, co C, enl 8/25/62 West Liberty, des 10/23/62 West Liberty, house 1-541, s 1,3,22.
BREWER, WILLIAM. reg 5, co C, enl 9/20/62 West Liberty, reg 10, co E, enl 3/1/63 Wolfe Co., cap Mt. Sterling 6/8/64, taken to Rock Island 6/22/64, joined US Army for frontier service 10/14/64, house 2-541, s 1,3,22.
BROOKS, CAMPBELL C. reg 5, co C, enl 9/18/62 Salyersville, left sick near Charleston TN 8/20/63, afterward wounded and taken prisoner, house 1-278, s 1,3,22.
BROWN, ALFRED. reg 5, co C, enr 9/7/62 West Liberty, des Lexington 10/10/62, house 1-124, s 1,3,22.
BROWN, EDWARD W. reg FR, enl 10/8/62 Johnson Co., des 10/18/62, house 1-341, s 1,3,22.
BROWN, FRANCIS A. reg FR, enl 10/8/62 Johnson Co., des 10/27/62, house 1-340, s 1,3,22.
BROWN, GEORGE W. reg 5, co H, enl 10/21/61 Prestonsburg, d camp hospital 3/25/62, cause and place unknown, house 1-321, s 1,3,22.
BROWN, ISAAC. reg 5, co B, enl 10/25/61 Prestonsburg, house 1-498, s 1,3,22.
BROWN, JOHN. reg 5, co B, enl 10/25/61 West Liberty, dark hair & skin, blue eyes, 5-10, cap Morgan Co., capture documents list Morgan Co. as residence, discharged on oath 3/28/64, house 1-491, 2-590, 1-70, 1-121, 1-284, 1-71, 2-330, or 1-126, s 1,3,22.
BROWN, NICHOLAS. reg 5, co B, enl 10/21/61 West Liberty, on roll of deserters from rebel army, received by Union army 1/1/64, died 2/7/64 of pneumonia, house 1-236, s 1,3,22.
BROWN, THOMAS. reg 5, co I, cap 5/12/63 Buchanan Co. VA, taken to Sandusky OH 11/14/63, exchanged Point Lookout 2/24/65, house 1-133, 1-493 or 2-584, s 1,22.

BROWN, WILEY J. reg 5, co B, enl 10/21/61 West Liberty, light hair, gray eyes, dark skin, 5-8, on roll of deserters from rebel army, received 1/1/64, place of residence Morgan Co., released on oath 7/9/64, house 1-236, s 1,3,22.

BROWN, WILLIAM. reg 1MR, co A, house 1-71, 1-284, 1-602, 1-628 or 2-370, s 1,22.

BROWN, WILLIAM A. reg 1BatCav, co A, enl 10/26/62 Prestonsburg, house 1-71, 1-284, 1-602, 1-628 or 2-170, s 3,22.

BROWN, WILLIAM W. reg 5, co C, enl 10/19/61 Prestonsburg, dis 10/20/62 Hazel Green, house 1-133, s 1,3.

BRYANT, ISAAC T. reg 5, co A, enl 1/7/62 Morgan Co., age 25, light hair & skin, blue eyes, 5-8, b Campbell Co. TN, dis for epilepsy, house 1-487, s 1.

BRYANT, JOSEPH H. reg 5, co K, enl 1/7/62 Morgan Co., age 19, light hair & skin, blue eyes, 5-9, b Campbell Co. TN, dis 7/30/62 for disability & bodily infirmity, house 1-489, s 1,22.

BUCHANAN, WILLIAM C. reg 6ConfCav, co D, cap Magoffin Co. 4/14/64, sent to Camp Morton 4/22/64, house 1-352, s 1.

BURKE, LEVI. reg 5, co F, enl 9/30/62 Licking Station, house 1-307, s 3,22.

BURNS, WILLIAM HARVEY. reg 5, co F&S, acs, app 11/1/61 near Pound Gap, house 1-677, s 1,22.

BURNS, WILLIAM W. reg 1MR, co A, enl 10/18/61 Prestonsburg, dis 11/20/62, house 2-728, s 1,3,34.

BURTON, JESSE. reg 5, co A, K, enl 1/1/62 Morgan Co., CSR: "sick at home in Morgan Co.", house 1-428, s 1,3,35.

BUSH, JOHN. reg 2MR, co A, enl 9/22/62 Wolfe Co., cap 10/18/62, house 2-707, s 1,3,22.

C

CANTRELL, JOHN. reg 5, co K, enl 12/14/61 camp on Middle Creek, near Prestonsburg, dis 10/20/62 Hazel Green, house 1-313, s 1,22.

CARPENTER, LEVI B. reg 5, co A, enl 10/21/61 West Liberty, dis 10/20/62 Hazel Green, house 2-451, s 1,3,22.

CARPENTER, WILLIS G. reg 5, co A, D, enl 10/22/61 Prestonsburg, dis 10/20/62 Hazel Green, light hair, gray eyes, fair skin, 5-8, wounded in battle and sent home, cap 7/22/63 Mt. Sterling, sent to Camp Chase 8/6/63, released 2/3/65 on oath of allegiance, Morgan Co. given as place of residence, house 2-452, s 1,3,22.

CARTER, ASA. reg 5, co B, r 3rd sgt, enl 10/21/61 West Liberty, dark hair, blue eyes, fair skin, 5-10, cap in Morgan Co. 1/28/64, CSR: "a notorious guerrilla and charged with murder", sent to Rock Island 2/12/64, house 2-748, s 1,3,22.

CARTER, FRANCIS M. reg 5, co A, enl 10/21/61 West Liberty, house 1-622, 1,3,22.

CARTER, GREENVILLE P. reg 5, co B, r 5th sgt, enl 10/21/61 West Liberty, cap 9/29/63 Morgan Co. sent to McLean Barracks, Cincinnati, released on oath, 10/16/63, house 1-593, s 1,3,22.

CARTER, JAMES. reg FR, enl 1/10/63 Morgan Co., reg 7ConfCav, co G, trans to Capt John T. Williams' Battalion Mounted Rifles, house 1-593 or 2-748, s 1,3,12,22.

CARTER, JAMES A. reg 5, co A, enl 10/21/61 West Liberty or Prestonsburg, took oath 2/17/64, house 1-593 or 2-748, s 1,2,35.

CARTER, JOEL W. J. reg 5, co A, enl 10/21/61 West Liberty, dis 10/20/62 Hazel Green, house 2-20, s 1,3,22.

CARTER, THOMAS. reg FR, enl 10/4/62 Morgan Co., cap 5/15/63, house 1-477, s 1,3,22.

CARTER, W. B. or WILSON. reg 2MR, co A, enl 9/15/62 Morgan Co., house 2-683, s 1,3,35.

CASKEY, HENRY. reg 5, co C, enl 9/1/62 West Liberty, des Paris 9/28/62 or 10/28/62, house 1-399, s 1,3,22.

CASKEY, ROBERT F. reg 1MR, co B, enl 10/26/61 Morgan Co., age 26, dark hair, gray eyes, cadaverous skin, 6-1, b Morgan Co., dis 4/19/62 for disability, liver disease, house 1-2, s 1,3,22.
CASSITY, JOHN S. reg 5, co C, enl 9/1/62 West Liberty, des 10/23/62 West Liberty, house 1-619 or 2-384, s 1,3.
CASSITY, WILLIAM H. reg 5, co B, r 4th cpl, enl 10/21/61 West Liberty, reg 10, co B, enl 1/18/63 Beaver Furnace KY, house 1-646, s 3,22.
CATRON, JOSEPH F. reg 10, co B, r 1st sgt, enl 1/28/63 West Liberty, prom to 1st sgt 5/1/63, cap 6/14/64 Cynthiana, taken to Camp Morton 6/25/64, to Point Lookout for exchange 2/14/65, house 2-412, s 1,3,35.
CHAMBERS, WILLIAM. reg 5, co I, enl 10/25/61 Prestonsburg, des 1/10/62 Middle Creek, house 2-207, s 1,3,22.
CLICK, JOHN. reg 2MR, co A, enl 9/8/62 Morgan Co., house 1-151, s 1,3,22.
COCK, ANDREW J. reg 5, co B, enl 10/21/61 West Liberty, house 1-480, s 1,3,22.
COCK, GEORGE. reg 5, co B, cap Morgan Co. 11/22/63, sent to Rock Island 12/3/63, enl US Army at Rock Island for frontier service, house 2-164, s 1, 22.
COCK, GORDON. reg 5, co B, enl 10/21/61 West Liberty, house 1-480, s 1,3,22.
COCK, JAMES. reg 5, co B, enl 10/21/61 West Liberty, house 2-655, s 1,3,22.
COLDIRON, FRANCIS. reg 5, co I, r musician, enl 10/25/61 Prestonsburg, dis 10/20/62 Hazel Green, house 2-193, s 1,3,22.
COLE, WILLIAM H. reg 5, co B, enl 10/25/61 Prestonsburg, house 1-274, s 3,22.
COLLINS, JOHN B. reg 5, co B, enl 5/25/63 Castlewood VA, des 8/10/63 Hansonville VA, house 1-132, s 1.
COLLINSWORTH, THOMAS P. reg 10, co B, enl 3/25/63 West Liberty, age 22, light hair & skin, blue eyes, 5-10, cap Morgan Co. 1/28/64, "a notorious guerrilla and charged with murder", sent to Rock Island 2/12/64, escaped from hospital, cap Floyd Co. 1/27/65, taken to Camp Chase 4/14/65, took oath 5/15/65, prison records state he is Floyd Co. resident, but best evidence is that he is Morgan Co. resident, house 2-565, s 1,3,10,22.
COLVIN, B. M. reg 3MR, co A, enl 10/18/62 Salyersville, house 2-727, s 1,22.
COLVIN, WILLIAM. reg 5, co F, C, enl 9/30/62 Licking Station, age 20, fair hair, blue eyes, dark skin, 5-8, cap Johnson Co. 5/27/63, taken to Camp Chase 6/9/63, to Johnson's Island 6/14/63, to Point Lookout, house 2-727, s 1,22.
COMBS, DAVIS. reg 5, co C, enl 8/22/62 Piketon, dis 10/20/62 Hazel Green, age 20, dark hair & eyes, 5-9, cap Estill Co., released on taking oath, house 2-443, s 1,2.
COMBS, PETER. reg 5, co I, enl 10/20/61 Prestonsburg, dis 10/20/62 Hazel Green, reg 10, co B, enl 4/8/63 Jackson, cap Magoffin Co. 3/14/64, d Camp Chase 5/11/64 of smallpox, house 2-431, s 1,3,10,22.
COMBS, STEPHEN. reg 5, co I, enl 12/28/61 Paintsville, des 2/7/62 Whitesburg, house 2-249, s 3,22.
CONGLETON, DAVIS. reg 5, co I, enl 12/28/61 Paintsville, des 1/10/62 Middle Creek, house 2-332, s 1,3,22.
CONLEY, ANDREW JACKSON. reg 5, co F, enl 9/30/62 Licking Station, house 7-725, s 1,22.
COOPER, JOHN. reg 2MR, co C, enl 9/5/62 Prestonsburg, house 2-385, s 1,3,22.
COTTLE, ISAAC. reg 10, co E, enl 1/7/63 Wolfe Co., house 1-246, s 3,22.
COTTLE, ISAAC N. reg 5, co A, r com. sgt, enl 10/21/61 West Liberty, dis 10/20/62 Hazel Green, reg 10, co E, enl 1/7/63 Wolfe Co., house 1-246, 1,3,22.
COTTLE, URIAH. reg 5, co A, enl 10/21/61 West Liberty, house 1-548, s 3,22.
COX, FIELDING. reg 5, co I, enl 10/21/61 Prestonsburg, des 5/5/62, reg 2MR, co A, enl 9/25/62 Wolfe Co., cap 10/2/62 Grayson, cap 4/17/64 Morgan Co., taken to Camp Morton 5/12/64, released on oath 2/10/65, house 2-526, s 1,3,22.

COX, GEORGE W. reg 5, co I, r 2nd lt, enl 10/25/61 Prestonsburg, killed at Middle Creek 1/10/62, house 2-354, s 1,3,22.

COX, HENRY C. reg 5, co A, enl 10/21/61 West Liberty, d Beaver Creek 1/21/62, house 2-752, s 1,3,22.

COX, JAMES. reg 5, co A, enl 8/29/62 Piketon, dis 10/20/62 Hazel Green, house 2-484, 2-514, 2-526 or 2-677, s 1,3,22.

COX, JAMES. reg 5, co I, enl 10/25/61 Prestonsburg, des 5/5/62, reg 2MR, co A, enl 8/25/62 Wolfe Co., house 2-484, 2-514, 2-526 or 2-677, s 1,3,22.

COX, JOHN. reg 2MR, co A, enl 8/25/62 Wolfe Co., house 2-526 or 2-573, s 1,3,22.

COX, JOHN J. reg 5, co C, enl 9/9/62 West Liberty, teamster, house 2-573, s 1,3,22.

COX, JOSHUA B. reg 5, co I, r 1st cpl, enl 10/25/61 Prestonsburg, des 5/5/62, reg 7ConfCav, co G, house 2-526, s 1,3,12,22.

COX, MILTON B. reg 5, co C, r 2nd lt, enl 9/6/62 West Liberty, elected 2nd lt 9/26/62, wounded Rocky Face Gap GA 5/10/64, house 1-30, s 1,3,22.

COX, THOMAS. reg 3MR, co B, enl 9/1/62 Mt. Sterling, house 1-263, s 1,3,22.

COX, WESTERN W. reg 5, co A, r 2nd lt, enl 10/27/61 Beaver KY, prom to Acting Asst. Quartermaster 1/9/62, relieved 12/15/62, reg 10, co B, r capt, app major 8/3/64, house 1-689, s 1,3,22.

COX, WILLIAM A. reg 1MR, co A, enl 1/28/62 Camp Johnson KY, house 2-753, s, 1,22.

COX, WILLIAM T. reg 5, co C, enl 9/12/62 West Liberty, chief artificer, wounded 5/28/64, house 2-753, s 1,3.

CRAIG, JAMES W. reg 5, co H, enl 10/26/61 Prestonsburg, des 1/26/62 near Rockhouse KY, house 1-659, s 1,3,22.

CULBERTSON, WILLIAM. reg 5, co H, enl 9/26/62 Mt. Sterling, reg 10, co B, enl 2/3/63 West Liberty, r 1st cpl, house 2-624, s 3,22.

CURTIS, JOHN. reg 5, co K, enl 9/12/62 Salyersville, des 10/21/62, house 1-358, s 1,3,22.

D

DAVIS, HARDIN. reg 5, co E, trans from 4th Ky. Cav. 8/27/63 by order of Gen. Preston, house 1-523, s 1,22.

DAVIS, HIRAM. reg 7ConfCav, co G, surrendered 4/30/65 Mt. Sterling, house 1-523, s 12,22.

DAVIS, JAMES B. reg 5, co C, enl 9/9/62 West Liberty, des Hurricane Mills, Pike Co., house 2-483, s 1,22.

DAVIS, JOHN B. reg 5, co C, enl 9/6/62 West Liberty, house 2-355, s 1,3,35.

DAVIS, SANFORD. reg 5, co C, r 2nd cpl, enl 9/9/62 West Liberty, age 27, red hair, gray eyes, ruddy skin, 5-7, prom to 2nd cpl 12/20/62, cap 22/23/63 near Marysville TN, remained in prison until the end of the war, released 6/9/65, prison records list Morgan Co. as residence, house 2-41, s 1,3,22.

DAY, BENJAMIN F. reg 10, co B, r 3rd sgt, enl 1/21/63 West Liberty or Hazel Green, prom to 3rd sgt 5/1/63, cap 6/12/64 Cynthiana, taken to Camp Morton 6/25/64, released on oath 2/10/65, house 2-535, s 1,3,22.

DAY, DANIEL. reg FR, enl 8/28/62 Morgan Co. or Carter Co., des 10/27/62 or 11/6/62, house 2-712, s 1,3,22.

DAY, JAMES W. reg 10, co B, H, r 2nd lt, enl 2/17/63 West Liberty, prom to 5th sgt 5/1/63, to 1st lt 5/15/63, house 1-255, s 1,3,22.

DAY, JOHN WALLACE. reg 5, co A, enl 10/21/61 West Liberty, reg 10, co B, enl 2/7/63 West Liberty, r 5th sgt, cap 1/2/64 West Liberty, took oath Camp Chase 5/13/65, house 2-133 or 2-771, s 1,3,22,28.

DEAL, WILLIAM aka JUNIOR. reg 7ConfCav, co G, cap 7/25/64 and ordered to be shot, house 1-473, s 12,22.

DEBOARD, JAMES. reg 10, co B, r 3d cpl, enl 12/31/62 West Liberty, cap 6/12/64 Cynthiana, 6/25/64 sent to Camp Morton, trans for exch 2/17/65, surr 4/25/65 Lynchburg, VA, prom to 3d cpl 5/1/63, house 2-66, rem listed on census under surname of Delvin, s 1.

DEBOARD, STEPHEN. reg 5, co A, enl 1/2/62 Paintsville, trans to co H 9/26/62, reg 10, co B, enl 12/31/63 West Liberty, cap 6/12/64 Cynthiana, sent to Rock Island, 6/22/64, admitted to hospital with phthisis pulmonalis 11/15/64, rem listed on census under surname of Delvin, house 2-66, s 1.

DENNIS, DAVID. reg 2MR, co F, enl 9/62, cap 6/14/64 Cynthiana, taken to Rock Island 6/24/64, trans for exchange 3/6/65, house 2-629, s 1,3,22.

DUNAWAY, JAMES. reg 5, co A, C, r 3rd sgt, enl 10/21/61 West Liberty, dis 10/20/62 Hazel Green, reg 2MR, co E, enl 10/20/62 Salyersville, reg 10, co C, enl 7/10/64 Liberty Hill VA, house 1-273, s 1,3,22.

DUNN, GEORGE. reg 5, co A, enl 10/25/61 Prestonsburg, reg 10, co E, enl 3/1/63 Wolfe Co., wounded in battle 11/8/61, sent home by regimental surgeon, rejoined 8/24/62, house 2-759, s 1,3,22.

DYER, JAMES. reg 5, co F, K, enl 12/14/61 Camp Recovery, reg 5, co K, enl 9/30/62 Licking Station, reg 7 ConfCav, co G, may be Lawrence Co. resident, house 1-546, s 1,3,12,22.

DYER, WILLIAM. reg 5, co A, enl 10/21/61 West Liberty, house 1-26 or 1-29, s 1,3,35.

E

EASTERLING, HENRY J. reg 5, co A, enl 9/29/61 West Liberty, house 1-300, s 1,3,22.

ELAM, JOSEPH C. reg 5, co A, r sgt, enl 10/21/61 West Liberty, dis 10/20/62 Hazel Green, made 2nd sgt 12/21/61, prom to 1st sgt 5/31/62, reg 2MR, co A, enl 10/2/62, app 2nd sgt 12/1/62, house 2-495, s 1,3,22.

ELAM, URIAH. reg 5, co A, r 4th cpl, enl 10/21/61 West Liberty, dis 10/20/62 Hazel Green, reg 2MR, co A, enl 10/21/62 Floyd Co., trans to Capt. J. D. Williams' co, house 2-769, s 1,3,22.

ELAM, WILLIAM W. reg 5, co A, enl 12/11/61 West Liberty, dis 10/20/62 Hazel Green, reg 2MR, co A, enl 10/21/62 Floyd Co., trans to Capt. J. D. Williams' co, house 2-769, s 1,3,22.

ELDRIDGE, ISAAC. reg 5, co B, r 3rd cpl, enl 10/21/62, dark hair, hazel eyes, florid skin, 5-8, cap 10/21/63 Lawrence or Morgan Co., taken to Camp Morton 11/3/63, released on oath 5/20/65, POW documents state he is a resident of Louisa, but he is not on Lawrence Co. census, house 1-626, s 1,3,22.

ELDRIDGE, JAMES. reg 10, co M, reg 13, co K, 10th Cav. service not on CSR, 13th Cav. service not on AG, paroled Cumberland Gap 4/30/65, house 1-330 or 1-626, s 3,22,34.

ELDRIDGE, JESSE. reg 5, co D, enl 10/1/62 Licking Station, light hair, blue eyes, fair skin, 6-0, wounded at Chickamauga GA 9/20/63, surrendered at Washington GA 5/6/65, took oath 5/21/65, place of residence stated as Morgan Co., house 1-606, s 1,3,22.

ELDRIDGE, JOSHUA. reg 5, co B, D, enl 10/21/61 West Liberty, dark hair, blue eyes, fair skin, 6-2, reg 5, co D, enl 10/1/62 Licking Station, wounded at Chickamauga GA 9/20/63, wounded battle of Jonesboro GA 8/31/64, surrendered Washington GA, 5/6/65, took oath 5/21/65, place of residence stated as Morgan Co., house 1-330, s 1,3,22.

ELDRDIGE, SAMUEL. reg 5, co B, enl 10/25/61 Prestonsburg, house 1-626, s 1,3,22.

ELLINGTON, JAMES W. reg 5, co C, enl 9/11/62 West Liberty, d Atlanta GA 6/2/64, house 1-280, s 1,3,35.

ELLIOTT, BENJAMIN F. reg 5, co D, enl 10/19/61 Carter Co., dis 10/20/62 Hazel Green, house 1-68, s 1,3,22.

ELLIOTT, GEORGE M. reg 7ConfCav, reg FR, enl 9/13/62 Morgan Co., des 10/27/62, cap 10/11/63 Greenup Co., house 1-566, s 12,22.

ELLIOTT, JAMES H. reg 5, co D, r 4th sgt, enl 10/19/61 Carter Co., dis 10/20/62 Hazel Green, made 4th sgt 10/19/61, reg FR, enl 5/22/63 Carter Co., house 1-566, s 1,3,22.

ELLIOTT, SAMUEL R. reg 5, co D, enl 10/19/61 Carter Co., dis 10/20/62 Hazel Green, age 49, gray hair, blue eyes, fair skin, 5-8, dis by reason of age and infirmity, house 1-68, s 1,3,22.

EVANS, WILLIAM F. reg 7ConfCav, co G, house 1-276, s 12,22.

F

FANNIN, DAVID. reg 5, co C, enl 9/1/62 West Liberty, des West Liberty 10/22/62, house 1-388, s 1,22.

FANNIN, GEORGE. reg 5, co B, enl 10/25/61 Prestonsburg, house 1-139, s 1,3,22.

FANNIN, JOHN. reg 5, co C, enl 9/20/62 West Liberty, des 10-23/62 West Liberty, house 1-139, 1-388 or 1-538, s 1,22.

FANNIN, JOHN T. reg 5, co C, enl 9/3/62 West Liberty, des 10/23/62 West Liberty, house 1-112 or 1-388, s 1,22.

FANNIN, MILTON G. reg 5, co C, enl 8/29/62 Piketon, cap Magoffin Co. 3/17/64, d in prison 11/2/64 of diarrhea, house 1-112, s 1,3,22.

FANNIN, PETER M. reg 5, co B, r 1st lt, enl 10/21/61 West Liberty, prom from 2nd lt 2/16/62, house 1-584, s 1,3,22.

FAULKNER, ALBERT C. reg 5, co I, enl 12/20/61 Prestonsburg, reg 10, co E, enl 4/15/63 Wolfe Co., house 2-417, s 1,3,22.

FAULKNER, WILLIAM L. reg 5, co A, trans from 4th Ky. Cav., co H 5/27/63, by order of Gen. Preston, house 2-340, s 1,22.

FERGUSON, HAYDEN. reg 5, co B, F, r 1st lt, enl 12/27/61 Camp Hager or 9/30/62 Licking Station, elected 1st lt 9/30/62, house 1-339, s 1,2.

FERGUSON, JOHN L. reg 5, co I, C, enl 10/6/62 Salyersville, trans from co I 11/18/62, wounded 7/22/64, house 2-48, s 1,2.

FERGUSON, WILLIAM J. reg 5, co C, enl 9/12/62 Salyersville, cap 7/22/64 near Atlanta GA, taken to Camp Chase 7/31/64, to Point Lookout 2/12/65, house 1-339, 2-48 or 2-54, s 1,2.

FIELDS, JONAS B. reg 5, co B, enl 12/27/61 Camp Hager, reg FR, enl 5/24/63 Morgan Co., house 1-448, s 1,3,22.

FLANNERY, ALBERT. reg FR, enl 9/25/62 Morgan Co., des 10/27/62, house 1-454, s 1,3,22.

FLANNERY, LITTLETON. reg FR, enl 3/27/63 Morgan Co., house 1-454, s 1,3,22.

FLANNERY, WILLIAM. reg 5, co B, enl 12/27/61 Camp Hager, house 1-512, s 1,2.

FOSTER, JOHN. reg 5, co B, enl 5/20/63 Jackson or Castlewood VA, less than 14 years old when enlisted, house 1-57, s 1,3,22.

FOSTER, ROBERT C. reg 5, co A, enl 10/21/61 West Liberty, des 1/10/62 from Prestonsburg, house 1-57, s 1,3,22.

FRALEY, ADAM C. reg 5, co B, enl 10/25/61 West Liberty, 5/62 left sick at home in Morgan Co., cap 9/28/63 Morgan Co., took oath 10/5/63, house 1-291, s 1,3,22.

FRALEY, GEORGE W. reg 5, co K, enl 12/25/61 Morgan Co., dis 10/20/62 Hazel Green, may be Floyd Co. resident, house 1-291, s 1,3,22.

FRALEY, MARCUS. reg 5, co B, K, enl 12/19/61 Camp Hager, age 20, brown hair, blue eyes, fair skin, 5-7, cap Morgan Co. 9/18/63, took oath of allegiance and released 10/16/63, b Morgan Co., CSR: "absent at home Morgan Co.", house 1-424, s 1,22.

FRISBY, CORNELIUS. reg 5, co A, enl 10/21/61 West Liberty, des 9/14/62 Camp Moccasin VA, house 2-33, s 1,3,34.

FRISBY, JASPER. reg 5, co A, B, C, enl 12/27/61 Camp Hager, reg 5, co C, enl 9/18/62 West Liberty, reg 2MR, co A, enl 10/21/62 Morgan Co. or Magoffin Co., trans to 2nd Ky. Cav. 3/1/63, wounded at Jonesboro GA 8/1/64, house 2-393, s 1,3,22.

FUGETT, FRANCIS M. reg 1MR, co A, enl 3/31/62 Camp Perry VA, cap 10/7/63 Farmington TN, sent to Camp Morton 10/15/63, released on oath 1/24/65, house 1-269, s 1,3,22.

FUGETT, GRANVILLE. reg 5, co A, enl 10/25/61 Prestonsburg, dis 10/20/62 Hazel Green, reg 10, co C, r 2nd sgt, enl 12/31/62 West Liberty, cap West Liberty or Little Stone Gap VA 3/12/64, taken to Camp Chase, to Ft. Delaware 3/14/64, took oath 6/9/65, house 1-245, s 1,3,10,22.

FUGETT, J. M. reg 10, co B, enl 3/25/63 West Liberty, clothing receipts 3rd quarter 1864, 9/25/64, house 1-269, s 1,3,35.

FUGETT, JOHN. reg 5, co A, B, enl 9/11/62 Breathitt Co., cap 12/10/_, house 2-498, s 1,22.

FUGETT, WILLIAM B. reg 5, co I, enl 12/28/61 Prestonsburg, dis 10/20/62 Hazel Green, cap Perry Co. 6/6/63, taken to Camp Chase 6/11/63, to Johnson's Island 6/20/13, to Point Lookout 11/30/63, released on oath 4/12/64, house 1-269 or 2-732, s 1,3,22.

FUGETT, ZACHARIAH. reg 5, co I, enl 12/28/61 Paintsville, dis 10/20/62 Hazel Green, house 2-11, s 1,3,22.

G

GARVEY, GEORGE W. reg 5, co K, enl 12/29/61 Camp Hager, dis 10/20/62 Hazel Green, reg FR, enl 3/9/63 Morgan Co., house 1-417, s 1,3,22.

GARVEY, HENRY J. reg 5, co C, r cpl, enl 1/5/62 Morgan Co., d Camp Moccasin VA 3/30/62, house 1-417, s 1,3,35.

GEORGE, ELIAS. reg 5, co F, enl 9/30/62 Licking Station, house 1-359, s 1,22.

GEVEDON, JOSEPH. reg 5, co A, enl 10/21/61 West Liberty or Prestonsburg, house 1-665, s 1,3,22.

GEVEDON, WILLIS GREEN. reg 5, co A, enl 10/25/61 Prestonsburg, dis 10/20/62 Hazel Green, house 1-277, s 1,3,22.

GIBBS, JAMES. reg 5, co c, enl 10/19/61 Prestonsburg, house 2-196, s 1,2.

GIBBS, JOHN H. reg 5, co A, enl 10/21/61 West Liberty or Prestonsburg, reg 10, co E, enl 4/1/63 Wolfe Co., house 2-643, s 1,3,22.

GIBBS, LOGAN G. reg 10, co E, enl 4/1/63 Wolfe Co., age 18, light hair, blue eyes, fair skin, 5-6, cap Morgan Co. 1/28/64, sent to Rock Island 2/12/64, took oath 2/22/64, d 3/22/64 of diphtheria & measles, buried Grave 82, Range 1, Cave Hill Cemetery, prison records list Morgan Co. as residence, house 2-643, s 1,3,22.

GIBBS, MILTON. reg 5, co I, enl 10/25/61 camp near Pound Gap, dis 10/20/62 Hazel Green, house 2-198, s 1,22.

GILLEM, JOHN. reg 2MR, co A, enl 8/25/62 Morgan Co., house 1-522, s 1,3,35.

GILLUM, JESSE. reg 5, co K, enl 1/1/62 Morgan Co., dis 10/20/62 Hazel Green, house 1-241, 1-216 or 1-352, s 1, 3, 35.

GILLUM, WILLIAM. reg FR, enl 9/23/62 Morgan Co., trans to reg 2MR, co A, enl 10/10/62 Morgan Co. or Floyd Co., house 1-522, s 1,3,22,35.

GIPSON, JAMES. reg FR, enl 9/13/62 Morgan Co., des 10/20/62, house 1-420, s 1,2.

GOAD or GOURD, RANSOM W. reg 5, co A, enl 9/1/62 Beaver Creek, dis 10/20/62 Hazel Green, reg 10, co B, enl 3/21/63 West Liberty, d 4/7/64, house 2-657, s 1,3,35.

GOODMAN, JAMES. reg 10, co A, enl 2/11/63 Prestonsburg, cap 3/63, CSR states that he was left home sick in Floyd Co., but he is not on Floyd Co. census, house 1-471, s 1,3,22.

GOODPASTER, JOHN YOUNG. reg 10, co B, enl 1/20/63 Hazel Green, des 7/20/63 or 8/20/63, house 2-448 or 2-650, s 1,3,22.

GOODPASTER, THOMAS J. reg 7ConfCav, co G, cap 2/2/64, house 3-446, s 12,22.

GOODPASTER, WILLIAM. reg 7ConfCav, co G, cap 2/2/64, house 2-446, s 12,22.

GORDON, ALFRED M. reg 2MR, co F, G, cap Bath Co. 9/2/63, sent to Camp Morton 11/2/63, trans to Ft. Delaware 3/14/64, house 1-544, s 1,22.

GRAY, SAMUEL. reg 5, co K, enl 1/6/62 Morgan Co., house 1-585, s 1,22.

GRAY, WILLIAM W. reg 2MR, co A, enl 9/15/62 Morgan Co., age 25, dark hair, blue eyes, fair skin, 6-1, cap Floyd Co., taken to Camp Chase 6/9/63, to Johnson's Island 6/14/63, house 1-231, s 1,3,35.

GREENWOOD, HENDERSON. reg 5, co B, enl 10/21/61 or 10/25/61 West Liberty or Prestonsburg, d Moccasin VA 4/3/62 of fever, "a good soldier", house 1-273, s 1,3,22.

GREENWOOD, JAMES. reg 5, co B, enl 10/25/61 Prestonsburg, house 1-197, s 1,3,22.

GRIFFITH, JAMES. reg 5, co C, enl 10/26/61 Prestonsburg, dis 10/20/62 Hazel Green, reg FR, enl 11/18/62 or 11/22/62 Lawrence Co., house 2-61, s 1,3,22.

GRIFFITH, JOHN T. reg 5, co C, dis 10/20/62 Hazel Green, reg FR, enl 11/22/62 Lawrence Co., may be Lawrence Co. resident, house 2-700, s 1,3,12.

H

HADDIX, HENRY C. reg 5, co B, enl 9/11/62 Jackson, des 10/1//62, house 2-200, s 1,3,22.

HALL, DAVID. reg 2MR, co A, enl 10/10/62 Morgan Co. or Wolfe Co., des 10/18/62, house 1-6, s 1,3,22.

HALL, ISAAC. reg 2MR, co A, enl 10/10/62 Morgan Co. or Wolfe Co., des 10/18/62, cap Rowan Co. 2/26/63, sent to Baltimore MD 5/12/63, house 1-131, s 1,3,22.

HAMILTON, JOHN M. reg 5, co K, r 1st sgt, enl 9/9/62 Beaver Hill, reg 7ConfCav, co G, taken prisoner 3/6/64, executed 8/15/64 pursuant to order of Brig. Gen. Stephen B. Burbridge, house 1-343, s 3,12.

HAMMONS, MORGAN B. reg 2MR, co A, enl 8/25/62 Wolfe Co., d in Wolfe Co., house 2-313, s 1,3,22.

HAMPTON, JEREMIAH. reg 5, co F, enl 11/1/61 Whitesburg, house 2-383, s 1,3,22.

HAMPTON, JOHN H. reg 5, co F, enl 11/1/61 Whitesburg, des 2/8/62, house 2-383, s 1,3,22.

HANEY, G. E. reg 10, co B, enl 3/29/63 West Liberty, house 2-3 or 2-31, s 1,3,35.

HANEY, JAMES M. reg 5, co C, 4th cpl, enl 9/6/62 West Liberty, black hair, blue eyes, dark skin, 5-11, prom to 4th cpl 12/1/63, wounded at Chickamauga GA, CSR lists Morgan Co. as residence, paroled Washington GA 5/6/65, house 2-16, s 1,22.

HANEY, LILBURN. reg 5, co A, enl 10/21/61 Prestonsburg or West Liberty, dis 10/20/62 Hazel Green, reg 10, co B, enl 12/9/62 Stone Creek VA, cap 6/12/64 Cynthiana, sent to Camp Morton 6/25/64, sent to Point Lookout for exchange 2/19/65, house 2-32, s 1,3,22.

HANEY, WILLIAM T. reg 13, co A, enl 6/1/62 Jeffersonville VA, rem des Whitesburg 10/10/62, house 2-50, s 1,31.

HANLEY, MADISON D. reg 5, co A, C, E, enl 12/13/61 West Liberty, dis 10/20/62 Hazel Green, reg 5, co C, enl 1/1/63 Holston VA, trans from 5th Ky. to 4th Ky. Cav, co H 11/24/63, trans from 5th Ky., co E, to 1MR, house 1-101, s 1,3,22.

HANNAH, JOHN. reg 2MR, co C, enl 9/12/62, house 1-423, s 1,22.

HARDIN, JOHN B. reg 10, co H, enl 5/15/63 Buchanan Co. VA, house 1-543, s 1,3,22.

HARGIS, JACOB. reg 5, co A, enl 9/11/62, des 10/12/62 Jackson, reg 10, co E, enl 9/1/63 Tazewell Co. VA, des 10/7/64, house 1-517, s 1,3,22.

HARGIS, JAMES R. reg 5, co K, C, enl 6/4/62 Jeffersonville VA, dis 10/20/62 Hazel Green, reg 5, co K, enl 6/4/62 Camp Recovery, trans from co K 10/20/62, re-enlisted, house 1-517, s 1,3,22.

HATTON, WILLIAM. reg 2MR, co E, enl 9/14/62 Powell Co., cap 11/5/62 Pike Co., house 2-268, s 1,3,22.

HAVENS, JAMES C. reg 1MR, co B, enl 10/19/61 West Liberty, reg 3MR, co E, enl 6/12/63 West Liberty, house 2-386, s 1,3,22.

HAVENS, SAMUEL J. reg 3MR, co E, enl 9/10/63 West Liberty, reg 10, co B, enl 9/10/63 West Liberty, trans to 1MR 5/31/64, house 2-386 or 2-393, s 1,22.

HAVENS, WILLIAM F. reg 5, co C, enl 9/17/62 West Liberty, wounded at Chickamauga GA 9/20/63 and at Dallas GA 5/28/64, cap 9/1/64 near Jonesboro GA and exchanged, house 2-456, s 1,3,22.

HAY, THOMAS. reg 5, co F, D, enl 9/30/62 Licking Station, may be Lawrence Co. resident, house 1-419, s 1,22.

HENRY, EDWIN V. reg 5, co A, enl 10/21/62 or reg 5, co B, enl 6/1/62 Morgan Co., reg 2MR, co A, enl 8/25/62 Morgan Co., wounded Dallas GA 5/28/64, mortally wounded Kennesaw Mtn. GA 6/30/64, d 7/4/64 Atlanta, house 1-693, s 1,3,22.

HENRY, JAMES S. reg 3MR, co E, enl 9/5/62 Mt Sterling, trans from 1MR, co B, house 2-740, s 1,3,22.

HENRY, LEWIS. reg 5, co C, A, enl 12/16/61 Paintsville, age 18, trans to co A, cap 6/18/62 West Liberty, sent to Camp Chase, exch 8/15/62, house 2-792, s 1,3,22.

HENRY, THOMAS J. reg 5, co A, C, r capt, enl 10/21/61 West Liberty, dis co A 10/20/62 Hazel Green, elected capt co C 9/26/62, wounded 8/28/64 & 8/31/64, house 1-693 or 2-740, s 1,3.

HENRY, WALTER S. reg 5, co A, C, r 2nd lt, enl 10/21/61 West Liberty, dis 10/20/62 Hazel Green, prom to 1st sgt and 2nd lt 10/20/64, wounded at Intrenchment Creek GA, trans from co A to co C 9/20/62, house 1-693, s 1,3,22.

HENSLEY, JOHN. reg 5, co A, I, enl 12/28/61 Paintsville, dis 10/20/62 Hazel Green, cap Murfreesboro TN 12/30/62, d 2/5/63 Camp Douglas of measles, house 2-415, s 1,22.

HIGGINBOTHAM, CHARLES. reg FR, enl 9/13/62 Morgan Co., des 10/30/62, house 2-678, s 1,3,22.

HILL, WILLIAM I. reg 5, co E, enl 10/23/61 Prestonsburg, reg FR, enl 10/7/62 Johnson Co., des 10/20/62 house 1-374, s 3.

HOLBROOK, LEWIS. reg 5, co A, K, enl 1/7/62 Morgan Co., d 5/21/62 Abingdon VA, house 1-441, s 1,3,35.

HOLBROOK, RICHARD. reg 5, co A, enl 1/1/62 Morgan Co., d 4/1/62 Camp Moccasin VA, house 1-430, s 1,3,22,35.

HOLBROOK, WILLIAM R. reg 2MR, co D, enl 8/26/62 Logan Co. WV or Lawrence Co., des 11/8/62 Johnson Co., house 1-442, s 1,3,22.

HORTON, GEORGE. reg 5, co K, enl 3/24/62 Moccasin VA, discharged, house 1-600, s 1,3,22.

HORTON, JAMES B. reg, co B, enl 10/26/61 Prestonsburg, cap Morgan Co. 11/22/63, sent to Rock Island 12/3/63, house 1-600, s 1,3,22.

HORTON, LORENZO D. reg 5, co A, D, enl 10/21/61, Morgan Co. dis 10/20/62 Hazel Green, reg 5, co D, enl 1/8/62 Carter Co., 5/62, CSR: "left home sick in Morgan Co., Ky.", house 1-652, s 1,3,22.

HORTON, RICHARD L. reg 5, co B, enl 10/25/61 Prestonsburg, deserted, house 1-571, s 1,3,22.

HORTON, WILLIAM. reg 10, co M, r capt, elected capt 7/4/64, reg FR, enl 9/15/62 Morgan Co., elected 2nd lt 12/24/62, house 1-574, s 1,3,10,22.

HOWARD, BOONE. reg 2MR, co A, enl 10/22/62 Morgan Co., trans from co B, 5th Ky., house 2-663, s 1,3,22.

HOWARD, GEORGE W. reg 5, co B, cap near Buffington OH 7/19/63, taken to Camp Douglas, house 1-650, s 1,22.
HOWARD, JESSE. reg 2MR, co A, enl 8/10/62 or 10/18/62 Morgan Co., des 11/1/62, house 1-189, s 1,3,22.
HOWARD, JOHN A. reg 5, co B, enl 10/21/61 West Liberty, took oath 10/1/63, CSR: "citizen of Morgan Co., Ky.", house 2-603, s 1,3,22.
HOWARD, JOHN B. reg 5, co A, enl 7/20/62 Liberty Hill VA, reg 2MR, co E, enl 9/14/62 Liberty Hill VA, trans from 5th Ky. Inf., co A 10/20/62, house 1-696, s 1,3,22.
HOWERTON, MATTHEW J. reg 5, co A, C, r 2nd cpl, enl 9/6/62 Piketon, prom from 3rd cpl 12/1/63, trans to Capt. Henry's company, 5th Ky. Inf., killed at Kennesaw Mtn. GA 6/22/64, house 1-265, s 1,3,22.
HUGHES, JAMES G. reg 10, co A, enl 4/21/64 Liberty VA, cap 6/64, house 2-534, s 1,3,22.
HUGHES, JOHN J. reg 3MR, co F, enl 11/22/62 Abingdon VA, house 2-534, s 1,3,22.
HUNTER, F. M. reg 3MR, clothing receipt 6/30/64, house 1-514, s 1,22.
HUNTER, JAMES K. reg 5, co B, r capt, enl 10/21/61 West Liberty, deserted, house 1-179, s 1,3,22.
HURST, CAMPBELL B. reg 5, co B, enl 10/25/61 Prestonsburg, house 1-413, s 1,3,22.
HURST, GEORGE. reg 5, co B, enl 12/25/61 Camp Hager, reg 7ConfCav, co G, r 1st lt, house 1-340, s 1,3,12,22.
HURST, ISAAC. reg 7ConfCav, co G, house 1-413, s 12,22.
HURST, JOHN. reg 5, co B, enl 10/25/61 Prestonsburg, reg 10, co B, enl 6/16/63 Liberty Hill VA, clothing receipt 3rd quarter 1864, house 1-329, s 1,3,22.

I

INGRAM, GEORGE W. reg 10, co B, enl 6/6/64 West Liberty, cap 6/12/64 Cynthiana, sent to Camp Morton 6/25/64, sent to Point Lookout for exchange 3/15/65, house 2-420 or 2-637, s 1,3,22.
INGRAM, JAMES N. reg 10, co B, enl 9/10/63 West Liberty, cap 6/12/64 West Liberty, sent to Camp Morton 6/25/64, trans to Point Lookout 3/15/65 for exchange, house 2-420, s 1,3,22.
INGRAM, WILLIAM J. reg 5, co I, enl 10/25/61 camp near Pound Gap or Prestonsburg, dis 10/20/62 Hazel Green, house 2-420, s 1,3,22.
ISOM, ARCHIBALD. reg 5, co B, enl 12/27/61 Camp Hager, house 1-329, s 1, 2.
ISON, DOCTOR. reg 5, co A, enl 1/22/62 Morgan Co., des 4/16/62, not on AG, house 1-329 or 1-421, s 1,22.
ISON, HAMILTON. reg FR, enl 10/8/62 Morgan Co., des 10/18/62 residence stated on s 36, house n/c, s 1,3,36.
ISON, MARTIN. reg 5, co K, enl 1/7/62 Morgan Co., dis 10/20/62 Hazel Green, re-enlisted 9/1/62, not on AG, reg FR, enl 1/6/62 Carter Co., trans from 5th Ky., co K, house 1-409, s 1,3,22.

J

JACKSON, JOHN H. reg 1MR, co A, enl 10/18/61 Prestonsburg, house 1-41, s 1,3,22.
JACKSON, WILLIAM. reg FR, enl 11/14/62 Carter Co., des 2/63, house 1-41, s 1,3,22.
JARRELL, GEORGE W. reg 5, co B, arrested 12/2/186_, house 1-207, s 1,22.
JARRELL, LEWIS. reg 5, co B, enl 10/26/61 Prestonsburg, 5/62 left sick at home in Morgan Co., house 1-586, s 1,22.
JENKINS, HENRY. reg FR, enl 10/14/62 Johnson Co., des 10/18/62, house 1-353, s 1,3,22.

JOHNSON, JAMES D. reg 5, co C, enl 9/1/62 West Liberty, not on CSR, cap 10/62, wounded 8/31/64 in hip & side, paroled 4/26/65 NC, house 1-49 or 1-345 s 1,3,35.
JOHNSON, JAMES DAVIS. reg 5, co C, enl 8/26/62 Piketon, not on CSR, house 1-49, 1-345 or 1-645, s 2,
JOHNSON, JAMES Z. reg 10, co M, clothing receipt 9/25/64, house 1-49 or 1-345, s 1,22.
JOHNSON, JOHN F. reg 5, co C, r 2nd lt, m/in 5/26/62, elected 2nd lt 9/22/62, house 1-23 or 1-629, s 1,22.
JOHNSON, JOSEPH. reg 5, co H, enl 8/25/62 Piketon, house 1-629, s 1,3,22.
JOHNSON, WILLIAM. reg FR, enl 9/15/62 Lawrence Co., des 10/25/62, house 1-629, s 1,3,22.
JOHNSON, WOODSON. reg 5, co C, r 2nd cpl, enl 9/19/62 West Liberty, app cpl 6/22/64, wounded in shoulder at Chickamauga GA, wounded again 8/31/64, hospital records list Morgan Co. as residence, house 1-249, s 1,3,35.
JONES, FRANCIS M. reg 5, co A, enl 10/21/61 Prestonsburg or West Liberty, dis 10/20/62 Hazel Green, house 1-107, s 1,3,22.
JONES, JOHN M. reg 5, co B, enl 1/3/62 Morgan Co., cap Rowan Co. 4/13/63, sent to City Point 4/29/63, house 1-59, s 1,3,22.
JONES, THOMAS N. reg 5, co A, musician, enl 10/21/61 West Liberty, dis 10/20/62 Hazel Green, house 2-61, s 1,3,22.

K

KASH, CALEB. reg 5, co A, B, enl 10/10/62 Jackson, des 10/24/62 Salyersville, house 2-238 or 2-713, s 1,22.
KASH, LEVI C. reg 5, co A, B, r 1st sgt, co B, enl 9/7/62 Jackson, app 1st sgt 11/18/62, des 12/28/63 Abingdon VA, house 2-713, s 1,22.
KEETON, HARVEY G. reg 5, co F, D, enl 9/8/62 Licking Station, trans by consolidation of co F, house 1-326, s 1,3,22.
KEETON, JOHN. reg 5, co F, enl 9/8/62 Licking Station, house 1-323, s 3,22.
KEETON, STEPHEN. reg FR, enl 3/27/63 Morgan Co., cap Morgan Co. 11/15/64, taken to Camp Chase 12/26/64, to City Point 2/25/65, house 1-397, s 1,3,35.
KENDALL, JAMES A. reg 5, co B, enl 10/25/61 Prestonsburg, house 1-426, s 1,3,22.
KENDALL, JOHN WICK. reg 5, co B, A, r ordinance sgt, enl 10/21/61 West Liberty, dis 10/20/62 Hazel Green, co A, enl 3/16/62 Mosley VA, reg 10, co B, enl 10/26/62 Osborne's Ford VA, house 1-426, s 1,3,22.
KENDALL, WILLIAM T. reg 5, co A, enl 10/21/61 West Liberty or Prestonsburg, dark hair & eyes, gray eyes, 6-0, des 2/15/62, reg 2MR, co A, enl 9/1/62 Morgan Co., cap Farmington TN 10/9/63, taken to Camp Morton 10/18/63, released on oath 12/22/64, house 1-680, s 1,3,22,35.
KIDD, AARON. reg 5, co C, enl 8/24/62 Piketon, mortally wounded at Jonesboro GA 8/31/64; d that day or 9/1/64, house 1-285, s 1,3,22.
KIDD, HARRISON. reg 13, co D, clothing receipts 4/7/64, 6/29/64, 9/1/64 & 9/15/64, house 1-285, s 1,22,31.

L

LACKEY, JOHN M. reg 2MR, co A, enl 10/10/62 Morgan Co., house 2-538, s 1,3,22.
LANDRUM, A. B. reg 10, co E, enl 1/1/63 Wolfe Co., clothing receipts 9/14/64, 10/25/64, house 2-156, s 1,3,22.

LANDRUM, JOSEPH A. reg 10, co E, enl 5/21/63 Wolfe Co., missing 6/12/64, house 2-156, s 1,3,22.

LAWRENCE, HENRY. reg 5, co A, I, enl 10/25/61 Prestonsburg or camp near Pound Gap, brown hair & eyes, dark skin, 5-8, cap Mt. Sterling 7/16/63, taken to Camp Chase 8/6/63, to Ft. Delaware 3/4/64, POW records list Morgan Co. as residence, house 2-659, s 1,3,22.

LEMASTER, RICHARD. reg FR, enl 9/18/62 Johnson Co., des 10/18/62, house 1-368, s 3,36.

LEWIS, ANDREW. reg 5, co B, K, enl 10/25/61 Prestonsburg, des 3/12/62 Gladesville, house 1-99, 1-102 or 1-142, s 1,3,22.

LEWIS, ANDREW. reg 7ConfCav, co G, house 1-99, 1-102 or 1-142, s 1,3,12,22.

LEWIS, HOWARD. reg 5, co K, enl 12/29/61 Camp Hager, dis 10/10/62 Hazel Green, reg 2MR, co A, enl 10/22/62 Morgan Co. or Licking Station, trans from 5th Ky., took oath 3/25/64, house 1-99, s 1,3,22.

LEWIS, JAMES. reg 5, co B, r 1st cpl, enl 10/25/61 Prestonsburg, reg 2MR, co A, enl 10/22/62 Morgan Co., house 1-167, 2-552 or 1-610, s 1,3,22.

LEWIS, JESSE C. reg 5, co K, enl 12/29/61 Camp Hager, des 4/16/62, house 1-24, s 1,22.

LEWIS, JOHN. reg 5, co B, enl 10/25/61 Prestonsburg, reg 2MR, co A, enl 10/22/62 Morgan Co., trans from 5th Ky. Inf., house 1-99, 1-102, 1-29, 1-22, 1-167 or 2-14, s 1,3,22,

LEWIS, JOHN C. reg 5, co B, enl 10/25/61 Prestonsburg, reg FR, enl 10/22/62 Morgan Co. or 10/29/62 Pike Co., trans from 5th Ky. Inf. 10/23/62, reg 7th ConfCav, co G, house 2-552, s 1,3,12,22.

LEWIS, JOHN S. reg 5, co D, enl 10/19/61 Carter Co., house 1-87, s 1,3,22.

LEWIS, SOLOMON. reg 5, co E, enl 10/20/61 Prestonsburg, des 1/10/62, house 1-99, s 1,3,22.

LEWIS, STEPHEN. reg 5, co B, enl 10/21/61 West Liberty, reg FR, enl 1/10/63 Carter Co., house 1-172, s 1,3,22.

LEWIS, THOMAS. reg 5, co A, enl 10/21/61 West Liberty, house 1-29, 1-635, 1-86, 1-210 or 1-24, s 1,3,22.

LEWIS, WILLIAM. reg 6ConvCav, co C, house 1-8, 1-67, 1-87 or 1-172, s 1,22.

LEWIS, WILLIAM W. reg 5, co C, r 1st cpl, enl 9/2/62 West Liberty, paroled 4/26/65 North Carolina, house 1-172, s 1,3,22,35.

LITTLE, JAMES. reg 5, co A, B, enl 9/14/62 Jackson, des 10/25/62 Salyersville, house 1-243 or 2-215, s 1,3,22.

LITTLE, JOHN C. reg 5, co A, B, enl 9/7/62 Jackson, trans to Capt. Bradshaw's cavalry company 12/1/62, killed by bushwhackers, house 2-187, s 1,3,22.

LITTLE, WILLIAM F. reg 5, co B, enl 9/11/62 Jackson, absent w/o leave 2/63 Jackson, house 2-576, s 1,3,22.

LONG, NOAH. reg 10, co B, enl 3/21/63 West Liberty, house 2-178, s 1,3,22.

LUCAS, ALLEN M. reg 5, co B, enl 10/21/61 or 10/25/61 West Liberty or Prestonsburg, house 1-208, s 1,3,22.

LUCAS, HARRISON A. reg 5, co B, enl 10/25/61 Prestonsburg, house 1-208, s 1,3,22.

LUMPKINS, WLEY. reg 5, co C, enl 9/1/62 West Liberty, des 10/23/62 West Liberty, house 2-495, s 1,3,35.

LYKINS, DAVID J. reg 5, co A, D, r capt, enl 10/21/61 or 10/25/61 West Liberty or Prestonsburg, age 28 (at capture), elected capt of co D 10/6/62, cap 12/6/62 Morgan Co., taken to Alton IL 1/10/63, released on oath 3/2/63, house 2-122, s 1,22.

LYKINS, DUDLEY C. reg 5, co C, r 5th sgt, enl 10/6/62 Salyersville, trans from co H 11/18/62, wounded in head 9/1/64, house 2-758, s, 1,3.

LYKINS, ELI S. reg 5, co A, 3rd lt, enl 10/21/61 West Liberty or Prestonsburg, elected 3rd lt 9/24/62, house 2-127, s 1,22.

LYKINS, ISAAC. reg 5, co A, enl 10/26/62 West Liberty, d 1/28/62 Rock House, KY, house 2-58 or 2-757, s 1,3,22.

LYKINS, ISAAC S. reg 5, co D, enl 9/16/62 Jackson, house 2-53, 2-58 or 2-757, s 1,3,22.
LYKINS, JAMES T. reg 5, co A, enl 10/21/61 or 10/25/61 West Liberty or Prestonsburg, house 2-75, s 1,3,22.
LYKINS, JOSEPH C. reg 5, co A, C, enl 8/25/62 Piketon, wounded severely in neck at Resaca GA 5/14/64 and in shoulder at Jonesboro GA 9/1/64, house 2-758, s 1,3,22.
LYKINS, JOSHUA W. reg 5, co A, enl 1/2/62 Paintsville, house 2-758, s 1,3,22.
LYKINS, WILLIAM. reg 5, co A, enl 10/21/61 West Liberty, dis 10/20/62 Hazel Green, musician, house 1-615, 2-52, 2-75, 2-118, 2-757 or 2-758, s 1,3,22.
LYKINS, WILLIAMSON B. reg 5, co A, fife major, enl 10/21/61 Prestonsburg or West Liberty, dis 10/20/62 Hazel Green, house 2-118, s 1,3,34.

M

MACKMILER, WILLIAM. reg 5, co G, K, enl 1/3/62 Morgan Co., house 1-449, s 1,3,35.
MANNIN, CHARLES. reg 5, co A, D, enl 1/4/62 Virginia, d Gladesville 3/8/62, house 2-679, s 1,3,22.
MANNIN or MANNING, WILLIAM H. reg 5, co I, C, enl 9/10/62 Salyersville, trans from co I 11/18/62, wounded in head 8/31/64, house 2-629 or 2-729, s 1,3.
MARTIN, JOHN. reg 2MR, co E, enl 9/14/62 Powell Co., house 1-14 or 2-121, s 1,3,22.
MASON, JOHN. reg 3MR, co A, enl 11/30/62 Rindershouse VA, house 2-738, s 1,3,22.
MAXIE, JACOB C. reg 3MR, co B, enl 9/1/62 Mt. Sterling, house 1-657, s 1,3,22.
MAXIE, RENEY C. reg 5, co I, enl 10/25/61 Prestonsburg, dis 10/20/62 Hazel Green, house 2-714, s 1,3,22.
MAY, ANDREW JACKSON. reg 5, co A, enl 11/17/61 West Liberty, prom from capt to lt col 11/7/61, to col 5/26/62, resigned 11/14/62, reg 10, col, resigned 8/3/64 because of bad health, house 1-672, s 1,3,22.
MAY, SAMUEL J. reg 5, co A, enl 10/21/61 or 10/25/61 West Liberty or Prestonsburg, dis 10/20/62 Hazel Green, house 1-635, s 1,22.
MAY, WILLIAM T. reg 5, co C, A, enl 8/24/62 Piketon, dis 10/20/62 Hazel Green, trans to co A 10/20/62, d 5/13/63 Guess Station, Wise Co. VA, house 2-461, s 1,3,22.
MAYS, DAVID. reg 5, co K, enl 1/3/62 Morgan Co., house 1-592, s 1,22.
MAYS, DAVIDSON. reg 5, co B, enl 1/6/62 Morgan Co., age 17, cap 12/2/62 Morgan Co., sent to Vicksburg MS for exchange, house 1-592, s 1,3,22.
MAYS, GEORGE W. reg 5, co H, enl 10/21/61 Prestonsburg, house 1-608, s 1,3,22.
MAYS, WILLIAM. reg 5, co B, enl 10/20/61 Prestonsburg, cap Morgan Co. 11/22/63, sent to Rock Island 12/11/63, died 4/22/64 of variola (smallpox), buried in grave no. 1077, house 1-230 or 1-591, s 1,3,22.
MAYS, WILLIAM DAVID, reg 5, co B, age 19 at capture, cap Morgan Co. 11/25/62, sent to Vicksburg MS 12/5/63 for exchange, house 1-230, s 1,22.
MCCLANAHAN or MCLANAHAN, JOHN. reg 1MR, co D, F, or reg 5, co B, enl 10/22/61 Prestonsburg, age 24, dark hair, eyes & skin, 6-0, reg 7 ConfCav, co G, cap 3/7/63 Rowan Co., taken to Sandusky OH 11/4/63, to Point Lookout 10/30/63, released on oath 4/12/64, house 1-588, s 1,3,12,22.
MCCLURE, MATTHEW. reg 5, co A, enl 10/21/61 or 10/25/61 West Liberty or Prestonsburg, house 1-5, s 1,3,22.
MCCLURE, WILLIAM. reg 5, co A, enl 10/21/61 or 10/25/61 West Liberty or Prestonsburg, house 1-5, s 1, 3.

MCCLURE, WILLIAM W. reg 1MR, co B, enl 10/18/61 or 10/26/61 Morgan Co. or Prestonsburg, age 23, light hair & skin, gray eyes, 6-0, cap 1/7/62 Jennys Creek, taken to Vicksburg MS for exchange, house 1-625, s 1,3,22.

MCGUIRE, JESSE F. reg 5, co C, enl 10/6/62 Salyersville, wounded at Chickamauga GA and at Jonesboro, GA 8/31/64, house 1-113, s 1,3,22.

MCGUIRE, JOEL FRANK. reg 5, co C, enl 10/1/62 Salyersville, wounded Dallas GA 5/28/64, house 1-115, s 1,3,22.

MCLAIN, JOHN S. reg 5, co C, enl 10/25/61 Prestonsburg, discharged, house 2-305 or 2-703, s 1,3,22.

MCLANAHAN, CORNELIUS H. reg 5, co B, enl 10/21/61 West Liberty 6/62, CSR: "left sick at home Morgan Co.", cap Morgan Co. 12/63, released 2/23/64 and sent north of Ohio River, house 1-553, s 1,3,35.

MCMILLEN, GEORGE W. reg 2MR co A, enl 9/15/62 Morgan Co., des 12/24/62, house 1-605, s 1,3,22.

MCPHERSON, JOHN. reg 5, co I, enl 12/28/61 Paintsville, des 2/13/62 Rock House, house 2-358 or 2-364, s 1,3,22.

MEADOWS, ELISHA. reg 5, co F, enl 9/11/62 Licking Station, house 1-361, s 1,22.

MILLER, JAMES M. reg 5, co D, enl 10/9/62 Licking Station, des 3/1/63, house 1-521, s 1,22.

MILLER, JOHN H. reg 1MR, co A, enl 10/18/61 Prestonsburg, dis 10/20/62, house 2-355, s 1,3,22.

MILLER, MARCUS L. reg 5, cap 1/27/62 at cliffs of Sandy, Morgan Co., house 1-521, s 1,22.

MILLER, ROBERT H. reg 5, co B, enl 10/21/61 or 10/25/61 West Liberty or Prestonsburg, reg 3MR, co D, enl 9/1/62 Piketon, house 1-521, s 1,3,22.

MILLER, WILLIAM. reg 1MR, co A, enl 9/15/62 Montgomery Co., dark hair, hazel eyes, light skin, cap Shelbyville TN 10/7/63, sent to Camp Morton 10/15/63, took oath of allegiance 12/22/64, house 2-355, s 1,22.

MILLER, WILLIAM C. reg 1BatCav, co A, enl 5/31/62, reg 3MR, co A, enl 7/5/62 or 7/29/62 Tazewell Co. VA, trans from Shawhan's Battalion 11/20/62, house 2-355, s 1,3,22.

MONTGOMERY, LEVI. reg 5, co A, enl 10/21/61 West Liberty, reg 10, co E, r cpl, enl 3/21/63 West Liberty, prom to cpl 5/1/63, cap 6/12/64 Cynthiana, sent to Rock Island 6/22/64, house 2-641, s 1,3,22.

MOORE, GEORGE. reg 5, co B, enl 1/1/62 Camp Hager, on list of prisoners shipped to Louisville 12/2/__. house 1-196, s 1,3,22.

MOORE, JOHN C. reg 5, co I, enl 10/25/61 Prestonsburg, house 2-354, s 1,3,22.

MOORE, SHADRACK. reg 5, co B, enl 10/26/61 Prestonsburg, on list of prisoners shipped to Louisville 12/2/__, house 1-528, s 1,3,22.

MOORE, WILLIAM W. reg 5, co I, enl 1/8/62 Beaver KY, des 2/4/62 Rockhouse KY, house 1-196, s 1,3,22.

MULLINS, JOHN A. reg 5, co F, enl 11/1/61 near Pound Gap, house 1-335, s 1,22.

MUNCY, JOHN. reg 5, co I, enl 12/28/61 Paintsville, dis 10/20/62 Hazel Green, cap Wolfe Co. 3/9/63, sent to Camp Butler IL 3/20/63, to City Point 3/27/63, house 2-247, s 1,3,22.

MURPHY, EDWARD. reg 5, co A enl 10/21/61 West Liberty, dis 10/20/62 Hazel Green, age 50, brown/gray hair, blue eyes, light skin, 5-5, reg 10, co B, enl 6/1/63 West Liberty, dis by reason of being too old for military service 5/31/64, house 1-552, s 1,3,22.

MURPHY, WILLIAM. reg 2MR, co D, enl 8/26/62 Logan Co. VA, reg 7 ConfCav, co G, cap 11/10/63 Morgan Co. taken to Camp Chase until 7/12/64 when he enlisted in U. S. Navy, house 2-426, s 1,3,12,22.

MURRAY, ADDISON W. reg 5, co B, enl 2/22/62 Moccasin VA, age 34, gray hair, blue eyes, fair skin, 5-10, arrested by Confederates as a spy, enlisted to save himself, served 3 months and deserted, cap Morgan Co. 5/10/63, taken to Johnson's Island 6/14/63, released 9/28/63 on oath of allegiance, house 1-193, s 1,3,22.

MYNHIER, WILLIAM. reg 5, co A, r major, enl 10/21/61 Prestonsburg, prom from 1st lt to capt 11/17/61, to major 11/14/62, wounded at Chickamauga GA 9/20/63, house 1-580, s 1,3,22.

N

NICKELL, ALEXANDER. reg 5, co A, enl 10/21/61 or 10/25/61 West Liberty or Prestonsburg, house 1-348, s 1,3,22.
NICKELL, HOLLOWAY P. reg 5, co A, r 2nd lt, enl 12/16/61 Middle Creek, dis 10/20/62 Hazel Green, app 2nd cpl 4/30/62, elected 2nd lt 9/24/62, cap Morgan Co. 5/19/63, taken to Camp Chase 7/20/63, to Johnson's Island 10/10/63, to City Point 2/24/65, house 2-3 or 2-755, s 1,3,22.
NICKELL, NAPOLEON B. reg 5, co A, enl 10/21/61 or 10/25/61 West Liberty or Prestonsburg, dis 10/20/62 Hazel Green, age 19, light hair, blue eyes, fair skin 5-7, cap 5/15/63 Morgan Co., sent to Camp Chase 5/31/63, to Johnson's Island 6/14/63, to Point Lookout 10/30/63, house 2-651, s 1,3,22.
NICKELL, ROBERT F. reg 2MR, co E, enl 8/7/62 Morgan Co., house 2-225, s 1,22.

O

OAKLEY, JOHNSON B. reg 2MR, pay receipt 3rd quarter 1863, house 1-36, s 1,22.
OAKLEY, WILLIAM G. reg 5, co A, enl 10/21/61 or 10/25/61 West Liberty or Prestonsburg, dis 10/20/62 Hazel Green, house 1-36, s 1,3,22.
ODITT, WILLIAM. reg 5, co C, enl 9/1/62 West Liberty, age 20, black hair & eyes, 5-8, cap 12/3/63 Anderson Co. TN, taken to Camp Chase 12/16/63, d 5/21/64 of smallpox or pneumonia, house 1-252, s 1.
OLDFIELD, GEORGE W. reg 2MR, co A, enl 11/8/62 Morgan Co., pay receipt for 9/30/63, house 2-395, s 1,3,22.
OLDFIELD, JESSE F. S. reg 1BatCav, co A, enl 4/18/62 Camp Center VA, house 2-396, s 1,3,22.
O'NEAL, GEORGE T. reg 7ConfCav, co G, took part in 1864 Paintsville raid, house 1-512, s 12,22.
O'NEAL, JAMES. reg 7ConfCav, co G, took part in 1864 Paintsville raid, house 1-530, s 12,22.
O'NEAL, JOHN. reg 7ConvCav, co G, took part in 1864 Paintsville raid, house 1-530, s 12,22.
ONEY, WILLIAM W. reg 5, co D, enl 10/19/61 Carter Co., dis 10/20/62 Hazel Green, reg FR, enl 5/27/63 Carter Co., house 2-373, s 1,3,22.
OSBORNE, JAMES S. reg FR, enl 10/12/62 Lawrence Co., house 1-11 or 1-294, s 1,3,22.
OSBORNE, JOHN W. reg 5, co G, enl 11/11/61 Pound Gap, des 2/1/62, reg 10, co E, enl 1/1/63 Wolfe Co., des 6/29/63, house 2-586, s 1,3,22.
OSBORNE, SAMUEL. reg 2MR, co A, enl 10/20/62 Morgan Co., house 1-11, s 1,3,22.
OSBORNE, WILLIAM JR. reg 10, co E, enl 1/1/63 Wolfe Co., des 6/29/63 in Kentucky, house 2-586, s 1,3,22.

P

PARKER, ANDREW J. reg 5, co A, r 1st lt, enl 10/21/61 West Liberty, dis 10/20/62 Hazel Green, elected 1st lt co E at re-enlistment, house 1-616, s 1,3,22.
PATTON, JOHN B. reg 1BatCav, co A, enl 10/21/61 Prestonsburg, dis 11/20/62, house 2-298, s 1,3,22.
PATRICK, ROBERT. reg 5, co B, enl 10/25/61, house 2-596, s 1,3,22.
PELFREY, DANIEL. reg 5, co F, D, enl 9/11/62 Licking Station, des 3/1/63, house 1-301, s 1,3,22.
PELFREY, WILLIAM R. reg 5, co I, enl 10/25/61 Prestonsburg, des 1/10/62 Middle Creek, house 2-303, s 1,3,22.

PENIX, JOHN. reg 5, co K, enl 12/14/61 Camp Recovery, near Prestonsburg, des 10/21/62, house 1-350, s 1,3,22.

PENNINGTON, ABEL. reg 13, r 2nd lt, light hair, hazel eyes, dark skin 5-10, cap and sent to Camp Chase, released 6/22/65 on oath of allegiance, CSR states Morgan Co. as residence, house 1-478, s 1,31.

PENNINGTON, ELI. reg 5, co B, enl 10/21/61 or 10/25/61 West Liberty or Prestonsburg, house 1-494, s 1,3,22.

PENNINGTON, HIRAM. reg FR, enl 10/8/62 Johnson Co., des 10/16/62, house 1-346, s 1,3,22.

PENNINGTON, JAMES H. reg 7ConfCav, co G, house 1-475, s 12,22.

PENNINGTON, NELSON. reg 5, co B, enl 10/25/61 Prestonsburg, house 1-594, s 1,3,22.

PERATT, JAMES T. reg 5, co I, enl 10/25/61 Prestonsburg, dis 10/20/62 Hazel Green, house 2-388 or 2-705, s 1,3,22.

PERATT, JOHN. reg 5, co A, enl 10/21/61 or 10/25/61 West Liberty or Prestonsburg, house 2-512, 2-638 or 2-708, s 1,3,22.

PERATT, SILAS. reg 5, co A, enl 10/21/61 or 10/25/61 West Liberty or Prestonsburg, dis 10/20/62 Hazel Green, house 2-183, s 1,3,22.

PERKINS, ISAAC S. reg 5, co C, enl 10/26/61 Prestonsburg, dis 10/20/62 Hazel Green, age 38, black hair, blue eyes, light skin, 5-8, arrested 12/2/62, b Morgan Co., house 1-119, s 1,22.

PERRY, ALLEN. reg 2MR, co A, enl 10/1/62 Morgan Co. or Rowan Co., cap 12/5/63 Morgan Co., sent to Camp Chase 8/10/64, enl in U.S. Army 4/22/65, house 1-619, s 1,3,22.

PERRY, BENJAMIN F. reg 5, co B, r 2nd lt, elected 9/2/62, house 1-676, s 1,22.

PERRY, HENRY. reg 5, co C, enl 8/25/62 West Liberty, des Mt. Sterling 10/9/62, house 2-321, s 1,3,21.

PERRY, JAMES W. reg 1MR, co B, enl 10/26/61 Morgan Co., des Piketon 11/9/61, reg 5, co C, enl 8/24/62 Piketon, des Lexington 10/9/62, house 2-144, s 1,3,22.

PERRY, THOMAS D. reg 5, co C, enl 9/9/62 Fleming Co., trans to 2nd Ky. Cav. 5/22/63, re-transferred 8/10/63, house 1-35, s 1,3,22.

PERRY, WILLIAM. reg 7ConfCav, co G, house 1-93, 2-321 or 2-646, s 12,22.

PEYTON, DANIEL. reg 5, co A, enl 1/1/62 Paintsville, house 2-108, s 1,3,22.

PHILLIPS, GEORGE W. reg 2MR, co A, enl 9/8/62 Morgan Co., dis 10/18/62, house 2-751, s 1,3,22.

PHILLIPS, TAZEWELL. reg 5, co I, enl 10/25/61 Prestonsburg, d Gladesville 2/18/62 or 2/19/62, house 2-678, s 1,3,22.

PIERCE, WILLIAM S. reg 5, co A, r 1st lt, enl 10/21/61 Prestonsburg, dis 10/20/62 Hazel Green, app 2nd lt 11/17/61, prom to 1st lt 6/6/62, reg 2MR, co A, enl 10/10/62 Rowan Co., des 10/15/62, arrested 12/2/__, on list of prisoners shipped to Louisville, house 1-551, s 1,3,22.

PORTER, HENRY D. reg 5, co D, enl 10/19/61 Carter Co., dis 10/20/62 Hazel Green, house 1-43, s 1,3,22.

PORTER, JAMES W. S. reg 5, co D, r 3rd cpl, enl 10/19/61 Carter Co., dis 10/20/62 Hazel Green, dark hair, blue eyes, ruddy skin, 5-10, prom to 3rd cpl 5/2/62, cap Morgan Co. 4/20/64, took oath 4/20/64, prison records list Morgan Co. as residence, house 1-463, s 1,3,22.

PRATER, HENRY. reg 2MR, co B, enl 10/3/62 Fleming Co., house 2-15, s 1,22.

PRATER, THOMAS. reg 2MR, co B, enl 9/14/62 or 10/14/62 Camp Bynum, Fleming Co., house 1-658, s 1,3,22.

PRATER, WILLIAM R. reg 5, co C, enl 10/26/61 Prestonsburg, house 2-427, s 1,2.

PUCKETT, JACOB C. reg 5, co C, enl 9/11/62 West Liberty, des Gladesville 4/20/63, house 1-30, s 1,3,22.

Q

QUICKSELL, JONATHAN E. reg 5, co A, enl 12/11/61 West Liberty, des 4/14/62 Moccasin VA, reg 10, co B, enl 2/2/63 West Liberty, house 2-489, s 1, 3,22,35.

R

RATLIFF, EZEKIEL M. reg 5, co C, enl 9/8/62 Salyersville, light hair, blue eyes, fair skin, 5-11, trans by consolidation of Capt. Lykins co G, wounded at Intrenchment Creek GA 7/22/74, CSR states Morgan Co. as residence, paroled Washington GA 5/6/65, house 1-12, s 1,3,22.

REED, WILLIAM H. reg 5, co C, enl 8/7/62 Bath Co. or Camp Barnett TN, brown hair, gray eyes, fair skin, 6-0, surrendered Washington GA 5/6/65, took oath 5/21/65, CSR lists Morgan Co. as residence, house n/c, s 1,3.

RICHARDSON, ROBERT W. reg 10, co B, enl 9/10/63 West Liberty, clothing receipt third quarter 1864, house 2-718, s 1,3,22.

ROBERTS, ANDREW J. reg 5, co C, enl 10/18/61 Prestonsburg, dis 10/20/62 Hazel Green, house 2-363, s 1,2.

ROBERTS, DAVID W. reg 5, co C, enl 9/15/62 West Liberty, age 40, dark hair, eyes & skin, 5-10, cap 5/15/63, taken to Johnson's Island 6/14/63, to Point Lookout 10/30/63, released on oath 1/10/64, house 1-95, s 1,3,22.

ROBERTS, HIRAM B. reg 5, co A, G, K, enl 3/13/62 Moccasin VA, trans to co G 5/26/62, house 1-104, s 1,3,22.

ROBERTS, JAMES. reg 5, co D, F, enl 10/9/62 Jackson or West Liberty, cap 10/16/63 Magoffin Co., taken to Camp Morton 11/2/63, d 8/8/64 of acute dysentery, buried grave 1040, Green Lawn Cemetery, house 1-104, s 1,3,22.

ROBBINS, JAMES. reg 5, co B, enl 10/25/61 Prestonsburg, des, house 1-380, s 1,3,22.

ROBBINS, JOHN. reg 5, co B, enl 10/25/61 Prestonsburg, des, house 1-380, s 1,3,22.

ROBBINS, JOSHUA. reg 5, co B, enl 10/25/61 Prestonsburg, des, house 1-283, s 1,3,22.

ROBBINS, WILLIAM C. reg 5, co B, enl 10/25/61 Prestonsburg, des, house 1-380, s 1,3,22.

ROBINSON, JAMES H. reg 7ConfCav, co G, participated in 1864 Paintsville raid, house 2-547, s 12,22.

ROSE, B. F. reg 10, co E, r cpl, enl 3/1/63 Wolfe Co., cap Rome TN 3/5/63, cap Flemingsburg or Cynthiana, 6/18/64, had received gunshot wound near hip joint, admitted to hospital at Lexington 6/20/64, taken to Camp Morton, paroled Camp Morton 3/15/65, house 2-759, s 1,22.

ROSE, JOHN. reg 2MR, co D, enl 8/26/62 Logan Co. VA, des Wayne Co. VA 10/3/62, house 2-299 or 2-222, s 1,3,22.

ROSE, ROBERT C. reg 5, co D, enl 11/13/61 Pound Gap VA, dis 10/20/62 Hazel Green, house 2-248, s 1,3,22.

ROSS, JOHN. reg 10, co D, enl 2/1/63 Rogersville TN, cap Morgan Co. 2/3/64, CSR: "notorious guerrilla and charged with murder", sent to Camp Chase 8/10/64, to Chicago 3/20/65, enlisted in U. S. Army 3/24/65, house 2-428 or 2-568, s 1,3,22.

RUSSELL, GEORGE C. reg 3MR, co B, r 1st sgt, enl 9/1/62 Mt. Sterling, house 2-610, s 1,22.

S

SEBASTIAN, WILLIAM S. reg 5, co A, G, r 1st lt, enl 10/25/61 Prestonsburg, dis 10/20/62 Hazel Green, app 2nd sgt 5/31/62, elected 2nd lt 10/6/62, house 2-67, s 1,3,22.

SHEPHERD, GEORGE. reg 3MR, co C, cap 10/7/63 Farmington TN, sent to Camp Morton 10/15/63, released on oath 2/14/65, house 2-348, s 1,22.
SHORT, JAMES. reg 5, co F, cap 10/16/63 Magoffin Co., sent to Camp Morton, 11/2/63, house 2-704, s 1,22.
SMITH, COVINGTON. reg 5, co F, enl 9/30/62 Licking Station, house 1-278, s 1,3,22.
SMITH, DAVID. reg 5, co F, K, enl 12/14/61 camp near Middle Creek, m/in co F 9/30/62 Licking Station, house 1-706, s 1,22.
SMITH, DAVID C. reg 2MR, co D, r 2nd lt, enl 8/26/62 Logan Co. VA, age 41, amber hair, blue eyes, fair skin, 5-10, paroled 5/65 Charleston WV, house 1-278, s 1,22.
SMITH, ELISHA. reg 5, co F, enl 9/30/62 Licking Station, house 1-206 or 1-316, s 1,3,22.
SMITH, HADEN. reg 5, co F, enl 9/19/62 or 9/30/62 Licking Station, house 1-538, s 1,3,22.
SMITH, JOHN. reg 5, co C, enl 11/18/62 Osborne's Ford VA, des 4/1/63 Scott Co. VA, house 1-312, 1-324 or 1-206, s 1,22.
SMITH, PETER. reg 5, co F, enl 9/30/62 Licking Station, house 1-314, s 1,3,22.
SPARKS, WILLIAM J. reg 5, co A, C, r cpl, enl 10/24/62 Paintsville, 5/8/63 Rockhouse VA, dis 10/20/62 Hazel Green, cap Harrison TN 11/26/63, to Louisville 12/9/63 to Rock Island IL 12/11/63, house 1-634, s 1,2.
SPENCER, JAMES. reg 2MR, co A, enl 9/12/62 Wolfe Co., cap 10/18/62, house 2-337, s 1,3,22.
STACY, GEORGE B. reg 10, co B, enl 2/6/63 West Liberty, cap Mt. Sterling 6/10/64, taken to Rock Island 6/22/64, house 2-114, s 1,3,22.
STACY, HENDERSON. reg 5, co A, enl 8/28/62 Piketon, dis 10/20/62 Hazel Green, house 2-39, s 1,3,22.
STACY, JAMES CAMPBELL. reg 5 co A, C, enl 2/1/61 Rockhouse VA, dis 10/20/62 Hazel Green, trans from co A, reenlisted, house 2-41, s 1,3.
STACY, JAMES CLAIBORNE. reg 5, co A, enl 12/23/61 Paintsville, dis 10/20/62 Hazel Green, house 2-114, s 1,3,22.
STACY, SAMUEL. reg 5, co A, r 1st cpl, enl 10/21/61 West Liberty or Prestonsburg, arrested 12/2/__, on list of prisoners sent to Louisville, house 2-114, s 1,3,22.
STACY, WILLIAM H. reg 10, co B, r 2nd cpl, enl 1/1/63 West Liberty, prom to 2nd cpl 5/1/63, cap 10/1/63 West Liberty, sent to Camp Douglas 10/2/63, house 2-114, s 1,3,22.
STAFFORD, JAMES. reg 5, co D, wounded in the arm at Middle Creek 1/10/62, house 1-450, s 1,22.
STAMPER, BENJAMIN C. reg 5, co C, enl 9/15/62 West Liberty, wounded in battle of Chickamauga GA 9/20/63, house 2-406, s 1,3,22.
STAMPER, HIRAM H. reg 5, co F, r 2nd lt, enl 11/1/61 camp near Pound Gap, prom to 2nd lt 5/10/62, house 2-22, s 1,22.
STAMPER, JAMES H. reg 1MR, co B, enl 10/19/61 Prestonsburg, reg 3MR, co E, r 2nd lt, enl 11/15/62 Abingdon VA, wounded Shelbyville TN 10/7/63, house 2-306, s 1,3,22.
STEPHENS, ANDREW J. reg 5, co K, enl 1/1/62 Morgan Co., des 4/16/62, house 1-432, s 1,22.
STEPHENS, DANIEL M. reg 10, co M, not on AG or CSR, house 1-383, 1-427 or 1-624, s 10,22,34.
STEPHENS, HENRY aka HAMILTON. reg FR, enl 5/24/63 Morgan Co., reg 10, co M, 10th Cav. service not on CSR, house 1-431, s 1,3,22,34,36.
STEPHENS, JOHN. reg 5, co K, enl 1/1/62 Morgan Co., reg 10, co M, reg FR, enl 9/18/62, paroled 5/65 Louisa, house 1-431, s 1,10,22.
STEPHENS, SOLOMON. reg 5, co A, K, r 3rd cpl, enl 12/29/61 Camp Hager, 3rd cpl from 5/1/62 to 5/26/62, house 1-431 or 1-434, s 1,22.
STEPHENS, STEPHEN. reg FR, enl 9/18/62 Morgan Co. house 1-383, 1-437 or 1-624, s 1,3,22.

STEPHENS, STEPHEN. reg 5, co K, enl 12/29/61 Camp Hager, des 4/16/62, house 1-383, 1-431 or 1-624, s 1.

STEVENS, D. K. reg FR, enl 9/18/62 Morgan Co., house 1-437 or 1-624, s 1,3, 35.

STEVENS, SOLOMON S. reg FR, enl 10/22/62, Morgan Co., house 1-431, 1-434 or 1-460, s 1,3,35,36.

STRICKLIN, JOHN ROBERT. reg 5, co A, C, enl 1/4/62 Paintsville, dis 10/20/62 Hazel Green, reg 10, co B, 6/2/63 West Liberty, cap 2/18/64 Booneville, taken to Ft. Delaware, paroled 9/28/64, returned to duty 12/31/64, house 2-658, s 1,3,10,22.

STRICKLIN, WILLIAM P. reg 5, co C, enl 9/10/62 West Liberty, des 10/5/62 Paris, may be a resident of another county, house 2-158, s 1,3,22.

STROTHER, ROBERT D. reg 5, co C, r 2nd lt, enl 9/6/62 West Liberty, elected 2nd lt 9/26/62, house 1-682, s 1,22.

SWANGO, DAVID FRANKLIN. reg 5, co I, r 1st lt, enl 10/25/61 Prestonsburg or camp near Pound Gap, dis 10/20/62 Hazel Green, reg 10, co E, r capt, killed at Mt. Sterling 6/8/64, house 2-191, s 1,3,22.

SWANGO, GREEN B. reg 5, co I, r 4th cpl, enl 10/25/61 Prestonsburg or camp near Pound Gap, dis 10/20/62 Hazel Green, prom to 4th cpl, reduced to ranks 1/1/62, reg 10, co E, r 3rd sgt, house 2-157, s 1,3,10,22.

SWANGO, WILLIAM HARRISON. reg 5, co I, musician, enl 2/1/62 Rockhouse KY, dis 10/20/62 Hazel Green, reg 10, co E, enl 10/20/62 Wolfe Co., killed Johnson City TN 9/20/63, house 2-191, s 1,3,22.

T

TAULBEE, WILLIAM H. reg 5, co A, r 2nd lt, enl 10/25/61 Prestonsburg, dis 10/20/62 Hazel Green, prom to sgt major 3/1/62, elected 2nd lt 5/1/62, house 2-97, s 1,3,22.

TAULBEE, WILLIAM W. reg 5, co D, enl 6/20/62 Jackson or Licking Station, des Rock House VA 5/12/63, house 2-200, s 1,3,22.

TERRY, ISAAC. reg 5, co K, enl 12/29/61 Camp Hager, CSR: "sick at home in Morgan Co.", house 1-253, s 1,22.

TERRY, JESSE. reg 5, co B, enl 10/25/61 Prestonsburg, cap Morgan Co. 5/27/63, house 1-253, s 1,3,22.

TERRY, MILES. reg 5, co A, age 16, light hair, blue eyes, fair skin, 5-6, cap Breathitt Co. 5/16/63, received Camp Chase 5/31/63, sent to Point Lookout 10/30/63, released on oath 11/10/64, age 28 on census, house 1-253, s 1,22.

THOMPSON, SAMUEL W. reg 5, co B, r 2nd lt, enl 10/25/61 Prestonsburg, prom from cpl 6/26/62, reg 13, co C, F, K, D, enl 3/1/63 Whitesburg, r 1st lt, elected 1st lt 4/9/64, paroled 5/3/65, prison records list Morgan Co. as residence, house 1-499, s 1,22,31.

THOMAS, WILLIAM. reg 5, co A, enl 10/27/61 Beaver Creek, dark hair, eyes & skin, 5-10, dis 4/7/62 Moccasin VA for lung disease, reg 3MR, co A, enl 8/19/62 Piketon, house 2-94, s 1,3,22.

TRIMBLE, JAMES. reg 1MR, co D, enl 10/22/61 Prestonsburg, dis 11/20/62, house 2-623 or 2-760, s 1,22.

TRIMBLE, WILLIAM H. reg 5, co A, G, enl 10/25/61 West Liberty or Prestonsburg, des 4/14/62 Camp Moccasin VA, could be Johnson Co. resident, house 2-623 or 2-761, s 1,3,35.

TURNER, HENRY C. reg 1MR, co B, enl 10/26/61 Morgan Co., des 11/9/61 Piketon, house 1-692, s 1,3,22.

TUTT, WILLIAM H. reg 2MR, co A, E, enl l8/25/62 Wolfe Co., age 17, cap near Shelbyville TN 10/7/63, taken to Camp Morton 10/15/63, took oath and released 3/31/65, house 2-721, s 1,3,22.

V

VANCE, WILLIAM H. reg 5, co C, enl 10/6/62 Salyersville, trans by consolidation from Lykins' company, house 2-469, s 1,3,22.

W

WAGGNOER, DAVID. reg FR, enl 10/4/62 or 11/4/62 Morgan Co., des 10/27/62, house 1-451, s 1,3,22.

WALDECK, JAMES M. reg 5, co A, enl 10/21/61 or 10/25/61 West Liberty or Prestonsburg, dis 10/20/62 Hazel Green, house 2-714, s 1,3,22.

WALTERS, ANDREW J. reg 13, co Kash's, rem not on CSR, house 2-85, s 1,31.

WARD, DAVID B. reg 5, co I, enl 12/28/61 Paintsville, dis 10/20/62 Hazel Green, house 2-631, s 1,3,22.

WATSON, WILLIAM RILEY. reg 5, co B, age 32, cap 11/26/62 Morgan Co., discharged on oath & bond 3/2/63, house 1-668, s 1,22.

WEBB, ISHAM G. reg 5, co A, enl 10/27/61 Beaver KY, d 5/61/62 Emory & Henry Hospital of disease, house 2-431, s 1,3,22.

WEBB, JAMES F. reg 2MR, co D, enl 8/26/62 Logan Co. VA, cap 9/10/63 Louisa by voluntary surrender, sent to Cincinnati 9/13/63, released on taking oath and giving bond, house 2-431, s 1,22.

WEBB, WILLIAM W. reg 5, co A, enl 10/21/61 or 10/25/61 West Liberty or Prestonsburg, house 2-431, s 1,3,22.

WEDDINGTON, HARVEY. reg 7ConfCav, co G, house 1-570, s 12,22.

WELLS, BENJAMIN F. SR. reg 5, co A, enl 10/19/61 Prestonsburg or Piketon, house 2-500, s 1,3,22.

WELLS, BENJAMIN F. JR. reg 5, co D, enl 10/19/61 Prestonsburg or Piketon, deserted, house 2-622, s 1,3,22.

WELLS, DANIEL P. reg 5, co A, enl 10/21/61 or 10/25/61 West Liberty or Prestonsburg, house 2-621, s 1,3,22.

WELLS, EDMOND. reg 5, co I, enl 12/28/61 Paintsville, age 20, light hair, blue eyes, fair skin, 5-10, dis for disability 4/30/62 of measles, house 2-750, s 1,22.

WELLS, JOHN M. reg 5, co H, enl 10/21/61 Prestonsburg, d 7/1/62, house 2-668, s 1,3,22.

WELLS, JOHN W. reg FR, r 1st sgt, enl 9/20/62 Morgan Co., elected sgt 10/23/62, cap 5/9/63 in Kentucky, house 1-465, s 1,3,22.

WELLS, WILLIAM. reg Ficklin's Batt. Cav., cap Owingsville, shipped to Louisville by provost marshal, house 1-43, s 1,22.

WHITT, GEORGE W. reg 5, co B, enl 10/25/61 Prestonsburg, house 1-150, s 1,3 .

WHITT, JAMES P. reg 5, co E, enl 10/23/61 Prestonsburg, house 1-598, s 1,22.

WHITT, MILES. reg 5, co B, age 60, brown hair, gray eyes, dark skin, 6-0, reg 2MR, co A, enl 9/8/62 Morgan Co., cap Morgan Co. 10/26/63, received at Louisville military prison 11/63, released on oath 11/3/63, prison records list Morgan Co. as residence, house 1-175, s 1,3,22.

WILLIAMS, DANIEL ALLEN. reg FR, enl 10/18/62 or 11/18/62 Morgan Co., des 10/25/62, house 1-266 or 2-69, s 1,3,22.

WILLIAMS, DIAL D. reg 5, co A, enl 10/25/61 Prestonsburg, house 2-462 or 2-463, s 1,22.

WILLIAMS, DIAL S. reg 5, co A, r 1st sgt, enl 10/21/61 West Liberty or Prestonsburg, made 1st sgt 12/25/61, resigned 5/31/62, dis 10/20/62 Hazel Green, house 2-462 or 2-463, s 1,3,22.

WILLIAMS, ELLIOTT. reg 5, co K, enl 12/14/61 Camp Recovery, Middle Creek, dis 10/20/62 Hazel Green, reg 2MR, co A, enl 10/10/62 Morgan Co., reg FR, enl 11/22/62 Morgan Co., house 1-378 or 1-386, s 1,3,22.

WILLIAMS, JAMES HADEN. reg 5, co A, enl 10/21/61 or 10/25/61 West Liberty or Prestonsburg, age 32, brown hair, hazel eyes, dark skin, 5-7, musician, dis 12/19/61 surgeon's certificate of disability, house 1-213 or 1-538, s 1,3,22.

WILLIAMS, JOHN T. reg 2MR, co A, r capt, enl 8/25/62 or 8/28/62 Morgan Co., resigned 3/12/65, house 2-495, s 1,3,22.

WILLIAMS, JOHN W. reg 5, co D, enl 9/16/62 Morgan Co. or Licking Station, reported deserted at Reingold GA 4/8/63, house 1-304, s 1,3,22.

WILLIAMS, MASON H. P. reg 5, co A, r 1st lt, enl 10/21/61 West Liberty or Prestonsburg, elected 1st 11/17/61, resigned 5/28/62, house 2-462, s 1,3,22.

WILLIAMS, THOMAS J. reg 5, co C, A, enl 10/19/61 Prestonsburg, dis 10/20/62 Hazel Green, chief musician, app drummer 3/10/62, drum major 7/1/63, trans to co A 7/1/63, house 1-261, s 1,3.

WILLIAMS, WILLIAM. reg 2MR, co A, house 1-660 or 2-160, s 1,22.

WILSON, ISAAC SHELBY. reg 13, co Kash's, rem not on AG or CSR, house 2-98, s 1,31.

WILSON, JACKSON. reg 13, co B, house 2-90, s 1,31.

WILSON, JOSEPH. reg 3MR, co B, enl 9/1/62 Mt. Sterling, house 2-74 or 2-189, s 1,3,22.

WILSON, THOMAS. reg 2MR, co A, enl 12/6/62 Camp Ross, house 2-98, s 1,3,22.

WILSON, WILLIAM H. reg 1MR, co A, enl 10/18/61 Prestonsburg, des 10/20/62 Salyersville, house 2-413, s 1,3,22.

WOMACK, JACKSON. reg 2MR, co A, enl 9/15/62 Piketon, trans from co C, 5th Ky. Inf. 10/20/62, house 2-360, s 1,22.

WOMACK or WORNACK, JAMES W. reg 5, co A, enl 10/21/61 or 10/25/61 West Liberty or Prestonsburg, dis 10/20/62 Hazel Green, house 1-296, s 1,3.

WYATT, HEZEKIAH. reg 5, co A, enl 10/28/61 Beaver KY, dis 10/20/62 Hazel Green, house 1-271, s 1,3,22.

WYATT, URIAH. reg 5, co A, enl 10/25/61 Prestonsburg, dis 10/20/62 Hazel Green, 1-271, s 1,3,22.

PIKE COUNTY CONFEDERATE SOLDIERS

A

ADAMS, JAMES W. reg 5, co G, enl 11/4/61 Pike Co. near Pound Gap, house 7-103, s 1,3.
ADAMS, WILLIAM E. reg 5, co G, enl 11/11/61 Pound Gap VA, rem des 1/1/62, house 7-103, s 1,3.
ADKINS, JAMES P. reg 5, co B, r musician, enl 10/21/61 West Liberty, house 7-76 or 7-372, s 3.
ADKINS, JAMES W. reg 5, co G, enl 11/11/61 Pound Gap VA, house 7-372, s 3.
ADKINS, JOSEPH. reg 5, co B, r capt, enl 10/21/61 West Liberty, black hair, gray eyes, dark skin, 6-2, prom to capt 2/16/62, house 7-29, s 1,3.
ADKINS, MOSES. reg 5, co G, enl 5/19/62 Princeton VA, 10, co C, enl 2/1/63 Pike Co., house 7-55, s 3,10,21.
ADKINS, NATHANIEL. reg 2MR, co D, enl 8/16/62 Logan Co. VA, house 7-279, s 1,3.
ADKINS, SAMUEL S. reg 5, co B, enl 10/23/61 Prestonsburg, house 1-83, s 3.
ADKINS, SPENCER. reg 5, co G, r 1st sgt, enl 10/28/61 Pike Co. near Pound Gap, rem prom to 1st sgt 5/30/62, reg 10, co C, r 1st lt, enl 2/1/63 Pike Co., rem prom from 2nd to 1st lt 6/8/64, house 7-5, s 1,3,10.
ADKINS, THOMAS. reg 10, co C, enl 12/20/63 Buchanan Co. VA, house 7-5, s 3,10.
ADKINS, WILLIAM. reg 10, co C, enl 12/20/62 Buchanan Co. VA, rem took oath at Louisa, 4/27/65, house 7-5 or 7-256, s 3,10.
ADKINS, WINRIGHT. reg 5, co G, enl 5/19/62 Princeton VA, age 24, black hair, gray eyes, fair skin, 5-4, reg 10, co C, r 5th sgt, enl 1/1/62 Pike Co., rem surr Mt. Sterling 4/30/65, house 7-56, s 1,3,10.
AKERS, JAMES W. reg 5, co G, enl 11/1/61 Pike Co. near Pound Gap, house 1-4, s 1,3.
ANDERSON, ALFRED. reg 5, co G, cpl, enl 11/4/61 Pike Co. near Pound Gap, rem prom from pvt 6/20/62, reg 10, co C, r sgt, enl 2/12/63 Pike Co., rem cap Floyd Co. 9/1/63 or 12/17/63, taken to Rock Island IL, trans to James River VA for exch 3/13/65, house 7-51, s 1,3,10.
ANDERSON, HIRAM. reg 5, co G, r cpl, enl 11/11/61 Pike Co. near Pound Gap, house 1-98, s 1,3.
ANDERSON, JEPTHA. reg 10, co C, enl 6/1/63 Pike Co., rem surr Louisa 4/26/65, house 7-51, s 3,10.
ANDERSON, SHADRACK. reg 10, co C, enl 12/21/62 Buchanan Co. VA, house 7-51, s 3,10.

B

BALL, WILLIAM. reg 10, co I, enl 7/1/63 Buchanan Co. VA, house 7-675, s 1,3,10.
BARTLEY, JAMES. reg 21VaBtnInf, co F, reg 5VSL, co C, reg 10, co K, enl 3/10/63 Liberty Hill VA, house 7-105, s 1,3,10,14.
BELCHER, BARTLEY. reg 10, co F, K, enl 2/28/63 Buchanan Co. VA, rem re-enlisted in co K 8/7/63 Liberty Hill VA, house 7-54, s 3,10.
BELCHER, ISAAC. reg 5, co C, enl 9/3/62 Pike Co., des 6/18/63, house 168, house 7-168, s 3.
BELCHER, JAMES W. reg 5, co G, enl 11/2/61 camp near Pound Gap, Pike Co., house 7-82, s 1,3.
BELCHER, JOHN M. reg 10, co K, enl 7/10/63 Liberty Hill VA, house 7-54, s 1,3,10.
BELCHER, LEWIS. reg 5, co G, enl 11/2/61 camp near Pound Gap, Pike Co., house 7-54, s 1,3.
BENTLEY, JOHN VENT. ret 13, co D, enl 10/4/62 Whitesburg, residence stated on muster roll, house 7-159, s 3,21,31.
BENTLEY, MOSES. reg 5, co F, enl 11/5/61 camp near Pound Gap, rem d 3/22/62 Camp Moccasin, Scott Co, VA, house 7-165, s 1,3.
BEVINS, JAMES MADISON. reg 10, co C, r 2nd lt, enl 12/20/62 Buchanan Co. VA, house 7-557, s 3,10.

BEVINS, JOHN J. reg VSL, reg 10, co C, enl 2/25/63 Pike Co., age 20, black hair, dark eyes, florid skin, 6-3, rem cap 3/13/65, took oath 6/10/65 Camp Chase OH, house 7-412, s 1,3,10,14.

BLACKBURN, JOHN. reg 1VSL, co A, enl 8/16/62 Tazewell VA, age 20, brown hair, black eyes, dark skin, 5-9, rem cap 5/9/63 Pike Co., rec'd Camp Chase 5/16/63, sent to Johnson's Island, OH, 6/14/63, sent to Point Lookout, MD & exch 11/30/63, house 7-837, s 3,14.

BLAIR, ANDERSON. reg 10, co D, enl 6/15/63 Pike Co., age 25, dark hair & skin, black eyes, 6-0, rem surr Charleston WV 5/4/65, house 7-854, s 1,3,10.

BLANKENSHIP, BENJAMIN. reg 34VaCav, co A, enl 11/1/62 Wise C.H., VA, house 7-490, s 2,15.

BLANKENSHIP, JOHN M. reg 2VSL, co E, reg 10, co H, enl 5/15/63 Buchanan Co. VA, house 7-489, s 1,3,10,14.

BLANKENSHIP, PRESLEY. reg 2VSL, co E, reg 10, co H, enl 5/15/63 Buchanan Co. VA, house 7-725, s 1,3,10,14.

BLANKENSHIP, WILLIAM. reg 2VSL, co E, reg 10, co H, enl 5/15/63 Buchanan Co. VA, house 7-720, s 1,3,10,14.

BRANHAM, JOHN C. reg 7ConfCav, age 45, dark hair, blue eyes, fair skin, 5-8, reg 5VSL, co H, enl 4/1/63, rem cap 4/15/63 Piketon, exch City Point VA 8/13/63, house 7-170, s 12,14.

BRANHAM, JOSEPH. reg 7ConfCav, co E, enl 7/12/63 rem served until unit disbanded, Scott Co. VA, house 7-170, s 12.

BRANHAM, RICHARD. reg 5, co K, r 5th sgt, enl 1/2/62 Carter Co., rem des 4/16/62 Camp Moccasin, reg 7ConfCav, co C, enl 1863, rem served until disbanded, house 7-170, s 1,12,14.

BRUNTY, JESSE. reg 10, co D, enl 9/16/62 Piketon, house 1-12, s 3,10.

BRYANT, JAMES B. reg 13, co D, enl 10/4/62 Whitesburg, rem des 11/20/62, reg 7ConfCav, co A, enl 1862, rem served until surrender, CSR and source 31 list him as Pike Co. resident, house 7-142, s 1,3,12,21,31.

BURGETT, JOHN. reg 1VSL, co E, enl 9/20/62 Logan Co., VA, dark hair & skin, hazel eyes, 5-6, rem des 12/20/62, paroled Charleston WV 4/28/65, house 7-565, s 14.

BURGETT, MOSES. reg 2VSL, co F, house 7-565, s 14.

BURKE, GREENVILLE. reg 5, co G or K, enl 11/21/61 camp near Pound Gap VA, house 1-124, s 1,21.

BURKE, JAMES. reg 5, co G, enl 10/29/61 camp near Pound Gap, Pike Co., house 7-924, s 1,3.

C

CANTRELL, REUBEN. reg 7ConfCav, age 28, brown hair, blue eyes, dark skin, 5-11, rem cap Piketon 4/15/63, paroled & exch, house 7-123, s 12,14.

CANTRELL, SHERWOOD. reg 5VSL, co C, reg 7ConfCav, co A, rem cap Gladesville 7/7/63, taken to Camp Chase OH, then to Camp Douglas, Chicago IL, house 7-141, s 12,14.

CAREY, BENJAMIN. reg 1VSL, co I, house 7-622, s 14.

CARY, LEWIS. reg 36VaInf, co D, H, K, r cpl, enl 7/3/61 Logan C.H., VA, age 27, rem prom to cpl 7/62, cap Winchester VA 9/19/64, sent of Point Lookout, MD, exch 3/13/65, house 7-622, s 3,24.

CASEBOLT, DAVID. reg 5, co G, enl 11/6/61 camp near Pound Gap, Pike Co., house 1-111, s 1,3.

CASEBOLT, HIRAM. reg 5, co G, enl 11/6/61 camp near Pound Gap, Pike Co., reg 7ConfCav, co C, enl 1863, rem present at disbandment at Roanoke VA, house 1-88, s 1,3,12.

CASEBOLT, WILLIAM. reg 5, co G, enl 11/6/61 camp near Pound Gap, Pike Co., rem d 5/6/62 Saltville VA of disease, house 1-88, s 1,3.

CECIL, SAMUEL. reg 2VSL, co G, house 7-441, s 14.

CECIL, THOMAS. reg 34VaCav, co A, enl 4/6/62 Lebanon, VA, rem trans to 1MR, co E, 6/1/62, reg 10, r surgeon, rem not on AG or CSR, house 7-974, s 2,14,15,21.

CHANEY, HENRY. reg 5, co D, brown hair, gray eyes, 5-8, rem cap Pike Co. 5/31/64, took oath & released 10/18/64, residence established by CSR, house n/c, s 1,21.

CHILDERS, DAVID. reg 13, co H, r 4th cpl, enl 10/18/62 Whitesburg, age 18, CSR states he is Letcher Co. resident, but he is not on Letcher Co. census, source 31 says he is Pike Co. resident, house 7-26 or 7-73, s 1, 3, 31.

CHILDERS, JOHN WESLEY. reg 1BatCav, co A, enl 5/19/62 Prestonsburg, reg 7ConfCav, co C, enl 1862, rem surr at Louisa 1865, house 7-71, s 3,12.

CLARK, DANIEL R. reg 36VaInf, co D, enl 7/3/61 Logan Co. VA, age 29, rem cap Winchester VA 9/19/64, sent to Point Lookout, MD, exch 3/15/65, house 7-619, s 3,24.

CLARK, GUY. reg 36VaInf, co D, K, enl 5/27/63 Logan Co. VA, age 47, light hair & eyes, 5-7, rem cap 5/9/63 Pike Co., took oath 1/10/64, house 7-604, s 24.

CLAY, ANDREW J. reg 5, co G, enr 10/29/61 Pound Gap, reg 10, co D, enl 2/10/63 Pike Co., rem cap Cynthiana 6/12/64, house 1-5, s 1,3,10.

CLAY, MITCHELL. reg 10, co D, enl 12/1/62 Pike Co., rem cap Morgan Co. 10/1/63, to Camp Morton, Indianapolis IN, took oath 2/29/64, house 7-980, s 3,10.

COLE, THOMPSON. reg 13, co H, enl 10/18/62 Whitesburg, rem des 12/12/62, s 31 says he is Pike Co. resident, house 7-164, s 3,21, 31.

COLEMAN, JAMES H. 1BatCav, co A, r 2nd sgt, enl 10/20/61 Prestonsburg, house 7-267, s 3.

COLEMAN, JAMES M. 1BatCav, co A, enl 10/20/61 Prestonsburg, house 7-266, s 3.

COLLINS, JOHN C. reg 10, co H enl 5/15/63 Buchanan Co. VA, age 18, rem may have been resident of Russell Co. VA, house 7-776, s 1,3,10.

COLLINS, THOMAS. reg 10, co D, enl 4/24/63 Pike Co., rem paroled Louisa 5/65, house 7-872, s 3,10.

COMPTON, JOHN W. reg 5, co G, r cpl, enl 11/15/61 Pound Gap VA, reg 10, co I, enl 7/1/63 Buchanan Co., VA, house 1-47, s 1,3,10.

COMPTON, WILLIAM F. reg 5, co G, enl 10/28/61 camp near Pound Gap, Pike Co., house 7-932, s 1,3.

COX, JAMES M. reg 5, co G, r 2nd lt, enl 10/28/61 Piketon, rem prom from 1st sgt 5/30/62, house 7-889, s 1,3.

D

DAMRON, JAMES. reg 10, co C, enl 2/11/63 Pike Co., house 1-40 or 1-57, s 3,10.

DAMRON, WRIGHT. reg 5, co G, enl 11/9/61 camp near Pound Gap, Pike Co., house 1-46, s 1,3.

DAWSON, BENJAMIN. reg 5, co E, enl 10/20/61 Prestonsburg, house 7-917, s 3.

DESKINS, HARRISON. reg 2VSL, co F, r 2nd lt, enl 1862, rem commissioned 2nd lt 10/4/62, house 7-576, s 14.

DESKINS, JAMES. reg 2VSL, reg 10, co G, enl 3/28/63 Grundy VA, house 7-591, s 1,3,10,14,21.

E

ELKINS, BOOKER. reg 7ConfCav, co C, enl 1863, house 1-152, s 7,12.

ELSWICK, JONATHAN. reg 10, co D, rem on co muster roll 6/30/63 to 2/29/64, house 7-128, s 1.

ENGLAND, JAMES. reg 5, co G, enl 11/1/61 Pike Co., rem des 5/6/62, house 1-118, s 3.

ENGLAND, RUEL (RUSSELL). reg 13, co C, rem cap Pike Co. 7/3/63, exch Point Lookout MD 2/24/65, house 7-121, s 21.

ESTEP, JAMES. reg 2VSL, co E, house 7-171, s 14.
ESTEP, JOSEPH. reg 2VSL, co E, house 7-751, s 14.
ETTER, JOHN H. reg 36VaInf, co D,K, r sgt, enl 5/27/61 Logan Co. VA, age 22, fair hair & skin, gray eyes, 5-11, reg, 1VSL, co A, r adjutant, enl 8/16/62 Tazewell Co. VA, rem prom to cpl 9/1/62, to 1st lt 11/18/62, to adjutant 1/63, wounded & left at Clarksville, TN 2/23/62, took oath & paroled 4/28/65, house 7-618, s 3,14,24.
ETTER, WILLIAM W. reg 36VaInf, co D, K, enl 10/14/61 Logan C.H. or Richmons Ferry, age 24, rem wounded Belle Grove 10/19/64, house 7-618, s 3,24.

F

FARLEY, JESSE. reg 36VaInf, co H, enl 7/3/61, age 34, CSR lists Pike Co. as residence, house n/c, s 24.
FARRIS, JAMES. reg 2VSL, co F, house 7-566, s 14.
FERRELL, SAMUEL R. reg 36VaInf, co D, enl 5/27/61 Logan C.H., age 23, dark skin & hair black eyes, 5-8, rem dis for disability, internal hemorrhoids, Princeton, VA, 11/20/62, house 7-979, s 3,7.
FERGUSON, JOHN. reg 1MR, co D, enl 10/22/61 Prestonsburg, house 7-865, s 3.
FLETCHER, JAMES W. reg 5, co G, enl 11/9/61 camp near Pound Gap, Pike Co., rem d Scott Co. VA 4/15/62, house 7-426, s 1,3.
FLETCHER, JOSEPH. reg 5, co G, r cpl, enl 11/9/61 Pike Co., red to pvt 2/12/62, house 7-426, s 3,21.
FRANCIS, JOHN W. reg 13, co A, enl 9/29/62 Whitesburg, rem cap Gladesville VA 7/7/63, d 8/19/64 of small pox Camp Douglas, Chicago IL, house 7-537, s 1,3,21.
FRANCISCO, PATRICK. reg 1VSL, co I, dark hair, hazel eyes, fair skin, 5-10, rem cap 7/8/63 Pike Co., house 7-648, s 14.
FRANCISCO, SAMUEL D. reg 5, co B, enl 3/28/62 Camp Moccasin VA, reg 1VSL, co I, rem cap 7/8/63 Pike Co., house 7-648, s 1,3,14.
FRANCISCO, WILLIAM P. reg 1VSL, co I, house 7-22, s 14.
FRY, ANDREW JACKSON. reg 7ConfCav, co F, r 2nd lt, house 7-207, s 12,14.
FULLER, HAWKINS. reg 5, co C, enl 6/62 or 8/22/62 Pike Co., reg 10, co D, enl 3/5/63 Piketon, rem des 4/1/63, 7-908, s 3,10,21.

G

GIBSON, JAMES. reg 10, co F, enl 7/24/63 Buchanan Co. VA, house 7-205 or 7-740, s 1,4.
GIBSON, JOEL. reg 5, co F, enl 12/10/61 Whitesburg, rem dark hair & skin, hazel eyes, 6-0, reg 13, co A, enl 12/10/62 Whitesburg, rem trans to reg 10, co C 2/12/63 Pike Co., reg FR, enl 2/25/63 Floyd Co., cap 5/20/63 Pike Co., taken to Camp Chase OH, took oath 5/15/65, house 7-91, s 1,3,10,21.
GIBSON, JOHN. reg 5VSL, co E, black hair & eyes, dark skin, 5-8, rem des reported to Louisa 3/30/64, took oath, house 1-30, 7-205 or 7-710, s 14.
GOFF, JOHN B. reg 2VSL, r capt, dark hair & skin, hazel eyes, 5-8, rem commissioned 10/4/62 cap Pike Co. 5/24/63, sent to Camp Chase OH, house 7-575, s 14.
GROSS, SOLOMON. reg 29VaInf, co I, enl 4/2/62 mouth of Indian Creek or Tazewell VA, house 7-591, s 3, Alderman, 29th Virginia Infantry.

H

HALE, JOHN JR. reg 10, co A, enl 9/11/62 Prestonsburg, rem cap Cynthiana 6/14/64, exch 2/19/65, house 7-470, s 3,10.

HALL, DAVID. reg 5, co G, enl 11/4/61 Pike Co., reg 10, co L, r cpl, enl 5/1/63 Pike Co., rem prom to cpl 2/15/64, house 1-44, s 1,3,10.

HALL, FLEMING. reg 5, co F, enl 11/11/61 camp near Pound Gap VA, house 7-183, s 1,21.

HALL, HENRY. reg 5, co G, r 4th sgt, enl 11/5/61 Piketon, reg 10, co L, enl 5/1/63 Pike Co., rem wounded at Piketon 8/20/63, house 1-44, s 1,3,10.

HALL, RICHARD. reg 10, co D, enl 6/1/63 Whitesburg, rem des Camp Bowen VA 8/10/63, house 1-135, s 3,10.

HALL, SAMUEL. reg 10, co C, enl 2/10/63 Pike Co., rem POW Camp Morton IN 3/28/65, house 1-44, s 3,10.

HAMILTON, WILLIAM. reg 5, co G, enl 11/861 camp near Pound Gap, Pike Co., reg 10, co L, enl 7/20/63 Saltville VA, rem d 7/7/64 Scott Co. VA, house 1-109, s 1,3,5,10.

HARRIS, ANDREW JACKSON. reg 5, co G, enl 11/2/61 Pike Co., house 7-962, s 3.

HENSON, PAUL. reg 13, co D, enl 10/4/62 Whitesburg, residence stated on CSR, cap Pike Co. 12/11/63, taken to Rock Island, released 10/13/64 on joining 3rd U.S. Vet. Inf., house 7-153, s 3, 31.

HOGSTON, WILLIAM J. reg 10, co C, enl 2/10/63 Pike Co., house 7-78, s 3,10.

HONAKER, JAMES. reg 10, co D, r capt, enl 9/10/62 Piketon, rem elected 1st lt, prom to capt 3/5/63, wounded in left leg Saltville VA, cap 12/9/64 Pike Co., house 7-240, s 3,10.

HOPKINS, JOSEPH. reg 10, co C, r cpl, enl 2/10/63 Pike Co., rem cap 10/1/64, executed 11/7/64 near Bloomfield by order of Brig. Gen. Burbridge, house 1-42, s 3,10.

HURLEY, JOHN B. reg 2VSL, co E, reg 10, co H, enl 5/25/63 Buchanan Co. VA, house 7-712 or 7-713, s 1,3,10,14.

HURLEY, JONATHAN. reg 2VSL, co E, reg 10, co H, enl 5/15/63 Buchanan Co. VA, house 7-711, s 1,3,10,14.

HURLEY, PEYTON. reg 2VSL, co E, reg 10, co H, enl 5/15/63 Buchanan Co. VA, house 7-714, s 1,3,10,14.

HURLEY, SAMUEL R. reg 2VSL, co E, reg 10, co H, r 1st sgt, enl 5/15/63 Buchanan Co. VA, house 7-722, s 1,3,10,14.

J

JACKSON, ROBERT LEE. reg 10, co D, r cpl, enl 10/5/62 Piketon, age 26 (at oath), dark hair, blue eyes, fair skin, 6-0, rem took oath at Charleston 4/28/65, house 7-482, s 1,3,10.

JOHNSON, ANDREW J. reg 5, co G, enl 3/20/62 Scott Co. VA, reg 13, co E, enl 10/5/62 or 10/14/62 Whitesburg, reg 10, co D, enl 10/25/63 Piketon, rem surr Louisa 4/65, house 7-867, s 1,3,10,21.

JOHNSON, JAMES WALTER. reg 5, co G, enl 11/1/61 camp near Pound Gap, Pike Co., reg 10, co D, enl 10/1/62 Piketon, house 1-78, s 1,21.

JOHNSON, THOMAS P. reg 63 Va. Inf., co E, enl 4/13/63 Saltville, Va., trans to Jeffress Battery 9/18/63, house 7-981, s 13,25.

JONES, NATHANIEL T. reg 10, co C, enl 1/15/63 Piketon, house 1-117, s 3,10.

JUSTICE, ANDREW. reg 10, co H, enl 5/15/63 Buchanan Co. VA, house 7-302, s 1,3,10.

JUSTICE, GILMORE. reg 10, co C, enl 3/7/63 Pike Co., rem cap Pike Co. 10/1/63, took oath McLean Barracks 11/11/63, house 7-262, s 3,10.

JUSTICE, HARVEY. reg 2VSL, co E, reg 10, co H, enl 5/15/63 Buchanan Co. VA, house 7-295, s 1,3,10,14.
JUSTICE, HIRAM. reg 2VSL, co E, r 2nd lt, reg 10, co H, r capt, enl 5/15/63 Buchanan Co. VA, light hair, blue eyes, fair skin, 5-11, rem des & took oath at Louisa 5/64 or 6/17/64, house 7-297, s 1,3,10,14.
JUSTICE, JOAB. reg 2VSL, co E, reg 10, co H, enl 5/15/63 Buchanan Co. VA, house 7-303, s 1,3,10,14.
JUSTICE, JOHN D. reg 10, co G, enl 3/28/63 Buchanan Co. VA, house 7-287, s 3,10.
JUSTICE, WILLIAM RILEY. reg 13, co E, enl 10/5/62, cap Gladesville 7/7/63, CSR states he is Letcher Co. resident, but he is not on Letcher Co. census, s 31 says he is Pike Co. resident, house 7-291, s 1,3,31.

K

KENDRICK, HARVEY P. reg 5VSL, co B, r 2nd lt, reg 10, co C, enl 1/1/63 Pike Co., rem cap 6/12/64 Cynthiana, d 3/21/65 Chimborazo Hospital, Richmond VA, chronic diarrhea, house 7-280, s 1,14,21.
KENDRICK, JAMES M. reg 10, co C, enl 2/24/63 Piketon, house 7-17, s 3,10.
KENDRICK, THOMAS J. reg 10, co C, enl 12/20/62 Buchanan Co. VA, rem des 10/12/64, house 7-257, s 3,10.
KENDRICK, WILLIAM H. reg 10, co C, r cpl, enl 2/28/63 Pike Co., rem prom to cpl 6/30/63, des 7/15/64, house 7-257, s 3,10.
KENNEY, HENRY. reg 5, co G, enl 11/12/61 Pound Gap VA, house 1-105, s 3.
KENNEY, JOHN W. reg 5, co G, enl 11/11/61 Pound Gap VA, house 1-104, s 3.
KENNEY, WILLIAM A. reg 5, co G, enl 11/11/61 Pound Gap VA, reg 4VSL, co F, reg 10, co L, enl 11/18/63 Bracken Co., house 1-104, s 3,14.

L

LAMBERT, HIRAM. reg 1VSL, co I, house 7-708, s 14.
LESLIE, KENAS F. reg 10, co D, enl 10/1/62 Piketon, rem cap 12/20/62, wounded 11/8/63 Rogersville TN, house 7-469, s 3,10.
LOCKHART, DAVID. reg 10, co L, r cpl, enl 1/1/63 Pike Co., rem prom to cpl 10/25/63, house 7-975, s 3,10.

M

MARRS, HARMON H. reg 5, co G, enl 3/19/62 Scott Co. VA, house 7-971, s 3.
MARRS, HENRY. reg 10, co D, r 3rd sgt, enl 9/19/62 Piketon, rem wounded Tazewell VA 8/30/64, surr Louisa 4/65, house 1-54, s 3,10.
MARRS, JAMES P. reg 10, co D, enl 9/19/62 Piketon, rem wounded Cynthiana 6/12/64, surr Louisa 4/65, house 1-54, s 3,10.
MARRS, NAPOLEON BONAPARTE. reg 5, co G, enl 9/5/62 Piketon, dis 10/20/62 Hazel Green, reg 10, co D, r cpl, enl 9/5/62 Piketon, rem reg 5 service not on AG or SCR, house 1-2, s 3,10,21.
MARRS, REESE T. reg 10, co D, r cpl, enl 8/27/62 Pike Co., rem took oath at Lexington, 4/5/65, house 7-898, s 3,10.
MARRS, SAMUEL R. reg 34VaCav, co B, enl 1/8/62 Martin's Mill, reg 4VSL, reg 10, co D, r 4th sgt, enl 6/10/63 Camp Bowen VA, house 1-54, s 3,10,14,15.

MARRS, SAMUEL W. reg 10, co D, r cpl, enl 9/10/62 Piketon, rem cap Cynthiana 6/11/64, taken to Camp Morton, Indianapolis IN, took oath 3/22/65 & 5/65, house 7-898, s 3,10.

MARRS, THOMAS. reg 2VSL, co I, r 2nd lt, enl 9/1/62, house 1-2, s 14.

MAY, DAVID. reg 4VSL, reg 10, co D, r 2nd sgt, enl 6/1/63 Pike Co., rem KIA Cynthiana 6/12/64, house 7-253, s 1,3,10,14,21.

MAY, HENRY. reg 4VSL, reg 10, co C, r 2nd lt, enl 12/20/62 Buchanan Co. VA, rem prom from pvt to 2nd lt 6/8/64, surr 5/65, house 1-31, s 3,10,14.

MAY, SOLOMON. reg 4VSL, rem KIA Mt. Sterling 6/9/64, house 1-45, s 3,10,14.

MAY, WILLIAM. reg 5, co E, r 1st sgt, enl 10/28/61 Prestonsburg, reg 10, co D, enl 11/1/62 Prestonsburg, rem cap 6/63 Floyd Co., house 7-561, s 3,10,21.

MAYO, THOMAS J. reg 10, co L, enl 7/4/64 Lebanon VA, rem not on AG or CSR, house 7-473, s 21.

MCCOWN, JAMES. reg 10, co D, enl 9/15/62 Piketon, rem wounded & cap 6/8/64 Mt. Sterling, d Camp Douglas, Chicago IL, 12/19/64 smallpox, house 7-904, s 3,10.

MCCOWN, THOMAS. reg 5, co G, r cpl, enl 11/15/61 Pound Gap VA, house 7-911, s 3.

MCCOY, SAMUEL. reg 5, co G, enl 12/7/61 Pike Co., rem d at Clinch River VA, house 7-462 or 7-801, s 1,3.

MCCOY, SELKIRK. reg 1VSL, co A, r 1st sgt, enl 12/31/62 Smyth Co. VA, fair hair & skin, hazel eyes, house 7-550, s 14.

MCCOY, SYLVESTER. reg 1VSL, co I, dark hair & skin, 5-7, rem cap 6/5/64, sent to Camp Morton, Indianapolis IN, rel 5/22/65, house 7-803, s 14.

MCCOY, WILLIAM M. reg 5, co G, enl 11/11/61 Pound Gap VA, rem d Scott Co. VA 4/19/62 erysipelas, house 7-855, s 3,22.

MCKENZIE, BALLARD. reg 5, co G, enl 10/25/61 Pike Co., reg 10, co L, r 4th sgt, enl 8/1/63 Pound Gap, rem prom to 4th sgt 2/18/64, wounded Blue Springs TN, 8/28/64, house 1-23, s 3,10.

MEAD, WILLIAM W. reg 10, co C, r 1st sgt, enl 12/20/62 Buchanan Co. VA, rem indicted in Pike Co. for horse stealing, house 1-29, s 3,10.

MILLER, ANDREW J. reg 5, co G, enl 11/2/61 camp near Pound Gap, Pike Co., house 7-601, s 1,3.

MILLER, SAMUEL H. reg 5, co G, r cpl, enl 11/11/61 Pound Gap VA., reg 2VSL, reg 10, co C, L, r 3rd sgt, enl 5/1/63 Pike Co., rem trans to co C, 10th Ky 8/2/64, house 1-165, s 1,3,10,14.

MOORE, PLATT S. reg 10, co D, enl 9/15/62 Piketon, rem cap 4/14/64, taken to Camp Morton, Indianapolis IN 4/22/64, house 1-20, s 1,3,10.

MOUNTS, HARRISON. reg 1VSL, co I, house 7-703, s 14.

MULLINS, ALEXANDER. reg 13, co E, r 1st lt, enl 11/2/62 Whitesburg, rem resigned, house 7-188, s 3,21.

MULLINS, ANDREW. reg 1VSL, co K, enl 9/20/62 Logan Co. VA., house 7-149, s 14.

MULLINS, JOHN A. reg 5, co F, enl 11/1/61 camp near Pound Gap, reg 5VSL, co C, reg 7ConfCav, co B, house 7-131, s 1,3,12,14.

MULLINS, JOHN W. reg 4VSL, reg 7ConfCav, reg 10, co K, enl 5/15/63 Buchanan Co. VA, house 1-149, s 3,10,12,14.

MULLINS, SHERWOOD. reg 7ConfCav, co C, dark hair, blue eyes, fair skin, 5-7, rem took oath 3/30/64 Louisville, house 7-124, s 12.

MULLINS, TILMAN. reg 34VaCav, co B, E, enl 7/15/62 Tazewell Co., VA, age 26, blue eyes, fair skin, 5-8, rem cap 6/20/64 McDowell Co. VA, d Camp Chase OH 11/12/64 pneumonia, buried grave 457, residence stated on roster of 34th Va. Inf., house n/c, s 2,15.

MULLINS, WILLIAM L. reg 7ConfCav, house 1-149, 7-156 or 7-187, s 1,3,12,14.

MURPHY, JAMES H. reg 2VSL, reg 10, co C, enl 3/1/63 Pike Co., rem des 5/15/63, house 7-68, s 3,10,14.

MURPHY, JOHN. reg 10, co C, enl 2/12/63 Pike Co., house 7-68, s 3,10.

N

NEWSOME, FREDERICK. reg 5, co G, enl 11/9/61 camp near Pound Gap, Pike Co., house 1-101, s 1,3.

NEWSOME, GEORGE WASHINGTON. reg 13, co D, enl 10/4/62 Whitesburg, CSR lists Letcher Co. as residence, s 31 lists Pike Co. as residence, house 1-73, s 3,21,31.

O

OSBURN, SHERWOOD. reg 10, co C, enl 3/25/63 Floyd Co., house 1-189, s 3,10.

P

PARSONS, JOHN J. reg 5, co G, enl 11/1/61 camp near Pound Gap, Pike Co, rem d 6/12/62 Jeffersonville VA, house 7-240, s 1,3.

PHILLIPS, ZACHARIAH. reg 34VaCav, co A, enl 12/11/61 Prestonsburg, reg 10, co C, enl 2/12/63 Pike Co., house 7-45 or 7-385, s 1,3,10,15.

PORTER, DRURY. reg 5, co E, enl 10/30/61 Prestonsburg, des 3/9/62, house 7-486, s 3,21.

POTTER, GEORGE. reg 10, co K, enl 8/7/63 Liberty Hill VA, house 7-86, s 3,10.

POTTER, HENRY. reg 10, co K, enl 8/7/63 Liberty Hill VA., house 7-87 or 7-90, s 3,10.

POTTER, SQUIRE. reg 10, co K, enl 7/10/63 Buchanan Co. VA, rem des 4/64, house 7-145, s 3,10.

POWELL, DAVID A. reg 10, co D, r 1st lt, enl 9/10/62 Piketon, rem elected 2nd lt 3/5/63, prom to 1st lt 10/22/63, house 7-51, s 3,10.

POWELL, JOHN W. reg 10, co C, r ord sgt, enl 12/20/62 Buchanan Co. VA, age 35(in 1865), rem prom to ordinance sgt 3/1/63, house 7-22, s 3,10.

R

RAINES, CHRISTOPHER. reg 10, co C, enl 2/23/63 Pike Co., rem cap 10/15/63 Floyd Co., taken to Rock Island IL 12/29/63, house 7-272, s 3,10.

RAMEY, HENRY. reg 5, co E, reg 10, co C, enl 3/1/63 Pike Co., rem reg 5 service not on AG or CSR, cap 7/3/63 Pike Co., trans to Camp Chase OH 7/24/63, trans to Camp Douglas IL 8/24/63, house 7-104, s 3,10,21.

RAMEY, LLOYD H. reg 10, co C, enl 2/1/63 Pike Co., house 7-98, s 3,10.

RAMEY, WILLIAM. reg 10, co C, enl 3/1/63 Pike Co., house 7-95, s 3,10.

RATLIFF, HARRISON. reg 10, co D, enl 9/19/62 Pike Co., rem d Kingsport TN 12/31/63 of fever, house 1-25, s 1,3,10.

RATLIFF, JACOB. reg 5, co G, enl 11/10/61 Pike Co., house 7-966, s 3.

RATLIFF, JAMES F. reg 10, co C, enl 2/12/63 Pike Co., rem des 9/20/64, house 7-65 or 7-66, s 3,10.

RATLIFF, JAMES L. reg 5, co G, r 2nd lt, enl 10/28/61 Piketon, age 30, dark hair & skin, gray eyes, 5-11, reg 10, co D, r 1st sgt, rem cap 4/15/63 Piketon, house 7-946, s 1,3,10.

RATLIFF, JOHN. reg 5, co G, enl 11/10/61 Pike Co., house 7-910 or 7-913, s 3.

RATLIFF, MOSES. reg 10, co I, enl 7/1/63 Buchanan Co. VA, house 7-430, s 1,3,10.

RATLIFF, SAMUEL. reg 7ConfCav, co C, enl 1863, rem took oath 6/65 Charleston WV, house 7-909, s 7,12.

RATLIFF, SILAS W. reg 10, co D, enl 9/20/62 Piketon, reg 2VSL, co D, house 7-119, 7-283 or 7-913, s 3,10,14.
RATLIFF, THOMPSON. reg 10, co C, enl 2/12/63 Pike Co., age 32, black hair & eyes, fair skin, 5-9, rem surr Charleston WV 5/15/65, house 7-50, s 3,10.
RATLIFF, WILLIAM. reg 10, co C, r capt, enl 2/12/63 Pike Co., rem prom from 1st lt to capt 8/31/64, house 7-21, 7-75 or 7-875, s 3,10.
RATLIFF, WILLIAM A. reg 10, co C, enl 1/1/62 Pike Co., rem des 9/1/63, house 7-67, s 3,10.
RATLIFF, WILLIAM O. B. reg 5, co G, r cpl, enl 10/28/61 Piketon, reg 10, co D, enl 9/22/62 Piketon, rem wounded & cap Mt. Sterling 6/9/64 or Cynthiana 6/12/64, taken to Camp Morton, Indianapolis IN, took oath 3/22/65, house 1-25, s 3,10.
RAY, ELI. reg 5, co E, enl 10/29/61 Pike Co., reg 10, co D, enl 2/10/63 Piketon, rem wounded, house 7-931, s 3,10.
RAY, JACKSON. reg 5, co G, enl 11/5/61 Pike Co., house 1-109, s 3.
RAY, JAMES L. reg 5, co G, enl 11/2/61 Pike Co., reg 10, co D, enl 4/24/63 Piketon, age 18, rem wounded in left ankle 6/11/64 Cynthiana, d 6/15/64, house 1-6, s 1,3,10.
ROBINETT, WILLIAM. reg 1VSL, co I, house 7-710, s 14.
ROBINSON, WILLIAM. reg 3MR, co G, cap Pike Co or Buffalo Furnace 10/11/63, rel from Louisville 10/31/63 on bond & oath, residence stated on CSR, house n/c, s 1,22.
ROMANS, WILLIAM APPERSON. reg 10, co C, enl 2/28/63 Pike Co., house 7-642, s 3,10.
ROSS, WILLIAM. reg 10, co D, enl 2/1/63 Rogersville TN, rem des 2/1/63, house 7-874, s 3,10.
RUNYON, JOHN COMPTON. reg 13, co B, enl 9/13/62 Whitesburg, des 9/10/63, house 7-681, s 3, 31.
RUNYON, THOMAS. reg 5, co G, enl 11/1/61 Pike Co., house 7-646, s 3.

S

SANDERS, JACOB. reg 7ConfCav, co C, r 1st lt, rem elected lt. 7/23/64, took oath 1865, service conflicts with U39D service, house 7-197, s 7,12.
SCOTT, HENRY. reg 5, co C, age 19, dark hair & skin, hazel eyes, 5-9, rem arrested Floyd or Pike Co. 5/14/623, received Camp Chase OH 5/26/63, taken to Johnson's Island 6/14/63, released on oath Point Lookout MD 1/10/64, house 7-474, s 1,21.
SHORTRIDGE, THOMAS R. reg 5, co E, enl 10/26/61 Prestonsburg, house 7-509, s 3.
SLONE, ARCH. reg 10, co C, rem not on AG or CSR, cap Mt. Sterling 6/14/64, taken to Camp Morton IN, trans for exch 2/19/65, house 7-26, s 21.
SLONE, ROBERT. reg 10, co C, enl 5/16/63 Pike Co., rem wounded & cap Mt. Sterling 6/14/64, taken to Camp Morton IN, trans to Point Lookout MD for exch 2/19/65, surr 4/15/65 Lynchburg VA, house 7-322, s 1,21.
SLONE, SIMEON. reg 10, co C, enl 2/26/63 Pike Co., rem des 9/20/64, house 7-259, s 1.
SLONE, SPOTSFORD. reg 10, co C, enl 5/16/63 Pike Co., rem wounded in TN 8/7/64, house 7-356, s 1.
SLONE, WILLIAM. reg 10, co C, enl 12/20/62 Buchanan Co. VA, age 24, light hair, hazel eyes, dark skin, 6-0, rem cap 4/15/63 Pike Co., exch 5/3/63, rejoined co 6/15/63, house 7-260, s 1.
SMITH, JOHN W. reg 1BatCav, co A, enl 10/20/61 Prestonsburg, house 7-826, s 3.
SMITH, JOSEPH M. reg 1BatCav, co A, enl 10/20/61 Prestonsburg, house 7-816, s 3.
SMITH, WILLIAM R. reg 5, co G, enl 11/11/61 Pound Gap VA, reg 2VSL, co E, reg 10, co H, enl 5/15/63 Buchanan Co. VA, house 7-782, s 1,3,10,14.
SPARKS, RICHARD. reg 5, co G, enl 11/10/61 camp near Pound Gap, Pike Co., house 7-467, s 1,3.
STACY, WILLIAM. reg 2VSL, co E, house 7-527, s 14.

STAFFORD, HARRISON. reg 1VSL, co I, r 2nd sgt, house 7-801, s 14.
STANLEY, GEORGE B. reg 2VSL, co E, reg 10, co H, enl 5/15/63 Buchanan Co. VA, house 7-833, s 1,3,10,14,21.
STEELE, JOHN. reg 1VSL, co I, house 7-704, s 14.
STONE, MOSES. reg 8VaCav, co K enl 8/1/62 Wayne Co, VA, age 27, fair skin, dark hair, gray eyes, 5-9, rem surr Charleston WV & took oath 3/24/65, house 7-878, s 2,16.
STURGILL, BLACKBURN. reg 5, co G, enl 10/30/61 Pike Co., house 1-8, s 3.
SWINEY, ELI. reg 5, co G, enl 11/4/61 camp near Pound Gap, Pike Co., reg 10, co D, enl 10/11/62 Piketon, rem not on AG or CSR, paroled 4/30/65, house 7-919, s 1,3,21.
SWORD, JAMES W. reg 5, co G, r 3rd sgt, enl 11/11/61 camp near Pound Gap, rem d Pound Gap VA 2/5/62, house 7-920, s 1,3.
SWORD, WILLIAM. reg 5, co G, enl 11/5/61 Pike Co., house 1-10, s 3.
SYKES, JAMES W. reg 5VSL, co B, house 7-206, s 14.

T

TACKETT, ABNER. reg 13, co B, enl 9/11/62 Middle Creek, dis 9/29/62 house 1-127, s 3,21.
TACKETT, GEORGE W. reg 5, co G, enl 11/11/61 Pound Gap VA, reg 13, co B, enl 9/6/62 Whitesburg, light hair, gray eyes, fair skin, 5-6, rem cap Pike Co. 10/6/63 rel on oath 10/31/63 Louisville, may be Floyd Co. resident, house 1-129, s 1,3,21.
TACKETT, HARVEY. reg 5, co G, enl 11/11/61 Pound Gap VA, house 1-114, s 3.
TACKETT, JOHN. reg 5, co C, G, enl 11/7/61 camp near Pound Gap, Pike Co., rem KIA 7/22/64, hospital record lists Robertson Creek, Ky. as post office, house 1-160, s 1,3.
TACKETT, MATTHEW. reg 13, co E, enl 10/5/62 Whitesburg, house 1-127, s 1,3,21.
TACKETT, SOLOMON. reg 5, co G, enl 11/11/61 Pound Gap VA, house 1-122, s 3.
TACKETT, WILLIAM. reg 5, co G, enl 11/11/61 Pound Gap VA, rem d 2/24/62 Gladesville, VA, house 1-108, s 1,3.
TAYLOR, BENJAMIN F. reg 1MR, co A, enl 10/18/61 Prestonsburg, house 7-589, s 3.
TAYLOR, JAMES. reg 10, co D, enl 8/1/61 Piketon, house 7-554 or 7-577, s 3,10.
THACKER, GEORGE W. reg 5, co G, enl 11/15/61 Pound Gap VA, reg 10, c o C, enl 2/23/63 Piketon, rem cap 12/11/63 Pike Co., taken to Rock Island IL 12/29/63, house 7-38, s 3,10.
THACKER, GREENVILLE. reg 10, co C, enl 8/1/63 or 8/15/63 Pike Co., rem des 9/9/63, house 7-247, s 3,10.
THACKER, JOSEPH. reg 5, co G, enl 11/11/61 Pound Gap VA, house 7-37, s 3.
THACKER, THOMAS. reg 10, co C, enl 8/15/63 Pike Co., rem cap Pike Co. 12/11/63 Pike Co., taken to Rock Island IL, house 7-37, s 3,10.
THOMPSON, SAMUEL W. reg 5, co B, r 2nd lt, enl 10/21/61 West Liberty, rem elected 2nd lt 6/16/62, house 7-944, s 3.

U

UNDERWOOD, JACK R. reg 2VSL, co F, house 7-573, s 14.

W

WALKER, HARVEY. reg 1VSL, co A, r 1st sgt, rem camp 6/23/63 Logan Co. VA, exch 2/23/65, house 7-598, s 14.

WALTERS, THOMAS. reg 5, co H, enl 9/1/61 Paintsville, house 7-899, s 1,3.

WARRIX, JOHN FOUNT. reg 5, co G, enl 11/9/61 Pike Co., reg 13, co D, enl 10/4/62 Whitesburg, rem reg 5 service not on AG or CSR, house 7-157, s 3,21.

WEDDINGTON, ANDREW JACKSON. reg 5, co G, enl 11/1/61 Pike Co., house 7-898, s 3.

WEDDINGTON, HENRY HARRISON. reg 5, co G, H, r 2nd lt, enl 10/8/62 Piketon, age 23, light hair, gray eyes, fair skin, 5-11, rem elected 2nd lt 10/8/62, reg 13, co K, r 2nd lt, enl 10/8/62, rem cap 7/7/63 Gladesville, rel Johnson's Island OH 6/28/65 on oath, house 7-897, s 1,21,31.

WEDDINGTON, JAMES M. reg 5, co C, enl 8/24/62 Pike Co., dark hair & skin, gray eyes, 6-0, rem took oath 6/20/64, house 7-891, s 1,3.

WEDDINGTON, KENAS F. reg 5, co G, enl 11/11/61 camp near Pound Gap VA, house 7-898, s 1,21.

WHITE, JAMES. reg 34VaCav, co B, enl 6/13/62 Tazewell Co. VA, age 22, fair hair & skin, hazel eyes, 5-9, rem took oath at Charleston WV 5/3/65, house 7-35, s 3,15.

WHITE, LEWIS. reg 10, co C, enl 3/1/63 Pike Co., house 7-64, s 3,10.

WILLIAMSON, FRANKLIN. reg 10, co D, enl 8/7/63 Piketon, rem took oath 8/12/65 Lexington, house 7-964, s 3,10.

WILLIAMSON, HARMON. reg 1VSL, co I, r 1st lt, house 7-811, s 14.

WILLIAMSON, JAMES. reg 1VSL, house 7-828 or 7-839, s 14.

WILLIAMSON, JAMES M. reg 5, co C, enl 9/6/62 Bath Co., rem wounded Dallas GA 5/28/64, d 7/1/64 Gilmon Hospital of vulvus oclopoticemus, house 7-828 or 7-839, s 1,3.

WILLIAMSON, JOHN H. reg 5, co G, r 3rd sgt, enl 11/25/61 Pound Gap VA, reg 10, co D, r 2nd lt, enl 9/10/62 Piketon, rem elected 2nd lt 3/5/63, wounded & cap Cynthiana 6/12/64, d of wounds, house 7-964, s 3,10.

WILLIAMSON, JONAH. reg 5, co G or H, cap Pike Co. 7/7/63, to Camp Chase, OH 7/20/63, d Camp Chase 8/20/63, not on AG or CSR, house 7-421, s 21.

WILLIAMSON, JULIUS G. reg 2VSL, co I, r capt, house 7-811, s 14.

WILLIAMSON, SAMUEL ROBERT. reg 10, co D, r cpl, enl 9/1/62 Piketon, house 7-964, s 3,10.

WILLIAMSON, ZACHARIAH TAYLOR. reg 10, co D, enl 8/7/63 Piketon, rem surr Louisa spring 1865, house 7-964, s 3,10.

WILSON, JAMES H. reg 5, co H, enl 10/21/61 Prestonsburg, dis 10/22/62 Salyersville, reg 2VSL, co E, reg 10, co H, enl 8/15/63 Buchanan Co. VA, house 7-694, s 1,3,10.

UNION SOLDIERS

BOYD COUNTY UNION SOLDIERS

A

ABNER, CAREY. reg 14, co A, enr 10/1/61 Louisa, enl 12/10/61 Louisa, dis 9/15/65 Louisville, age 26, trans to 14th Ky. Vet. Inf., b Wayne Co., residence stated on muster roll, house n/c, s 1,2,4.

ABSHIRE, ALLEN. reg 5Va, co G, enr & enl 9/26/11 Ceredo, dis 10/3/64 Wheeling, re-enlisted as Vet. Volunteer 12/25/63, b Boyd Co., CSR: enrolled in 9th District of Ky., house 21, s 1,27.

ACKERSON, THOMAS. reg 5Va, co C, enr 8/30/61 Ceredo, enl 9/2/61 Ceredo, dis 9/21/64 Wheeling, age 22, house 590, s 1,26,27.

ADAMS, JOHN. reg 5Va., co E, enr 8/6/61 Ceredo, enl 9/2/61 Ceredo, dis 10/4/64 Wheeling, age 21 or 33, brown hair, blue eyes, light skin, 5-8, dis 2/3/63 Fairfax VA for disability of inguinal hernia, b Lawrence Co. OH, house 24, s 1,27.

ADAMS, JOSHUA. reg 39, co A, enr 10/18/62 Peach Orchard, enl 2/16/63 Peach Orchard, dis 9/15/65 Louisville, age 18, light hair, blue eyes, fair skin, 5-5, b Memphis TN, residence stated on muster roll, house n/c, s 1,2,4.

ADAMS, MONTGOMERY. reg 2Cav, co E, enr 7/14/61 Camp Jo Holt, enl 9/9/61 Muldraugh Hill, dis 10/12/64 Nashville TN, age 22, house 676, s 1,2.

ADAMS, NATHAN S. reg 14, co C, enr 10/10/61 Louisa, enl 12/10/61 Catlettsburg, dis 9/15/65 Louisville, age 33, trans to 14th Vet. Inf., b Scioto Co. OH, age 25 on census, house 283, s 1,2,4.

ADAMS, ROBERT. reg 10Cav, co F, enl 8/9/62 Boyd Co., enl 9/9/62 Covington, dis 9/17/63 Maysville, age 19, taken prisoner & paroled at Mt. Sterling 3/22/63, residence stated on muster roll, house n/c, s 1,2,4.

ADKINS, RILEY. reg 45, co I, enl 10/19/63 Ashland, dis 2/4/64 Mt. Sterling, age 18, light hair & skin, blue eyes, 5-9, trans to 4th Vet. Inf., b Boyd Co., d 2/27/64 Richmond VA of disease, age 23 on census, house 395, s 1,2.

ALEXANDER, JOSEPH. reg 22EM, co B, r sgt, enl 5/26/64 Catlettsburg, dis 6/28/64, age 24, dark hair & skin, gray eyes, 5-8, b Chester Co. PA, house C9, s 2,4.

ALLEY, FLOYD H. reg 10Cav, co F, enr 8/9/62 Boyd Co., enl 9/9/62 Covington, dis 9/17/63 Maysville, age 22, house 47, s 1,2,4.

ALLEY, LORENZO D. reg 14, co C, enr 10/10/61 Louisa, enl 12/10/61 Louisa, dis 1/31/65 Louisa, age 32, wounded in shoulder 6/22/64 Kennesaw Mtn. GA, CSR: 3/63, at home sick in Boyd Co., house 46, s 1,2,4.

ALLEY, MARCUS L. reg 14, co C, enr 10/10/61 Louisa, enl 12/10/61 Louisa, dis 12/31/62 Lexington, age 28, dark hair, blue eyes, fair skin, 5-10, CSR: 12/61 at home sick in Boyd Co., dis for disability of partial paralysis, house 39, s 1,2,4.

ALLEY, WILLIAM. reg 22EM, co A, enl 5/26/64, dis 6/28/64, age 17, light hair & skin, blue eyes, 5-10, house 31, s 2,4.

ALLISON, THEODORE R. reg 54, co A, enr & enl 9/5/64 Greenupsburg, dis 9/1/65 Louisville, r 1st sgt, age 24, dark hair, blue eyes, light skin, 5-6, prom to 1st sgt 12/31/64, b Lawrence Co. OH, house 364, s 1,2,26.

ANDERSON, WILLIAM. reg 5Va, co K, enr 11/2/63 Ceredo, enl 1/12/63, dis 10/3/64 Wheeling, age 18, brown hair, gray eyes, dark skin, 5-8, residence stated as Boyd Co., wounded Battle of Cedar Creek VA 10/19/64, house 573, s 1,27.

ANDERSON, WILLIAM C. reg 10Cav, co F, enr 8/9/62 Boyd Co., enl 9/9/62 Covington, age 19, not on AG, house 325, s 1,25.
ANDREWS, NELSON P. reg 22EM, co A, enl 5/26/64, dis 6/28/64, age 38, dark hair, blue eyes, light skin, 5-6, b Scioto Co. OH, house A4, s 2,4,5.
ARMSTRONG, CHARLES M. reg 14, co C, enr 10/10/61 Paintsville, enl 12/10/61 Louisa, dis 1/31/65 Louisa, age 27, house A34, s 1,2,4.
ARTHUR, GEORGE D. reg 14, co A, musician, enr 10/1/61 Louisa, enl 12/10/61 Louisa, dis 1/31/65 Louisa, age 20, residence stated on muster roll, house n/c, s 1,2,4.
ARTHUR, JAMES. reg 14, co C, enr 10/1/61 Ashland, age 18, d 2/6/62 Paintsville of disease, age 11 on census, house 416, s 1,2.
ARTHUR, JOSEPH. reg 14, co A, enr 10/1/61 Louisa, enl 12/10/61 Louisa, dis 9/15/65 Louisville, age 37, trans to 14th Vet. Inf. 3/15/64, house 595, s 1,2,4.
ARTHUR, LEVI. reg 53, co I, enl & m/in 3/29/65 Greenupsburg, dis 9/15/65 Louisville, age 19, light hair, hazel eyes, fair skin, 5-4, b Boyd Co., house 54, s 1, 2,5.
ARTHUR, SIMEON. reg 50th Ohio Infantry, co K, enr 8/16/62, dis 1/25/65 Salisbury NC, age 18, house 487, s 5,33.
ARTHUR, THOMAS. reg 14, co A, enr 10/1/61 Louisa, enl 12/10/61 Louisa, dis 1/31/65 Louisa, age 22, house 401, s 1,2,4.
ARTHUR, WILEY. reg 14, co A, enr 10/1/61 Ashland, enl 12/10/61 Louisa, dis 1/31/65 Louisa, age 18, sandy hair, gray eyes, light skin, 5-7, house 400, s 1,2,4.
ARTHUR, WILLIAM. reg 14, co C, enr 10/1/61 Catlettsburg, enl 12/10/61 Louisa, dis 1/31/65 Louisa, age 38, residence stated as Boyd Co., age 53 on census, house 402, s 1,2,4.
ARTIS, HENRY H. reg 14Cav, co C, enr 8/16/62 Star Furnace, m/in 11/6/62 Mt. Sterling, m/out 9/16/63 Maysville, reg 54, co A, enl 9/5/64 Greenupsburg, dis 9/1/65 Louisville, age 19, dark hair, gray eyes, fair skin, 5-10, credited to Boyd Co, b Greenup Co., cap in Virginia 1/65, house n/c, s 1.
ARTIST or ARTEST, HENRY. reg 14, co A, enr 10/1/61 Louisa, enl 12/10/61 Louisa, dis 9/15/65 Louisville, r cpl, age 35, trans to 14th Vet. Inf., prom to cpl 8/8/63, wounded in right arm between 7/2/64 & 8/13/64, house 635, s 1,2,4.
ARTRIP, ENOCH D. reg 14, co C, A, enr 10/1/61 Louisa, enl 12/10/61 Louisa, dis 9/15/65, age 26, trans to 14th Vet. Inf., enr 2/19/64, m/in 3/19/64, cap 9/4/62 or 2/15/63, residence stated on muster roll, house n/c, s 1,2,4.

B

BAILEY, WILEY. reg 40, co C, enr 7/27/63 Grayson, enl 9/26/63 Grayson, age 18, wounded in action in Virginia and supposed to have been captured, residence stated on muster roll, house n/c, s 1,2,4.
BALDWIN, DAVID. reg 10Cav, co F, enr 8/9/62 Boyd Co., enl 9/9/62 Covington, dis 9/17/63 Maysville, age 22, residence stated on muster roll, house n/c, s 1, 2,4.
BALDWIN, JOHN. reg 14, co C, enr 10/10/61 Louisa, enl 12/10/61 Louisa, age 28, des 5/4/62 Lexington, CSR lists Lawrence Co. OH as residence, but he is not on Lawrence Co. OH census, house 28, s 1,2,4.
BARBER, REUBEN. reg 45, co K, enr 10/1/63 Catlettsburg, enl 12/9/63 Louisa, dis 2/14/65 Catlettsburg, age 30, house 169, s 1,2,26.
BARBER, ROBERT. reg 45, co K, enr 10/1/63 Catlettsburg, enl 12/9/63 Louisa, dis 2/14/65 Catlettsburg, age 21, house 173, s 1,2.
BARTON, JONAS. reg 14, co I, r com. sgt, enr 11/10/61 Louisa, enl 12/1061 Louisa, dis 9/15/65 Louisville, age 24 or 27, fair hair, blue eyes, dark skin, 5-6, trans to 14th Vet. Inf., enr 2/29/64, m/in

3/15/64, prom to sgt 9/8/63, app com. sgt 2/28/65, b Morgan Co., residence stated on muster roll, house n/c, s 1,2,4.

BARTRUM, FREDERICK. reg 45, co B, r cpl, enr 6/8/63 Catlettsburg, enl 10/10/63 Catlettsburg, age 18, d 6/1/64 in Ohio of disease, house 6, s 1,2,26.

BARTRUM, JAMES. reg 5Va, co F, enr 9/2/61 Camp Pierpont, enl 9/2/61 Ceredo, dis 9/23/64 Wheeling, age 26, d 12/15/61 of measles while on furlough at Catlettsburg, house 391, s 1,26,27.

BARTRUM, THOMAS. reg 10Cav, co F, enr 8/9/62 Boyd Co., enl 9/9/62 Covington, dis 9/17/63 Maysville, age 44, house 7, s 1,2,4.

BARTRUM, WILLIAM. reg 75th Ohio Infantry, co K, enl 12/30/61, dis 1/20/63, age 52, house 13, s 26,33.

BATES, CAREY PATTERSON. reg 14, co E, r 1st sgt, enr 10/15/61 Ashland, enl 12/10/61 Louisa, dis 1/31/65 Louisa, age 23, prom from cpl to sgt 7/1/62, to 1st sgt 5/1/64, may have been prom to 2nd lt, 40th Ky. Inf. but no record of service on AG, house 447, s 1,2,4.

BATES, SAMUEL B. reg 14, co E, r cpl, enr 10/19/63 Louisa, enl 10/29/63 Louisa, dis 9/15/65 Louisville, age 19, dark hair, black eyes, fair skin, 5-8, trans to 14th Vet. Inf., app cpl 2/1/65, house 447, s 1,2,4.

BATES, WILLIAM HIRAM. reg 14, co A, E, enr 10/15/61 Ashland, enl 12/10/61 Louisa, dis 9/15/65 Louisville, age 21, brown hair, blue eyes, fair skin, 5-11, trans to 14th Vet. Inf., enr 2/29/64, m/in 3/19/64, house 447, s 1,2,4.

BELL, JOHN W. reg 54, co A, enr & enl 9/5/64 Greenupsburg, dis 9/1/65 Louisville, age 29, dark hair, blue eyes, light skin, 5-10, b Monongalia Co. VA, credited 9th Congressional District of Ky., age 17 on census, house 373, s 1,2.

BELLAMY, JOSEPH. reg 14, co A, enr 10/1/61 Louisa, enl 12/10/61 Louisa, dis 1/31/65 Louisa, age 18, house 405, s 1,2,4.

BELLAMY, THOMAS J. reg 14, co A, enr 10/1/61 Louisa or Ashland, enl 12/10/61 Louisa, age 21, dark hair, hazel eyes, light skin, 5-9, b Wayne Co., d 1/13/62 Lexington of typhoid fever, house 434, s 1,2,4.

BLACK, JAMES. reg 54, co A, r cpl, enr 9/5/64, enl 9/5/64 Greenupsburg, dis 9/1/65 Louisville, age 18, light hair, gray eyes, light skin, 5-4, b Lawrence Co. OH, credited to 9th Congressional District of Ky., age 22 on census, house 364, s 1,2.

BLACK, WILLIAM. reg 14, co A, C, enr 8/30/63 Ashland, enl 8/29/63 Louisa, dis 9/15/65 Louisville, age 18, trans to 14th Vet. Inf., house 526, s 1,2,4.

BLANKENSHIP, JOHN. reg 22EM, co A, enl 5/26/64, dis 6/28/64, age 18, light hair & skin, blue eyes, b Carter Co., house 62, s 2,4,5.

BLANKENSHIP, WILLIAM H. reg 5Va, co G, enr 10/2/61 Ceredo, dis 10/3/64 Wheeling, age 19, house 55, s 1,27.

BLEVINS, JAMES P. reg 10Cav, co F, enr 8/9/62 Boyd Co., enl 9/9/62 Covington, dis 9/17/63 Maysville, age 32, residence stated on muster roll, CSR: "absent sick in Boyd Co.", house n/c, s 1,2,4.

BOBBETT, THOMAS. reg 189th Ohio Infantry, co I, house 550, s 26,33.

BOCOOK, ALLEN. reg 40, co C, enl 7/15/63 Grayson, enl 9/26/63 Grayson, dis 12/30/64 Catlettsburg, age 18, cap by enemy at Mt. Sterling 6/8/64, residence stated on muster roll, house n/c, s 1,2,4.

BOCOOK, RUDOLPH. reg 5Va, co G, enr 8/20/61 Camp Pierpont, m/in 9/2/61 Ceredo, wounded 8/29/62, des 5/29/63 Camp White WV, m/out 10/3/64 Wheeling, reg 40, co C, r sgt, enr 7/15/63 Grayson, enl 9/26/63 Grayson, age 20 or 26, des from co G, 5th Va. Inf. 5/24/63, arrested for desertion 2/29/64, residence stated on muster roll, house n/c, s 1,2,4.

BOCOOK, WILLIAM. reg 5Va, co G, enr 8/20/61 Camp Pierpont, enl 9/2/61 Ceredo, dis 2/13/63 Convalescent Camp VA, age 23 or 33, brown hair, blue eyes, light skin, 5-8, b Lawrence Co., age 44 on census, dis for disability of loss of thumb and heart disease, house 100, s 1,27.
BOND, HENRY M. reg 39, co D, E, enr 11/2/62 Peach Orchard, enl 2/16/63 Peach Orchard, dis 9/15/65 Louisville, age 21, cap 12/4/62 Floyd Co., paroled City Point 4/3/63, trans to co D 6/1/63, house A115, s 1,2,4.
BOND, HENRY M. reg 14, co C, A, r sgt, enr 10/10/61 Louisa, enl 12/10/61 Louisa, age 9/15/65 Louisville, age 21, trans to 14th Vet. Inf., enr 2/29/64 Catlettsburg, m/in 3/19/64, prom from cpl to sgt 2/27/62, house A115, s 1,2,4. Note: Only one Henry M. Bond was found on the Boyd Co. census, and no Henry M. Bond was found on other local census records. One man could not have served in both the 14th and 39th Kentucky Infantries, as indicated by the previous two service records.
BOWLING, THOMAS. reg 14, co E, enr 10/15/61 Ashland, enl 12/10/61 Louisa, age 37, brown hair, gray eyes, fair skin, 5-10, dis for disability 12/31/62, nearly blind, severe cornitis incurred in forced march from Cumberland Gap, residence stated on muster roll, house n/c, s 1,2,4.
BRADLEY, WILLIAM A. reg 14, co F, enr 11/19/61 Louisa, enl 12/10/61 Louisa, age 21, des 4/1/63 Louisa, residence stated on muster roll, house n/c, s 1, 2,4.
BRANHAM, EDWARD. reg 45, co G, enr 9/15/63 Ashland, enl 11/30/63 Ashland, age 23, d 3/1/64 Flemingsburg of measles, house 280, s 1,2.
BRANHAM, RILEY. reg 54, co A, enr & enl 9/5/64 Greenupsburg, dis 9/1/65 Louisville, age 35, dark hair, gray eyes, fair skin, 5-6, credited to 9th Congressional District of Ky., b Pike Co., age 24 on census, house 284, s 1,2,25.
BRODESS, HENRY B. reg 14, co A, r 1st lt, enr 10/1/61 Louisa, enl 12/10/61 Louisa, age 30, resigned 11/12/61 Winchester, house C23, s 1,2,4.
BROWN, ANDREW H. reg 45, co B, enr 7/6/63 Catlettsburg, enl 10/10/63 Catlettsburg, age 20, black hair, blue eyes, fair skin, 6-4, des 9/24/64 Prestonsburg, b Greenup Co., house 19, s 1,2.
BROWN, HENRY R. reg 10Cav, co F, r 1st sgt, enr 8/9/62 Boyd Co, enl 9/9/62 Covington, dis 9/17/63 Maysville, age 18, app com. sgt 8/18/62, ord. sgt 7/28/63, reg 39, co A, r capt, enr & enl 11/17/64 Lexington, dis 9/15/65 Louisville, commissioned from civilian life, house 329, s 1,2,4.
BROWN, HIRAM. reg 14, co E, F, enr 11/19/61 Louisa, enl 12/10/61 Louisa, dis 1/31/65 Louisa, age 38, trans from co F to co E 8/28/63, back to co F 1/20/65, house A22, s 1,2,4.
BROWN, ISHAM. reg 22EM, co A, enl 5/26/64, dis 6/28/64, age 35, black hair, dark eyes & skin, 5-10, b Scott Co. VA, house 20, s 2,4,5.
BROWN, JESSE. reg 14, co C, enr 10/10/61 Louisa, enl 12/10/61 Louisa, dis 9/15/65 Louisville, age 24, trans to 14th Vet. Inf., enr 2/29/64, m/in 3/19/64, July-Aug. 1864: wounded in left arm, in hospital at Knoxville TN, residence stated on muster roll, CSR: "at home sick in Boyd Co.", house n/c, s 1,2,4.
BROWN, JOHN. reg 14, co I, enr 9/17/62 Catlettsburg, enl 12/12/62 Richmond, dis 8/2/65 Lexington, age 18, trans to 14th Vet. Inf., house 81, s 1,2.
BROWN, JOSEPH R. reg 14, F&S, r lt. col., enr 11/19/61 Louisa, enl 12/10/61 Louisa, age 45, died 5/9/62 Lexington of camp fever, house 329, s 1,2,4.
BROWN, WESLEY. reg 5Va, co G, r sgt, enr 8/12/61 Ceredo, enl 9/10/61 Ceredo, dis 10/3/64 Wheeling, age 23, prom to 3rd sgt 2/7/62, house 40, s 1,27.
BROWN, WILLIAM C. reg 14, co A, r 1st lt, enr 10/1/61 Louisa, enl 12/10/61 Louisa, dis 1/31/65 Louisa, age 25, prom from sgt to 2nd lt 11/17/62, to 1st lt 2/26/63, residence on List of Officers, house A7, s 1,2,4,32.
BROWNSTED, GEORGE. reg 91st Ohio Infantry, co H, r com. sgt, enr 8/22/62, enl 9/7/62, dis 6/24/65 Cumberland MD, age 18, app com sgt 1/1/65, house 543, s 26, R. M. Windsor, History of the 91st Regiment, O.V.I.

BRUCE, JAMES. reg 10Cav, co F, enr 8/9/62 Boyd Co., enl 9/9/62 Covington, age 19, not on AG, house 176, s 1,25.

BRUCE, WILLIAM. reg 54, co D, enr 10/26/64, enl 11/2/64 Covington, des 11/12/64 Covington, not on CSR, house 176, s 2.

BRUNER, GEORGE. reg 14, co F, enr 11/19/61 Louisa, enl 12/10/61 Louisa, age 29, died 2/17/62 Camp Buell, Paintsville of typhoid fever, house 208, s 1,2, 4.

BRUNING, FRANK H. reg 22EM, co A, enl 5/26/64, dis 6/28/64, age 20, fair hair, blue eyes, light skin, 5-7, house A37, s 2,4.

BRYANT, JOHN. reg 22EM, co A, enl 5/26/64, dis 6/28/64, age 21, light hair, blue eyes, dark skin, 5-9, b Lawrence Co., house 50, s 2,4,5.

BURDETTE, JOSEPH F. reg 14, co A, enr 10/1/61 Louisa, enl 12/10/61 Louisa, dis 3/31/64, age 40, light hair & skin, blue eyes, 5-9, dis for disability, imperfect vision & wounded under right side rib, house C62, s 1,2,4.

BURKE, WILLIAM B. reg 14, co F&S, r major, enr 11/19/61 Louisa, enl 12/10/61 Louisa, age 22, d 4/15/62 Catlettsburg of disease, residence stated on List of Officers, house A2, s 1,2,4,32.

C

CALDER, JOHN. reg 2Cav, co E, r 1st lt, enr 7/14/61 Ashland or Camp Jo Holt, enl 9/27/61 Camp Muldraugh Hill, dis 3/1/64, age 26, prom to sgt 2/7/63 or 5/1/63, to 1st lt 9/1/63, wounded at Chickamauga GA 9/20/63, dis for wounds received in combat, right leg amputated; his address was listed as Ashland, Boyd Co., house C30, s 1,2,5.

CALDWELL, MARSHALL. reg 14, co F, A, enr 11/19/61 Louisa, enl 12/10/61 Louisa, dis 1/31/65 Louisa, age 24, trans to co A 11/12/63, back to co F 1/20/65, wounded in left hand between 7/2/64 & 8/13/64, residence stated on muster roll, house n/c, s 1,2,4.

CALDWELL, WILLIAM. reg 14, co F, r cpl, enr 11/19/61 Louisa, enl 12/10/61 Louisa, dis 1/31/65 Louisa, age 36, house 121, s 1,2,4.

CAMPBELL, CALVIN A. reg 14, co F, r sgt, enr 11/19/61 Louisa, enl 12/10/61 Louisa, dis 1/31/65 Louisa, age 18, light hair, blue eyes, fair skin, 5-8, prom to cpl 11/20/62, to sgt 5/10/63, to 4th sgt 11/63, house 117, s 1,2,4.

CAMERON, JOHN A. reg 2Cav, co I, r cpl, enr 8/27/61 Camp Jo Holt, enl 9/9/61 Muldraugh Hill, dis 7/17/65 Lexington NC, age 22, dark hair, eyes & skin, 5-8, enl Vet. Vol. 2/1/64, m/in 3/7/64, cap Newnan GA 7/30/64, paroled N.E. Ferry NC 2/27/65 reduced to ranks 4/8/63, hospital records state he is Greenup Co. resident, but he is not on Greenup Co. census, house 650, s 1,2.

CAMERON, MARCELLUS. reg 22, co C, r cpl, enr 12/2/61 Camp G. D. Prentice, enl 1/10/62 Louisa, dis 1/20/65 Louisville, age 20, light hair, gray eyes, fair skin 5-11, trans to 7th Vet. Inf,, enl & m/in 3/16/64 Baton Rouge LA, b. Franklin Co., house 658, s 1,2,26.

CARNAHAN, ALSENIOUS. reg 5Va, co G, r cpl, enr 8/24/61 Camp Pierpont, enl 9/2/61 Ceredo, dis 10/3/64 Wheeling, age 23, house 95, s 1,26,27.

CARNAHAN, ALONZO B. reg 5Va, co H, F&S, r sgt, hospital steward, enr & enl 9/14/61 Ceredo, dis 10/5/64 Wheeling, age 24, house 95, s 1,26,27.

CASTNER, CASPER. reg 10Cav, co F, r 1st lt, enr 8/9/62 Boyd Co., enl 9/9/62 Covington, dis 9/17/63, age 54, resigned 4/30/63 for disability, house A116, s 1, 2,4.

CASTNER, JAMES K. P. reg 10Cav, co F, r 1st sgt & com sgt, enr 8/9/62 Boyd Co., enl 9/9/62 Covington, dis 9/17/63 Maysville, age 18, app 1st sgt 8/18/62, house A116, s 1,2,4.

CASTNER, JOHN M. O. reg 5Va, co B, K & F&S, r sgt major, enr 7/20/61 or 8/14/61 Ceredo, enl 8/14/61 Ceredo, dis 9/13/64 Charleston, age 22 or 26, reduced to ranks 6/63, trans to co K 8/14/61, to co H 8/14/62, house A116, s 1,27.
CAZARD, NELSON E. reg 14, co A, enr 10/1/61 Louisa, enl 12/10/61 Louisa, dis 9/15/65 Louisville, age 34, trans to 14th Vet. Inf., enr 2/29/64, m/in 3/15/64, residence stated on muster roll, house n/c, s 1,2,4.
CHADWICK, DAVID A. reg 14, co F, wagoner, enr 11/19/61 Louisa, enl 12/10/61 Louisa, dis 1/31/65 Louisa, age 21, house 135, s 1,2,4.
CHADWICK, JAMES. reg 14, co A, F, enr 10/25/61 Louisa, enl 12/10/61 Louisa, dis 1/31/65 Louisa, age 18, dark hair & skin, blue eyes, 5-10, trans to co A 11/12/63, residence stated on muster roll, house n/c, s 1,2,4.
CHANEY, JOHN. reg 14, co A, enr 10/1/61 Louisa, enl 12/10/61 Louisa, dis 1/31/65 Louisa, age 32 or 34, residence stated on muster roll, house n/c, s 1,2,4.
CHAPMAN, WILLIAM FLOYD. reg 22EM, co B, enl 5/26/64, dis 6/28/64, age 42, dark hair, eyes & skin, 5-8, b Gallia Co. OH, house A68, s 2,4.
CHEAP, JOSEPH. reg 14, co A, enr 10/1/61 Louisa, enl 12/10/61 Louisa, dis 1/31/65 Louisa, age 18, house C139, s 1,2,4.
CLAIR, DARIUS M. reg 14, co A, enr 10/1/61 Louisa or Ashland, enl 12/10/61 Louisa, dis 1/31/65 Louisa, age 20, dark hair, blue eyes, light skin, 5-10, house 418, s 1,2,4.
CLARK, JOEL. reg 45, co D, H, r 4th sgt, enr 7/14/63 Catlettsburg, enl 10/17/63 Ashland, dis 12/24/64 Catlettsburg, age 35, trans to co H 2/1/64, back to co D 5/20/64, age 26 on census, house 551, s 1,2,5.
CLARK, JOHN. reg 22EM, co B, enl 5/26/64, dis 6/28/64, age 18, light hair, gray eyes, fair skin, 5-4, house 200, s 2,4.
CLARK, THOMAS. reg 45, co I, enr 10/23/64 Ashland, enl 2/4/64 Mt. Sterling, dis 2/14/65 Catlettsburg, age 18, light hair & skin, blue eyes, 5-6, b Lawrence Co. OH, house 445, s 1,2.
CLARK, WILLIAM. reg 54, co F, enr & enl 9/3/64 Greenupsburg, dis 9/1/65 Louisville, age 30, brown hair, hazel eyes, fair skin, 5-9, b Lewis Co., credited to 9th Congressional District, house A131, s 1,2.
CLAY, HENRY. reg 45, co B, r 4th sgt, enr 6/24/63 Catlettsburg, enl 10/10/63 Catlettsburg, dis 12/24/64 Catlettsburg, age 22, house 154, s 1,2.
CLAY, WILLIAM R. reg 40, co K, r cpl, enr 7/27/63 Grayson, enl 9/29/63 Grayson, dis 1/30/64 Catlettsburg, age 18, house 161, s 1,2.
CLAY, WYATT L. reg 40, co K, enr 1/7/64, enl 4/13/64 Lexington, dis 12/30/64 Catlettsburg, age 20, light hair, blue eyes, fair skin, 5-11, b Raleigh Co. VA, missing Mt. Sterling 6/9/64, house 161, s 1,2,5.
CLUTTS, JAMES H. reg 14, co E, r sgt, enr 10/15/61 Ashland, enl 12/10/61 Louisa, dis 1/31/65 Louisa, age 25, prom from cpl to sgt 1/1/62, residence stated on muster roll, house n/c, s 1,2,4.
COATS, LYSANDER. reg 5Va, co A, enr 8/10/61 Ceredo, enl 9/2/61 Ceredo, dis 10/3/64 Wheeling, age 46, brown hair, dark eyes, light skin, 5-10, b Buffalo NY, discharged for right inguinal hernia, house C130, s 1,26,27.
COBURN, LEANDER. reg CG, co E, enl 5/28/64 Catlettsburg, enl 7/4/64 Frankfort, age 18, light hair & skin, hazel eyes, 5-5, b Lawrence Co., house A70, s 2,4.
COLE, ARCHIBALD. reg 14, co C, F, enr 12/19/61 Louisa, enl 12/10/61 Louisa, age 21 or 23, dark hair & skin, blue eyes, 5-9, died 12/11/63 Ashland of acute rheumatism, b Scott Co. VA, trans to co F 1/20/65, house 76, s 1,2,4.
COLE, ELISHA. reg 22EM, co A, r cpl, enl 5/26/64, dis 6/28/64, age 19, light hair, dark eyes & skin, 6-0, b Wayne Co., house 11, s 2,4,5.
COLE, GEORGE W. reg 22EM, co A, r sgt, enl 5/26/64, dis 6/28/64, age 22, dark hair, eyes & skin, 6-0, b Wayne Co. VA, house 11, s 2,4.

COLEGROVE, JOHN. reg 2Cav, co I, r cpl, enr 8/27/11, Camp Jo Holt, enl 9/2/61 Muldraugh Hill, dis 7/17/65 Lexington NC, age 28, light hair, gray eyes, fair skin 5-8, b Greenup Co., enl veteran volunteers 2/1/64, m/in 3/7/64, house 362, s 1,2,5.

COLEGROVE, JOHN T. reg 14, co F, r cpl, enr 11/19/61 Louisa, enl 12/10/61 Louisa, dis 1/31/65 Louisa, age 35, prom from 2nd cpl to 1st cpl, house 355, s 1, 2,4.

COLLIER, AARON. reg 5Va, co E, K, r cpl, enr & enl 9/2/61 Ceredo, age 18, dark hair, blue eyes, fair skin, 5-8, re-enlisted as veteran volunteer 12/19/63, b Lawrence Co. OH, des 8/4/64 Middleton MD, house A90, s 1,26,27.

COLLINS, WILLIAM. reg 68EM, co H, enl 5/21/64, dis 6/22/64, age 34, dark hair, eyes & skin, 5-10, b Pike Co., house 645, s 2,4.

COOK, WILLIAM H. H. reg 2Cav, co E, r cpl, enr 7/14/61 Camp Jo Holt, enl 9/9/61 Muldraugh Hill, dis 7/17/65 Lexington NC, age 22, dark hair, blue eyes, dark skin, 6-2, b Scioto Co. OH, enl Vet. Vol. 2/7/64, m/in 3/7/64, cap Georgia 10/64 & exch, drowned on steamer Sultana on Mississippi River 4/27/65, house C150, s 1,2.

COOKE, THERON D. reg 14, co A, r sgt, enr 10/1/61 Louisa, enl 12/10/61 Louisa, dis 1/31/65 Louisa, age 26 or 35, dark hair, eyes & skin, 5-9, prom from cpl to sgt 7/5/62, reduced to ranks 8/3/63, b Fayette Co. PA, residence stated on muster roll, house n/c, s 1,2,4.

CRAFT, ROBERT. reg 14, co C, B, enr 2/21/63 Louisa, enl 10/31/63 Catlettsburg, dis 9/15/65 Louisville, age 18 or 19, trans to 14 Vet. Inf., wounded Chattanooga TN, residence stated on muster roll, house n/c, s 1,2,4.

CRAFT, THOMAS. reg 14, co C, enr 10/10/61 Louisa, enl 12/10/61 Louisa, dis 1/31/65 Louisa, age 45, residence stated on muster roll, house n/c, s 1,2,4.

CRAFT, TILMAN. reg CG, co E, enr 5/31/64, enl 7/4/64 Frankfort, dis 3/11/65 Catlettsburg, age 19, dark hair, gray eyes, fair skin, 5-7, reg 39, co G, enr 3/10/65 Catlettsburg, enl 3/16/65 Greenupsburg, dis 9/15/65 Louisville, age 18, b Johnson Co., house 223, s 1,2.

CRAFT, WILEY JR. reg 14, co B, C, enr 2/21/63 Louisa, enl 10/31/63 Catlettsburg, dis 9/15/65, age 22, trans to 14 Vet. Inf., residence stated on muster roll, house n/c, s 1,2,4.

CRAFT, WILEY SR. reg 14, co C, enr 10/10/61 Louisa, enl 12/10/61 Louisa, dis 1/31/65 Louisa, age 45, house 223, s 1,2,4.

CRANE, JOHN. reg 14Cav, co C, enr 8/4/62 Boyd Co., enl 8/21/62 Mt. Sterling, dis 9/16/63 Maysville, age 34, cap & paroled by Col. Roy Cluke 3/22/63 Mt. Sterling, residence stated on muster roll, house n/c, s 1,2,4.

CROOKS, C. EDWARD. reg 22EM, co B, enl 5/26/64, dis 6/28/64, age 30, dark hair & skin, gray eyes, 5-9, house 478, s 2,4.

CROOKS, GEORGE W. reg 5Va, co G, H, enr 9/2/61 Camp Pierpont, enl 9/2/61 Ceredo, dis 9/21/64 Wheeling, age 18 or 21, black hair & eyes, fair skin, 5-3, trans to co H 11/29/61, b Boyd Co., enrolled in 9th Congressional District, cap Lynchburg VA 8/18/64, confined at Andersonville GA, paroled Vicksburg MS 4/6/65, house 394, s 1,27.

CROSS, JOHN M. reg 39, co G, enr 7/4/63 Pikeville, enl 8/30/63 Louisa, dis 9/15/65 Louisville, age 18, age 27 on census, house 94, s 1,2.

CROUSE, JOHN B. reg 14, co A, r 1st sgt, enr 10/1/61 Louisa, enl 12/10/61 Louisa, dis 1/31/65 Louisa, age 23, prom to cpl 6/1/62, to sgt 11/17/62, to 1st sgt 4/1/64, house C151, s 1,2,4.

CULVER, ABRAHAM R. reg 14, co D, enr 10/20/61 Louisa, enl 12/10/61 Louisa, dis 1/31/65 Louisa, age 43, residence stated on muster roll, house n/c, s 1, 2,4.

CULVER, CHARLES C. reg 14, co A, E, F&S, r hospital steward, enr 10/1/61 Louisa, enl 12/10/61 Louisa, dis 1/31/65 Louisa, age 34 or 35, prom to hospital steward 11/17/61, returned to pvt, co A

3/19/62, prom to com. sgt 6/1/62, trans from co A to co E, back to co A 1/20/65, reduced to ranks 2/19/64, house C12, s 1,2,4.

CULVERT, ISAAC. reg 14, co E, enr 10/15/61, enl 12/10/61 Louisa, dis 1/31/65 Louisa, age 32, not on CSR, residence stated on muster roll, house n/c, s 2,4.

CUNNINGHAM, JOSEPH. reg 2Cav, co E, enr 7/14/61 Camp Jo Holt, enr 9/9/61 Muldraugh Hill, dis 10/12/64 Nashville TN, age 23, house 615, s 1,2,5.

D

DAMRON, JOHN M. reg 14, co C, enr 10/10/61 Louisa, enl 12/10/61 Louisa, dis 1/31/65 Louisa, age 18, "at home sick in Boyd Co." 2/62, house 70, s 1,2,4.

DAMRON, SAMUEL. reg 14, co F, C, enr 11/19/61 Louisa, enl 12/10/61 Louisa, dis 1/31/65 Louisa, age 26, trans from co F to co C 8/28/63, back to co F 1/20/65, house 278, s 1,2,4.

DAMRON, WILLIAM P. reg 14, co C, enr 10/10/61 Catlettsburg, enl 12/10/61 Louisa, dis 1/31/65 Louisa, age 21, light hair, dark eyes & skin, 5-8, b Cabell Co. VA, wounded in action 6/22/64, house 70, s 1,2,4.

DARBY, GEORGE. reg 14, co E, enr 10/15/61 Ashland, enl 12/10/61 Louisa, dis 1/31/65 Louisa, age 21, house 672, s 1,2,26.

DARBY, HUGH. reg 14, co E, r cpl, enr 10/15/61 Ashland, enl 12/10/61 Louisa, dis 1/31/65 Louisa, age 44, house 672, s 1,2.

DAUGHERTY, ANDREW J. reg 10Cav, co F, enr 8/9/62 Boyd Co., enl 9/9/62 Covington, dis 9/17/63 Maysville, age 33, app teamster 12/10/62, cap & paroled 3/22/63 Mt. Sterling by Col. Roy Cluke, residence stated on muster roll, house n/c, s 1,2,4.

DAVIS, EDWARD. reg 40, co C, age 18, deserted before muster, residence stated on muster roll, house n/c, s 1,4.

DAVIS, EDWARD. reg 14, co F, A, enr 8/28/63 Louisa, enl 10/31/63 Louisa, dis 9/15/65 Louisville, age 17 or 18, trans from co F to co A 11/12/63, back to co F 1/20/65, age 13 on census, house 142, s 1,2,4.

DAVIS, HICKMAN. reg 5Va, co B, enr 7/18/61 or 9/2/61 Camp Pierpont, enl 9/2/61 Ceredo, age 31, black hair & eyes, dark skin, 5-4, cap Winchester VA 7/24/64, confined at Richmond VA 3/7/65, paroled Cox's Wharf, VA 3/10/65, d at home 4/20/65 while on furlough, re-enlisted as veteran volunteer, b Tazewell Co. VA, enlisted at Catlettsburg, enrolled 9th Congressional District, house A67, s 1,27.

DAVIS, HIRAM. reg 45, co I, r sgt, enr 1/1/64 Mt. Sterling, enl 2/4/64 Mt. Sterling, dis 2/14/65 Catlettsburg, age 30, dark hair & eyes, light skin, 5-7, prom to sgt 11/30/63, b Morgan Co., house A132, s 1,2.

DAVIS, JAMES. reg 14, co F, E, r sgt, enr 11/19/63 Louisa, enl 12/10/61 Louisa, dis 1/31/65 Louisa, age 26, trans from co F to co B 8/28/63, back to co F 1/20/65, reduced to ranks 7/1/62, CSR: "at home sick in Boyd Co.", house 681, s 1,2,4.

DAVIS, JESSE W. reg 14, co A, enr 10/1/61 Louisa, enl 12/10/61 Louisa, age 20, des 7/1/62 Cumberland Gap, residence stated on muster roll, house n/c, s 1,2, 4.

DAVIS, ROBERT. reg 14, co A, enr 10/1/61 Louisa, enl 12/10/61 Louisa, dis 1/31/65 Louisa, age 25, residence stated on muster roll, house n/c, s 1,2,4.

DAVIS, SOLOMON. reg 14, co F, r capt, enr 11/19/61 Louisa, enl 12/10/61 Louisa, age 26, resigned 3/27/62, house 131, s 1,2,4.

DAY, JOHN. reg 14, co F, E, A, enr 11/17/61 Louisa, enl 12/10/61 Louisa, dis 9/15/65 Louisville, age 18, trans to 14th Vet. Inf., enr 2/29/64, m/in 3/14/64, trans from co F to co E 8/28/63, back to co F 1/20/65, wounded left arm 6/22/64 Kennesaw Mtn. GA, b Grant Co. Wisconsin, residence stated on muster roll, house n/c, s 1,2,4.

DEBORD, ANDREW J. reg 5Va, co G, r cpl, enr & enl 9/2/61 Ceredo, age 19, cap Summersville WV 11/5/63, confined at Richmond VA 11/14/63, taken to Andersonville GA 3/1/64, died of typhoid, buried #110, grave 24, house 84, s 1,27.

DEGANS, COLUMBUS C. reg 10Cav, co F, enr 8/9/62 Boyd Co., enl 9/19/62 Covington, dis 9/17/63/Maysville, age 25, house 65, s 1,2,4.

DICKISON, JOHN. reg 40, co C, enr 7/29/63 Grayson, enl 9/26/63 Grayson, dis 12/30/64 Catlettsburg, b Carter Co., residence stated on muster roll, house, n/c, s 1,2,4.

DIXON, HARDEN S. reg 40, co C, r sgt, enr 8/8/63, enl 8/19/64 Lexington, dis 12/30/64 Catlettsburg, age 18, light hair, blue eyes, fair skin, 6-0, b Boyd Co., prom to sgt 9/1/64, age 13 on census, credited to Boyd Co., house 438, s 1,2,4.

DIXON, JAMES. reg 45, co E, enr 11/3/63, enl 11/6/63 Ashland, dis 12/24/64 Catlettsburg, not on CSR, house 384, s 2.

DIXON, JAMES F. reg 14, co A, F&S, r Quartermaster sgt, enr 10/1/61 Louisa, enl 12/10/61 Louisa, dis 1/31/65 Louisa, age 25, prom from sgt 6/1/62, house 438, s 1,2,4.

DIXON, JOHN A. reg 14, co A, enr 10/1/61 Ashland, enl 12/10/61 Louisa, dis 12/31/64 Richmond, age 45, gray hair, blue eyes, light skin, 5-8, b Bedford Co. VA, dis for disability of weakness of back & legs and lumbago, house 385, s 1,2, 4.

DIXON, JOHN N. reg 14, co C, A, enr 10/10/61 Louisa, enl 12/10/61 Louisa, dis 9/15/65 Louisville, trans to 14th Vet. Inf., enl & m/in 3/19/64, age 22, CSR: "sick at home in Boyd Co.", age 30 on census, house 597, s 1,2,4.

DIXON, JOHN WILLIAM. reg 14, co A, enr 10/1/61 Louisa, enl 12/10/61 Louisa, dis 1/31/65 Louisa, age 22, residence stated on muster roll, house n/c, s 1, 2,4.

DIXON, LEWIS. reg 14, co A, enr 10/1/61 Ashland, enl 12/10/61 Louisa, dis 1/31/65 Louisa, age 22, sandy hair, blue eyes, light skin, 6-0, b Wayne Co., residence stated on muster roll, house n/c, s 1,2,4.

DIXON, MEREDITH. reg 14, co A, enr 10/1/61 Louisa, enl 12/10/61 Louisa, dis 9/15/65 Louisville, age 18, trans to 14th Vet. Inf., enr 2/29/64, m/in 3/19/64 Louisa, age 10 on census, house 385, s 1,2,4.

DIXON, WILLIAM. reg 14, co A, enr 10/1/61 Louisa, enl 12/10/61 Louisa, dis 12/31/62 Richmond, age 40, black hair, blue eyes, light skin, 5-11, dis 12/31/62 Richmond for disability, weakness in back & legs, rheumatism, reg 22 EM, co B, enr 5/26/64, dis 6/28/64, b Bedford Co. VA, house 597, s 1,2,4.

DIXON, WILLIAM L. reg 5Va, co A, enr 10/16/62 Ceredo, dis 10/3/64 Wheeling, age 17, 18 or 20, dark hair, black eyes, fair skin, 5-6, accidentally wounded & in hospital at Philadelphia, b Boyd Co., age 14 on census, house 452, s 1,27.

DIXON, WILLIAM T. reg CG, co E, enr 5/30/64 Catlettsburg, enl 7/4/64 Frankfort, dis 3/1/65 Catlettsburg, age 19, light hair, blue eyes, fair skin, 5-8, b Greenup Co., house 452, s 2,4.

E

EASTHAM, HARTWELL C. reg CG, co E, enr 5/30/64 Catlettsburg, enl 7/4/64 Frankfort, dis 3/11/65 Catlettsburg, age 20, dark hair, brown eyes, fair skin, 5-8, b Greenup Co., house 684, s 2,4.

EASTWOOD, JESSE. reg 22EM, co A, r 2nd lt, enl 5/26/64, dis 6/28/64, age 37, black hair & eyes, dark skin, 5-10, house A58, s 2,4,5.

EBA, WILLIAM F. reg 14, co C, r musician, enr 10/10/61 Louisa, enl 12/10/61 Louisa, dis 1/31/65 Louisa, age 18, age 12 on census, house A24, s 1,2,4.

EBA, WILLIAM H. H. reg 5Va, co I, F, F& S, r 1st lt, enr 9/14/61 Ceredo, dis 5/6/63, age 20, 28 or 32, app sgt major 12/22/61, prom to 1st lt 3/26/62, resigned 4/12/63 disability of prostate disease, house A108, s 1,27.

EDMONDS, BALLARD. reg 14, co C, r musician, enr 10/10/61 Louisa, enl 12/10/61 Louisa, dis 1/31/65 Louisa, age 18, residence stated on muster roll, house n/c, s 1,2,4.

ELKINS, SAMUEL H. reg 39, co A, r cpl, enr 10/17/62 Peach Orchard, enl 2/16/63 Peach Orchard, dis 9/15/65 Louisville, age 18, house 388, s 1,2,4.

ELLIOTT, ROBERT. reg 40, co C, enr 7/31/63 Grayson, enl 9/26/63 Grayson, dis 12/30/64 Catlettsburg, age 21, residence stated on muster roll, house n/c, s 1, 2.

ELY, JAMES C. reg 14, co C, A, r 2nd lt, enr 10/10/61 Louisa, enl 12/10/61 Louisa, dis 9/15/65 Louisville, trans to 14th Vet. Inf., enr 2/29/64, m/in 3/19/64, prom to 1st lt 7/1/65, house A7, s 1,2.

EVANS, GEORGE W. reg 40, co C, enr 9/10/63 Grayson, enl 9/25/63 Grayson, dis 12/30/64 Catlettsburg, age 20, b Carter Co., residence stated on muster roll, house n/c, s 1,4.

EVANS, JAMES. reg 14, co D, F, enr 10/14/63 Salyersville, enl 12/31/63 Louisa, dis 9/15/65, age 21, light hair, blue eyes, fair skin, 5-8, trans to 14th Vet. Inf., b Magoffin Co., residence stated on muster roll, house n/c, s 1,2,4,25.

EVANS, JAMES. reg 14, co F, E, enr 11/19/61 Louisa, enl 12/10/61 Louisa, dis 1/31/65 Louisa, age 18, fair skin, 5-8, prom to cpl 9/20/62, reduced to ranks 8/28/63, trans from co F to co E, back to co F 1/20/65, residence stated on muster roll, house n/c, s 1,2,4.

EVERMAN, SANDERS. reg 40, co C, r cpl, enr 8/31/63 Grayson, enl 9/26/63 Grayson, dis 12/30/64 Catlettsburg, age 20, residence stated on muster roll, house n/c, s 1,2,4.

EVICH, HENRY. reg 2Cav, co E, enr 7/14/61 Camp Jo Holt, enl 9/9/61 Camp Muldraugh Hill, dis 6/17/65 Camp Chase, age 20, m/in as veteran volunteer, enl 2/7/64, m/in 3/7/64, cap near Milledgeville GA 11/24/64, b Wood Co. VA, house A76, s 1,26.

EVICH, WILLIAM C. reg 5Va. co B, H, enr 7/18/61 Ceredo, dis 9/21/64 Wheeling, age 18 or 21, trans to co H 10/31/61, wounded left arm Cross Keys WV 6/8/62, house A76, s 1,26.

EWING, THOMAS J. reg 5Va, co G, r capt, enl 9/2/61, age 21, resigned 1/3/63, resigned to become colonel of 39th Ky. Inf., but no record of service in that unit, reg 22EM, r col, enl 5/26/64, dis 6/28/64, house 34, s 1,2,5,20.

F

FANNIN, JOHN D. reg 14, co C, F, D, enr 9/8/62 Catlettsburg, enl 10/10/62 Portland OH, dis 8/4/65 Lexington, age 21, 26, 31 or 34, trans to 14th Vet. Inf., trans to co C 7/63, trans to co F, house 11, s 1,2,4.

FARMER, EDWARD F. reg 173 Ohio Infantry, co A, enl 9/15/64, dis 6/26/65 Nashville TN, age 18, house 326, s 26,33.

FARMER, JOHN W. reg 14, co A, F, r cpl, enr 11/19/61 Louisa, enl 12/10/61 Louisa, dis 9/15/65 Louisville, age 18 or 20, light hair, blue eyes, fair skin, 5-8, trans to 14 Vet. Inf., enr 2/19/64, m/in 3/31/64, prom to cpl 11/1/64, b Lawrence Co., trans from co F to co A 11/12/63, back to co F 1/20/65, house 521, s 1,2,4.

FIELDS, JOSEPH. reg 68EM, co B, enr 5/21/64, dis 6/22/64, age 28, black hair & eyes, dark skin, 6-0, b Lawrence Co., house A62, s 2,4.

FINN, JACOB. reg 14, co A, F, enr 10/25/61 Louisa, enl 12/10/61 Louisa, dis 1/31/65 Louisa, age 29, trans from co F to co A 8/28/63, back to co F 1/26/65, house 601, s 1,2,4.

FINN, JAMES H. reg 14, co A, enr 10/1/61 Louisa, enl 12/10/61 Louisa, dis 9/15/65 Louisville, age 24, dark hair, gray eyes, light skin, 5-8, trans to 14th Vet. Inf., enr 2/29/64, m/in 3/15/64, house 598, s 1,2,4.

FINN, WILLIS. reg 14, co A, enr 10/1/61 Louisa, enl 12/10/61 Louisa, dis 1/31/65 Louisa, age 21, house 598, s 1,2,4.

FITCH, CHAMPLAIN H. reg 14, co C, r sgt, enr 10/10/61 Louisa, enl 12/10/61 Louisa, dis 1/31/65, age 23 or 27, age 43 on census, house 311, s 1,2,4.

FITCH, JAMES. reg 14, co C, r sgt, enr 10/10/61 Louisa, enl 12/10/61 Louisa, dis 1/31/65 Louisa, age 21, house 311, s 1,2,4.

FLOYD, JACKSON F. reg 5Va, co E, enr 8/2/61 Ceredo, enl 9/2/61 Ceredo, dis 10/4/64 Wheeling, age 30, des Ceredo, broke guard after being tried for desertion, took up arms with rebels, sentenced to be shot to death, sentence set aside, house A32, s 1,27.

FORD, CHARLES W. reg 22EM, co B, enl 5/26/64, dis 6/28/64, house A56, s 2,5.

FOSTER, JAMES D. reg 14, co F&S, r reg Quartermaster & 1st lt, enr 10/15/61 Ashland, enl 12/10/61 Louisa, dis 1/31/65 Louisa, age 20, 21 or 27, prom from com. sgt to reg. quartermaster 6/3/62, residence stated on List of Officers, house n/c, s 1,2,4,32.

FOSTER, NOAH W. reg 10Cav, co F, r cpl, enr 8/9/62 Boyd Co., enl 9/9/62 Covington, dis 9/17/63 Maysville, age 27, app 2nd cpl 8/18/62, house 299, s 1,2, 4.

FREEMAN, EFFORT. reg 14, co E, C, enr 3/27/62 Ashland, enr 2/18/63 Louisa, dis 1/31/65 Louisa, age 19, light hair, gray eyes, light skin, 6-0, trans to 14th Vet. Inf., b Estill Co., residence stated on muster roll, house n/c, s 1,2,4.

FULTS, HARRISON. reg 54, co A, enr & enl 9/5/64 Greenupsburg, dis 9/1/65 Louisville, age 42, dark hair & skin, blue eyes, 5-10, b Lawrence Co., age 32 on census, house 647, s 1,2.

FULTS (FULTZ), HEZEKIAH. reg 53, co K, enr & enl 4/11/65 Covington, dis 9/15/65 Louisville, age 19, dark hair & skin, gray eyes, 5-8, b Greenup Co., credited to Kenton Co., but he is not on Kenton Co. census, house 178, s 1,2.

FULTS, HIRAM. reg 2Cav, co E, enr 7/14/61 Camp Jo Holt, enl 9/9/61 Muldraugh Hill, dis 7/17/65 Lexington NC, age 18, dark hair & skin, gray eyes, 5-9, enl Vet. Vol. 2/7/64, m/in 3/7/64, may have also served in reg 14, co A, enr 10/6/62 Portland OH, b Greenup Co., house 178, s 1,2,6.

G

GALLOWAY, JOHN. reg 5Va, co G, enr 10/2/61 Ceredo, enl 9/2/61 Ceredo, dis 10/3/64 Wheeling, age 22, house 59, s 1,27.

GARD, JOHN. reg 53, co I, enr & enl 4/11/65 Covington, dis 9/15/65 Louisville, age 18, light hair, blue eyes, fair skin, 5-8, b Greenup Co., credited to Bracken Co., but he is not on Bracken Co. census, house 511, s 1,2,5.

GARRETT, FLETCHER. reg 10Cav, co F, enr 8/9/62 Boyd Co., enl 9/9/62 Covington, dis 9/17/63 Maysville, reg 45, co G, enr 11/25/63, m/in 10/30/63 Mt. Sterling, trans to 4th Ky. Vet. Inf., age 18, house A74, s 1,2,4.

GARTHEE, JOSEPH. reg 14, co C, F, enr 10/25/61 Louisa, enl 12/10/61 Louisa, dis 1/31/65 Louisa, age 26, trans from co F to co C 8/28/63, back to co F 1/20/65, house 346, s 1,2,4.

GIBSON, DAVID. reg 10Cav, co F, enr 8/9/62 Boyd Co., enl 9/9/62 Covington, dis 9/17/63 Maysville, age 26, residence stated on muster roll, house n/c, s 1,2,4.

GIBSON, JAMES. reg 10Cav, co F, enr 8/9/62 Boyd Co., enl 9/9/62 Covington, dis 9/17/63, age 18, residence stated on muster roll, house n/c, s 1,2,4.

GILKERSON, NOBLE. reg 10Cav, co F, enr 8/9/62 Boyd Co., enl 9/9/62 Covington, dis 9/17/63 Maysville, age 44, cap & paroled 3/2/63 Mt. Sterling by Col. Roy Cluke, house A46, s 1,2,4.

GILKERSON, PETER. reg 53, co I, r sgt, enr & enl 3/29/65 Greenupsburg, dis 9/15/65 Louisville, age 18, auburn hair, blue eyes, fair skin, 5-9, b Boyd Co., credited to Boyd Co., house A46, s 1,2,5.

GILLESPIE, JOHN. reg 5Va, co H, K, enr & enl 2/12/63 Ceredo, dis 9/28/65 St. Louis MO, missing Lynchburg VA 6/18/64, CSR: "at home Boyd Co., Ky.", house 589, s 1,27.

GILLESPIE, SAMUEL reg 5Va, co A, enr & enl 9/2/61 Ceredo, dis 10/3/65 Wheeling, age 20 or 22, brown hair, hazel eyes, dark skin, 5-10, dis 2/20/63 on surgeon's certificate of disability of phthisis pulmonalis (tuberculosis), reg 45, co H, enr 7/14/63, enl 10/17/63 Ashland, d date & place unknown, reg 45 service not on CSR, b Mason Co. VA, house 589, s 1,2,27.

GLOVER, JOSHUA R. reg 22, co B, enr 11/9/61 Camp Swigart, enl 1/10/62 Louisa, dis 8/6/63 Vicksburg MS, age 24, sandy hair, gray eyes, ruddy skin, 5-10, dis surgeon's certificate of disability for acute pleurisy, b Greenup Co., residence stated on muster roll, house n/c, s 1,2,4.

GOULSBERRY, ISAAC. reg 14, co E, A, enr 10/15/61 Ashland, enl 12/10/61 Louisa, dis 9/15/65 Louisville, age 24, trans to 14th Vet. Inf, enr 2/29/64, m/in 3/19/64, house 476, s 1,2,4.

GRAHAM, ANDREW. reg 14, co D, enr 10/20/61, enl 12/10/61 Louisa, dis 1/31/65 Louisa, age 23, light hair & skin, black eyes, 6-2, muster roll lists Lawrence Co. as residence, but he is not on Lawrence Co. census, house 240, s 1,2.

GRAHAM, BENJAMIN. reg 14, co D, enr 10/20/61, enl 12/10/61 Louisa, dis 1/31/65 Louisa, age 49, light hair & skin, gray eyes, 6-0, muster roll lists Lawrence Co. as residence, but he is not on Lawrence Co. census, house 240, s 1,2.

GRAHAM, JACOB P. reg 14, co F, enr 11/19/61 Louisa, enl 12/10/61 Louisa, dis 1/31/65 Louisa, age 31, residence stated on muster roll, house n/c, s 1,2,4.

GRAHAM, HARDIN O. B. reg 14, co D, B, enr 9/15/63 Louisa, enl 10/30/63 Louisa, dis 9/15/65 Louisville, age 15, trans to 14th Vet. Inf., house 240, s 1,2, 25.

GRAHAM, OLIVER PERRY. reg 14, co D, B, enr 9/15/63 Louisa, enl 10/30/63 Louisa, dis 9/15/65 Louisa, age 17, light hair & skin, gray eyes, 5-8 trans to 14th Vet. Inf., b Lawrence Co., house 240, s 1,2.

GRAY, ISAAC A. reg 14, co E, A, enr 10/15/61 Ashland, enl 12/10/61 Louisa, dis 9/15/65 Louisville, age 20, light hair & skin, hazel eyes, 5-7, trans to 14th Vet. Inf., enr 2/29/64, m/in 3/19/64, cap Cumberland Gap 9/15/62 & paroled Aikens Landing VA 10/6/62, b Scott Co. VA, house C52, s 1,2,4.

GRAY, ISAAC ELLINGTON. reg 14, co E, r capt, enr 10/15/61 Ashland, enl 12/10/61 Louisa, age 23, prom from cpl to sgt 11/1/62, dis 11/6/63 discharged to accept commission, prom to 2nd lt, reg 39, co D, enl 5/20/65 Lexington, dis 9/15/65 Louisville, List of Officers lists Pike Co. as residence, but he is not on Pike Co. census, muster roll lists Boyd Co. as residence, house 410, s 1,2,4.

GRAY, JOHN M. reg 2Cav, co E, r 5th sgt, enr 7/8/61 or 7/14/61 Ashland or Camp Jo Holt, enl 9/9/61 Muldraugh Hill, age 25 auburn hair, blue eyes, light skin, 5-10, prom from cpl to sgt 10/18/61, may have also served in reg 192nd Ohio Infantry, co F, r sgt major, dis 9/1/65 Winchester VA, age 27, was sgt at enlistment, prom to sgt major, b Floyd Co., house C52, s 1,2,26,33.

GROSBECK, GEORGE. reg 22EM, co B, enl 5/26/64, dis 6/28/64, age 38, light hair, gray eyes, fair skin, 5-7, b Bavaria, Germany, house C150, s 2,4.

GROSS, OSCAR. reg 14, co C, wagoner, enr 10/10/61 Louisa, enl 12/10/61 Louisa, dis 1/31/65 Louisa, age 21, residence stated on muster roll, house n/c, s 1, 2,4.

GUSTIN, JAMES W. reg 14, co A, r cpl, enr 10/1/61 Louisa, enl 12/10/61 Louisa, dis 1/31/65 Louisa, age 19, prom to cpl 11/17/61, age 10 on census, house C12, s 1,2,4.

H

HACKWORTH, CHARLES H. reg 14, co A, enr 10/1/61 Louisa, enl 12/1/61 Louisa, dis 1/31/65 Louisa, age 20, dark hair, gray eyes, light skin, 5-11, b Boyd Co., house 417, s 1,2,4.

HACKWORTH, JAMES H. reg 14 co A, B, r sgt, enr 10/1/61 Louisa, enl 12/10/61 Louisa, dis 9/15/65 Louisville, age 25, dark hair, gray eyes, light skin, 5-9, trans to 14th Vet. Inf., enr 2/29/64, m/in 3/31/64, house 413, s 1,2,4.

HACKWORTH, REUBEN E. reg 14, co A, enr 10/1/61, enl 12/10/61 Louisa, dis 1/31/65 Louisa, age 22, not on CSR, residence stated on muster roll, house n/c, s 2,4.

HACKWORTH, WILLIAM. reg 22EM, co B, enr 5/22/64, dis 6/28/64, age 37, brown hair, blue eyes, fair skin, b Bedford Co. VA, house 417, s 2.

HAILEY, ALFRED C. reg 39, co D, E, r capt, enr 9/27/62 Boyd Co. enl 2/16/63 Peach Orchard, dis 9/15/65 Louisville, age 27, 1st lt of co D; prom to capt co E 3/21/65, residence stated on List of Officers, house A107, s 1,2,4,32.

HAILEY, JAMES T. reg 5Va, co A, r sgt, enr 7/17/61 Ceredo, enl 9/12/61 Ceredo, dis 10/3/64 Wheeling, age 19, sandy hair, blue eyes, fair skin, 6-0, b Greenup Co., prom to cpl 9/2/61, prom to com sgt 11/1/62, enrolled in 9th Congressional District, re-enlisted as veteran volunteer 12/23/63, house 692, s 1,27.

HALEY, JAMES A. reg 45, co B, enr 6/8/63 Catlettsburg, enl 10/10/63 Catlettsburg, dis 12/24/64 Catlettsburg, age 18, b Russell Co. VA, house 243, s 1,2.

HALL, WILLIAM. reg 39, co I, enr 12/12/63, enl 12/28/63 Louisa, dis 9/15/65 Louisville, age 18, dark hair & skin, blue eyes, 5-11, b Tazewell Co. VA, house 457, s 1,2.

HAMILTON, JOHN J. reg 14, co B, enr 10/10/61 Louisa, enl 12/10/61 Louisa, dis 1/31/65 Louisa, age 18, residence stated on muster roll, house n/c, s 1,2,4.

HAMMOND, CHARLES. reg 53, co I, enr & enl 4/3/65 Greenupsburg, dis 9/15/65 Louisville, age 18, brown hair, hazel eyes, fair skin, 5-7, b Greenup Co., credited to Boyd Co., house 586, s 1,2,26.

HAMMOND, JOHN. reg 53, co E, enr 3/28/65, enl 3/29/65 Greenupsburg, died 6/1/65 Mt. Sterling, not on CSR, house 512, s 2.

HAMPTON, LEVI J. reg 14, co H, enr 10/25/61 Catlettsburg, enl 12/10/61 Louisa, reg 39, enr 10/27/62, r adjutant, age 45, KIA 12/5/62 Floyd Co., house A14, s 1,2,4.

HAMPTON, MILLARD F. reg 22EM, enl 5/26/64, dis 6/28/64, age 17, light hair & skin, blue eyes, 5-9, b Greenup Co., house A14, s 2,4.

HAMPTON, WILLIAM OLIVER. reg 45, co E, enr 8/23/63 Catlettsburg, enl Louisa 11/6/63, m/out 12/24/64 Catlettsburg, 22EM, co A, r 1st lt, enl 5/26/64, dis 6/28/64, age 29, light hair & skin, blue eyes, 5-9, b Greenup Co., house A65, s 2,4.

HARRIS, GEORGE. reg 14, co G, A, enr 11/9/61 Louisa, enl 12/10/61 Louisa, dis 9/15/65 Louisville, age 31, dark hair, black eyes, fair skin, 5-7, trans to 14th Vet. Inf., enl 2/29/64, m/in 3/15/64, house 75, s 1,2,4.

HART, GEORGE. reg 45, co G, enr 10/3/63 Ashland, enl 11/30/63 Ashland, dis 2/14/65 Catlettsburg, age 36, light hair, blue eyes, fair skin, 6-1, b Greenup Co., age 32 on census, house 564, s 1,2.

HART, HENRY C. reg 45, co G, enr 10/31/63 Ashland, enl 11/30/63 Ashland, dis 2/14/65 Catlettsburg, age 28, house 564, s 1,2,5.

HATTON, HIRAM. reg 14, co C, enr 10/10/61 Louisa, enl 12/10/61 Louisa, dis 1/31/65 Louisa, age 18, age 13 on census, house 299, s 1,2,4.

HAZELETTE, WILLIAM. reg 14, co F, enr 11/19/61 Louisa, enl 12/10/61 Louisa, dis 1/31/65 Louisa, age 21, wounded in chest, house 148, s 1,2,4.

HENDERSON, JOHN C. reg 14, co F&S, r quartermaster sgt, 1st lt, enr 11/19/61 Louisa, enl 12/10/61 Louisa, age 25, prom to 1st lt co D 6/8/62, house A14, s 1,2,4.

HENSLEY, HENRY W. reg 5Va, co F, enr 8/10/61 Camp Anthony or Camp Pierpont, enl 9/2/61 Ceredo, dis 9/3/64 Wheeling, age 32, d 3/9/62 Parkersburg VA of fever, house 456, s 1,27.

HENSLEY, JACKSON. reg 14, co F, C, enr & enl 10/17/62 Portland OH, age 18, dark hair & skin, brown eyes, 5-1 or 5-3, trans to 14th Vet. Inf., trans to co E 8/29/63, back to co F 1/20/65, residence stated on muster roll, b Carter, Greenup or Boyd Co., house n/c, s 1,2,4.

HENSLEY, JACOB. reg 14, co E, E, enr & enl 10/7/62 Portland OH, dis 7/24/64 Marietta GA, age 19, light hair, blue eyes, fair skin, 5-6, trans from co F to co E 8/28/63, back to co F 1/20/65, died Marietta GA 7/23/64 of typhoid fever, house 231, s 1,2,4.

HENSLEY, JAMES W. reg CG, co E, enr 3/8/63 Catlettsburg, enl 7/4/64 Frankfort, dis 3/11/65 Catlettsburg, age 18, dark hair & skin, hazel eyes, 5-5, b Greenup Co., house 143, s 2,4.

HENSLEY, JOHN. reg 14, co E, F, enr 10/25/61 Louisa, enl 12/10/61 Louisa, dis 1/31/65 Louisa, age 39, trans from co F to co E 8/29/63, back to co F 1/20/65, house 229, s 1,2,4.

HENSLEY, LEWIS. reg 14, co F, E, enr 7/20/63 Louisa, enl 8/29/63 Louisa, dis 9/15/65 Louisville, age 18, sandy hair, blue eyes, fair skin, 5-2, trans to 14th Vet. Inf., trans from co F to co E 8/28/63, back to co F 1/20/65, b Greenup Co., house 229 or 246, s 1,2,4.

HENSLEY, MORDECAI. reg 14, co C, F, enr 10/25/61 Louisa, enl 12/10/61 Louisa, dis 1/31/65 Louisa, age 19 or 21, light hair & skin, brown hair, 5-11 or 6-1, trans to co C 8/28/63, b Carter Co., CSR: "at home sick in Boyd Co.", house 143, s 1,2,4.

HENSLEY, WILEY. reg 5Va, co G, enr 8/24/61 Camp Pierpont, enl 9/2/61 Ceredo, dis 10/3/64 Wheeling, age 20, des 3/25/63 Ceredo, house 194, s 1,27.

HENSLEY, WILLIAM R. reg 5Va, co G, enr 10/2/61 Ceredo, dis 10/3/64 Wheeling, age 18, age 21 on census, des 6/25/63 Ceredo, house 247, s 1,27.

HITE, LEMUEL STROTHER. reg 14, co C, enr 10/10/61 Catlettsburg, enl 12/10/61 Louisa, dis 1/31/65 Louisa, age 32, dark hair, eyes & skin, 5-7, b Cabell Co. VA, house A94, s 1,2,4.

HOLBROOK, HARRISON. reg 14, co F, r cpl, enr 11/19/61 Louisa, enl 12/10/61 Louisa, dis 1/31/65 Louisa, age 28, prom to cpl 9/15/63, residence stated on muster roll, house n/c, s 1,2,4.

HOLLINGSWORTH, ISAAC. reg 14, co H, r capt, enr 10/25/61 Catlettsburg, enl 12/10/61 Louisa, age 23, died 2/25/62 Catlettsburg of typhoid fever, residence stated on muster roll & List of Officers, house n/c, s 1,2,4.

HOLT, WADE H. reg 14, co F, r 1st sgt, enr 11/19/61 Louisa, enl 12/10/61 Louisa, age 28, app 1st sgt 11/19/61, reduced to ranks 4/28/62, died 5/30/62 Camp Broadus of typhoid fever, residence stated on muster roll, house n/c, s 1,2,4.

HONAKER, JOHN W. reg 10Cav, co F, r 5th cpl, enr 8/9/62 Boyd Co., enl 9/9/62 Covington, dis 9/17/63 Maysville, age 26, app 5th cpl 8/18/62, house 58, s 1,2,4.

HOOD, CHARLES E. reg 2Cav, co E, r co QM sgt, enr 7/14/61 Camp Jo Holt, enl 9/9/61 Muldraugh Hill, dis 10/12/64 Nashville TN, age 26, house 186, s 1,2.

HOOD, JAMES T. reg 2Cav, co E, r saddler, enr 7/14/61 Camp Jo Holt, enl 9/9/61 Muldraugh Hill, dis 7/24/62, age 27, dark hair & skin, black eyes, 5-9, dis for tuberculosis, b Greenup Co., CSR indicated records to be addressed to Mount Savage, Carter Co., but he is not on Carter Co. census, house 183, s 1,2.

HOPKINS, GEORGE W. reg 14, co A, r 2nd lt, enr 10/1/61 Louisa, enl 12/10/61 Louisa, age 22, d 7/4/62 Pine Mountain, Whitley Co. KY of camp fever, residence stated on List of Officers, house C29, s 1,2,4,32.

HOPKINS, WILLIAM. reg 5Va, co H, enr 9/16/61 Ceredo, dis 9/21/61, dis immediately after enlistment at Ceredo 9/16/61, house C29, s 1,27.

HOWARD, JACOB. reg 14, co H, enr 2/28/63 Louisa, enl 8/29/63 Louisa, dis 9/15/65 Louisville, age 30 or 31, trans to 14th Vet. Inf., residence stated on muster roll, house n/c, s 1,2,4.

HOWELL, ALEX C. reg CG, co E, r cpl, enr 6/6/64 Catlettsburg, enl 7/4/64 Frankfort, dis 3/11/65 Catlettsburg, age 23, dark hair, hazel eyes, light skin, 5-10, b Greenup Co., house 481, s 2,4,5.

HOWELL, CHRISTIAN OR CHARLESTON. reg 14, co A, enr 10/1/61 Ashland, enl 12/10/61 Louisa, age 18, d 1/8/62 at home in Ashland of disease, residence stated on muster roll, house n/c, s 1,2,4.

HOWELL, EDWARD. reg 14, co A, enr 10/1/61 Louisa, enl 12/10/61 Louisa, dis 1/31/65 Louisa, age 21, house 416, s 1,2,4.

HOWELL, EVAN P. reg 45, co D, H, r 2nd cpl, enr 7/4/63 Catlettsburg, enl 10/17/63 Ashland, age 18, trans to co H 1/1/64, back to co D 2/1/65, d 5/27/64 Lexington hospital of disease, house 594, s 1,2.

HOWELL, GEORGE W. reg 5Va, co C, G, enr 10/25/62 Ceredo, enl 12/13/62 Ceredo, dis 9/21/64 Wheeling, age 18, house 221, s 1,5,20,27.

HOWELL, HENDERSON. reg 5Va, co C, G, enr Ceredo or Lawrence Co., enl 10/21/61 Ceredo, dis 9/21/64 Wheeling, age 18 or 20, dark hair, hazel eyes, fair skin, 5-8, re-enlisted as veteran volunteer 2/14/64, b Pike Co., house 221, s 1,26,27.

HOWELL, JOHN. reg 10Cav, co F, enr 8/9/62 Boyd Co., enl 9/9/62 Covington, dis 9/17/63 Maysville, age 22, sandy hair, blue eyes, dark skin, 5-9, cap & paroled 3/22/63 Mt. Sterling by Col. Roy Cluke, b Pike Co., house 221, s 1,2,4.

HOWELL, SAMUEL. reg 10Cav, co F, enr 8/9/62 Boyd Co., enl 9/9/62 Covington, dis 9/17/63 Maysville, age 45, cap & paroled 3/22/63 Mt. Sterling by Col. Roy Cluke, house 221, s 1,2,4.

HUNT, THOMAS. reg 14, co F, C, enr 11/19/61 Louisa, enl 12/10/61 Louisa, dis 1/31/65 Louisa, age 18, trans to co C 8/28/63, back to co F 1/20/65, residence stated on muster roll, house n/c, s 1,2,4.

HUTCHINSON, DAVID. reg 5Va, co G, r 5th sgt, enr 8/20/61 Camp Pierpont, enl 9/20/61 Ceredo, dis 10/3/64 Wheeling, age 24, prom to 5th sgt 1/3/63, house 467, s 1,27.

HUTCHINSON, HENRY L. reg 22EM, co A, r cpl, enl 5/26/64, dis 6/28/64, age 18, light hair & skin, dark eyes, 5-7, b Lawrence Co., house 608, s 2,4,5.

HYATT, JOHN R. reg 14, co A, r sgt, enr 10/1/61 Louisa, enl 12/10/61 Louisa, dis 1/31/65 Louisa, age 40, prom from cpl to sgt 2/26/63, house C122, s 1,2,4.

HYDEN, CLAIBORNE. reg 22EM, co A, enl 5/26/64, dis 6/28/64, age 35, light hair & skin, blue eyes, 5-10, b Lee Co. VA, house A133, s 2,4.

HYLTON, WILLIAM R. reg 14, co F, r 2nd sgt, enr 11/19/61 Louisa, enl 12/10/61 Louisa, dis 1/31/65 Louisa, age 27, app 5th sgt 5/1/62, prom to 2nd sgt 1863, residence stated on muster roll, 9/63 on detached duty with sappers & miners in TN, house n/c, s 1,2,4.

I

IRVINE, JAMES. reg 14Cav, co C, enr 8/16/62 Maysville, enl 8/21/62 Mt. Sterling, age 25, 35 or 38, cap & paroled 2/24/63 Mt. Sterling by Col. Roy Cluke, residence stated on muster roll, house n/c, s 1,2,4.

J

JACKSON, JOHN. reg 14, co E, enr 10/15/61 Ashland, enl 12/10/61 Louisa, dis 1/31/65 Louisa, age 25, house 587, s 1,2,4.

JACKSON, SAMUEL. reg 14, co E, r cpl, enr 10/15/61 Ashland, enl 12/10/61 Louisa, dis 1/31/65 Louisa, age 32, prom to cpl 7/1/62, house 587, s 1,2,4.

JOHNSON, CALVIN. reg 14, co C, F, enr 11/19/61 Louisa, enl 12/10/61 Louisa, dis 1/31/65 Louisa, age 26 or 29, light hair, brown eyes, dark skin, 5-9, trans from co F to co C 8/28/62, back to co F 1/20/65, b Washington Co. VA, house 235, s 1,2,4.

JOHNSON, GEORGE W. reg 40, co D, r 4th sgt, enr 6/26/63 or 7/4/63 Grayson, enl 9/25/63 Grayson, dis 12/30/64 Catlettsburg, age 23, reduced to ranks 11/14/63, house 119, s 1 2.

JOHNSON, HARRISON. reg 14, co F, enr 11/19/61 Louisa, enl 12/10/61 Louisa, dis 1/31/65 Louisa, age 20, residence stated on muster roll, house n/c, s 1, 2,4.

JOHNSON, HIRAM. reg 10Cav, co F, enr 8/9/62 Boyd Co., enl 9/9/62 Covington, dis 9/17/63 Maysville, age 18, d 3/8/63 or 3/10/63 Danville of kidney disease, house 237, s 1,2,4.

JOHNSON, ISAAC. reg 22EM, co B, enl 5/26/64, dis 6/28/64, age 26, dark hair & skin, gray eyes, 5-9, age 33 on census, house 475, s 2,4.

JOHNSON, JAMES. reg 10Cav, co F, enr 8/9/62 Boyd Co. enl 9/9/62 Covington, dis 9/17/63 Maysville, age 18, reg 22EM, enr 5/26/64, dis 6/28/64, light hair & skin, gray eyes, 5-6, b Greenup Co., house 236, 1,2,4.

JOHNSON, JAMES. reg 5Va, reg F, enr 8/10/61 Camp Anthony, enl 9/2/61 Ceredo, age 23, died 9/11/62 vulnus sclopetarium (gunshot wound), buried grave 281, Milton cemetery, Alexandria VA, house A69, s 1,27.

JOHNSON, JESSE. reg 14, co C, enr 10/10/61 Louisa, enl 12/10/61 Louisa, age 20, des 2/1/64 Catlettsburg, residence stated on muster roll, house n/c, s 1,2,4.

JOHNSON, JOHN. reg 14, co F, enr 11/19/61 Louisa, enl 12/10/61 Louisa, age 29, des 9/28/62 on the march or 10/3/62 Carter Co., house 119, s 1,2,4.

JOHNSON, JOHN. reg 5Va, co D, enr 8/18/61 or 9/2/61 Camp Pierpont, Ceredo, dis 9/20/64 Wheeling, age 32 or 44, dark hair, blue eyes, light skin, 5-10, dis 11/8/62 Cumberland MD 11/8/62 for disability of hydrocele caused by exertion, b Stokes Co. NC, house 340, s 1,27.

JOHNSON, JOHN H. reg 14, co E, enr 10/15/61 Ashland, enl 12/10/61 Louisa, dis 1/31/65 Louisa, age 26, light hair & skin, blue eyes, 5-9, des Cumberland Gap 9/10/62, b Monongalia Co. VA, residence stated on muster roll, house n/c, s 1,2, 4.

JOHNSON, ROBERT L. reg 5Va., co C, enr 10/25/62 Ceredo, dis 9/21/64 Wheeling, age 18, age 10 on census, house 340, s 1,27.

JONES, JOHN PAUL. reg 22, co G, F&S, r capt, enr 10/25/61 Grayson, enl 1/10/62 Louisa, dis 1/20/65 Louisville, age 38, made reg. QM 1/18/62, resigned 6/5/62, residence stated on List of Officers, house 532, s 1,2,4,32.

JONES, WILLIAM. reg 2Cav, co E, r wagoner, enr 7/6/61 or 7/14/61 Ashland or Camp Jo Holt, enl 9/9/61 Muldraugh Hill, age 33, dark hair & skin, blue eyes, 5-8, des Savannah TN 7/62, b Greenup Co., house C10, s 1,2.

JORDAN, JOHN W. reg 22EM, co B, enl 5/26/64, dis 6/28/64, age 33, dark hair, eyes & skin, 5-5, b North Carolina, house 316, s 2,4.

K

KEESEE, BENJAMIN. reg 14, co A, enr 10/1/61 Ashland or Louisa, enl 12/10/61 Louisa, dis 1/31/65 Louisa, age 20, black hair, gray eyes, light skin, 5-6, b Greenup Co., residence stated on muster roll, house n/c, s 1,2,4.

KEESEE, GEORGE. reg 22EM, co A, enr 5/26/64, dis 6/28/64, age 28, black hair, dark eyes & skin, 6-0, b Wayne Co., house 43, s 2,4.

KELLEY, JOHN. reg 5Va, co K, enr & enl 6/15/62 Piedmont VA, dis 10/64 Wheeling, age 43, KIA Lynchburg VA 6/18/64 or 6/21/64, house 397, s 1,27.

KELLEY, JOSEPH V. reg CG, co enr 6/20/64, enl 7/4/64 Catlettsburg, m/out 3/11/65 Catlettsburg, reg 53, co I, enr & enl 4/11/65 Covington, dis 9/15/65 Louisville, age 18, dark hair, blue eyes, fair skin, 5-4, b Boyd Co., credited to Bracken Co., but he is not on Bracken Co. census, house 397, s 1,2,26.

KELLEY, WESLEY. reg 14, co C, enr 10/10/61 Louisa, enl 12/10/61 Louisa, dis 1/31/65 Louisa, age 23, cap in Lawrence 10/1/62 and paroled, CSR: "at home sick in Boyd Co.", house 82, s 1,2,4.

KELLEY, WILLIAM A. reg CG, co E, enr 6/20/64, m/in 7/4/64 Frankfort, m/out 3/1/65 Catlettsburg, reg 53, co I, enr 3/27/65 Catlettsburg, enl 3/29/65 Greenupsburg, dis 9/15/65 Louisville, age 18, dark hair, blue eyes, fair skin, 5-7, b Lawrence Co., credited to Boyd Co., house 397, s 1,2,26.

KIBBE, LOUIS L. reg 10Cav, co F, r sgt, enr 8/9/62 Boyd Co., enl 9/9/62 Covington, dis 9/17/63 Maysville, age 23, app 3rd cpl 8/18/62, prom to sgt 5/1/63, residence stated on muster roll, house n/c, s 1,2,4.

KILBOURN, ROLLAND B. reg 45, co F, enr 10/21/63, enl 11/2/63 Ashland, dis 12/24/63 Catlettsburg, not on CSR, house A84, s 2.

KILGORE, WILLIAM. reg 14, co C, r 1st lt, enr 10/10/61 Louisa, enl 12/10/61 Louisa, age 23, resigned 8/13/62 for poor health, List of Officers lists address as Steubenville OH; muster roll lists Boyd Co. as residence, house n/c, s 1,2,4.

KILLEN, WILLIAM WELLINGTON. reg 14, co C, musician, enr 10/10/61 Louisa, enl 12/10/61 Louisa, dis 1/31/65 Louisa, age 18, CSR: "at home sick Catlettsburg", house A21, s 1,2,4.

KINCAID, JAMES D. reg 22EM, r surgeon, enl 5/26/64, dis 6/28/64, house A5, s 2,4,5.

KING, JOSEPH R. reg 14, co A, musician, enr 2/29/64 Louisa, enl 3/15/64 Louisa, dis 9/15/65 Louisville, age 18, sandy hair, gray eyes, light skin, 5-5, trans to 14th Vet. Inf., house C63, s 1,2,4.

KING, LAWRENCE. reg 5Va, co A, enr 7/17/61 Ceredo, enl 8/15/61 Ceredo, dis 10/3/64 Wheeling, age 32, sandy hair, blue eyes, fair skin, 5-4, musician, CSR states Boyd Co. as residence, house C68, s 1,27.

KING, LEWIS N. reg 5Va, co A, enr 7/17/61 Ceredo, enl 9/2/61 Ceredo, dis 10/3/64 Wheeling, age 22 or 25, member of regimental band, house C63, s 1,27.

KING, ROBERT H. reg 14, co A, enr 10/1/61 Louisa, enl 12/10/61 Louisa, dis 1/31/65 Louisa, age 45, house C63, s 1,2,4.

KIRBY, CHARLES. reg 14, co F, A, D, enr 7/16/63 Louisa, enl 10/31/63 Louisa, dis 9/15/65 Louisa, age 15 or 17, trans to 14th Vet. Inf., trans from co A to co F 8/26/63, back to co F 1/20/65, house 361, s 1,4.

KIRBY, CURTIS. reg 14, co F, enr 11/19/61 Louisa, enl 12/10/61 Louisa, dis 1/31/65 Louisa, age 28, house 258, s 1,2,4.

KIRBY, GEORGE. reg 14, co A, F, enr 11/19/61 Louisa, enl 12/10/61 Louisa, dis 9/15/65 Louisville, age 21, light hair, blue eyes, fair skin, 5-8, trans from co F to co C 11/12/63, back to co F 1/20/65, house 361, s 1,2,4.

KIRK, GEORGE W. reg 14, co F, r cpl, enr 11/19/61 Louisa, enl 12/10/61 Louisa, dis 1/31/65 Louisa, age 40 or 44, app cpl 11/19/61, reduced to ranks 6/2/64, house 114, s 1,2,4.

KIRK, SOLOMON. reg 45, co K, enr 10/10/63 Ashland, enl 12/19/63 Louisa, age 18, d 4/17/64 Ashland or Flemingsburg of measles & lung inflammation, house 114, 1,2,26.

KISSINGER, WILLIAM. reg 18th Ohio Infantry, co A, house 654, s 26,33.

KOUNS, ABRAHAM. reg 45, co K, enr 10/18/63 Ashland, enl 12/9/63 Louisa, dis 2/14/65 Catlettsburg, age 18, house 519, s 1,2.

KOUNS, JOHN M. reg 45, co H, enr 7/14/63 Catlettsburg, enl 2/6/64 Mt. Sterling, dis 2/14/65 Catlettsburg, age 22, light hair, gray eyes, dark skin, 5-6, b Greenup Co., house 504, s 1,2.

KOUNS, WILLIAM H. ret 53, co I, r cpl, enr & enl 4/3/65 Greenupsburg, dis 9/15/65 Louisville, age 20, black hair, blue eyes, dark hair, 5-7, b Boyd Co., credited to Boyd Co., house 504, s 1,2.

KROUSE, PAUL L. reg 40, co E, r QM sgt, enr 8/5/63 Grayson, enl 9/28/63 Grayson, age 19, prom to QM sgt 7/1/64, cap by Gen. Morgan 5/6/64, residence stated on muster roll, b Ohio, house n/c, s 1,2,4.

L

LAKIN, JAMES C. reg 14, co F, r sgt, enr 11/19/61 Louisa, enl 12/10/61 Louisa, age 30, d 2/4/62 or 2/17/62 Ashland hospital of disease, app sgt 11/19/61, house 106, s 1,2,4.

LAKIN, JOHN R. reg 14, co C, r cpl, enr 10/10/61 or 10/25/61 Louisa or Catlettsburg, enl 12/10/61 Louisa, dis 1/31/65 Louisa, age 40 or 45, dark hair, eyes, & skin, 5-6, b Cabell Co. VA, cap Lawrence Co. 12/23/62 & paroled, house 97, s 1,2,4.

LAMBERT, JOB or JOAB. reg 5Va, co G, enr 9/5/61 Ceredo, dis 10/3/64 Wheeling, age 30, reg 53, co K, enr & enl 4/11/65 Covington, dis 9/15/65 Louisville, age 39, dark hair, gray eyes, fair skin, 5-7, b Lawrence Co., credited to Kenton Co., but not on Kenton Co. census, house 90, s 1,2,4,27.

LARGE, SOLOMON. reg 6th Ohio Cavalry, co H, enr 12/4/61, dis 8/7/65 Petersburg VA, age 32, house 399, s 26,27.

LARGE, VINSON. reg 10Cav, co F, enr 8/9/62 Boyd Co., enl 9/9/62 Covington, dis 9/17/63 Maysville, age 34, cap & paroled 3/22/63 Mt. Sterling by Col. Roy Cluke, house 219, s 1,2,4.

LARK, ALEXANDER. reg 22EM, co B, enl 5/26/64, dis 6/28/64, age 35, brown hair, blue eyes, fair skin, 5-9, b Virginia, house A52, s 2,4.

LAUGHERY, ROBERT. reg 14, co A, enr 10/1/61 Louisa, enl 12/10/61 Louisa, dis 4/15/63 Louisa, age 26, dark hair, gray eyes, light skin, 5-8, b Fayette Co. PA, dis for oblique inguinal hernia sustained while drilling at Camp deCourcey in May 1862, residence stated on muster roll, house n/c, s 1,2,4.

LAYNE, JAMES H. reg 5Va, co K, enr 7/24/63 Ceredo, enl 1/4/64 Charleston, dis 10/3/64 Wheeling, age 21, house A131, s 1,27.

LAYNE, JOHN N. reg 5Va, co H, A, r sgt, enr & enl 9/18/61 Ceredo, dis 6/20/64, age 40, light hair & skin, blue eyes, 5-6, cap Guyandotte VA 12/10/61, confined at Richmond VA 11/22/61, sent to Salisbury NC 12/24/61, paroled 5/28/62 Salisbury NC, dis surgeon's certificate of disability for chronic opthalmia (eye inflammation) with granulated lids, b Lawrence Co. OH, house A131, s 1,27.

LEFFINGWELL, DWIGHT A. reg 14, co E, F, r capt, enr 10/15/61 Ashland, enl 12/10/61 Louisa, dis 1/31/65 Louisa, age 19, light hair, blue eyes, fair skin, 5-10, prom from 1st sgt co E to 1st lt co F 6/12/62, prom from 1st co F to capt co E 11/1/62, b Chautauqua Co. NY, house C56, s 1,2,4.

LEHMAN, VALENTINE. reg 14, co A, r cpl, enr & enl 10/6/62 Portland OH, dis 9/15/65 Louisville, age 18, brown hair, hazel eyes, dark skin, 5-5, trans to 14th Vet. Inf., app cpl 2/65, b Germany, residence stated on muster roll, house n/c, s 1, 2,4.

LESLIE, JOHN B. reg 5Va, co G, enr 8/20/61 Camp Pierpont, enl 9/2/61 Ceredo, age 31, age 21 on census, house 163, s 1,27.

LESLIE, ROBERT T. reg 5Va, co G, r cpl, enr 8/2/61 Ceredo, enl 9/2/61 Ceredo, dis 10/3/64 Wheeling, age 23, house 169, s 1,26 27.

LEWIS, ALLEN. reg 14, co F, A, enr 10/25/61 or 11/19/61 Louisa, enl 12/10/61 Louisa, age 18, 22 or 23, trans to co C 11/12/63, trans back to co F 1/20/65, house 348, s 1,2,4.

LEWIS, BENJAMIN F. JR. reg 5Va, co G, enr 1/23/63 Ceredo, age 19, not mustered into U. S. service, CSR: "absent sick with leave at home in Ky.", age 13 on census, house 515, s 1,27.

LEWIS, CHARLES. reg 14, co F, enr 11/1/61 Louisa, enl 12/10/61 Louisa, age 42, 44 or 56, dis 12/31/62 Lexington for age & injury to great toe, house 348, s 1, 2,4.

LEWIS, CHARLES. reg 14, co F, A, D, enr 8/8/63 Louisa, enl 1/10/63, Louisa, dis 9/15/65 Louisville, age 17, trans from co F to co A 8/28/63, back to co F 1/20/65, wounded in left arm July or August 1864, house 348, s 2,4.

LEWIS, GIDEON. reg 14, co F, E, enr 11/19/61 Louisa, enl 12/10/61 Louisa, dis 1/31/65 Louisa, age 18, trans from co F to co E 8/28/63, back to co F 1/20/65, age 18, age 13 on census, house 348, s 1,2,4.

LEWIS, HUGH. reg 5Va, co G, enr 8/20/61 Camp Pierpont, enl 9/2/61 Ceredo, dis 10/3/64 Wheeling, age 19, des 5/8/62 Petersburg VA, house 181, s 1,27.

LEWIS, JAMES C. reg 10Cav, co F, enr 8/9/62 Boyd Co., enl 9/9/62 Covington, dis 9/16/64 Maysville, age 22, cap & paroled 3/22/63 Mt. Sterling by Col. Roy Cluke, residence stated on muster roll, house n/c, s 1,2,4.

LEWIS, STEPHEN. reg CG, co G, enr 5/28/64 Louisa, enl 7/6/64 Frankfort, dis 3/11/65 Catlettsburg, age 27, black hair, gray eyes, dark skin, 5-8, house 348, s 2, 4.

LOCK, JOHN. reg 14, co F, enr 10/25/61 or 11/19/61 Louisa, enl 12/10/61 Louisa, dis 1/31/65 Louisa, age 19, black hair & eyes, dark skin, 5-8, b Preston Co. VA, house 120, s 1,2,4.

LOCK, WILLIAM. reg 14, co F, enr 11/19/61 Louisa, enl 12/10/61 Louisa, dis 1/31/65 Louisa, age 26, house 295, s 1,2,4.

LOCKWOOD, DAVID. reg 22EM, co A, enl 5/26/64, dis 6/28/64, age 22, light hair & skin, blue eyes, 5-10, b Lawrence Co., house 467, s 2,4.

LOCKWOOD, JACOB. reg 5Va., co G, enr 8/23/61 Camp Pierpont, enl 9/2/61 Ceredo, dis 3/23/63 Washington DC, age 25, black hair, brown eyes, fair skin, 5-9, dis on account of wounds received at Bull Run 8/29/62, amputation of right leg, b Lawrence Co., house 150, s 1,27.

LOCKWOOD, JAMES. reg 22EM, co A, enl 5/26/64, dis 6/28/64, age 19, black hair, dark eyes & skin, 5-4, b Lawrence Co., house 460, s 2,4.

LOCKWOOD, WILLIAM. reg 14, co C, A, enr 10/10/61 Louisa, enl 12/10/61 Louisa, dis 9/15/65 Louisville, age 20, trans to 14th Vet. Inf., enl 2/29/64, m/in 3/15/64, house 460, s 1,2,4.

LOWMAN, GEORGE W. reg 14, co C, enr 10/10/61 Louisa, enl 12/10/61 Louisa, dis 9/15/65 Louisville, age 20, trans to 14th Vet. Inf., enl 2/29/64, m/in 3/19/64, b Monongalia Co. WV, residence stated on muster roll, house n/c, s 1,2, 4.

LOVEJOY, LAFAYETTE. reg 14, co C, enr 10/10/61 or 10/25/61 Louisa, enl 12/10/61 Louisa, dis 1/31/65 Louisa, age 24, gray hair, light eyes, fair skin, 5-4, b Lawrence Co., cap Lawrence Co. 9/25/64, paroled in eastern Ky., residence stated on muster roll, house n/c, s 1,2,4.

LOWTHER, JOHN M. reg 14, co A, r 2nd lt, enr 10/1/61 Louisa, enl 12/10/61 Louisa, dis 1/31/65 Louisa, age 26, app 1st sgt 7/5/62, prom from 1st sgt to 2nd lt 2/26/63, house C46, s 1,2,4.

LUNSFORD, ANDREW. reg 40, co K, enr 8/7/63 Grayson, enl 9/29/63 Grayson, dis 12/31/64 Catlettsburg, age 21, trans to 24 Ky. Inf. 1/24/64, d 7/8/64 Lexington of acute dysentery, house 290, s 1,2.

LUNSFORD, MARTIN. reg 40, co K, enr 6/27/63 Carter Co., enl 9/29/63 Grayson, dis 12/30/64 Catlettsburg, age 23, fair hair, eyes & skin, 6-0, trans to 24th Ky. Inf. 1/15/64, b Carter Co., house 289, s 1,2.

LUNSFORD, PETER. reg 5Va. co K, enr & enl 11/15/61 Ceredo, age 18, reg 40, co D, K, enr 6/27/63 Grayson, enl 9/27/63 Grayson, dis 12/30/64 Catlettsburg, house 288, 1,4,27.

LUNSFORD, SOLOMON. reg 5Va, co K, enr 11/15/61 Ceredo, des 12/15/62, m/out 10/3/64 Wheeling, reg 40, co D, K, enr 8/17/63 Grayson, enl 9/29/63 Grayson, dis 12/30/64 Catlettsburg, age 21, light hair & skin, blue eyes, 5-6, b Carter Co., house 288, s 1,4,5,20,27.

LYNCH, MICHAEL. reg 5th West Virginia Cavalry, co H, enr 6/10/61 Ironton or Wheeling, enl 6/28/61 Wheeling, dis 6/29/64, age 21 or 26, red hair, gray eyes, fair skin, 5-6, re-enlisted 1/15/64, b Lawrence Co. or Ireland, house C118, s 1,26.

M

MACAULEY, CULBERT. reg 10Cav, co F, enr 8/9/62 Boyd Co., enl 9/9/62 Covington, dis 9/17/63 Maysville, age 20, cap & paroled 3/22/63 Mt. Sterling by Col. Roy Cluke, residence stated on muster roll, house n/c, s 1,2,4.

MALLOY, DABNEY C. reg 14, co C, enr 10/10/61 Louisa, enl 12/10/61 Louisa, dis 1/31/65 Louisa, age 45 or 46, CSR: "at home sick in Boyd Co.", house A96, s 1,2,4.

MANN, JOHN H. reg 5Va. co G, enr 8/20/61 Camp Pierpont, enl 9/2/61 Ceredo, dis 10/3/64 Wheeling, dis 9/5/63 Newark NJ, for general disability and feebleness, b Grayson Co. VA, CSR: "soldier desires to be addressed at Catlettsburg, Boyd Co.", reg 22EM, co B, enl 5/26/64, dis 6/28/64, age 28, dark hair, eyes & skin, 5-10, house 111, s 1,2,4,27.

MARSHALL, MOSES M. reg 5Va, co I, enr 9/14/61 Ceredo, age 43 or 49, light hair & skin, blue eyes, 5-11, dis 7/3/62 Strasburg VA for irritated spinalis vide, b Pike Co. PA, house 178, s 1,27.

MARTIN, ALBERT C. reg 5Va, co C, G, enr 4/6/63 Ceredo, dis 9/21/64 Wheeling, age 18, age 26 on census, house C17, s 1,27.

MARTIN, JOHN M. reg 5Va, co C, enr 8/12/61 Ceredo, enl 9/2/61 Ceredo, age 25, brown hair, blue eyes, fair skin, 5-9, dis 2/13/63 Washington DC for disability of deformity and lameness from a burn received before enlistment, age 20 on census, house 523, s 1,27.

MARTIN, WILLIAM F. reg 14, co F, r sgt, enr 11/9/61 Louisa, enl 12/10/61 Louisa, age 25, d 2/14/62 Ashland of typhoid fever, app sgt 11/19/61, house 523, s 1,2,4.

MAY, MARION. reg 14, co A, enr 10/1/61 Louisa, enl 12/10/61 Louisa, age 22, d 4/19/62 or 4/21/62 Lexington of heart disease, residence stated on muster roll, house n/c, s 1,2,4.

MAY, WILLIAM C. reg 10Cav, co F, enr 8/9/62 Boyd Co., enl 9/9/62 Covington, dis 9/17/63 Maysville, age 25, cap & paroled 3/22/63 Mt. Sterling by Col. Roy Cluke, reg 22EM, co A, r cpl, enl 5/26/64, dis 6/28/64, dark hair & skin, black eyes, 5-11, b Pike Co., house 18, s 1,2,4,27.

MAYHEW, WILLIAM C. reg 45, co L, r 2nd sgt, enr 10/7/63 Ashland, enl 12/9/63 Louisa, dis 2/14/65 Catlettsburg, age 21, prom to sgt 1/1/64, house 160, s 1,2.

MAYS, WILLIAM. reg 5Va, co C, enr 8/13/61 Ceredo, enl 9/2/61 Ceredo, dis 9/21/64 Wheeling, age 27, age 18 on census, house 567, s 1,27.

MCBRAYER, JAMES RILEY. reg 22EM, co B, r 1st sgt, enl 5/26/64, dis 6/28/64, age 32, brown hair, light eyes, fair skin, 6-3, age 55 on census, b Greenup Co., house 139 or 141, s 2,4.

MCBRAYER, LEWIS P. reg 39, co D, r 4th sgt, enr 10/22/62 Boyd Co., enl 2/16/63 Peach Orchard, dis 9/15/65 Louisville, age 34, house 218, s 1,2,4.

MCBRAYER, SOLOMON. reg 39, co D, enr 10/17/62 Boyd Co., enl 2/16/63 Peach Orchard, age 37, dark hair, blue eyes, fair skin, 6-2, d 4/13/64 Louisa of lung inflammation, b Floyd Co., effects sent to wife at Catlettsburg, house A36, s 1,2,26.

MCBRAYER, WILLIAM P. reg 45, co G, enr 11/22/63 Catlettsburg, enl 11/30/63 Ashland, dis 2/14/65, age 25, b Greenup Co., house 220, s 1,2.

MCCALL, ROBERT B. reg 5Va, co B, r capt, enr & enl 9/2/61 Ceredo, dis 9/25/64 Wheeling, age 31, prom from 2nd lt to 1st lt 4/9/62, from 1st lt to capt 5/19/62, house A135, s 1,5,20,27.

MCCLELLAND, JOHN. reg 22EM, co B, enl 5/26/64, dis 6/28/64, age 43, dark hair & skin, gray eyes, 5-11, b Lee Co. VA, house 319, s 2,4.

MCGHEE, DAVID H. reg 14, co C, r 1st lt, enr 10/10/61 Louisa, enl 12/10/61 Louisa, dis 1/31/65 Louisa, age 32, dark hair, blue eyes, fair skin, 5-8, prom to ord sgt 5/1/62, prom to 2nd lt 11/1/62, to 1st lt 2/27/63, b Bedford Co. VA, residence stated on muster roll & List of Officers, house n/c, s 1,2,4,32.

MCGINNIS, JASPER N. reg 14, co F, r sgt, enr 11/19/61 Louisa, enl 12/10/621 Louisa, dis 1/31/65 Louisa, age 21, dark hair & skin, blue eyes, 5-9, prom to cpl 5/12/63, to sgt 11/17/63, b Carter Co., house 132, s 1,2,4.

MCKNIGHT, JOHN. reg 5Va, co A, enr 7/17/61 Ceredo, enl 9/2/61 Ceredo, dis 10/3/64 Wheeling, age 18, sandy hair, blue eyes, fair skin, 5-4 or 5-6, enrolled 9th Congressional District, b Lawrence Co. OH, house 557, s 1,27.

MCKNIGHT, THOMAS. reg 5Va, co A, r sgt, enr & enl 9/2/61 Ceredo, dis 10/3/64 Wheeling, age 21 or 24, black hair & eyes, dark skin, 5-5, re-enlisted as veteran volunteer, enl & m/in 12/23/63 Charleston WV, prom to cpl 2/26/63, b Clarion Co. PA, enrolled 9th Congressional District, house 557, s 1,5,20,27.

MCMILLEN, ALEXANDER E. reg 14, co C, enr 10/10/61 Louisa, enl 21/10/61 Louisa, dis 1/31/65 Louisa, age 28, house A120, s 1,2,26.

MCMULLEN, JESSE SR. reg 5Va, co C, r cpl, enr 8/29/61 Ceredo, enl 9/2/61 Ceredo, dis 9/2/64 Wheeling, age 44, age 53 on census, house 454, s 1,27.

MCMULLEN, JESSE JR. reg 5Va. co C, G, enr 8/24/61 Ceredo, enl 9/29/61 Ceredo, dis 9/21/64 Wheeling, age 19 or 21, light hair & skin, blue eyes, 5-5, enrolled 11th Congressional District of Ohio, but he is not on Lawrence Co. OH census, b Mercer Co. OH, house 454, s 1,27.

MCWHORTER, BENJAMIN. reg 14, co F, D, enr & enl 10/8/62 Portland OH, dis 9/15/65 Louisville, age 18, dark hair & eyes, fair skin, 5-5, trans to 14th Vet. Inf., b Carter Co., house 129, s 1,2,4.

MCWHORTER, JAMES W. reg 14, co F, A, r 1st sgt, enr 11/19/61 Louisa, enl 12/10/61 Louisa, dis 1/31/65 Louisa, age 19, brown hair, blue eyes, dark hair, 5-5, prom to 2nd sgt 11/11/62, to 1st sgt 11/17/63, house 129, s 1,2,4.

MEAD, WILLIAM R. reg 14Cav, co C, r 5th sgt, enr 8/16/62 Boyd Co., enr 8/21/62 Mt. Sterling, dis 9/16/63 Maysville, age 21, app sgt 8/16/62, house 380, s 1,2,4.

MEANS, ARCHIBALD. reg 14, co E, r capt, enr 10/15/61 Ashland, enl 12/10/61 Louisa, age 28, dark hair, black eyes, light skin, 5-9, resigned 12/18/62, b Alleghany Co. PA, house C96, s 1,2,4.

MILLER, ABRAHAM. reg 14, co E, F, enr 10/25/61 or 11/19/61 Louisa, enl 12/10/61 Louisa, dis 1/31/65 Louisa, age 18, trans to co E 8/29/63, to co F 1/20/65, age 14 on census, house 649, s 1,2,4.

MILLER, GEORGE W. reg 14, co F, musician, enr 11/19/61 Louisa, enl 12/10/61 Louisa, age 20, light hair & skin, blue eyes, 5-8, dis 12/21/62 for disability of back weakness, house 649, s 1,4.

MILLER, JACOB C. reg 45, co B, c cpl, enr 7/21/63 Catlettsburg, enl 10/16/63 Catlettsburg, age 18, wounded on picket duty 6/9/64 Lexington, d of wounds 6/14/64, house 468, s 1,2,26.

MILLER, JOHN C. reg 5Va, co G, r sgt, enr 7/29/61 Camp Pierpont, enl 9/2/61 Ceredo, dis 10/3/64 Wheeling, age 22, CSR: "on sick furlough Boyd Co., Ky.", house C8, s 1,27.

MILLER, JOSEPH. reg 14, co F, E, enr 10/25/61 or 11/19/61 Louisa, enl 12/10/61 Louisa, dis 1/31/65 Louisa, age 18, trans from co F to co E 8/28/63, back to co F 1/20/65, residence stated on muster roll, house n/c, s 1,2,4.

MILLER, MARTIN. reg 36 Ohio Infantry, co A, drowned in Virginia 9/18/62, house 468, s 26,33.

MILLER, ROBERT. reg 45, co B, enr 7/27/63 Catlettsburg, enl 10/10/63 Catlettsburg, dis 12/24/64 Catlettsburg, age 18, house 468, s 1,2.

MILLER, STEPHEN. reg 14, co F, enr 11/19/61 Louisa, enl 12/10/61 Louisa, age 31, light hair & skin, blue eyes, 5-8, dis 12/31/62 Lexington for disability, piles, rheumatism & back weakness, b Greenup Co., residence stated on muster roll, house n/c, s 1,2,4.

MILLER, WILLIAM. reg 5Va, co D, G, K, enr 4/8/63 Ceredo, dis 9/20/64 Wheeling, age 18, house 468, s 1,27.

MILLER, WILLIAM. reg 14, co F, E, enr 11/19/61 Louisa, enl 12/10/61, dis 1/31/65 Louisa, age 35, trans from co F to co E 8/29/63, back to co F 1/20/65, house 644, s 1,2,4.

MIMS, DAVID A. reg 14, co C, r capt, enr 10/10/61, enl 12/10/61 Louisa, age 28, reg 39, r F&S, col, enr 1/21/63 Frankfort, enl 2/16/63 Peach Orchard, dis 9/15/65 Louisville, 7/16/64 placed in command of forces at Louisa, house A124, s 1,2,4.

MITCHUM, JAMES. reg 14, co C, enr 10/10/61 Louisa, enl 12/10/61 Louisa, dis 1/31/65 Louisa, age 30 or 32, light hair, blue eyes, fair skin, 5-7, b Tazewell Co. VA, CSR: "resides in Boyd Co.", house 68, s 1,2,4.

MORGAN, EDWARD. reg 5Va, co I, K, enr & enl 9/14/61 Ceredo, dis 10/4/64 Wheeling, age 34, light hair & skin, dark eyes, 5-5, b United Kingdom, enrolled 9th Congressional District, house 688, s 1,26,27.

MORGAN, EVAN. reg 45, co E, enr 9/29/63 Catlettsburg, enl 11/6/63 Ashland, dis 12/24/64 Catlettsburg, age 37, house 688, s 1,2.

MORGAN, NATHAN. reg 10Cav, co F, enr 8/9/62 Boyd Co., enl 9/9/62 Covington, dis 9/17/63 Maysville, age 31, app teamster 11/1/62, CSR: "absent sick in Boyd Co.", residence stated on muster roll, house n/c, s 1,2,4.

MOTT, FRANK reg 10Cav, co F, r capt, enr 8/9/62 Boyd Co., enl 9/9/62 Covington, dis 9/17/63 Maysville, age 30, commissioned as capt 8/22/62, reg 45, co C, enr 2/29/64 Mt. Sterling, enl 2/29/64 Flemingsburg, dis 12/24/64 Catlettsburg, residence on muster roll & List of Officers, house n/c, s 1,2,4,32.

MURPHY, JAMES. reg 22EM, co B, r capt, enl 5/26/64, dis 6/28/64, age 28, light hair, blue eyes, fair skin, 5-8, b Ireland, house 266, s 2,4.

MURPHY, JOHN W. D. reg 14, co F, r 2nd lt, enr 11/19/61 Louisa, enl 12/10/61 Louisa, age 25, resigned 6/10/62, residence stated on muster roll, house n/c, s 1, 2,4.

MURPHY, THOMAS. reg CG, co E, enr 7/30/64 Catlettsburg, enl 7/30/64 Frankfort, dis 3/11/65 Catlettsburg, reg 53, co I, enr 3/5/65 Catlettsburg, enl 3/29/65 Greenupsburg, dis 9/15/65 Louisville, age 18, brown hair, green eyes, fair skin, 5-9, b Madison Co., CSR lists him as Boyd Co. resident, house C112, s 1,2.

MUTTER, JOHN W. reg 39, co D, enr 8/18/63 Pike Co., enl 8/30/63 Louisa, dis 9/15/65 Louisville, age 20, age 27 on census, house 291, s 1,2.

MUTTERS, ALEXANDER. reg 14, co F, C, enr 11/19/61 Louisa, enl 12/10/61 Louisa, dis 1/31/65 Louisville, age 33, dark hair & skin, black or blue eyes, 5-11 or 6-2, trans from co F to co C 8/28/63, back to co F, b Pike Co. or Boyd Co., house 262, s 1 2,4.

MUTTERS, FRANKLIN. reg 14, co F, A, enr 10/25/61 or 11/19/61 Louisa, enl 12/10/61 Louisa, dis 1/31/65 Louisa, age 32, trans from co F to co C 11/12/63, back to co F 1/26/65, wounded in Battle of Tazewell TN, left at Cumberland Gap, taken prisoner & paroled, house 250, s 1,2,4.

MYERS, MARTIN. reg 14, co C, B, enr 6/20/63 Cumberland Gap, dis 9/15/65 Louisville, age 18, trans to 14th Vet. Inf., residence stated on muster roll, house n/c, s 1,2,4.

N

NEAL, ELIJAH. reg 75th Ohio Infantry, co K, enl 12/30/61, age 23, house 492, s 26,33.

NELSON, JACOB. reg 10Cav, co K, enr & enl 7/26/62 Louisville, resigned 7/7/63, r capt, comm. 2nd lt 7/29/62, prom to capt 9/9/62, reg CG, co E, r capt, enr 7/4/64 Catlettsburg, enl 7/4/64 Frankfort, age 32, auburn hair, blue eyes, fair skin, 5-8, resigned 11/23/64, residence stated on List of Officers, b Ireland, house n/c, s 2,4,32.

NICHOLSON, HARRISON BOONE. reg 2Cav, co E, enr 7/14/61, m/in 7/9/61 Muldraugh Hill, des, reg 40, co C, r 2nd sgt, enr 6/2/63 Grayson, enl 9/26/63 Grayson, dis 12/30/64 Catlettsburg, age 45, app 2nd sgt 2/29/64, house C66, s 1, 2,4.

NICHOLSON, JOHN J. reg 2Cav, co E, r cpl, enr 7/1/61 or 7/14/61 Ashland or Camp Jo Holt, enl 9/9/61 Muldraugh Hill, dis 7/17/65 Lexington NC, age 19, light hair, gray eyes, fair skin, 5-4, enl Vet. Vol. 2/7/64, m/in 3/7/64, prom to cpl 1/1/63, b Maysville, house C66, s 1,2.

NUNLEY, BENJAMIN F. reg CG, co E, enr 5/17/64 Catlettsburg, enl 7/4/64 Frankfort, dis 3/11/65 Catlettsburg, age 18, light hair, blue eyes, fair skin, 5-6, b Greenup Co., house 336, s 2,4.

NUNLEY, JOHN. reg 45, co B, enr 7/23/63 Catlettsburg, enl 10/10/63 Catlettsburg, dis 12/24/64 Catlettsburg, age 18, house 336, s 1,2.

NUNLEY, WILLIAM. reg 45, co B, enr 7/14/63 Catlettsburg, enl 10/10/63 Catlettsburg, dis 12/24/64 Catlettsburg, age 42, age 30 on census, house 230, s 1,2.

O

O'BRIAN, GEORGE. reg 14, co K, enr 11/8/61, enl 12/10/61 Louisa, age 28, sandy hair, blue eyes, fair skin, 5-8, muster roll lists Lawrence Co. as residence, but he is not on Lawrence Co. census, des Ashland 3/27/63, shot & killed trying to escape, house 623, 1,2.

O'BRIAN, JOHN. reg 5Va, co I, enr & enl 9/14/61 Ceredo, dis 10/4/64 Wheeling, age 25, light hair & skin, blue eyes, 5-6, wounded at Cross Keys 6/8/62, enrolled 9th Congressional District, b Lawrence Co., house 335, s 1,27.

ORMSTEAD, RALPH. reg 5Va, co F&S, r major, enr & enl 9/14/61 Camp Pierpont, Ceredo, age 26, KIA 9/21/61 by rebels Cassville VA, house A135, s 26, 27.

OVENDORF, ELISHA. reg 10Cav, co F, enr 8/9/62 Boyd Co., enl 9/9/62 Covington, dis 9/17/63 Maysville, age 42, cap & paroled 3/22/63 Mt. Sterling by Col. Roy Cluke, house 177, s 1,2,4.

OTEY, JORDAN. reg 14, co C, enl 12/10/61 Louisa, age 28 or 31, dark hair & skin, gray eyes, 6-1, trans to 14th Vet. Inf., enl 2/29/64, m/in 3/19/64, d 6/23/64 of wounds near Marietta GA, residence stated on muster roll, house n/c, s 1,2,4.

P

PATTON, GEORGE B. reg 14, co C, F&S, r com sgt, 2nd lt, enr 11/19/61 Louisa, enl 1/10/61 Louisa, dis 1/31/65 Louisa, age 18 or 22, prom from cpl to 1st sgt 11/1/62, from 1st sgt to 2nd lt 2/27/63, CSR: "at home sick in Boyd Co. Ky.", house A100, s 1,2,4.

PATTON, WILLIAM. reg 45, co E, K, enr 10/20/63 Ashland, enl 11/6/63 Ashland or Louisa, dis 12/24/64 Catlettsburg, trans from co E to co K 2/1/64, des 3/10/64 Flemingsburg, 22EM, co A, enl 5/26/64, dis 6/28/64, age 17, light hair & skin, dark eyes, 5-5, b Greenup Co., house A100, s 1,2,4.

PAYNE, BENJAMIN. reg 14, co A, enr 4/22/63, enl 5/7/63 Louisa, age 18, sandy hair, blue eyes, light skin, 5-7, died 8/12/64 Louisville of chronic diarrhea, b Boyd Co., house 424, s 1,2,4.

PAYNE, EDMUND. reg 14, co F, E, r 3rd sgt, enr 11/19/61 Louisa, enl 12/10/61 Louisa, dis 1/31/65 Louisa, age 25, reduced to ranks 4/21/63, trans to co E 8/28/63, back to co F 1/20/65, house 66, s 1,2,4.

PAYNE, NOAH L. reg 14, co A, r cpl, enr 10/1/61 Louisa, enl 12/10/61 Louisa, dis 1/31/65 Louisa, age 20, prom to cpl 6/1/62, wounded in face 5/28/64, house 424, s 1,2,4.

PAYNE, RICHARD F. reg 14, co A, enr 10/1/61 Louisa, enl 12/10/61 Louisa, dis 1/31/65 Louisa, age 20, house 424, s 1,2,4.

PAYNE, WILLIAM A. reg 39, co I, enr 1/6/64 Louisa, enl 3/20/64 Greenupsburg, dis 9/15/65 Louisville, age 18, dark hair, black eyes, fair skin, 5-11, b Tazewell Co. VA, house 424, s 1,2.

PENIX, ISAAC WILLIAM. reg 39, co D, enr 5/14/63 Louisa, enl 6/10/63 Louisa, dis 9/15/65 Louisville, age 18 or 19, light hair, gray eyes, fair skin, 5-6, b Greenup Co., residence stated on muster roll, house n/c, s 1,4.

PENNINGTON, HENDERSON. reg 5Va. co I, enr & enl 9/14/61 Ceredo, dis 10/4/64 Wheeling, age 18, drummer, age 11 on census, house A110, s 1,5,20,27.

PETERMAN, BURGESS. reg 14, co C, enr 10/25/61 Louisa, enl 12/10/61 Louisa, dis 1/31/65 Louisa, age 21 or 27, light hair, blue eyes, fair skin, 5-7, b Lawrence Co., CSR: "at home sick in Boyd Co.", residence stated on muster roll, house n/c, s 1,2,4.

PETERMAN, JACOB. reg 14, co C, enr 10/25/61 Louisa, enl 12/10/61 Louisa, dis 1/31/65 Louisa, age 26 or 27, residence stated on muster roll, house n/c, s 1, 2,4.

PITTS, JOHN N. reg 53, co K, enr & enl 3/25/65 Greenupsburg, dis 9/15/65 Louisville, age 18, brown hair, hazel eyes, fair skin, 5-8, b Greenup Co., credited to Greenup Co., but he is not on Greenup Co. census, house 165, s 1,2.

POAGE, AUGUSTUS. reg 22EM, co B, enl 5/26/64, dis 6/28/64, age 41, light hair, blue eyes, fair skin, 5-4, b Greenup Co., house 479, s 2,4.

POAGE, JACOB M. reg 14, co E, r 2nd lt, enr 10/15/61 Ashland, enl 12/10/61 Louisa, dis 1/31/65 Louisa, age 26, prom from 1st sgt to 2nd lt 11/7/62, residence stated on List of Officers, house C73, s 1,2,4,32.

POPE, HENRY P. reg 14, co F, r cpl, enr 11/19/61 Louisa, enl 12/10/61 Louisa, dis 1/31/65 Louisa, age 21, CSR: "at home sick Boyd Co.", house 146, s 1,2,4.

PORTER, GREENVILLE. reg 22EM, co B, enl 5/26/64, dis 6/28/64, age 18, light hair & eyes, fair skin, 5-6, b Floyd Co., house 689, s 2,4.

PORTER, JAMES L. reg 22EM, co B, enl 5/26/64, dis 6/28/64, age 19, light hair & skin, blue eyes, 6-0, b Johnson Co., house 689, s 2,4.

PORTER, JOHN W. reg 14, co C, r sgt, enr 10/25/61 Catlettsburg, enl 12/10/61 Louisa, age 21, light hair, blue eyes, dark skin, 5-9, trans to 14th Vet. Inf., enl 2/29/64, m/in 3/19/64, prom from cpl to sgt 3/23/65, house 689, s 1,2,4.

PORTER, MARTIN VAN BUREN. reg CG, co E, r sgt, enr 5/17/64 Catlettsburg, enl 7/4/64 Frankfort, dis 3/11/65 Catlettsburg, age 21, light hair, gray eyes, fair skin, 5-7, b Grayson Co. VA, house 347, s 2,4.

PORTER, WILLIAM R. reg 14Cav, co C, enr 8/16/62 Boyd Co., enl 8/21/62 Mt. Sterling, dis 9/16/63 Maysville, age 23, cap & paroled 3/22/63 Mt. Sterling by Col. Roy Cluke, house 339, s 1,2,4.

PORTER, ZEPHANIAH. reg 14, co F, enr 11/19/61 Louisa, enl 12/10/61 Louisa, age 37, brown hair & eyes, dark skin, 5-10, dis 3/13/62 Camp Buell disability of scorbutus (scurvy), residence stated on muster roll, house n/c, s 1,2,4.

POTEET, WILLIAM. reg 22EM, co B, enl 5/26/64, dis 6/28/64, age 21, dark hair, eyes & skin, 5-6, b Boyd Co., house A20, s 2,4.

POWER, THOMAS. reg 14, co A, r cpl, enr 10/1/61 Louisa, enl 12/10/61 Louisa, dis 1/31/65 Louisa, age 30, house 34, s 1,2,4.

POWERS, BENJAMIN F. reg 14, co E, r cpl, enr 10/15/61 Ashland, enl 12/10/61 Louisa, dis 1/31/65 Louisa, age 34, prom to cpl 1/1/62, house C161, s 1, 2,4.

PRICE, JACOB L. reg 14, co A, enr 10/1/61 Louisa, enl 12/10/61 Louisa, dis 1/31/65, age 36, house C135, s 1,2,4.

PRICE, WILLIAM. reg 14, co E, r 1st lt, enr 10/15/61 Ashland, enl 12/10/61 Louisa, dis 1/31/65 Louisa, age 27, prom from 2nd lt to 1st lt 11/1/62, C135, s 1, 2,4.

PRICHARD, ANDREW L. reg 45, co G, r 1st sgt, enr 10/1/63 Ashland, enl 11/30/63 Ashland, dis 2/14/65 Catlettsburg, age 21, black hair, blue eyes, fair skin, 5-9, prom from sgt to 1st sgt 2/27/64, reg 53, co K, enr & enl 4/11/65 Greenupsburg, dis 9/15/65 Louisville, b Greenup Co. or Letcher Co., 53rd Ky. Inf. service credited to Kenton Co., but he is not on Kenton Co. census, house 198, s 1,2.

PRICHARD, CHARLES N. reg 10Cav, co F, r QM sgt, enr 8/9/62 Boyd Co., enl 9/9/62 Covington, dis 9/17/63 Maysville, age 23, app QM sgt 8/18/62, residence stated on muster roll, house n/c, s 1,2,4.

PRICHARD, WILLIAM R. reg 45, co G, enr 10/1/63 Ashland, enl 11/30/63 Ashland, dis 2/14/65 Catlettsburg, age 23, black hair, blue eyes, fair skin, 5-10, age 35 on census, house 87, s 1,2.

PUGH, LEMUEL. reg 2Cav, co E, enr 7/14/61 Camp Jo Holt, enl 9/9/61 Muldraugh Hill, dis 10/12/64 Nashville TN, age 25, house C48, s 1,2.

R

RANDALL, PERES R. reg 5Va, co F&S, r surgeon, enr & enl 9/14/61 Ceredo, dis 9/20/64, age 57, house A79, s 1,27.

RANKIN, JOSEPH P. reg 2Cav, co E, r sgt, enr 7/14/61 Camp Jo Holt, enl 9/9/61 Muldraugh Hill, age 28 or 30, black hair, hazel eyes, dark skin, 5-8, b Philadelphia PA, trans to Invalid Corps, house C62, s 1,2.

RAUSCH, JOHN. reg 14, co A, enr 10/1/61 Louisa, enl 12/10/61 Louisa, dis 1/31/65 Louisa, age 35, wounded right arm between 7/2/64 & 8/13/64, residence stated on muster roll, house n/c, s 1,2,4.

REYNOLDS, REUBEN N. reg CG, co E, enr 5/31/64 Catlettsburg, enl 7/4/64 Frankfort, dis 3/11/65 Catlettsburg, age 18, light hair & skin, blue eyes, 5-8, b Greenup Co., house 404, s 2,4.

RICE, CHARLES. reg 10Cav, co F, enr 8/9/62 Boyd Co., enl 9/9/62 Covington, dis 9/17/63 Maysville, age 45, residence stated on muster roll, house n/c, s 1,2,4.

RICE, HIRAM. reg 5Va, co K, enr & enl 9/18/61 Ceredo, dis 10/3/65 Wheeling, age 26, house 317, s 1,2,5,27.

RICHARDSON, JAMES E. reg 14, co B, C, r sgt, enr 9/8/62 Catlettsburg, enl 10/10/62 Portland OH, dis 9/15/65 Louisville, age 18, trans to 14th Vet. Inf., prom from cpl to sgt 2/1/65, house A130, s 1,2,4.

RICHARDSON, WILLIAM. reg 22EM, co A, r cpl, enr 5/26/64, dis 6/28/64, age 18, black hair, blue eyes, light skin, 5-6, b Pike Co., house A130, s 2,4.

RIFFE, PETER. reg 45, co K, r cpl, enr 10/15/63 Ashland, enl 12/9/63 Louisa, dis 2/14/65 Catlettsburg, age 18, prom to cpl 1/1/64, house 175, s 1,2.

RILEY, WILLIAM. reg 45, co I, enr 11/16/63 Ashland, enl 2/4/64 Mt. Sterling, dis 2/14/65 Catlettsburg, age 30, brown hair, blue eyes, light skin, 5-8, b Lawrence Co. OH, house 538, s 1,2.

RINGGOLD, WILLIAM WALLACE. reg 14Cav, co C, r saddle sgt, enr 8/5/62 Ashland, enl 8/21/62 Mt. Sterling, dis 9/16/63 Maysville, age 41 or 42, prom from pvt to saddle sgt 4/10/63, house C78, s 1,2,4.

ROBERTS, EDWARD J. reg 14, r adjutant, enr 11/19/61 Louisa, enl 12/10/61 Camp Wallace, Louisa, dis 1/31/65 Louisa, age 43, prom from sgt major to adjutant 3/1/62, wounded in right arm between 7/2/64 & 8/13/64, house 675, s 1,2,4.

ROBERTSON, DAVID. reg 22EM, co B, r cpl, enl 5/26/64, dis 6/28/64, age 25, dark hair & skin, gray eyes, 6-1, b Cabell Co. VA, house 678, s 2,4.

ROBERTSON, MILTON. reg 54, co A, enr & enl 9/5/64 Greenupsburg, dis 9/1/65 Louisville, not on CSR, house 491, s 2.

ROBERSON, WILLIAM J. reg 39, co A, enr 9/18/62, enl 2/16/63 Peach Orchard, dis 9/15/65 Louisville, age 18, residence stated on muster roll, house n/c, s 1,2,4.

ROBINSON, MARION. reg 14, co F, enr 11/19/61 Louisa, enl 12/10/61 Louisa, age 18, brown hair, black eyes, fair skin, 5-4, d 11/19/64 Camp Nelson, b Carter Co., residence stated on muster roll, house n/c, s 1,2,4.

ROBINSON, SAMUEL. reg 14Cav, co C, enr 8/16/62 Boyd Co., enl 8/21/62 Mt. Sterling, dis 9/16/63 Maysville, age 26, cap & paroled 3/22/63 by Col. Roy Cluke, residence stated on muster roll, house n/c, s 1,2,4.

ROBISON, LOUIS. reg 10Cav, co F, enr 8/9/62 Boyd Co., enl 9/9/62 Covington, dis 9/17/63 Maysville, age 20, cap & paroled 3/22/63 Mt. Sterling, residence stated on muster roll, but he may be on Johnson Co. census, reg 39 co A, enr 10/11/63 Louisa, enl 10/29/63 Louisa, dis 9/15/65 Louisville, black eyes, fair skin, 5-8, b Johnson Co., house n/c, s 1,2,4.

ROLLINS, WILLIAM. reg 14, co C, enr 10/25/61 Louisa, enl 12/10/61 Louisa, dis 1/31/65 Louisa, age 35 or 37, house 82, s 1,2,4.

ROSE, ISRAEL. reg 14, co C, enr 9/8/62 Catlettsburg, enl 10/10/62 Portland OH, age 38, light hair, blue eyes, dark skin, 5-6, d 12/26/62 Richmond of typhoid fever, b Tazewell Co. VA, residence stated on muster roll, house n/c, s 1,2,4.

ROSS, JOHN S. reg 45, co K, r sgt, enr 10/10/63 Ashland, enl 12/9/63 Louisa, dis 2/14/65 Catlettsburg, age 18, prom to sgt 1/1/64, house 169, s 1,2.
ROSS, WILLIAM. reg 2Cav, co E, enr 7/14/61 Camp Jo Holt, enl 9/9/61 Muldraugh Hill, dis 7/17/65 Lexington, age 20, dark hair, blue eyes, fair skin, 5-4, m/in as veteran volunteer 3/7/64, b Fayette Co. PA, house 169, s 1,2.
ROTHWELL, JOHN B. reg 14, co E, enr 10/15/61 Ashland, enl 12/10/61 Louisa, dis 1/31/65 Louisa, age 26, residence stated on muster roll, house n/c, s 1, 2,4.
ROUS, GEORGE M. reg 14, co A, enr 10/1/61 Louisa, enl 12/10/61 Louisa, dis 9/15/65 Louisville, age 19, dark hair, blue eyes, light skin, 5-7, trans to 14th Vet. Inf., enl 2/29/64, m/in 3/15/64, b Greenup Co., residence stated on muster roll, house n/c, s 1,2,4.
ROUSE, JOHN. reg 14Cav, co M, r com sgt, enr 12/25/62 Owsley Co., enl 2/13/63 Irvine, age 25, killed 8/16/63 Lost Creek, Breathitt Co., age 33 on census, prom to sgt 2/14/63, house 547, s 1,2.
ROUSE, RICHARD M. reg 14, co A, r sgt, enr 10/1/61 Louisa, enl 12/10/61 Louisa, dis 9/15/65 Louisville, age 25, dark hair, gray eyes, light skin, 5-9, trans to 14th Vet. Inf., enl 2/29/64, m/in 3/15/64, app sgt 6/1/62, reduced to ranks 6/1/63, house 429, s 1,2,4.
ROUSE, SAMUEL W. reg 14, co A, enr 10/1/61 Louisa, enl 12/10/61 Louisa, dis 9/15/65 Louisville, age 20, sandy hair, blue eyes, light skin, 5-7, trans to 14th Vet. Inf., enl 2/29/64, m/in 3/15/64, wounded in cheek between 7/2/64 & 8/13/64, b Greenup Co., house 429, s 1,2,4.
ROUSE, WILLIAM F. reg 14, co A, enr 8/8/62 Ashland, enl 10/6/62 Portland OH, dis 9/15/65 Louisville, age 32 or 35, dark hair, gray eyes, light skin, 5-10, trans to 14th Vet. Inf., b Greenup Co., residence stated on muster roll, house n/c, s 1,2.
RULE, ANDREW J. reg 14, co A, C, enr 8/5/63 Louisa, enl 8/27/63 Louisa, dis 9/15/65 Louisville, age 18, trans to 14th Vet. Inf., age 18, house 435, s 1,2,4.
RULE, ANDREW W. reg 14, co E, enr 10/15/61 Ashland, enl 12/10/61 Louisa, dis 1/31/65 Louisa, age 20, house 436, s 1,2,4.
RUNYON, GEORGE W. reg 5Va, co G, enr 10/25/62 Ceredo, dis 10/3/64 Wheeling, age 23, trans to Invalid Corps 12/15/63, house 60, s 1,27.
RUNYON, HARVEY. reg 14, co C, enr 10/25/61 Louisa, enl 12/10/61 Louisa, dis 1/31/65 Louisa, age 31, light hair, blue eyes, fair skin, 5-6, b Pike Co., house 56, s 1,2,4.
RUNYON, JOHN MILTON. 22EM, co B, enl 5/26/64, dis 6/28/64, age 18, dark hair & skin, gray eyes, 5-4, b Boyd Co., house 315, s 2,4.
RUSSELL, MATHIES. reg 14, co D, A, enr 10/20/61 Louisa, enl 12/10/61 Louisa, dis 9/15/65 Louisville, age 18, dark hair, eyes & skin, 5-5, trans to 14th Vet. Inf., enl 2/29/64, m/in 3/15/64, b Wayne Co. VA, residence stated on muster roll, house n/c, s 1,2,4.

S

SADDLER, ANDREW. reg CG, co K, enr 7/3/64 Boyd Co., enl 7/28/64 Frankfort, dis 3/11/65 Catlettsburg, age 18, light hair, blue eyes, fair skin, 5-5, b Russell Co. VA, house 212, s 2,4.
SCOTT, JAMES. reg 14, co A, C, enr 10/15/61 Louisa, enl 12/10/61 Louisa, dis 9/15/65 Louisville, age 18, light hair, gray eyes, dark skin, 5-1, trans to 14th Vet. Inf., enr 2/29/64, m/in 3/15/64, b Lawrence Co. OH, residence stated on muster roll, house 513, s 1,2,4.
SEATON, JAMES. reg 45, co F&S, r adjutant, enr 11/9/63 Ashland, enl 11/10/63 or 12/9/63 Louisa, dis 12/24/64 Catlettsburg, age 28, house A136, s 1,2.
SEXTON, GREENVILLE or GREENBURY. reg 14, co C, B, enr 8/7/63 Louisa, enl 10/31/63 Catlettsburg, dis 9/15/65 Louisville, age 19, trans to 14th Vet. Inf., house 188, s 1,2,5.

SEXTON, PASCHAL. reg 5Va., co G, enr & enl 10/19/61 Ceredo, dis 10/3/64 or 7/22/65 Wheeling, age 19, dark hair, hazel eyes, fair skin, 5-7, re-enlisted as veteran volunteer, enl & m/in 12/25/63, wounded in finger near Manassas VA 8/29/62, wounded in foot in Battle of Lynchburg VA 6/17/64, b Boyd Co., house 188, s 1,5,20,27.

SHALL, GEORGE. reg 14, co F, enr 11/19/61 Louisa, enl 12/10/61 Louisa, age 38, black hair, hazel eyes, dark skin, 5-2, dis 2/16/62 for disability of ruptured hernia, b Bavaria, house 353, s 1,2,4.

SHINER, DENNIS. reg 22EM, co A, r sgt, enl 5/26/64, dis 6/28/64, age 23, light hair & skin, dark eyes, 5-3, b Providence RI, house C62, s 2,4.

SHOCKEY, GEORGE W. reg 14, co C, enr 10/25/61 Louisa, enl 12/10/61 Louisa, age 18, light hair, blue eyes, fair skin, 5-2, dis by civil authorities 3/62 as a minor, age 13 on census, b Carter Co., house 48, s 1,2.

SHOCKEY, WILLIAM H. reg 22EM, co A, enl 5/26/64 Catlettsburg, dis 6/28/64, age 20, light hair & skin, blue eyes, b Carter Co., house 48, s 2,4.

SHUFF, SAMUEL. reg 2Cav, co E, enr 7/14/61 Camp Jo Holt, Boyd Co., enl 9/9/61 Muldraugh Hill, dis 3/20/63, age 19, light hair, blue eyes, fair skin, 5-10, on detached duty with 1st Ky. Artillery, wounded right shoulder, Battle of Chaplin Hills (Perryville) 10/8/62, dis on surgeon's certificate of disability, b Fayette Co. PA, house 641, s 1,2.

SINGER, BENJAMIN W. reg 2Cav, co E, enr 7/14/61 Camp Jo Holt, enl 9/9/61 Muldraugh Hill, dis 4/27/64 Camp Chase, age 18, brown hair, hazel eyes, dark skin, 5-4, wounded right shoulder with clavicle fracture Battle of Steven's Gap GA 9/11/63 or 9/20/63, cap Steven's Gap 9/19/63, paroled City Point 10/28/63, residence stated as Ashland, KY, house C72, s 1,2,5.

SLING, ROBERT. reg 14Cav, co C, enr 8/6/62 Boyd Co., enl 8/21/62 Mt. Sterling, dis 9/16/63 Maysville, age 30, residence stated on muster roll, house n/c, s 1,2,4.

SMITH, ELIJAH. reg 14, co E, enr 10/15/61 Ashland, enl 12/10/61 Louisa, dis 1/31/65 Louisa, age 34, residence stated on muster roll, house n/c, s 1,2,4.

SMITH, HENRY. reg 14, co C, enr 10/25/61 Louisa, enl 12/10/61 Louisa, dis 1/31/65, CSR: "resides in Boyd Co.", house 433, s 1,2,4.

SMITH, JAMES. reg 91st Ohio Infantry, co F, r cpl, enr 8/1/62, dis 1/24/65, app cpl 6/18/64, house A104, s 5, A. H. Windsor, History of the 91st Regiment, O.V.I.

SMITH, JOHN H. reg 14, co C, enr 10/225/61 Louisa, enl 12/10/61 Louisa, dis 1/31/65 Louisa, age 23 or 24, house A102, s 1,2,4.

SMITH, PETER. reg 5Va, co G, enr 10/2/61 Ceredo, age 28, brown hair, blue eyes, light skin, 5-9, dis 9/12/62 on surgeon's certificate of disability of deformity of right foot, b Wayne Co. VA, house C33, s 1,27.

SMITH, SAMUEL. reg 14, co C, H, enr 10/29/63 Louisa, enl 10/30/63 Louisa, dis 9/15/65 Louisville, age 18 or 20, house 486, s 1,4.

SMITH, WILLIAM. reg 14th Ohio Heavy Artillery, co F, enr 1862, dis 1865, house 566, s 5,33.

SNEAD, JAMES A. reg 40, co F&S, r chaplain, enr 10/15/63 Grayson, enl 10/15/63 Cincinnati, dis 12/30/64 Catlettsburg, house C31, s 1,2,4.

SNEAD, ROBERT C. reg 40, co C, E, F&S, r 2nd lt, enr 8/1/63 Grayson, enl 9/28/63 Grayson, dis 12/30/64 Catlettsburg, age 20, prom to QM sgt 9/28/63, app 2nd lt 12/1/63 or 5/17/64, house C31, s 1,2,4.

SNODDY, WILLIAM M. reg 14, co E, r sgt, enr 10/15/61 Ashland, enl 12/10/61 Louisa, dis 1/31/65 Louisa, age 22 or 26, prom from cpl to sgt 7/1/62, "shell stunned" between 7/2/64 & 8/13/64, house 593, s 1,2,4.

SPARKS, HENRY. reg 14, co A, C, enr 10/1/61 or 4/22/63 Ashland, enl 4/22/63 Louisa, dis 7/10/65 Camp Dennison OH, age 32, trans to 14th Vet. Inf., house 379, s 1,2,4.

SPARKS, THOMAS J. reg 2Cav, co E, r farrier, enr 7/14/61 Camp Jo Holt, enl 9/9/61 Muldraugh Hill, dis 9/26/64 Nashville TN, age 24, house 266, s 1,2.

SPEICHT, FRANCIS. reg 5Va, co B, F&S, r sgt, drum major, enr & enl 9/2/61 Camp Pierpont, Ceredo, dis 9/23/64 Wheeling, age 23 or 29, trans to NCO staff 6/63, prom to drum major 8/63, reduced to ranks 7/24/64, house 686, s 1,27.

SPERRY, JAMES H. reg 14, co F, A, r capt, enr 11/19/61 Louisa, enl 12/10/61 Louisa, dis 9/15/65 Louisville, age 26 or 29, trans to 14th Vet. Inf., app 3rd sgt 4/21/62, prom to 2nd lt 5/12/63, prom to 1st lt 8/11/64 or 9/12/64, 8/23/65 mustered out as 1st lt, co H, to accept captain's rank, CSR: "12/61 at home sick Boyd Co.", house 102, s 1,2,4.

SPURLOCK, MARINE F. reg CG, co E, enr 6/5/64 Catlettsburg, enl 7/4/64 Frankfort, dis 3/11/65 Catlettsburg, age 18, light hair, blue eyes, fair skin, 5-2, age 24 on census, b Boone Co. VA., house A117, s 2.

STARKEY, CHARLES. reg 26, co D, enl 9/26/64 Greenupsburg, dis 7/10/65 Salisbury NC, age 29, dark hair, blue eyes, fair skin, 5-10, b Floyd Co., house 552, s 1,5.

STARKEY, JOHN H. reg CG, co E, enr 5/31/64 Catlettsburg, enl 7/4/64 Frankfort, dis 10/29/64 Frankfort, age 32, dark hair, blue eyes, fair skin, 6-1, b Floyd Co., house 552, s 2,4.

STARKEY, ROBERT. reg 22EM, co B, enl 5/26/64, dis 6/28/64, age 35, dark hair, eyes & skin, 6-3, b Floyd Co., house 484, s 2,4.

STEED, AARON. reg 189th Ohio Infantry, co I, house C54, s 26,33.

STEELE, DANIEL W. reg 22, co B, r 1st lt, enr 11/9/61 Camp Swigart, enl 1/10/62 Louisa, dis 1/31/65 Louisville, age 24, app 2nd sgt 11/9/61, prom to 1st sgt 2/12/62, prom to 2nd lt 10/21/62, prom to 1st lt 12/14/63, house 228, s 1,2,4.

STEPHENS, JAMES M. reg 2Cav, co E, r sgt, enr 8/27/61 Camp Jo Holt, enl 9/9/61 Muldraugh Hill, dis 7/17/65 Lexington NC, age 30, dark hair, blue eyes, light skin, 6-0, reduced to ranks 11/1/62, enl Vet. Vol. 2/1/62, m/in 3/7/64, cap & paroled Rough & Ready GA 9/18/64, cap Waynesboro GA 11/21/64, paroled Sisters Ferry GA 5/4/65, right arm amputated from injury received in battle 11/28/64 Waynesboro GA, hospital records indicate he was Boyd Co. resident, b Ashland, house 671, s 1,2.

STEPHENSON, CALVARY. reg 14, co C, enr 10/25/61 Catlettsburg, enl 12/10/61 Louisa, dis 1/31/65 Louisa, age 23, dark hair, eyes & skin, 5-6, b Wayne Co., residence stated on muster roll, house n/c, s 1,2,4.

STEWART, ANDREW J. reg 40, co C, r sgt, enr 8/14/63 Grayson, enl 9/26/63 Grayson, dis 1/30/64 Catlettsburg, age 23, residence stated on muster roll, house n/c, s 1,2,4.

STEWART, THOMAS L. reg 14, co A, enr 10/1/61 Louisa, enl 12/10/61 Louisa, dis 12/31/62 Richmond, age 36, dark hair, eyes & skin, 5-8, dis 12/31/62 for disability of leg ulcer, b Fayette Co. PA, house 539, s 1,2,4.

STEWART, WILLIAM. reg 40, co K, enr 7/30/63 Grayson, enl 9/29/63 Grayson, dis 12/20/64 Catlettsburg, age 44, missing Mt. Sterling 6/9/64, house 660, s 1,2.

SULLIVAN, JOHN. reg 5Va, co F, enr & enl 9/2/61 Camp Pierpont, Ceredo, dis 6/19/65 Wheeling, age 21, cap Salem VA 6/21/64, confined Andersonville GA, escaped 5/7/65, reported to Camp Chase 6/15/65, house 134, s 1,26,27.

SULLIVAN, THOMAS. reg 22EM, co B, enl 5/26/64, dis 6/28/64, age 18, dark hair, eyes & skin, 6-0, b Wayne Co., house 134, s 2,4.

T

TABB, GEORGE S. reg 146th Ohio Infantry, co I, enl 5/2/64, dis 9/7/64 Camp Dennison OH, age 22, house 529, s 26,33.

TAYLOR, GEORGE W. reg 14, co A, C, enr & enl 10/6/62 Portland OH, dis 9/15/65 Louisville, age 16 or 18, brown hair, blue eyes, light skin, 5-6, trans to 14th Vet. Inf., b Floyd Co., house 254, s 1,2,4.

TAYLOR, WILLIAM. reg 14, co A, r cpl, enr 10/1/61 Louisa, enl 12/10/61 Louisa, dis 1/31/65 Louisa, age 20, light hair, gray eyes, fair skin, 5-11, b Greenup Co., app cpl 4/64, house 254, s 1,2,4.

THOMAS, ALFRED J. reg 14, co A, enr 10/1/61 Louisa, enl 12/10/61 Louisa, dis 1/31/65 Louisa, age 18 or 19, house C144, s 1,2,4.

THOMAS, DAVID C. reg 14, co A, F&S, r 1st lt, enr 10/1/61 Louisa, enl 12/10/61 Louisa, dis 9/15/65 Louisville, age 18, trans to 14th Vet. Inf., enl 2/29/64, m/in 3/15/64, prom to 1st sgt 2/26/63, app sgt major 1/1/64, m/in as 1st lt 8/12/65, house C121, s 1,2,4.

THOMAS, EVAN D. reg 22, co G, r capt, enr 10/25/61 Grayson, enl 1/10/62 Louisa, age 28, prom from 1st lt to capt 1/6/63, app aide de camp to Col. deCoursey 8/62, wounded in explosion of munitions 5/1/63 or 5/16/63, d 12/20/63 Plaquemine LA of chronic diarrhea, residence stated on muster roll & List of Officers, house n/c, s 1,2,4,32.

THOMAS, HARRISON. reg 10Cav, co F, enr 8/9/62 Boyd Co., enl 9/9/62 Covington, dis 9/17/63 Maysville, age 20 or 23, age 14 on census, house 268, s 1,2,4.

THOMAS, JAMES A. reg 54, co A, r sgt, enr & enl 9/5/64 Greenupsburg, dis 9/1/65 Louisville, age 21, dark hair & skin, blue eyes, 5-8, b Rowan Co., credited 9th Congressional District, prom to sgt 2/28/65, house 268, s 1,2.

THOMAS, RHYS M. reg 14, co A, F&S, r lt col, enr 10/1/61 Louisa, enl 12/10/61 Louisa, age 29, prom from capt co A to major 1/28/63, to lt col 9/29/64, residence stated on muster roll & List of Officers, house n/c, s 1,2,4,32.

THORNTON, JOHN WESLEY. reg 10Cav, co F, r 2nd sgt, enr 8/9/62 Boyd Co., enl 9/9/62 Covington, dis 9/17/63 Maysville, app 2nd sgt 8/18/62 reg 45, co B, r 1st lt, enr 5/8/64 Lexington, enl 5/11/64 Catlettsburg, dis 12/24/64 Catlettsburg, age 20, commissioned by Governor, reg 53, co I, r 1st lt, enl 4/19/65, m/in 6/27/65 Louisville, dis 9/15/65 Louisville, residence stated on muster roll & List of Officers, house A54, s 1,2,32.

TILSLEY, HERBERT. reg 14, co C, r cpl, enr 10/15/61 Louisa, enl 12/10/61 Louisa, dis 1/31/65 Louisa, age 24, prom to cpl 2/27/63, CSR: "Staffordshire, England, mine engineer", residence stated on muster roll, house n/c, s 1,2,4.

TILSLEY, WILLIAM. reg 22EM, co B, r sgt, enl 5/26/64, dis 6/28/64, age 23, dark hair & skin, blue eyes, 5-7, age 16 on census, b Boyd Co., house 680, s 2,4.

TINSLEY, THOMAS. reg 10Cav, co F, enr 8/9/62 Boyd Co., enl 9/9/62 Covington, dis 9/17/63 Maysville, age 19, residence stated on muster roll, house n/c, s 1,2,4.

TOLER, LEWIS. reg 14, co A, enr 10/1/61 Louisa, enl 12/10/61 Louisa, dis 1/31/65 Louisa, age 18, house 407, s 1,2,4.

TRIPLETT, JOSEPH. reg 5Va, co G, H, enr 8/24/61 Ceredo, enl 9/2/61 Ceredo, dis 9/21/64 Wheeling, age 19, auburn hair, blue eyes, fair skin, 5-7, trans to co H 11/29/61, house 503, s 1,27.

TURMAN, JAMES W. reg 14, co C, r sgt, enr 10/10/61 Louisa, enl 12/10/61 Louisa, dis 1/31/65 Louisa, age 22, prom from cpl to sgt 10/16/63, house 91, s 1, 2,4.

TWIMAN, WILLIAM. reg 14, co E, enr 8/1/63 Louisa, enl 8/29/62 Louisa, age 18, light hair & skin, blue eyes, 5-7, b Greenup Co., d 7/31/64 Chattanooga TN of disease, house 367, s 1,2,4.

U

ULIN, LEWIS R. reg 40, co K, r 5th sgt, enr 8/21/63 Grayson, enl 9/29/63 Grayson, dis 12/20/64 Catlettsburg, age 18, missing Mt. Sterling 6/9/64, house 356, 1, 2.

V

VAUGHAN, BENJAMIN. reg 22EM, co A, enl 5/26/64, dis 6/28/64, age 22, black hair, gray eyes, dark hair, 5-11, house 13, s 2,4 5.

W

WALKER, WILLIAM. reg 10Cav, co F, enr 8/9/62 Boyd Co., enl 9/9/62 Covington, dis 9/17/63 Maysville, age 21, residence stated on muster roll, house n/c, s 1,2,4.
WALTERS, EMANUEL. reg5Va, co G, r sgt, enr 8/8/61 Camp Pierpont, enl 9/2/61 Ceredo, dis 10/3/64 Wheeling, age 27, prom to cpl 1/23/62, to sgt 9/1/63, d 8/5/64 army hospital, Charleston WV, house 622, s 1,27.
WARD, WILLIAM P. reg 14, co F r cpl, enr 11/19/61 Louisa, enl 12/10/61 Louisa, age 43, dark hair & skin, gray eyes, 5-8, app cpl 11/19/64, reduced to ranks, b Columbiana Co. OH, d 11/24/64 Ashland of chronic nephritis, house 267, s 1,2,4.
WAYMER, JAMES P. reg 5Va, co G, r capt, enr 8/12/61 Camp Pierpont, enl 9/2/61 Ceredo, dis 10/3/64 Wheeling, age 20, prom from 1st sgt to 2nd lt 1/3/63, prom to capt 9/8/63, house 226, s 1,27.
WEAVER, JOHN. reg 9th Ohio Infantry, enl 2/22/64, dis 8/15/65, house 685, s 5,33.
WEISE, JOHN W. reg 14, co E, r cpl, enr 10/15/61 Ashland, enl 12/10/61 Louisa, dis 1/31/65 Louisa, age 26, residence on muster roll, house n/c, s 1,2,4.
WELLS, JOSEPH. reg 14, co C, enr 10/25/61 Louisa, enl 12/10/61 Louisa, dis 1/31/65 Louisa, age 20, residence on muster roll, house n/c, s 1,2,4.
WENCH or WENSH, GEORGE. reg 2Cav, co E, enr 9/3/61 Camp Jo Holt, enl 9/9/61 Muldraugh Hill, dis 7/17/65 Lexington NC, age 42, regimental teamster, enl Vet. Vol. 2/1/64, m/in 3/7/64, CSR: "absent sick at home in Greenup Co., Ky.", but he is not on Greenup Co. census, house 670, s 1,2.
WEST, JAMES R. reg 14, co A, r cpl, enr 10/1/61 Louisa, enl 12/10/61 Louisa, age 20, died 7/2/62 Camp Baird, Cumberland Gap of lung congestion & heart failure, house 540, s 1,2,4.
WEST, JOEL. reg 14, co A, enr 10/1/61 Louisa, enl 12/10/61 Louisa, dis 1/31/65 Louisa, age 26, age 35 on census, house 541, s 1,2,4.
WHITE, ALFRED F. reg 5Va, co G, r sgt, enr 8/20/61 Camp Pierpont, enl 9/2/61 Ceredo, dis 10/3/64 or 7/22/65 Wheeling, age 21, yellow hair, gray eyes, light skin, 6-2, wounded in action 8/29/62, prom to cpl 9/1/63, prom to sgt 6/13/64, re-enlisted as veteran volunteer, b Cabell Co. VA, age 29 on census, house 113, s 1, 5,20,27.
WHITE, HENRY. reg 14, co F, A, r 2nd lt, enr 10/25/61, Camp Wallace, Louisa, enl 12/10/61 Louisa, dis 1/31/65 Louisa, age 23, prom to 2nd lt 11/1/62, trans from co F to co A & reduced to ranks 11/12/63, back to co F 1/26/65, house 113, s 1,2.
WHITE, JAMES. reg 5Va, co G, r cpl, enr 8/29/61 Camp Pierpont, enl 9/2/61 Ceredo, dis 7/21/65 Cumberland MD, age 23 or 25, light hair & skin, blue eyes, prom to cpl 1/3/63, reduced to ranks 10/5/63, prom to cpl 6/13/64, killed in battle 9/22/64, b Carter Co., house 466, s 1,27.
WHITE, JAMES K. POLK. reg 45, co G, r cpl, enr 11/2/63 Ashland, enl 11/30/63 Ashland, dis 2/14/65 Catlettsburg, age 19, black hair, blue eyes, fair skin, 5-8, prom to cpl 8/31/64, b Greenup Co., house 369, s 1,2,5.
WHITE, JOHN. reg 39, co H, I, enr 12/14/62 Pike Co., enl 6/10/63 Louisa, dis 9/15/65 Louisville, age 23 or 30, trans to co H 7/1/63, house C114, 1,2.
WHITE, SYLVESTER. reg 14, co H, enr 10/25/61 Catlettsburg, enl 12/10/61 Louisa, age 30, light hair, blue eyes, fair skin, died 8/8/64 of wounds near Marietta GA, muster roll lists Lawrence Co. as residence, but he is not on Lawrence Co. census, house 636, s 1,2,4.

WHITMORE, WIILIAM T. reg 14, co A, enr Ashland, enl 12/10/61 Louisa, dis 9/17/64 Ashland, age 24, dark hair & skin, black eyes, 5-6, dis for disability of conjunctivitis, b Westmoreland Co. VA, house 545, s 1,2,4.

WHITTEN, JAMES C. reg 14 co A, r capt, enr 10/1/61 Louisa, enl 12/10/61 Louisa, dis 1/31/65 Louisa, age 22, prom from 1st sgt to 2nd lt 7/5/62, to 1st lt 11/17/62, to capt 6/20/64, wounded 6/20/64 Foster's farm in right hip, residence stated on muster roll & List of Officers, house n/c, s 1,2,4,32.

WILLIAMS, THADDEUS. reg 14Cav, enr 8/16/62 Boyd Co., enl 8/21/62 Mt. Sterling, dis 9/16/63 Maysville, age 22, cap & paroled 3/2/63 Mt. Sterling by Col. Roy Cluke, residence stated on muster roll, house n/c, s 1,2,4.

WILLIAMSON, RICHARD. reg 45, co F, r 1st lt., enr 8/25/63 Peach Orchard, enl 11/2/63 Ashland, dis 12/24/64 Catlettsburg, age 35, dark hair, eyes & skin, 5-6, residence stated on List of Officers, house n/c, s 1,2,6.

WILLIAMSON, RICHARD C. reg 39, co E, enr 10/25/62, reg 14, co H, enr 5/1/63 Louisa, enl 8/29/63 Louisa, age 18, light hair, blue eyes, fair skin, 5-5, died 11/29/64 New Albany IN phthisis pulmonalis (tuberculosis), b Lawrence Co., house A112, s 1,4.

WILLIAMSON, RICHARD T. reg 39, co E enr 10/25/62 Catlettsburg, age 18 rem d 10/29/62 Catlettsburg, house A112, s 1,4.

WILMORE, MARTIN. reg 5Va, co A, r cpl, enr 8/10/61 Ceredo, enl 9/2/61 Ceredo, dis 10/3/64 Wheeling, age 21 or 26, light hair, blue eyes, fair skin, prom to cpl 1/1/62, dis Washington DC for disability from gunshot wound in left hand 9/22/62, b Lawrence Co. OH, house C160, s 1,27.

WILSON, GEORGE. reg 45, co G, enr 11/4/63 Ashland, enl 11/30/63 Ashland, dis 4/13/65 Louisville, age 18 or 20, dark hair, blue eyes, fair skin, 5-6, cap near Gessey Station VA, released Aiken's Landing VA 2/17/65, b Ohio, house A29, s 1,2.

WILSON, LLOYD. reg 22, co B, enr 11/9/61 Camp Swigart, enl 1/10/62 Louisa, dis 1/20/65 Louisville, pow from 6/2/64 to 11/8/64, CSR refers to home in Greenup Co., but he is not on Greenup census, house 558, s 1,2,26.

WILSON, RICHARD. reg 14, co C, r cpl, enr 10/10/61 Louisa, enl 12/1/61 Louisa, dis 1/31/65 Louisa, age 32, house 23, s 1,2,4.

WILSON, WILLIAM. reg 45, co D, H, enr 7/14/63 Catlettsburg, enl 10/17/63 Ashland, dis 12/24/64 Catlettsburg, age 18, trans from co D to co H 2/1/64, back to co D 5/20/64, house A29, s 1,2.

WISE, EDWARD C. reg 45, co E, r 1st sgt, enr 9/1/63 Catlettsburg, enl 11/6/63 Ashland, dis 12/24/64 Catlettsburg, age 18, prom from sgt to 1st sgt 1/1/64, house A55, s 1,2.

WITHROW, AFLRED. reg 54 co F, enr & enl 9/3/64 Greenupsburg, dis 9/1/65 Louisville, age 29, light hair, blue eyes, fair skin, 5-8, b Greenup Co., credited to 9th Congressional District, house 618, s 1,2.

WOLFF, AUGUSTUS HENRY. reg 5Va, co E, r sgt, enr 8/2/61 Ceredo, enl 9/2/61 Ceredo, dis 10/4/64 Wheeling, age 22, app sgt 12/27/61, house C159, s 1, 27.

WOLFF, DAVID B. reg 5Va, co E, enr & enl 9/15/61 Ceredo, dis 10/3/64 Wheeling, age 26, dis 9/2/63 to accept promotion in 3rd Va. Cav., reg 3rd Va. Cav., co K, m/in Charleston WV, commissioned by West Virginia governor as captain, dismissed from service 10/27/64 by order of the President, b Scioto Co. OH, house C158, s 1,27.

WORKMAN, HARMON. reg 14, co F, A, D, enr 5/20/63 Louisa, enl 10/31/63 Louisa, dis 9/15/65 Louisville, trans to 14th Vet. Inf., trans from co F to co A 11/12/63, back to co F 1/20/65, residence stated on muster roll, house n/c, s 1,2, 4.

WORTHINGTON, CHARLES S. reg 40, co C, enr 8/8/63 Grayson, enl 9/26/62 Grayson, dis 12/30/64 Catlettsburg, age 20, house C108, s 1,2,4.

WORTHINGTON, DAVID L. reg 14, co F, r capt, enr 11/19/61 Louisa, enl 12/10/61 Louisa, age 31, app 2nd lt 11/19/61, prom to capt 5/8/62, resigned 6/12/62 because of bad health, residence stated on muster roll, house n/c, s 1,2,4, 32.

Y

YORK, ANDREW E. reg 68EM, co C, enl 5/21/64, dis 6/22/64, age 25, dark hair, blue eyes, fair skin, 5-10, reg CG, co L, enl 6/8/64, m/in 7/6/64 Frankfort, m/out 3/11/65 Catlettsburg, b Ohio, credited to Lawrence Co., but he is not on Lawrence Co. census, house A40, s 1,2,4,5.

YORK, GLAUCUS H. reg 10Cav, co F, enr 8/9/62 Boyd Co., enl 9/9/62 Covington, dis 9/17/63 Maysville, reg 22EM, co B, enl 5/26/64, dis 6/28/64, age 22, dark hair & skin, blue eyes, 5-2, b Boyd Co., house A73, s 1,2,4.

YORK, JAMES M. reg 45, co E, r 5th sgt, enr 9/5/63 Catlettsburg, enl 11/6/63 Ashland, dis 12/24/64 Catlettsburg, age 16 or 18, light hair, dark eyes, fair skin, reduced to ranks from sgt 5/1/64, b Wayne Co., house A73, s 1,2,26.

YORK, THOMAS. reg 10Cav, co F, enr 8/9/62 Boyd Co., enl 9/9/62, dis 9/17/63 Maysville, reg 22EM, co A, r sgt, enl 5/26/64, dis 6/28/64, age 18, dark hair & eyes, light skin, b Wayne Co., house A40, s 1,2,4.

YOUNG, DAVID G. R. reg 10Cav, co F, enr 8/9/62 Boyd Co., enl 9/9/62 Covington, age 18, name not found on subsequent rolls of the company, residence stated on muster roll, house n/c, s 1,4.

YOUNG, JAMES. reg 14, co C, enr 10/25/61 Louisa, enl 12/10/61 Louisa, age 18, d 2/22/63 Louisa or Ashland of disease, residence stated on muster roll, house n/c, s 1,2,4.

Z

ZEIGLER, JOHN. reg 22EM, co B, enl 5/26/64, dis 6/28/64, age 19, light hair & eyes, fair skin, 6-0, b Wayne Co., house n/c, s 2.

FLOYD COUNTY UNION SOLDIERS

A

ADAMS, ALFRED. reg 14, co I, enr 11/10/61 Louisa, enl 12/10/61 Louisa, age 19, fair hair, blue eyes, 5-10, dark skin, rem d 8/19/62 Cumberland Gap typhoid fever, house F171, s 1,2,4.

ADAMS, JAMES. reg 39, co A, r cpl, enr 10/11/62 Johnson Co., enl 2/16/63 Peach Orchard, dis 9/15/65 Louisville, age 37, light hair, blue eyes, fair skin, 5-10, house F50, s 1,2,4.

ADAMS, WILLIAM. reg 39, co K, enr 11/16/62, enl 2/16/63 Peach Orchard, dis 9/15/65 Louisville, age 25, light hair, blue eyes, fair skin, 6-1, house W268, s 1,2,4.

ADKINS, GEORGE A. reg 39, co C, enr 9/30/62, enl 2/16/63 Peach Orchard, dis 9/15/65 Louisville, age 25, residence stated on muster roll, house n/c, s 2,4.

AKERS, ANDREW J. reg 39, co B, r 1st sgt, enr 11/16/62 Floyd Co., enl 2/16/63 Peach Orchard, dis 9/15/65 Louisville, age 18, dark hair & skin, hazel eyes, 5-4, prom to sgt 8/1/63, red to pvt 9/1/64, app sgt 11/4/64, house W291, s 1,2,4,8.

AKERS, JAMES. reg 39, co A, enr 9/6/62 Johnson Co., enl 2/16/63 Peach Orchard, dis 9/15/65 Louisville, age 18, light hair, gray eyes, fair skin, 5-3, house W42, s 1,2,4.

AKERS, JAMES M. reg 39, co B, enr 9/6/62 Louisa, enl 2/16/63 Peach Orchard, age 16 or 24, light hair, blue eyes, fair skin, 5-7, rem d 4/5/63 Ashland of disease, residence stated on muster roll, house n/c, s 1,2,4.

AKERS, WILLIAM. reg 39, co A, enr 9/6/62 Johnson Co., enl 2/16/63 Peach Orchard, dis 9/15/65 Louisville, age 27, black hair, gray eyes, dark skin, 5-10, residence stated on muster roll, house n/c, s 1,2,4.

ALDRIDGE, ALI. reg 167WV, co Sampson Kirk, reg 39, co C, I, enr 11/5/62 or 10/20/62 Pike Co., enl 2/16/63 Peach Orchard, dis 9/15/65 Louisville, age 27 or 31, dark hair & skin, black eyes, 5-8, trans to co I, house W341, s 1,2,4,23.

ALLEN, ANDREW J. reg 39, co F, enr 12/5/62, enl 7/16/63 Peach Orchard, dis 9/15/65 Louisville, age 19, black hair, blue eyes, fair skin, 5-8, house F221, s 1,2,4.

ALLEN, DAVID. reg 39, co F, enr 5/16/63 Louisa, enl 6/11/63 Louisa, rem des 6/20/63 Paintsville, house F221 or F616, s 1.

ALLEN, GEORGE J. reg 39, co F, r 1st lt, enr 12/18/62, enl 2/16/63, Peach Or-chard, age 43, rem cap 1/28/63 Floyd Co., dis 11/4/64 for rheumatism, house F293, s 1,2,4.

ALLEN, JOHN. reg 45, co G, enr 11/8/63 Louisa, enl 11/30/63 Ashland, dis 2/14/65 Catlettsburg, age 22 or 24, black hair, dark eyes, fair skin, 5-9, rem b Johnson Co., house F321, s 1,2,6.

AUSTIN, THOMAS. reg 39, co B, enr 11/16/62 Pike Co., enl 2/16/63 Peach Orchard, dis 9/15/65 Louisville, age 21, light hair, blue eyes, dark skin, 5-6, residence stated on muster roll, house n/c, s 1,2,4.

B

BALDWIN, ALEXANDER. reg 39, co B, r cpl, enr 11/7/62 Floyd Co., enl 2/16/63 Peach Orchard, dis 9/15/65 Louisville, age 28, dark hair, blue eyes, fair skin, 5-8, house W255, s 1,2,4.

BALDWIN, JARVY. reg 39, co B, enr 2/6/63, enl 2/16/63 Peach Orchard, dis 9/15/65 Louisville, age 23, black hair & eyes, dark skin, 6-1, house W164, s 1,2,4.

BALDWIN, JOHN W. reg 39, co B, enr 11/7/62 Floyd Co., enl 2/16/63 Peach Orchard, dis 9/15/65 Louisville, age 26, light hair, blue eyes, fair skin, 5-7, residence stated on muster roll, house n/c, s 1,2,4.

BANDY, THOMAS. reg 14, co K, enr 5/25/63, enl 5/28/63 Louisa, age 23, des 5/11/64 Louisa, residence stated on muster roll, house n/c, s 2,4.

BANKS, WILLIAM. reg CG, co G, enr 6/9/64, enl 7/6/64 Frankfort, dis 3/11/65 Catlettsburg, age 18, light hair, blue eyes, fair skin, 5-9, house F175, s 2,4.

BARNETT, JOHN L. reg 14, co H, enr 10/25/61 Catlettsburg, enl 12/10/61 Louisa, age 25, dark hair, blue eyes, fair skin, 6-0, des 3/10/62 Paintsville; supposed to be dead, residence stated on muster roll, house n/c, s 1,2,4.

BARNETT, NELSON. reg 39, co F, enr 6/4/63 Lawrence Co., enl 6/11/63 Lawrence Co., dis 9/15/65 Louisville, age 21, dark hair, gray eyes, fair skin, 6-1 residence stated on muster roll, house n/c, s 1,2,4.

BEGLEY, JOHN. reg 39, enr 12/8/62 Floyd Co., age 35, dark hair and skin, black eyes, cap 2/10/63 Floyd Co., house F275, s 1,4.

BENTLEY, JAMES. reg 14, co H, enr 10/25/61 Catlettsburg, enl 12/10/61 Louisa, dis 1/31/65 Louisa, age 32, dark hair & skin, gray eyes, 5-10, cap & paroled at Richmond 8/30/62, residence stated on muster roll, house n/c, s 1,2,4.

BENTLEY, WILLIAM. reg 39, co K, enr 10/10/63, enl 10/30/63 Louisa, dis 9/15/65 Louisville, age 19, black hair & eyes, dark skin, 5-9, house F504, s 1,2,4.

BLANKENSHIP, MITCHELL. reg 39, co K, 11/16/62 Pike Co., enl 2/16/63, dis 9/15/65 Louisville, age 22, light hair, blue eyes, fair skin, 5-10, cap 12/4/62 Floyd Co., returned 5/20/63, house W267, s 1,2,4.

BOLIN, ENOCH. reg 39, co F, enr 12/8/62 Floyd Co., enl 7/16/63 Peach Orchard, dis 9/15/65 Louisville, age 18, black hair & eyes, dark skin, 5-9, cap 1/28/63 Floyd Co., house F311, s 1,2,4.

BOLIN, RICE. reg 39, co F, enr 12/8/62 Floyd Co., enl 7/16/63 Peach Orchard, dis 9/15/65 Louisville, age 20, black hair & eyes, dark skin, 5-8, cap 6/27/63 Breathitt Co., house F311, s 1,2,4.

BOND, JOHN. reg 167 WV, co Sampson Kirk, house W344, s 23.

BOOTH, HARRISON. reg 65, co B, enl 5/21/64, dis 6/12/64, age 40, dark eyes, hair & skin, 5-6, house W215, s 1.

BOOTH, JAMES. reg CG, co K, enr 6/9/64, enl 7/28/64 Frankfort, dis 3/11/65 Catlettsburg, age 18, black hair & eyes, dark skin, 5-7, house W215, s 2,4.

BOW, ANDREW J. reg 14, co B, enr 10/10/61 Louisa, enl 12/10/61 Louisa, dis 1/31/65 Louisa, age 21, dark hair, blue eyes, fair skin, 5-5, house W41, s 1,2,4.

BOW, HARGIS. reg 39, co A, enr 9/6/62, Johnson Co., enl 6/11/63 Louisa, dis 9/15/65 Louisville, age 44, black hair, blue eyes, dark skin, 5-10, house W41, s 1,2,4.

BOW, JAMES. reg 39, co A, enr 10/18 or 10/23/62 Johnson Co., enl 2/16/63 Peach Orchard, dis 9/15/65 Louisville, age 28, light hair, blue eyes, fair skin, 5-9, house W41, s 1,2,4.

BOW, WILLIAM. reg 39, co A, enr 9/6/62 Johnson Co., enl 2/16/63 Peach Orchard, dis 9/15/65 Louisville, age 18, light hair, blue eyes, fair skin, 5-4, house W41, s 1,2,4.

BRADLEY, ELIAS. reg 39, co F, enr 11/16/62 Floyd Co., enl 10/30/63 Louisa, dis 9/15/65 Louisville, age 23, black hair & eyes, dark skin, 5-8, house F229, s 1,2,4.

BRANHAM, GEORGE W. reg 39, co C, enr 11/8/62 Pike Co., enl 2/16/63 Peach Orchard, dis 9/15/65 Louisville, age 18, black hair & eyes, dark skin, 5-11, cap 12/8/62 Floyd Co., returned to duty, house W147, s 1,2,4,8.

BROWN, GEORGE R. reg 14, co H, enr 10/25/61, enl 12/10/61 Louisa, age 41, black hair, blue eyes, fair skin, 6-0, des 1/12/62 at Louisa or Paintsville, house F189, s 1,2,4.

BROWN, MARION. reg 39, co K, enr 11/16/62, enl 2/16/63 Peach Orchard, dis 9/15/65 Louisville, age 20, dark hair & skin, black eyes, 5-9, residence stated on muster roll, house n/c, s 1,2,4.

BROWN, SAMUEL. reg 14, co K, enr 11/8/61 Louisa, enl 12/10/61 Louisa, age 35, dark hair, blue eyes, red skin, 5-10, d Lost Mountain GA 6/3/64 of wounds received 6/2/64, house W12, s 1,2,4.

BURCHETT, LEWIS. reg 39, co C, enr 8/6/63 Louisa, enl 8/30/63 Louisa, dis 9/15/65 Louisville, age 45, dark hair & skin, gray eyes, 5-11, house W106, s 1,2,4.

BURCHETT, RICHARD L. reg 39, co A, r 2nd lt., enr 10/11/62 Johnson Co., enl 4/12/64 Lexington, dis 9/15/65 Louisville, age 21, light hair, gray eyes, fair skin, 5-11, prom from sgt to 2nd lt 4/12/64, house W29, s 1,2,4.

BURCHETT, WILLIAM. reg 14, co H, r wagoner, enr 10/25/61 Catlettsburg, enl 12/10/61 Louisa, dis 1/31/65 Louisa, age 42, gray hair, blue eyes, fair skin, 5-7, house W301, s 1,2,4.

BUSKIRK, CLINTON VAN. reg 39, co H, enr 9/5/62 Pike Co., enl 2/16/63 Peach Orchard, dis 9/15/65 Louisville, age 41, dark hair & skin, black eyes, 5-9, house F26, s 1,2,4.

C

CLARK, ISAAC LEE. reg 39, co B, enr 10/1/63 Louisa, enl 10/30/63 Louisa, dis 9/15/65 Louisville, age 19, black hair & eyes, dark skin, 5-6, house W197, s 1,2,4.

CLARK, JOHN E. reg 39, co C, r sgt, enr 9/26/62 Floyd Co., enl 2/16/63 Peach Orchard, dis 9/15/65 Louisville, age 21, light hair, gray eyes, fair skin, 5-11, cap Pike Co. 9/1/63, paroled Richmond VA 9/22/63, house W197, s 1,2,4.

CLARK, MORGAN. reg 14, co H, r cpl, enr 10/25/61 Catlettsburg, enl 12/10/61 Louisa, dis 1/31/65 Louisa, age 21 or 26, dark hair, blue eyes, fair skin, 5-10, app cpl 7/6/64, house W217, s 1,2,4.

CLARK, REUBEN. reg 45, co I, enr 12/12/63 Louisa, enl 2/4/64 Mt. Sterling, dis 2/14/65 Catlettsburg, age 18, light hair & skin, gray eyes, 5-6, rem b Pike Co., house W107, s 1,2.

CLARK, SAMUEL. reg 14, co A, enr 7/27/63, enl 8/29/63 Louisa, dis 9/15/65 Louisville, age 18, black hair & eyes, fair skin, 5-4, trans to 14 Ky Vet Inf, Co C, enr 7/27/63, m/in 8/29/63 Louisa, house W43, s 1,2,4.

CLAY, FLEMING. reg 39, r cpl, co G, enr 11/15/62, enl 2/16/63 Peach Orchard, rem d 5/28/63 Louisa, house W98, s 2,4.

CLICK, JAMES. reg 39, co F, enr 11/15/62 Floyd Co., age 25 or 35, black hair & eyes, dark skin, rem cap 2/10/63 Floyd Co., house F586, s 1,4.

CLICK, WILLIAM H. reg 39, co F, enr 5/23/64 Louisa, enl 8/30/64 Lexington, dis 9/15/65 Louisville, age 32, dark hair & skin, black eyes, 6-0, house F243, s 1,2,4.

COBURN, GEORGE. reg 39, co F, enr 7/6/63 enl 8/20/64 Louisa, age 20, light hair, blue eyes, fair skin, 5-8, rem des 8/12/64 Louisa, house F295, s 1,2,4.

COBURN, JOHN. reg 39, co F, enr 12/7/62, enl 2/16/63 Peach Orchard, age 26, rem cap 1/1/63 in Floyd Co., des 7/18/63 Floyd Co. and joined rebel army, house F324 or F325, s 1,2,4.

COLLINS, JOHN. reg 22, co F, enr 12/2/61, enl 1/10/62 Louisa, rem des 9/1/62 Cumberland Gap, house F97, s 2.

COLLINS, SANFORD. reg 45, co C, enr 11/3/63 Ashland, enl 11/4/63 Ashland, dis 12/24/64 Catlettsburg, age 16 or 18 or 20, light hair, blue eyes, fair skin, 5-5, trans to co E 5/20/64, house F97, s 1,2,6.

COLLINS, SIMON. reg 39, co F, enr 4/1/63 Lawrence Co., enl 6/11/63 Louisa, dis 9/15/65 Louisville, age 44, black hair, blue eyes, fair skin, 5-8, residence stated on muster roll, house n/c, s 1,2,4.

CONLEY, GEORGE W. reg 45, co I, enr 1/1/64 Mt. Sterling, enl 2/4/64 Mt. Sterling, dis 2/14/65 Catlettsburg, age 17 or 19, sandy hair, blue eyes, light hair, 5-8, house F94, s 1,2.

CRISP, BAILEY. reg 14, co H, enr 10/25/61 Catlettsburg, enl 12/10/61 Louisa, dis 1/31/65 Louisa, age 30, dark hair, eyes & skin, 5-8, rem des 1/28/62, returned to duty 10/1/62, house F181, s 1,2,4.

D

DAVENPORT, THOMAS. reg 39, co A, enr 10/8/62 Johnson Co., enl 2/16/62 Peach Orchard, dis 10/5/65 Louisville, age 22, light hair, blue eyes, fair skin, 5-8, residence stated on muster roll, house n/c, s 1,2,4.

DAVIS, HARVEY. reg 167 WV, co Sampson Kirk, house W354, s 23.

DAVIS, HENRY. reg 167 WV, co Sampson Kirk, house W354, s 23.

DAVIS, JAMES D. reg 45, co G, r sgt, enr 11/2/63 Ashland, enl 11/30/63 Ashland, dis 2/14/65 Catlettsburg, age 21 or 23, rem prom to sgt 5/1/64, house W354, s 1,2.

DINGUS, DAVID C. reg 39, co F, enr 11/26/62 Floyd Co., enl 2/16/63 Peach Orchard, age 24, dark hair, blue eyes, dark skin, 6-0, rem d 8/23/64 Mt. Sterling typhoid fever, house F587, s 1,2,4.

DINGUS, JAMES H. reg 39, co F, r sgt, enr 10/11/62, enl 2/16/63 Peach Orchard, dis 9/15/65 Louisville, age 26, light hair, blue eyes, fair skin, 5-9, house F239, s 1,2,4.

DOTSON, WILLIAM H. reg 39, co E, enr 3/8/63 Louisa, enl 12/24/63 Catlettsburg, dis 9/15/65 Louisville, age 26, dark hair & skin, gray eyes, 5-9, rem cap 12/28/64 Wise Co. VA, house F154, s 1,2,4.

DRAPER, JAMES N. reg 39, r surgeon, enr 9/1/63, enl 9/30/63 Lexington, dis 9/15/65 Louisville, age 59, rem prom to surgeon 6/15/64, house F26, s 1,2,4.

DUTTON, GEORGE W. reg 39, co E, r cpl, enr 11/10/62, Piketon, enl 2/16/63 Peach Orchard, age 29, dark hair, blue eyes, fair skin, 5-9, rem des Mt. Sterling 10/15/64, house W361, s 1,2,4.

DYER, WILLIAM. reg 14, co K enr 11/8/61, enl 12/10/61 Louisa, dis 1/31/65 Louisa, age 25, dark hair, gray eyes, fair skin, 5-9, residence stated on muster roll, house n/c, s 1,2,4.

E

ELLIOTT, GRANVILLE. reg 39, co K, enr 11/16/62 Piketon, enl 2/16/63 Peach Orchard, age 29, dark hair, blue eyes, fair skin, 5-9, rem d 4/9/63 Ashland typhoid fever, house W243, s 1,2,4.

ELLIOTT, ROBERT D. reg 39, co B, enr 11/6/62, enl 2/16/63 Peach Orchard, dis 9/15/65 Louisville, age 35, light hair, gray eyes, fair skin, 5-7, house W270, s 1,2,4.

ESTEP, JOEL. reg 45, co G, enr 11/20/63 Greenup Co., enl 11/30/63 Ashland, age 31 or 32, dark hair, blue eyes, fair skin, 5-6, rem d 9/10/64 Lexington of consumption, house W38, s 1,2.

F

FITZPATRICK, WILLIAM. reg 45, co F, enr 11/3/63 Peach Orchard, enl 11/30/63 Ashland, dis 12/24/64 Catlettsburg, age 22 or 28 or 32, light hair, eyes & skin, 5-11, rem trans to co G 5/20/64, house F98, s 1,2,6.

FLANERY, JOHN L. reg 39, co F, enr 11/16/62 Floyd Co., enl 8/30/63 Louisa, dis 9/15/65 Louisville, age 25, light hair, blue eyes, fair skin, 5-7, house F238, s 1,2,4.

FRASURE, CYRUS. reg 39, co B, enr 12/3/62, enl 2/16/63 Peach Orchard, dis 9/15/65 Louisville, age 24, residence stated on muster roll, house n/c, s 2,4.

FRASURE, GEORGE. reg 39, co F, enr 11/15/62 Floyd Co., age 22, light hair, blue eyes, fair skin, 5-10, cap 2/10/63 Floyd Co., residence stated on muster roll, house n/c, s 1,4.

FRASURE, WILLIAM. reg 39, co B, enr 8/12/63 Louisa, enl, 8/29/63 Louisa, dis 9/15/65 Louisville, age 23, dark hair & skin, blue eyes, 5-8, house F236, s 1,2,4.

FRAZIER, JOHN. reg 39, co F, enr 11/15/62 Floyd Co., enl 2/16/63 Peach Orchard, dis 9/15/65 Louisville, age 21, light hair, blue eyes, fair skin, 5-8, house W235, s 1,2,4.

FRILEY, WILLIAM. reg 39, co D, enr 11/5/62 Pike Co., enl 8/30/63 Louisa, age 29, light hair, blue eyes, fair skin, 5-9, des 6/12/64 returned 4/17/65 under President's proclamation, house W93, s 1,2,4.

G

GEORGE, ALBERT G. reg 14, co K, r cpl, enr 11/8/61 Louisa, enl 12/10/61 Louisa, dis 1/31/65 Louisa, age 32, dark hair, gray eyes, fair skin, 5-9, rem app cpl 12/31/62, residence stated on muster roll, house n/c, s 1,2,4.

GEORGE, JAMES H. reg 14, co K, r sgt, enr 11/8/61 Louisa, enl 12/10/61 Louisa, age 25, rem killed 8/11/64 in skirmish near Atlanta GA, house F47, s 1,2,4.

GEORGE, JOHN M. reg 14, co K, enr 4/20/63 Louisa, enl 7/28/63 Louisa, dis 9/15/65 Louisville, age 36, dark hair & eyes, fair skin, 5-10, rem trans to co C, 14 Ky Vet Inf, enr 4/30/63, m/in 7/28/63 Louisa, residence stated on muster roll, house n/c, s 1,2,4.

GEORGE, ROBERT. reg 14, co K, enr 12/10/61 Louisa, enl, 12/10/61 Louisa, dis 1/31/65 Louisa, age 31, dark hair, blue eyes, fair skin, 6-1, house F48, s 1,2,4.

GEORGE, THOMAS J. reg 14, enr 4/20/63 Louisa, enl 5/28/63 Louisa, age 18, rem des 9/7/63, presumed to have joined rebel army, residence stated on muster roll, house n/c, s 1,4.

GIBSON, RILEY. reg 39, co F, enr 11/16/62, Floyd Co., enl 2/16/63 Peach Orchard, age 44, black hair & eyes, dark skin, 6-0, rem des 6/3/65 Paintsville, residence stated on muster roll, house n/c, s 1,2,4.

GILLIAM, LILBURN. reg 39, co K, enr 10/22/62 Piketon, enl 2/16/63 Peach Orchard, age 36, dark hair, blue eyes, fair skin, 5-10, rem d 12/5/64 Louisa smallpox, residence stated on muster roll, house n/c, s 1,2,4.

GOODMAN, ANDREW J. reg 39, co F, enr 11/14/63 Floyd Co., enl 12/29/63 Louisa, dis 9/15/65 Louisville, age 43, black hair & eyes, dark skin, 5-9, residence stated on muster roll, house n/c, s 1,2,4.

GOODMAN, JOHN. reg 39, co F, enr 12/6/62 Floyd Co., enl 2/16/63 Peach Orchard, dis 9/15/65 Louisville, age 26, black hair & eyes, dark skin, 5-9, rem cap 2/10/63 Floyd Co., house F272, s 1,2,4.

GOODMAN, PLEASANT. reg 39, co F, enr 11/26/63, enl 12/29/63 Louisa, dis 9/15/65 Louisville, age 19, black hair & eyes, dark skin, 5-5, house F272, s 1,2,4.

GOODMAN, WILLIAM C. reg 39, co F, enr 6/4/63 Floyd Co., enl 6/11/63 Louisa, age 21, light hair, blue eyes, fair skin, 5-7, rem cap Floyd Co. 2/10/63, house F262, s 1,2,4.

GOODMAN, WILLIAM K. reg 39, co F, enr 12/6/62 Floyd Co., enl 12/29/63 Louisa, dis 9/15/65 Louisville, age 24, light hair, blue eyes, fair skin, 5-10, rem cap Floyd Co. 2/10/63, residence stated on muster roll, house n/c, s 1,2,4.

GREER, SAMUEL K. reg 14, co H, enr 10/25/61 Catlettsburg, enl 12/10/61 Louisa, dis 1/31/65 Louisa, age 30 or 50, gray hair, dark eyes & skin, 5-8, rem trans to co G, 39th Ky 3/11/63, trans back to original reg & co 1/20/65, trans to 14th Ky Vet Inf 1/65, house W290, s 1,2,4.

GREER, WILLIAM W. reg 39, co B, enr 8/20/63, enl 8/29/63 Louisa, dis 9/15/65 Louisville, age 18, black hair, blue eyes, dark hair, 5-7, house W290, s 1,2,4.

GUNNELL, JAMES M. reg 39, co C, enr 9/10/63 Louisa, enl 2/16/63 Peach Orchard, age 26, light hair, blue eyes, fair skin, 5-4, rem d 4/13/63 Ashland typhoid, house W219, s 1,2,4.

GUNNELS, GEORGE W. reg 39, co G, enr 12/28/63, enl 12/30/63 Louisa, dis 9/15/65 Louisville, age 18, dark hair, eyes & skin, 5-8, house W219, s 1,2,4.

H

HACKWORTH, JAMES. reg 39, co F, enr 10/15/63, enl 10/30/63 Louisa, age 18, dark hair, black eyes, fair skin, 5-5, rem des 11/8/63 Louisa, house F153, s 1,2,4.

HALE, GEORGE W. reg 14, co K, enr 11/8/61 Louisa, enl 12/10/61 Louisa, dis 9/15/65, age 19, sandy hair, blue eyes, fair skin, 5-4, rem trans to 14th Ky Vet Inf, co A, enr 2/29/64, m/in 3/15/64, wounded 9/64 and sent to hospital at Knoxville TN, house W46, s 1,2,4.

HALL, GRANVILLE. reg 39, co K, enr 2/28/64 Louisa, enl 3/29/64 Greenupsburg, age 27, dark hair & skin, black eyes, 5-6, houses W233, s 1,2,4.

HALL, HARMON. reg 39, enr 11/16/62 Pike Co., enl 2/16/63 Peach Orchard, dis 9/15/65 Louisville, age 32, black hair & eyes, dark skin, 5-9, house F507, s 1,2,4.

HALL, HENDERSON. reg 39, co B, enr 9/6/62, enl 6/10/63 Louisa, dis 9/15/65 Louisville, age 20, house W256, s 2,4.

HALL, OWEN. reg 39, co B, enr 11/6/62, enl 2/16/63 Peach Orchard, dis 9/15/65, age 29, black hair, blue eyes, dark skin, 6-1, house F503, s 1,2,4.

HALL, PRESTON. reg 39, co K, enr 10/27/62 Pike Co., enl 2/16/63 Peach Orchard, dis 9/15/65 Louisville, age 35, dark hair & eyes, fair skin, 5-9, house F72, s 1,2,4.

HALL, RILEY. reg 39, co K, enr 11/16/62 Pike Co., enl 2/16/63 Peach Orchard, dis 9/15/65 Louisville, age 25 or 35 or 38, black hair & eyes, dark skin, 5-7, house F447, s 1,2,4.

HALL, ROBERT. reg 39, co B, enr 11/18/62 Pike Co., enl 2/16/63 Peach Orchard, dis 9/15/65 Louisville, age 38, black hair & eyes, dark skin, 5-5, house W261, s 1,2,4.

HALL, SAMUEL. reg 39, co K, enr 11/16/62 Pike Co., enl 2/16/63 Peach Orchard, dis 9/15/65 Louisville, age 37, black hair & eyes, dark skin, 6-2, residence stated on muster roll, house n/c, s 1,2,4.

HALL, WILLIAM. reg 45, co G, enr 7/28/63, enl 11/30/63 Ashland, dis 2/14/65 Catlettsburg, age 18 or 34, black hair & eyes, dark skin, 5-1, house F444, s 1,2.

HALL, WILLIAM. reg 39, co B, enr 9/6/63 Louisa, enl 12/30/63 Louisa, dis 9/15/65 Louisville, age 19, dark hair, skin & eyes, 5-6, house W501, s 1,2,4.

HAMILTON, ANDREW J. reg 39, co F, enr 6/5/63, dis 12/29/64, house F201, s 5.

HAMILTON, BENJAMIN. reg 14, co H, enr 10/25/61 Catlettsburg, enl 12/10/61 Louisa, dis 1/31/65 Louisa, age 30 or 35, black hair & eyes, dark skin, 5-11, house F204, s 1,2,4.

HAMILTON, CRAIG. reg 39, co B, enr 11/6/62 Piketon, enl 2/16/63 Peach Orchard, dis 9/15/65 Louisville, age 24, black hair & eyes, dark skin, 6-0, house W245, s 1,2,4.

HAMILTON, DAVID. reg 14, co K, enr 11/8/61 Louisa, enl 12/10/61 Louisa, dis 1/31/65 Louisa, age 25, sandy hair, blue eyes, fair skin, 5-7, CSR indicates he may have moved to Lawrence Co., house F208, s 1,2,4.

HAMILTON, FREEMAN. reg 39, co B, enr 2/3/63 Piketon, enl 2/16/63 Peach Orchard, dis 9/15/65 Louisville, age 20 or 22, dark hair & skin, black eyes, 5-8, house W274, s 1,2,4.

HAMILTON, IRA. reg 14, co K, enr 11/8/61 Louisa, enl 12/10/61 Louisa, dis 9/15/65 Louisville, age 26, dark hair, eyes & skin, 5-8, served in co C, 14th Vet. Inf., house F232, s 1,2,4.

HAMILTON, JAMES. reg 39, co F, r cpl, enr 12/5/62 Floyd Co., enl 2/16/63 Peach Orchard, dis 9/15/65 Louisville, age 19, black hair & eyes, dark skin, 5-7, cap 2/10/63 in Floyd Co., house F208, s 1,2,4.

HAMILTON, JAMES J. reg 14, co I, enr & enl 3/24/62 Paintsville, dis 9/15/65 Louisville, age 21, black hair & eyes, dark skin, 5-10, served in co B, 14th Vet. Inf., house F201, s 1,2,4.

HAMILTON, JOHN. reg CG, co G, enr 8/1/64, des 9/12/64, House W292, s 2,4.

HAMILTON, JOHN. reg 39, co B, enr 12/3/62, enl 2/16/63 Peach Orchard, dis 9/15/65 Louisville, age 25, black hair & eyes, dark skin, 5-7, house W262, s 1,2,4.

HAMILTON, KENAS F. reg 39, co K, enr 10/22/62 Piketon, enl 2/16/63 Peach Orchard, age 18, black hair, dark eyes, fair skin, 5-9, rem d 12/5/64 of smallpox at Louisa regimental hospital, house W275, s 1,2,4.

HAMILTON, LEONARD. reg 39, co K, enr 2/1/63 Piketon, enl 2/16/63 Peach Orchard, dis 9/15/65 Louisville, age 21, light hair, blue eyes, fair skin, 5-11, house W279, s 1,2,4.

HAMILTON, SAMUEL. reg 39, co K, enr 11/15/62 Piketon, enl 2/16/63 Peach Orchard, age 24, dark hair, blue eyes, fair skin, 5-10, rem cap 12/5/62 Floyd Co., d in prison in Richmond VA, 2/5/63, house W262, s 1,2,4,8.

HAMILTON, WILLIAM. reg 39, co F, enr 12/5/62 Floyd Co., enl 2/16/63 Peach Orchard, age 22, light hair, blue eyes, fair skin, 5-8, rem killed 4/26/63 Louisa by accidental shot from fellow soldier's gun, house F200, s 1,2,4.

HAMILTON, WILLIAM. reg 14, co K, enr 11/8/61 Louisa, enl 12/10/61 Louisa, dis 1/31/65 Louisa, age 23 (at discharge), CSR for 5/62: "sick at home in Floyd Co.", house F214, s 1, 2.

HAMPTON, EDWARD. reg 14, co K, r cpl, enr 11/8/61 Louisa, enl 12/10/61 Louisa, dis 1/31/65 Louisa, age 26, prom to cpl 9/29/64, residence stated on muster roll, house n/c, s 1,2,4.

HANDSHOE, ADAM. reg 39, co F, enr 11/11/62 Floyd Co., enl 2/16/63 Peach Orchard, age 21, light hair, blue eyes, fair skin, 5-10, rem des 6/18/63 at Louisa, house F314, s 1,2,4.

HANDSHOE, ANDREW. reg 39, co F, enr 10/23/63, enl 10/30/63 Louisa, age 18, dark hair & skin, blue eyes, 6-0. rem des 6/1/64 at Louisa, house F124, s 1,2,4.

HANDSHOE, HARRISON. reg 39, co F, enr 11/11/62 Floyd Co., enl 2/16/63 Peach Orchard, age 21 or 46, light hair, blue eyes, fair skin, 6-3, rem des 7/18/63 at Louisa, house F314, s 1,2,4.

HARDIN, HARVEY. reg 167 WV, co Sampson Kirk, reg 68, co H, enl 5/21/64, dis 6/22/64, age 34, black eyes, dark hair & skin, 5-6, house W315, s 2,4,23.

HARKINS, JOHN J. reg 39, co B, r 2nd lt, enr 1/1/64 Paintsville, enl 3/29,64 Greenupsburg, dis 9/15/65 Louisville, age 27, light hair, blue eyes, fair skin, 5-7, rem commissioned 2nd Lt by Governor of KY 9/18/64, house F13, s 1,2,8.

HARMON, DAN. reg 167 WV, co Sampson Kirk, house F672 or W203, s 23.

HARMON, JAMES W. reg 39, co G, enr 9/13/62, enl 2/16/63 Peach Orchard, dis 9/15/65 Louisville, age 36, light hair, blue eyes, dark skin, 5-6, house W21, s 1,2,4.

HARMON, LORENZO D. reg 39, co G, r cpl, enr 9/30/62 Peach Orchard, enl 2/16/63 Peach Orchard, dis 9/15/65 Louisville, age 30, dark hair & skin, blue eyes, 5-6, house W20, s 1,2,4.

HATFIELD, OWEN. reg 39, co A, enr 10/11/62 Johnson Co., enl 1/11/63 Louisa, dis 9/15/65 Louisville, age 43, black hair, gray eyes, dark skin, 5-10, rem cap Pike Co. 12/6/62 and taken to Richmond VA, paroled 4/3/63, house F71, s 1,2,4,8.

HATFIELD, SAMUEL. reg 14, co K, enr 11/8/61 Louisa, enl 12/10/61 Louisa, dis 1/31/65 Louisa, age 27, house W59, s 1,2,4,5.

HATFIELD, SHADRACK. reg 14, co K, enr 2/14/63 Louisa, enl 2/17/63 Louisa, dis 9/15/65 Louisville, age 23, dark hair eyes & skin, 5-10, rem trans to 14th Vet Inf, enr 2/14/63, m/in 2/17/63 Louisa, house W58, s 1,2,4.

HATFIELD, WILLIAM. reg 14, co K, enr 11/8/61 Louisa, enl 12/10/61 Louisa, dis 1/31/65 Louisa, age 19, dark hair, black eyes, fair skin, 6-0, house W2, s 1,2,4.

HAYWOOD, HENRY C. reg CG, co E, enr 5/7/64, enl 7/4/64 Frankfort, dis 3/11/65 Catlettsburg, age 28, light hair, blue eyes, fair skin, 6-1, house F133, s 2,4.

HEREFORD, BEVERLY W. reg 14, r hospital steward, enr 12/17/62 Richmond KY, enl 2/18/63 Louisa, dis 10/11/63 for disability, tuberculosis, age 32, light hair, gray eyes, fair skin, 5-9, residence stated on muster roll, house n/c, s 1,2,4

HEREFORD, JAMES. reg 68, co E, enl 5/21/64, age 25, dark hair & skin, gray eyes, 5-8, house F67, s 4.

HEREFORD, JAMES H. reg 39, r surgeon, enr 2/17/63, enl 6/10/63 Louisa, rem dismissed 1/31/63, house F67, s 2,4.

HITE, ANDREW J. reg 14, co K, enr 11/8/61 Louisa, enl 12/10/61 Louisa, dis 1/31/65 Louisa, age 21, sandy hair, gray eyes, fair skin, 5-9, house W55, s 1,2,4.

HITE, CHARLES ROBERT. reg 39, co A, enr 10/11/62 Johnson Co., enl 8/30/63 Louisa, dis 9/15/65 Louisville, age 28, rem CSR states he was sick at home in Lawrence Co. on 9/10/64, residence stated on muster roll, house n/c, s 1,4.

HOLBROOK, RANDOLPH. reg 39, co F, enr 12/11/62, enl 8/30/63 Louisa, age 23, black hair & eyes, dark skin, 6-0, rem des 8/12/64 at Louisa, house F168, s 1,2,4.

HOWARD, ELIJAH. reg 14, co H, enr 9/20/63, Louisa, enl 10/30/63 Louisa, dis 9/15/65 Louisville, age 26, dark hair & eyes, fair skin, 5-11, rem trans to 14th Vet Inf, co C, enr 9/20/63, m/in 10/30/63 Louisa, house F196, s 1,2,4.

HOWARD, ELIJAH. reg 16, co A, enl 4/3/62 Prestonsburg, dis 7/24/65 Lexington, age 25 or 26, residence stated on muster roll, house n/c, s 1,4.

HOWARD, ELISHA. reg 167 WV, co Sampson Kirk, reg 14, co H, enr 9/9/63 Louisa, enl 10/30/63 Louisa, dis 9/15/65 Louisville, age 30, dark hair, eyes & skin, 5-8, rem trans to 14th Vet Inf, co C, enr 9/9/63, m/in 10/30/63 Louisa, house W330, s 1,2,4,23.

HOWELL, JOHN. reg 39, co B, enr 9/6/62 Louisa, enl 8/29/63 Louisa, dis 9/15/65 Louisa, age 20, light hair, blue eyes, dark skin, 5-9, house F429, s 1,2,4.

HUEY, ROBERT S. reg 39, r adjutant, enr 8/1/63, enl 10/29/63 Louisa, dis 9/15/65 Louisville, age 50, rem prom to quartermaster sgt 10/1/63, to adjutant 1/22/65, residence stated on list of officers, house n/c, s 1,2,4,8.

HUGHES, WALTER. reg 39, co F, enr 12/4/62 Floyd Co., enl 2/16/63 Peach Orchard, dis 9/15/65 Louisville, age 21, light hair, blue eyes, fair skin, 6-3, rem cap 1/28/63 Floyd Co., house F194, s 1,2,4.

J

JACKSON, DAVID. reg 167 WV, co Sampson Kirk, house W336, s 23.

JAMES, WILLIAM C. reg 39, co C, enr 7/18/63 Floyd Co., enl 8/30/63 Louisa, age 30, dark hair, blue eyes, fair skin, 5-9, rem d 5/10/64 at Ashland of measles & pneumonia, house W96, s 1,2,4.

JOHNSON, JAMES E. reg 14, co K, enr 11/8/61 Louisa, enl 12/10/61 Louisa, age 36, black hair, blue eyes, fair skin, 6-0, rem des 3/27/62 Ashland, house F144, s 1,2,4.

JOHNSON, JAMES M. reg 45, co K enr 11/24/63 Relief, enl 12/9/63 Louisa, dis 2/19/65, age 45, house F563, s 1,2.

JOHNSON, WILLIAM W. reg 14, co K, enr 11/8/61 Louisa, age 20, rem d 12/8/61 Louisa of measles, house F233, s 1,4.

JONES, AMBROSE. reg 39, co B, enr 11/7/62 Piketon, enl 2/16/63 Peach Orchard, dis 9/15/65 Louisville, age 26, light hair, blue eyes, fair skin, 5-8, house W266, s 1,2,4.

JOSEPH, NELSON. reg 14, co F, enr l8/3/63 Salyersville, enl 8/3/63 Louisa, age 19, rem des 5/12/64 Louisa, house F206, s 1,2,4.

JUSTICE, CAMBRIDGE. reg 14, co E, enr 10/15/63 Louisa, enl 10/29/63 Louisa, age 18, black hair, blue eyes, fair skin, 5-9, rem d 8/17/64 Knoxville TN of disease, house F376, s 1,2,4.

JUSTICE, EDMUND. reg 39, co F, enr 1/1/62 Floyd Co., enl 2/16/63 Peach Orchard, dis 9/15/65 Louisville, age 27, dark hair, blue eyes, fair skin, 5-9, house F266, s 1,2,4.

JUSTICE, JACKSON. reg 39, co F, enr 4/15/64, age 38, light hair, blue eyes, fair skin, 5-8, rem cap 4/24/64 Floyd Co., d 9/2/64 at Andersonville GA prison of anasarca (swelling), house F245, s 1,2,4,8.

JUSTICE, THOMAS. reg 14, co E, enr 8/1/63 Louisa, enl 8/29/63 Louisa, dis 9/15/65 Louisville, age 18, dark hair, gray eyes, light hair, 5-9, rem trans to 14th Vet Inf, co C, enr 8/1/63, m/in 10/29/63 Louisa, house F376, s 1,2,4.

K

KEATHLEY, OLIVER G. reg 39, co B, enr 9/16/62, enl 2/16/63 Peach Orchard, dis 9/15/65 Louisville, age 23, dark hair, gray eyes, fair skin, 5-9, house W212, s 1,2,4.

KELLEY, HARVEY. reg 39, co C, enr 11/4/62, enl 2/16/63 Peach Orchard, dis 9/15/65 Louisville, age 18, dark hair, gray eyes, fair skin, 5-8, residence stated on muster roll, house n/c, s 1,2,4.

KELLEY, WILLIAM. reg 39, co C, enr 11/4/62 Pike Co., enl 2/16/63 Peach Orchard, dis 9/15/65 Louisville, age 39, dark hair & skin, blue eyes, 6-0, residence stated on muster roll, house n/c, s 1,2,4.

KENDRICK, AUGUSTUS E. reg 39, co F, r 1st lt, enr 10/2/63 Louisa, enl 10/30/63 Louisa, dis 9/15/65 Louisville, age 32, rem prom from sgt to 1st lt 11/21/64, List of Officers gives Lawrence Co. as residence, house F287, s 1,2,4.

KIDD, JAMES. reg 39, co C, enr 11/8/62, enl 2/16/63 Peach Orchard, dis 9/15/65 Louisville, age 18, light hair, gray eyes, fair skin, 5-8, rem cap 12/4/62, house W224, s 1,2,4.

KIDD, WILLIAM. reg 39, co C, enr 11/8/62 Floyd Co., enl 2/16/63 Peach Orchard, age 21, light hair, gray eyes, fair skin, 5-9, rem cap 12/4/62 Floyd Co. & exchanged, d 5/1/64 Louisa of measles & pneumonia, house W224 or W225, s 1,2,4.
KILE, ROBERT. reg 39, co F, enr 11/8/62 Floyd Co., enl 2/16/63 Peach Orchard, dis 9/15/65 Louisville, age 25, light hair, blue eyes, fair skin, 6-0, residence stated on muster roll, house n/c, s 1,2,4.
KIRK, JAMES T. reg 167 WV, co Sampson Kirk, house W356, s 23.
KIRK, SAMPSON, reg 167 WV, co Sampson Kirk, r capt., reg 68, co H, enl 5/21/64, dis 6/22/64, age 35, dark eyes, hair & skin, 5-10, house W335, s 2,4,23.
KIRK, THOMAS. reg 167 WV, co Sampson Kirk, reg 68, co H, enl 5/21/64, dis 6/22/64, age 26, gray eyes, dark hair, light skin, 5-8, house W357, s 2,4,23.

L

LAFERTY, JAMES. reg 65, co A, enl 5/21/64, rem des 5/64, house F540, s 4.
LAYNE, JAMES C. reg 68, co C, enl 5/21/64, age 24, fair hair & skin, blue eyes, 5-10, house F542, s 4.
LAYNE, JOHN L. reg 68, co I, enl 5/21/64, dis 6/22/64, age 25, light hair, blue eyes, fair skin, 5-8, house W148, s 2,4.
LAYNE, LINDSEY. reg 39, r quartermaster, co C, enr 11/1/62, enl 2/16/63 Peach Orchard, dis 9/15/65 Louisville, age 44, dark hair & skin, gray eyes, 5-6, rem prom from quartermaster sgt to regimental quartermaster 7/1/63, house W300, s 1,2,4.
LAYNE, SAMUEL. reg 68, co C, r cpl, enl 4/7/64, 5/21/64, dis 4/16/64, 6/22/64, age 18, blue eyes, dark hair, fair skin, 5-8, house W300, s 2,4.
LAYNE, TANDY M. reg 39, co C, r Quartermaster sgt, enr 10/18/62 Pike Co., enl 2/16/63 Peach Orchard, dis 9/15/65 Louisville, age 19, light hair, blue eyes, fair skin, 6-0, rem prom from pvt co C to Q.M. sgt. 7/1/65, house W300, s 1,2,4.
LEEK, THOMPSON. reg 65, co A, enl 5/21/64, rem des 6/30/64, house F53, s 4.
LEWIS, JAMES MARION. reg 39, co B, enr 11/7/62 Pike Co., enl 2/16/63 Peach Orchard, dis 9/15/65 Louisville, age 23, dark hair, blue eyes, fair skin, 5-6, house W220, s 1,2,4.
LEWIS, WILLIAM. reg 45, co F, enr 8/21/63 Peach Orchard, enl 11/2/63 Ashland, dis 12/24/64 Catlettsburg, age 19 or 28, light hair, eyes & skin, 5-10, house W302, s 1,2.
LITTON, JAMES H. reg 1st U.S.Vol. Inf., co D, enl 1/29/64 Point Lookout, MD, m/in 5/1/64 Norfolk, VA, m/out Ft. Leavenworth, KS 11/27/65, age 35, light skin, dark hair, blue eyes, 5-11, house W82, s 2,25.

M

MARCUM, THOMAS. reg 39, co I, enr 11/23/62 Pike Co., enl 2/16/63 Peach Orchard, dis 9/15/65 Louisville, age 35, light hair, blue eyes, fair skin, 5-5, house W347, s 1,2,4.
MARSHALL, HENRY. reg 65, co A, enl 5/21/64, rem des 6/64, house F625, s 4.
MARTIN, GEORGE. reg 39, co F, enr 8/8/63, enl 8/30/63 Louisa, dis 9/15/65 Louisville, age 30, dark hair, blue eyes, fair skin, 5-9, house F415, s 1,2,4.
MARTIN, SIMPSON. reg 39, co F, enr 12/12/63 Louisa, enl 12/29/63 Louisa, dis 9/15/65 Louisville, age 18, light hair, blue eyes, fair skin, 5-10, house F419, s 1,2,4.
MARTIN, WILLIAM. reg 39, co F, enr 12/5/62 Floyd Co., enl 2/16/63 Peach Orchard, age 24, light hair, blue eyes, fair skin, 6-0, rem des 4/10/63 Peach Orchard, house F372, s 1,2,4.
MARTIN, WYATT. reg 39, co F, enr 10/3/63, enl 10/30/63 Louisa, dis 9/15/65 Louisville, age 19, light hair, blue eyes, fair skin, 6-0, house F419, s 1,2,4.

MAYNARD, ISAAC. reg 39, co E, enr 11/10/62 Pike Co., enl 2/16/63 Peach Orchard, dis 9/15/65 Louisville, age 43, dark hair & skin, blue eyes, 5-8, residence stated on muster roll, house n/c, s 1,2,4.

MCCOY, ANDREW J. reg 39, co E, enr 9/10/62, enl 2/16/63 Peach Orchard, trans from co C 10/29/63, age 44, light hair, blue eyes, fair skin, 6-0, CSR: died at home in Floyd Co. of fever 12/11/63, house n/c, s 1,2,4,8.

MCCOY, ANDREW J. reg 68, co H, enl 5/21/64, dis 6/22/64, age 25, black eyes, dark hair & skin, 5-10, house W311, s 2,4.

MCCOY, PLEASANT. reg 68, co H, enl 5/21/64, dis 6/22/64, age 44, black eyes, dark hair & skin, 5-6, house W311, s 2,4.

MCGUIRE, DAVID. reg 45, co K, enr 12/8/63 Louisa, enl 12/9/63 Louisa, dis 2/14/65 Catlettsburg, age 17 or 22 or 23, dark hair, blue eyes, fair skin, 5-10, house F620, s 1,2,6.

MCGUIRE, WILLIAM. reg 39, co F, enr 3/27/64 Louisa, enl 3/29/64 Greenupsburg, age 26, black hair, blue eyes, dark skin, 6-3, rem d 6/15/64 of wounds received in action 6/12/64 Cynthiana, house F611, s 1,2,4.

MEAD, JOHN P. reg 39, co K, enr 5/5/64 Greenupsburg, enl 2/16/65, dis 9/15/65 Louisville, age 18, light hair, blue eyes, fair skin, 5-11, house W298, s 2,4.

MEADE, LORENZO D. reg 39, co A, enr 5/20/63 Johnson Co., enl 6/11/63 Louisa, dis 9/15/65 Louisville, age 24, black hair, gray eyes, dark skin, 5-6, house W43, s 1,2,4.

MEADE, RODES. reg 45, co E, enr 9/20/63 Catlettsburg, enl 11/6/63 Ashland, dis 12/14/64 Catlettsburg, age 19, gray hair, light eyes, fair skin, 5-6, rem cap Wayne Co. WV 4/17/64, house W298, s 1,2,6.

MEAD, RHODES. reg CG, co K, enr 6/9/64, enl 7/28/64 Frankfort, dis 3/11/65 Catlettsburg, house W299, s 2,4.

MEAD, RHODES W. reg 39, co K, enr 3/10/64 Louisa, enl 3/29/64 Greenupsburg, dis 9/15/65 Louisville, age 18, light hair, blue eyes, fair skin, house W298 or F481, 5-8, s 1,2,4.

MEAD, ROBERT. reg 39, co B, enr 11/6/62, enl 2/16/63 Peach Orchard, dis 9/15/65 Louisville, age 20, dark hair & skin, black eyes, 5-10, house W298, s 1,2,4.

MOLES, FRANCIS M. reg 14, co K, enr 11/8/61, enl 12/10/61 Louisa, dis 1/31/65, age 21, dark hair, black eyes, fair skin, 6-1, rem wounded in thigh between 6/4 & 7/4/64, house F60, s 1,2,4.

MOORE, SAMPSON. reg 39, co C, enr 11/4/62 Pike Co., enl 2/16/63 Peach Orchard, age 32 or 45, light hair, blue eyes, fair skin, 5-9, rem d 4/9/65 at Ashland of consumption, house F314, s 1,2,4.

MOORE, SAMUEL. reg 167 WV, co Sampson Kirk, house W312, s 23.

MORGAN, HIRAM. reg 39, co F, enr 11/15/62 Floyd Co., enl 2/16/63 Peach Orchard, dis 9/15/65 Louisville, age 22, black hair & eyes, dark skin, 5-11, house F603, s 1,2,4.

MORGAN, WILLIAM. reg 14, co H, rem des before muster, reg 39, co F, enr 12/8/62 Floyd Co., enr 2/16/63 Peach Orchard, dis 9/15/65 Louisville, age 22, black hair & eyes, dark skin, 5-10, rem cap 2/11/63 in Floyd Co., house F229, s 1,2,4.

MOSLEY, SAMUEL. reg 39, co F, enr 9/23/63 Floyd Co., enl 10/30/63 Louisa, dis 9/15/65 Louisville, age 19, light hair, blue eyes, fair skin, 5-9, house F613, s 1,2,4.

MOSLEY, WILLIAM. reg 39, co G, enr 12/4/62, enl 2/16/63 Peach Orchard, age 22, rem cap 12/4/62 Floyd Co., des 7/2/63 at Piketon, house F538, s 2,4.

MULLINS, ISHAM. reg 39, co C, enr 11/5/62 Johnson Co., enl 6/11/63 Louisa, dis 9/15/65 Louisville, age 18, black hair & eyes, dark skin, 5-8, house W313, s 1,2,4.

MULLINS, MARSHAL. reg 39, co C, enr 4/21/63 Pike Co., enl 6/11/63 Louisa, dis 9/15/65 Louisville, age 39, black hair, gray eyes, dark skin, 5-8, house W313, s 1,2,4.

MUNCY, JAMES H. reg 167WV, co Sampson Kirk, reg 45 co E, enr 11/4/63 Ashland, enl 11/6/63 Ashland, dis 12/24/64 Catlettsburg, age 16 or 20 or 21, light hair, gray eyes, fair skin, 5-10, rem trans to co F, 2/21/64, back to co E, 5/20/64, house W346 or W352, s 1,2,23.
MUNCY, THOMAS. reg 167WV, co Sampson Kirk, reg CG, co L, enr 6/8/64, enl 7/6/64 Frankfort, dis 3/11/65 Catlettsburg, age 28, dark hair & skin, blue eyes, 5-11, house W350, s 2,4,23.
MUNCY, WILLIAM. reg 167WV, co Sampson Kirk, house W345 or W346, s 23.
MUSIC, GEORGE W. reg 39, co A, enr 9/11/62, enl 1/11/63 Louisa, dis 9/15/65 Louisville, age 44, rem cap and paroled, house F58, s 1,2.
MUSIC, JOHN W. reg 14, co K, enr 11/8/61 Louisa, enl 12/10/61 Louisa, dis 1/31/65 Louisa, age 21, black hair & eyes, fair skin, 5-9, house F58, s 1,2,4.
MUSIC, THOMAS W. reg 39, co A, enr 10/11/62 Peach Orchard, enl 2/16/63 Peach Orchard, dis 9/15/65 Louisville, age 34, rem captured and paroled, residence stated on muster roll, house n/c, s 1,2,4.

N

NELSON, JACOB. reg 39, co F, enr 11/13/62 Floyd Co., enl 2/13/63 Peach Orchard, dis 9/15/65 Louisville, age 26, light hair, blue eyes, fair skin, 5-10, house F157, s 1,2,4.
NESBITT, WILLIAM H. reg 39, co C, enr 11/8/62 Floyd Co., enl 2/16/63 Peach Orchard, dis 9/15/65 Louisville, age 18, dark hair, blue eyes, fair skin, 5-8, rem cap 12/8/62 Floyd Co., residence stated on muster roll, house n/c, s 1,2,4.
NEWSOM, HENRY. reg 39, co C, enr 11/4/62 Peach Orchard, enl 2/16/63 Peach Orchard, dis 9/15/65 Louisville, age 25, dark hair, blue eyes, fair skin, 6-2, house W322, s 1,2,4.

O

ONEY, JOHN C. U.S. Army, house F326, s 31.
ONEY, THEOPHILUS. reg 39, co F, enr 12/3/62 Floyd Co., age 21, light hair, blue eyes, fair skin, 5-11, rem cap 2/10/63 in Floyd Co., residence stated on muster roll, house n/c, s 1,4.
OSBORN, DAVID. reg 39, co C, enr 11/26/62, enl 10/30/63 Louisa, dis 9/15/65 Louisville, age 24, red hair, blue eyes, fair skin, 6-0, rem cap 1/1/63 in Floyd Co., house F590, s 1,2,4.
OSBORN, JAMES. reg 45, co K, enr 12/2/63 Ashland, enl 12/9/63 Louisa, dis 2/14/65 Catlettsburg, age 18 or 22, light hair, gray eyes, dark skin, 5-4, house F631, s 1,2,6.
OSBORNE, JONAS. reg CG, co E, enr 5/14/64, enl 7/4/64 Frankfort, dis 3/11/65 Catlettsburg, house F285, s 2,4.
OSBORNE, REPTS. reg 39, co F, enr 6/5/63 Louisa, age 31, light hair, blue eyes, fair skin, 5-9, house F590, s 1.
OSBURN, THOMAS. reg 39 co F, enr 6/3/63 Lawrence Co., enl 6/11/63 Louisa, dis 9/15/65 Louisville, age 22, light hair, blue eyes, fair skin, 5-10, house F590, s 1,2,4.
OSBORN, WILLIAM. reg 39, co F, enr 12/6/63, enl 2/16/63 Peach Orchard, dis 9/15/65 Louisville, age 22, light hair, blue eyes, fair skin, 5-9, house F285, s 1,2,4.
OUSLEY, HAGER. reg 39, co F, enr 12/28/62 Floyd Co., age 19, light hair, blue eyes, fair skin, 5-10, rem cap 2/10/63 in Floyd Co., residence stated on muster roll, house n/c, s 1,4.
OUSLEY, JOHN. reg 39, co F, enr 12/27/62 Floyd Co., age 33, light hair, blue eyes, fair skin, 5-9, rem cap 2/10/63 Floyd Co., house F289, s 1,4.
OUSLEY, THOMAS. reg 39, co F, enr 12/28/62 Floyd Co., age 21, black hair, blue eyes, fair skin, 6-0, rem cap 2/10/63 Floyd Co., residence stated on muster roll, house n/c, s 1,4.

OWENS, JOHN. reg 39, co F, enr 2/2/63 Lawrence Co, enl 2/16/63 Peach Orchard, dis 9/15/65 Louisville, age 22, light hair, blue eyes, fair skin, 6-0, house F322, s 1,2,4.

P

PARSLEY, JOHN. reg 167 WV, co Sampson Kirk, house W344, s 23.
PARSLEY, MOSES. reg 167 WV, co Sampson Kirk, reg 68, co H, enl 5/21/64, age 36, dark hair & eyes, light skin, 6-0, house W343, s 4,23.
PARSLEY, SAMUEL. reg 167 WV, co Sampson Kirk; reg 39 co I, enr 10/4/62, enl 2/16/63 Peach Orchard, dis 9/15/65 Louisville, age 21, black hair, dark eyes, fair skin, 6-0, house W359, s 1,2,4.
PATTON, HARVEY. reg 39, co F, enr 12/5/62 Floyd Co., enl 2/16/63 Peach Orchard, dis 9/15/65 Louisville, age 32, black hair & eyes, dark skin, 5-11, rem cap 1/28/63 in Floyd Co., house F274, s 1,2,4.
PATTON, HENRY. reg 39, co F, enr 12/5/62 Johnson Co., enl 2/16/63 Peach Orchard, age 22, dark hair, black eyes, fair skin, 6-0, rem cap 6/27/63 Breathitt Co., d of typhoid or pneumonia at Andersonville GA or Richmond VA, house F259, s 1,2,4,8.
PATTON, HIRAM B. reg 39, co F, enr 12/5/62 Floyd Co., enl 2/16/63 Peach Orchard, dis 9/15/65 Louisville, age 35, black hair & eyes, dark skin, 5-10, rem cap 2/10/63 in Floyd Co., house F263, s 1,2,4.
PATTON, JOHN SR. reg 39, co F, enr 12/6/62 Floyd Co., enl 6/11/63 Louisa, dis 9/15/65 Louisville, age 25 or 33, black hair & eyes, dark skin, 5-10, rem cap 2/10/63 Floyd Co., residence stated on muster roll, house n/c, s 1,2,4.
PATTON, JOHN. reg 39, co F, enr 12/4/63, enl 12/29/63 Louisa, dis 9/15/65 Louisville, age 24, rem cap 2/10/63 in Floyd Co., house F244, s 1,4.
PATTON, JOHN P. reg 39, co F, enr 11/15/62 Floyd Co., enl 2/16/63 Peach Orchard, dis 9/15/65 Louisville, age 19, dark hair, black eyes, dark skin, 5-7, residence stated on muster roll, house n/c, s 1,2,4.
PATTON, JOHN R. reg 39, co F, enr 12/5/62, enl 2/16/63 Peach Orchard, dis 9/15/65 Louisville, age 18, black hair & eyes, dark skin, 6-0, rem cap 2/10/63 in Floyd Co., residence stated on muster roll, house n/c, s 1,2,4.
PATTON, ROBERT. reg 39, co F, enr 12/3/62 Peach Orchard, enl 2/16/63 Peach Orchard, dis 9/15/65 Louisville, age 18, residence stated on muster roll, house n/c, s 1,2,4.
PATTON, SAMUEL. reg 39, co F, enr 12/15/62 Floyd Co., enl 2/16/63 Peach Orchard, age 20, black hair & eyes, dark skin, 6-1, rem cap 2/10/63 in Floyd Co., house F244, s 1,2,4.
PATTON, STEPHEN. reg 39, co F, enr 12/8/62 Floyd Co., enl 2/16/63 Peach Orchard, dis 9/15/65 Louisville, age 20, light hair, blue eyes, fair skin, 5-11, residence stated on muster roll, house n/c, s 1,2,4.
PATTON, WILLIAM. reg 39, co F, enr 11/27/62, enl 2/16/63 Peach Orchard, dis 9/15/65 Louisville, age 35, rem cap 2/10/63 in Floyd Co., house F261, s 2,4.
PATTON, WILLIAM. reg 39, co F, enr 12/11/62 Floyd Co., enl 2/16/63 Peach Orchard, age 22, black hair & eyes, dark skin, rem cap Breathitt Co. 6/27/63, d at Andersonville GA, residence stated on muster roll, house n/c, s 1,2,4,8.
PITTS, ALFRED. reg 39, co F, enr 6/25/63 Louisa, enl 8/30/63 Louisa, age 22, light hair, blue eyes, fair skin, 5-8, rem des 2/1/64 from Louisa, house F71, s 1,2,4.
PORTER, SAMUEL. reg 39, co E, enr 9/16/62 Piketon, enl 2/16/63 Peach Orchard, dis 9/15/65 Louisville, age 30, dark hair, eyes, & skin, 5-11, house F8, s 1,2,4.
PRATER, ELIAS. reg 45, co, enr 11/30/63 Ashland, enl 11/30/63 Ashland, age 18 or 32, rem trans to 4th Ky Vet Inf. 5/5/64, house F121, s 1,2.
PRATER, GEORGE. reg 45, co C, enr 10/5/63 Ashland, enl 11/30/63 Ashland, dis 2/19/65 Catlettsburg, age 13 or 18, house F211, s 1,2.

PRATER, JAMES. reg 39, co F, enr 7/20/63, enl 8/30/63, dis 5/25/65 Covington, age 33, dark hair, blue eyes, fair skin, 6-0, rem dis for disability, house F307, s 1,2,4.

PRATER, JOHN. reg 45, co G, enr 7/28/63 Mt. Sterling, enl 11/30/63 Ashland, age 14 or 20, rem d 3/20/64 in Bath or Rowan Co. of fever or measles, house F296, s 1,2.

PRATER, JOHN. reg 39, co D, enr 7/30/64, enl 8/25/64 Greenupsburg, dis 9/15/65 Louisville, age 24, light hair, blue eyes, fair skin, 5-4, house F298, s 2,4.

PRATER, NEWMAN. reg 39, co F, enr 12/5/62 Floyd Co., enl 6/1/63 Louisa, dis 9/15/65 Louisville, age 24, light hair, blue eyes, fair skin, 6-0, house F300, s 1,2,4.

PRATER, WILEY G. reg 39, co F, enr 5/27/64 Louisa, enl 6/29/64 Lexington, dis 9/15/65 Louisville, age 18 or 35, light hair, blue eyes, dark skin, 5-10, house F216, s 1,2,4.

PRATER, WILLIAM. reg 39, co F, enr 12/7/62 Floyd Co., enl 6/11/63 Louisa, dis 9/15/65 Louisville, age 40, light hair, blue eyes, fair skin, 6-0, house F296, s 1,2,4.

PRESTON, CALVIN. reg 39, co F, r 2nd lt., enr 12/18/62 Floyd Co., enl 2/16/63 Peach Orchard, dis 9/15/65 Louisville, age 30, light hair, blue eyes, fair skin, 5-10, house F591, s 1,2,4.

R

RATLIFF, JAMES. reg 39, co F, r cpl, enr 12/5/62 Floyd Co., enl 2/16/63 Peach Orchard, dis 9/15/65 Louisville, age 25, black hair & eyes, dark skin, 5-9, rem cap 1/28/63 in Floyd Co., residence stated on muster roll, house n/c, s 1,2,4.

RATLIFF, ROBERT J. reg 39, co F, r cpl, enr 12/20/62, dis 9/15/65, house F271, s 1,5.

RATLIFF, WILLIAM. reg 39, co F, enr 12/6/62 Floyd Co., enl 2/16/63 Peach Orchard, age 22, black hair & eyes, dark skin, 6-1, rem d 5/1/63 at Ashland of typhoid fever, house F226, s 1,2,4.

REFFETT, DANIEL. reg 39, co F, enr 12/6/62 Floyd Co., enl 2/16/63 Peach Orchard, dis 9/15/65 Louisville, age 28, black hair & eyes, dark skin, 5-7, house F269, s 1,2,4.

REFFETT, JOSEPH. reg 39, co F, enr 1/7/63 Floyd Co., enl 2/16/63 Peach Orchard, dis 9/15/65 Louisville, age 25, dark hair, blue eyes, fair skin, 5-8, rem cap 1/28/63 in Floyd Co., residence stated on muster roll, house n/c, s 1,2,4.

RILEY, JOHN. reg 39, co C, enr 11/6/62, enl 2/16/63 Peach Orchard, dis 9/15/65 Louisville, age 22, dark hair, blue eyes, fair skin, 5-7, residence stated on muster roll, house n/c, s 1,2,4.

RILEY, THOMAS. reg 39, co K, enr 11/23/62, enl 2/16/63 Peach Orchard, dis 9/15/65 Louisville, age 20, dark hair, eyes & skin, 5-9, residence stated on muster roll, house n/c, s 1,2,4.

ROBERSON, GEORGE W. reg 14, co K, r 1st sgt, enr 11/8/61 Louisa, enl 12/10/61 Louisa, dis 1/31/65 Louisa, age 24, rem prom from cpl to sgt 7/1/63, to 1st sgt 2/29/64, residence stated on muster roll, house n/c, s 1,2,4.

ROBINSON, HARRISON. reg 45, co K, enr 12/8/63, enl 12/9/63 Louisa, rem trans to 4th Ky Vet Inf 7/19/64, house F611, s 1,2.

ROBINSON, HARVEY H. reg 39, co F, enr 11/10/62 Floyd Co., enl 2/16/63 Peach Orchard, age 31, black hair & eyes, dark skin, 6-0, rem cap 1/1/63 in Floyd Co., des 9/11/65 at Louisa, house F608, s 1,2,4.

ROBINSON, HENRY. reg 14, co K, enr & enl 5/28/63 Louisa, dis 9/15/65 Louisville, age 18, rem trans to 14th Vet Inf, co C, enr & m/in 5/28/63 Louisa, house F54, s 1,2,4.

ROBINSON, JOHN O. reg 14, co K, enr 11/8/61, Louisa, enl 12/10/61 Louisa, dis 1/31/65 Louisa, age 20, dark hair, black eyes, fair skin, 5-8, residence stated on muster roll, house n/c, s 1,2,4.

ROBINSON, THOMAS J, JR. reg 14, co K, enr 7/6/63, enl 8/28/63 Louisa, age 30, d 8/20/64 Nashville TN, residence stated on muster roll, house n/c, s 2, 4.

S

SALISBURY, WILLIAM T. reg 39, co B, enr 10/15/62 Catlettsburg, enl 2/16/63 Peach Orchard, dis 9/15/65 Louisville, age 21, dark hair, blue eyes, fair skin, 5-9, house F527, s 1,2,4.

SALMONS, THOMAS. reg 68, co H, enl 5/21/64, dis 6/22/64, house F577, s 2,4.

SALMONS, WILLIAM R. reg 39, co G, enr 11/17/62, enl 2/17/63 Peach Orchard, age 21, rem d 5/15/63 at Ashland, house F583, s 2,4.

SALYER, RILEY. reg 39, co F, enr 6/26/63 Floyd Co., enl 8/30/63 Louisa, dis 9/15/65 Louisville, age 18, light hair, blue eyes, fair skin, 6-0, house F317, s 1,2,4.

SAMMONS, JOHN. reg 39, co F, enr 11/15/62 Floyd Co., age 22, black hair & eyes, dark skin, 5-8, rem cap 2/10/63 in Floyd Co., house F575, s 1,4.

SELLARDS, DRURY L. reg 1ST U.S. Vol. Inf., co D, enl 1/29/64 Point Lookout MD, m/in 5/1/64 Norfolk, VA, m/out Ft. Leavenworth, KS 12/27/65, age 23, light skin, sandy hair, gray eyes, 6-0, rem joined U.S. service after cap 4/15/63, house W108, s 2,21.

SELLARDS, JAMES. reg 39, co G, r sgt, enr 1/15/62, enl 2/16/63 Peach Orchard, age 28, light hair & skin, blue eyes, 5-10, rem d 4/10/63 at Ashland of fever, house W89, s 1,2,4.

SHEPHERD, WILLIAM. reg 14, co H, enr 10/25/61 Catlettsburg, enl 12/10/61 Louisa, age 21, dark hair, blue eyes, fair skin, 6-0, rem des 1/10/62 at Prestonsburg, house F191, s 1,2,4.

SIZEMORE, APPERSON. reg 39, co F, enr 11/9/62 Peach Orchard, enl 2/16/63 Peach Orchard, dis 9/15/65 Louisville, age 18, black hair & eyes, dark skin, 5-5, residence stated on muster roll, house n/c, s 1,2,4.

SIZEMORE, FARRIS. reg 39, co F, enr 11/16/62 Peach Orchard, enl 2/16/63 Peach Orchard, dis 9/15/65 Louisville, age 18, red hair, blue eyes, fair skin, 5-8, rem cap 1/28/63 in Floyd Co., residence stated on muster roll, house n/c, s 1,2,4.

SIZEMORE, JEFFERSON. reg 39, co F, enr 11/9/62, enl 2/16/63 Peach Orchard, dis 9/15/65 Louisville, age 20, red hair, blue eyes, fair skin, 5-7, rem was 5th sgt; returned to ranks, residence stated on muster roll, house n/c, s 1,2,4.

SIZEMORE, JOHN. reg 39, co F, enr 11/13/62 Peach Orchard, enl 2/16/63 Peach Orchard, age 44, dark hair, blue eyes, fair skin, 5-9, rem killed 12/7/62 in Magoffin Co. by accidental shot, house F517, s 1,2,4.

SIZEMORE, LINDSEY. reg 39, co F, enr 12/3/62 Floyd Co., enl 12/29/63 Louisa, dis 9/15/65 Louisville, age 26, dark hair & skin, black eyes, 6-2, rem cap 6/27/63 Breathitt Co., or cap 7/2/63 Pike Co., confined Richmond VA, paroled City Point VA, 7/14/63, house F335, s 1, 2,4.

SKEENS, GEORGE. reg 14, co H, enr 10/25/61 Catlettsburg, enl 12/10/61 Louisa, dis 1/31/65 Louisa, age 23, dark hair & eyes, fair skin, 5-9, house F193, s 1,2,4.

SKEANS, JONATHAN. reg 14, co H, enr 10/25/61 Catlettsburg, enl 12/10/61 Louisa, dis 1/31/65 Louisa, age 26, dark hair, gray eyes, fair skin, 5-9, house F197, s 1,2,4.

SKEANS, JOSEPH. reg 14, co K, enr 11/8/61 Louisa, enl 12/10/61 Louisa, age 45, sandy hair, blue eyes, fair skin, 5-10, rem d 6/30/62 Floyd Co. of cancer, house F198, s 1,2,4.

SKEANS, THOMAS P. reg 39, co F, enr 11/7/63 Louisa, enl 12/29/63 Louisa, dis 9/15/65 Louisville, age 20 or 26, dark hair, blue eyes, fair skin, 5-9, rem cap 12/12/64 and taken to Richmond VA, paroled Richmond VA 2/15/65, house F198, s 1,2,4.

SLONE, GEORGE W. reg 45, co G, enr 11/30/63, enl 11/30/63 Ashland, dis 2/14/65 Catlettsburg, house F377, s 2.

SLONE, JOHN P. reg 39, co F, enr 1/7/64, enl 3/29/64 Greenupsburg, dis 9/15/65 Louisville, age 18, dark hair, black eyes, dark skin, 6-0, house F379, s 1,2.

SLONE, SPENCER. reg 39, co F, enr 11/16/62 Peach Orchard, age 20, rem cap 1/1/63 in Floyd Co., house F408, s 1,4.

SLONE, TANDY. reg 39, co F, enr 11/16/62 Peach Orchard, age 25, rem cap 1/1/63 or 2/1/63 in Floyd Co., house F407, s 1,4.

SMITH, GEORGE. reg 45, co G, enr 12/7/63 Louisa, enl 11/30/63 Ashland, age 21, rem des 12/15/63 Louisa, house F416, s 1,2.

SMITH, JOHN. reg 45, co C, enr 8/3/63 Paintsville, enl 10/10/63 Catlettsburg, dis 12/24/64 Catlettsburg, age 27, house W83 or W101, s 1,2.

SPARKS, WILLIAM. reg 39, co F, enr 4/15/62, dis 9/15/65, house W26, s 5.

STANLEY, JOHN R. reg 39, co B, enr 9/6/62 Louisa, enl 2/16/63 Peach Orchard, age 37, dark hair, blue eyes, fair skin, 5-11, rem d 3/31/63 Ashland of typhoid fever, house F520, s 1,2,4.

STEPP, MOSES. reg 167 WV, co Sampson Kirk, house W351, s 23.

STONE, JAMES. reg 14, co H, enr 10/25/61 Catlettsburg, enl 12/10/61 Louisa, age 30, light hair, blue eyes, fair skin, 5-9, rem des 2/62 at Paintsville, house F203, s 1,2,4.

STURGEON, JOHN. reg 39, co B, enr 11/9/62 Peach Orchard, enl 2/16/63 Peach Orchard, dis 9/15/65 Louisville, age 32, black hair, dark skin, 6-3, house W44, s 1,2,4.

STURGEON, WILLIAM. reg 39, co F, enr 6/4/63 Louisa, enl 6/11/63 Louisa, dis 9/15/65 Louisville, age 18, black hair & eyes, dark skin, 5-4, house W155, s 1,2,4.

T

TACKETT, GREENVILLE. reg 39, co B, enr 11/16/62 Piketon or Peach Orchard, enl 2/16/63 Peach Orchard, dis 9/15/65 Louisville, age 30, dark hair & skin, blue eyes, 5-8, rem wounded by premature discharge of cannon, house W281, s 1,2,4,8.

TACKETT, JOHN. reg 39, co K, enr 11/16/62 Pike Co., enl 2/16/63 Peach Orchard, age 24, black hair, blue eyes, fair skin, 5-6, rem cap 12/4/62 in Floyd Co., des 6/30/63 at Louisa, residence stated on muster roll, house n/c, s 1,2,4.

THACKER, JOHN. reg 45, co D, enr 7/14/63 Catlettsburg, enl 10/17/63 Ashland, dis 12/24/64 Catlettsburg, age 18, house F319, s 1,2.

TIPTON, DAVID. reg 39, co K, enr 11/15/63 Louisa, enl 12/30/63 Louisa, dis 9/15/65 Louisville, age 18, light hair, red eyes, fair skin, 5-4, house W283, s 1,2,4.

TIPTON, JAMES M. reg 39, co K, enr 11/6/62 Peach Orchard, enl 2/16/63 Peach Orchard, dis 9/15/65 Louisville, age 19, dark hair, blue eyes, fair skin, 5-11, house W283, s 1,2,4.

TIPTON, JOHN C. reg 39, co K, enr 9/6/62 Peach Orchard, enl 2/16/63 Peach Orchard, age 44, dark hair, blue eyes, fair skin, 6-2, house W283, s 1,2,4,

TIPTON, REUBEN. reg 39, co K, enr 11/7/62 Floyd Co., enl 2/16/63 Peach Orchard, dis 9/15/65 Louisville, age 24, dark hair, blue eyes, fair skin, 6-0, house W283, s 1,2,4.

TIPTON, WILEY. reg 39, co B, r cpl, enr 9/6/62 Peach Orchard, enl 2/16/63 Peach Orchard, dis 9/15/65 Louisville, age 24, light hair, gray eyes, fair skin, 5-8, residence stated on muster roll, house n/c, s 1,2,4.

TURNER, JOHN B. reg 45, co F, enr 11/1/63 Ashland, enl 11/2/63 Ashland, dis 12/24/64 Catlettsburg, age 17, house F515, s 1,2.

TUSSEY, JONATHAN. reg 39, co F, enr 9/26/63 Floyd Co., enl 10/30/63 Louisa, dis 9/15/65 Louisville, age 30, light hair, blue eyes, fair skin, 5-9, house F211, s 1,2,4.

V

VANOVER, WILLIAM. reg 14, co H, enr 7/12/63 Louisa, enl 8/29/63, age 18, light hair, blue eyes, fair skin, 5-7, house F382, s 1,2,4.

VAUGHN, JOHN. reg 45, co K, enr 10/26/63 Catlettsburg, enl 12/9/63 Louisa, age 18, light hair, blue eyes, fair skin, 5-9, rem d Lexington 4/30/64 of fever, house F90, s 1,2.

W

WARD, THOMAS. reg 39, co G, enr 11/21/62 Peach Orchard, enl 2/16/63 Peach Orchard, dis 9/15/65 Louisville, age 28, dark hair & skin, hazel eyes, 5-11, house F618, s 1,2,4.

WATKINS, WILLIAM. reg 14, co K, enr 5/28/63 Louisa, enl 5/28/63 Louisa, dis 9/15/65 Louisville, age 22, red hair, gray eyes, fair skin, 5-11, rem trans to 14th Vet Inf, co C, enr & m/in 5/28/63, residence stated on muster roll, house n/c, s 1,2,4.

WATSON, JOHN P. reg 39, co I, enr 11/12/62 Pike Co. or Peach Orchard, enl 2/16/63 Peach Orchard, dis 9/15/65 Louisville, age 18, light hair, blue eyes, fair skin, 5-4, rem cap at Cynthiana 6/21/64 and confined at Richmond VA, escaped and returned near Savannah GA, residence stated on muster roll, house n/c, s 1,2,4.

WEBB, HEZEKIAH. reg 39, co F, r capt, enr 12/18/62 Peach Orchard, enl 2/16/63 Peach Orchard, age 37, rem resigned 3/16/65 for disability of chronic bronchitis & rheumatism; slightly wounded at Cynthiana, house F287, s 1,2,4.

WEBB, JONATHAN. reg 39, co E, enr 10/30/62 Piketon, enl 2/16/63 Peach Orchard, age 43, light hair, gray eyes, fair skin, 5-8, rem d 7/10/64 at Louisa of accidental gun shot, house F542, s 1,2,4.

WEBB, JOSEPH M. reg 39, co F, r sgt, enr 1/16/63 Floyd Co., enl 2/16/63 Peach Orchard, dis 9/15/65 Louisville, age 18, light hair, blue eyes, fair skin, 5-6, rem prom to sgt 1/30/65, house F287, s 1,2,4.

WEBB, RICHARD. reg 39, co F, enr 11/11/62 Floyd Co., enl 2/16/63 Peach Orchard, dis 9/15/65 Louisville, age 35, black hair, blue eyes, dark skin, 5-9, rem wounded 8/22/64 Morgan Co., house F288, s 1,2,4.

WEBB, SYLVESTER. reg 39, co G, enr 11/10/62 Peach Orchard, enl 2/16/63 Peach Orchard, dis 9/15/65 Louisville, age 19, dark hair & skin, hazel eyes, 5-7, rem cap 12/4/62 in Floyd Co., confined at Richmond VA, paroled City Point VA, 4/3/63, house W39, s 1,2,4.

WHITAKER, WILLIAM R. reg 14, co F, D, enr 9/4/63 Salyersville, enl 10/31/63 Louisa, dis 9/15/65 Louisville, age 18, 28 or 33, trans to 14th Vet Inf, house F209, s 1,2,28.

WHITE, WILLIAM HARVEY. reg 39, co A, enr 10/20/62 Peach Orchard, enl 2/16/63 Peach Orchard, dis 9/15/65 Louisville, age 19, dark hair, blue eyes, fair skin, 5-9, rem wounded at Saltville VA 10/2/64 & left in hands of enemy, paroled 2/21/65, house W28, s 1,2.

WHITT, JAMES P. reg 39, co F, enr 5/17/64 Louisa, enl 7/24/65 Greenupsburg, dis 9/15/65 Louisville, age 21, light hair, blue eyes, fair skin, 6-0, house F277, s 1,2,4.

WHITT, JOHN B. reg 39, co F, enr & enl 12/29/63 Louisa, dis 9/15/65 Louisville, age 23, light hair, blue eyes, fair skin, 6-0, house F277, s 1,2,4.

WILCOX, GEORGE W. reg 39, co A, enr 9/6/62 Johnson Co., enl 2/16/63 Peach Orchard, dis 9/15/65 Louisville, age 18, red hair, blue eyes, fair skin, 5-8, residence stated on muster roll, house n/c, s 1,2,8.

WILCOX, OWEN. reg 39, co A, enr 9/6/62 Johnson Co., enl 2/16/63 Peach Orchard, age 44, dark hair & skin, blue eyes, 5-6, rem d 3/16/65 at Paintsville of pneumonia, house F49, s 1,2,4,8.

WILLIAMS, HARRISON. reg 23, co K, enl 10/5/64 Greenupsburg, age 19, light hair, fair skin, hazel eyes, 5-8, rem des 12/25/64 Pulaski TN, house W222, s 2.

WILLIS, GEORGE. reg 39, co F, r 1st sgt, enr 11/9/62 Floyd Co., enl 2/16/63 Peach Orchard, age 35, dark hair & skin, blue eyes, 5-10, rem killed in action 1/12/65 in Lawrence Co., house F264, s 1,2,4.

Y

YATES, ALEXANDER. reg 39, co A, enr 1/18/64 Johnson Co., enl 3/28/64 Greenupsburg, dis 9/15/65 Louisville, age 24, light hair, blue eyes, fair skin, 5-9, rem cap Kingsport TN 12/12/64, paroled at Aiken's Landing 2/15/65, house F61, s 1,2,4,8.

YATES, ANDREW J. reg 39, co K, enr 8/27/63 Louisa, enl 8/30/63 Louisa, dis 9/15/65 Louisville, age 18, dark hair & eyes, fair skin, 5-8, house F601, s 1,2,4.

JOHNSON COUNTY UNION SOLDIERS

A

ADAMS, HARMON. reg 39, co A, enr 1863, dis 9/15/65 Louisville, reg 45, enr 8/26/63 Paintsville, enl 10/10/63 Catlettsburg, dis 12/24/64 Catlettsburg, age 18, dark hair, gray eyes, fair skin, 5-10, house 129, s 1,2,5,6,8.

ADAMS, JAMES. reg 14, co G, enr 11/19/61 Catlettsburg, enl 12/10/61 Louisa, dis 1/31/65 Louisa, age 35, black hair & eyes, dark skin, 5-6, rem wounded in left foot 5/30/64, residence stated on muster roll, house n/c, s 1,2,4.

ADAMS, JAMES M. reg 39, co A, enr 9/6/62 Johnson Co., enl 2/16/63 Peach Orchard, dis 9/15/65 Louisville, age 18, light hair, blue eyes, dark skin, 5-6, residence stated on muster roll, house n/c, s 1,2,4.

ADAMS, THOMAS. reg 39, co A, enr 11/1/62 Johnson Co., enl 2/16/63 Peach Orchard, dis 9/15/65 Louisville, age 38, black hair & eyes, dark skin, 5-5, house 366, s 1,2,4.

AKERS, JOHN R. reg 45, co C, enr 5/27/63 Paintsville, enl 10/10/63 Catlettsburg, dis 12/24/64 Catlettsburg, age 22, house 284, s 1,2.

AKERS, ROBERT. reg 65, co C, r 2d lt, enl 5/21/64, dis 6/21/64, age 31, blue eyes, light hair, fair skin, 5-8, house 284, s 2,4.

ALLEY, ROBERT. reg 65, co B, enl 5/21/64, rem des 5/30/64, house 97, s 4.

ARMS, ELIJAH B. reg 14, co K, enr 11/8/61 Louisa, enl 12/10/61 Louisa, dis 1/31/65 Louisa, age 18, sandy hair, blue eyes, fair skin, 5-7, house 96, s 1,2,4.

ARMS, JAMES. reg 45, co C, enr 9/27/63 Paintsville, enl 10/10/63 Catlettsburg, age 18, fair hair & skin, blue eyes, 5-3, rem d 2/14/64 at Mt. Sterling, house 96, s 1,2.

ARMS, WALLACE B. reg 65, co E, r cpl, enl 5/21/64, dis 6/21/64, age 27, blue eyes, light hair, fair skin, 5-9, rem in camp, house 100, s 2,4.

ARTHINGTON, ISAAC. reg 14, co K, enr 11/8/61 Louisa, enl 12/10/61 Louisa, age 19, sandy hair, blue eyes, fair skin, 5-3, rem dis 1/13/63 for disability from ulcers, residence stated on muster roll, house n/c, s 1,2,4.

AUXIER, ANDREW. reg 65, co C, enl 5/21/64, rem des 5/30/64, house 651, s 4.

AUXIER, DAVID VALENTINE. reg 39, co A, r capt, age 22, black hair & eyes, dark skin, 5-7, rem prom from 2nd lt to capt, 2/24/64, cap 12/4/62 Floyd Co. and taken to Richmond VA, wounded in right lung at Saltville VA, 10/2/64, d 10/4/64, house 651, s 1,2,4.

AUXIER, GEORGE W. reg 39, co A, enr 4/25/63 Johnson Co., enl 8/30/63, dis 9/15/65 Louisville, age 21, dark hair, black eyes, fair skin, 5-10, house 651, s 1,2,4.

AUXIER, HENRY J. reg 65, co C, enl 5/21/64, rem des 6/64 from push boats while on detached duty, house 166, s 4.

AUXIER, HIRAM. reg 14, co K, enr 2/29/64, enl 3/15/64 Louisa, dis 9/15/65 Louisville, age 19, dark hair & skin, black eyes, 5-7, rem trans to 14th Vet Inf. Co A, enr 2/29/64, m/in 3/15/64 Louisa, house 438, s 1,2,4.

AUXIER, JAMES K. P. reg 65, co C, enl 5/21/64, rem des 5/30/64, house 158, s 4.

AUXIER, JOHN B. reg 39, co A, r major, enr 9/6/62 Louisa, enl 2/16/63 Peach Orchard, age 46, black hair & eyes, dark hair, 5-10, rem prom from capt co. A to major 12/22/63, resigned 11/17/64 because of disability, house 165, s 1,2,4.

AUXIER, JOHN J. reg 14, co G, r cpl, enr 11/19/61 Louisa, enr 12/10/61 Louisa, dis 9/15/65 Louisville, age 34, black hair & eyes, dark skin, 5-8, rem trans to 14th Vet Inf., co A, r cpl, enr 2/28/64, m/in 3/15/64 Louisa, wounded between 7/2/64 & 8/13/64 in right arm, dis 2/28/64 for scorbutus(scurvy), residence stated on muster roll, house n/c, s 1,2,4.

AUXIER, JOSEPH D. reg 39, co A, enr 9/25/63 Johnson Co., age 18, light hair, blue eyes, fair skin, 5-6, house 156, s 1.

AUXIER, SAMUEL W. reg 65, co C, enl 5/21/64, dis 6/21/64, age 24, blue eyes, light hair, fair skin, 5-8, rem in camp, house 159 or 651, s 2,4.

AUXIER, WILLIAM L. reg 65, co C, enl 5/21/64, rem des 5/30/64, house 158, s 4.

B

BADGETT, AMERICUS J. reg 39, co A, enr 9/6/62 Johnson Co., enl 2/16/63 Peach Orchard, age 34, black hair & eyes, dark hair, 5-7, rem d 2/24/64 or 2/24/65, house 163, s 1,2,4.

BALDRIDGE, ANDREW J. reg 39, co A, enr 10/11/62, enl 2/16/63 Peach Orchard, dis 9/15/65 Louisville, age 18, black hair & eyes, dark skin, 5-10, house 181, s 1,2,4.

BALDRIDGE, JAMES. reg 39, co A, enr 9/6/62 Johnson Co., enl 2/16/63 Peach Orchard, dis 6/15/65 Covington, age 18, black hair, gray eyes, dark skin, 5-7, house 180, s 1,2,4.

BALDRIGE, JOHN. reg 39, co A, enr 10/11/62 Johnson Co., enl 8/30/63 Louisa, dis 9/15/65 Louisville, age 40, black hair, blue eyes, dark skin, 6-1, house 181, s 1,2,4.

BALDRIDGE, THOMAS. reg 39, co A, enr 7/25/63 Johnson Co., enl 8/30/63 Louisa, dis 9/15/65, age 32, light hair, blue eyes, dark skin, 6-2, house 164, s 1,2,4.

BALDRIDGE, WILLIAM. reg 65, co C, enl 5/21/64, rem des 5/30/64, house 181, s 4.

BALDWIN, GEORGE. reg 65, co A, enl 5/21/64, dis 6/21/64, age 21, black eyes, red hair, dark skin, 5-10, rem in camp, house 26, s 2,4.

BANNISTER, ANDERSON. reg 65, co D, r 2nd lt, enl 5/21/64, dis 6/1/64, age 21, blue eyes, light hair, fair skin, 5-9, rem in camp, house 250, s 2,4.

BARNETT, JOHN B. reg 65, co E, r cpl, enl 5/21/64, dis 6/21/64, age 26, blue eyes, light hair, fair skin, 5-11, rem in camp, house 437, s 2,4.

BAYES, JOSHUA H. reg 14, co G, enr 11/19/61 Louisa, enl 12/10/61 Louisa, dis 1/31/65 Louisa, age 24, sandy hair, blue eyes, fair skin, 5-11, house 552, s 1,2,4.

BAYES, SAMUEL E. reg 14, co G, enr 11/19/61 Louisa, enl 12/10/61 Louisa, dis 1/31/65 Louisa, age 18, light hair, blue eyes, fair skin, 5-8, residence stated on muster roll, house n/c, s 1,2,4.

BAYES, WILLIAM A. reg 65, co E, enl 5/21/64, age 30, light hair, blue eyes, fair skin, 5-6, rem AWOL, house 752, s 4.

BAYES, WILLIAM R. reg 14, co G, enr 11/19/61 Louisa, enl 12/10/61 Louisa, dis 1/31/65 Louisa, age 20, sandy hair, blue eyes, fair skin, 5-6, rem wounded 8/6/64 near Atlanta GA in left leg, residence stated on muster roll, house n/c, s 1,2,4.

BAYS, JAMES J. reg 14, co I, enr 10/10/61 Louisa, enl 12/10/61 Louisa, dis 9/15/65 Louisville, age 34, dark hair, blue eyes, fair skin, 5-8, rem trans to 14th Vet Inf, co A, enr 2/29/64, m/in 3/15/64 Louisa, house 777, s 1,2,4.

BLAIR, AMOS. reg 65, co A, enl 5/21/64, dis 6/21/64, age 21, blue eyes, black hair, dark skin, 6-0, rem in camp, house 103, s 2,4.

BLAIR, ANDREW J. reg 65, co A, enl 5/21/64, dis 6/21/64, age 22, blue eyes, black hair, dark skin, 6-0, house 128, s 2,4.

BLAIR, ASA J. reg 45, co C, enr 11/3/63 Ashland, enl 11/4/63 Catlettsburg, dis 12/24/64 Catlettsburg, age 21 or 26, rem trans to co E 5/20/64, house 98, s 1,2.

BLAIR, BRITTON F. reg 45, co C, r cpl, enr 9/29/63 Paintsville, enl 10/10/63 Catlettsburg, dis 12/24/64 Catlettsburg, age 21, house 92, s 1,2.

BLAIR, GENERAL JACKSON. reg CG, co K, enr 6/9/64, enl 10/20/64 Frankfort, dis 3/11/65 Catlettsburg, age 18, light hair, blue eyes, fair skin, 5-9, house 123, s 2,4.

BLAIR, GEORGE N. reg 65, co A, enl 5/21/64, dis 6/21/64, age 28, blue eyes, light hair & skin, 5-10, rem in camp, house 102, s 2,4.

BLAIR, JAMES H. reg 65, co A, enl 5/21/64, dis 6/21/64, reg CG, co K, enr 6/9/64, enl 7/28/64 Frankfort, dis 3/11/65 Catlettsburg, age 37, light hair, blue eyes, fair skin, 5-10, rem in camp, house 146, s 2,4.

BLAIR, JOHN L. reg 65, co E, enl 5/21/64, dis 6/21/64, age 30, blue eyes, light hair, fair skin, 5-8, rem in camp, house 101, s 2,4.

BLAIR, SAMUEL. reg 65, co A, enl 5/21/64, dis 6/21/64, age 20, gray eyes, black hair, dark skin, 5-11, rem in camp, house 103, s 2,4.

BLAIR, WILLIAM P. J. reg CG, co E, enr 6/9/64, enl 10/20/64 Frankfort, dis 3/1/65 Catlettsburg, age 20, light hair, blue eyes, fair skin, 5-9, house 123, s 2,4.

BLANTON, JAMES. reg 65, co E, enl 5/21/64, dis 6/21/64, age 18, blue eyes, light hair, fair skin, 5-9, house 845, s 2,4.

BLANTON, JAMES. reg 14, co I, enr 11/10/61 Louisa, enl 12/10/61 Louisa, age 19, black hair & eyes, dark skin, 5-9, d 5/4/62 London KY of typhoid, residence stated on muster roll, house n/c, s 1,2,4.

BLANTON, JAMES. reg 14, co K, enr 11/8/61, enl 12/10/61 Louisa, dis 1/31/65 Louisa, age 25, sandy hair, gray eyes, fair skin, 5-11, residence stated on muster roll, house n/c, s 1,2,4.

BLANTON, JOHN. reg 14, co K, enr 11/8/61 Louisa, enl 12/10/61 Louisa, dis 9/15/65 Louisville, age 24, sandy hair, blue eyes, fair skin, 5-7, rem trans to 14th Vet Inf, co A, enr 2/29/64, m/in 3/15/64 Louisa, house 840, s 1,2,4.

BLEVINS, DANIEL. reg 65, co D, enl 5/21/64, dis 6/21/64, age 35, blue eyes, dark hair, fair skin, 5-11, house 717, s 2,4.

BLEVINS, HENDERSON. reg 14, co G, enr 6/18/63 Louisa, enl 6/30/63 Louisa, dis 9/15/65 Louisville, age 17, dark hair, blue eyes, fair skin, 5-0, rem trans to 14th Vet Inf, co D, enr 6/13/63, m/in 6/30/63, house 328, s 1,2,4.

BLEVINS, JEFFERSON. reg 14, co K, enr 9/21/62 Paintsville, enl 5/28/63 Louisa, dis 9/15/65 Louisville, age 20, dark hair, blue eyes, fair skin, 5-10, rem trans to 14th Vet Inf, co C, 9/21/62, m/in 5/28/63 Louisa, residence stated on muster roll, house n/c, s 1,2,4.

BLEVINS, LEWIS. reg 65, co E, enl 5/21/64, age 32, black hair, blue eyes, fair skin, 6-0, rem AWOL, house 441, s 4.

BLEVINS, MARTIN. reg 65, co E, enl 5/21/64, age 20, black hair & eyes, dark skin, 5-6, rem AWOL, house 767, s 4.

BLEVINS, WILLIAM. reg 65, co F, enl 5/21/64, dis 6/21/64, age 34, blue eyes, dark hair, fair skin, 5-2, house 612, s 2,4.

BLEVINS, WILLIAM. reg 14, co K, enr 4/4/63 Louisa, enl 5/28/63 Louisa, dis 9/15/65 Louisville, age 18, light hair, blue eyes, dark skin, 5-7, rem trans to 14th Vet Inf, co C, enr 10/10/62, m/in 5/28/63 Louisa, wounded in left thigh 10/64 in Georgia, residence stated on muster roll, house n/c, s 1,2,4.

BORDERS, HEZEKIAH. reg 68, co K, r 1st sgt, enl 4/7/64, 5/21/64, dis 4/16/64, 6/22/64, age 34, black eyes & hair, fair skin, 6-0, rem residence established by filing divorce action in Johnson Circuit Court in 1861, residence shown on enrolled militia list, house n/c, s 2,4.

BORDERS, JOHN. reg 14, co D, enr 10/20/61 Louisa, enl 12/10/61 Louisa, dis 9/15/65 Louisville, age 18, black hair, dark eyes, light skin, 5-6, rem trans to 14th Vet Inf, co A, enr 2/29/64, m/in 3/15/64 Louisa, descriptive index gives Johnson Co. as residence, house 602, s 1,2,4.

BORDERS, WILLIAM. reg 65, co A, enl 5/21/64, dis 6/21/64, age 39, blue eyes, black hair, dark skin, 6-1, rem in camp, house 53, s 2,4.

BOWEN, JOHN. reg 39, co G, enr 8/11/63 Louisa, enl 8/30/63 Louisa, dis 9/15/65 Louisville, age 18, dark hair & skin, blue eyes, 5-6, house 277, s 1,2,4.

BOYD, JOHN J. reg 14, co D, enr 10/1/61 or 11/19/61 Louisa, enl 12/10/61 Louisa, dis 1/31/65 Louisa, age 24, sandy hair, gray eyes, fair skin, 6-2, rem trans to co G 1/24/65, house 388, s 1,2,4.

BOYD, WILLIAM D. reg CG, co E, enr 6/4/64, enl 7/4/64 Frankfort, dis 3/11/65 Catlettsburg, house 388, s 2,4.

BRANHAM, TURNER. reg 14, co I, age 37, house 58 or 834, s 4.

BROWN, DAVID K. reg 65, co B, enl 5/21/64, dis 6/21/64, age 44, dark eyes, hair & skin, 5-9, rem in camp, house 495, s 2,4.

BROWN, JOHN J. reg 65, co B, enl 5/21/64, dis 6/21/64, age 24, dark eyes, light hair, fair skin, 6-0, rem in camp, house 497, s 2,4.

BROWN, THOMAS S. reg 45, co C, r sgt, enr 9/22/63 Paintsville, enl 10/10/63 Catlettsburg, age 20, house 13, s 1,2.

BROWN, WILLIAM. reg 65, co B, enl 5/21/64, dis 6/21/64, age 32, black eyes & hair, dark skin, 6-0, house 496, s 2,4.

BURCHETT, JAMES. reg 45, co C, enr 8/20/63 Paintsville, enl 10/10/63 Catlettsburg, age 19, rem d 1/4/64 at Paintsville of typhoid fever, house 690, s 1,2.

BURGESS, JOHN S. reg 65, co B, enl 5/21/64, dis 6/9/64, reg CG, co K, enr 6/9/64, enl 7/28/64 Frankfort, dis 3/11/65 Catlettsburg, age 21, blue eyes, light hair, fair skin, 5-0, house 473, s 2,4.

BUTCHER, HENDERSON H. reg 65, co B, enl 5/21/64, dis 6/21/64, age 22, dark eyes, hair & skin, 6-0, rem in camp, house 323, s 2,4.

BUTCHER, WILLIAM. reg 65, co C, enl 5/21/64, dis 6/21/64, age 45, black eyes, sandy hair, fair skin, 5-10, rem in camp, house 173, s 2,4.

BUTLER, JAMES F. reg 14, co K, r cpl, enr 11/8/61 Louisa, enl 12/10/61 Louisa, dis 1/31/65 Louisa, age 21, sandy hair, blue eyes, red skin, 5-9, rem prom cpl 9/29/64, house 661, s 1,2,4.

BUTLER, JOHN T. reg 14, co K, enr & enl 2/17/63 Louisa, age 25, dark hair, blue eyes, fair skin, 6-0, rem dis for disability 4/13/65, house 354, s 1,4.

C

CASSADY, HENRY. reg 39, co D, enr 11/19/62 Pike Co., enl 2/6/63 Peach Orchard, age 20, light hair, blue eyes, fair skin, 5-6, rem cap 12/5/62, paroled City Point VA 4/3/63, d 9/10/63 at Louisa of disease, house 229, s 1,2,4.

CASSADY, PHILIP. reg 65, co D, enl 5/21/64, dis 6/21/64, age 36, blue eyes, red hair, fair skin, 5-8, house 230, s 2,4.

CASTLE, AMOS. reg 39, co G, enr 10/10/62 Peach Orchard, enl 2/16/63 Peach Orchard, dis 9/15/65 Louisville, age 20, light hair & skin, blue eyes, 5-6, house 504, s 1,2,4.

CASTLE, APPERSON. reg 65, co B, enl 5/21/64, dis 6/21/64, age 21, blue eyes, light hair, fair skin, 5-8, house 507, s 2,4.

CASTLE, BENJAMIN. reg 39, co G, enr 9/13/62, enl 2/16/63 Peach Orchard, dis 9/15/65 Louisville, age 19, dark hair & skin, black eyes, 5-9, house 511, s 1,2,4.

CASTLE, BENJAMIN F. reg 39, co A, enr 9/12/62, enl 2/16/63 Peach Orchard, dis 9/15/65 Louisville, age 23, fair hair & skin, blue eyes, 6-2, house 374, s 1,2,4.

CASTLE, CHARLES. reg 65, co A, enl 5/21/64, dis 6/21/64, rem in camp, residence shown on militia list, house n/c, s 2,4,19.

CASTLE, CHARLES J. reg 45, co C, enr 9/1/63 Paintsville, enl 10/10/63 Catlettsburg, dis 12/24/64 Catlettsburg, age 18, house 532, s 1,2.

CASTLE, EMERY. reg 65, co B, enl 5/21/64, dis 6/21/64, age 22, dark eyes, hair & skin, 5-7, rem in camp, house 501, s 2,4.

CASTLE, GEORGE W. reg 65, co A, enl 5/21/64, rem des 6/64, house 48, s 4.
CASTLE, HENDERSON. reg 65, co B, enl 5/21/64, dis 6/21/64, age 23, dark eyes, hair & skin, 5-7, rem in camp, house 501, s 2,4.
CASTLE, ISRAEL. reg 65, co A, enl 5/21/64, rem des 6/64, house 532, s 4.
CASTLE, JAMES. reg 65, co B, enl 5/21/64, dis 6/21/64, age 40, blue eyes, light hair, fair skin, 5-6, house 379, s 2,4.
CASTLE, JAMES. reg CG, co K, enr 6/9/64, enl 7/28/64 Frankfort, dis 3/11/65 Catlettsburg, age 18, light hair, blue eyes, fair skin, 5-0, house 368, s 2,4.
CASTLE, JEFFERSON. reg 65, co A, enl 5/21/64, age 25, blue eyes, light hair, fair skin, 5-8, rem des 6/29/64, house 384, s 4.
CASTLE, JOHN. reg 39, co A, enr 9/6/62 Johnson Co., enl 2/16/63 Peach Orchard, age 18, fair hair & skin, blue eyes, 5-7, rem d 4/4/63 at Ashland of typhoid fever, house 373, s 1,2,4,8.
CASTLE, JOHN S. reg 65, co B, enl 5/21/64, dis 6/21/64, rem in camp, house 412 or 500, s 2,4.
CASTLE, MADISON, reg 39, co G, enr 9/13/62, age 26, rem killed by guerrillas 12/8/62 in Floyd Co., house 531, s 2,4.
CASTLE, THOMAS. reg 65, co B, r cpl, enl 5/21/64, dis 6/21/64, age 24, blue eyes, light hair, fair skin, 6-0, rem in camp, house 511 or 532, s 2,4.
CASTLE, WILLIS. reg 65, co B, enl 5/21/64, dis 6/21/64, reg CG, co K, enr 6/9/64, enl 7/28/64 Frankfort, dis 3/11/65 Catlettsburg, age 18, light hair, blue eyes, fair skin, 5-8, house 504, s 2,4.
CAUDILL, ABNER C. reg 14, co G, enr 8/21/63 Louisa, enl 8/30/63 Louisa, dis 9/15/ 65, age 34, black hair, dark eyes & skin, 5-7, rem trans to 14th Vet Inf, co D, enr 8/21/63, m/in 8/30/63 Louisville, app cpl 2/1/65, house 557, s 1,2,4.
CAUDILL, JESSE. reg 65, co F, enl 5/21/64, dis 6/21/64, reg CG, co K, enr 6/9/64, enl 7/28/64 Frankfort, dis 3/1/65 Catlettsburg, age 20, light hair, blue eyes, fair skin, 5-8, house 567, s 2,4.
CAUDILL, JOHN H. reg 45, co C, enr 8/15/63 Paintsville, enl 10/10/63 Catlettsburg, age 20, dark hair, eyes & skin, 5-6, rem d 4/15/64 Flemingsburg of measles, house 769, s 1,2.
CAUDILL, STEPHEN. reg 45, co C, enr 9/27/63 Paintsville, enl 10/10/63 Catlettsburg, dis 12/24/63 Catlettsburg, age 20, house 769, s 1,2.
CAUDILL, THOMAS. reg 39, co E, enr 4/8/65, enl 5/22/65 Lexington, dis 9/15/65 Louisville, age 19, light hair, blue eyes, fair skin, 5-10, house 121, s 2,4.
CHANDLER, HENRY C. reg 65, co B, enl 5/21/64, dis 6/21/64, age 24, blue eyes, light hair, fair skin, 5-8, rem in camp, house 488, s 2,4.
CHANDLER, ISAAC. reg 65, co F, enl 5/21/64, dis 6/21/64, age 36, blue eyes, dark hair, fair skin, 5-9, house 534, s 2,4.
CHANDLER, JAMES. reg 14, co G, enr 11/19/61 Louisa, enl 12/10/61 Louisa, dis 1/31/65 Louisa, age 23 or 28, sandy hair, blue eyes, fair skin, 5-9, house 542, s 1,2,4.
CHANDLER, THOMAS. reg 65, co F, enl 5/21/64, dis 6/21/64, age 29, black eyes, light hair, fair skin, 5-10, house 535, s 2,4.
CHANDLER, WILLIAM W. reg 65, co F, r 2d lt, enl 5/21/64, dis 6/21/64, age 18, blue eyes, light hair, fair skin, 5-2, house 540, s 2,4.
CHILDERS, JOHN. reg 14, co C, enr 10/10/61 Louisa, enl 12/10/61 Louisa, dis 1/31/65 Louisa, age 26, dark hair, eyes & skin, 5-11, rem wounded in right thigh between 7/2/64 and 8/13/64 in Georgia, residence stated on muster roll, house n/c, s 1,2,4.
CHILDERS, WILLIAM H. reg 14, co K, enr 11/8/61 Louisa, enl 12/10/61 Louisa, dis 9/15/65 Louisville, age 23, dark hair, gray eyes, fair skin, 5-11, rem trans to 14th Vet Inf, co A, enr 2/29/64, m/in 3/15/64 Louisa, residence stated on muster roll, house n/c, s 1,2,4.

CHRISTIAN, LEWIS. reg 39, co A, r sgt, enr 12/8/62 Johnson Co., enl 2/16/63 Peach Orchard, dis 9/15/65 Louisville, age 28 or 31, dark hair, blue eyes, fair skin, 6-0, residence stated on muster roll, house n/c, s 1,2,4.

CLAY, DANIEL J. reg CG, co K, enr 6/9/64, enl 10/20/64 Frankfort, dis 3/11/65 Catlettsburg, age 18, light hair, blue eyes, fair skin, 5-2, house 674, s 2,4.

CLAY, GEORGE H. reg 39, co A, enr 10/11/62, enl 2/16/63 Peach Orchard, dis 9/15/65 Louisville, age 18, black hair, gray eyes, dark skin, 5-5, house 364, s 1,2,4.

CLAY, HENRY M. reg 16, co C, enr 11/2/61 Camp Guthrie, enl 12/8/61 Camp Lee, dis 7/24/65 Lexington, died 12/27/61 Camp Lee of fever, residence stated on muster roll, house 660 or 674, s1,2,4.

CLAY, JOHN. reg 45, co F, enr 9/13/63 Rockcastle, enl 11/2/63 Ashland, age 20, light hair, eyes & skin, 5-4, rem d 4/14/64 Flemingsburg, house 239, s 1,2,6.

CLAY, JORDAN. reg 65, co D, r cpl, enl 5/21/64, dis 6/21/64, age 26, gray eyes, light hair, fair skin, 5-7, rem in camp, house 239, s 2,4.

CLAY, THOMAS J. reg 45, co F, enr 9/13/63 Rockcastle, enl 11/2/63 Ashland, dis 12/24/64 Catlettsburg, age 18, light hair, eyes & skin, 5-4, house 239, s 1,2,6.

COLLINS, ALLEN. reg 14, co K, enr 11/8/61 Louisa, enl 12/10/61 Louisa, dis 1/31/65 Louisa, age 22, black hair & eyes, dark skin, 5-9, rem wounded, in Knoxville TN hospital in 8/64, house 74, s 1,2,4.

COLLINS, ANDREW J. reg 65, co C, enl 5/21/64, dis 6/21/64, age 20, gray eyes, dark hair & skin, 5-8, rem in camp, house 190, s 2,4.

COLLINS, ELIJAH. reg 14, co I, enr 11/10/61 Louisa, enl 12/10/61 Louisa, dis 1/31/65 Louisa, age 31, black hair & eyes, dark skin, 5-10, rem cap by enemy while in desertion, house 435, s 1,2,4.

COLLINS, G. W. reg 65, co E, enl 5/21/64, dis 6/21/64, age 34, dark eyes, hair & skin, 5-6, rem in camp, house 433 or 440, s 2,4.

COLLINS, HIRAM. reg 14, co K, enr 11/8/61 Louisa, enl 12/10/61 Louisa, age 26, black hair & eyes, dark skin, 5-8, rem d 4/23/63 at Louisa of typhoid fever, residence stated on muster roll, house n/c, s 1,2,4.

COLLINS, JAMES M. reg CG, co K, r sgt, enr 6/9/64, enl 7/28/64 Frankfort, dis 3/1/65 Catlettsburg, age 20, black hair & eyes, fair skin, 5-6, house 352, s 2,4.

COLLINS, PETER. reg 65, co E, enl 5/21/64, dis 6/21/64, age 27, black eyes, hair & skin, 5-11, rem in camp, house 69, s 2,4.

COLLINS, WILLIAM. reg 14, co I, enr 11/10/61 Louisa, enl 12/10/61 Louisa, dis 1/31/65 Louisa, age 33, black hair & eyes, dark skin, 5-11, house 69, s 1,2,4.

COLLINS, WILLIAM W. reg 14, co G, enr 11/19/61 Louisa, enl 12/10/61 Louisa, age 28, rem des 6/19/62 at Catlettsburg, house 205, s 1,2,4.

COLVIN, JOHISHA. reg 14, co I, enr 10/10/61 Louisa, enl 12/10/61 Louisa, dis 9/15/65 Louisa, age 22, light hair, blue eyes, fair skin, 5-11, rem trans to 14th Vet Inf, co B, enr 2/29/64, m/in 3/15/64 Louisa, house 108, s 1,2,4.

CONLEY, ABSALOM. reg 65, co E, enl 5/12/64, dis 6/21/64, reg CG, co K, enr 6/9/64, enl 10/20/64 Frankfort, dis 3/11/65 Catlettsburg, age 30, black hair & eyes, fair skin, 5-9, house 831, s 2,4.

CONLEY, DAVID H. reg 65, co E, enl 5/21/64, dis 6/21/64, age 30, black eyes & hair, dark skin, 5-6, house 789, s 2,4.

CONLEY, EDMOND. reg 45, co K, enr 11/24/63 Relief, enl 12/9/63 Louisa, age 21, light hair, blue eyes, fair skin, 5-5, KIA 6/9/64 Lexington, b Morgan Co., house 789, s 1,2.

CONLEY, HENRY J. reg 65, co A, enl 5/31/64, dis 6/21/64, age 20, blue eyes, light hair, fair skin, 6-0, rem in camp, house 126, s 2,4.

CONLEY, ISAAC. reg 65, co E, enl 5/21/64, age 28, black hair, blue eyes, fair skin, 6-0, rem AWOL, house 808, s 4.

CONLEY, JAMES H. reg 65, co A, enl 5/21/64, dis 6/21/64, age 24, blue eyes, black hair, dark skin, 6-0, rem in camp, house 133, s 2,4.

CONLEY, JOHN. reg CG, co K, enr 6/9/64, age 18, black hair & eyes, dark skin, 5-8, house 126, s 4.

CONLEY, JOHN. reg 45, co D, enr 10/11/63 Salyersville, enl 10/17/63 Ashland, dis 12/24/64 Catlettsburg, age 18, black hair & eyes, red skin, 5-5, house 805, s 1,2,6.

CONLEY, LEVI. reg 14, co F, enr 8/3/63 Salyersville, enl 8/30/63 Louisa, dis 9/15/65 Louisa, age 19, trans to 14VetInf, co D, cap Salyersville 11/29/63, d Richmond VA 7/11/64 of variola, house 604, s 1,2.

CONLEY, THOMAS J. reg 65, co A, enl 5/21/64, dis 6/21/64, age 21, blue eyes, dark hair, light skin, 5-9, rem in camp, house 94, 620 or 1122, s 2,4.

CONLEY, WILLIAM J. reg 65, co C, enl 5/21/64, dis 6/21/64, age 32, black eyes, dark hair, fair skin, 6-1, rem in camp, residence shown on militia list, house n/c, s 2,4,19.

CONLEY, WILLIAM W. reg 45, co E, enr 10/30/63 Ashland, enl 11/6/63 Ashland, age 36, rem mia Saltville VA 10/2/64, residence shown on militia list, house n/c, s 2,4,19.

CONLEY, WINSTON M. reg 68, co C, enl 4/7/64, 5/21/64, dis 4/16/64, 6/22/64, age 22, fair hair & skin, blue eyes, 6-2, residence shown on militia list, house n/c, s 2,4.

CRAFT, HENDERSON. reg 14, co D, enr 10/20/61 Louisa, enl 12/10/61 Louisa, dis 1/31/65 Louisa, age 21, light hair & skin, blue eyes, 5-5, rem cap, paroled at Cumberland Gap, 10/2/62, residence stated on muster roll, house n/c, s 1,2,4.

CRAFT, WILLIAM Z. reg 14, co D, enr 10/20/61 Louisa, enl 12/10/61 Louisa, age 25, light hair & skin, blue eyes, 5-8, rem d 10/10/64 Marietta GA of typhoid fever, house 568, s 1,2,4.

CRUM, ADAM. reg 65, co D, enl 5/21/64, dis 6/21/64, age 23, blue eyes, dark hair, fair skin, 5-6, house 246 or 334, s 2,4.

CRUM, ELI. reg 65, co D, enl 5/21/64, dis 6/21/64, age 37, blue eyes, light hair, fair skin, 5-8, rem in camp, house 254, s 2,4.

CRUM, MOSES. reg 45, co C, enr 9/22/63, enl 10/10/63 Catlettsburg, age 20, rem d 4/5/64 at Flemingsburg, house 334, s 1,2.

CRUM, PLEASANT. reg 39, co H, r musician, enr 12/18/62 Peach Orchard, enl 2/16/63 Peach Orchard, dis 9/15/65 Louisville, age 40, dark hair, blue eyes, fair skin, 6-0, house 238, s 1,2,4.

CRUM, WILLIAM. reg 65, co D, enl 5/21/64, dis 6/21/64, age 30, black eyes & skin, dark hair, 6-1, rem in camp, house 246, s 2,4.

CRUM, WILLIAM. reg CG, co K, enr 6/9/64, age 25, black hair & eyes, fair skin, 5-11, house 222, s 4.

CRUM, WILLIAM. reg 45, co C, enr 11/3/63 Ashland, enl 11/4/63 Ashland, dis 12/24/64 Catlettsburg, age 18, rem trans to co E 5/20/64, house 334, s 1,2.

CUNNINGHAM, PETER G. reg 65, co C, enl 5/21/64, dis 6/21/64, age 43, blue eyes, light hair, fair skin, 5-11, rem in camp, house 291, house 167, s 2,4.

CUNNINGHAM, ROBERT. reg 65, co C, enl 5/21/64, dis 6/21/64, age 37 gray eyes, dark hair & skin, 5-10, residence shown on militia list, house n/c, s 2,4,19.

CUNNINGHAM, TIMOTHY. reg 65, co C, enl 5/21/64, dis 6/21/64, age 27, gray eyes, light hair, fair skin, 5-8, residence shown on militia list, house n/c, s 2,4,19.

CUNNINGHAM, WILLIAM. reg 65, co C, enl 5/21/64, dis 6/21/64, age 39, blue eyes, light hair, fair skin, 6-1, rem in camp, house 292, s 2,4.

D

DALE, BERRY. reg 14, co K, enr 11/8/61 Louisa, enl 12/10/61 Louisa, dis 1/31/65, age 26, black hair & eyes, dark skin, 5-9, house 350, s 1,2,4.

DALE, PLEASANT. reg 14, co K, enr 11/8/61 Louisa, enl 12/10/61 Louisa, dis 1/31/65, age 22, black hair, gray eyes, dark skin, 5-11, residence stated on muster roll, house n/c, s 1,2,4.

DAMRON, JOHN J. reg 14, co K, enr 11/8/61, enl 12/10/61 Louisa, age 20, rem dis 1/13/63 for disability, house 268, s 2,4.

DAMRON, MOSES. reg 14, co K, enr 11/8/61, enl 12/10/61 Louisa, dis 1/31/65 Louisa, age 18, house 269, s 2,4.

DAMRON, SAMUEL. reg 14, co C, enr 10/25/61 Louisa, enl 12/10/61 Louisa, age 27, black hair, gray eyes, dark skin, 5-8, rem trans to co F 1/20/65, house 484, s 1,2,4.

DANIEL, DAVID. reg 65, co B, enl 5/21/64, dis 6/2/64, age 21, blue eyes, light hair, fair skin, 6-0, rem in camp, house 453, 562 or 708, s 2,4.

DANIEL, FLEMING. reg 65, co B, enl 5/21/64, dis 6/21/64, age 26, blue eyes, light hair, fair skin, 5-8, rem in camp, residence stated on militia list, house n/c, s 2,4,19.

DANIELS, GEORGE. reg 65, co D, enl 5/21/64, dis 6/21/64, age 38, blue eyes, light hair, fair skin, 5-11, rem in camp, house 271, s 2,4.

DANIEL, GEORGE W. reg 65, co B, enl 5/21/64, dis 6/21/64, age 20, dark eyes, hair & skin, 5-6, rem in camp, house 378, s 2,4.

DANIEL, GEORGE W. reg 14, co B, r cpl, enr 10/20/61 Louisa, enl 12/10/61 Louisa, dis 9/15/65 Louisville, age 18, light hair & skin, blue eyes, 5-4, rem trans to 14th Vet Inf, Co A, r cpl, enr 2/29/64, m/in 3/15/64 Louisa, house 408, s 1,2,4.

DANIEL, GEORGE W. reg 39, co G, enr 11/16/62, enl 8/30/63 Louisa, dis 9/15/65 Louisville, age 18, light hair & skin, blue eyes, 5-6, house 457, s 1,2,4.

DANIEL, HENRY J. reg 14, co D, enr 10/20/61 Louisa, enl 12/10/61 Louisa, dis 1/31/65 Louisville, age 22, black hair & eyes, light skin, 6-0, house 561, s 1,2,4.

DANIEL, ISOM. reg 65, co F, r 1st lt, enl 5/21/64, dis 6/12/64, age 41, blue eyes, black hair, dark skin, 6-0, house 561, s 2,4.

DANIEL, JAMES J. reg 14, co G, enr 11/19/61 Louisa, enl 12/10/61 Louisa, dis 1/31/65 Louisa, age 18, black hair, blue eyes, dark skin, 5-10, house 559, s 1,2,4.

DANIEL, JASPER. reg 65, co B, enl 5/21/64, dis 6/21/64, age 21, dark eyes, hair & skin, 5-10, house 520, s 2,4.

DANIELS, JOHN. reg 39, co G, enr 11/15/62, enl 2/16/63 Peach Orchard, dis 9/15/65, age 18, dark hair, blue eyes, light skin, 5-6, house 453 or 559, s 1,2,4.

DANIELS, NEWTON. reg 39, co G, enr 11/10/62, enl 2/16/63 Peach Orchard, dis 9/15/65 Louisville, age 19, light hair & skin, blue eyes, 5-11, house 408 or 520, s 1,2,4.

DANIEL, PETER. reg 65, r major, enl 5/21/64, dis 6/21/64, rem in camp, house 457, s 2,4.

DANIEL, THOMAS B. reg 65, co A, enl 5/2/64, dis 6/21/64, age 33, black eyes, light hair, dark skin, 5-9, house 382, s 2,4.

DANIEL, THOMAS J. reg 39, co G, enr 10/11/62 Peach Orchard, enl 2/16/63 Peach Orchard, dis 9/15/65 Louisville, age 22, black hair & eyes, dark skin, 5-10, house 446, s 1,2,4.

DANIEL, WYATT. reg 65, co B, enl 5/21/64, dis 6/21/64, age 22, dark eyes, hair & skin, 5-11, rem in camp, house 471, s 2,4.

DAVENPORT, DAVID. reg 39, co A, enr 12/30/63 Johnson Co., enl 3/28/64 Greenupsburg, dis 9/15/65 Louisville, age 26, light hair, gray eyes, fair skin, 5-6, rem residence stated on CSR, house n/c, s 1,2.

DAVENPORT, ISHAM. reg 39, co A, enr 2/1/63 Johnson Co., enl 2/16/63 Peach Orchard, dis 10/5/65 Louisville, age 20, dark hair & skin, black eyes, 5-8, residence stated on muster roll, house n/c, s 1,2,4.

DAVENPORT, WILLIAM. reg 39, co A, Enr 3/13/64 Johnson Co., enl 3/28/64 Greenupsburg, dis 9/15/65 Louisville, age 22, dark hair & skin, gray eyes, 5-8, rem residence stated on CSR, house n/c, s 1,2.

DAVIS, APPERSON. reg 39, co G, enr 11/3/62 Peach Orchard, enl 2/16/63 Peach Orchard, dis 9/15/65 Louisville, age 18, dark hair & skin, hazel eyes, 5-8, house 477, s 1,2,4.

DAVIS, BRACKEN L. reg 65, co A, enl 5/21/64, dis 6/21/64, age 25, gray eyes, light hair, dark skin, 5-11, rem in camp, house 304, s 2,4.

DAVIS, DANIEL. reg 65, co A, enl 5/21/64, age 18, house 66, s 4.

DAVIS, HENRY. reg 65, co E, enl 5/21/64, dis 6/21/64, age 30, blue eyes, light hair, fair skin, 6-0, house 100 or 419, s 2,4.

DAVIS, JAMES. reg 45, co G, enr 7/28/63, Mt. Sterling, enl 11/30/63 Ashland, age 18, rem des 12/7/64 at Mt. Sterling, residence shown on militia list, house n/c, s 1,2.

DAVIS, JOHN. reg 65, co A, enl 5/21/64, dis 6/21/64, house 66, s 2,4.

DAVIS, JOHN M. reg 14, co C, enr 10/10/61, enl 12/10/61 Louisa, dis 1/31/65 Louisa, age 18, house 545, s 2,4.

DAVIS, JOHN W. reg 65, co A, enl 5/21/64, dis 6/21/64, age 18, blue eyes, light hair & skin, 5-9, house 66, s 2,4.

DAVIS, JOSEPH. reg 65, co B, enl 5/21/64, rem des 5/30/64, house 467 or 477, s 4.

DAVIS, MICHAEL. reg 39, co G, r cpl, enr 11/15/62 Peach Orchard, enl 2/16/63 Peach Orchard, dis 9/15/65 Louisville, age 38, dark hair & skin, black eyes, 5-8, house 477, s 1,2,4.

DELONG, DAVID. reg 14, co G, r cpl, enr 11/19/61, enl 12/10/61 Louisa, dis 1/31/65 Louisa, age 23, dark hair, blue eyes, fair skin, 5-9, house 212, s 1,2,4.

DELONG, EMERY. reg 14, co G, enr 11/19/61 Louisa, enl 12/10/61 Louisa, age 20, dark hair, blue eyes, fair skin, 6-0, rem d 6/7/64 of wounds received 5/30/64, house 210, s 1,2,4.

DELONG, HARVEY. reg 14, co D, enr 10/1/61 Louisa, enl 12/10/61 Louisa, dis 3/21/64 Louisa, age 32, dark hair, blue eyes, fair skin, 6-1, rem dis for disability, chronic diarrhea, house 209, s 1,2,4.

DELONG, JEFFERSON. reg 65, co D, enl 5/21/64, dis 6/21/64, age 21, blue eyes, light hair, fair skin, 5-10, rem in camp, house 208, s 2,4.

DELONG, JOHN P. reg 14, co K, enr 11/8/61 Louisa, enl 12/10/61 Louisa, dis 1/1/65 Louisa, age 18, dark hair, blue eyes, fair skin, 5-10, house 212, s 1,2,4.

DELONG, SAMUEL. reg 14, co G, enr 11/8/61 Louisa, enl 12/10/61 Louisa, dis 1/31/65 Louisa, age 43, black hair, blue eyes, dark skin, 5-9, rem trans to co K 1/20/65, house 212, s 1,2,4.

DELONG, WILLIAM J. reg 65, co D, enl 5/21/64, dis 6/21/64, age 23, blue eyes, light hair, fair skin, 5-7, house 208, s 2,4.

DIALS, ELI R. reg 39, co A, enr 9/26/62 Johnson Co., enl 1/11/63 Louisa, dis 9/15/65 Louisville, age 19, light hair, gray eyes, dark skin, 5-6, rem cap 12/4/62 in Floyd Co. and taken to Richmond, paroled City Point VA 4/3/63, house 666, s 1,2,4.

DIXON, FARMER. reg 14, co H, enr 11/8/61 Louisa, enl 12/10/61 Louisa, dis 9/15/65 Louisville, age 26, light hair, blue eyes, fair skin, 6-0, rem trans to 14th Vet Inf, co A, enr 2/29/64, m/in 3/5/64, residence shown on militia list, house n/c, s 1,2,4.

DIXON, ISAAC. reg 14, co I, enr 9/4/62 Catlettsburg, enl 12/12/62 Richmond, dis 8/2/65 Lexington, age 22, dark hair, gray eyes, dark skin, 6-0, rem trans to 14th Vet Inf, co B, enr 9/4/62, m/in 12/12/62 Louisa, house 355, s 1,2,4.

DIXON, JAMES H. reg 14, co I, enr 11/10/61 Louisa, enl 12/10/61 Louisa, dis 4/18/63, age 23, dark hair & eyes, fair skin, 5-6, rem dis for disability, consumption, house 386, s 1,2,4.

DIXON, JOHN H. reg 65, co A, enl 5/21/64, dis 6/21/64, age 18, blue eyes, light hair & skin, 5-10, rem in camp, house 353, s 2,4.

DIXON, JOSEPH. reg 14, co F, r sgt, enr 8/1/63 Salyersville, enl 8/30/63 Louisa, dis 9/15/65 Louisville, age 19 at muster out, rem trans to co D, 14th Vet. Inf., prom from cpl to sgt 2/1/65, house 355, s 1,3.

DIXON, THOMAS J. reg 14, co K, enr 11/8/61 Louisa, enl 12/10/61 Louisa, dis 1/31/65 Louisa, age 19, sandy hair, blue eyes, red skin, 5-9, residence stated on muster roll, house n/c, s 1,2,4.

DUTTON, ELIAS. reg 39, co E, enr 12/17/62, enl 2/16/63 Peach Orchard, dis 9/15/65 Louisville, age 32, light hair, gray eyes, fair skin, 5-8, rem cap 12/4/62 in Floyd Co., house 232, s 1,2,4.

E

ELAM, R. D. reg 65, co E, enl 5/21/64, age 35, black hair, blue eyes, fair skin, 5-8, rem AWOL, house 847, s 4.

ELLIOTT, ABRAHAM M. reg 39, co A, enr 1/10/64 Johnson Co., enl 3/20/64 Greenupsburg, dis 9/15/65 Louisville, age 20, light hair, blue eyes, fair skin, 5-5, house 184, s 1,2,4.

ELLIOTT, JAMES. reg CG, co K, enr 6/9/64, enl 7/28/64 Frankfort, dis 3/11/65 Catlettsburg, age 20, black hair, blue eyes, fair skin, 5-7, house 184 or 345, s 2,4.

ELLIOTT, JAMES. reg 65, co B, enl 5/21/64, dis 6/21/64, age 22, blue eyes, light hair, fair skin, 5-8, house 345, s 2,4.

ELLIOTT, JAMES W. reg 39, co A, enr 9/6/62 Johnson Co., enl 2/16/63 Peach Orchard, age 21, black hair, blue eyes, fair skin, 5-4, rem d 2/26/63 of fever at regimental hospital at Louisa, house 345, house 184 or 345, s 1,2,4.

ELLIOTT, THOMAS W. reg 39, co A, enr 1/13/64 Johnson Co., enl 3/26/64 Greenupsburg, dis 9/15/65 Louisville, age 18, light hair, blue eyes, fair skin, 5-4, house 184, s 1,2,4.

ELY, DANIEL. reg 45, co C, enr 8/19/63 Paintsville, enl 10/10/63 Catlettsburg, age 19, dark hair, eyes & skin, 5-7, rem d 5/6/64 at Lexington of pulmonalis, house 420, s 1,2.

ELY, WILLIAM. reg 45, co C, enr 8/19/63 Paintsville, enl 10/10/63 Catlettsburg, dis 12/24/64 Catlettsburg, age 18, house 420, s 1,2.

ESTEP, LILBURN. reg 45, co C, enr 8/22/63 Paintsville, enl 10/10/63 Catlettsburg, dis 12/24/64 Catlettsburg, age 27, house 422, s 1,2.

ESTEP, SAMUEL. reg 65, co A, enl 5/21/64, dis 6/21/64, age 40, blue eyes, light hair & eyes, 5-11, house 55, s 2,4.

EWING, JAMES A. reg 39, co A, enr 1/5/63, enl 2/16/63 Peach Orchard, age 20, dark hair, gray eyes, fair skin, 5-6, rem d 4/25/63 Louisa of typhoid fever, residence stated on muster roll, house n/c, s 1,2,4,8.

F

FAIRCHILD, JESSE. reg 14, co D, enr 10/20/61 Louisa, enl 12/10/61 Louisa, dis 1/31/65 Louisa, age 18, light hair & skin, blue eyes, 5-8, rem cap near Louisa 3/24/63 and exchanged, house 589, s 1,2,4.

FAIRCHILD, LEVI. reg 65, co A, enl 5/21/64, dis 6/21/64, age 34, blue eyes, light hair & skin, 5-9, rem in camp, house 81, s 2,4.

FAIRCHILD, MOSES. reg 65, co F, enl 5/21/64, dis 6/21/64, age 36, blue eyes, black hair, fair skin, 6-0, house 573, s 2,4.

FAIRCHILD, SHADRACK. reg 65, co A, enl 5/21/64, dis 6/21/64, age 42, blue eyes, black hair, light skin, 5-10, rem in camp, house 85, s 2,4.

FAIRCHILD, WILLIAM. reg CG, co K, enr 6/9/64, enl 7/28/64 Frankfort, dis 3/11/65 Catlettsburg, age 24, light hair, blue eyes, fair skin, 6-0, house 832, s 2,4.

FAIRCHILD, WILLIAM. reg 65, co E, enl 5/21/64, dis 6/12/64, age 28, blue eyes, light hair, fair skin, 5-11, house 81, s 2,4.

FAIRCHILD, WILLIAM H. reg 45, co C, enr 8/22/63 Paintsville, enl 10/10/63 Catlettsburg, dis 12/24/64 Catlettsburg, age 26, residence shown on militia list, house 832, s 1,2.

FANNIN, HENRY. reg 65, co B, enl 5/21/64, dis 6/21/64, age 38, blue eyes, light hair, fair skin, 6-0, house 479, s 2,4.

FANNIN, SAMUEL. reg 65, co B, enl 5/21/64, dis 6/21/64, reg CG, co K, enr 6/9/64, enl 7/28/64 Frankfort, dis 3/11/65 Catlettsburg, age 25, black hair, blue eyes, fair skin, 6-0, house 529, s 2,4.

FITZPATRICK, CHARLES. reg 65, co A, enl 5/21/64, dis 6/21/64, age 31, blue eyes, black hair, dark skin, 5-10, rem in camp, house 111, s 2,4.

FITZPATRICK, CIVILAR. reg 65, co A, enl 5/21/64, rem des 5/30/64, house 120, s 4.

FITZPATRICK, HENRY. reg 65, co A, enl 5/21/64, dis 6/21/64, age 34, blue eyes, light hair & skin, 5-10, rem in camp, house 111, s 2,4.

FITZPATRICK, ISAAC. reg 65, co A, enl 5/21/64, dis 6/21/64, age 25, black eyes & hair, dark skin, 5-10, rem in camp, house 134, s 2,4.

FITCHPATRICK, JAMES. reg 14, co G, enr 11/19/61 Louisa, enl 12/10/61 Louisa, dis 1/24/64 Louisa, age 45 or 52, dark hair, blue eyes, fair skin, 6-0, rem dis for rheumatism, deafness and being 52 years old, house 558, s 1,2,4.

FITCHPATRICK, JOHN. reg 65, co C, enl 5/21/64, dis 6/21/64, age 30, blue eyes, light hair, fair skin, 5-10, rem in camp, house 395, s 2,4.

FITCHPATRICK, SAMPSON. reg 14, co G, enr 11/19/61 Louisa, enl 12/10/61 Louisa, dis 1/31/65 Louisa, age 20, black hair, blue eyes, fair skin, 5-11, house 558, s 1,2,4.

FITZPATRICK, MARION. reg 45, co C, enr 8/21/63 Paintsville, enl 10/10/63 Catlettsburg, age 23, light hair, eyes & skin, 5-10, rem d 3/17/64 Flemingsburg of measles, house 83, s 1,2.

FLETCHER, SYLVESTER. reg 39, co G, enr 11/13/62 Peach Orchard, enl 2/16/63 Peach Orchard, dis 9/15/65 Louisville, age 18, light hair & skin, blue eyes, 5-8, rem cap 12/18/64 Bristol, TN, rel 2/14/65, residence stated on muster roll, house n/c, s 1,2,4.

FLETCHER, WALTER. reg 39, co G, enr 9/13/62 Peach Orchard, enl 2/16/63 Peach Orchard, dis 9/15/62 Louisville, age 18, light hair & skin, hazel eyes, 506, residence stated on muster roll, house n/c, s 1,2.4.

FLETCHER, WINSTON. reg 39, co G, enr 12/24/62 Peach Orchard, enl 2/16/63 Peach Orchard, dis 9/15/65 Louisville, age 18, light hair & skin, hazel eyes, 5-10, residence stated on muster roll, house n/c, s 1,2,4.

FOX, ANDREW J. reg 14, co K, r 1st lt, enr 11/8/61 Louisa, enl 12/10/61 Louisa, dis 1/31/65 Louisa, age 25, rem prom from 2nd lt to 1st lt 3/1/62, house 2, s 1,2,4.

FRANKLIN, BIRD. reg 65, co C, enl 5/21/64, dis 6/21/64, age 35, gray eyes, light hair, fair skin, 5-5, house 301, s 2,4.

FRANKLIN, FREDERICK. reg 39, co A, enr 9/12/62 Johnson Co., enl 2/16/63 Peach Orchard, dis 9/15/65 Louisville, age 18, light hair, blue eyes, fair skin, 5-5, residence stated on muster roll, house n/c, s 1,2,4.

FRANKLIN, WILLIAM J. reg 39, co A, enr 10/11/62, enl 2/16/63 Peach Orchard, age 19, light hair, gray eyes, fair skin, 5-8, rem d 7/14/63 Louisa of typhoid fever, residence stated on muster roll, house n/c, s 1,2,4.

FRAZIER, ALEXANDER. reg 14, co I, enr 10/12/62 Paintsville, enl 6/10/63 Louisa, dis 9/15/65 Louisville, age 42, dark hair, black eyes, fair skin, 5-10, rem trans to 14th Vet Inf, co B, enr 10/12/62, m/in 6/10/63 Louisa, residence stated on muster roll, house n/c, s 1,2,4.

FRAZIER, JAMES. reg 45, co C, enr 9/30/63 Ashland, enl 11/4/63 Ashland, dis 12/24/63 Catlettsburg, age 18, dark hair, blue eyes, fair skin, 5-0, house 51, s 1,2,6.

FRAZIER, WILLIAM. reg 65, co E, enl 5/21/64, age 21, black hair, blue eyes, fair skin, 5-8, rem AWOL, house 424, s 4.

G

GIBBS, ABRAHAM. reg 14, co G, enr 11/10/62 Louisa, enl 6/10/63 Louisa, dis 6/12/65 Covington, age 19, light hair, blue eyes, swarthy skin, 5-6, rem trans to 14th Vet Inf, co D, enr 11/10/62, m/in 6/10/63 Louisa, dis for pulmonary disability, house 764, s 1,2,4.

GIBSON, ABRAHAM. reg 14, co G, enr 1/1/62 Johnson Co., enl 1/1/62 Louisa, dis 1/31/65 Louisa, age 18, dark hair, gray eyes, dark skin, 5-8, house 503, s 1,2,4.

GIBSON, ANDREW J. reg 14, co K, enr 11/8/61 Louisa, enl 12/10/61 Louisa, dis 1/31/65 Louisa, age 19, black hair & eyes, red skin, 5-9, rem wounded in face between 7/2/64 and 8/13/64, house 436, s 1,2,4.

GIBSON, IRA. reg 14, co I, age 37, residence stated on muster roll, house n/c, s 4.

GIBSON, SAMUEL. reg 39, co G, enr 9/13/62, enl 2/16/63 Peach Orchard, age 24, light hair, blue eyes, fair skin, 6-0, rem d 6/15/63 at Ashland of pneumonia, residence stated on muster roll, house n/c, s 1,2,4.

GILLESPIE, ANDREW J. reg 14, co G, enr 6/1/63 Louisa, enl 6/10/63 Louisa, age 15, light hair, black eyes, fair skin, 5-1, rem d 11/12/64 at Nashville of pneumonia and wounds received near Kennesaw Mountain GA 6/26/64, residence stated on muster roll, house n/c, s 1,2,4.

GOBLE, ANDREW J. reg 39, co A, enr 1/5/63 Johnson Co., enl 2/16/63 Peach Orchard, dis 9/15/65 Louisville, age 21, black hair, gray eyes, dark skin, 5-6, house 202, s 1,2,4.

GOBLE, DAVID. reg 65, co D, enl 5/21/64, age 35, light hair, blue eyes, dark skin, 5-10, rem des 6/12/64, house 204, s 4.

GOBLE, DRURY. reg 45, co F, enr 9/18/63 Peach Orchard, enl 11/2/63 Ashland, dis 12/24/64 Catlettsburg, age 27, dark hair & eyes, light skin, 5-6, house 245, s 1,2,6.

GOBLE, HIRAM. reg 14, co B, enr 10/10/61 Louisa, enl 12/10/61 Louisa, age 21, light hair & skin, dark eyes, 5-8, rem d 4/18/62 Lexington of lung fever, house 171, s 1,2,4.

GOBLE, ISAAC. reg 39, co A, r 1st lt., enr 9/6/62 Johnson Co., enl 2/16/63 Peach Orchard, dis 9/15/65 Louisville, age 31, black hair & eyes, fair skin, 5-6, rem cap 12/4/62 at Wireman's Shoals, prisoner at Richmond VA five months, paroled City Point VA 5/5/63, house 171, s 1,2,4,8.

GOBLE, JEREMIAH. reg 14, co B, enr 10/10/61 Louisa, enl 12/10/61 Louisa, dis 1/31/65 Louisa, age 30, dark hair, blue eyes, fair skin, 5-6, residence stated on muster roll, house n/c, s 1,2,4.

GOBBLE, JOHN. reg 14, co B, r sgt, enr 10/10/61 Louisa, enl 12/10/61 Louisa, dis 1/31/65 Louisa, age 19, light hair, blue eyes, fair skin, 5-1, rem app sgt 6/20/62, house 207, s 1,2,4.

GOBLE, JOHN L. reg 14, co B, enr 6/9/63 Louisa, enl 6/6/63 Louisa, age 26, dark hair & eyes, fair skin, 5-9, rem d 6/15/64 at Chattanooga TN of measles & chronic diarrhea, house 203, s 1,2,4.

GOBLE, WILLIAM. reg 14, co B, enr 10/10/61 Louisa, enl 12/10/61 Louisa, dis 1/31/65 Louisa, age 23, light hair, blue eyes, fair skin, 5-8, house 201, s 1,2,4.

GRACE, JAMES E. reg 39, co A, r sgt major, enr 2/5/63 Johnson Co., enl 2/16/63 Peach Orchard, age 22, black hair, blue eyes, fair skin, 5-10, rem prom to sgt major 11/1/63, des 6/16/64, reduced to ranks, residence stated on muster roll, house n/c, s 1,2,4,8.

GREEN, DAVID D. reg 65, co B, enl 5/21/64, dis 6/21/64 age 36, blue eyes, dark hair & skin, 6-0, house 403, s 2,4.

GREEN, FRANCIS M. reg 45, co D, enr 7/14/63 Catlettsburg, enl 10/17/63 Ashland, dis 4/15/65 Louisville, age 18, rem trans to co H 1/1/64, house 99, s 1,2.

GREEN, JOHN. reg 14, co G, r cpl, enr 11/19/61 Louisa, enl 12/10/61 Louisa, dis 1/31/65 Louisa, age 23, dark hair, blue eyes, fair skin, 5-10, house 544, s 1,2,4.

GREEN, WILLIAM. reg 65, co F, enl 5/21/64, dis 6/21/64, age 31, black eyes, light hair, fair skin, 6-0, rem in camp, house 99 or 543, s 2,4.

GRIM, C. J. reg 65, co F, enl 5/21/64, dis 6/21/64, age 26, light hair, blue eyes, fair skin, 5-2, house 533, s 2,4.

H

HAGER, DANIEL. reg 14, co K, enr 5/20/63 Louisa, enl 5/28/63 Louisa, age 18, gray hair, dark eyes & skin, 5-8, rem KIA at Altoona Mtn. or Lost Mtn. GA 5/31/64, house 159, s 1,2,4.

HAGER, DANIEL M. reg 45, co D, r sgt, enr 8/23/63 Salyersville, enl 10/17/63 Ashland, dis 12/24/64 Catlettsburg, age 23, black hair & eyes, dark skin, 5-5, house 443, s 1,2,6.

HALL, JOHN M. reg 14, co D, G, enr 11/19/61 Louisa, enl 12/10/61 Louisa, dis 1/31/65 Louisa, age 32 or 38, dark hair, blue eyes, fair skin, 5-8, rem trans to co D 8/31/63, back to co G, 1/20/65, house 206, s 1,2,4.

HALL, WILLIAM. reg 39, co G, enr 10/1/62, enl 2/16/63, age 30, black hair & eyes, dark skin, 5-6, rem cap 12/4/62 in Floyd Co., d 3/15/63 of fever at Richmond VA while a prisoner, house 456, s 1,2,4.

HAMMOND, JAMES M. reg 45, co C, enr 3/6/64 Paintsville, enl 3/12/64 Flemingsburg, age 21, light hair, eyes & skin, 6-0, rem CSR lists Johnson Co. as residence, house 33, s 1,2.

HAMMOND, WILEY W. reg 65, co A, enl 5/21/64, dis 6/21/64, age 18, blue eyes, red hair, red skin, 5-10, rem in camp, residence established by 6/27/64 letter to Governor, house n/c, s 2,4.

HANNA, EBENEZER. reg 65, co E, enl 5/21/64, dis 6/21/64, age 43, blue eyes, light hair, fair skin, 5-8, rem in camp, house 86, s 2,4.

HANNAH, ISAAC H. reg 14, co I, enr & enl 3/8/62 Camp Buell, dis 2/7/65 or 3/24/65 Cleveland OH, age 19, black hair, blue eyes, dark skin, 5-9, rem trans to 14th Vet Inf, Co B, enr 3/8/62, wounded 5/28/64 Altoona Mtn. GA, house 87, s 1,2,4.

HANNA, JOHN S. reg 14, co B, enr 10/10/61 Louisa, enl 12/10/61 Louisa, age 21, dark hair, blue eyes, fair skin, 5-10, rem des 5/28/64 Altoona Mtn. GA, house 168, s 1,2,4.

HANNAH, SAMUEL B. reg 39, co A, enr 5/10/64 Louisa, enl 3/28/64 Greenupsburg, dis 9/15/65 Louisville, age 25, dark hair & skin, gray eyes, 5-8, house 168, s 1,2,4.

HARLESS, VAN L. reg 39, co G, enr 12/1/62, enl 2/16/63 Peach Orchard, dis 9/15/65 Louisville, age 19, dark hair, eyes & skin, 5-6, residence stated on muster roll, house n/c, s 1,2,4.

HELTON, JEFFERSON. reg 14, co G, enr 10/10/61 Louisa, enl 1/1/62 Johnson Co., dis 1/31/65 Louisa, age 21, sandy hair, blue eyes, fair skin, 5-9, rem trans from co G, 14th to co G, 39th 4/1/63 and back to 14th 1/20/65, app cpl 9/1/62, residence stated on muster roll, house n/c, s 1,2,4.

HERNDON, MOSES. reg 39, co A, enr 12/30/63 Johnson Co., enl 3/28/64 Greenupsburg, dis 9/15/65 Louisville, age 28, light hair, blue eyes, fair skin, 5-9, residence stated on CSR, house n/c, s 1,2,4.

HILL, BENJAMIN F. reg 39, co A, enr 9/16/62 Johnson Co., enl 2/16/63 Peach Orchard, dis 9/15/65 Louisville, age 19, light hair, gray eyes, fair skin, 5-6, house 585, s 1,2,4.

HILL, HENRY H. reg 14, co D, r 2nd lt, enr 11/19/61 Louisa, enl 12/10/61 Louisa, dis 9/15/65 Louisville, age 23, light hair, blue eyes, fair skin, 5-6, prom from Sgt major to 2nd lt 10/1/64, trans to co B, 14th VetInf 11/1/64, m/in 1/30/65 Louisa, residence stated on list of officers, house 585, s 1,2,4.

HILL, THOMAS. reg 45, co E, enr 10/30/63 Louisa, enl 11/6/63 Ashland, dis 12/24/64 Catlettsburg, age 21, house 152, s 1,2.

HILL, WILLIAM E. reg 39, co A, enr 9/12/62 Johnson Co., enl 2/16/63 Peach Orchard, dis 9/15/65 Louisville, age 26, black hair, gray eyes, fair skin, 6-1, house 585, s 1,2,4.

HITCHCOCK, JOHN. reg 65, co F, enl 5/21/64, dis 6/21/64, reg CG, co K, enr 6/9/64, age 31, light hair, blue eyes, fair skin, 5-7, house 753, s 2,4.

HITCHCOCK, PARKER. reg 65, co E, enl 5/21/64, dis 6/21/64, reg CG, co K, enr 6/9/64, enl 10/28/64 Frankfort, dis 3/11/65 Catlettsburg, age 35, light hair, blue eyes, fair skin, 5-5, house 785, s 2,4.

HITCHCOCK, ROLAND G. reg 65, co E, enl 5/21/64, dis 6/21/64, age 26, black eyes & hair, dark skin, 6-0, residence stated on militia list, house n/c, s 2,4,19.

HITE, CHARLES ROBERT. reg 39, co A, enr 10/11/62 Johnson Co., enl 8/30/63 Louisa, dis 9/15/65 Louisville, age 28, black hair, gray eyes, dark skin, 5-8, house 321, s 1,2,4,8.

HITE, NICHOLAS. reg 39, co A, enr 1/10/64 Johnson Co., enl 3/28/64 Greenupsburg, dis 9/15/65 Louisville, age 18, dark hair & skin, black eyes, 5-8, house 320, s 1,2,4.

HORN, JOHN W. reg 14, co K, enr 11/8/61 Louisa, enl 12/10/61 Louisa, dis 1/31/65 Louisa, age 28, sandy hair, blue eyes, fair skin, 5-8, house 80, s 1,2,4.

HORN, THOMAS J. reg 65, co E, enl 5/21/64, dis 6/21/64, age 18, blue eyes, light hair, fair skin, 5-6, rem in camp, house 437, s 2,4.

HORN, WILLIAM R. reg 14, co K, enr 11/8/61 Louisa, enl 12/10/61 Louisa, dis 1/31/65 Louisa, age 19, sandy hair, blue eyes, fair skin, 6-0, residence stated on muster roll, house n/c, s 1,2,4.

HOWES, JAMES H. reg 65, co F, r cpl, enl 5/21/64, dis 6/21/64, age 34, black eyes & hair, fair skin, 6-0, house 363 or 663, s 2,4.

HOWES, SAMUEL. reg 39, co A, r cpl, enr 9/15/62 Johnson Co., enl 2/16/63 Peach Orchard, age 18, dark hair, black eyes, fair skin, 5-5, rem slightly wounded Battle of Cynthiana 6/11/64, house 363, s 1,2,4.

HUFF, JOHN. reg 45, co C, enr 3/6/64 Paintsville, enl 3/12/64 Flemingsburg, age 18, light hair & skin, dark eyes, 5-8, reg CG, co E, enr 5/7/64, enl 7/4/64 Frankfort, rem des 9/12/64 Frankfort, house 54, s 1,2,4.

HURT, CHRISTOPHER C. reg 39, co A, r cpl, enr 9/6/62 Johnson Co., enl 2/16/63 Peach Orchard, dis 9/15/65 Louisville, age 20, black hair & eyes, dark skin, 5-3, house 160, s 1,2,4.

HURT, FRANCIS. reg CG, co K, enr 6/9/64, enl 7/28/64 Frankfort, dis 3/11/65 Catlettsburg, house 160, s 2,4.

J

JACKSON, JASPER. reg 39, co K, enr 10/9/62 Piketon, enl 2/16/63 Peach Orchard, dis 9/15/65 Louisville, age 20, red hair, blue eyes, fair skin, 5-10, rem prom from cpl to sgt 4/10/63, reduced to ranks 1/64, house 68, s 1,2,4.

JAMES, JOHN L. H. reg 65, co D, r sgt, enl 5/21/64, dis 6/21/64, age 22, gray eyes, light hair, fair skin, 5-8, rem in camp, house 240, s 2,4,5.

JENKINS, FRANCIS. reg 45, co K, enr 11/24/63 Relief, enl 12/9/63 Louisa, age 18, rem des 2/12/64 at Mt. Sterling, house 812, s 1,2.

JENKINS, W. HARRISON. reg 45, co K, enr 11/24/63 Relief, enl 12/9/63 Louisa, age 18, rem des 2/12/64 at Mt. Sterling, house 812, s 1,2.

JENKINS, ROBERT. reg 45, co K, enr 11/24/63 Relief, enl 12/9/63 Louisa, age 23, rem des 2/12/64 at Mt. Sterling, house 819, s 1,2.

JOHNSON, ISAAC. reg 14, co B, enr 10/10/61 Louisa, enl 12/10/61 Louisa, age 22, light hair, blue eyes, fair skin, 6-0, rem d 3/3/62 at Paintsville of lung congestion, residence stated on muster roll, house n/c, s 1,2,4.

JOHNSON, JOEL. reg 45, co C, r cpl, enr 8/21/63 Paintsville, enl 10/10/63 Catlettsburg, dis 12/24/64 Catlettsburg, age 36, house 768, s 1,2.

JOHNSON, WILLIAM. reg 14, co G, enr 4/7/63 Louisa, enl 6/10/63 Louisa, dis 9/15/65 Louisville, age 18, sandy hair, blue eyes, fair skin, 5-10, rem trans to 14th Vet Inf, co C, enr 4/7/63, m/in 6/10/63 Louisa, wounded in right arm between 7/2/64 & 8/13/64, residence stated on muster roll, house n/c, s 1,2,4.

JONES, FRANCIS. reg 14, co D, enr 9/8/62 Catlettsburg, enl 10/8/62 Portland OH, dis 9/15/65 Louisville, age 18, light hair, dark eyes & skin, 5-5, rem trans to 14thVet Inf, co B, enr 9/17/62, m/in 10/8/62 Portsmouth OH, house 574, s 1,2,4.

JONES, LEMUEL. reg 14, co D, enr 10/10/61 Louisa, enl 12/10/61 Louisa, dis 1/31/65 Louisa, age 23, dark hair, blue eyes, light skin, 5-7, house 574, s 1,2,4.

JONES, WILLIAM P. reg 65, co F, enl 5/21/64, dis 6/21/64, age 25, blue eyes, light hair, fair skin, 5-10, house 700, s 2,4.

JUSTICE, ABRAHAM. reg 65, co A, enl 5/21/64, rem des 5/30/64, house 549, s 4.

JUSTICE, ANDREW. reg 14, co D, enr 10/20/61 Louisa, enl 12/10/61 Louisa, dis 1/31/65 Louisa, age 20, light hair, gray eyes, dark skin, 5-9, rem wounded in arm 6/28/64, residence established by descriptive muster roll, house 549, s 1,2,4.

JUSTICE, EDMUND. reg 14, co D, enr 10/20/61 Louisa, enl 12/10/61 Louisa, dis 1/31/65 Louisa, age 18, light hair & skin, blue eyes, 5-6, house 553, s 1,2,4.

K

KIMBLER, HIRAM. reg 14, co G, enr 11/29/62, enl 6/10/63 Louisa, age 19, light hair, blue eyes, fair skin, 5-8, rem d 7/6/64 at Chattanooga TN of typhoid fever, residence stated on muster roll, house n/c, s 1,2,4.

KIMBLER, JOSEPH. reg 14, co G, enr 11/29/62 Louisa, enl 6/10/63 Louisa, dis 9/15/65 Louisville, age 21, sandy hair, blue eyes, fair skin, 5-8, rem trans to 14th Vet Inf, co C, enr 11/29/62, m/in 6/10/63 Louisa, residence stated on muster roll, house n/c, s 1,2,4.

KIMBLER, SILAS P. reg 14, co K, enr 11/8/61 Louisa, enl 12/10/61 Louisa, dis 1/31/65 Louisa, age 28, light hair, blue eyes, fair skin, 5-10, house 669, s 1,2,4.

KIMBLER, SOLOMON. reg 14, co K, enr 11/8/61, age 30, rem d 12/4/61 or 12/22/61 of measles, mustered into state service 11/19/61, never mustered into federal service, house 657, s 1,4.

KIMBLER, WILLIAM. reg 14, co G, enr 11/1/61 Louisa, enl 12/10/61 Louisa, dis 1/31/65 Louisa, age 27, light hair, blue eyes, fair skin, 5-8, house 683, s 1,2,4.

KING, CHOCKLET. reg 39, co A, enr 9/6/62 Johnson Co., enl 1/11/63 Louisa, dis 9/15/65 Louisville, age 24, black hair, dark eyes & skin, 5-7, rem cap 12/4/62 and sent to Richmond VA, paroled 4/6/63, residence stated on muster roll, house n/c, s 1,2,4,8.

L

LAWSON, GEORGE W. reg 14, co G, enr 7/27/63 Louisa, enl 8/30/63 Louisa, dis 9/15/65 Louisville age 18, light hair, gray eyes, fair skin, 5-3, rem trans to 14th Vet Inf, co D, enr 7/29/63, m/in 8/30/63 Louisa, house 660, s 1,2,4.

LEMASTER, ARCHIBALD. reg 65, co F, enl 5/21/64, dis 6/21/64, age 21, blue eyes, light hair, fair skin, 6-0, house 596, s 2,4,19.

LEMASTER, DANIEL JR. reg 65, co F, enl 5/21/64, dis 6/21/64, age 28, blue eyes, dark hair, fair skin, 5-9, house 597, s 2,4.

LEMASTER, DANIEL SR. reg 65, co F, enl 5/21/64, dis 6/21/64, age 44, blue eyes, dark hair, fair skin, 5-10, house 569 or 771, s 2,4.

LEMASTER, ELEAZER. reg 65, co F, enl 5/21/64, dis 6/21/64, age 25, blue eyes, light hair, fair skin, 5-4, house 591, s 2,4.

LEMASTER, ELEAZER. reg 39, co G, enr 9/17/62 Peach Orchard, enl 10/27/63 Louisa, dis 9/15/65 Louisville, age 35, light hair, blue eyes, fair skin, 5-6, house 591, s 1,2,4.

LEMASTER, ELIAS. reg 14, co K, enr 9/19/62 Paintsville, enl 5/28/63 Louisa, dis 1/31/65 Louisa, rem trans to co G, 39th Ky Inf, 9/30/63, residence stated on muster roll, house n/c, s 1,4.

LEMASTER, FRANCIS M. reg 65, co F, enl 5/21/64, dis 6/21/64, age 29, black eyes, dark hair, fair skin, 5-10, house 591, 596 or 772, s 2,4.

LEMASTER, JAMES. reg 14, co K, enr 12/23/62 Paintsville, enl 5/28/63 Louisa, dis 9/15/65 Louisville, age 18, red hair, blue eyes, fair skin, 5-7, rem trans to 14th Vet Inf, co C, enr 12/23/62, m/in 5/28/63 Louisa, house 743, s 1,2,4.

LEMASTER, JAMES P. reg 45, co C, enr 8/22/63 Paintsville, enl 10/10/63 Catlettsburg, dis 12/24/63 Catlettsburg, age 23, house 423, s 1,2.

LEMASTER, LEWIS SR. reg 65, co F, enl 5/21/64, dis 6/1/64, age 37, blue eyes, light hair, fair skin, 6-0, house 590, s 2,4.

LEMASTER, LEWIS J. reg 65, co F, enl 5/1/64, dis 6/21/64, age 18, blue eyes, red hair, fair skin, 5-6, house 593, s 2,4.

LEMASTER, MARCUS. reg 14, co D, enr 10/20/61 Catlettsburg, 12/10/61 Louisa, age 18, dark hair, blue eyes, light skin, 5-10, rem d 4/13/62 Ashland, house 569, s 2,4.

LEMASTER, WILLIAM C. reg 65, co F, enl 5/21/64, dis 6/21/64, age 43, blue eyes, red hair, fair skin, 6-0, rem in camp, house 593 or 688, s 2,4.

LITTERAL, FLEMING. reg 65, co E, enl 5/21/64, dis 6/21/64, reg CG, co K, r sgt, enr 6/9/64, enl 7/28/64 Frankfort, dis 3/11/65 Catlettsburg, age 20, light hair, blue eyes, fair skin, 5-9, house 794, s 2,4.

LITTERAL, FLEMING. reg 14, co F, enr 6/15/63 Salyersville, enl 8/30/63 Louisa, dis 9/15/65 Louisville, age 19, dark hair, blue eyes, light skin, 6-0, rem trans to 14th Vet Inf, co D, enr 6/20/63, m/in 8/30/63 Louisa, house 788, s 1,2,4.

LITTERAL, GEORGE WASHINGTON. reg 65, co B, enl 5/21/64, rem des 5/30/64, house 349, s 4.

LITTERAL, JAMES W. reg 14, co I, enr 11/10/61 Louisa, enl 12/10/61 Louisa, dis 1/31/65 Louisa, age 23, residence stated on muster roll, house n/c, s 1,2,4.

LITTERAL, ROWLAND. reg 45, co D, enr 8/22/63 Catlettsburg, enl 10/17/63 Ashland, age 24, dark hair & eyes, red skin, 5-10, rem d 4/5/64 Flemingsburg of camp fever, house 790, s 1,2,6.

LYONS, JAMES. reg CG, co E, enr 6/7/64, enl 7/4/64 Frankfort, dis 3/11/65 Catlettsburg, house 634, s 2,4.

M

MAHAN, JOHIAL H. reg 45, co C, enr 8/9/63 Paintsville, enl 10/10/63 Catlettsburg, dis 12/24/64 Catlettsburg, age 36, house 24, s 1,2.

MAHAN, MASON. reg 45, co C, enr 8/7/63 Paintsville, enl 10/10/63 Catlettsburg, dis 12/24/64 Catlettsburg, age 21, house 131, s 1,2.

MAHAN, WILLIAM. reg 45, co C, enr 10/30/63 Ashland, enl 11/4/63 Ashland, dis 12/24/64 Catlettsburg, age 24 or 25, light hair & skin, blue eyes, 6-0, rem trans to co E 5/20/64, house 24, s 1,2,6.

MARSHALL, HIRAM. reg 39, co B, enr 10/11/63 Pike Co., enl 10/30/63 Louisa, dis 9/15/65 Louisville, age 19, dark hair & skin, blue eyes, 5-9, house 416, s 1,2,4.

MARSHALL, JOHN. reg 45, co C, enr 9/28/63 Paintsville, enl 10/10/63 Catlettsburg, age 30, rem d 4/6/64 Flemingsburg, house 417, s 1,2.

MARSHALL, JOHN. reg 39, co K, enr 4/18/64 Paintsville, enl 8/30/64 Louisa, dis 9/15/65 Louisville, age 30, dark hair, blue eyes, fair skin, 6-1, house 760, s 1,2,4.

MAYES, HENLEY C. reg 14, co G, enr 11/19/61 Louisa, enl 1/10/61 Louisa, dis 1/31/65 Louisa, age 28, dark hair, blue eyes, fair skin, 5-10, rem wounded in right foot 5/30/64, residence stated on muster roll, house n/c, s 1,2,4.

MAYNARD, THOMAS. reg 39, co D, enr 11/19/62, enl 2/16/63 Peach Orchard, dis 9/15/65 Louisville, age 18, residence stated on muster roll, house n/c, s 1,2,4.

MCCLOUD, JONATHAN. reg 14, co K, enr 11/8/61, enl 1/10/61 Louisa, dis 1/31/65 Louisa, age 44, dark hair, blue eyes, fair skin, 5-7, house 63, s 1,2,4.

MCDALE, LEWIS. reg 65, co F, enl 5/21/64, dis 6/21/64, reg CG, co K, enr 6/9/64, age 33, dark hair, blue eyes, fair skin, 6-0, house 684, s 2,4.

MCFARLAND, WILLIAM. reg 65, co E, enl 5/21/64, dis 6/21/64, age 40, blue eyes, light hair, fair skin, 6-0, house 826, s 2,4.

MCGINNIS, GEORGE. reg 14, co G, enr 11/19/61 Louisa, enl 12/10/61 Louisa, dis 1/30/65 Louisa, age 23, dark hair, blue eyes, fair skin, 6-0, rem d 2/5/62 at Louisville of heart disease, house 211, s 1,2,4.

MCGINNIS, JACKSON. reg 14, co G, r cpl, enr 11/19/61 Louisa, enl 12/10/61 Louisa, dis 1/30/65 Louisa, age 22, light hair, blue eyes, fair skin, 6-1, rem prom to cpl 5/1/63, wounded in shoulder near Kennesaw Mtn. GA 6/22/64, house 211, s 1,2,4.

MCINTIRE, JOHN. reg 39, co A, enr 9/10/62 Johnson Co., enl 2/16/63 Peach Orchard, dis 9/15/65 Louisville, age 27, light hair, blue eyes, fair skin, 5-11, rem cap 12/4/62 in Floyd Co., house 35, s 1,2,4.

MCKENZIE, ANDREW. reg 65, co F, enl 5/21/64, dis 6/21/64, reg CG, co I, enr 6/15/64, enl 10/20/64 Frankfort, dis 3/11/65 Catlettsburg, age 18, blue eyes, light hair, fair skin, 5-10, house 727, s 2,4.

MCKENZIE, GEORGE. reg 14, co G, cpl, enr 11/19/61 Louisa, enl 1/10/61 Louisa, dis 1/31/65 Louisa, age 18, dark hair & skin, black eyes, 5-7, house 681, s 1,2,4.

MCKENZIE, HENRY. reg 14, co D, enr 9/13/63 Louisa, enl 10/10/63 Louisa, dis 9/15/65 Louisville, age 30, light hair, blue eyes, dark skin, 6-2, rem trans to 14th Vet Inf, co B, enr 9/13/63, m/in 10/30/63 Louisa, house 679, s 1,2,4.

MCKENZIE, HIRAM E. reg 39, co B, enr 7/2/64, enl 8/30/64 Lexington, dis 9/15/65 Louisville, age 19, light hair, blue eyes, fair skin, 5-9, house 678, s 2,4.

MCKENZIE, JOHN W. reg 65, co F, enl 5/21/64, dis 6/21/64, age 20, blue eyes, black hair, dark skin, 5-0, house 670, 737 or 824, s 2,4.

MCKENZIE, JOSEPH. reg 14, co D, enr 12/13/63 Louisa, enl 12/28/63 Louisa, dis 9/15/65 Louisville, age 27, light hair & skin, blue eyes, 6-0, rem trans to 14th Vet Inf, enr 12/13/63, m/in 12/28/63 Louisa, house 671, s 1,2,4.

MCKENZIE, MARTIN. reg 14, co D, enr 10/20/61 Catlettsburg, enl 12/10/61 Louisa, dis 1/31/65 Louisa, age 23, light hair & skin, blue eyes, 6-1, residence stated on muster roll, house n/c, 1,2,4.

MCKENZIE, WILLIAM F. reg 65, co F, enl 5/21/64, dis 6/21/64, age 20, blue eyes, black hair, dark skin, 5-0, house 670, s 2,4.

MCKENZIE, WILLIAM J. reg 65, co A, enl 5/21/64, dis 6/21/64, age 34, black eyes, light hair & skin, 5-10, house 664, s 2,4.

MEAD, JAMES K. reg 65, co E, r cpl, enl 5/21/64, dis 6/21/64, age 20, blue eyes, light hair, fair skin, 5-7, house 797, s 2,4.

MEADE, JOSEPH. reg 14, co K, enr 5/27/63 Louisa, enl 5/28/63 Louisa, dis 9/15/65 Louisville, age 18, light hair, blue eyes, fair skin, 6-1, rem trans to 14th Vet Inf, co C, enr 5/27/63, m/in 5/28/63 Louisa, wounded in right arm between 7/2/64 & 8/13/64, residence stated on muster roll, house n/c, s 1,2,4.

MEAD, RHODES. reg 65, co E, enl 5/21/64, dis 6/21/64, house 797, s 2,4.

MEAD, ROBERT A. reg 45, co C, enr 8/20/63 Paintsville, enl 10/10/63 Catlettsburg, dis 12/24/63 Catlettsburg, age 23, house 797, s 1,2.

MEADE, SAMUEL. reg 45, co C, enr 9/15/63 Paintsville, enl 10/10/63 Catlettsburg, dis 12/24/64 Catlettsburg, age 18, house 524, s 1,2.

MEADOWS, ELIJAH. reg 45, co C, enr 7/26/63 Paintsville, enl 10/10/63 Catlettsburg, dis 12/24/63 Catlettsburg, age 19, house 411, s 1,2.

MEADOWS, SEYMOUR. reg 45, co C, enr 8/9/63 Paintsville, enl 10/10/63 Catlettsburg, dis 12/24/64 Catlettsburg, age 19, house 411, s 1,2.

MEEK, ELIAS. reg 65, co B, r sgt, enl 5/21/64, dis 6/21/64, age 21, black eyes & hair, dark skin, 6-0, house 326, s 2,4.

MEEK, JAMES. reg 65, co B, enl 5/21/64, dis 6/21/64, age 29, dark eyes, light hair, fair skin, 5-6, house 340, s 2,4.

MEEK, JOHN. reg 65, co B, enl 5/21/64, dis 6/21/64, reg CG, co K, enr 6/9/64, enl 7/28/64 Frankfort, dis 3/11/65 Catlettsburg, age 23, light hair, blue eyes, fair skin, 6-0, house 326, s 2,4.

MEEK, NATHANIEL. reg 65, co B, enl 5/21/64, dis 6/21/64, age 27, blue eyes, dark hair, fair skin, 6-0, house 327, s 2,4.

MEED, SHADRACK. reg 65, co B, enl 5/21/64, rem des 5/30/64, house 28, s 4.

MELVIN, ANDREW. reg 65, co A, enl 5/21/64, dis 6/21/64, age 25, black eyes & hair, dark skin, 5-5, house 68, s 2,4.

MELVIN, GEORGE. reg 45, co C, enr 10/13/63 Paintsville, enl 10/10/63 Catlettsburg, dis 12/24/64 Catlettsburg, age 18, house 658, s 1,2.

MELVIN, LEWIS. reg 14, co G, r cpl, enr 1/1/62 Johnson Co., enl 1/1/62 Louisa, dis 1/31/65 Louisa, age 21, light hair, gray eyes, fair skin, 5-8, rem prom to cpl 6/5/62, house 658, s 1,2,4.

MILAM, HENRY J. reg 39, co A, enr 11/29/62 Johnson Co., enl 2/16/63 Peach Orchard, dis 9/15/65 Louisville, age 18, dark hair, blue eyes, fair skin, 5-2, rem trans to co F, 3/1/64, residence stated on muster roll, house n/c, s 1,2,4,8.

MILAM, JOHN. reg 39, co A, enr 4/18/63 Johnson Co., enl 8/30/63 Louisa, dis 9/15/65 Louisville, age 19, black hair & eyes, dark skin, 5-8, residence stated on muster roll, house n/c, s 1,2,4,8.

MILAM, SAMUEL. reg 39, co A, enr 11/29/62 Johnson Co., enl 1/11/63 Louisa, dis 6/15/65 Covington, age 20, dark hair & skin, black eyes, 5-9, residence stated on muster roll, house n/c, s 1,2,4.

MILLER, JOHN S. reg 65, co B, enl 5/21/64, dis 6/21/64, age 32, blue eyes, light hair, fair skin, 6-1, house 485, s 2,4.

MILLER, SYLVESTER B. reg 39, co G, enr 12/1/62, enl 2/16/63 Peach Orchard, age 26, rem des 6/21/64 at Louisa, house 482, s 2,4.

MOLLETT, BENJAMIN. reg 45, co C, enr 9/18/63 Paintsville, enl 10/10/63 Catlettsburg, age 19, rem absent sick at muster out, house 278, s 1,2.

MOLLETT, DAVID. reg 14, co G, enr 11/19/61 Louisa, enl 12/10/61 Louisa, dis 1/31/65 Louisa, age 45, house 483, s 1,2,4.

MOLLETT, DAVID B. reg 14, co G, enr 11/19/61 Louisa, enl 12/10/61 Louisa, dis 1/31/65 Louisa, age 21, house 267, s 1,4.

MOLLETT, ELIAS B. reg 39, co G, enr 12/24/62, enl 2/16/63 Peach Orchard, dis 9/15/65 Louisville, age 21, light hair, black eyes, dark skin, 5-10, house 276, s 1,2,4.

MOLLETT, JAMES. reg 39, co G, enr 11/18/62, enl 2/16/63 Peach Orchard, dis 9/15/65 Louisville, age 22, light hair, blue eyes, fair skin, 5-10, rem cap in Floyd Co. 12/4/62 or 1/15/63 or 2/1/63, house 278, s 1,2,4.

MOLLETT, JAMES H. reg 65, co B, enl 5/21/64, dis 6/21/64, age 23, blue eyes, light hair, fair skin, 6-0, rem in camp, house 258, s 2,4.

MOLLETT, JOHN. reg 65, co D, enl 5/21/64, dis 6/21/64, age 34, blue eyes, light hair, fair skin, 5-8, house 264, s 2,4.

MOLLETT, JOHN C. reg 39, co G, enr 8/1/63 Louisa, enl 8/30/63 Louisa, dis 9/15/65 Louisville, age 18, light hair, blue eyes, dark skin, 5-8, house 276, s 1,2,4.

MOLLETT, LEVI. reg 14, co G, enr 8/20/63, reg 65, co D, enl 5/21/64, dis 6/21/64, age 24, gray eyes, dark hair, fair skin, 5-11, rem in camp, house 259, s 2,4,19.

MOLLETT, THOMAS. reg 14, co B, enr 10/10/61 Catlettsburg, enl 2/16/63 Louisa, dis 9/15/65 Louisville, age 20, light hair, blue eyes, fair skin, 5-4, rem trans to 14th Vet Inf, co A, enr 2/29/64, m/in 3/15/64 Louisa, residence stated on muster roll, house n/c, s 1,2,4.
MOLLETT, WILLIAM. reg 65, co B, enl 5/21/64, dis 6/21/64, age 25, blue eyes, light hair, fair skin, 5-10, house 276, s 2,4.
MONTGOMERY, JILSON. reg 65, co B, enl 5/21/64, dis 6/1/64, age 38, blue eyes, light hair, fair skin, 5-8, rem in camp, house 322, s 2,4.
MONTGOMERY, WILEY. reg 65, co C, enl 5/21/64, dis 6/21/64, age 35, blue eyes, light hair, fair skin, 5-5, rem in camp, house 285, s 2,4.
MOORE, JOHN. reg 65, co D, enl 5/21/64, dis 6/21/64, age 39, black eyes, dark hair, fair skin, 5-10, rem in camp, house 213, s 2,4.
MORRIS, PARDON A. reg 45, co G, r cpl, enr 11/29/63 Louisa, enl 11/30/63, dis 4/14/65 Catlettsburg, age 19, house 701, s 1,2.
MURPHY, ALEXANDER. reg 39, co A, enr 9/16/62, enl 2/16/63 Peach Orchard, dis 9/15/65 Louisville, age 21, light hair, blue eyes, fair skin, 5-7, rem residence established by descriptive muster roll, house 313, s 1,2,4.
MURPHY, JAMES C. reg 39, co A, enr 11/29/62, enl 2/16/63 Peach Orchard, dis 9/15/65 Louisville, age 26, dark hair & skin, black eyes, 5-6, house 313, s 1,2,4.
MURPHY, ROBERT. reg 65, co C, enl 5/21/64, rem des 6/17/64, house 314, s 4.
MURRAY, FREDERICK. reg 14, co D, enr 10/20/61, enl 12/10/61 Louisa, dis 1/31/65 Louisa, age 21, house 393, s 2,4
MURRAY, JESSE. reg 65, co F, enl 5/21/64, dis 6/21/64, age 42, blue eyes, dark hair & skin, 6-0, house 480, s 2,4.
MURRAY, SAMUEL. reg 14, co D, r cpl, enr 10/20/61 Louisa, enl 1/10/61 Louisa, dis 1/31/65 Louisa, age 18, red hair, blue eyes, fair skin, 5-8, rem wounded in hospital at Louisa 6/64, house 570, s 1,2,4.
MUSIC, ANDREW B. reg 65, co B, enl 5/21/64, dis 6/21/64, age 30, dark eyes, hair & skin, 5-6, rem in camp, residence shown on militia list, house n/c, s 2,4,19.
MUSIC, ANDREW H. reg 14, co B, enr 10/10/61 Louisa, enl 12/10/61 Louisa, age 27, rem d 12/28/61 Catlettsburg of measles, house 199, s 1,2,4.
MUSIC, ANDREW J. reg 39, co A, r sgt, enr 10/11/62 Johnson Co., enl 6/11/63 Louisa, age 24, black hair & eyes, fair skin, 5-10, rem prom from pvt, cap & paroled, house 296, s 1,2,4.
MUSIC, JOHN. reg 65, co C, enl 5/21/64, dis 6/21/64, house 298, s 2,4.
MUSIC, MICHAEL. reg 39, co A, enr 10/11/62 Johnson Co., enl 8/2/063 Louisa, dis 9/15/65 Louisville, age 36, light hair, blue eyes, fair skin, 5-10, house 169, s 1,2,4.

N

NEWSOM, JAMES. reg 39, co C, enr 9/10/62 Louisa, enl 2/16/63 Peach Orchard, age 35, dark hair & skin, gray eyes, 6-3, rem trans to co E 10/30/63, residence stated on muster roll, house n/c, s 1,2,4.
NIBERT, JAMES. reg 65, r quartermaster, enl 5/21/64, dis 6/21/64, house 407, s 2,4.
NICHOL, GEORGE J. reg 65, co F, enl 5/21/64, dis 6/21/64, age 33, blue eyes, light hair, fair skin, 6-0, house 571, s 2,4.
NICKELL, ALEX W. reg CG, co K, r capt, enr & enl 8/9/64 Frankfort, dis 3/11/65 Frankfort, rem residence established by List of Officers, house n/c, s 2.

O

O'BRYAN, JAMES. reg CG, Co K, enr 6/9/64, enl 7/28/64 Frankfort, dis 3/11/65 Catlettsburg, age 28, dark hair, black eyes, fair skin, 5-9, house 536, s 2,4.

O'BRYAN, JAMES. reg 14, co K, enr 11/8/61, enl 12/10/61 Louisa, dis 1/31/65, age 20, house 24, s 2,4.

O'BRYAN, JAMES V. reg 65, co E, enl 5/21/64, dis 6/21/64, age 36, blue eyes, dark hair, fair skin, 6-0, rem in camp, house 59, s 2,4.

OSBORN, ALFRED. reg 65, co C, enl 5/21/64, dis 6/21/64, age 40, blue eyes, dark hair, fair skin, 5-10, rem in camp, house 310, s 2,4.

OSBORNE, CALVIN. reg 65, co B, enl 5/21/64, dis 6/21/64, age 35, blue eyes, light hair, fair skin, 6-0, house 316, s 2,4.

P

PACK, CHARLES. reg 14, co G, r sgt, enr 11/19/61 Louisa, enl 12/10/61 Louisa, dis 1/31/65 Louisa, age 28, sandy hair, blue eyes, red skin, 5-9, rem prom to cpl 5/25/62, app sgt 8/31/62, house 541, s 1,2,4.

PACK, WILLIAM. reg 14, co G, enr 11/19/61 Louisa, enl 1/10/61 Louisa, age 26, dark hair, eyes & skin, 5-9, cap Lawrence Co. 3/24/63, paroled in eastern Ky., d 8/22/64 Marietta GA of chronic diarrhea, residence stated on muster roll, house n/c, s 1,2,4.

PATRICK, GREENVILLE. reg 39, co A, enr 10/11/62 Johnson Co., enl 8/30/63 Louisa, dis 9/15/65 Louisville, age 18, black hair & eyes, dark skin, 5-6, house 288, s 1,2.

PATRICK, JACKSON M. reg 65, co A, r 1st lt, enl 5/21/64, dis 6/21/64, rem in camp, house 109, s 2,4.

PATRICK, JILSON P. reg 65, co A, enl 5/21/64, dis 6/21/64, age 36 or 43, gray eyes, light hair & skin, 6-0, rem in camp, house 117, s 2,4.

PELPHREY, DANIEL. reg 65, co B, enl 5/21/64, dis 6/21/64, reg CG, co K, enr 6/9/64 Lawrence Co., age 22, dark hair, blue eyes, fair skin, 5-4, house 749, s 4.

PELPHREY, DANIEL. reg 65, co E, enl 5/21/64, age 36, red hair, blue eyes, fair skin, 5-10, rem AWOL, house 781, s 4.

PELPHREY, DAVID. reg 45, co C, enr 9/28/63 Paintsville, enl 10/10/63 Catlettsburg, dis 12/24/64 Catlettsburg, age 26, house 851, s 1,2.

PELPHREY, JAMES. reg 65, co F, enl 5/21/64, dis 6/21/64, age 20, blue eyes, light hair, fair skin, 5-10, house 751, s 2,4.

PELPHREY, JOHN W. reg 65, co E, enl 5/21/64, dis 6/21/64, age 30, blue eyes, black hair, fair skin, 6-0, house 853, s 2,4.

PELPHREY, JOSEPH. reg 65, co E, enl 5/21/64, dis 6/12/64, age 19, blue eyes, light hair, fair skin, 5-8, house 749, s 2,4.

PELPHREY, WILLIAM A. reg 65, co E, enl 5/21/64, dis 6/21/64, age 43, blue eyes, light hair, fair skin, 5-11, house 749, s 2,4,19.

PENIX, ALLEN. reg 45, co D, enr 10/25/63 Salyersville, enl 2/3/64 Mt. Sterling, age 26, dark hair & skin, gray eyes, 5-6, rem trans to co H, 5/20/64, house 492, s 1,2,6.

PENNINGTON, MILTON. reg 14, co K, enr 9/2/62, enl 5/8/63 Louisa, dis 8/2/65 Lexington, age 18, light hair, blue eyes, fair skin, 6-0, rem trans to 14th Vet Inf, co C, enr 9/2/62, m/in 5/28/63 Louisa, house 721, s 1,2,4.

PERRY, GEORGE WASHINGTON. reg 65, co B, enl 5/21/64, rem des 5/30/64, house 335 or 628, s 4.

PHILLIPS, JOHN. reg 14, co H, enr 7/12/63 Louisa, enl 8/29/63 Louisa, dis 9/15/65 Louisville, age 28, residence stated on muster roll, house n/c, s 1,4.

PICKLESIMER, GEORGE N. reg 14, co I, enr 11/10/61 Louisa, enl 12/10/61 Louisa, dis 1/31/65 Louisa, age 26, black hair, blue eyes, dark skin, 5-10, house 70, s 1,2,4.

PICKLESIMER, JASPER. reg 45, co C, enr 8/19/63 Paintsville, enl 10/10/63 Catlettsburg, dis 12/24/64, age 19, house 775, s 1,2.

PICKLESIMER, JOHN. reg 14, co G, enr 11/19/61 Louisa, enl 12/10/61 Louisa, dis 1/31/65 Louisa, age 32, black hair & eyes, dark skin, 5-10, house 680, s 1,2,4.

PICKLESIMER, NATHANIEL. reg 65, co E, r 1st sgt, enl 5/21/64, dis 6/21/64, age 36, blue eyes, dark hair, fair skin, 5-7, rem in camp, house 774, s 2,4.

PICKLESIMER, SAMUEL. reg 65, co E, enl 5/21/64, age 25, light hair, blue eyes, fair skin, 5-8, rem AWOL, house 827, s 4.

PICKLESIMER, WALLACE. reg 45, co C, E, enr 10/30/63 Louisa, enl 11/4/63 Ashland, dis 12/24/64 Catlettsburg, age 18, house 775, s 1,2.

PORTER, BENJAMIN. reg 45, co E, enr 9/11/63 Catlettsburg, enl 11/1/63 Ashland, age 22, yellow hair, light eyes, fair skin, 6-2, rem cap 9/64 in Pike Co., house 251, s 1,2,6.

PORTER, BENJAMIN B. reg 65, co D, enl 5/21/64, dis 6/21/64, age 27, blue eyes, light hair, fair skin, 5-7, rem in camp, house 223, s 2,4.

PORTER, JOHN M. reg 65, co C, enl 5/21/64, dis 6/21/64, age 31, black eyes & hair, dark skin, 5-11, rem in camp, house 283, s 2,4.

PORTER, JOSEPH. reg 65, co D, enl 5/21/64, dis 6/21/64, age 32, blue eyes, light hair, fair skin, 6-3, house 214, s 2,4

PORTER, WILLIAM G. reg CG, co G, r 1st lt, enr 8/9/64, enl 9/29/64, age 28, light hair & skin, blue eyes, 6-2, rem resigned 11/28/64, house 281, s 2,4.

POSTON, HARVEY. reg 39, co A, enr 12/28/63 Johnson Co., enl 3/28/64 Greenupsburg, dis 9/15/65 Louisville, age 22, black hair & eyes, dark skin, 6-0, residence stated on CSR, house n/c, s 1,2,4.

PRATER, GEORGE W. reg 14, co K, enr & enl 5/28/63 Louisa, dis 9/15/65 Louisville, age 18, dark hair & eyes, fair skin, 5-4, rem trans to 14th Vet Inf, co C, enr & m/in 5/28/63, residence stated on muster roll, house n/c, s 1,2,4.

PRESTON, BATEMAN. reg 68, co C, enl 4/7/64, 5/21/64, dis 4/16/64, 6/22/64, age 28, blue eyes, fair skin & hair, 6-1, house 392, s 2,4.

PRESTON, BURGESS. reg 65, r col, enl 5/21/64, dis 6/21/64, house 522, s 2,4.

PRESTON, E. E. reg 65, co B, enl 5/21/64, dis 6/21/64, age 39, blue eyes, light hair, fair skin, 5-8, house 345, s 2,4.

PRESTON, ELIPHUS. reg 65, co A, enl 5/21/64, rem des 6/64, house 391, s 4.

PRESTON, GREENVILLE. reg 65, co B, enl 5/21/64, rem des 5/30/64, house 405, s 4.

PRESTON, HARRISON. reg 45, co F, enr 8/25/63 Peach Orchard, enl 11/2/63 Ashland, dis 12/24/64 Catlettsburg, age 28, dark hair, light eyes & skin, 5-10, house 391, s 1,2,6.

PRESTON, HENRY. reg 65, co A, enl 5/21/64, rem des 6/28/64, house 32, s 4.

PRESTON, JESSE. reg 65, co B, enl 5/21/64, dis 6/21/64, reg CG, co K, enr 6/9/64, enl 7/28/64 Frankfort, dis 3/11/65 Catlettsburg, age 20, black hair & eyes, fair skin, 5-7, house 345, s 2,4.

PRESTON, JOHN D. reg 39, co G, r 1st sgt, enr 11/10/62, enl 2/16/63 Peach Orchard, dis 9/15/65 Louisville, age 18, dark hair, gray eyes, fair skin, 6-1, house 32, s 2,4.

PRESTON, LAFAYETTE. reg 65, co B, r 1st lt, enl 4/7/64, 5/21/64, dis 4/16/64, 6/22/64, age 18, gray eyes, light hair, fair skin, 5-11, house 393, s 2,4.

PRESTON, MARTIN. reg 65, co A, enl 5/21/64, rem des 6/28/64, house 15, s 4.

PRESTON, MONTRAVILLE. reg 65, co A, enl 5/21/64, rem des 6/10/64 from push boats, house 302, s 4.

PRESTON, NATHAN. reg 39, co A, enr 12/12/62 Johnson Co., enl 2/16/63 Peach Orchard, dis 9/15/65 Louisville, age 42, black hair, gray eyes, dark skin, 5-6, house 9, s 1,2,4.

PRESTON, SAMUEL. reg 65, co B, enl 5/21/64, age 25, blue eyes, light hair, fair skin, 6-0, house 397, s 2,4.

PRESTON, SAMUEL WILLIAM. reg 18 Inf, co I, enr 10/25/61 Morgan Co., enl 2/8/62 Cynthiana, KIA 8/30/62 Richmond, house 522, s 1,2.

PRESTON, SHADRACK. reg 65, co B, enl 5/21/64, dis 6/21/64, age 24, black eyes, dark hair & skin, 5-9, house 345 or 389, s 2,4.

PRESTON, THOMAS J. reg 45, co C, enr 9/10/63 Paintsville, enl 10/10/63 Catlettsburg, dis 12/24/64 Catlettsburg, age 19, house 391, s 1,2.

PRESTON, WALLACE. reg 45, co F, enr 8/25/63 Peach Orchard, enl 11/2/63 Ashland, dis 12/24/64 Catlettsburg, age 18, dark hair & eyes, light skin, 5-6, house 345, s 1,2,6.

PRICE, CHRISTOPHER C. reg 65, co A, enl 5/21/64, dis 6/21/64, age 27, blue eyes, light hair & skin, 6-0, rem in camp, house 28, s 2,4.

PRICE, FRANKLIN. reg 65, co C, r sgt, enl 5/21/64, dis 6/21/64, age 22, blue eyes, light hair, fair skin, 5-10, rem in camp, house 312, s 2,4.

PRICE, JESSE. reg 65, co C, enl 5/21/64, dis 6/21/64, rem in camp, age 18, blue eyes, light hair, fair skin, 5-10, house 312, s 2,4.

PRICE, JESSE. reg 39, co G, enr 12/2/62, enl 2/16/63 Peach Orchard, dis 1/2/65 Lexington, age 38, dark hair & skin, black eyes, 5-9, rem cap 12/4/62 Floyd Co, paroled 9/3/63 City Point VA, dis for chronic bronchitis, house 315, s 1,2,4.

PRICE, KINGSTON F. reg 45, co C, enr 9/6/63 Paintsville, enl 10/10/63 Catlettsburg, dis 12/24/64 Catlettsburg, age 20, house 306, s 1,2.

PRICE, MARTIN L. reg 45, co C, enr 9/11/63 Paintsville, enl 10/10/63 Catlettsburg, dis 12/24/64, age 18, house 303, s 1,2.

PRIEST, CORNELIUS W. reg 65, co D, enl 5/21/64, dis 6/21/64, age 39, gray eyes, dark hair, fair skin, 5-8, house 220, s 2,4.

PRIEST, HENRY H. reg 14, co H, r sgt, enr 10/25/61 Louisa, enl 12/10/61 Louisa, dis 1/31/65 Louisa, age 21, dark hair & skin, blue eyes, 5-9, rem app cpl 5/1/62, app sgt 7/5/63, wounded in right wrist between 7/2/64 & 8/13/64, house 216, s 1,2,4.

PRIEST, HIRAM J. reg 14, co H, r cpl, enr 10/25/61 Catlettsburg, enl 12/10/61 Louisa, age 23, dark hair & skin, blue eyes, 6-1, rem d 9/5/64 Knoxville TN of dysentery & chronic diarrhea, house 216, s 1,2,4.

PUCKETT, LEVI. reg 14, co I, age 42, residence stated on muster roll, house n/c, s 4.

PUCKETT, WILLIAM. reg 14, co I, age 18, residence stated on muster roll, house n/c, s 4.

Q

QUILLEN, SOLOMON. reg 14, co K, enr 11/8/61 Louisa, enl 12/10/61 Louisa, age 25, sandy hair, blue eyes, fair skin, 5-6, rem d 3/6/62 Paintsville of fever, house 78, s 1,2,4.

R

RAMEY, JOHN. reg 65, co F, enl 5/21/64, dis 6/21/64, age 43, blue eyes, dark hair, fair skin, 5-8, rem in camp, house 686, s 2,4.

RAMEY, SAMUEL. reg 65, co A, enl 5/21/64, dis 6/21/64, age 25, blue eyes, light hair & skin, 5-10, rem in camp, house 434, s 2,4,19.

RAMEY, TAYLOR. reg 45, co C, enr 10/13/63 Paintsville, enl 10/10/63 Catlettsburg, dis 12/24/64 Catlettsburg, age 18, house 686, s 1,2.

RAMEY, THOMAS. reg 65, co F, r sgt, enl 5/21/64, dis 6/21/64, age 40, black eyes, dark hair, fair skin, 5-0, rem in camp, house 686, s 2,4.

RAMEY, WILLIAM R. reg CG, co E, enr 5/28/64, enl 7/4/64 Frankfort, dis 3/11/65 Catlettsburg, house 686, s 2,4.

RANDOLPH, WILLIAM N. reg 39, r comm sgt, enr 9/8/62, enl 2/16/63 Peach Orchard, dis 9/15/65 Louisville, age 38, dark hair & skin, black eyes, 5-9, rem prom from pvt, co A, 7/1/63, house 6, s 1,2,4.

RATLIFF, HENRY. reg 14, co K, enr 11/8/61 Louisa, enl 12/10/61 Louisa, dis 1/31/65 Louisa, age 27, dark hair, blue eyes, fair skin, 5-11, house 426, s 1,2,4.

RATLIFF, JAMES. reg 65, co E, enl 5/21/64, dis 6/21/64, age 27, blue eyes, dark hair, fair skin, 5-9, rem in camp, house 432, s 2,4.

RATLIFF, JOHN. reg 14, co K, enr 11/8/61 Louisa, enl 12/10/61 Louisa, age 22, black hair & eyes, fair skin, 5-11, rem killed at Lost Mtn. GA 5/28/64, house 432, s 1,2,4.

REED, WILLIAM T. reg 45, co D, enr 10/27/63 Salyersville, enl 2/3/64 Mt. Sterling, dis 2/14/65 Catlettsburg, age 18, dark hair, blue eyes, fair skin, 5-5, rem trans to co H, 5/20/64, residence shown on militia list, house n/c, s 1,2,19.

REYNOLDS, JOHN C, reg 14 KyCav, co B, enr 8/16/62, m/in 11/6/62 Mt. Sterling, reg 39, co A, enr 3/13/64 Johnson Co., enl 3/28/64 Greenupsburg, dis 9/15/65 Louisville, age 24, dark hair & skin, black eyes, 5-10, residence shown on CSR, house n/c, s 1,2,4.

REYNOLDS, NOAH. reg 39, co A, enr 11/28/62 or 12/28/62 Peach Orchard, enl 2/16/63 Peach Orchard, age 24, rem killed 2/21/63 in Johnson Co. in an affray by a citizen, residence stated on muster roll, house n/c, s 1,2,4.

REYNOLDS, OLIVER. reg 39, co A, r cpl, enr 11/29/62 Peach Orchard, enl 2/16/63 Peach Orchard, age 22, black hair & eyes, fair skin, 6-0, rem des 4/25/64 at Louisa, residence stated on muster roll, house n/c, s 1,2,4.

RICE, ALEXANDER. reg 65, co A, enl 5/1/64, dis 6/21/64, age 22, black eyes, light hair & skin, 5-11, house 360, s 2,4.

RICE, ANDREW J. reg 65, co A, enl 5/21/64, dis 6/21/64, house 116, s 2,4.

RICE, ANDREW JACKSON. reg 65, co E, enl 5/21/64, age 33, light hair, blue eyes, fair skin, 6-0, rem AWOL, residence shown on militia list, house n/c, s 4,19.

RICE, ANDREW W. reg 39, co A, enr 9/6/62 Johnson Co., enl 2/16/63 Peach Orchard, dis 9/15/65 Louisville, age 18, light hair, blue eyes, fair skin, 5-9, house 360, s 1,2,4.

RICE, GEORGE W. reg 39, co A, r cpl, enr 9/6/62 Johnson Co., enl 2/16/63 Peach Orchard, dis 9/15/65, age 31, light hair, gray eyes, fair skin, 6-0, house 584, s 1,2,4.

RICE, HARRISON. reg CG, co K, enr 6/9/64 Lawrence Co., age 32, light hair, blue eyes, fair skin, 5-11, house 127, s 4.

RICE, ISAAC. reg 39, r hospital steward, enr 9/6/62 Johnson Co., enl 2/16/63 Peach Orchard, dis 9/15/65 Louisville, age 40, dark hair, blue eyes, fair skin, 6-0, rem prom from pvt co A, 3/21/63, house 360, s 1,2,4.

RICE, JAMES. reg 65, co A, enl 5/21/64, dis 6/21/64, age 18, blue eyes, light hair & skin, 5-9, rem in camp, house 113 or 360, s 2,4.

RICE, JOHN. reg 14, co D, enr 10/20/61 Louisa, enl 12/10/61 Louisa, dis 3/19/64 Louisa, age 41, dark hair, eyes & skin, 6-0, rem dis for disability, rheumatism, house 554, s 1,2,4.

RICE, JOHN H. reg 65, co A, enl 5/21/64, dis 6/21/64, age 18, black eyes & hair, light skin, 5-10, rem in camp, house 116, s 2,4.

RICE, JOHN J. reg 65, co A, enl 5/21/64, dis 6/21/64, age 31, gray eyes, light hair & skin, 5-10, rem in camp, house 115, s 2,4,19.
RICE, JOHN P. M. reg 45, co C, r cpl, enr 8/21/63 Paintsville, enl 10/10/63 Catlettsburg, dis 12/24/64 Catlettsburg, age 22, house 82, s 1,2.
RICE, JOHN R. reg 65, co A, enl 5/21/64, dis 6/21/64, age 27, black eyes & hair, dark skin, 5-10, house 110, s 2,4.
RICE, MARTIN. reg 14, co I, enr 10/10/61 Louisa, age 22, black hair & eyes, dark skin, 5-7, rem d 12/10/61 Louisa of pneumonia, house 114, s 1,2,4.
RICE, SAMUEL. reg 14, co D, enr 9/1/63 Louisa, enl 10/30/63 Louisa, dis 9/15/65 Louisville, age 16, dark hair & eyes, fair skin, 5-10, rem trans to 14th Vet Inf, co B, enr 9/21/63, m/in 10/30/63 Louisa, house 554, s 1,2,4.
RICE, SAMUEL J. reg 65, co A, r sgt, enl 5/21/64, dis 6/21/64, age 26, black eyes & hair, dark skin, 5-9, rem in camp, house 107, s 2,4.
RICE, SAMUEL K. reg 14, co I, enr 11/10/61 Louisa, enl 12/10/61, dis 1/31/65 Louisa, age 36, dark hair & skin, black eyes, 5-10, house 106, s 1,2,4.
RICE, SAMUEL M. reg 14, co I, enr 11/10/61 Louisa, enl 12/10/61 Louisa, dis 1/31/65 Louisa, age 19, fair hair & skin, blue eyes, 5-8, house 360, s 1,2,4.
RICE, WALLACE. reg 14, co I, r cpl, enr 11/10/61 Louisa, enl 12/10/61 Louisa, dis 1/31/65 Louisa, age 25, fair hair & skin, blue eyes, 6-0, rem prom to cpl 6/30/64, house 662, s 1,2,4.
RICE, WILEY. reg 65, co A, enl 5/21/64, dis 6/21/64, age 23, black eyes, light hair & skin, 5-9, rem in camp, house 118, s 2,4.
RICE, WILLIAM M. reg 14, co D, enr 10/20/61 Louisa, enl 12/10/61, age 20, dark hair & eyes, fair skin, 5-9, rem 14th Vet Inf, co B, enr 2/29/64, m/in 3/15/64 Louisa, d 7/18/64 Nashville TN of typhoid fever, house 554, s 1,2,4.
ROBERSON, LOUIS. reg 10 KyCav, enr 8/9/62, m/in 9/9/62 Covington, m/out 9/17/63 Maysville, reg 39, co A, r cpl, enr 10/11/63 or 10/19/63 Louisa, enl 10/29/63 Louisa, dis 9/15/65 Louisville, age 20 or 22, hair, black eyes, fair skin, 5-8, house 286, s 1,2.
ROBERTS, GEORGE W. reg 39, co A, enr 10/17/62, enl 2/16/63 Peach Orchard, dis 9/15/65 Louisville, age 26, residence stated on muster roll, house, house 297, s 2, 4.
ROBERTS, JAMES. reg 45, co C, enr 8/7/63 Paintsville, enl 10/10/63 Catlettsburg, dis 12/24/64 Catlettsburg, age 23, house 3, s 1,2.
ROBERTS, REUBEN. reg 14, co G, enr 11/19/61 Louisa, enl 12/10/61 Louisa, dis 1/31/65, age 18, light hair, blue eyes, fair skin, 5-9, residence stated on muster roll, house, n/c, s 1,2,4.
ROBERTS, RICHARD. reg 39, co A, enr 11/14 or 18/62 Peach Orchard, enl 2/16/63 Peach Orchard, age 24, black hair, gray eyes, fair skin, 5-9, rem cap 12/4/62 Floyd Co., sent to Richmond, VA, d 11/2/64 Lexington of fever, residence stated on muster roll, house n/c, s 1,2,4.
ROBERTS, STROTHER W. reg 14, co G, enr 11/19/61 Louisa, enl 12/10/61 Louisa, dis 1/31/65 Louisa, age 19, dark hair, blue eyes, fair skin, 5-8, rem cap 2/15/63 in Lawrence Co., paroled in Eastern Kentucky, residence stated on muster roll, house n/c, s 1,2,4.
ROBERTS, WILLIAM. reg 65, co A, enl 5/21/64, dis 6/21/64, age 33, blue eyes, red hair, light skin, 5-8, rem in camp, house 22, s 2,4.
ROBERTSON, GEORGE W. (SR.). reg 39, co A, enr 10/11/62, enl 2/16/63 Peach Orchard, dis 9/15/65 Louisville, age 44, house 286, s 2,4.
ROBERTSON, GEORGE W. (JR.). reg 39, co A, enr 1/8/64 Johnson Co., enl 3/28/64 Greenupsburg, dis 9/15/65 Louisville, age 23, fair hair & skin, blue eyes, 5-6, residence shown on CSR, house n/c, s 1,2,4.

ROBERTSON, JOHN J. reg 14, co K, enr 11/8/61 Louisa, enl 12/10/61 Louisa, age 31, rem des 9/4/62, residence stated on muster roll, house n/c, s 1,2,4.

ROBERTSON, WALTER M. reg 65, co A, enl 5/21/64, dis 6/21/64, residence shown on militia list, house n/c, s 2,4,19.

ROBINSON, THOMAS. reg 14, co K, enr 4/20/63 Louisa, enl 5/28/63 Louisa, dis 9/15/65 Louisville, age 30, dark hair, gray eyes, fair skin, 5-10, rem trans to 14th Vet Inf, co C, enr 4/20/63, m/in 5/28/63, r sgt, house 144, s 1,2,4.

ROBINSON, WILLIAM. reg 14, co K, enr 9/2/63 Louisa, enl 10/29/63 Louisa, dis 9/15/65 Louisville, age 22, dark hair, blue eyes, fair skin, 5-10, rem trans to 14th Vet Inf, co C, enr 9/2/63, m/in 10/29/63 Louisa, r cpl, house 142, s 1,2,4.

ROTON, JONATHAN. reg 39, co A, r 2nd sgt, enr 9/6/62 Johnson Co., enl 2/16/63 Peach Orchard, dis 9/15/65 Louisville, age 18, fair hair & skin, gray eyes, 5-9, residence stated on muster roll, house n/c, s 1,2,4.

ROWLAND, ARMSTRONG. reg CG, co K, enr 6/9/64, age 32, light hair, blue eyes, fair skin, 5-6, house 76, s 4.

ROWLAND, FINNEY. reg 65, co A, enl 5/21/64, dis 6/21/64, age 20, black hair & eyes, fair skin, 5-10, rem in camp, house 654, s 2,4.

ROWLAND, JOHN. reg 45, co E, enr 10/4/63 Catlettsburg, enl 11/6/63 Ashland, dis 12/24/64 Catlettsburg, age 33, house 77, s 1,2.

ROWLAND, JOHN JR. reg 65, co A, enl 5/21/64, dis 6/21/64, age 36, blue eyes, light hair & skin, 5-7, house 77, s 2,4.

ROWLAND, JOSEPH C. reg 45, asst surgeon, enr 9/25/63 Paintsville, enl 10/10/63 Catlettsburg, dis 2/14/65 Catlettsburg, age 28, trans from co C to F&S 4/12/64, house 76, s 1,2.

RULE, CHARLES G. reg 65, co A, enl 5/21/64, dis 6/21/64, age 30, blue eyes, black hair, dark skin, 5-9, rem in camp, house 516, s 2,4.

RULE, HANKLIN F. reg 14, co G, enr 9/4/62 Catlettsburg, enl 9/4/62 Portland OH, dis 8/2/65 Lexington, age 20, light hair, blue eyes, fair skin, 5-6, rem trans to 14th Vet Inf co D, enr 9/4/62, m/in 9/4/62 Portsmouth OH, app cpl 2/1/65, residence stated on muster roll, house n/c, s 1,2,4.

RULE, JESSE C. reg 65, co A, r sgt, enl 5/21/64, dis 6/21/64, age 23, blue eyes, light hair & skin, 5-10, rem in camp, house 655, s 2,4.

S

SALYER, BENJAMIN. reg 65, co F, enl 5/21/64, dis 6/21/64, age 23, blue eyes, black hair, fair skin, 6-0, house 587 or 648, s 2,4.

SALYER, B. F. reg 65, co F, r cpl, enl 5/21/64, dis 6/21/64, age 34, blue eyes, light hair, fair skin, 5-10, house 790, s 2,4.

SALYER, GENERAL F. reg 45, co C, r cpl, enr 8/22/63 Paintsville, enl 10/10/63 Catlettsburg, age 21, dark hair & skin, blue eyes, 5-11, rem d 6/4/64 Ft. Beaver KY, house 783, s 1,2.

SALYER, JACKSON. reg 65, co F, enl 5/21/64, dis 6/21/64, age 36, blue eyes, light hair, fair skin, 5-10, house 691, s 2,4.

SALYER, JACOB. reg 45, co D, enr 9/28/63 Salyersville, enl 10/17/63 Ashland, age 18, dark hair, blue eyes, red skin, 5-5, rem d 11/22/63 Salyersville, house 790, s 1,2.

SALYER, JONATHAN H. reg 65, co F, enl 5/21/64, dis 6/12/64, age 27, black eyes & hair, fair skin, 6-2, house 576, s 2,4.

SALYER, LEVI. reg 65, co F, enl 5/21/64, dis 6/21/64, reg CG, co K, enr 6/9/64, enl 10/20/64 Frankfort, dis 3/11/65 Catlettsburg, age 24, dark hair, black eyes, fair skin, 5-10, house 588, s 2,4.

SALYER, SAMUEL B. reg 14, co G, enr 11/19/61 Louisa, enl 12/10/61 Louisa, dis 1/31/65, age 30, sandy hair, dark eyes, fair skin, 5-9, trans to co E, 39th Ky 5/1/63, trans back to 14th Ky 1/20/65, house 694, s 1,2,4.

SALYER, WILEY. reg 65, co F, enl 5/21/64, dis 6/21/64, age 26, black eyes & hair, fair skin, 6-0, house 692, s 2,4.

SALYER, WILLIAM. reg 14, co D, r wagoner, enr 10/20/61 Louisa, enl 12/10/61 Louisa, dis 1/31/65 Louisa, age 23, dark hair & eyes, fair skin, 5-7, house 551, s 1,2,4.

SALYER, WILLIAM. reg 45, co C, enr 8/22/63 Paintsville, enl 10/10/63 Catlettsburg, dis 12/24/63 Catlettsburg, age 18, house 576, s 1,2.

SALYER, ZACHARIAH. reg 45, co C, enr 9/27/63 Paintsville, enl 10/10/63 Catlettsburg, age 18, light hair, blue eyes, dark skin, 5-6, rem d 7/6/64 at Lexington of wounds received in action at Cynthiana, house 783, s 1,2.

SANSOM, THOMAS B. reg 39, co G, r cpl, enr 11/14/62 Peach Orchard, enl 2/16/63 Peach Orchard, dis 9/15/65 Louisville, age 20, light hair, hazel eyes, dark skin, 5-10, residence stated on muster roll, house n/c, s 1,2,4.

SEGRAVES, THOMAS. reg 65, co F, enl 5/21/64, dis 6/21/64, age 44, blue eyes, black hair, fair skin, 6-0, residence shown on militia list, house n/c, s 2,4.

SHAVERS, RANSOM. reg 45, co C, enr 3/6/64 Paintsville, enl 3/12/64 Flemingsburg, age 33, light hair, eyes & skin, 5-11, house 767, s 1,2.

SHERMAN, JOHN M. E. reg 45, co C, enr 10/16/63 Paintsville, enl 2/6/64 Mt. Sterling, dis 2/14/65 Catlettsburg, age 18, light hair & skin, gray eyes, 5-3, rem trans to co H, house 652, s 1,2.

SHERMAN, NATHAN. reg 65, co A, enl 5/21/64, rem des 5/30/64, house 652, s 4.

SHERMAN, THOMAS J. reg 14, co D, r cpl, enr & enl 5/24/63 Louisa, dis 9/15/65 Louisville, age 26, dark hair, gray eyes, fair skin, 6-0, rem trans to 14th Vet Inf, co B, enr & m/in 5/24/63, app cpl 3/1/65, house 652, s 1,2,4.

SHERMAN, WILLIAM. reg 45, co C, r sgt, enr 8/22/63 Paintsville, enl 10/10/63 Catlettsburg, dis 12/24/64 Catlettsburg, age 28, house 652, s 1,2.

SHORT, GRANDERSON. reg 65, co F, enl 5/21/64, dis 6/21/64, age 43, black eyes & hair, dark skin, 5-8, house 290, s 2,4.

SHORT, ISAAC. reg 65, co C, enl 5/21/64, dis 6/21/64, age 21, black eyes & hair, dark skin, 5-10, rem in camp, house 311, s 2,4.

SHORT, SILAS. reg 65, co C, enl 5/21/64, dis 6/21/64, age 33, gray eyes, dark hair, fair skin, 5-10, rem in camp, house 290, s 2,4.

SLOAN, JOHN. reg 14, co G, enr 11/19/61 Louisa, enl 12/10/61 Louisa, dis 1/31/65 Louisa, age 43, light hair, blue eyes, fair skin, 6-0, house 547, s 1,2,4.

SMITH, DAVID J. reg 14, co K, enr 10/2/62 Paintsville, enl 5/28/63 Louisa, dis 9/15/65 Louisville, age 18, light hair, blue eyes, fair skin, 5-6, rem trans to 14th Vet Inf, co C, enr 10/10/62, m/in 5/28/63 Louisa, r cpl, house 98, s 1,2,4.

SMITH, JAMES. reg 65, co E, enl 5/21/64, dis 6/21/64, age 30, blue eyes, dark hair, fair skin, 6-0, house 810, s 2,4.

SMITH, JOSIAH J. reg 14, co D, enr 10/20/61 Louisa, enl 12/10/61 Louisa, dis 3/26/63 Camp Chase OH, age 28, dark hair & skin, blue eyes, 5-9, rem dis for chronic diarrhea & bronchitis, residence stated on muster roll, house n/c, s 1,2,4.

SPARKS, ALLEN. reg 14, co G, enr 11/19/61 Louisa, enl 12/10/61 Louisa, age 21, dark hair, eyes & skin, 6-0, rem trans to 14th Vet Inf 3/15/64, d 6/29/64 at Chattanooga TN of chronic diarrhea, house 617, s 1,2,4.

SPARKS, ELISHA. reg 14, co D, enr 10/20/61 Louisa, enl 12/10/61 Louisa, age 21, black hair & eyes, dark skin, 5-8, rem d 2/10/63 Ashland of typhoid, house 580, s 1,2,4.

SPARKS, NATHAN. reg 14, co D, enr 8/5/63 Louisa, enl 8/30/63 Louisa, dis 9/15/65 Louisville, age 24, dark hair & skin, blue eyes, 5-7, rem trans to 14th Vet Inf, co B, enr 8/5/63, m/in 8/30/63 Louisa, house 605, s 1,2,4.

SPARKS, WILLIAM. reg 14, co D, enr 10/20/61 Louisa, enl 12/10/61 Louisa, dis 1/31/65 Louisa, age 23, black hair & eyes, dark skin, 5-8, rem wounded in right foot between 7/2/64 & 8/13/64, residence established by descriptive muster roll, house 579, s 1,2,4.

SPEARS, ENOCH. reg 65, co A, enl 5/21/64, dis 6/21/64, age 19, gray eyes, black hair, dark skin, 5-6, house 150, s 2,4.

SPEARS, MORGAN. reg 14, co K, enr 11/8/61 Louisa, enl 12/10/61 Louisa, age 30, black hair, gray eyes, fair skin, 5-10, rem d 8/64 at Chattanooga TN of disease, house 140, s 1,2,4.

SPEARS, SAMUEL. reg 65, co C, r capt, enl 5/21/64, dis 6/21/64, age 36, blue eyes, dark hair, fair skin, 5-10, house 309, s 2,4.

SPEARS, THOMAS J. reg 39, co A, enr 8/3/63 Johnson Co., enl 8/30/63 Louisa, age 24, fair hair, gray eyes, dark skin, 5-8, rem d 8/26/64 Mt. Sterling, house 195, s 1,2,4.

SPEARS, THOMAS W. reg 65, co C, r sgt, enl 5/21/64, dis 6/12/64, age 34, gray eyes, dark hair & skin, 5-10, house 192, s 2,4.

SPEARS, VINCENT F. reg 39, co A, enr 10/11/62 Peach Orchard, enl 2/16/63 Peach Orchard, dis 9/15/65 Louisville, age 39, light hair, gray eyes, fair skin, 5-7, residence stated on muster roll, house n/c, s 1,2,4,8.

SPEARS, WALLACE W. reg 65, co C, r cpl, enl 5/21/64, dis 6/21/64, age 26, blue eyes, dark hair, fair skin, 5-8, rem in camp, residence shown on militia list, house n/c, s 2,4.

SPRADLIN, ANDREW J. reg 14, co K, r cpl, enr 11/8/61 Louisa, enl 12/10/61 Louisa, dis 9/15/65 Louisville, age 18, sandy hair, gray eyes, fair skin, 5-9, rem trans to 14th Vet Inf, co C, enr 2/29/64, m/in 3/15/64 Louisa, r sgt, house 88, s 1,2,4.

SPRADLIN, BENJAMIN F. reg 65, co A, r 2nd lt, enl 5/21/64, dis 6/21/64, age 32, blue eyes, light hair & skin, 6-2, rem in camp, house 89, s 2,4,19.

SPRADLIN, DANIEL. reg 14, co K, enr 5/1/63 Louisa, enl 5/28/63 Louisa, dis 9/15/65 Louisville, age 21, dark hair, gray eyes, fair skin, 5-11, rem trans to 14th Vet Inf, co C, enr 5/1/63, m/in 5/28/63 Louisa, house 95, s 1,2,4.

SPRADLIN, EVAN. reg 65, co C, r cpl, enl 5/21/64, dis 6/21/64, age 42, blue eyes, light hair, fair skin, 5-11, rem in camp, residence shown on militia list, house n/c, s 2,4.

SPRADLIN, JAMES. reg 14, co K, enr 9/2/63 Louisa, enl 10/29/63 Louisa, dis 9/15/65 Louisville, age 22, black hair & eyes, fair skin, 6-0, rem trans to 14th Vet Inf, co C, enr 9/2/63, m/in 10/29/63 Louisa, house 95, s 1,2,4.

SPRADLIN, JAMES H. reg 65, co A, r capt, enl 5/21/64, dis 6/21/64, age 36, blue eyes, black hair, fair skin, 5-11, rem in camp, house 49, s 2,4.

SPRADLIN, JOHN. reg 65, co A, enl 5/21/64, dis 6/21/64, age 35, black eyes & hair, dark skin, 5-11, rem in camp, house 90, s 2,4.

SPRADLIN, JOHN M. reg 14, co K, enr 11/8/61 Louisa, enl 12/10/61 Louisa, age 19, sandy hair, blue eyes, fair skin, 6-1, rem KIA 8/6/64 Atlanta GA, residence stated on muster roll, house n/c, s 1,2,4.

SPRADLIN, MICHAEL. reg CG, co K, r cpl, enr 6/9/64, enl 7/28/64 Frankfort, dis 3/11/65 Catlettsburg, age 47, dark hair, blue eyes, fair skin, 5-10, residence shown on militia list, house n/c, s 2,4.

SPRADLIN, SOLOMON. reg 39, co A, enr 9/15/62 Peach Orchard, enl 2/16/63 Peach Orchard, dis 9/15/65 Louisville, age 24, residence stated on muster roll, house n/c, s 1,2,4.

SPRADLIN, WILLIAM. reg 45, co C, enr 3/6/64 Paintsville, enl 3/12/64 Flemingsburg, dis 2/14/65 Catlettsburg, age 27, dark hair, eyes & skin, 5-11, CSR gives residence as Johnson Co., house 105, s 1,2.

SPRIGGS, ROBERT. reg 65, co B, enl 5/21/64, age 24, blue eyes, light hair, fair skin, 6-0, house 329, s 2,4

STACY, ADAM. reg 14, co H, enr 10/25/61 Catlettsburg, enl 12/10/61 Louisa, dis 1/31/65 Louisa, age 23, light hair, blue eyes, fair skin, 5-5, house 307, s 1,2,4.

STAFFORD, FRANCIS M. reg 65, co A, enl 5/21/64, dis 6/21/64, age 26, blue eyes, dark hair, light skin, 5-9, rem in camp, house 43, s 2,4.

STAFFORD, JAMES. reg 65, co A, enl 5/1/64, dis 6/21/64, age 38, blue eyes, light hair & skin, 5-8, rem in camp, house 35, s 2,4.

STAFFORD, JEFFERSON. reg 14, co G, r 2nd lt, enr 11/19/61 Louisa, enl 12/10/61 Louisa, dis 1/31/65 Louisa, age 20, black hair & eyes, dark skin, 5-7, rem prom from cpl to sgt 2/1/62, from sgt to 2nd lt 8/2/62, wounded 6/22/64 in finger & hand, house 473, s 1,2,4.

STAFFORD, JOHN. reg 14, co D, enr 9/4/62 Portland OH, enl 9/4/62 Catlettsburg, dis 8/2/65 Lexington, age 25, light hair, blue eyes, fair skin, 6-1, rem trans to 14th Vet Inf, co D, enr 9/4/62, m/in 9/4/62 Portsmouth OH, house 473, s 1,2,4.

STAFFORD, THOMAS. reg CG, co K, enr 6/3/64, enl 7/28/64 Frankfort, dis 12/5/64 Frankfort, age 23, brown hair, blue eyes, dark skin, 6-0, house 473, s 2,4.

STAFFORD, THOMAS. reg 65, co B, r capt, enl 5/21/64, dis 6/21/64, age 25, blue eyes, light hair, fair skin, 6-0, house 474, s 2,4.

STAFFORD, WILLIAM. reg 39, co G, enr 2/4/64 Louisa, enl 3/29/64 Greenupsburg, dis 9/15/65 Louisville, age 16, light hair, dark eyes, fair skin, 5-4 or 5-9. house 474, s 1,2,4.

STAMBAUGH, FREDERICK SR. reg 65, co F, enl 5/12/64, dis 6/21/64, reg CG, co K, r 2nd lt, enr 8/9/64, enl 8/9/64 Frankfort, dis 3/11/65 Catlettsburg, age 33, dark hair, blue eyes, fair skin, 5-11, house 374, s 2,4.

STAMBAUGH, JEFFERSON. reg CG, co K, enr 6/9/64 Lawrence Co., age 33, dark hair, blue eyes, fair skin, 5-9, house 702, s 4.

STAMBAUGH, JONATHAN. reg 65, co F, r cpl, enl 5/21/64, dis 6/12/64, age 30, black eyes, dark hair, fair skin, 6-2, house 533, s 2,4.

STAMBAUGH, PHILIP. reg 65, co F, enl 5/21/64, dis 6/21/64, reg CG, co K, enr 6/9/64, enl 7/28/64 Frankfort, dis 3/11/65 Catlettsburg, age 33, dark hair, black eyes, fair skin, 6-0, house 667, s 2,4.

STAMBAUGH, SAMUEL. reg 65, co F, enl 5/21/64, dis 6/21/64, age 22, blue eyes, black hair, fair skin, 6-0, house 533, s 2,4.

STAPLETON, EDWARD. reg CG, co K, enr 6/9/64, enl 7/28/64 Frankfort, dis 3/11/65 Catlettsburg, age 18, dark hair, black eyes, fair skin, 5-6, house 698, s 2,4.

STAPLETON, ELI. reg 39, co G, enr 10/17/62 Peach Orchard, enl 2/16/63 Peach Orchard, dis 9/15/65 Louisville, age 23, dark hair & skin, blue eyes, 5-11, house 400, s 1,2,4.

STAPLETON, ISRAEL. reg CG, co E, enl 5/29/64 Catlettsburg, age 27, light hair, blue eyes, fair skin, 5-6, rem des 9/12/64 at Frankfort, house 275, s 2,4.

STAPLETON, ISAAC. reg 65, co B, enl 5/21/64, dis 6/21/64, age 25, blue eyes, light hair, fair skin, 5-0, rem in camp, house 512, s 2,4.

STAPLETON, ISAAC. reg 39, co G, enr 11/14/62 Peach Orchard, enl 2/16/63 Peach Orchard, dis 9/15/65 Louisville, age 18, light hair, blue eyes, fair skin, 5-10, house 471, s 1,2,4.

STAPLETON, JACKSON. reg CG, co E, enr 6/1/64, enl 7/4/64 Frankfort, dis 3/11/65 Catlettsburg, age 21, light hair, brown eyes, fair skin, 6-0, house 274, s 2,4.

STAPLETON, JOHN. reg 39, co G, r cpl, enr 11/18/62 Peach Orchard, enl 2/16/63 Peach Orchard, age 18, light hair, blue eyes, fair skin, 5-8, rem d 4/15/63 or 4/27/63 in Johnson Co. of fever, residence stated on muster roll, house n/c, s 1,2,4.

STAPLETON, WILLIAM. reg 45, co E, enr 9/8/63 Catlettsburg, enl 11/6/63 Ashland, dis 12/24/64 Catlettsburg, age 18, gray hair, dark eyes, fair skin, 5-7, house 274 or 698, s 1,2,6.

STAPLETON, ZION. reg 65, co B, enl 5/21/64, age 24, blue eyes, light hair, fair skin, 6-0, residence shown on militia list, house n/c, s 2,4,19.

STEPP, JAMES M. reg 65, co D, enl 5/21/64, dis 6/21/64, age 28, blue eyes, dark hair & skin, 5-9, house 237, s 2,4.

STEPP, MOSES. reg 65, co D, enl 5/21/64, dis 6/21/64, age 32, blue eyes, light hair, fair skin, 6-2, house 227, s 2,4.

STEPP, WILLIAM. reg 65, co D, enl 5/21/64, dis 6/21/64, age 37, gray eyes, dark hair, fair skin, 6-2, house 224, s 2,4.

STEWART, JAMES E. reg 65, r comm sgt, enl 5/21/64, dis 6/21/64, house 1, s 2,4.

STURGILL, JEFFERSON. reg 65, co A, enl 5/21/64, dis 6/1/64, age 25, black eyes & hair, light skin, 6-6, house 832, s 2,4.

STURGILL, JOSEPH. reg 65, co F, enl 5/21/64, dis 6/21/64, house 660, s 2,4.

SWETNAM, C. HAMILTON. reg 65, r surgeon, enl 5/21/64, dis 6/21/64, house 19, s 2,4.

T

TACKETT, ISAAC. reg CG, co K, enr 6/9/64, enl 7/28/64 Frankfort, dis 3/11/65 Catlettsburg, age 18, light hair, blue eyes, fair skin, 5-7, house 425, s 2,4

TACKETT, JAMES M. reg 65, co E, enl 5/21/64, age 28, light hair, blue eyes, fair skin, 6-0, rem AWOL, house 773, s 4.

TACKETT, LEVI. reg 14, co I, enr 11/16/62 Paintsville, enl 6/10/63 Louisa, dis 9/15/65 Louisville, age 42, light hair & skin, blue eyes, 5-3, rem trans to 14th Vet Inf, co B, enr 11/16/62, m/in 6/10/63 Louisa, house 852, s 1,2,4.

TACKETT, WILLIAM. reg CG, co E, enr 5/9/64, enl 7/4/64 Frankfort, dis 3/11/65 Catlettsburg, age 20, light hair & skin, blue eyes, 5-10, house 852, s 2,4.

TACKETT, WILLIAM. reg 14, co I, enr 10/5/62 Paintsville, enl 6/10/63 Louisa, dis 9/15/65 Louisville, age 18, light hair, blue eyes, fair skin, 5-11, rem trans to 14th Vet Inf, co B, enr 10/5/62, m/in 6/10/63 Louisa, house 722, s 1,2,4.

TAYLOR, DAVID W. reg 14, co G, enr 11/19/61 Louisa, enl 12/10/61 Louisa, dis 1/31/65 Louisa, age 25, red hair, blue eyes, fair skin, 5-10, residence shown on militia list, house n/c, s 1,2,4.

TRAVIS, JOSEPH. reg 14, co G, enr 10/11/61 Catlettsburg, enl 1/10/61 Louisa, age 20, black hair & eyes, dark skin, 5-8, rem trans to 14th Vet Inf, co A, enr 2/29/64, m/in 3/15/64 Louisa, d 3/9/65 Louisa of gunshot wound in the chest, residence stated on muster roll, house n/c, s 1,2,4.

TRIMBLE, JAMES. reg 65, co E, r cpl, enl 5/21/64, dis 6/1/64, age 40, blue eyes, light hair, fair skin, 5-10, house 829, s 2,4.

TRIMBLE, JOHN G. reg 45, co C, enr 3/6/64 Paintsville, enl 3/12/64 Flemingsburg, dis 2/14/65 Catlettsburg, age 18, light hair, eyes & skin, 5-6, rem CSR gives residence as Johnson Co., house 829, s 1,2.

TRIMBLE, WILLIAM. reg 65, co E, enl 5/21/64, age 25, light hair, blue eyes, fair skin, 5-10, rem AWOL, house 776, s 4.

TURNER, EDWIN S. reg 45, co C, r 1st lt, enr 6/20/63 Paintsville, enl 10/10/63 Catlettsburg, dis 12/24/64 Catlettsburg, age 37, house 656, s 1,2.

TURNER, ISAAC R. reg 45, co C, enr 8/18/63 Paintsville, enl 10/10/63 Catlettsburg, dis 12/2/4/64 Catlettsburg, age 22, house 36, s 1,2.
TURNER, JOHN. reg 65, co A, enl 5/21/64, dis 6/21/64, age 22, black eyes, light hair & skin, 5-8, rem in camp, house 65, s 2,4,19.
TURNER, JOSEPH. reg 65, co A, enl 5/21/64, dis 6/21/64, age 27, black eyes & hair, dark skin, 5-5, rem in camp, house 352, s 2,4.
TURNER, SAMUEL. reg 65, co A, enl 5/21/64, dis 6/1/64, age 29, black eyes & hair, dark skin, 5-6, rem in camp, house 442, s 2,4.

V

VANHOOSE, GEORGE W. reg 45, co C, enr 8/22/63 Paintsville, enl 10/10/63 Catlettsburg, age 20, light hair & eyes, fair skin, 6-0, d 3/22/64 at Flemingsburg of measles, house 764, s 1,2.
VANHOOSE, HENRY J. reg 65, co B, enl 5/21/64, dis 6/21/64, age 25, blue eyes, light hair, fair skin, 6-0, house 450, s 2,4,19.
VANHOOSE, JAMES, reg 65, co B, enl 5/21/64, dis 6/21/64, age 44, blue eyes, light hair, fair skin, 6-0, rem in camp, house 448, s 2,4.
VANHOOSE, JESSE. reg 65, co B, enl 5/21/64, age 40, blue eyes, light hair, fair skin, 6-0, rem in camp, house 763, s 2,4.
VANHOOSE, JOHN. reg 65, F&S, r sgt major, enl 5/21/64, dis 6/21/64, house 764, s 2,4.
VANHOOSE, JOHN B. reg 65, co B, enl 5/21/64, dis 6/21/64, age 26, blue eyes, light hair, fair skin, 6-0, rem in camp, house 450, s 2,4,19.
VANHOOSE, JOHN B. reg 39, co G, r 1st lt, enr 10/17/62 Peach Orchard, enl 2/16/63 Peach Orchard, age 30, rem res 5/29/63 for disability of right hand contraction, house 486, s 1,2,4.
VANHOOSE, LEVI. reg 65, co B, enl 5/21/64, dis 6/21/64, age 35, blue eyes, light hair, fair skin, 5-7, rem in camp, house 385, s 2,4.
VANHOOSE, LEVI J. reg 45, co C, r cpl, enr 8/22/63 Paintsville, enl 10/10/63 Catlettsburg, dis 12/24/64 Catlettsburg, age 22, rem prom to cpl 6/1/64, house 764, s 1,2.
VANHOOSE, MARTIN. reg 45, co C, enr 7/7/63 Paintsville, enl 10/10/63 Catlettsburg, dis 12/24/64 Catlettsburg, age 18, house 653, s 1,2.
VANHOOSE, MOSES D. reg 65, co B, enl 5/21/64, dis 6/21/64, age 32, blue eyes, dark hair & skin, 6-0, rem in camp, house 530, s 2,4.
VANHOOSE, WILLIAM. reg 65, co E, r sgt, enl 5/21/64, dis 6/21/64, age 43, blue eyes, red hair, fair skin, 5-8, house 765, s 2,4.
VANHOOSE, WILLIAM. reg 45, co C, enr 10/2/63 Paintsville, enl 10/10/63 Catlettsburg, dis 12/24/64 Catlettsburg, age 26, house 764, s 1,2.
VANHOOSE, WILLIAM J. reg 45, co C, r sgt, enr 8/3/63 Paintsville, enl 10/10/63 Catlettsburg, dis 12/24/64 Catlettsburg, age 21, house 653, s 1,2.
VAUGHN, ALEXANDER J. reg 14 Ky Cav, co B, enr 8/1/62, enl 11/6/62 Mt. Sterling, house 4, s 2.
VAUGHAN, WILLIAM W. reg 14, co G, enr 11/19/61 Louisa, enl 12/10/61 Louisa, dis 1/31/65 Louisa, age 35, red hair, dark eyes, fair skin, 5-11, house 7, s 1,2,4.
VERMILLION, SAMUEL. reg 14, co H, enr 10/25/61 Catlettsburg, enl 12/10/61 Louisa, age 20, light hair, blue eyes, fair skin, 5-9, rem d 2/26/62 at Paintsville of camp fever, residence stated on muster roll, house n/c, s 1,2,4.
VERMILLION, WALLACE. reg 14, co H, enr 10/2/62 Catlettsburg, enl 2/16/63 Peach Orchard, dis 9/15/65 Louisville, age 21, light hair, blue eyes, fair skin, 5-8, rem trans to co E, 39th Ky Inf 1/20/65, house 236, s 1,2,4.

VERMILLION, WILLIAM. reg 45, co F, r cpl, enr 8/25/63 Peach Orchard, enl 11/2/63 Ashland, dis 12/24/64 Catlettsburg, age 51, light hair, eyes & skin, 5-10, rem app cpl 11/1/63, cap in Lawrence by Rebel Bill Smith 10/2/64, released Aiken's Landing VA 2/5/65, house 236, s 1,2,6.

W

WALKER, ELEXIOUS H. reg 65, co A, r cpl, enl 5/21/64, dis 6/21/64, age 27, black eyes & hair, dark skin, 6-0, rem in camp, house 649, s 2,4.

WALKER, GEORGE R. reg 65, co A, enl 5/21/64, dis 6/21/64, age 29, gray eyes, black hair, light skin, 6-0, rem in camp, house 67, s 2,4.

WALKER, JAMES F. reg 14, co I, enr 11/10/61 Louisa, enl 12/10/61 Louisa, dis 1/31/65 Louisa, age 20, light hair, blue eyes, fair skin, 6-0, house 649, s 1,2,4.

WALKER, JOHN W. reg 14, co I, r cpl, enr 11/10/61 Louisa, enl 12/10/61 Louisa, dis 1/31/65 Louisa, age 22, dark hair & skin, blue eyes, 6-2, rem app cpl 5/1/62, house 23, s 1,2,4.

WALTER, WINFREY. reg 65, co B, enl 5/21/64, age 34, blue eyes, dark hair, fair skin, 5-7, house 463, s 2,4.

WALTERS, SHADRACK. reg 65, co B, enl 5/21/64, rem des 5/30/64, house 464, s 4.

WARD, ADAM. reg 39, co A, enr 10/11/62 Johnson Co., enl 8/30/63 Louisa, dis 9/15/65 Louisville, age 26, light hair, blue eyes, fair skin, 5-5, house 367, s 1,2,4.

WARD, ANDREW J. reg 65, co B, enl 5/21/64, dis 6/21/64, age 32, blue eyes, light hair, fair skin, 6-0, house 255, s 2,4.

WARD, ARTHUR A. reg 65, co D, enl 5/21/64, dis 6/21/64, age 21, blue eyes, dark hair, fair skin, 5-7, house 248, s 2,4.

WARD, DANIEL A. reg 65, co A, enl 5/21/64, dis 6/21/64, age 23, black eyes & hair, dark skin, 5-10, rem in camp, house 73, s 2,4.

WARD, EMANUEL. reg 14, co B, enr 10/10/61 Louisa, enl 12/10/61 Louisa, age 22, light hair, blue eyes, fair skin, 6-0, rem d 6/23/64 of wounds received 6/22/64 near Marietta GA, residence stated on muster roll, house n/c, s 1,2,4.

WARD, FRANCIS MARION. reg 45, co C, enr 8/28/63 Paintsville, enl 10/10/63 Catlettsburg, dis 12/24/64 Catlettsburg, age 19, house 513, s 1,2.

WARD, GEORGE W. reg 65, co B, enl 5/21/64, age 19, blue eyes, light hair, fair skin, 5-0, rem in camp, house 244, s 2,4.

WARD, GEORGE WASHINGTON. reg 14, co G, enr 8/5/63 Louisa, enl 8/30/63 Louisa, dis 9/15/65 Louisville, age 18, red hair, blue eyes, fair skin, 5-9, trans to 14th Vet Inf, co D, enr 8/5/63, m/in 8/30/63 Louisa, house 248, s 1,2,4.

WARD, GREENVILLE. reg 65, co B, r cpl, enl 5/21/64, dis 6/21/64, age 23, blue eyes, light hair, fair skin, 5-10, house 318, s 2,4.

WARD, JACKSON. reg 65, co B, enl 5/21/64, dis 6/21/64, age 34, blue eyes, light hair, fair skin, 5-4, house 333, s 2,4.

WARD, JAMES. reg 14, co G, enr 11/19/61 Louisa, enl 12/10/61 Louisa, dis 1/31/65 Louisa, age 45, dark hair, blue eyes, fair skin, 5-8, house 515, s 1,2,4.

WARD, JAMES G. reg 45, co C, enr 8/23/63 Paintsville, enl 10/10/63 Catlettsburg, dis 12/24/64, age 25, residence shown on militia list, house n/c, s 1,2,5.

WARD, JAMES W. reg 14, co K, enr 11/8/61 Louisa, enl 12/10/61 Louisa, age 25, black hair, gray eyes, dark skin, 5-10, rem des 3/15/62 in Johnson Co., house 344, s 1,2,4.

WARD, JOHN M. reg 65, co B, enl 5/21/64, age 32, blue eyes, light hair, fair skin, 6-0, house 465, s 2,4,19.

WARD, JOHN T. reg 65, co A, enl 5/1/64, dis 6/21/64, age 35, black eyes & hair, dark skin, 5-11, rem in camp, house 460, s 2,4.

WARD, JONATHAN. reg 65, co B, enl 5/21/64, age 26, blue eyes, light hair, fair skin, 5-6, house 342, s 2,4.

WARD, JONATHAN. reg 45, co C, enr 7/13/63, enl 10/10/63 Catlettsburg, dis 12/24/64 Catlettsburg, age 19, house 513, s 1,2.

WARD, JONATHAN. reg 65, co B, enl 5/21/64, age 22, blue eyes, light hair, fair skin, 5-8, house 469, s 2,4.

WARD, JOSEPH. reg 14, co G, enr 11/19/61 Louisa, enl 12/10/61 Louisa, dis 9/15/65 Louisville, age 18, light hair, blue eyes, fair skin, 5-9, rem trans to 14th Vet Inf, co A, enr 2/29/64, m/in 3/15/64 Louisa, house 330, s 1,2,4.

WARD, SAMPSON. reg 39, co G, enr 12/28/63 Louisa, enl 12/30/63 Louisa, dis 9/15/65 Louisville, age 18, light hair & eyes, fair skin, 5-8, house 272, s 1,2,4.

WARD, SHADRACK. reg 65, co B, enl 5/21/64, rem des 5/30/64, house 343, s 4.

WARD, SOLOMON. reg 65, co D, enl 5/21/64, dis 6/21/64, age 34, gray eyes, dark hair & skin, 6-1, house 252, s 2,4.

WARD, SOLOMON. reg 14, co G, enr 4/1/63 Louisa, enl 6/10/63 Louisa, age 30, black hair, blue eyes, dark skin, 5-9, rem killed at Kennesaw Mt. GA 6/22/64, house 398, s 1,2,4.

WARD, STEPHEN. reg 65, co B, enl 5/21/64, dis 6/9/64, age 37, blue eyes, light hair, dark skin, 6-0, house 465, s 2,4.

WARD, THOMPSON. reg 65, co B, enl 5/21/64, dis 6/21/64, age 33, blue eyes, light hair, fair skin, 5-6, rem in camp, house 332, s 2,4.

WARD, WASHINGTON. reg 65, co D, r cpl, enl 5/21/64, dis 6/21/64, age 37, blue eyes, light hair, fair skin, 5-8, house 513, s 2,4.

WARD, WILLIAM. reg 39, co A, enr 8/22/63 Johnson Co., enl 8/30/63 Louisa, dis 9/15/65 Louisville, age 36, fair hair, blue eyes, fair skin, 5-8, house 64, s 1,2,4.

WARD, WILLIAM. reg 65, co B, enl 5/21/64, rem des 5/30/64, house 64, house 331, 466, 490, or 515, s 4.

WARD, WILLIAM D. reg 45, co C, enr 8/28/63 Paintsville, enl 10/10/63 Catlettsburg, dis 12/24/64 Catlettsburg, age 18, house 342, s 1,2.

WATKINS, REECE. reg 14, co K, enr 11/8/61 Louisa, enl 12/10/61 Louisa, dis 1/31/65 Louisa, age 34, sandy hair, blue eyes, fair skin, 5-8, house 125, s 1,2,4.

WEBB. EDMUND R. reg 14, co B, r cpl, enr 10/10/63 Louisa, enl 12/10/61 Louisa, dis 1/31/65 Louisa, age 18, dark hair, black eyes, fair skin, 5-7, rem app cpl 7/1/62, house 179, s 1,2,4.

WEBB, JACOB. reg 65, co C, enl 5/21/64, rem des 5/30/64, house 178, s 4.

WEBB, JAMES. reg 39, co A, enr 10/11/61 Johnson Co., enl 2/16/63 Peach Orchard, dis 9/15/65 Louisville, age 18, black hair & eyes, fair skin, 5-2, house 179, s 1,2,4.

WEBB, JAMES A. reg 39, co A, r cpl, enr 10/20/62 Johnson Co., enl 2/16/63 Peach Orchard, dis 9/15/65 Louisville, age 19, black hair, blue eyes, fair skin, 5-9, house 179, s 1,2,4.

WEBB, JOHN R. reg 45, co C, enr 8/9/63 Paintsville, enl 10/10/63 Catlettsburg, age 19, rem d 3/4/64 at Mt. Sterling, house 712, s 1,2.

WEBB, JOSEPH H. reg 39, co A, enr 10/11/62 Johnson Co., enl 2/16/63 Peach Orchard, dis 9/15/65 Louisville, age 20, dark hair, black eyes, fair skin, 5-7, house 179, s 1,2,4.

WEBB, THOMAS. reg 65, co C, enl 5/21/64, dis 6/21/64, age 34, blue eyes, black hair, dark skin, 5-9, house 183, s 2,4.

WEBB, WILLIAM J. reg 65, co C, r cpl, enl 5/21/64, dis 6/21/64, age 27, black eyes, dark hair & skin, 5-11, rem in camp, house 178, s 2,4.

WEBB, WILLIAM W. reg 39, co A, enr 10/20/62 Johnson Co., enl 2/16/63 Peach Orchard, dis 9/15/65 Louisville, age 22, dark hair, blue eyes, fair skin, 5-6, residence stated on muster roll, house n/c, s 1,2,4.

WELCH, JAMES M. reg 39, co A, r sgt, enr 10/20/62 Johnson Co., enl 2/16/63 Peach Orchard, dis 9/15/65 Louisville, age 24, black hair & eyes, dark skin, 5-9, house 68, s 1,2.

WELCH, PETER S. reg 39, co A, enr 9/6/62 Johnson Co., enl 2/16/63 Peach Orchard, dis 9/15/65 Louisville, age 21, black hair & eyes, dark skin, 5-6, house 188, s 1,2,4.

WELCH, THOMAS J. reg 65, co C, r 1st sgt, enl 5/21/64, dis 6/21/64, age 29, gray eyes, dark hair & skin, 5-8, house 188, s 2,4.

WELCH, WILLIAM H. H. reg 39, co A, r cpl, enr 9/6/62 Peach Orchard, enl 2/16/63 Peach Orchard, dis 9/15/65 Louisville, age 18, light hair, blue eyes, fair skin, 5-9, rem wounded at Saltville VA & left in hands of enemy, cap 10/2/64, paroled Cox's Wharf VA 2/5/65, residence stated on muster roll, house n/c, s 1,2,4.

WELLS, AARON. reg 65, co B, enl 5/21/64, dis 6/21/64, age 22, blue eyes, light hair, fair skin, 5-0, rem in camp, house 325, s 2,4.

WELLS, ALEXANDER G. reg 65, co C, enl 5/21/64, rem des 5/30/64, house 187, s 4.

WELLS, ALLEN S. reg 65, co C, enl 5/21/64, dis 6/21/64, age 18, black eyes, dark hair, fair skin, 5-8, house 193, s 2,4.

WELLS, GEORGE W. reg 65, co C, enl 5/21/64, dis 6/21/64, age 33, gray eyes, dark hair & skin, 5-11, rem in camp, house 194, s 2,4.

WELLS, HENRY C. reg 65, co C, r cpl, enl 5/21/64, dis 6/21/64, rem in camp, house 186, s 2,4.

WELLS, HIRAM. reg 39, co A, enr 9/23/62 or 10/23/62 Boyd Co. or Louisa, enl 2/16/63 or 10/29/63 Louisa or Peach Orchard, dis 9/15/65 Louisville, age 26 black hair & eyes, dark skin, 5-10, residence stated on muster roll, house n/c, s 1,2,4.

WELLS, JAMES. reg 65, co C, enl 5/21/64, dis 6/21/64, age 33, black eyes & hair, dark skin, 6-1, rem in camp, house 191, s 2,4.

WELLS, MARCUS L. K. reg 45, co C, r cpl, enr 9/18/63 Paintsville, enl 10/10/63 Catlettsburg, dis 12/24/64 Catlettsburg, age 18, rem prom to cpl 6/1/64, house 325, s 1,2.

WELLS, MORGAN. reg 65, co C, r sgt, enl 5/21/64, dis 6/21/64, age 25, gray eyes, dark hair, fair skin, 5-10, rem in camp, house 185, s 2,4.

WELLS, MOSES. reg 65, co D, r 1st sgt, enl 5/21/64, dis 6/21/64, age 21, blue eyes, light hair, fair skin, 5-6, house 325, s 2,4.

WELLS, RICHARD M. reg 65, co B, r 1st sgt, enl 5/21/64, dis 6/21/64, age 24, black eyes & hair, dark skin, 5-10, rem in camp, house 325, s 2,4.

WELLS, WILLIAM. reg 65, co C, enl 5/21/64, dis 6/21/64, age 37, gray eyes, dark hair & skin, 6-0, rem in camp, house 174, s 2,4.

WELLS, WILLIAM. reg 45, co E, enr 9/6/63 Catlettsburg, enl 11/6/63 Ash-land, dis 12/24/64 Catlettsburg, age 18, house 325, s 1,2.

WELLS, WILLIAM ALLEN. reg 65, co B, r cpl, enl 5/21/64, dis 6/21/64, age 19, dark eyes, hair & skin, 5-11, rem in camp, residence shown on militia list, house n/c, s 2,4.

WEST, CALEB A. reg 14, co H, enr 10/25/61 Catlettsburg, enl 1/10/61 Louisa, age 24, rem des 1/10/62 Prestonsburg, residence stated on muster roll, house n/c, s 1,2,4.

WHEELER, DANIEL. reg 65, co F, r sgt, enl 5/21/64, dis 6/21/64, age 28, black eyes, dark hair, fair skin, 5-10, rem in camp, house 40 or 598, s 2,4.

WHEELER, JAMES. reg 14, co G, enr 11/19/61 Louisa, enl 12/10/61 Louisa, dis 1/31/65 Louisa, age 29, sandy hair, blue eyes, fair skin, 5-8, house 659, s 1,2,4.

WHEELER, JOHN B. reg 65, co F, enl 5/21/64, dis 6/21/64, age 33, black eyes & hair, fair skin, 5-10, house 659, s 2,4,19.

WHEELER, JOHN J. reg 14, co G, enr 11/19/61 Louisa, enl 12/10/61 Louisa, dis 1/31/65 Louisa, age 27, sandy hair, blue eyes, fair skin, 5-5, house 602, s 1,2,4.

WHEELER, MARTIN. reg 65, co A, r 1st sgt, enl 5/21/64, dis 6/21/64, age 23, blue eyes, black hair, dark skin, 5-10, rem in camp, house 389, s 2,4.

WHEELER, SAMUEL G. reg 65, co A, r sgt, enl 5/21/64, dis 6/21/64, age 22, blue eyes, light hair & skin, 5-10, rem in camp, residence shown on militia list, house n/c, s 2,4,19.

WHEELER, STEPHEN. reg 65, co F, r cpl, enl 5/21/64, dis 6/21/64, age 31, black eyes, light hair, fair skin, 5-8, house 600, s 2,4.

WHEELER, STEPHEN H. reg 14, co B, enr 10/10/61 Louisa, enl 12/10/61 Louisa, dis 1/31/65 Louisa, age 44, light hair, blue eyes, fair skin, 6-2, house 637, s 1,2,4.

WHEELER, WILLIAM P. reg 14, co G, enr 11/19/61 Louisa, enl 1/10/61 Louisa, dis 1/31/65 Louisa, age 26, sandy hair, blue eyes, fair skin, 5-7, house 659, s 1,2,4.

WHITE, GEORGE. reg 39, co A, enr 1/29/64 Johnson Co., enl 3/28/64, dis 9/15/65 Louisville, light hair, black eyes, dark skin, 5-11, residence shown on CSR, house n/c, s 1.

WHITE, HARVEY. reg 39, co A, enr 10/20/62 Peach Orchard, enl 2/16/63 Peach Orchard, dis 9/15/65 Louisville, age 19, rem wounded and captured Saltville, VA 10/2/64, confined at Richmond, VA, paroled at Aikens Landing, 2/21/65, residence stated on muster roll, house n/c, s 1,2,4.

WHITE, RUFUS. reg 39, co A, enr 10/11/62 Peach Orchard, enl 2/16/63 Peach Orchard, dis 9/15/65 Louisville, age 26, residence stated on muster roll, house n/c, s 1,2,4.

WILEY, ANDREW J. reg 65, co B, enl 5/21/64, dis 6/21/64, age 32, dark eyes, hair & skin, 5-8, rem in camp, house 401, s 2,4.

WILEY, ANDREW J. reg 39, co A, enr 10/10/62 Peach Orchard, enl 2/16/63 Peach Orchard, dis 9/15/65 Louisville, age 27, dark hair, eyes & skin, 5-9, house 526, 1,2,4.

WILLIAMS, ANDREW H. reg 14, co H, age 31, residence stated on muster roll, house n/c, s 4.

WILLIAMS, WILEY J. reg 65, co A, r cpl, enl 5/21/64, dis 6/21/64, age 25, black eyes, light hair & skin, 5-10, rem in camp, house 60, s 2,4.

WILLIAMS, WILLIAM. reg 65, co A, enl 5/21/64, dis 6/21/64, age 32, black eyes & hair, dark skin, 5-8, rem in camp, house 233, s 2,4.

WILLIAMSON, ASA. reg 45, co F, enr 8/25/63 Peach Orchard, enl 11/2/63 Ashland, dis 12/24/64 Catlettsburg, age 18 or 23, light hair, eyes & skin, 6-0, house 249, s 1,2.

WILLIAMSON, KENUS. reg 14, co G, enr 11/19/61 Louisa, enl 12/10/61 Louisa, age 24, dark hair, blue eyes, fair skin, 5-11, rem d 8/5/64 at Marietta GA of chronic diarrhea, residence stated on muster roll, house n/c, s 1,2,4.

WITTEN, FRANCIS M. reg 14, co K, enr 11/8/61 Louisa, enl 12/10/61 Louisa, age 18, dark hair, gray eyes, fair skin, 5-10, rem d 7/27/64 at Knoxville TN of wounds received 6/22/64 near Kennesaw Mtn. GA, residence stated on muster roll, house n/c, s 1,2,4.

WITTEN, GEORGE HAMILTON. reg 14, co K, enr 11/8/61 Louisa, enl 12/10/61 Louisa, dis 1/31/65 Louisa, age 38, sandy hair, blue eyes, fair skin, 5-9, rem given leave of absence on 12/5/63 to attend the General Assembly, of which he was a member, residence stated on muster roll, house n/c, s 1,2,4.

WITTEN, ISAAC. reg 65, co A, enl 5/21/64, dis 6/21/64, age 38, blue eyes, light hair & skin, 5-11, rem in camp, house 761, s 2,4.

WITTEN, JOHN W. reg 65, co F, enl 5/21/64, dis 6/21/64, reg CG, co K, enr 6/2/64, enl 7/28/64 Frankfort, dis 3/11/65 Catlettsburg, age 44, light hair, blue eyes, fair skin, 5-6, house 577, s 2,4.

WITTEN, THOMAS FLOYD. reg 14, co K, enr 9/4/62 Catlettsburg, enl 9/4/62 Portland OH, dis 9/15/65 Louisville, age 22, black hair & eyes, fair skin, 5-6, rem trans to 14th Vet Inf, enr 9/4/62, m/in 9/4/62 Portsmouth OH, r cpl, house 358, s 1,2,4.

WITTEN, WILLIAM PRESTON. reg 14, co K, r cpl, enr 11/8/61 Louisa, enl 12/10/61 Louisa, dis 1/31/65 Louisa, age 24, sandy hair, blue eyes, fair skin, 5-11, rem prom to cpl 9/29/64, wounded in shoulder near Dallas GA 6/2/64, residence stated on muster roll, house n/c, s 1,2,4.

WOLFE, REUBEN D. reg 14, co H, enr 10/25/61 Catlettsburg, enl 12/10/61 Louisa, dis 1/31/65 Louisa, age 40, fair hair & skin, blue eyes, 5-7, rem wounded in action 6/64, house 262, s 1,2,4.

WOODS, WILLIAM. reg 65, co A, enl 5/21/64, dis 6/21/64, age 35, blue eyes, light hair & skin, 5-10, rem in camp, house 57, s 2,4.

Y

YATES, GEORGE W. reg 14, co G, r cpl, enr 11/9/61 Louisa, enl 12/10/61 Louisa, dis 1/31/65 Louisa, age 20, sandy hair, blue eyes, fair skin, 5-9, rem prom to cpl 5/25/62, wounded by grapeshot in left hip 7/23/64, house 543, s 1,4.

YATES, JOHN. reg 14, co G, enr 11/19/61 Louisa, enl 12/10/61 Louisa, dis 1/31/65 Louisa, age 27, dark hair, blue eyes, fair skin, 5-10, residence stated on muster roll, house n/c, s 1,2,4.

LAWRENCE COUNTY UNION SOLDIERS

A

ADAMS, ARTHUR. reg 68, co G, r cpl, enl 5/21/64, dis 6/21/64, age 20, blue eyes, light hair, fair skin, 5-10, house 540, s 2,4.

ADAMS, CORY. reg 68, co G, enl 4/7/64, 5/21/64, dis 4/16/64, 6/22/64, reg CG, co L, enr 6/18/64, enl 7/6/64 Frankfort, dis 3/11/65 Catlettsburg, age 18, black hair, dark eyes & skin, 5-10, house 540, s 2,4.

ADAMS, JAMES. reg 68, co G, enl 4/7/64, 5/21/64, dis 4/16/64, 6/22/64, age 40, black eyes & hair, dark skin, 5-10, house 115 or 674, s 2,4.

ADAMS, JAMES JR. reg 68, co G, r cpl, enl 4/7/64, 5/21/64, dis 4/16/64, 6/22/64, age 20, blue eyes, light hair, fair skin, 5-5, house 115 or 540, s 2,4.

ADAMS, MARTIN. reg 68, co G, enl 4/7/64, 5/21/64, dis 4/16/64, 6/22/64, age 38, black eyes & hair, dark skin, 5-10, house 352, s 2,4.

ADAMS, WILLIAM E. reg 45, co C, r sgt, enr 8/15/63 Paintsville, enl 10/10/63 Catlettsburg, age 24, rem des 2/25/64 at Mt. Sterling, house 541, s 1,2.

ADKINS, H. H. reg 68, co G, enl 4/7/64, 5/21/64, dis 4/16/64, 6/22/64, age 35, black eyes & hair, dark skin, 6-0, house 289, s 2,4.

ADKINS, JOHN. reg 14, co K, enr 8/18/63 Louisa, enl 8/28/63 Louisa, dis 9/15/65 Louisville, age 20, dark hair, eyes & skin, 5-7, rem trans to 14th Vet Inf, co C, enr 8/18/63, m/in 8/28/63 Louisa, house 988, s 1,2,4.

ADKINS, JONAH. reg 14, co K, enr 8/17/63 Louisa, enl 8/28/63 Louisa, dis 9/15/65 Louisville, age 18, light hair, blue eyes, fair skin, 5-6, rem trans to 14th Vet Inf, co C, enr 8/17/63, m/in 8/28/63 Louisa, house 988, s 1,2,4.

ADKINS, WASHINGTON. reg 68, co A, enl 5/21/64, dis 6/22/64, age 25, blue eyes, light hair, fair skin, 5-7, house 1063, s 2,4.

ADKINS, WILLIAM. reg 68, co I, enl 4/7/64, 5/21/64, dis 4/16/64, 6/22/64, age 25, blue eyes, light hair, fair skin, 5-6, house 123, s 2,4.

ADKINS, WILLIAM. reg 14, co H, r musician, enr 10/25/61 Catlettsburg, enl 12/10/61 Louisa, dis 1/31/65 Louisa, age 28, dark hair, blue eyes, fair skin, 5-11, house 123, s 1,2,4.

ADKINS, WILLIAM H. reg 14, co D, enr 10/20/61, enl 12/10/61 Louisa, dis 1/31/65 age 30, house 1063, s 2,4.

AKERS, BURWELL. reg 14, co F, enr 11/19/61 Louisa, enl 12/10/61 Louisa, dis 1/31/65 Louisa, age 34, light hair & skin, blue eyes, rem trans to co E, 8/29/63 and back to co F, 1/21/65, wounded in action 6/22/64, residence stated on muster roll, house n/c, s 1,2,4.

ALDRIDGE, JAMES A. reg 167WV, co Ira Copley, enl 8/62 to 2/64, dis 5/2/64, reg 68, co H, enl 5/21/64, dis 6/21/64, age 36, blue eyes, dark hair, house 1142, s 2,4,23.

ALEXANDER, JOHN. reg 68, co C, enl 5/21/64, dis 6/21/64, reg CG, co L, enr 6/8/64, enl 7/6/64 Frankfort, dis 3/1/65 Catlettsburg, age 19 or 22, light hair, gray eyes, fair skin, 5-9, house 930, s 2,4.

ALEXANDER, LEWIS. reg 68, enl 5/21/64, dis 6/21/64, reg CG, co C, enr 7/18/64, enl 8/30/64 Frankfort, dis 3/11/65 Catlettsburg, age 21 or 23, light hair, blue eyes, dark skin, 5-6, house 917, s 2,4.

ALLEN, WILLIAM L. reg 14, co K, enr 11/8/61 Louisa, enl 12/10/61 Louis, dis 1/31/65 Louisa, age 22, rem wounded in right side between 7/64 & 8/13/64, house 1213, s 1,2,4.

ALLISON, HIRAM H. reg 109USCT, co H, enl 10/24/64 Baltimore, dis 3/4/66 Louisville, house 162, s 2.

ALLISON, JAMES L. reg 68, co C, r cpl, enl 4/7/64, 5/21/64, dis 4/16/64, 6/22/64, age 22, blue eyes, fair hair & skin, 5-8, house 194, s 2,4.

ATHERTON, ANDREW. reg 68, co K, enl 5/21/64, dis 6/21/64, age 25, blue eyes, light hair, fair skin, 5-3, house 1093, s 2,4,18.

AUSTIN, JOHN. reg 39, co B, enr 10/3/62, enl 2/16/63 Peach Orchard, age 27, fair hair & skin, gray eyes, 6-0, rem trans to co G 3/15/63, turned over to civilian authorities to be tried for murder committed prior to enlistment, house 736, s 1,2,4.

AUSTIN, THOMAS. reg 68, co K, enl 4/7/64, 5/21/64, dis 4/16/64, 6/22/64, age 30, blue eyes, light hair, fair skin, 6-0, house 1050, s 2,4.

B

BACK, SAMUEL M. reg 14, co D, enr 10/20/61 Louisa, enl 12/10/61 Louisa, age 33, light hair & skin, blue eyes, 6-1, rem d 10/11/64 at Marietta GA of typhoid, residence stated on muster roll, house n/c, s 1,2,4.

BAISDEN, JAMES. reg 5VA, co F, r 2nd lt, enl 9/14/61, age 31 or 41, rem killed in action near Cassville VA 9/23/61, house 1158, s 20.

BAKER, A. J. reg 68, co A, enl 4/7/64, 5/21/64, dis 4/16/64, 6/21/64, age 28, blue eyes, light hair, fair skin, 5-2, residence shown on militia list, house n/c, s 2,4,18.

BALL, CALVIN. reg 68, co I, enl 5/21/64, age 30, light hair, blue eyes, fair skin, 5-6, house 155, s 4.

BALL, DAVID. reg 14, co D, enr 10/20/61 Louisa, enl 12/10/61 Louisa, age 21, rem d 2/24/62 Paintsville of typhoid fever, house 730, s 1,2,4.

BALL, ELIHU. reg 68, co G, enl 4/7/64, 5/21/64, dis 4/16/64, 6/22/64, age 38, blue eyes, light hair, fair skin, 5-6, house 1003, s 2,4.

BALL, ELSEY. reg 68, co G, enl 4/7/64, 5/21/64, dis 4/16/64, 6/22/64, age 18, light hair, fair skin, 5-5, house 988, s 2,4.

BALL, GEORGE. reg 14, co D, enr 10/20/61 Louisa, enl 12/10/61 Louisa, dis 9/15/65 Louisville, age 18, brown hair, black eyes, dark skin, 5-7, rem trans to 14th Vet Inf, co A, enr 2/29/64, m/in 3/14/64 Louisa, house 730, s 1,2,4.

BALL, GREENVILLE. reg 14, co G, enr 12/10/61 Louisa, enl 3/11/62 Paintsville, dis 1/30/65 Louisa, age 20, light hair, blue eyes, fair skin, 5-7, rem trans to 14th Vet Inf, co C, enr 3/11/62, m/in 4/5/63 Lexington, cap 8/8/64 near Atlanta, paroled 12/10/64 at Charleston SC, house 284 or 989, s 1,2,4.

BALL, SILAS. reg 167WV, co Ira Copley Scouts, enl 8/62 to 2/64, dis 5/2/64, reg 68, co H, enl 5/21/64, dis 6/21/64, age 32, dark eyes & hair, light skin, 5-5, house 1159, s 2,4,23.

BALL, THOMPSON. reg 14, co G, enr 11/19/61 Louisa, enl 12/10/61 Louisa, dis 1/31/65 Louisa, age 24, sandy hair, dark eyes, fair skin, 5-6, house 229, s 1,2,4.

BALL, WILLIAM L. reg 14, co D, r sgt, enr 10/20/61 Louisa, enl 12/10/61 Louisa, dis 1/31/65 Louisa, age 22, dark hair, blue eyes, light skin, 5-10, house 996, s 1,2,4.

BALL, WILLIAM M. reg 14, co D, enr 10/20/61 Catlettsburg, enl 12/10/61 Louisa, dis 1/31/65 Louisa, age 19, brown hair, black eyes, dark skin, 5-6, house 730, s 1,2,4.

BANKS, DAVID C. reg 68, co A, enl 4/7/64, 5/21/64, dis 4/16/64, 6/21/64, age 34, dark eyes & hair, fair skin, 5-6, house 385, s 2,4.

BARNETT, JAMES. reg 40, co C, enr 8/4/63, enl 9/26/63 Grayson, rem d 3/17/64 at Grayson, house 920, s 2,4.

BARRETT, CHARLES R. reg 14, co E, enr 10/25/61 Louisa, enl 12/10/61 Louisa, dis 9/15/65 Louisville, age 18, light hair & skin, blue eyes, 5-8, rem trans to 14th Vet Inf, co A, enr 2/29/64, m/in 3/15/64 Louisa, trans to co F 1/20/65, house 79, s 1,2,4.

BARRETT, WILLIAM H. reg 14, co E, enr 10/25/61 Louisa, enl 12/10/61, age 19, dark hair, brown eyes, fair skin, 6-1, rem trans from co F to co E 8/28/63, wounded 6/2/64 near Marietta GA, d 7/14/64 at Knoxville TN, house 79, s 1,2,4.

BARTRUM, WILLIAM H. reg 14, co H, r capt, enr 10/25/61, enl Louisa, dis 1/31/65 Louisa, age 23, rem prom from 1st lt to capt 2/26/63, house 911, s 1,2.

BAUGH, ALEXANDER. reg 68, co D, enl 4/7/64, 5/21/64, dis 4/16/64, 6/22/64, age 22, black eyes & hair, dark skin, 6-0, house 14, s 2,4.

BERRY, GEORGE A. reg 68, co G, r cpl, enl 4/7/64, 5/21/64, dis 4/16/64, 6/22/64, age 30, blue eyes, black hair, dark skin, 6-0, house 1002, s 2,4,18.

BERRY, JOHN. reg 68, co F, enl 4/7/64, 5/21/64, dis 4/16/64, 6/22/64, age 26, hazel eyes, dark hair, fair skin, 5-0, house 355, 675 or 683, s 2,4.

BERRY, JOHN M. reg 68, co G, enl 4/7/64, 5/21/64, dis 4/16/64, 6/22/64, age 25, blue eyes, light hair, fair skin, 6-0, house 1000, s 2,4.

BERRY, JOHN W. reg 14, co D, enr 10/20/61 Catlettsburg, enl 12/10/61 Louisa, dis 4/11/63 Louisa, age 19, light hair & skin, black eyes, 5-6, rem dis for tuberculosis, residence stated on muster roll, house n/c, s 1,2,4.

BERRY, REUBEN. reg 14, co D, r cpl, enr 10/20/61 Catlettsburg, enl 12/10/61 Louisa, dis 1/31/65 Louisa, age 23, dark hair, eyes & skin, 5-6, house 1000, s 1,2,4.

BERRY, REUBEN F. reg 68, co G, enl 4/7/64, 5/21/64, dis 4/16/64, 6/22/64, age 18, blue eyes, light hair, fair skin, 6-0, house 535, s 2,4.

BERRY, WILEY. reg 68, co D, r cpl, enl 5/21/64, dis 6/21/64, age 19, blue eyes, light hair, fair skin, 5-8, house 683, s 2,4.

BERRY, WILLIAM H. reg 14, co H, r musician, enr 10/25/61 Catlettsburg, enl 12/10/61 Louisa, dis 1/31/65 Louisa, age 25, light hair, blue eyes, fair skin, 5-9, residence stated on muster roll, house n/c, s 1,2,4.

BERRY, WILLIAM T. reg 39, co G, enr 12/4/62, enl 2/16/63 Peach Orchard, dis 9/15/65 Louisville, age 24, light hair, blue eyes, fair skin, 5-9, reg 39, co E, r 1st lt, enr 4/27/65, enl 4/27/65 Louisa, rem trans from co G, 14th Ky Inf to 39th 1/20/65, app lt by Governor of Ky. 4/13/65, residence stated on muster roll, house n/c, s 1,2,4.

BEVINS, DAVID. reg 14, co F, enr 11/19/61 Louisa, enl 12/10/61 Louisa, dis 1/31/65 Louisa, age 28, dark hair & skin, blue eyes, 5-8, rem 8/63 trans to co D, back to co F 1/20/65, house 1095, s 1,2,4.

BILLUPS, JOSEPH S. reg 68, co C, r 1st lt, enl 4/7/64, 5/21/64, dis 4/16/64, 6/21/64, age 35, blue eyes, black hair, dark skin, 5-9, residence shown on militia list, house n/c, s 2,4,18.

BISHOP, DAVID R. reg 14, co B, 1st sgt, enr 10/10/61 Lawrence Co., enl 12/10/61 Louisa, dis 1/31/65 Louisa, age 21, dark hair, hazel eyes, fair skin, 6-1, rem app sgt 10/10/61, app 1st sgt 8/28/63, cap 2/15/63 in Lawrence Co, paroled in eastern KY, residence stated on muster roll, house n/c, s 1,2,4.

BISHOP, GATHER. reg 14, co B, enr 10/10/61 Louisa, enl 12/10/61 Louisa, dis 1/31/65 Louisa, age 33, dark hair & eyes, fair skin, 5-9, house 568, s 1,2,4.

BISHOP, GEORGE. reg 39, co G, r musician, enr 12/19/62 Peach Orchard, enl 2/16/63 Peach Orchard, dis 9/15/65 Louisville, age 44, black hair & eyes, dark skin, 5-4, house 569, s 1,2,4.

BISHOP, THOMAS. reg 68, co B, enl 4/7/64, 5/21/64, dis 4/16/64, 6/22/64, age 35, black eyes, light hair, dark skin, 5-10, house 566, s 2,4.

BLACKBURN, ALLEN. reg 39, co C, enr 7/1/63 Pike Co., enl 8/30/63 Louisa, dis 9/15/65 Louisville, age 27, dark hair, gray eyes, fair skin, 6-2, house 874, s 1,2,4.

BLANKENSHIP, JOHN W. reg 45, co F, enr 8/25/63 Peach Orchard, enl 11/2/63 Ashland, dis 12/24/64 Catlettsburg, age 21, light hair, eyes & skin, 6-0, house 298, s 1,2.

BLANKENSHIP, WILLIAM M. reg 68, co I, r capt, enl 4/7/64, 5/21/64, dis 4/16/64, 6/22/64, age 30, blue eyes, dark hair & skin, 5-10, house 959, s 2,4.

BLANKENSHIP, WILLIAM R. reg 68, co F, r cpl, enl 4/7/64, 5/21/64, dis 4/16/64, 6/22/64, age 25, hazel eyes, dark hair, fair skin, 5-6, house 297, s 2,4.

BOGGS, ALFRED. reg 68, co B, enl 4/7/64, 5/21/64, dis 4/16/64, 6/21/64, age 30, black eyes & hair, fair skin, 5-8, house 399, s 2,4.

BOGGS, ELIPHUS. reg 14, co B, enr 10/10/61 Louisa, enl 12/10/61 Louisa, dis 1/31/65 Louisa, age 26, dark hair, blue eyes, fair skin, 5-10, house 442, s 1,2,4.

BOGGS, HENDERSON. reg 68, co A, enl 4/7/64, 5/21/64, dis 4/16/64, 6/21/64, age 38, gray eyes, dark hair, fair skin, 6-3, house 371, s 2,4.

BOGGS, HUGH. reg 68, co A, enl 4/7/64, 5/21/64, dis 4/16/64, 6/21/64, age 24, dark eyes, dark hair, fair skin, 5-4, house 386, s 2,4.

BOGGS, HUGH. reg 14, co B, enr 7/7/63, enl 8/10/63 Louisa, dis 9/15/65 Louisville, age 18, light hair, blue eyes, dark skin, 5-6, rem trans to14th Vet Inf, co B, enr 7/7/63, m/in 8/10/63 Louisa, house 398, s 2,4.

BOGGS, JAMES. reg 40, co D, enr 10/6/63 Carter Co., enl 3/16/64 Paris, dis 12/30/64 Catlettsburg, age 22, dark hair, blue eyes, fair skin, 6-0, house 400, s 1,2,4.

BOGGS, JAMES H. reg 14, co B, enr 10/10/61 Louisa, enl 12/10/61 Louisa, dis 1/31/65 Louisa, age 31, dark hair, blue eyes, light skin, 6-0, rem app cpl 4/12/63, later red to ranks, house 380, s 1,2,4.

BOGGS, JOHN D. reg 68, co A, enl 4/7/64, 5/21/64, dis 4/16/64, 6/21/64, age 37, blue eyes, dark hair, fair skin, 5-6, house 383, s 2,4.

BOGGS, JOHN H. reg 14, co B, enr 10/10/61, enl 12/10/61 Louisa, dis 4/30/63 Louisa, reg 40, co D, enr 10/1/63 enl 3/16/64 Paris, dis 12/30/64 Catlettsburg, age 33 or 35, dark hair, blue eyes, fair skin, 6-2, house 372, s 1,2,4.

BOGGS, NELSON T. reg 14, co B, r sgt, enr 10/10/61 Louisa, enl 12/10/61 Louisa, age 24 or 26, dark hair, blue eyes, fair skin, 6-1, rem killed in action at Middle Creek 1/10/62, house 379, s 1,2,4.

BOGGS, RANDOLPH. reg 68, co A, r cpl, enl 4/7/64, 5/21/64, dis 4/16/64, 6/21/64, age 30, blue eyes, dark hair & eyes, 5-10, house 382, s 2,4.

BOGGS, WASHINGTON. reg 68, co A, r cpl, enl 4/7/64, 5/21/64, dis 4/16/64, 6/21/64, age 20, blue eyes, light hair, fair skin, 5-11, house 387, s 2,4.

BOGGS, WILLIAM SR. reg 14, co B, enr 10/10/61 Louisa, enl 12/10/61 Louisa, dis 1/31/65 Louisa, age 21, dark hair, blue eyes, fair skin, 5-7, rem cap & paroled near Louisa 1/15/63, house 371, s 1,2,4.

BOGGS, WILLIAM JR. reg 14, co B, enr 10/10/61 Louisa, enl 12/10/61 Louisa, dis 1/31/65 Louisa, age 19, light hair, blue eyes, dark skin, 5-9, rem cap and paroled near Louisa 2/15/63, wounded in elbow between 7/2/64 & 8/13/64, house 379 or 398, s 1,2,4.

BOLT, ISAAC N. reg 68, co D, r sgt, enl 4/7/64, 5/21/64, dis 4/16/64, 6/22/64, age 23, blue eyes, light hair, fair skin, 5-11, house 60, s 2,4.

BOLT, WILLIAM C. reg 14, co F, enr 11/19/61, enl 12/10/61 Louisa, dis 1/31/65, age 20, house 60, s 2,4.

BOLT, WILLIAM D. reg 14, co A, enr 10/25/61 Louisa, enl 12/10/61 Louisa, dis 1/31/65 Louisa, age 18, dark hair, blue eyes, light skin, 5-11, rem trans from co F 1/26/65 residence stated on muster roll, house n/c, s 1,2,4.

BOND, JOHN M. reg 39, co E, enr 11/16/62, enl 12/26/62 Catlettsburg, dis 9/15/65 Louisville, age 26, dark hair, blue eyes, fair skin 5-8, residence stated on muster roll, house n/c, s 1,2,4.

BOOTH, ELLIS. reg 5VA, co I, enr 10/1/61 Ceredo, enl 10/1/61 Ceredo, dis 10/6/64 Wheeling WV, age 33, house 785, s 1,20.

BORDERS, DANIEL reg 39, co G, enr 9/13/62 Peach Orchard, enl 2/16/63 Peach Orchard, dis 9/15/65 Louisville, age 38, black hair & eyes, dark skin, 5-9, house 1076, s 1,2,4.

BORDERS, HENRY. reg 68, co K, enl 4/7/64, 5/21/64, dis 4/16/64, 6/22/64, age 35, black eyes & hair, dark skin, 6-0, house 1079, s 2,4.

BORDERS, HENRY A. reg 14, co D, r 1st lt, enr 10/20/61 Louisa, enl 12/10/61 Louisa, age 21, brown hair, blue eyes, light skin, rem app cpl 3/1/62, prom from 1st sgt to 2nd lt 1/10/63, to 1st lt 3/9/64, d 8/1/64 Marietta GA of disease, house 836, s 1,2,4.

BORDERS, HEZEKIAH. reg 5VA, co I, enr 9/14/61 Ceredo, enl 9/14/61 Ceredo, age 23, dark hair, gray eyes, light skin, 5-10, rem dis 5/22/62 for disability, reg 39, co G, enr 7/20/63, enl 8/29/63 Louisa, age 24, rem d 9/6/64 at Ashland of diarrhea, house 1094, s 1,2,4.

BORDERS, MARTIN. reg 5VA, co I, enr 9/14/61 Ceredo, enl 9/14/61, dis 10/4/64 Wheeling WV, age 18, house 784, s 1,20.

BORDERS, WALLACE. reg 45, co F, r cpl, enr 8/25/63 Peach Orchard, enl 11/2/63 Ashland, dis 12/24/64 Catlettsburg, age 18, dark hair, eyes & skin, 5-5, house 784, s 1,2,6.

BORDERS, WILLIAM. reg 68, co K, r capt, enl 4/7/64, 5/21/64, dis 4/16/64, 6/22/64, age 37, blue eyes, dark hair, fair skin, 5-8, house 1096, s 2,4.

BOTNER, COLUMBUS. reg 68, co G, enl 4/7/64, 5/21/64, dis 4/16/64, 6/22/64, age 19, blue eyes, light hair, fair skin, 5-10, house 251, s 2,4.

BOTNER, OLIVER D. reg 14, co G, r capt, enr 11/19/61 Louisa, enl 12/10/61 Louisa, age 42, rem res 6/5/62 for disability, house 251, s 1,2,4.

BOW, WILLIAM. reg 68, co C, enl 4/7/64, 5/21/64, dis 4/16/64, 6/22/64, age 34 or 39, blue eyes, light hair, fair skin, 5-10, residence shown on militia list, house n/c, s 2,4,18.

BOWEN, ALFRED. reg 167WV, co Ira Copley, enl 8/62 to 2/64, dis 5/2/64, house 876, s 23.

BOWEN, ASA. reg 167WV, co George W. Murray, reg 68, co H, enl 5/24/64, age 22, dark hair, eyes & skin, 5-6, house 1133, s 4,23.

BOWEN, FRANKLIN. reg 167WV, co Ira Copley, enl 8/62 to 2/64, dis 5/2/64, reg 45, co F, enr 10/1/63 Ashland, enl 11/2/63 Ashland, dis 12/24/64 Catlettsburg, age 22, light hair, eyes & skin, house 896, s 1,2,23.

BOWEN, HENRY. reg 39, co G, enr 9/13/62 Peach Orchard, enl 2/16/63 Peach Orchard, dis 9/15/65 Louisville, age 41, black hair & eyes, dark skin, house 1075, s 1,2,4.

BOWEN, NATHANIEL. reg 167WV, co George W. Murray, reg 68, co H, enl 5/21/64, dis 6/22/64, age 19, gray eyes, light hair & skin, 6-0, house 1133, s 2,4,23.

BOWEN, OLIVER. reg 167WV, co George W. Murray, house 1133, s 23.

BOWEN, WILLIAM. reg 68, co H, r sgt, enl 4/7/64, 5/21/64, dis 4/16/64, 6/22/64, age 24, blue eyes, light hair & skin, 5-10, house 878, s 2,4.

BOWLAND, WILLIAM. reg 68, co K, enl 5/21/64, dis 6/2/64, age 21, light eyes, hair & skin, 6-0, house 262, s 2,4.

BOWLING, WILLIAM N. reg 68, co E, r sgt, enl 4/7/64, 5/21/64, dis 4/16/64, 6/22/64, residence shown on militia list, house n/c, s 2,4,18.

BOYD, ANDERSON. reg 39, co G, enr 9/13/62 Peach Orchard, enl 2/16/63 Peach Orchard, dis 9/15/65 Louisville, age 20, light hair, blue eyes, fair skin, 5-11, house 1070, s 1,2,4.

BOYD, ANDREW. reg 68, co K, enl 4/7/64, 5/21/64, dis 4/16/64, 6/22/64, age 40, blue eyes, light hair, fair skin, 6-0, house 1069, s 2,4.

BOYD, ARTHUR. reg 39, co G, r sgt, enr 9/13/62 Peach Orchard, enl 2/16/63 Peach Orchard, dis 9/15/65 Louisville, age 18, dark hair & skin, black eyes, 5-1, house 818, s 1,2,4.

BOYD, GREENVILLE. reg 14, co G, enr 11/19/61 Louisa, enl 12/10/61 Louisa, dis 1/31/65 Louisa, age 37, gray hair, blue eyes, fair skin, 5-9, house 818, s 1,2,4.

BOYD, HIRAM. reg 68, co K, r sgt, enl 4/7/64, 5/21/64, dis 4/16/64, 6/22/64, age 38, black eyes & hair, fair skin, 5-10, house 1038, s 2,4.

BOYD, HUGH. reg 68, co E, enl 4/7/64, 5/21/64, dis 4/16/64, 6/22/64, age 35, dark eyes, hair & skin, 6-2, house 844, s 2,4.

BOYD, ISOM. reg 68, co E, enl 5/21/64, dis 6/22/64, age 32, light eyes, fair hair & skin, 6-6, house 850, s 2,4.

BOYD, JAMES. reg 14, co D, enr 3/20/62 Camp Buell, enl 3/20/62 Camp Buell, dis 3/17/63 Lexington, age 26, light hair, blue eyes, dark skin, 5-6, rem dis for tuberculosis, residence established by descriptive muster roll, house 1094, s 1,2,4.

BOYD, JAMES. reg 45, co F, enr 9/21/63 Peach Orchard, enl 11/2/63 Ashland, dis 12/24/64 Catlettsburg, age 18, light hair, eyes & skin, 6-0, house 1070, s 1,2,6.

BOYD, WILLIAM H. reg 45, co A, enr 7/6/63 Clarksburg, enl 10/10/63 Catlettsburg, dis 12/24/64 Catlettsburg, age 18, house 1069, s 1,2.

BRADLEY, DANIEL reg 39, co C, enr 9/10/62 Louisa, enl 2/16/63 Peach Orchard, dis 9/15/65 Louisville, age 34, dark hair & skin, blue eyes, 5-11, residence stated on muster roll, house n/c, s 1,2,4.

BRADLEY, WILLIAM. reg 68, co I, enl 4/7/64, 5/21/64, dis 4/16/64, 6/22/64, age 35, blue eyes, light hair, fair skin, 5-6, house 175, s 2,4.

BRANHAM, HENDERSON. reg 167WV, co Ira Copley Scouts, r 2nd lt, enl 8/62 to 2/64, dis 5/2/64 reg 68, co H, r 2nd lt, enl 5/21/64, dis 6/22/64, age 36, blue eyes, dark hair & skin, 5-10, house 905, s 2,4,23.

BRANHAM, WILBURN. reg 167WV, co Ira Copley, enl 8/62 to 2/64, dis 5/2/64, reg 68, co H, r cpl, enl 4/7/64, 5/21/64, dis 4/16/64, 6/22/64, age 32, dark eyes, hair & skin, 6-0, house 909, s 2,4,23.

BROWN, DANIEL H. reg 14, co G, r 1st lt, enr 11/8/61 Louisa, enl 12/10/61 Louisa, dis 1/31/65 Louisa, age 24, rem prom from sgt major to 1st lt 6/5/62, residence stated on muster roll, house n/c, s 1,2,4.

BROWN, THOMAS. reg 68, co E, enl 4/7/64, 5/21/64, dis 4/16/64, 6/22/64, reg CG, co K, enr 6/9/64, enl 7/28/64 Frankfort, dis 3/11/65 Catlettsburg, age 20, light hair, blue eyes, fair skin, 5-9, house 1097, s 2,4.

BRUMFIELD, WILLIAM. reg 68, co D, r cpl, enl 4/7/64, 5/21/64, dis 4/16/64, 6/22/64, age 22, black eyes, dark hair, fair skin, 5-11, house 344, s 2,4.

BRYAN, DAVID. reg 10Cav, co F, enr 8/9/62 Boyd Co., enl 9/9/62 Covington, dis 9/17/63 Maysville, age 23, residence stated on muster roll, house, residence stated on muster roll, house n/c, s 1,2,4.

BRYANT, HARRISON. reg 5VA, co G, enr 1/19/63 Ceredo, enl1/19/63, dis 10/3/64 Wheeling WV, house 18, s 1,20.

BRYANT, JOHNSON. reg 5VA, co G, enr 1/19/63 Ceredo, enl 1/19/63, dis 10/3/64 Wheeling WV, house 18, s 1,20.

BRYANT, SYLVESTER. reg 68, co D, enl 5/21/64, dis 6/22/64, age 20, black eyes & hair, dark skin, 6-0, house 953, s 2,4.

BURCHETT, ARMSTEAD. reg 14, co K, r sgt, enr 11/8/61 Louisa, enl 12/10/61 Louisa, age 44, gray hair, blue eyes, fair skin, 5-11, rem dis 1/13/63 for disability of rheumatism, house 1201, s 1,2,4.

BURCHETT, BENJAMIN. reg 68, co I, enl 5/21/64, age 27, light hair, blue eyes, fair skin, 5-6, house 964, s 4.

BURCHETT, DRURY J. reg 14, co K, r major, enr 11/8/61 Louisa, enl 11/10/61 Louisa, dis 1/31/65 Louisa, age 19, rem prom from 1st lt to capt 3/1/62, to major 9/29/64, house 1201, s 1,2,4.

BURCHETT, FLEMING. reg 68, co I, enl 4/7/64, 5/21/64, dis 4/16/64, 6/22/64, age 30, blue eyes, light hair, fair skin, 5-6, house 965, s 2,4.

BURCHETT, HENRY. reg 68, co I, enl 5/21/64, age 23, light hair, blue eyes, fair skin, 6-0, house 129, s 4.

BURCHETT, JAMES. reg 68, co I, enl 5/21/64, age 25, light hair, blue eyes, fair skin, 5-6, house 129, s 4.

BURGESS, CORNELIUS. reg 68, co E, enl 5/21/64, dis 6/22/64, age 30, blue eyes, light hair & skin, 5-10, house 733, s 2,4.

BURGESS, ELLIOTT. reg 65, co C, enl 5/21/64, dis 6/22/64, age 34, light hair, gray eyes, fair skin, 5-9, house 746, s 2,4.

BURGESS, FRANCIS M. reg 14, co H, r 1st lt, enr 3/25/63 Catlettsburg, enl 8/7/63 Louisa, age 27, dark hair, gray eyes, fair skin, 5-8, rem prom from sgt to 2nd lt 3/28/63, wounded 6/22/64, d of wounds 8/10/64, house 745, s 1,2,4.

BURGESS, GEORGE T. reg 39, co G, enr 11/3/62 Peach Orchard, enl 2/16/63 Peach Orchard, dis 9/15/65 Louisville, age 19, light hair, blue eyes, fair skin, 5-11, rem trans to co H, 14th Ky Inf 3/12/63, back to co G, 39th Ky Inf 1/20/65, house 747, s 1,2,4.

BURGESS, HENRY. reg 68, F&S, r major, enl 4/7/64, dis 4/16/64, house 745, s 4.

BURGESS, JOHN F. reg 14, co H, r 1st sgt, enr 10/25/61 Catlettsburg, enl 12/10/61 Louisa, dis 1/31/65 Louisa, age 27, light hair, blue eyes, fair skin, 5-9, rem prom to sgt 12/1/62, to 1st sgt 9/7/64, house 745, s 1,2,4.

BURGESS, PETER. reg 68, co K, enl 4/7/64, 5/21/64, dis 4/16/64, 6/22/64, age 23, blue hair, light hair, fair skin, 5-8, house 251, s 2,4.

BURGESS, THOMAS J. reg 68, co C, r cpl, enl 4/7/64, 5/21/64, dis 4/16/64, 6/22/64, age 27, black eyes, fair hair & skin, 6-1, house 733, s 2,4.

BURK, CHARLES. reg 68, co I, enl 5/21/64, age 30, light hair, blue eyes, fair skin, 5-8, house 958, s 4.

BURKE, JAMES H. reg 68, co I, enl 5/21/64, dis 6/22/64, age 21, dark eyes, hair & skin, 5-10, house 199, s 2,4.

BURK, JAMES N. reg 10Cav, co F, r 2nd lt, enr 8/9/62 Boyd Co., enl 9/9/62 Covington, dis 9/17/63 Maysville, age 21, app orderly sgt 8/18/62, prom from 1st sgt 5/1/63, reg 68, F&S, r sgt. major, enl 5/21/64, dis 6/22/64, residence stated on muster roll, house 199, s 1, 2, 4.

BURTON, ALLEN M. C. reg 68, co K, r 1st sgt, enl 4/7/64, 5/21/64, dis 4/16/64, 6/22/64, age 28, black eyes & hair, fair skin, 6-0, house 1089, s 2,4.

BURTON, ANDREW. reg 14, co B, enl 10/10/61 Louisa, enl 12/10/61 Louisa, dis 1/31/65 Louisa, age 46, dark hair & skin, blue eyes, 5-10, house 324, s 1,2,4.

BURTON, ANDREW J. reg 53, co I, enr 4/3/65, enl 4/3/65 Greenupsburg, age 18, sandy hair, blue eyes, florid skin, 5-7, dis 9/15/65 Louisville, house 324, s 2.

BURTON, BENNETT W. reg 14, co B, enr 10/10/61 Louisa, enl 12/10/61 Louisa, dis 1/31/65 Louisa, age 18, light hair, blue eyes, fair skin, 5-10, house 324, s 1,2,4.

BURTON, SAMUEL. reg 68, co G, enl 4/7/64, 5/21/64, dis 4/16/64, 6/22/64, age 40, blue eyes, light hair, fair skin, 6-0, house 153, s 2,4.

BURTON, THOMAS. reg 14, co G, enr 11/19/61 Louisa, enl 12/10/61 Louisa, dis 1/31/65 Louisa, age 20, dark hair, blue eyes, fair skin, 5-7, rem cap & paroled Lexington 9/62, residence stated on muster roll, house n/c, s 1,2,4.

BURTON, WILLIAM J. reg 14, co B, enr 11/22/61 Louisa, enl 12/10/61 Louisa, dis 1/31/65 Louisa, age 19, dark hair, blue eyes, fair skin, 5-9, house 324, s 1,2,4.

BUTLER, ANDREW. reg 68, co E, enl 4/7/64, 5/21/64, dis 4/16/64, 6/22/64, age 34, light eyes, hair & skin, 5-10, house 775, s 2,4.

C

CAINS, PERRY. reg 14, co K, enr 11/8/61, enl 12/10/61 Louisa, dis 1/31/65 Louisa, age 19, house 202, s 2,4.

CAINS, THOMAS. reg 14, co K, enr 11/8/61, enl 12/10/61 Louisa, dis 1/31/65 Louisa, age 20, house 202, s 2,4.

CAPERTON, JAMES J. reg 14, co H, r cpl, enr 10/25/61 Catlettsburg, enl 12/10/61 Louisa, dis 1/31/65 Louisa, age 26, dark hair, eyes & skin, 5-3, rem app cpl 9/7/64, residence stated on muster roll, house n/c, s 1,2,4.

CAREY, JAMES H. reg 14, co H, r 2nd lt, enr 10/25/61 Catlettsburg, enl 12/10/61 Louisa, dis 1/31/65 Louisa, age 24, light hair, blue eyes, fair skin, 5-5, rem app 1st sgt 2/26/63, prom to 2nd lt 8/14/64, residence stated on muster roll, house n/c, s 1,2,4.

CARROWAY, ALLEN. reg 68, co E, enl 4/7/64, 5/21/64, dis 4/16/64, 6/22/64, age 35, dark eyes, hair & skin, 6-2, residence shown on militia list, house n/c, s 2,4,18.

CARROWAY, WILLIAM. reg 68, co E, enl 4/7/64, 5/21/64, dis 4/16/64, 6/22/64, age 38, dark eyes, hair & skin, 6-0, residence shown on militia list, house n/c, s 2,4,18.

CARTER, ANDREW J. reg 68, co I, enl 4/7/64, 5/21/64, dis 4/16/64, 6/22/64, age 29, blue eyes, light hair, fair skin, 5-6, house 138, s 2,4.

CARTER, COVEY. reg 68, co G, enl 5/21/64, dis 6/22/64, age 35, black eyes & hair, dark skin, 6-0, house 285, s 2,4.

CARTER, GEORGE, reg 68, co I, enl 4/7/64, 5/21/64, dis 4/16/64, 6/22/64, age 30, light hair, blue eyes, fair skin, 6-0, house 118, s 2,4.

CARTER, JAMES. reg 68, co G, enl 5/21/64, dis 6/22/64, age 40, blue eyes, light hair, fair skin, 6-0, house 990, s 2,4.

CARTER, JAMES H. reg 68, co I, enl 4/16/64, 5/21/64, dis 4/16/64, 6/22/64, age 30, blue eyes, light hair, fair skin, 6-0, house 136, s 2,4.

CARTER, JAMES W. reg 14, co D, enr 10/26/61 Catlettsburg, enl 12/10/61 Louisa, dis 1/31/65 Louisa, age 21, brown hair, blue eyes, light skin, 5-11, rem wounded near Marietta GA 8/18/64, residence stated on muster roll, house n/c, s 1,2,4.

CARTER, JOHN B. reg 68, co I, enl 4/7/64, 5/21/64, dis 4/16/64, 6/22/64, age 28, blue eyes, light hair, fair skin, 6-0, house 205, s 2,4.

CARTER, JOHN W. reg 68, co I, enl 5/21/64, dis 6/22/64, age 32, blue eyes, light hair, fair skin, 5-10, house 134, s 2,4.

CARTER, LANDON. reg 68, co I, enl 4/7/64, 5/21/64, dis 4/16/64, 6/22/64, age 22, blue eyes, light hair, fair skin, 5-10, house 132, s 2,4.

CARTER, ROBERT H. reg 14, co D, enr 10/20/61 Louisa, enl 12/10/61 Louisa, age 19, brown hair, blue eyes, light skin, 5-5, rem d 9/3/65 or 9/5/65 at Marietta GA, of concussion of shell explosion to head & typhoid fever, house 357, s 1,2,4.

CARTER, THOMAS. reg 14, co G, enr 10/1/61 Catlettsburg, enl 12/10/61 Louisa, dis 1/31/65 Louisa, age 20, black hair, blue eyes, dark skin, 5-9, rem red from cpl to pvt 5/11/63, house 531, s 1,2,4.

CARTER, WILLIAM. reg 14, co D, r cpl, enr 10/20/61 Louisa, enl 12/10/61 Louisa, dis 1/31/65 Louisa, age 19, brown hair, black eyes, dark skin, 5-9, rem slightly wounded at Culp's farm Kennesaw Mtn. GA 6/22/64, residence stated on muster roll, house n/c, s 1,2,4.

CASEY, WILLIAM. reg 14, co H, enr 10/25/61, enl 12/10/61 Louisa, dis 1/31/65 Louisa, age 18, residence stated on muster roll, house n/c, s 2,4.

CASSEL, ANDREW JACKSON. reg 68, co E, r cpl, enl 4/7/64, 5/21/64, dis 4/16/64, 6/22/64, age 38, dark eyes, hair & skin, 5-10, house 754, s 2,4.

CASTEEL, GEORGE. reg 68, co A, enl 5/21/64, dis 6/22/64, age 24, dark eyes & skin, black hair, 5-11, house 377, s 2,4.

CASTEEL, JAMES. reg 14, co B, enr 10/10/61 Louisa, enl 12/10/61 Louisa, dis 1/31/65 Louisa, age 28, dark hair & skin, blue eyes, 5-10, house 377, s 1,2,4.

CASTEEL, JAMES R. reg 14, co D, enr 10/20/61 Catlettsburg, enl 12/10/61 Louisa, dis 1/31/65 Louisa, age 18, brown hair, black eyes, dark skin, 5-11, house 244, s 1,2,4.

CASTEEL, JOHN. reg 68, co G, enl 4/7/64, 5/21/64, dis 4/16/64, 6/22/64, age 40, black eyes & hair, dark skin, 6-0, house 244, s 2,4.

CASSELL, JOSHUA Z. reg 39, co E, enr 11/3/62 Piketon, enl 2/16/63 Peach Orchard, dis 9/15/65, Louisville, age 18, dark hair, gray eyes, dark skin, 5-7, house 898, s 1,2,4.

CASTEEL, SAMPSON. reg 14, co B, enr 10/10/61 Louisa, enl 12/10/61 Louisa, dis 1/31/65 Louisa, age 26, dark hair, eyes, & skin, house 377, s 1,2,4.

CASTEEL, WILLIAM. reg 14, co B, enr 10/10/61 Louisa, enl 12/10/61 Louisa, dis 1/31/65 Louisa, age 28, dark hair & skin, blue eyes, 5-11, house 377, s 1,2,4.

CASTLE, DANIEL. reg 39, co G, enr 9/13/62 Peach Orchard, enl 2/16/63 Peach Orchard, dis 9/15/65 Louisville, age 22, light hair & skin, hazel eyes, 5-8, house 1083, s 1,2,4.

CASTLE, FOREST M. reg 14, co G, enr 10/10/61 Catlettsburg, enl 12/10/61 Louisa, dis 1/31/65 Louisa, age 18, dark hair, blue eyes, fair skin, 5-11, residence stated on muster roll, house n/c, s 1,2,4.

CASTLE, HENRY. reg 68, co B, enl 4/7/64, 5/21/64, dis 4/16/64, 6/22/64, age 30, black eyes, light hair, fair skin, 6-0, house 570, s 2,4.

CASTLE, JAMES F. reg 14, co G, r sgt, enr 11/19/61 Louisa, enl 1/10/61 Louisa, dis 5/9/65 Louisville, age 18, brown hair, blue eyes, light skin, 5-8, rem prom to cpl 6/5/62, to sgt 9/1/62, cap Lawrence Co. 3/14/63, cap at Atlanta 8/8/64, released Wilmington NC 2/24/65, house 141, s 1,2,4.

CASTLE, MARION. reg 39, co G, enr 11/20/62, enl 8/30/63 Louisa, dis 9/15/65 Louisville, age 18, dark hair, blue eyes, light skin, 5-8, house 141, s 1,2,4.

CASTLE, MILES H. reg CG, co K, enr 6/9/64, enl 7/28/64 Frankfort, dis 3/11/65 Catlettsburg, age 33, black hair & eyes, fair skin, 5-4, house 1098, s 2,4.

CASTLE, SOLOMON. reg 45, co F, enr 8/25/63 Catlettsburg, enl 11/2/63 Ash-land, dis 12/24/64 Catlettsburg, age 19, light hair, eyes & skin, 5-8, house 898, s 1,2,6.

CASTLE, WILLIAM. reg 68, co E, r sgt, enl 4/7/64, 5/21/64, dis 4/16/64, 6/22/64, age 40, dark eyes & hair, light skin, 5-11, house 753, s 2,4.

CASTLE, WOOTEN. reg 39, co B, age 33, residence stated on muster roll, house n/c, s 4.

CASTLE, ZEDEKIAH. reg 45, co F, enr 11/1/63 Ashland, enl 11/2/63 Ashland, dis 12/24/64 Catlettsburg, age 31, light hair, eyes & skin, 6-2, house 817, s 1,2,6.

CAUDLE, JESSE. reg 68, co G, enl 4/7/64, 5/21/64, dis 4/16/64, 6/22/64, age 28, black eyes & hair, dark skin, 6-0, house 265, s 2,4.

CEARSER, BAPTIST. reg 14, co A, enr 10/1/61 Louisa, enl 12/10/61 Louisa, dis 1/3/65 Louisa, age 39, black hair & eyes, light hair, 5-5, residence stated on muster roll, house n/c, s 1,2,4.

CHAFFFINS, MICHAEL. reg 5VA, co F, enr 9/2/61 Ceredo, enl 9/14/61, dis 9/23/64 Wheeling, age 20, rem cap near Winchester VA 7/24/64, paroled James River VA 2/22/65, house 1137, s 1,20.

CHAFIN, FRANKLIN M. reg 68, co G, enl 4/7/64, 5/21/64, dis 4/16/64, 6/22/64, age 28, black eyes & hair, dark skin, 6-0, house 227, s 2,4.

CHAFIN, HARVY. reg 14, co B, enr 10/10/61 Louisa, enl 12/10/61 Louisa, dis 1/31/65 Louisa, age 29, dark hair, blue eyes, fair skin, 5-11, house 225, s 1,2,4.

CHAFIN, JAMES. reg 68, co H, enl 5/21/64, dis 6/22/64, age 18, blue eyes, light hair & skin, 5-4, house 117, s 2,4.

CHAFIN, JAMES. reg 68, co G, enl 5/21/64, dis 6/22/64, age 35, blue eyes, light hair & skin, 6-0, house 224, s 2,4.

CHAFIN, JAMES H. reg 14, co B, r sgt, enr 10/10/61 Louisa, enl 12/10/61 Louisa, dis 1/31/65 Louisa, age 23, dark hair & skin, blue eyes, 5-8, app sgt 6/20/62, house 225, s 1,2,4.

CHAFIN, JAMES W. reg 14, co B, r 1st lt, enr 9/9/64, dis 1/31/65 Louisa, residence stated on list of officers, house n/c, s 2,4,32.

CHAFIN, JOHN B. reg 68, co I, enl 4/7/64, 5/21/64, dis 4/16/64, 6/22/64, age 40, blue eyes, light hair, fair skin, 6-0, house 333 or 984, s 2,4.

CHAFIN, JOHN W. reg 68, co F, enl 5/21/64, dis 6/22/64, age 29, blue eyes, dark hair, fair skin, 5-8, house 978 s 2,4.

CHAFIN, KENAS M. reg 68, co F, enl 4/7/64, 5/21/64, dis 4/16/64, 6/22/64, age 25, blue eyes, dark hair & skin, 5-7, house 975, s 2,4.

CHAFIN, THADDEUS. reg 68, co D, enl 4/7/64, 5/21/64, dis 4/16/64, 6/22/64, age 30, black eyes & hair, dark skin, 5-11, house 44, s 2,4.

CHAFIN, WILLIAM. reg 14, co H, enr 9/19/63 Louisa, enl 10/30/63 Louisa, dis 9/15/65 Louisville, age 18, light hair, blue eyes, fair skin, 5-7, rem trans to 14th Vet Inf, co C, enr 9/14/63, m/in 10/30/63 Louisa, house 45, s 1,2,4.

CHAMBERS, ROBERT. reg 68, co C, enl 4/7/64, 5/21/64, dis 4/16/64, 6/22/64, age 42, black eyes, dark hair & skin, 5-11, house 930, s 2,4.

CHANDLER, WILLIAM. reg 68, co K, enl 4/7/64, 5/21/64, dis 4/16/64, 6/22/64, age 30, black eyes & hair, dark skin, 5-8, residence shown on militia list, house n/c, s 2,4,18.

CHAPMAN, ALBERT. reg 39, co F, enr 4/15/63 Louisa, enl 6/11/63 Louisa, dis 9/15/65 Louisa, age 18, light hair, blue eyes, fair skin, 5-6, rem trans to co G, house 998, s 1,2,4.

CHAPMAN, EZEKIEL G. reg 14, co H, enr 10/25/61 Catlettsburg, enl 12/10/61 Louisa, dis 1/31/65 Louisa, age 19, light hair, blue eyes, fair skin, 5-5, house 181, s 1,2,4.

CHAPMAN, GEORGE. reg 14, co D, enr 10/20/61 Louisa, enl 12/10/61 Louisa, dis 10/11/63 Louisa, age 24, black hair & eyes, dark skin, 5-3, rem dis for disability of unsound mind, house 1012, s 1,2,4.

CHAPMAN, GEORGE. reg 167WV, co George W. Murray, reg 68, co H, enl 5/24/64, age 38, dark hair & skin, blue eyes, 6-0, house 1143, s 4,23.

CHAPMAN, GEORGE R. B. reg 14, co H, r 1st lt, enr 10/25/61 Catlettsburg, enl 12/10/61 Louisa, age 32, rem prom from 2nd lt to 1st lt 1/24/63, res 3/27/63 or 4/3/63 for bronchitis & pneumonia, reg 68, co C, enl 4/7/64, 5/21/64, dis 4/16/64, 6/22/64, age 34, blue eyes, black hair, fair skin, 5-9, house 181, s 1,2,4.

CHAPMAN, GREEN. reg CG, co L, enr 6/8/64, enl 7/6/64 Frankfort, dis 3/11/65 Catlettsburg, age 18, dark hair & skin, blue eyes, 5-0, house 998, s 2,4.

CHAPMAN, JAMES. reg 167WV, co Geo. Murray, house 1117, s 23.

CHAPMAN, JOHN R. reg 68, co C, enl 4/7/64, 5/21/64, dis 4/16/64, 6/22/64, age 31, blue eyes, dark hair & skin, 6-5, house 1117, s 2,4.

CHAPMAN, ROBERT. reg 14, co G, enr 11/19/61 Louisa, enl 12/10/61 Louisa, age 23, dark hair, blue eyes, fair skin, 5-8, rem trans to 14th Vet Inf, co A, enr 2/29/64, m/in 3/15/64 Louisa, des 2/26/65 Louisa, residence stated on muster roll, house n/c, s 1,2,4.

CHAPMAN, RYBURN. reg 68, co K, enl 4/7/64, 5/21/64, dis 4/16/64, 6/22/64, age 30, black eyes & hair, dark skin, 6-0, house 1094, s 2,4.

CHAPMAN, WILLIAM. reg 14, co H, enr 10/25/61 Catlettsburg, enl 12/10/61 Louisa, dis 5/27/63 Louisa, age 33, black hair, dark eyes & skin, 5-8, rem for disability of heart disease & weak lungs, house 180, s 1,2,4.

CHAPMAN, WILLIAM S. reg 68, co C, r sgt, enl 4/7/64, 5/21/64, dis 4/16/64, 6/22/64, reg CG, co L, r sgt, enr 6/8/64, enl 7/6/64 Frankfort, dis 3/11/65 Catlettsburg, age 23, dark hair, blue eyes, fair skin, 5-8, house 180, s 2,4.

CHILDERS, HENRY. reg 39, co G, enr 11/30/62 Peach Orchard, enl 2/16/63 Peach Orchard, dis 9/15/65 Louisville, age 18, dark hair & skin, black eyes, 5-9, house 756, s 1,2,4.

CHILDERS, JAMES. reg 68, co E, r cpl, enl 4/7/64, 5/21/64, dis 4/16/64, 6/22/64 age 32, dark eyes, hair & skin, 5-6, house 811, s 2,4.

CHILDERS, JOHN A. reg 5VA, co I, enr 10/1/61 Ceredo, enl 10/1/61, dis 10/12/64 Wheeling WV, age 34, house 827, s 1,20.

CHILDERS, MOSES. reg 68, co E, enl 4/7/64, 5/21/64, dis 4/16/64, 6/22/64 age 28, dark eyes, hair & skin, 6-2, house 827, s 2,4.

CHILDERS, OLIVER PERRY. reg 68, co E, enl 5/21/64, dis 6/22/64, age 19, dark eyes, hair & skin, 6-0, house 827, s 2,4.

CHILDERS, RUSSELL. reg 68, co E, r cpl, enl 4/7/64, 5/21/64, dis 4/16/64, 6/22/64, age 37, dark eyes, hair, & skin, 6-0, house 790, s 2,4.

CHILDERS, WALLACE. reg 45, co F, r cpl, enr 8/25/63 Peach Orchard, enl 11/2/63 Ashland, dis 12/24/64 Catlettsburg, age 20, light hair, eyes & skin, 6-2, house 827, s 1,2,6.

CHILDERS, WESLEY. reg 5VA, co I, r 4th sgt, enr 9/14/61 Ceredo, enl 9/14/61, dis 10/4/64 Wheeling WV, age 21, rem prom to sgt 8/31/63, red to ranks 7/23/64, house 827, s 1,20.

CHILDERS, WILLIAM. reg 5VA, co I, enr 9/14/61 Ceredo, age 21, dark hair & skin, blue eyes, 5-5, rem dis 10/1/62 for disability, reg 39, co G, r musician, enr 6/13/63 Louisa, enl 8/30/63 Louisa, dis 9/15/65 Louisville, age 21, dark hair & skin, blue eyes, 5-9, house 756, s 1,2,4,9,20.

CLARK, JOSEPH M. reg 14, co D, enr 10/20/61 Louisa, enl 10/20/61 Louisa, dis 1/31/65 Louisa, age 43, black hair & eyes, dark skin, 5-9, house 502, s 1,2,4.

CLAYTON, JOHN M. reg 68, co C, enl 4/7/64, 5/21/64, dis 4/16/64, 6/22/64, age 44, black eyes & hair, dark skin, 5-8, house 162, s 2,4.

CLEVENGER, ALEXANDER. reg 14, co G, enr 11/19/61 Louisa, enl 12/10/61 Louisa, dis 1/31/65 Louisa, age 18, sandy hair, blue eyes, fair skin, 5-6, rem wounded between 7/2/64 & 8/13/64, residence stated on muster roll, house n/c, s 1,2,4.

CLEVENGER, JOSHUA. reg 14, co G, enr 11/19/61 Louisa, enl 12/10/61 Louisa, age 20, sandy hair, blue eyes, fair skin, 5-6, rem d 12/28/64 in Lawrence Co. of smallpox, house 230, s 1,2,4.

CLEVENGER, MATHIAS. reg 14, co G, enr 11/19/61 Louisa, enl 12/10/61 Louisa, dis 1/31/65 Louisa, age 27, light hair, blue eyes, fair skin, 5-6, house 230, s 1,2,4.

CLEVENGER, THOMAS C. reg 14, co G, enr 4/3/63 Louisa, enl 6/10/63 Louisa, age 22, light hair, blue eyes, fair skin, 5-6, rem KIA Kennesaw Mtn. GA 6/22/64, house 230, s 1,2,4.

COBURN, JOSEPH. reg 14, co K, enr 11/8/61 Louisa, enl 12/10/61 Louisa, dis 1/31/65 Louisa, age 35, black hair & eyes, dark skin, 5-7, residence stated on muster roll, house n/c, s 1,2,4.

COBURN, RUFUS. reg 68, co D, enl 4/7/64, 5/21/64, dis 4/16/64, 6/22/64, age 23, black eyes & hair, dark skin, 5-11, house 94, s 2,4.

COLEMAN, JOHN P. reg 14, co B, enr 10/10/61 Louisa, enl 12/10/61 Louisa, dis 9/15/65 Louisville, age 18, light hair, blue eyes, fair skin, 5-7, rem trans to 14th Vet Inf, co A, enr 2/29/64, m/in 3/15/64 Louisa, residence stated on muster roll, house n/c, s 1,2,4.

COLYER, DAVID. reg 14, co B, enr 10/10/61, age 30, rem d 11/10/61 at Blaine, house 382, s 2,4.

COLYER, WILLIAM D. reg 45, co C, r cpl, enr 9/4/63, enl 10/10/63 Catlettsburg, dis 12/24/64 Catlettsburg, age 30, house 390, s 2.

COMPTON, JACOB. reg 68, co D, enl 5/21/64, dis 6/22/64, age 19, blue eyes, light hair, fair skin, 5-10, house 103, s 2,4.

COMPTON, JAMES H. reg 53, co I, enr 3/29/65, enl 3/29/65 Greenupsburg, age 18, light hair, fair skin, blue eyes, 5-8, m/out 11/4/65 Lexington, rem absent sick at muster-out of company, house 698, s 2.

COMPTON, MOORE. reg 68, co C, enl 4/7/64, 5/21/64, dis 4/16/64, 6/22/64, age 35, blue eyes, dark hair, fair skin, 5-10, house 697, s 2,4,18.

COMPTON, SAMUEL. reg 68, co D, r 2nd lt, enl 4/7/64, dis 4/16/64, age 20, black hair, blue eyes, dark skin, 5-10, house 103, s 4.

COMPTON, WILLIAM. reg 39, co B, enr 9/6/62 Louisa, enl 2/16/63 Peach Orchard, age 29, light hair, gray eyes, fair skin, 6-0, rem d 5/31/63 at Ashland of typhoid fever, house 1061, s 1,2,4.

COOKSEY, ALBERT. reg 14, co G, enr 11/19/61 Louisa, enl 12/10/61 Louisa, age 32, sandy hair, blue eyes, fair skin, 5-7, rem d 10/24/63 in Lawrence Co. of consumption, house 986, s 1,2,4.

COOKSEY, ANDREW. reg 68, co F, enl 4/7/64, 5/21/64, dis 4/16/64, 6/22/64, age 41, blue eyes, light hair, fair skin, 5-8, house 328, s 2,4.

COOKSEY, GREENVILLE. reg 68, co F, enl 5/21/64, dis 6/22/64, age 22, blue eyes, light hair, fair skin, 5-6, house 329, s 2,4.

COOKSEY, MONTRAVILLE. reg 45, co G, enr 11/28/63 Ashland, enl 11/30/63 Ashland, dis 2/14/65 Catlettsburg, age 19, light hair, blue eyes, fair skin, 5-4, house 985, s 1,2.

COOKSEY, SOLOMON. reg 68, co G, enl 4/7/64, 5/21/64, dis 4/16/64, 6/22/64, age 35, blue eyes, light hair, fair skin, 5-8, house 1169, s 2,4.

COPLEY, JAMES D. reg 5VA, co F, r sgt, enr 9/2/61 Ceredo, enl 9/14/61, dis 10/23/64 Wheeling WV, age 41, rem prom to sgt 5/1/64, house 1136, s 1,20.

COPLEY, STANLEY. reg 167WV, co Geo. Murray, reg 14, co H, enr 9/19/63 Louisa, enl 10/30/63 Louisa, age 18, light hair, blue eyes, fair skin 5-10, rem trans to 14th Vet Inf, co C, enr 9/19/63, m/in 10/30/63 Louisa, r sgt, house 1136, s 1,2,4,23.

CORDIAL, AMOS. reg 68, co G, enl 4/7/64, 5/21/64, dis 4/16/64, 6/22/64, age 33, black eyes & hair, dark skin, 5-5, house 243, s 2,4.

CORDLE, HOLLY. reg 39, co D, enr 12/13/62, enl 2/16/63 Peach Orchard, age 18, black hair, blue eyes, fair skin, 5-6, rem d 3/22/63 at Louisa, house 576, s 1,2,4.

CORDLE, JOHN. reg 14, co D, r cpl, enr 10/20/61 Louisa, enl 12/10/61 Louisa, dis 1/31/65 Louisa, age 32, black hair & eyes, dark skin, 5-11, house 242, s 1,2,4.

CORDLE, RALPH. reg 14, co D, enr 10/20/61 Louisa, enl 12/1/61 Louisa, dis 1/31/65 Louisa, age 18, black hair & eyes, dark skin, 5-9, house 576, s 1,2,4.

CORDLE, RUSSELL, reg CG, co L, enr 7/25/64, enl 8/30/64 Frankfort, dis 3/1/65 Catlettsburg, age 18, house 577, s 2,4.

CORDIAL, WILLIAM. reg 68, co B, enl 4/7/64, 5/21/64, dis 4/16/64, 6/22/64, age 30, dark skin, black hair & eyes, 6-4, house 578, s 2,4.

COX, BENNETT. reg 167WV, co Ira Copley, enl 8/62 to 2/64, dis 5/2/64, reg 14, co H, enr 8/14/63 Louisa, enl 8/29/63 Louisa, age 42, light hair, blue eyes, fair skin, 5-7, rem trans to 14th Vet Inf, co C, enr 8/14/63, m/in 8/29/63 Louisa, house 924, s 1,2,4,23.

COX, JEREMIAH. reg CG, co G, enr 8/13/64, enl 7/6/64 Frankfort, rem d 9/23/64 at Frankfort, house 924, s 2,4.

COX, MARION. reg 5VA, co F, enr 9/26/61 Ceredo, enl 9/14/61, dis 9/23/64 Wheeling WV, age 18, house 924, s 1,20.

CRABTREE, JOHN. reg 39, co A, B, enr 11/18/62, enl 2/16/63 Peach Orchard, dis 9/15/65 Louisville, age 35 or 36, rem trans to co A, 1/1/64, house 1176, s 1,2.

CRANK, JOHN. reg CG, co L, enr 7/18/64, enl 8/30/64 Frankfort, dis 3/11/65 Catlettsburg, age 16, light hair & skin, black eyes, 5-3, house 1171, s 2,4.

CREECH, ENOCH P. reg 14, co B, enr 10/10/61 Louisa, enl 12/10/61 Louisa, age 19, light hair, blue eyes, fair skin, 5-8, rem d 8/16/64 Chattanooga TN of typhoid fever, house 491, s 1,2,4.

CREECH, GEORGE T. reg 14, co B, enr 10/10/61 Louisa, enl 12/10/61 Louisa, age 23, light hair, blue eyes, fair skin, 5-8, rem d 8/2/64 at Atlanta GA, of wound in right leg received 7/21/64 near Atlanta, house 491, s 1,2,4.

CREECH, HENRY. reg 14, co B, enr 10/10/61 Louisa, enl 12/10/61 Louisa, dis 1/31/65 Louisa, age 30, light hair, blue eyes, fair skin, 5-10, rem cap Lawrence Co., 2/15/63, paroled in eastern Kentucky, house 469, s 1,2,4.

CREECH, JOHN S. reg 14, co B, enr 10/10/61 Louisa, 12/10/61 Louisa, dis 1/31/65 Louisa, age 35, light hair, blue eyes, fair skin, 5-10, rem app cpl 10/10/61, red to ranks 6/20/62, cap Lawrence Co. 7/10/63, paroled in Eastern Kentucky, house 492, s 1,2,4.

CROSS, JOHN. reg 68, co D, r cpl, enl 5/21/64, dis 6/22/64, age 28, blue eyes, light hair, fair skin, 5-11, residence shown on militia list, house n/c, s 2,4,18.

CRUM, ADAM. reg 39, co G, enr 2/12/63 Peach Orchard, enl 2/16/63 Peach Orchard, dis 9/15/65, age 20, dark hair & skin, hazel eyes, 5-8, residence shown on muster roll, house n/c, s 1,2,4.

CRUM, JESSE. reg 5VA, co F, enr 9/2/61 Ceredo, enl 9/14/61, age 26, sandy hair, hazel eyes, light skin, 5-8, rem dis 5/3/62 Wheeling WV for disability, house 1149, s 1,20.

CRUM, JOHN C. reg 45, co F, enr 9/1/63 Catlettsburg, enl 11/2/63 Ashland, dis 12/24/64 Catlettsburg, age 27, dark hair, eyes & skin, 5-5, rem d 12/26/64 of lung inflammation, house 1148, s 1,2,6.

CUMMINS, WILLIAM. reg CG, co E, enr & enl 7/30/64 Frankfort, dis 3/11/65 Catlettsburg, house 795, s 2,4.

CURNUTTE, DAVID T. reg 68, co G, enl 4/7/64, 5/21/64, dis 4/16/64, 6/22/64, age 25, blue eyes, light hair, fair skin, 5-8, house 234, s 2,4.

CURNUTT, ELISHA. reg 14, co G, enr 4/18/63 Louisa, enl 6/10/63 Louisa, age 18, black hair, dark eyes, fair skin, 5-5, rem trans to 14th Vet Inf, co D, enr 4/26/63, m/in 6/10/63 Louisa, cap Atlanta GA 8/8/64 or 8/17/64, paroled Vicksburg MS 4/29/65, d 4/27/65 in explosion of steamer Sultana, house 537, s 1,2,4.

CURNUTTE, JAMES. reg 68, co G, enl 5/21/64, dis 6/22/64, age 18, blue eyes, dark hair & skin, 5-5, house 233, s 2,4.

CURNUTTE, JAMES. reg 14, co G, enr 11/19/61 Louisa, enl 12/10/61 Louisa, dis 1/31/65 Louisa, age 25, light hair, blue eyes, fair skin, 5-6, rem wounded in face between 7/2/64 & 8/13/64, house 229, s 1,2,4.

CURNUTTE, JAMES H. reg 14, co B, r sgt, enr 10/10/61 Louisa, enl 12/10/61 Louisa, dis 1/31/65 Louisa, age 24, black hair & eyes, dark skin, 6-1, rem app sgt 8/10/63, house 677, s 1,2,4.

CURNUTTE, JOHN. reg 14, co G, enr 1/19/61 Louisa, enl 12/10/61 Louisa, dis 1/31/65 Louisa, age 32, light hair, blue eyes, fair skin, 5-8, house 538, s 1,2,4.

CURNUTTE, JOHN H. reg 68, c G, r cpl, enl 4/7/64, 5/21/64 dis 4/16/64, 6/22/64, age 25, blue eyes, black hair, dark skin, 5-8, house 232, s 2,4.

CURNUTT, JOHN T. reg 68, co F, r 1st sgt, enl 4/7/64, 5/21/64, dis 4/16/64, 6/22/64, age 39, blue eyes, light hair, fair skin, 6-0, house 682, s 2,4.

CURNUTT, STEPHEN. reg 68, co D, enl 5/21/64, dis 6/22/64, age 44, black eyes & hair, dark skin, 5-11, house 1175, s 2,4.

CURNUTT, THOMPSON B. reg 14, co G, enr 7/29/63 Louisa, enl 8/30/63 Louisa, dis 9/15/65 Louisville, age 18, light hair, blue eyes, fair skin, 5-0, rem trans to 14th Vet Inf, co C, enr 7/29/63, m/in 8/30/63, Louisa, wounded in knee 6/27/64, house 537, s 1,2,4.

CURNUTTE, WILLIAM W. reg 14, co G, enr 11/19/61 Louisa, enl 12/10/61 Louisa, dis 1/31/65 Louisa, age 21, light hair, black eyes, fair skin, 5-4, house 537, s 1,2,4.

D

DANIELS, THOMAS. reg 68, co A, enl 5/21/64, dis 6/22/64, age 19, blue eyes, light hair, fair skin, 5-6, house 547, s 2,4.

DAVENPORT, LAWRENCE P. reg 14, co D, r 2nd lt, enr 11/19/61, enl 12/10/61 Louisa, age 28 or 35, rem res 7/24/62, reg 68, co C, r sgt, enl 4/7/64, 5/21/64, dis 4/16/64, 6/22/64, blue eyes, light hair, dark skin, 5-10, house 144, s 2,4.

DAVIS, BEALS. reg 45, co K, enr 11/24/63 Louisa, enl 12/9/63 Louisa, age 18, light hair, blue eyes, fair Skin, 5-6, rem d 1/28/65 at Ashland of consumption, house 88, s 1,2.

DAVIS, DAVID D. reg 39 co D, r cpl, enr 9/10/62 enl 2/16/63 Peach Orchard, age 20, light hair, blue eyes, fair skin, 508, rem 3/64 red to ranks, d 8/1/64 Mt. Sterling, skin, 5-8, house 1073, s 1,2,4.

DAVIS, HARVEY. reg 68, co H, enl 5/21/64, dis 6/10/64, age 20, light eyes, hair & skin, 5-8, residence shown on militia list, house n/c, s 2,4,18.

DAVIS, HENRY. reg 14, co H, r cpl, enr 10/25/61 Catlettsburg, enl 12/10/61 Louisa, dis 1/31/65 Louisa, age 21, dark hair, blue eyes, fair skin, 5-8, residence stated on muster roll, house n/c, s 1,2,4.

DAVIS, HEZEKIAH. reg 68, co K, enl 5/21/64, dis 6/22/64, age 38, black eyes & hair, dark skin, 6-0, house 1071, s 2,4.

DAVIS, JAMES. reg 14, co H, r 5th sgt, enr 10/25/61 Louisa, enl 12/10/61 Louisa, dis 1/31/65 Louisa, age 24, rem red to ranks 7/1/62, residence stated on muster roll, house n/c, s 1,2,4.

DAVIS, JAMES SR. reg 39, co H, enr 10/9/63 Louisa, enl 10/29/63 Louisa, dis 9/15/65 Louisa, age 30 or 38, dark hair, blue eyes, fair skin, 5-11, house 1174, s 1,2,4.

DAVIS, JEDEDIAH. reg 14, co D, enr 10/20/61 Catlettsburg, enl 12/10/61 Louisa, dis 1/31/65 Louisa, age 18, dark hair & skin, black eyes, 5-8, reg 39, co G, r sgt, enr 4/6/65, dis 9/15/65 Louisville, rem trans to 39th Ky Inf 4/1/63, house 1073, s 1,2,4.

DAVIS, MARTIN P. M. reg 68, co K, r 1st lt, enl 4/7/64, 5/21/64, dis 4/16/64, 6/22/64, age 27, black eyes & hair, fair skin, 5-7, house 1053, s 2,4.

DAVIS, MICHAEL. reg 68, co K, r cpl, enl 4/7/64, 5/21/64, dis 4/16/64, 6/22/64, age 30, black eyes & hair, dark skin, 6-0, house 1072, s 2,4.

DAVIS, SAMUEL B. reg 39, co G, enr 2/22/64 Louisa, enl 3/29/64 Greenupsburg, dis 9/15/65 Louisville, age 18, light hair, gray eyes, fair skin, 5-9, house 1073, s 1,2,4.

DAVIS, WILLIAM. reg 68, co C, r 1st sgt, enl 4/7/64, 5/21/64, dis 4/16/64, 6/22/64, age 22, blue eyes, fair hair, dark skin, 5-8, house 1074, s 2,4.

DAVIS, WILLIAM H. reg 10KyCav, co F, enr 8/9/62, enl 9/9/62 Covington, dis 9/17/63 Maysville, reg 45, co F, r sgt, enr 10/21/63 Catlettsburg, enl 11/2/63 Ashland, dis 12/24/64 Catlettsburg, age 34, dark hair, light eyes & skin, 5-11, residence stated on muster roll, house 803, s 1,2,4.

DAVIS, WILLIAM M. reg 68, co K, r cpl, enl 4/7/64, 5/21/64, dis 4/16/64, 6/22/64, age 31, blue eyes, light hair, fair skin, 5-6, house 1124, 5s 2,4.

DAWSON, ISAAC. reg 68, co E, enl 4/7/64, 5/21/64, dis 4/16/64, 6/22/64, age 29, light eyes, hair & skin, 5-6, residence shown on militia list, house n/c, s 2,4,18.

DEAN, JOHN T. reg 14, co D, enr 9/10/63 Louisa, enl 10/31/63 Louisa, dis 9/15/65 Louisville, age 30, black hair & eyes, dark skin, 6-0, rem trans to 14th Vet Inf, co B, enr 9/10/63, m/in 10/20/63 Louisa, house 1212, s 1,2,4.

DEAN, MARSHALL. reg 68, co D, enl 4/7/64, 5/21/64, dis 4/16/64, 6/22/64, age 24, blue eyes, dark hair, fair skin, 5-11, residence shown on militia list, house n/c, s 2,4.

DEAN, THOMAS. reg 14, co D, enr 10/20/61 Louisa, enl 12/10/61 Louisa, dis 3/19/64 Louisa, age 20, dark hair, eyes & skin, 5-9, rem dis for disability of heart disease, residence stated on muster roll, house n/c, s 1,2,4.

DEAN, WILLIAM E. reg 68, co D, enl 5/21/64, dis 6/22/64, age 32, blue eyes, dark hair & skin, 5-9, residence shown on militia list, house n/c, s 2,4.

DEBOARD, JOHN. reg 39, co G, r cpl, enr 9/13/62 Peach Orchard, enl 2/16/63 Peach Orchard, dis 9/15/65 Louisville, age 19, light hair & skin, blue eyes, 6-0, rem prom to cpl 9/1/64, house 1077, s 1,2,4.

DEBOARD, WILLIAM. reg 39, co G, r sgt, enr 9/13/62 Peach Orchard, enl 2/16/63 Peach Orchard, dis 9/15/65 Louisville, age 24, light hair, blue eyes, fair skin, 6-0, house 1067, s 1,2,4.

DEMPSEY, ANDREW. reg 14, co H, enr 12/23/63 Louisa, enl 12/28/63 Louisa, dis 9/15/65 Louisville, age 21, light hair, blue eyes, fair skin, 5-7, rem trans to14th Vet Inf, co C, enr 12/23/63, m/in 12/28/63 Louisa, house 1129, s 1,2,4.

DEMPSEY, JOSEPH B. reg 39, co E, r sgt, enr 12/10/62 Piketon, enl 2/16/63 Peach Orchard, dis 9/15/65 Louisville, age 27, dark hair, blue eyes, fair skin, 5-10, rem app sgt 8/3/64, house 1129, s 1,2,4.

DERIFIELD, DAVID. reg 14, co D, enr 9/28/63 Louisa, enl 10/31/63 Louisa, dis 9/15/65 Louisville, age 35, dark hair, eyes & skin, 6-2, rem trans to 14th Vet Inf, co B, enr 9/28/63, m/in 10/31/63 Louisa, r cpl, residence shown on militia list, house n/c, s 1,2,4.

DERIFIELD, DERASCUS H. reg 14, co D, enr 10/20/61 Louisa, enl 12/10/61 Louisa, dis 1/31/65 Louisa, age 19, brown hair, blue eyes, light skin, 5-10, house 212, s 1,2,8.

DERIFIELD, SYLVESTER. reg 68, co G, enl 4/7/64, 5/21/64, dis 4/16/64, 6/22/64, age 18, black eyes, light hair, fair skin, 5-5, house 212, s 2,4.

DIAMOND, CHARLES D. reg 68, co I, enl 4/7/64, 5/21/64, dis 4/16/64, 6/22/64, age 28, blue eyes, dark hair, fair skin, 6-0, house 161, s 2,4.

DIAMOND, DAVID D. reg 68, co I, enl 4/7/64, 5/21/64, dis 4/16/64, 6/22/64, age 27, dark eyes & hair, fair skin, 5-8, house 157, s 2,4.

DIAMOND, HENRY CHRISTIAN. reg 68, co I, enl 4/7/64, 5/21/64, dis 4/16/64, 6/22/64, age 30, dark eyes, red hair, fair skin, age 19, r, fair skin, 5-10, house 154, s 2,4.

DIAMOND, HENRY J. reg 68, co I, r sgt, enl 4/7/64, 5/21/64, dis 4/16/64, 6/22/64, age 30, dark eyes, hair & skin, 5-10, house 151, s 2,4.

DIAMOND, JOHN. reg 68, co I, enl 4/7/64, 5/21/64, dis 4/16/64, 6/22/64, age 24, blue eyes, red hair, fair skin, 5-8, house 151, 157 or 160, s 2,4.

DIAMOND, JOHNAH. reg 68, co I, enl 5/21/64, age 35, red hair, blue eyes, fair skin, 6-0, house 165, s 4.

DIAMOND, MILES K. reg 14, co K, r sgt, enr 11/8/61 Louisa, enl 12/10/61 Louisa, dis 1/31/65 Louisa, age 23, black hair & eyes, dark skin, 5-9, rem prom from cpl to sgt 9/20/64, house 151, s 1,2,4.

DIAMOND, RUFUS. reg 68, co I, enl 4/7/64, 5/21/64, dis 4/16/64, 6/22/64, age 18, dark eyes & hair, fair skin, 5-8, house 151, s 2,4.

DINGUS, FREDERICK. reg 68, co H, enr 4/7/64, 5/21/64, dis 4/16/64, 6/22/64, age 25, dark eyes, hair & skin, 5-4, residence shown on militia list, house n/c, s 2,4,18.

DINGUS, JOHN. reg 68, co H, enl 5/24/64, age 34, dark hair, eyes, & skin, 5-8, house 1130, s 4.

DOBINS, FRANCIS. reg 68, co E, enl 5/21/64, dis 6/22/64, age 28, dark eyes, hair & skin, 6-0, house 723, s 2,4.

DOBINS, WASHINGTON. reg 68, co E, enl 5/21/64, dis 6/22/64, age 25, dark eyes, hair & skin, 5-10, residence shown on militia list, house n/c, s 2,4,18.

DOBINS, WILLIAM H. reg 14, co H, enr 10/25/61 Catlettsburg, enl 12/10/61 Louisa, dis 1/31/65 Louisa, age 21, dark hair & eyes, fair skin, 5-8, house 723 or 1028, s 1,2,4.

DOOLEY, HARRISON. reg 68, co K, r cpl, enl 4/7/64, 5/21/64, dis 4/16/64, 6/22/64, age 35, black eyes & hair, dark skin, 6-0, house 1034, s 2,4.

DOWDEN, MARLIN. reg 14, co D, enr 10/25/61, m/in 12/10/61, age 28, black eyes & hair, dark skin, 5-111/2, rem trans to co D 8/30/63, killed Cassville, WV 10/30/63 by guerrillas, house 1131, s 1,2.

DRAKE, MATTHEW. reg CG, co L, enr 6/10/64, enl 7/6/64 Frankfort, dis 3/11/65 Catlettsburg, age 44, light hair, dark eyes, fair skin, 5-5, house 1223, s 2,4.
DULIN, JAMES W. reg 22, co D, enr 1/30/62, age 17, rem transferred to 7th Ky. Vet. Inf., residence stated on muster roll, house n/c, s 2,4.
DUTTON, GEORGE W. reg 39, co E, enr 11/18/62, enl 2/16/63 Peach Orchard, dis 9/15/65 Louisville, age 29, residence stated on muster roll, house n/c, s 4.
DYER, JAMES. reg 68, co D, enl 4/7/64, 5/21/64, dis 4/16/64, 6/22/64, house 345, s 2,4,18.
DYER, PATRICK, reg 5VA, co I, enr 10/1/61 Ceredo, enl 10/1/61, dis 10/14/64 Harper's Ferry WV, age 18, house 769, s 1,20.

E

EDWARDS, CHARLES S. reg 10Cav, co F, r 6th cpl, enr 8/9/62 Boyd Co., enl 9/9/62 Covington, dis 9/17/63 Maysville, age 38, app 6th cpl 8/18/62, residence stated on muster roll, house n/c, s 1, 2, 4.
EDWARDS, EDMUND. reg 68, co A, r sgt, enl 4/7/64, 5/21/64, dis 4/16/64, 6/22/64, age 24, blue eyes, dark hair & skin, 5-9, house 367, s 2,4.
EDWARDS, ISAAC. reg 68, co A, r cpl, enl 4/7/64, 5/21/64, dis 4/16/64, 6/22/64, age 43, blue eyes, light hair & skin, 5-7, house 630, s 2,4.
EDWARDS, JOEL G. reg 39, co G, enr 9/13/62 Peach Orchard, enl 2/16/63 Peach Orchard, dis 9/15/65 Louisville, age 21 or 31, light hair & skin, blue eyes, 6-0, rem trans to co D, 14th Ky Inf 4/1/63 back to co G, 39th Ky Inf 1/20/65, residence stated on muster roll, house n/c, s 1,2,4.
EDWARDS, JOHN. reg 14, co D, enr 10/20/61 Louisa, enl 12/10/61 Louisa, dis 1/31/65 Louisa, age 20, black hair & eyes, light skin, 6-0, house 1054, s 1,2,4.
EDWARDS, JOSEPH. reg 39, co G, enr 9/26/61, dis 9/15/65, house 1054, s 5.
EDWARDS, WILLIAM. reg 68, co B, r sgt, enl 4/7/64, 5/21/64, dis 4/16/64, 6/22/64, age 42, black eyes & hair, fair skin, 5-6, house 628, s 2,4.
ELDRIDGE, JAMES. reg 45, co E, enr 10/20/63 Catlettsburg, enl 11/6/63 Ashland, dis 12/24/64 Catlettsburg, age 24, dark hair, gray eyes, fair skin, 5-10, house 435, s 1,2,6.
ELKINS, MARVEL. reg 14, co H, enr 10/25/61 Catlettsburg, enl 12/10/61 Louisa, age 28, light hair, blue eyes, fair skin, 5-7, rem KIA 6/22/64 Marietta GA, house 913, s 1,2,4.
ELSWICK, RICH. reg 39, co B, enr 9/12/62 Pike Co., enl 2/16/63 Peach Orchard, dis 9/15/65 Louisville, age 25, black hair & eyes, dark skin, 6-2, prom to 5th sgt 6/15/63, drummed out of camp 3/24/64, residence stated on muster roll, house n/c, s 1,4.
ENDICOTT, FRANCIS. reg 14, co H, enr 10/25/61 Catlettsburg, enl 12/10/61 Louisa, dis 2/24/64 Louisa, age 21, light hair, blue eyes, fair skin, 5-8, rem dis for disability Louisa 12/2/63 for ulcer of hip & thigh, house 1164, s 1,2,4.
ENDICOTT, GABRIEL. reg 68, co H, enl 4/7/64, 5/21/64, dis 4/16/64, 6/22/64, age 36, light eyes, hair & skin, 6-0, house 902, s 2,4.
ENDICOTT, JOSEPH. reg 14, co H, enr 10/25/61 Catlettsburg, enl 12/10/61 Louisa, age 23, dark hair, blue eyes, fair skin, 5-9, rem d 1/1/64 Wayne Co. WV by accidental fall of tree while on scout, house 909, s 1,2,4.
ENDICOTT, JOSHUA. reg 167WV, co Ira Copley, enl 8/62 to 2/64, dis 5/2/64, house 1164, s 23.
ENDICOTT, JOSHUA. reg 14, co H, enr 6/1/63 Louisa, enl 8/29/63 Louisa, dis 9/15/65 Louisville, age 19, dark hair, eyes & skin, 5-8, rem trans to 14th Vet Inf, co C, enr 6/1/63, m/in 8/29/63 Louisa, house 1165, s 1,2,4.
ENDICOTT, SAMUEL. reg 167WV, co Ira Copley, enl 8/62 to 2/64, dis 5/2/64, house 903, s 23.

ENDICOTT, SAMUEL. reg 68, co H, enl 4/7/64, 5/21/64, dis 4/16/64, 6/22/64, age 35, light eyes, hair & skin, 6-0, house 1165, s 2,4.

ESTEP, CORBIN. reg 68, co F, enl 4/7/64, 5/21/64, dis 4/16/64, 6/22/64, reg CG, co L, enr 6/8/64, enl 7/6/64 Frankfort, age 38, light hair, black eyes, fair skin, 6-0, rem des, house 48, s 2,4.

EVANS, BENJAMIN. reg 167WV, co Ira Copley, enl 8/62 to 2/64, dis 5/2/64, house 901, s 23.

EVANS, HENRY C. reg 14, co B, enr 2/16/63 Louisa, enl 6/10/63 Louisa, dis 9/15/65 Louisville, age 24, dark hair, blue eyes, fair skin, 5-11, rem trans to 14th Vet Inf, co B, enr 2/18/63, m/in 6/10/63 Louisa, house 611, s 1,2,4.

EVANS, JAMES G. reg 167WV, co Geo. Murray, reg 14, co E, r cpl, enr 10/25/61 Louisa, enl 12/10/61 Louisa, age 19, light hair & skin, brown eyes, 5-5, rem prom to cpl 8/28/63, trans from co F to co E 8/28/63, trans to 14th Vet Inf, co D, enr 10/14/63, m/in 12/31/63 Louisa, trans to co F 1/20/65, house 901, s 2,4,23.

F

FANNIN, JACKSON. reg 68, co E, enl 4/7/64, 5/21/64, dis 4/16/64, 6/22/64, age 40, dark eyes, hair & skin, 5-10, house 842, s 2,4.

FANNIN, JOHN. reg 68, co D, enl 5/21/64, dis 6/22/64, age 27, blue eyes, dark hair, fair skin, 5-6, house 62, s 2,4.

FANNIN, LEWIS. reg 68, co D, enl 4/7/64, 5/21/64, dis 4/16/64, 6/22/64, age 30, blue eyes, dark hair, fair skin, 6-0, house 77, s 2,4.

FERGUSON, ELISHA. reg 5VA, co I, enr 9/14/61 Ceredo, enl 9/14/61, dis 10/4/64 Wheeling WV, rem d 10/10/61 or 10/14/61 of flux, house 629, s 1,20.

FERGUSON, MEREDITH. reg 14, co B, r cpl, enr 10/10/61 Louisa, enl 12/10/61 Louisa, dis 1/31/65 Louisa, age 24, light hair, blue eyes, fair skin, 6-0, rem app sgt 10/10/61, red to ranks 6/20/62, app cpl 1/10/63, residence stated on muster roll, house n/c, s 1,2,4.

FERGUSON, SAMUEL. reg 45, co G, r cpl, enr 12/7/63 Louisa, enl 11/30/63 Ashland, dis 2/14/65 Catlettsburg, age 18, rem prom to cpl 11/30/63, house 639, s 1,2.

FITZPATRICK, ARTHUR. reg 45, co F, enr 8/21/63 Lawrence Co., enl 11/2/63 Ashland, dis 12/24/64 Catlettsburg, age 41, light hair, eyes & skin, 5-7, house 851, s 1,2,6.

FITZPATRICK, BENJAMIN. reg 45, co F, enr 8/21/63 Peach Orchard, enl 11/2/63 Ashland, dis 12/24/64 Catlettsburg, age 18, light hair, eyes & skin, 5-4, house 851, s 1,2,6.

FITZPATRICK, GEORGE W. reg 45, co F, enr 8/21/63 Peach Orchard, enl 11/2/63 Ashland, dis 12/24/64 Catlettsburg, age 19, light hair, eyes & skin, 5-4, house 851, s 1,2,6.

FIRZPATRICK, JOHN. reg 45, co F, enr 8/21/63 Peach Orchard, enl 11/2/63 Ashland, dis 12/24/64 Catlettsburg, age 26, light hair, eyes & skin, 5-7, house 852, s 1,2,6.

FITZPATRICK, REASON. reg 68, co E, enl 4/7/64, 5/21/64, dis 4/16/64, 6/22/64, age 26, light eyes, hair & skin, 5-6, house 852, s 2,4.

FITZPATRICK, ULYSSES. reg 68, co C, enl 5/21/64, dis 6/22/64, reg CG, co L, r cpl, enr 6/8/64, enl 7/6/64 Frankfort, dis 3/11/65 Catlettsburg, age 19, dark hair & skin, gray eyes, 5-10, house 917, s 2,4.

FITZPATRICK, WILLIAM F. reg 45, co F, enr 8/21/63 Ashland, enl 11/2/63 Ashland, dis 12/24/64 Catlettsburg, age 39, residence shown on militia list, house n/c, s 1,2.

FLUTY, AARON. reg 5VA, co F, enr 9/2/61 Ceredo, enl 9/14/61, dis 9/23/64 Wheeling WV, age 34, house 1157, s 1,20.

FLUTY, FRANCIS. reg 5VA, co F, enr 9/2/61 Ceredo, enl 9/14/61, dis 9/23/64 Wheeling WV, age 44, light hair & skin, gray eyes, 5-7, rem dis Washington DC 9/20/62 for disability of advanced age of 71 years, house 1160, s 1,20.

FLUTY, FRANCIS. reg 167WV, co Ira Copley, r 1st lt, enl 7/62 to 2/64, dis 5/2/64, reg 68, co H, r 1st lt, enl 5/21/64, dis 6/22/64, age 35, blue eyes, dark hair & skin, 5-10, house 1161, s 2,4,23.

FLUTY, JOHN. reg 167WV, co Ira Copley, enl 8/62 to 2/64, dis 5/2/64, house 1161, s 23.

FORRESTER, JOHN W. reg 3KyCav, co G, r sgt, enr 10/3/61 Louisville, m/in McLean Co., KY., reg 5th KyCav, co K, r capt, enr 4/3/63, enl 4/4/63 Nashville TN, age 21, light skin, gray eyes, brown hair, 5-7, rem prom f sgt co G, 3rd Ky Cav, wounded 11/28/64 Buckhead Creek, GA, d 11/29/64, residence established by List of Officers, house n/c, s 1,2.

FORSHEE, CALEB. reg 14, co D, enr 10/20/61 Louisa, enl 12/10/61 Louisa, age 23, dark hair & skin, blue eyes, 5-7, rem KIA 6/22/64 near Marietta GA, residence stated on muster roll, house n/c, s 1,2,4.

FOSTER, WILLIAM S. reg 68, co I, enl 5/21/64, dis 6/22/64, age 30, blue eyes, fair hair & skin, 5-8, house 116, s 2,4.

FOWLER, JAMES. reg 68, co D, r cpl, enl 5/21/64, dis 6/22/64, residence shown on militia list, house n/c, s 2,4,18.

FRALEY, SAMUEL. reg 14, co H, r cpl, enr 10/25/61 Catlettsburg, enl 12/10/61 Louisa, dis 1/31/65 Louisa, age 26 or 36, light hair, blue eyes, fair skin, 5-7, rem wounded in right hand 6/22/64 near Marietta GA, house 812, s 1,2,4.

FRANCIS, WILIAM. reg 68, co K, enl 4/7/64, 5/21/64, dis 4/16/64, 6/22/64, age 26, black eyes & hair, dark skin, 6-0, residence shown on militia list, house n/c, s 2,4,18.

FRASHER, CHUSHINGBURY. reg 68, co C, enl 5/21/64, dis 6/22/64, age 32, blue eyes, light hair, fair skin, 6-2, house 910, s 2,4.

FRASHER, ERVIN. reg 68, co G, enl 4/7/64, 5/21/64, dis 4/16/64, 6/22/64, age 40, blue eyes, light hair, fair skin, 5-10, house 996, s 2,4.

FRASHER, OLIVER M. reg 14, co C, r capt, enr 10/10/61 Louisa, enl 12/10/61 Louisa, dis 1/3/65 Louisa, age 23, rem prom from 1st lt to capt 2/21/63, residence stated on muster roll, house n/c, s 1,2,4.

FRASHER, WILLIAM D. reg 68, co C, enl 5/21/64, dis 6/22/64, age 23, blue eyes, fair hair & skin, 6-0, house 916, s 2,4.

FRILEY, MC. reg 39, co K, enr 12/6/64 Louisa, enl 2/16/65 Greenupsburg, dis 9/15/65 Louisville, age 18, dark hair, blue eyes, fair skin, 5-9, residence stated on CSR, house n/c, s 1,2,4.

FUGITT, JAMES. reg 14 co G, enr 11/19/61 Louisa, enl 12/10/61 Louisa, dis 3/19/62 Paintsville, age 28, dark hair, blue eyes, fair skin, 6-2, house 204, s 1,2,4.

FUGITT, KENUS. reg 14, co G, enr 11/19/61 Louisa, enl 12/10/61 Louisa, dis 1/31/65 Louisa, age 21, light hair, blue eyes, fair skin, 5-4, house 156, s 1,2,4.

FUGITT, WILLIAM. reg 14, co G, enr 11/19/61 Louisa, enl 12/10/61 Louisa, dis 1/31/65 Louisa, age 20, light hair, blue eyes, fair skin, 5-10, rem wounded by shell contusion between 7/2/64 & 8/15/64, residence stated on muster roll, house n/c, s 1,2,4.

FYFFE, HENRY. reg 68, co B, r cpl, enl 4/7/64, 5/21/64, dis 4/16/64, 6/22/64, age 29, black eyes & hair, fair skin, 6-6, house 424, s 2,4.

G

GALLUP, GEORGE W. reg 14, r col, enr 11/19/61 Louisa, enl 12/10/61 Louisa, dis 1/31/65 Louisa, age 31, rem prom from regimental Q.M. to lt col 5/11/62, to col 1/13/63, to commander Eastern District of Ky., 7/30/63, to brevet brig. gen. 3/13/65 by order of 7/16/67, house 1218, s 1,2,4.

GAMBILL, ADISON. reg 68, co A, enl 4/7/64, 5/21/64, dis 4/16/64, 6/22/64, age 30, blue eyes, light hair, fair skin, 5-6, house 388, s 2,4.

GAMBILL, JOHN. reg 68, co B, enl 4/7/64, 5/21/64, dis 4/16/64, 6/22/64, age 39, blue eyes, light hair, fair skin, 5-8, house 404, s 2,4.

GAMBILL, WILLIAM H. reg 14, co B, enr 10/10/61 Louisa, enl 12/10/61 Louisa, dis 1/31/65 Louisa, age 21, light hair, blue eyes, fair skin, 5-8, residence stated on muster roll, house n/c, s 1,2,4.

GAMBLE, HENRY H. reg 14, co B, enr 4/10/63 Louisa, enl 6/1/63 Louisa, age 18, light hair & skin, blue eyes, 5-7, rem trans to 14th Vet Inf, co B, enr 4/10/63, m/in 6/10/63 Louisa, cap near Adairsville GA, 8/10/64, released 3/31/65, house 405, s 1,2,4.

GAMBLE, JESSE. reg 14, co B, enr 8/9/63 Louisa, enl 8/10/63 Louisa, dis 9/15/65 Louisville, age 29, dark hair & eyes, fair skin, 5-7, rem trans to 14th Vet Inf, co B, enr 8/9/63, m/in 8/10/63, house 389, s 1,2,4.

GAMBLE, NATHAN O. reg 14, co B, enr 7/7/63 Louisa, enl 8/0/63 Louisa, dis 9/15/65 Louisville, age 18, light hair, dark eyes, fair skin, 5-5, rem trans to 14th Vet Inf, co B, enr 7/7/63, m/in 8/10/63 Louisa, house 403, s 1,2,4.

GAMBRELL, JOHN J. reg 14, co B, r cpl, enr 10/10/61 Louisa, enl 12/10/61 Louisa, dis 1/31/65 Louisa, age 19, light hair, blue eyes, fair skin, 5-9, rem app cpl 6/20/62, wounded by shell to right shoulder between 7/26/64 & 8/13/64, house 405, s 1,2,4.

GARRED, DAVID. reg 68, co E, enl 4/7/64, 5/21/64, dis 4/16/64, 6/22/64, age 40, dark eyes, hair & skin, 5-10, house 731, s 2,4.

GILLIAM, PETER. reg 68, co B, enl 4/7/64, 5/21/64, dis 4/16/64, 6/22/64, age 44, blue eyes, light hair, fair skin, 6-0, house 420, s 2,4.

GLAUSNER, NICHOLAS. reg 5VA, co I, enr 10/1/61 Ceredo, enl 10/1/61, dis 10/4/64 Wheeling WV, age 30, house 757, s 1,20.

GODBEY, PRESTON. reg 14, co H, enr 10/25/61 Catlettsburg, enl 12/10/61 Louisa, dis 1/31/65 Louisa, age 24, light hair, blue eyes, fair skin, 5-10, house 913, s 1,2,4.

GOODWIN, CHARLES. reg 5VA, co I, enr 9/19/61 Ceredo, enl 9/14/61, dis 10/4/64 Wheeling WV, age 23, light hair & skin, blue eyes, 5-11, rem dis 8/12/62 for disability relating to a leg problem, house 776, s 1,20.

GRAHAM, ANDREW. reg 14, co D, enr 10/20/61 Louisa, enl 12/10/61 Louisa, dis 1/31/65 Louisa, age 23, light hair & skin, black eyes, 6-2, residence stated on muster roll, house n/c, s 1,2,4.

GRAHAM, BENJAMIN. reg 14, co D, enr 10/20/61 Louisa, enl 12/10/61 Louisa, dis 1/31/65 Louisa, age 49, light hair & skin, gray eyes, 6-0, residence stated on muster roll, house n/c, s 1,2,4.

GRAHAM, GREENVILLE. reg 68, co A, enl 4/7/64, 5/21/64, dis 4/16/64, 6/22/64, age 28, blue eyes, light hair, fair skin, 5-5, house 219, s 2,4.

GRAHAM, J. P. reg 68, co A, enl 4/7/64, 5/21/64, dis 4/16/64, 6/22/64, age 31, black eyes, dark hair & skin, 6-2, house 220, s 2,4.

GRAHAM, MARTIN V. reg 68, co A, enl 4/7/64, 5/21/64, dis 4/16/64, 6/22/64, age 28, blue eyes, light hair, fair skin, 6-0, house 219, s 2,4.

GRAHAM, RICHARD F. reg 68, co G, enl 4/7/64, 5/21/64, dis 4/16/64, 6/22/64, age 18, blue eyes, light hair, fair skin, 5-10, residence shown on militia list, house n/c, s 2,4,18.

GRAHAM, WILLIAM. reg 68, co F, enl 5/21/64, dis 6/22/64, age 28, blue eyes, light hair, fair skin, 5-6, house 633, s 2,4.

GRANT, JOHN. reg CG, co L, m/in 7/6/64 Frankfort, enl 6/8/64, dis 3/11/65 Catlettsburg, reg 39, co B, enr 3/27/65 Louisa, enl 4/13/65 Greenupsburg, dis 9/15/65 Louisville, age 24, light hair, blue eyes, fair skin, 6-3, rem credited to Lawrence Co. as per CSR, house n/c, s 1,2,4.

GREEN, BURWELL. reg 68, co K, enl 5/21/64, dis 6/22/64, age 30, light eyes, hair & skin, 5-10, residence shown on militia list, house n/c, s 2,4,18.

GREEN, GEORGE N. W. reg 14, co B, enr 10/10/61 Louisa, enl 12/10/61 Louisa, dis 9/6/65 Lexington, age 20, light hair & skin, blue eyes, 5-7, rem trans to 14th Vet Inf, enr 10/16/61, m/in 12/10/61 Louisa, cap near Marietta GA 6/22/64, paroled Richmond VA 2/14/65, house 581, s 1,2,4.

GREEN, GEORGE W. reg 14, co B, r capt, enr 10/10/61 Louisa, enl 12/10/61 Louisa, dis 3/1/64, age 27, rem prom to 2nd lt 10/30/61, to capt 6/22/63, resigned 3/1/64 for disability, house 571, s 1,2,4.

GREEN, JOHN. reg 68, co B, r cpl, enl 4/7/64, 5/21/64, dis 4/16/64, 6/22/64 age 25, black eyes & hair, fair skin, 6-0, house 572, s 2,4.

GREEN, THOMAS. reg 68, co B, enl 5/21/64, dis 6/22/64, age 43, black eyes & hair, dark skin, 6-0, house 581, s 2,4.

GRIFFITH, ABRAHAM. reg 68, co A, enl 4/7/64, 5/21/64, dis 4/16/64, 6/22/64, age 35, blue eyes, dark hair & skin, 6-0, residence stated on muster roll, house n/c, s 2,4,18.

GRIFFITH, DAVID. reg 14, co B, enr 8/9/63 Louisa, enl 8/10/63 Louisa, dis 9/15/65 Louisville, age 21, light hair, blue eyes, fair skin, 5-5, rem trans to 14th Vet Inf, co B, enr 8/9/63, m/in 8/10/63, house 645, s 1,2,4.

GRIFFITH, ELZA. reg 68, co A, enl 5/21/64, dis 6/22/64, age 30, blue eyes, light hair, fair skin, 5-6, house 575, s 2,4.

GRIFFITH, GABRAEL. reg 68, co B, enl 4/7/64, 5/21/64, dis 4/16/64, 6/22/64, age 34, blue eyes, black hair, dark skin, 5-8, house 608, s 2,4.

GRIFFITH, GEORGE W. reg 14, co B, enr 8/9/63 Louisa, enl 8/10/63 Louisa, dis 9/15/65 Louisville, age 25, light hair, blue eyes, fair skin, 5-6, rem trans to 14th Vet Inf, co B, enr 8/9/63, m/in 8/10/63, dis for chronic rheumatism, house 622, s 1,2,4.

GRIFFITH, J. HARRISON. reg CG, co L, enr 6/13/64, enl 7/6/64 Frankfort, dis 3/11/65 Catlettsburg, age 17, dark hair & eyes, fair skin, 6-0, house 621, s 2,4.

GRIFFITH, JAMES A. reg 14, co B, enr 10/10/61 Louisa, enl 12/10/61 Louisa, dis 1/31/65 Louisa, age 30, dark hair & skin, blue eyes, 5-9, rem cap Lawrence Co., 2/15/63, paroled in eastern Ky., residence stated on muster roll, house n/c, s 1,2,4.

GRIFFITH, JOHN J. reg 14, co B, r cpl, enr 10/10/61 Louisa, enl 12/10/61 Louisa, dis 1/31/65 Louisa, age 24, dark hair & skin, black eyes, 5-9, rem red to ranks 6/20/62, house 321, s 1,2,4.

GRIFFITH, JOHN R. reg 14, co B, r cpl, enr 10/10/61 Louisa, enl 12/10/61 Louisa, dis 1/31/65, age 19, dark hair & eyes, fair skin, 5-8, rem cap Lawrence Co. 2/15/63 & paroled, app cpl 8/28/63, house 622 or 693, s 1,2,4.

GRIFFITH, MEREDITH. reg 5VA, co I, enr 9/14/61 Ceredo, enl 9/14/61, age 22, brown hair, gray eyes, dark skin, 5-11, rem des 2/12/63 Ceredo WV, house 587, s 1,20.

GRIFFITH, MEREDITH. reg 14, co B, enr 8/9/63 Louisa, enl 8/10/63 Louisa, dis 9/15/65 Louisville, age 21, light hair, blue eyes, fair skin, 5-5, rem trans to 14th Vet Inf, co B, enr 8/9/63, m/in 8/10/63 Louisa, house 645, s 1,2,4.

GRIFFITH, RICHARD. reg 5VA, co I, enr 9/14/61 Ceredo, enl 9/14/61, dis 10/4/64 Wheeling WV, age 29 or 32, dark hair, eyes & skin, 5-10, rem prom to sgt 7/5/62, red to ranks 8/31/63, house 587, s 1,20.

GRIFFITH, WALTER O. reg 14, co B, enr 10/10/61 Louisa, enl 12/10/61 Louisa, dis 2/26/64 Louisa, age 32, light hair, blue eyes, fair skin, 6-0, rem cap Lawrence Co. 2/15/63, paroled in eastern Ky., dis for disability, tuberculosis, house 621, s 1,2,4.

GRUBB, GEORGE WASHINGTON. reg 68, co D, enl 4/7/64, 5/21/64, dis 4/16/64, 6/22/64, age 36, black eyes & hair, dark skin, 5-11, house 678, s 2,4,18.

GRUBB, ISAAC. reg 68, co I, enl 4/7/64, 5/21/64, dis 4/16/64, 6/22/64, age 26, blue eyes, fair hair & skin, 6-0, house 332, s 2,4.

GRUBB, JOSEPHUS. reg 14, co B, enr 7/28/63 Louisa, enl 8/1/63 Louisa, age 19, light hair, blue eyes, fair skin, 5-6, rem drowned 3/30/64 in Tug Fork, Big Sandy River, house 332, s 1,2,4.

H

HAGER, FERNANDEZ. reg 14, co G, r musician, enr 11/19/61 Louisa, enl 12/10/61 Louisa, dis 9/15/65 Louisville, age 18, sandy hair, blue eyes, fair skin, 5-6, rem trans to 14th Vet Inf, co A, enl 2/29/64, m/in 3/15/64 Louisa, prom to musician 5/1/62, stunned by shell between 7/2/64 & 8/13/64, residence stated on muster roll, house n/c, s 1,2,4.

HAGER, WILLIAM. reg 14, co G, enr 11/19/61 Louisa, enl 12/10/61 Louisa, age 20, dark hair, blue eyes, fair skin, 5-11, rem d 7/18/64 Knoxville TN of wounds received in action 6/22/64, residence stated on muster roll, house n/c, s 1,2,4.

HALE, GREENVILLE. reg 68, co G, enl 4/7/64, 5/21/64, dis 4/16/64, 6/22/64, age 21, black eyes, fair hair, dark skin, 5-6, house 999, s 2,4.

HALE, BLUFORD F. reg 14, co D, r 1st lt, enr 10/20/61 Louisa, enl 12/10/61 Louisa, age 30, black hair & eyes, dark skin, 5-10, rem res 1/10/63, reg 68, r adjutant, enl 4/7/64, 5/21/64, dis 4/16/64, 6/22/64, house 261, s 1,2,4.

HALE, IRA. reg 14, co D, enr 10/20/61 Louisa, enl 12/10/61 Louisa, dis 1/31/65 Louisa, age 18, black hair, blue eyes, dark skin, 5-8, rem in hospital at Louisville 6/64 from wound, residence stated on muster roll, house n/c, s 1,2,4.

HALL, ELISHA M. reg 68, co K, enl 4/7/64, 5/51/64, dis 4/16/64, 6/22/64, age 35, black hair & eyes, dark skin, 6-0, house 228, s 2,4.

HALL, JONATHAN. reg 68, co H, enl 5/21/64 Louisa, dis 6/22/64, age 40, dark hair, eyes & skin, 5-10, credited to Lawrence Co. on CSR, house n/c, s 1,2.

HALL, SAMUEL. reg 39, co B, enr 5/27/64, enl 4/27/65 Lexington, dis 9/15/65 Louisville, age 37, light hair, gray eyes, fair skin, 6-0, residence shown on CSR, house n/c, s 1,2,4.

HALL, SQUIRE. reg 39, co B, enr 9/6/62, enl 4/27/65 Lexington, dis 9/15/65 Louisville, age 32, dark hair & skin, blue eyes, 5-10, residence shown on CSR, house n/c, s 1,2,4.

HALLEY, EDGAR. reg 14, co D, r cpl, enr 10/20/61, enl 12/10/61 Louisa, dis 1/31/65 Louisa, age 22, residence stated on muster roll, house n/c, s 2,4.

HAMMONDS, JOHN. reg 14, co H, enr 10/25/61 Catlettsburg, enl 12/10/61 Louisa, dis 1/31/65 Louisa, age 42, black hair & eyes, dark skin, 5-9, residence stated on muster roll, house n/c, s 1,2,4.

HAMMONDS, WILLIAM S. reg 167WV, co Ira Copley, enl 8/62 to 2/64, dis 5/2/64, reg 68, co H, enl 4/7/64, 5/21/64, dis 4/16/64, 6/22/64, age 34, dark eyes, hair & skin, 5-10, house 1162, s 2,4,23.

HAMMONS, JOHN. reg 68, co E, enl 4/7/64, 5/21/64, dis 4/16/64, 6/22/64, age 23, dark eyes, hair & skin, 6-2, residence shown on militia list, house n/c, s 2,4,18.

HANEY, JAMES F. reg 39, co E, enr 11/5/62 Piketon, enl 2/16/63 Peach Orchard, dis 9/15/65 Louisville, age 19, black hair, gray eyes, fair skin, 5-7, house 882, s 1,2,4.

HANEY, JOHN B. reg 45, co F, enr 8/25/63 Peach Orchard, enl 11/2/63 Ashland, age 18, dark hair, eyes & skin, 5-8, rem d 8/8/64 at Ashland of diarrhea, house 882, s 1,2,6.

HANEY, WILLIAM. reg 68, co H, enl 5/24/64, age 41, light hair & skin, blue eyes, 6-0, house 882, s 4.

HANNAH, GEORGE W. reg 39, co A, enr 9/13/62 Lawrence Co., enl 2/16/63 Peach Orchard, age 32, dark hair, eyes & skin, 5-8, rem dis 10/7/64 at Covington for wounds suffered in Battle of Cynthiana 6/12/64, house 1000, s 1,2,4,8.

HARDWICK, GEORGE. reg 14, co H, enr 10/25/61 Catlettsburg, enl 12/10/61 Louisa, dis 6/63 Louisa, age 23, light hair, blue eyes, fair skin, 5-11, rem dis for disability of epilepsy, house 921, s 1,2,4.

HARDWICK, JOHN. reg 14, co H, r sgt, enr 10/25/61 Catlettsburg, enl 12/10/61 Louisa, dis 1/31/65 Louisa, age 24, light hair, dark eyes, fair skin, 5-9, rem app sgt 1/1/62, wounded in right side 7/20/64, house 921, s 1,2,4.

HARDWICK, RICHARD. reg 14, co H, enr 7/5/63 Louisa, enl 8/29/63 Louisa, age 18, light hair, blue eyes, fair skin, 5-9, rem d 7/8/64 at Knoxville TN of chronic diarrhea, house 921, s 1,2,4.

HARMAN, WILLIAM F. reg 68, co D, r cpl, enl 5/21/64, dis 6/22/64, age 21, black eyes, dark hair, light skin, 6-0, house 21, s 2,4.

HARRIS, JOHN. reg 68, co I, enl 4/7/64, 5/21/64, dis 4/16/64, 6/22/64, age 25, blue eyes, dark hair, fair skin, 5-8, house 768, s 2,4.

HARRIS, WILLIAM A. reg 14, co B, enr 10/10/61 Louisa, enl 12/10/61 Louisa, dis 2/2/63 Lexington, age 39, dark hair, eyes & skin, 5-8, rem dis for disability of rheumatism, residence stated on muster roll, house n/c, s 1,2,4.

HARRISON, CALVIN. reg 39, co I, r sgt, enr 12/18/62, enl 2/16/63 Peach Orchard, dis 9/15/65 Louisville, age 20 or 23, dark hair, blue eyes, fair skin, 5-9, rem prom from cpl to sgt 9/22/64, residence stated on muster roll, house n/c, s 1,2,4.

HATCHER, JOHN B. reg 68, co F&S, r comm. sgt, enl 4/7/64, 5/21/64, dis 4/16/64, 6/22/64, residence shown on militia list, house n/c, s 2,4,18.

HATTON, JASPER C. reg 45, co E, r 2nd lt, enr 8/8/63, enl 11/6/63 Ashland, dis 12/24/64 Catlettsburg, age 21, rem residence established by List of Officers, house n/c, s 1,2,32.

HATTON, JOSEPH F. reg 68, co D, r capt, enl 4/7/64, 5/21/64, dis 4/16/64, 6/22/64, age 27, blue eyes, light hair, fair skin, 5-10, house 27, s 2,4.

HAWS, ALLEN P. reg 5VA, co I, r 2nd lt, enr 9/9/61 Ceredo, age 38, rem res 3/62 for poor health, reg 39, co G, r capt, enr 1/12/63, enl 2/16/63 Peach Orchard, dis 9/15/65 Louisville, age 39, house 814, s 1,2,4,20.

HAWS, ARTHUR W. reg 68, co I, r cpl, enl 4/7/64, 5/21/64, dis 4/16/64, 6/10/64, reg CG, co L, r sgt, enr 6/9/64, enl 7/16/64 Frankfort, dis 3/11/65 Catlettsburg, age 17, light hair, blue eyes, fair skin, 5-8, house 204, s 2,4.

HAWS, JOHN W. reg 68, co G, r sgt, enl 4/7/64, 5/21/64, dis 4/16/64, 6/22/64, reg CG, co L, enr 6/15/64, enl 7/6/64 Frankfort, dis 3/1/65 Catlettsburg, age 18, dark hair, eyes & skin, 6-1, house 227, s 2,4.

HAYS, ISAAC. reg 14, co G, r sgt, enr 11/19/61 Louisa, enl 12/10/61 Louisa, dis 1/31/65 Louisa, age 32, dark hair, blue eyes, fair skin, 5-7, house 256, s 1,2,4.

HAYS, JOHN. reg 68, co K, enr 4/7/64, 5/21/64, dis 4/16/64, 6/22/64, age 28, black eyes & hair, dark skin, 5-8, house 1043, s 2,4.

HENSLEY, DANIEL B. reg CG, co E, enr 5/16/64, enl 7/4/64 Frankfort, dis 3/11/65 Catlettsburg, age 18, dark hair, hazel eyes, dark skin, 5-6, house 666, s 2,4.

HENSLEY, ISOM. reg 68, co F, r sgt, enl 4/7/64, 5/21/64, dis 4/16/64, 6/22/64, age 33, blue eyes, light hair, fair skin, 5-5, house 662, s 2,4.

HENSLEY, JACOB. reg CG, co K, enr 6/9/64, enl 7/18/64 Frankfort, dis 3/11/65 Catlettsburg, house 930, s 2,4.

HENSLEY, JOHN W. reg 68, co F, r 2nd lt, enl 4/7/64, 5/21/64, dis 4/16/64, 6/22/64, age 35 or 39, dark eyes, hair & skin, 5-5, house 652, s 2,4.

HENSLEY, THOMAS (THOMPSON). reg 68, co F, enr 4/7/64, 5/21/64, dis 4/16/64, 6/22/64, age 34, blue eyes, light hair, fair skin, 5-3, house 665, s 2,4.

HENSON, DAVID. reg 68, co D, enl 4/7/64, 5/21/64, dis 4/16/64, 6/22/64, age 35, blue eyes, light hair & skin, 6-0, residence shown on militia list, house n/c, s 2,4,18.

HICKMAN, JOHN W. reg 39, co G, r sgt, enr 9/29/62 Peach Orchard, enl 2/16/63 Peach Orchard, dis 9/15/65 Louisville, age 18, black hair & eyes, dark skin, 5-6, house 1068, s 1,2,4.

HICKS, CHARLES. reg 68, co F, enl 5/21/64, dis 6/22/64, age 30, blue eyes, light hair, fair skin, 6-0, house 671 or 690, s 2,4.

HICKS, CLAIBORNE. reg 14, co B, enr 8/30/63 Louisa, enl 8/31/63 Louisa, dis 9/15/65 Louisville, age 19, light hair, blue eyes, fair skin, 6-0, rem trans to 14th Vet Inf, co B, enr 8/30/63, m/in 8/31/63 Louisa, house 671, s 1,2,4.

HICKS, ELIHU. reg 14, co A, enr 10/4/63 Louisa, enl 10/31/63 Louisa, dis 9/15/65 Louisville, age 18, dark hair, gray eyes, fair skin, 5-11, rem trans to 14th Vet Inf, co C, enr 10/4/63, m/in 10/31/63 Louisa, slightly wounded in hand between 6/4/64 & 7/4/64 near Atlanta, house 671, s 1,2,4.

HICKS, GEORGE W. reg 14, co E, enr 8/11/63 Louisa, enl 8/29/63 Louisa, dis 9/15/65 Louisville, age 20, sandy hair, blue eyes, fair skin, 5-8, rem trans to 14th Vet Inf, co C, enr 8/1/63, m/in 8/29/63 Louisa, house 551, s 1,2,4.

HICKS, JOHN. reg 14, co A, enr 10/4/63 Louisa, enl 10/31/63 Louisa, dis 9/15/65 Louisville, age 25, light hair & skin, blue eyes, rem trans to 14th Vet Inf, co C, enr 10/4/63, m/in10/31/63 Louisa, house 670, s 1,2,4.

HINKLE, ALLEN. reg 68, co K, enl 4/7/64, 5/21/64, dis 4/16/64, 6/22/64, age 30, black eyes & hair, dark skin, 5-8, house 1055, s 2,4.

HINKLE, HANSFORD. reg 68, co E, enl 5/21/64, dis 6/22/64, age 26, gray eyes, dark hair & skin, 6-2, house 1105, s 2,4.

HINKLE, JAMES. reg 68, co E, enl 4/7/64, 5/21/64, dis 4/16/64, 6/22/64, age 27, dark eyes, hair & skin, 5-8, house 1104, s 2,4.

HINKLE, JOHN. reg 39, co H, enr 1/15/63, enl 2/16/63 Peach Orchard, age 44, dark hair, blue eyes, fair skin, 5-5, rem dis 11/21/64 at Louisa for disability of epilepsy, house 897, s 1,2,4.

HINKLE, WESLEY. reg 68, co E, enl 4/7/64, 5/21/64, dis 4/16/64, 6/22/64, age 42, dark eyes, hair & skin, 5-6, house 1106, s 2,4.

HOBBS, JOHN. reg 5VA, co F, enr 9/2/61 Ceredo, enl 9/14/61, dis 9/23/64 Wheeling WV, age 34, brown hair, blue eyes, light skin, 5-8, rem dis 9/28/62 Washington DC for old rib fracture, house 1146, s 1,20.

HODGE, GABRIEL. reg 14, co K, enr 11/8/61 Louisa, enl 12/10/61 Louisa, dis 1/31/65 Louisa, age 30, house 149, s 1,2,4.

HODGE, JAMES H. reg 14, co D, enr 9/2/63 Louisa, enl 10/30/63 Louisa, dis 9/15/65 Louisville, rem trans to 14th Vet Inf, co B, house 149, s 1,2.

HOLBROOK, ALBERT. reg 14, co G, enr 4/9/63 Louisa, enl 6/10/63 Louisa, dis 9/15/65 Louisville, age 47, sandy hair, blue eyes, fair skin, 5-7, rem trans to 14th Vet Inf, co C, enr 4/9/63, m/in 6/10/63 Louisa, house 236, s 1,2,4.

HOLBROOK, CALVIN. reg 68, co D, enl 4/7/64, 5/21/64, dis 4/16/64, 6/22/64, age 35, blue eyes, light hair & skin, 6-0, house 96, s 2,4.

HOLBROOK, CAMPBELL. reg 68, co A, enl 4/7/64, 5/21/64, dis 4/16/64, 6/22/64, age 32, blue eyes, dark hair & skin, 5-6, house 460, s 2,4.

HOLBROOK, DAVID. reg 68, co B, enl 4/7/64, 5/21/64, dis 4/16/64, 6/22/64, age 24, blue eyes, light hair, fair skin, 6-0, house 406, s 2,4.

HOLBROOK, HARGUS. reg 68, co B, enl 4/7/64, 5/21/64, dis 4/16/64, 6/22/64, age 35, blue eyes, light hair, fair skin, 6-0, house 445, s 2,4.

HOLBROOK, JOHN H. reg 68, co B, enl 5/21/64, dis 6/22/64, age 21, blue eyes, light hair, fair skin, 5-8, house 406, s 2,4.

HOLBROOK, JOHN K. reg 68, co B, enl 5/21/64, dis 6/22/64, age 44, blue eyes, light hair, fair skin, 6-0, house 604, s 2,4.

HOLBROOK, PHILANDER. reg 14, co B, enr 10/10/61 Catlettsburg, enl 12/10/61 Louisa, dis 4/30/63 Louisa, age 22, light hair, blue eyes, fair skin, 5-10, rem dis for rheumatism, house 610, s 1,2,4.

HOLBROOK, RALPH W. reg 14, co B, r 2nd lt, enr 10/10/61 Louisa, enl 12/10/61 Louisa, dis 8/17/64, age 28 or 38, light hair, blue eyes, fair skin, 6-0, rem cap Lawrence Co. 2/15/63, prom from 1st sgt to 2nd lt 8/28/63, res for disability of tuberculosis, house 361, s 1,2,4.

HOLBROOK, ROBERT. reg 68, co G, enl 4/7/64, 5/21/64, dis 4/16/64, 6/22/64, age 35, blue eyes, light hair, fair skin, 5-10, house 214, s 2,4.

HOLBROOK, SQUIRE. reg 68, co G, enl 5/21/64, dis 6/22/64, age 40, blue eyes, light hair, fair skin, 5-10, residence shown on militia list, house n/c, s 2,4,18.

HOLBROOK, WILLIAM C. reg 40, co K, enr 12/25/63 Grayson, enl 4/14/64 Lexington, dis 8/31/64 Catlettsburg, age 18, florid hair, blue eyes, fair skin, 5-9, residence stated on muster roll, house n/c, s 1,2,4.

HOLBROOK, WILLIAM L. reg 68, co A, enl 4/7/64, 5/21/64, dis 4/16/64, 6/22/64, age 44, dark eyes & hair, fair skin, 6-0, house 396, s 2,4.

HOLBROOK, WILLIAM R. reg 14, co B, enr 10/10/61 Louisa, enl 12/10/61 Louisa, dis 1/31/65 Louisa, age 32, light hair, blue eyes, fair skin, 5-11, house 362, s 1,2,4.

HORN, JAMES. reg 167WV, co Geo. Murray, house 1138, s 23.

HOWARD, JAMES. reg 14, co H, enr & enl 3/12/62 Paintsville, dis 4/5/65 Lexington, age 28, black hair & eyes, dark skin, 6-1, rem trans to 14th Vet Inf, co C, enr 3/12/62, residence stated on muster roll, house n/c, s 1,2,4.

HOWARD, LEWIS. reg 14, co H, enr 10/25/61 Catlettsburg, enl 12/10/61 Louisa, dis 1/31/65 Louisa, age 27, black hair & eyes, dark skin, 5-10, residence stated on muster roll, house n/c, s 1,2,4.

HUFF, HIRAM. reg 14, co H, enr 10/25/61 Catlettsburg, enl 12/10/61 Louisa, dis 3/12/62 Paintsville, age 38, dark hair & skin, gray eyes, 6-0, rem dis for disability, residence stated on muster roll, house n/c, s 1,2,4.

HUFF, JAMES. reg 68, co E, enl 5/21/64, dis 6/22/64, age 26, dark eyes, hair & skin, 6-0, house 1108, s 2,4.

HUFF, WASHINGTON. reg 14, co H, age 35, rem KIA before being mustered, house 952, s 4.

HUGHES, GARRED. reg 68, co I, enl 4/7/64, 5/21/64, dis 4/16/64, 6/22/64, age 21, blue eyes, light hair, fair skin, 5-4, residence shown on militia list, house n/c, s 2,4,18.

HULETT, JAMES T. reg 68, co I, age 21, fair hair, blue eyes, light skin, 5-6, house 197, s 4.

HULETT, WILLIAM JR. reg 68, co I, enl 5/21/64, dis 6/22/64, age 19, blue eyes, light hair, fair skin, 5-6, house 943, s 2,4.

HULETT, WILLIAM (SR.). reg 68, co I, enl 5/21/64, age 27, dark hair, eyes & skin, 6-0, house 197, s 4.

HUNTINGDON, EDWARD. reg 39, co G, enr 1/19/63, enl 2/16/63 Peach Orchard, age 24, light hair, blue eyes, dark skin, 5-6, rem d 4/10/63 Louisa of fever, residence stated on muster roll, house n/c, s 1,2,4.

HUTCHISON, ALLEN C. reg 14, co H, r 1st sgt, enr 10/15/61 Catlettsburg, enl 12/10/61 Louisa, dis 3/5/62 Paintsville, age 25, black hair, hazel eyes, dark skin, 6-3, rem dis for disability of heart & lungs, house 1205, s 1,2,4.

HUTCHISON, GEORGE W. reg 14, r com sgt, enr 10/25/61 Catlettsburg, enl 12/10/61 Louisa, dis 1/31/65 Louisa, age 21, dark hair, blue eyes, fair skin, 6-0, rem app com sgt 2/19/64, cap & paroled 8/62 Lexington, house 339, s 1,2,4.

HUTCHISON, GEORGE W. reg 5VA, co G, r cpl, enr 9/2/61 Ceredo, enl 9/2/61, dis 10/3/64 Wheeling WV, age 18, reg 68, co I, r cpl, enl 4/7/64, 5/21/64, dis 4/16/64, 6/10/64, reg CG, co L, r 1st sgt, enr 6/8/64, enl 7/6/64 Frankfort, dis 3/11/65 Catlettsburg, age 21, light hair, gray eyes, fair skin, 6-1, house 135, s 1,2,4,20.

HUTCHISON, HARVEY. reg 68, co I, enl 4/7/64, 5/21/64, dis 4/16/64, 6/22/64, age 25, dark eyes & hair, fair skin, 5-6, house 339, s 2,4.

HUTCHISON, HENDERSON. reg 68, co I, r sgt, enl 4/7/64, 5/21/64, dis 4/16/64, 6/22/64, age 21, blue eyes, dark hair, fair skin, 6-0, residence shown on militia list, house n/c, s 2,4.

HUTCHISON, IRAD B. reg 68, co C, r capt, enl 4/7/64, 5/21/64, dis 4/16/64, 6/22/64, reg CG, co L, r capt, enr 6/8/64, enl 7/6/64 Frankfort, dis 3/11/65 Catlettsburg, age 31, dark hair, blue eyes, fair skin, 6-2, house 1222, s 2,4.

HUTCHISON, JOHN. reg 68, co I, enl 4/7/64, 5/21/64, dis 4/16/64, 6/22/64, age 35, blue eyes, dark hair, fair skin, 5-8, house 119, s 2,4.

HUTCHISON, THOMAS B. reg 68, co A, enl 5/21/64, dis 6/22/64, age 25, blue eyes, dark hair & skin, 6-0, house 339, s 2,4.

J

JACKSON, DAVID. reg 39, co I, r cpl, enr 9/25/62 Pike Co., enl 2/16/63 Peach Orchard, dis 9/15/65 Louisville, age 35, dark hair, blue eyes, fair skin, 5-10, rem prom to cpl 5/12/65, residence stated on muster roll, house n/c, s 1,2,4.

JACKSON, JAMES. reg 40, co K, r cpl, enr 7/30/63, enl 9/29/63 Grayson, dis 12/30/64 Catlettsburg, age 26, house 1182, s 1,2,4.

JACKSON, JOHN. reg 39, co C, enr 9/10/64 or 10/4/62 Louisa, enl 2/16/63 Peach Orchard, age 24, dark hair & skin, gray eyes, 5-10, rem cap 12/4/62 Floyd Co., des 12/21/62 Floyd Co., residence stated on muster roll, house n/c, s 1,2,4.

JAMES, SOLOMON. reg 68, co E, enl 4/7/64, 5/21/64, dis 4/16/64, 6/22/64, age 35, light eyes, hair & skin, 6-0, house 860, s 2,4.

JARRELL, GEORGE. reg 45, co F, enr 10/24/63 Ashland, enl 11/2/63 Ashland, dis 12/24/64 Catlettsburg, age 18, dark hair & skin, light eyes, 5-6, house 1147, s 1,2,6.

JARRELL, HIRAM W. reg 68, co D, enl 4/7/64, 5/21/64, dis 4/16/64, 6/22/64, age 30, black eyes, dark hair & skin, 5-11, house 1155, s 2,4.

JARRELL, WILLIAM R. reg 5VA, co F, enl 9/14/61 age 25, reg 45, co F, r cpl, enr 10/4/63 Catlettsburg, enl 11/2/63 Ashland, dis 12/24/64 Catlettsburg, age 25, house 1155, s 1,2,20.

JOB, ELISHA. reg 68, co F, r sgt, enl 4/7/64, 5/21/64, dis 4/16/64, 6/22/64, age 30, blue eyes, light hair, fair skin, 5-5, house 981, s 2,4.

JOB, JAMES H. reg 68, co F, r cpl, enl 4/7/64, 5/21/64, dis 4/16/64, 6/22/64, age 28, blue eyes, light hair, fair skin, 6-3, house 982, s 2,4.

JOB, WILLIAM. reg 68, co F, enl 4/7/64, 5/21/64, dis 4/16/64, 6/22/64, age 35, blue eyes, light hair, fair skin, 6-0, house 983, s 2,4.

JOHNS, MARTIN H. reg 68, r lt col, enl 4/7/64, 5/21/64, dis 4/16/64, 6/22/64, house 1191, s 2,4.

JOHNSON, GEORGE F. reg 14, co H, r 1st lt, enr 10/25/61 Catlettsburg, enl 12/10/61 Louisa, dis 1/21/65 Louisa, age 22, black hair, dark eyes & skin, 5-9, rem residence established by List of Officers, prom to 2nd lt 2/26/63, to 2nd lt 3/28/63, trans to 14th Vet Inf, co D, r capt, enr 8/12/65, m/in 8/12/65 Louisville, m/out 9/15/65 Louisville, residence shown on list of officers, house n/c, s 1,2,32.

JOHNSON, JAMES J. reg 14, co G, enr 11/19/61 Louisa, enl 12/10/61 Louisa, dis 1/31/65 Louisa, age 23, light hair, blue eyes, fair skin, 5-4, house 1041, s 1,2,4.

JOHNSON, JOHN. reg 68, co B, enl 5/21/64, dis 6/22/64, age 25, blue eyes, light hair, fair skin, 5-6, house 501 or 592, s 2,4.

JOHNSON, JOHN. reg 68, co A, enl 5/21/64, dis 6/22/64, age 26, blue eyes, dark hair, fair skin, 5-8, house 501 or 592, s 2,4.

JOHNSON, JOHN. reg 68, co E, enl 4/7/64, 5/21/64, dis 4/16/64, 6/22/64, age 30, light eyes, hair & skin, 5-7, residence shown on militia list, house n/c, s 2,4,18.

JOHNSON, JOHN. reg 14, co F, enr 11/19/61, enl 12/10/61 Louisa, age 29, rem des 9/28/62 on march from Cumberland Gap, house 501, s 1,2.

JOHNSON, JOHN. reg 167WV, co Ira Copley, enl 8/62 to 2/64, dis 5/2/64, house 501 or 592, s 23.

JOHNSON, JOSEPH. reg 14, co G, enr 1/5/64 Louisa, enl 3/29/64 Greenupsburg, dis 9/15/65 Louisville, age 18, light hair, gray eyes, fair skin, 5-5, rem trans to 14th Vet Inf, co C, enr 2/5/64, m/in 2/5/64 Greenupsburg, house 808, s 1,2,4.

JOHNSON, SAMUEL. reg 68, co I, enl 4/7/64, 5/21/64, dis 4/16/64, 6/22/64, age 40, blue eyes, red hair, fair skin, 6-0, house 173, s 2,4.

JOHNSON, THOMAS. reg 14, co G, enr 11/19/61 Louisa, enl 12/10/61 Louisa, dis 1/31/65 Louisa, age 31, dark hair, blue eyes, fair skin, 5-8, house 773, 1,2,4.

JONES, WILLIAM R. reg 68, r major, enl 4/7/64, 5/21/64, dis 4/16/64, 6/22/64, house 1231, s 2,4.

JORDAN, ABSALOM. reg 68, co D, enl 4/7/64, 5/21/64, dis 4/16/64, 6/22/64, age 22, blue eyes, light hair & skin, 6-0, residence shown on militia list, house n/c, s 2,4,18.

JORDAN, DAVID. reg 14, co G, enr 11/19/61 Louisa, enl 12/10/61 Louisa, dis 9/15/65 Louisville, age 24, black hair, dark eyes & skin, 5-1, rem trans to 14th Vet Inf, co A, enr 2/29/64, m/in 5/15/64 Louisa, residence established by descriptive muster roll, house n/c, s 1,2,4.

JORDAN, FLEMING. reg 14, co B, enr 5/24/63 Louisa, enl 6/10/63 Louisa, dis 9/15/65 Louisville, age 18, light hair, dark eyes, fair skin, 5-3, rem trans to 14th Vet Inf, co B, enr 5/24/63, m/in 6/10/63 Louisa, residence stated on muster roll, house n/c, s 1,2,4.

JORDAN, GEORGE. reg 68, co G, enl 4/7/64, 5/21/64, dis 4/16/64, 6/22/64, age 40, black eyes & hair, dark skin, 5-5, house 993, s 2,4,18.

JORDAN, GEORGE W. reg 68, co G, r cpl, enl 4/7/64, 5/21/64, dis 4/16/64, 6/22/64, age 30, black eyes & hair, dark skin, 6-0, house 991, s 2,4,18.

JORDAN, GEORGE W. reg 39, co A, enr 9/12/62, enl 2/16/63 Peach Orchard, dis 9/15/65 Louisville, age 18, black hair, gray eyes, dark skin, 5-6, residence stated on muster roll, house n/c, s 1,2,4.

JORDAN, GREENVILLE. reg 14, co D, enr 10/20/61 Louisa, enl 12/10/61 Louisa, dis 1/31/65 Louisa, age 20, black hair, blue eyes, dark skin, 5-8, house 314, s 1,2,4.

JORDAN, GREENVILLE. reg 68, co F, r cpl, enl 4/7/64, 5/21/64, dis 4/16/64, 6/22/64, age 21, blue eyes, dark hair, fair skin, 5-6, residence shown on militia list, house n/c, s 2,4,18.

JORDAN, HIRAM. reg 68, co G, r cpl, enl 5/21/64, dis 6/22/64, age 32, blue eyes, black hair, dark skin, 5-5, house 261, s 2,4,18.

JORDAN, HIRAM. reg 68, co F, r capt, enl 4/7/64, 5/21/64, dis 4/16/64, 6/22/64, age 26, blue eyes, dark hair, fair skin, 6-0, house 314, s 2,4.

JORDAN, JAMES H. reg 68, co G, r sgt, enl 5/21/64, dis 6/22/64, age 30, blue eyes, black hair, dark skin, 5-10, residence shown on militia list, house n/c, s 2,4,18.

JORDAN, JEREMIAH. reg 68, co G, enl 4/7/64, 5/21/64, dis 4/16/64, 6/22/64, age 28, black eyes & hair, dark skin, 5-5, house 993, s 2,4.

JORDAN, JESSE. reg 68, co I, enl 5/21/64, dis 6/22/64, age 40, blue eyes, light hair, fair skin, 6-0, house 125, s 2,4.

JORDAN, JESSE. reg 68, co G, enl 4/7/64, 5/21/64, dis 4/16/64, 6/22/64, age 20, black eyes & hair, dark skin, 5-5, house 114, s 2,4.

JORDAN, JOHN. reg 14, co F, enr 9/10/63 Salyersville, enl 10/31/63 Louisa, dis 9/15/65 Louisville, age 20, black hair & eyes, dark skin, 5-8, rem trans to 14th Vet Inf, co D, enr 10/10/63, m/in 10/31/63 Louisa, house 356, s 1,2,4.

JORDAN, JOHN. reg 14, co G, enr 11/19/61 Louisa, enl 12/10/61 Louisa, dis 1/31/65 Louisa, age 33, dark hair, blue eyes, fair skin, 5-10, house 124, s 1,2,4.

JORDAN, JONAS. reg 14, co G, enr 2/27/63 Louisa, enl 6/10/63 Louisa, dis 9/15/65 Louisville, age 42, sandy hair, blue eyes, fair skin, 5-4, rem trans to 14th Vet Inf, co D, enr 2/27/63, m/in 6/10/63 Louisa, house 210, s 1,2,4.

JORDAN, PLEASANT. reg 14, co G, K, enr 10/10/61 Catlettsburg, enl 12/10/61 Louisa, age 46, dark hair, blue eyes, fair skin, 5-8, rem trans to co K 3/62, back to co G 1/20/65, house 238, s 2,4.

JORDAN, WILLIAM JR. reg 68, co G, enl 4/7/64, 5/21/64, dis 4/16/64, 6/22/64, age 18, black eyes & hair, dark skin, 5-5, house 356, s 2,4.

JORDAN, WILLIAM SR. reg 68, co G, enl 4/7/64, 5/21/64, dis 4/16/64, 6/22/64, age 30, black eyes & hair, dark hair, 5-5, house 995, s 2,4.

JUDE, HIRAM. reg 14, co H, enr 3/12/63 Louisa, enl 8/29/63 Louisa, age 19, light hair, blue eyes, fair skin, 5-8, rem trans to 14th Vet Inf, co C, enr 3/26/63, m/in 8/29/63 Louisa, cap 8/9/64 at Atlanta, paroled 11/20/64, d 6/21/65 of fever at Louisa, residence stated on muster roll, house n/c, s 1,2,4.

JUSTICE, ALLEN. reg 14, co H, r cpl, enr 10/25/61 Catlettsburg, enl 12/10/61 Louisa, age 33, dark hair & skin, blue eyes, 5-9, rem d 6/10/62 at Ironton OH of measles, house 908, s 1,2,4.

JUSTICE, CALEB. reg 39, co B, enr 2/11/63 Peach Orchard, enl 2/16/63 Peach Orchard, dis 9/15/65 Louisville, age 32, light hair, blue eyes, fair skin, 5-8, house 877, s 1,2,4.

JUSTICE, ELZY M. reg 14, co D, enr 10/20/61 Louisa, enl 12/10/61 Louisa, age 18, dark hair & skin, blue eyes, 5-6, rem KIA 3/26/63 in skirmish on Little Blaine near Louisa, house 246, s 1,2,4.

JUSTICE, GEORGE T. reg 39, co B, enr 11/17/62, enl 2/16/63 Peach Orchard, dis 9/15/65 Louisville, age 26, light hair, blue eyes, fair skin, 5-5, house 890, s 1,2,4.

JUSTICE, JESSE. reg 39, co B, enr 10/17/62 Catlettsburg, enl 2/16/63 Peach Orchard, age 21, dark hair, blue eyes, fair skin, 5-9, rem d 5/20/63 Ashland, house 872, s 1,2,4.

JUSTICE, MERIDA. reg CG, co L, enr 7/21/64, enl 8/30/64 Frankfort, dis 3/11/65 Catlettsburg, age 18, dark hair & skin, black eyes, 5-2, house 295, s 2,4.

JUSTICE, TIMOTHY. reg 68, co H, r sgt, enl 5/21/64, dis 6/22/64, age 35, dark eyes, hair & skin, 5-11, residence shown on militia list, house n/c, s 2,4,18.

JUSTICE, WILLIAM. reg 68, co G, enl 5/21/64, dis 6/22/64, age 25, blue eyes, dark hair, fair skin, 5-10, residence shown on militia list, house n/c, s 2,4,18.

JUSTICE, WILLIAM. reg 39, co B, enr 10/17/62 Catlettsburg, enl 2/16/63 Peach Orchard, age 24, dark hair, blue eyes, fair skin, 5-10, rem dis 6/12/65 for disability of puncture of cornea, house 268, s 1,2,4.

K

KAZEE, JEREMIAH. reg 39, co G, enr 10/13/62 Peach Orchard, enl 2/16/63 Peach Orchard, dis 9/15/65 Louisville, age 40 or 44, dark hair & skin, blue eyes, 5-6, house 755, s 1,2,4.

KAZEE, JESSE. reg 45, co G, enr 11/1/63 Greenup Co., enl 11/30/63 Ashland, age 38, rem des 2/10/64 at Flemingsburg, house 525, s 1,2.

KAZEE, OLIVER R. reg 39, co G, enr 12/25/62 Peach Orchard, enl 2/16/63 Peach Orchard, dis 9/15/65 Louisville, age 18, dark hair & skin, hazel eyes, 5-3, house 755, s 1,2,4.

KEESEE, JOHN. reg 68, co C, enl 4/7/64, 5/21/64, dis 4/16/64, 6/22/64, reg CG, co L, enr 6/8/64, enl 7/6/64 Frankfort, dis 3/1/65 Catlettsburg, age 18, dark hair & eyes, fair skin, 5-8, house 755, s 2,4,18.

KEESEE, WILLIAM. reg 14, co A, enr 10/1/61 Louisa, enl 12/10/61 Louisa, dis 1/31/65 Louisa, age 25, house 526, s 1,2,4.

KEITH, TOLIVER. reg 14, co C, age 22, residence stated on muster roll, house n/c, s 4.

KELLY, DARBY A. reg 14, co E, r sgt, enr 11/19/61 Louisa, enl 12/10/61 Louisa, dis 1/31/65 Louisa, age 24, dark hair & skin, blue eyes, 5-6, rem prom from cpl to sgt 2/17/62, house 60, s 1,2,4.

KELLY, GEORGE W. reg CG, co G, enr 8/11/64, enl 7/6/64 Frankfort, dis 3/11/65 Catlettsburg, age 22, dark hair, eyes & skin, 5-7, house 410, s 2,4.

KELLY, JAMES. reg 14, co B, enr 10/10/61 Catlettsburg, enl 12/10/61 Louisa, dis 1/31/65 Louisa, age 32, red hair, blue eyes, fair skin, 6-1, residence shown on militia list, house n/c, s 1,2,4.

KELLY, JOHN. reg CG, co G, enr 5/11/64, enl 7/6/64 Frankfort, dis 3/11/65 Catlettsburg, age 25, dark hair & skin, gray eyes, 5-7, house 410 or 643, s 2,4.

KELLY, WILLIAM W. reg 40, co D, enr 11/17/63, enl 11/25/63 Catlettsburg, dis 12/30/64 Catlettsburg, age 19, house 410, s 1,2,4.

KENNEDY, JOHN. reg 39, co K, enr 5/23/64 Louisa, enl 8/30/64 Louisa, dis 9/15/65 Louisville, age 18, light hair, blue eyes, fair skin, 5-9, residence shown on CSR, house n/c, s 1,2,4.

KICKHUYFUL, ERNEST. reg 39, co D, enr 7/28/64 Louisa, enl 8/28/64 Greenupsburg, dis 9/15/65 Louisville, age 44, light hair, blue eyes, fair skin, 5-5, residence shown on CSR, house n/c, s 1,2,4.

KING, MARCUS L. reg 39, r chaplain, enl 2/6/64 Louisa, dis 9/15/65 Louisville, age 43, rem residence established by List of Officers, house n/c, s 2,4,32.

KINNER, LAFAYETTE. reg 68, co D, enl 5/21/64, dis 6/22/64, age 24, blue eyes, light hair & skin, 5-11, house 26, s 2,4.

KINNER, OLIVER. reg 68, co D, enl 5/21/64, dis 6/22/64, age 19, blue eyes, light hair & skin, 5-11, house 25, s 2,4.

KIRK, JAMES A. reg 14, co H, enr 10/25/61 Catlettsburg, enl 12/10/61 Louisa, dis 1/31/65 Louisa, age 24, dark hair, blue eyes, fair skin, 5-6, residence stated on muster roll, house n/c, s 1,2,4.

KIRK, JAMES D. reg 167WV, co Geo. Murray, reg 39, co I, r 1st sgt, enr 8/28/63, enl 8/29/63 Louisa, dis 9/15/65 Louisville, age 26 at muster out, rem prom from pvt 9/1/64, prom from 3rd sgt to 1st sgt 5/13/65, residence shown on militia list, house n/c, s 1,2,9,23.

KIRK, JOSEPH M. reg 5VA, co F, r capt, enr 9/2/61 Ceredo, age 39, rem res 2/7/62 Parkersburg WV, reg 39, co I, enr 1/15/63, enl 2/16/63 Peach Orchard, age 41, rem dismissed from service 3/31/64, house 1132, s 1,2,4,20.

KIRK, THOMAS. reg 68, co H, enl 5/21/64, dis 6/22/64, age 34, black eyes, dark hair & skin, 6-0, residence shown on militia list, house n/c, s 2,4,18.

KIRK, WILLIAM. reg 68, co H, enl 5/21/64, dis 6/22/64, age 45, dark eyes, hair & skin, 6-0, residence shown on militia list, house n/c, s 2,4,18.

KIRK, WILLIAM. reg 14, co H, enr 10/25/61 Catlettsburg, enl 12/10/61 Louisa, age 22, dark hair, eyes & skin, 5-2, rem d 5/9/64 Knoxville TN of wounds, chronic diarrhea & typhoid, residence stated on muster roll, house n/c, s 1,2,4.

KISE, BENJAMIN F. reg 68, co E, enl 5/21/64, dis 6/22/64, age 23, dark eyes, hair & skin, 6-0, house 734, s 2,4.

KISE, DAVID. reg 68, co E, enl 5/21/64, dis 6/22/64, age 18, dark eyes & hair, light skin, 5-6, house 734, s 2,4.

KISE, THOMAS B. reg 14, co H, enr 10/25/61 Catlettsburg, enl 12/10/61 Louisa, dis 1/31/65 Louisa, age 18, dark hair, eyes & skin, 5-7, house 734, s 1,2,4.

KITCHEN, ARTHUR. reg 14, co B, enr 4/25/63 Louisa, enl 6/10/63 Louisa, dis 9/15/65 Louisville, age 18, light hair, blue eyes, fair skin, 5-7, rem trans to 14th Vet Inf, co B, enr 4/25/63, m/in 6/10/63, residence stated on muster roll, house n/c, s 1,2,4.

KITCHEN, GEORGE. reg 14, co B, enr 10/10/61 Louisa, enl 12/10/61 Louisa, dis 1/31/65 Louisa, age 41, dark hair, blue eyes, fair skin, 6-1, house 663, s 1,2,4.

KITCHEN, JAMES. reg 14, co B, enr 3/10/63 Louisa, enl 6/10/63 Louisa, dis 9/15/65 Louisville, age 18, dark hair, blue eyes, fair skin, 5-8, rem trans to 14th Vet Inf, co B, enr 3/10/63, m/in 6/10/63 Louisa, house 664, s 1,2,4.

KITCHEN, JOHN. reg 14, co B, enr 10/10/61 Louisa, enl 12/10/61 Louisa, age 28, dark hair & eyes, fair skin, 6-0, rem d 6/23/64 of wounds received 6/22/64 near Marietta GA, residence stated on muster roll, house n/c, s 1,2,4.

KITCHEN, JOHN. reg 14, co K, enr 11/8/61, enl 12/10/61 Louisa, dis 1/31/65 Louisa, age 42, dark hair, blue eyes, fair skin, 5-7, house 325, s 1,2,4.

KITCHEN, LEVI. reg 14, co B, enr 10/10/61 Louisa, enl 12/10/61 Louisa, dis 1/31/65 Louisa, age 18, dark hair, blue eyes, fair skin, 5-8, house 663, s 1,2,4.

KITCHEN, NEHEMIAH. reg 68, co F, enl 4/7/64, 5/21/64, dis 4/16/64, 6/22/64, age 39, blue eyes, light hair, fair skin, 5-6, house 663, s 2,4.

KITCHEN, WILLIAM SR. reg 14, co B, enr 10/10/61 Louisa, enl 12/10/61 Louisa, dis 1/31/65 Louisa, age 39, rem residence established by descriptive muster roll, house 240, s 2,4.

KITCHEN, WILLIAM JR. reg 14, co B, r cpl, enr 3/10/63 Louisa, enl 6/10/63 Louisa, dis 9/15/65 Louisville, age 20, dark hair, blue eyes, fair skin, 5-9, rem trans to 14th Vet Inf, co B, enr 3/10/63, m/in 6/10/63, Louisa, app cpl 2/1/65, residence established by descriptive muster roll, house n/c, s 1,2,4.

L

LACEY, KENNETH F. reg 39, co D, enr 9/22/62 Lawrence Co., enl 2/16/63 Peach Orchard, age 23, dark hair, blue eyes, fair skin, 5-9, rem trans to co H, 14th Ky. Inf. 3/16/63, drowned 3/16/65 Middle Creek, Floyd Co., residence stated on muster roll, house n/c, s 1,2,4.

LAKIN, GEORGE. reg 68, co D, enl 4/7/64, 5/21/64, dis 4/16/64, 6/22/64, age 22, black eyes, dark hair & skin, 5-11, house 954, s 2,4.

LAKIN, THOMAS. reg 68, co D, enl 4/7/64, 5/21/64, dis 4/16/64, 6/22/64, age 20, black eyes, dark hair & skin, 5-8, house 954, s 2,4.

LAMBERT, ABNER M. reg 14, co F, enr 11/19/61 Louisa, enl 12/10/61 Louisa, age 22, light hair, blue eyes, fair skin, 5-9, rem d 6/18/62 at home in Lawrence Co. of typhoid fever, house 67, s 1,2,4.

LAMBERT, BENJAMIN F. reg 14, co C, enr 10/10/61 Louisa, enl 12/10/61 Louisa, dis 9/15/65 Louisville, age 24, light hair, dark eyes & skin, 5-7, rem trans to 14th Vet Inf, co A, enr 2/29/64, m/in 3/19/64 Louisa, house 66, s 1,2,4.

LAMBERT, HIRAM T. reg 14, co F, enr 9/10/63 Louisa, enl 10/11/63 Louisa, dis 9/15/65 Louisville, age 20, fair hair & skin, blue eyes, 5-11, rem trans to 14th Vet Inf, co H, house 66, s 1,2,4.

LAMBERT, JEREMIAH. reg 68, co D, enl 5/21/64, dis 6/22/64, house 70, s 2,4.

LAMBERT, POLEMUS. reg 14, co F, enr 11/19/61 Louisa, enl 12/10/61 Louisa, dis 1/31/65 Louisa, age 20, brown hair, blue eyes, dark skin, 5-3, house 66, s 1,2,4.

LANG, JOHN. reg 14, r hospital steward, enr 10/25/61, enl 12/10/61 Louisa, dis 1/31/65 Louisa, age 29, house 187, s 1,4.

LARGE, JOHN FRANKLIN. reg 14, co G, enr 11/19/61 Louisa, enl 12/10/61 Louisa, age 19, light hair, blue eyes, fair skin, 5-8, rem trans to 14th Vet Inf 3/15/64, KIA at Atlanta 7/21/64, house 673, s 1,2,4.

LARGE, JOHN JR. reg 68, co F, enl 4/7/64, 5/21/64, dis 4/16/64, 6/22/64, age 18, black eyes, dark hair & skin, 5-6, house 973, s 2,4.

LARGE, SAMUEL. reg 14, co K, enr 7/9/63, enl 8/28/63 Louisa, age 18, rem trans to 14th Vet Inf, co C, house 673, s 1,2.

LARGE, WALTER. reg 14, co G, enr 11/19/61, enl 12/10/61 Louisa, age 19, sandy hair, blue eyes, fair skin, 5-5, rem des 3/9/63 at Louisa, house 979, s 2,4.

LARGE, WILLIAM F. reg 14, co G, enr 11/19/61 Louisa, enl 12/10/61 Louisa, dis 9/15/65 Louisville, age 18, sandy hair, blue eyes, fair skin, 5-5, rem trans to 14th Vef Inf, co A, enr 2/29/64, m/in 3/15/64 Louisa, house 673, s 1,2,4.

LARGE, WILLIAM G. reg 68, co G, enl 4/7/64, 5/21/64, dis 4/16/64, 6/22/64, age 40, black eyes & hair, dark skin, 6-0, house 137, s 2,4.

LAYNE, JAMES C. reg 68, co C, r cpl, enl 4/7/64, 5/21/64, dis 4/16/64, 6/22/64, residence shown on militia list, house n/c, s 2,4,18.

LEWIS, BENJAMIN F. reg 5VA, co G, enr 9/2/61 Ceredo, enl 1/25/62, dis 9/23/64 Wheeling WV, age 19 or 23, house 829, s 1,20.

LEWIS, DAVID. reg 14, co B, enr 10/10/61 Louisa, enl 12/10/61 Louisa, dis 1/31/65 Louisa, age 23, dark hair, eyes & skin, 5-7, house 644, s 1,2,4.

LEWIS, WILLIAM P. reg CG, co K, enr 6/9/64, enl 7/28/64 Frankfort, dis 3/11/65 Catlettsburg, house 717, s 2,4.

LIMINGS, ANDERSON. reg 68, co A, enl 4/7/64, 5/21/64, dis 4/16/64, 6/22/64, age 35, blue eyes, light hair, fair skin, 5-4, house 656, s 2,4.

LIMINGS, JAMES. reg 68, co A, enl 4/7/64, 5/21/64, dis 4/16/64, 6/22/64, age 29, blue eyes, light hair, fair skin, 5-3, house 304, s 2,4.

LIMINGS, JOHN. reg 68, co A, enl 4/7/64, 5/21/64, dis 4/16/64, 6/21/64, reg CG, co L, r cpl, enr 6/12/64, enl 7/6/64 Frankfort, dis 3/11/65 Catlettsburg, age 20, dark hair, yellow eyes, light skin, 5-9, house 656, s 2,4.

LITTERAL, WILLIAM. reg 14, co K, enr 5/28/63 Louisa, enl 8/28/63 Louisa, dis 9/15/65 Louisville, age 19, black hair, blue eyes, fair skin, 5-8, rem trans to 14th Vet Inf, co C, enr & m/in 5/28/63 Louisa, house 300, s 1,2,4.

LOW, JOHN. reg 68, co K, enl 5/21/64, dis 6/22/64, reg CG, co L, enr 6/9/64, enl 7/6/64 Frankfort, dis 3/11/65 Catlettsburg, age 26, fair hair & skin, blue eyes, 5-6, house 1082, s 2,4.

LOW, WILLIAM. reg 68, co K, enl 4/7/64, 5/21/64, dis 4/16/64, 6/22/64, age 27, blue eyes, light hair, fair skin, 5-6, house 843 or 1085, s 2,4.

LUSTER, DAVID. reg 68, co B, enl 5/21/64, dis 6/22/64, age 30, black eyes, dark hair & skin, 6-0, house 364, s 2,4.

LUSTER, HARVEY. reg 68, co A, enl 5/21/64, dis 6/22/64, age 29, dark eyes, hair & skin, 5-2, house 450, s 2,4.

LUSTER, ISAAC. reg 68, co B, r cpl, enl 5/21/64, dis 6/2/64, age 27, black eyes, dark hair & skin, 5-8, house 574, s 2,4.

LUSTER, LINSEY. reg 68, co B, r 2nd lt, enl 4/7/64, 5/21/64, dis 4/16/64, 6/22/64, age 28, black eyes & hair, fair skin, 6-0, house 607, s 2,4.

LUSTER, THOMAS J. reg 68, co B, r 1st lt, enl 5/21/64, dis 6/22/64, age 36, black eyes & hair, fair skin, 6-0, house 407 or 563, s 2,4.

LUSTER, WILLIAM. reg 68, co B, enl 4/7/64, 5/21/64, dis 4/16/64, 6/22/64, age 20, blue eyes, light hair, fair skin, 5-6, house 564, s 2,4.

LYON, COLBY. reg 68, co B, r cpl, enl 4/7/64, 5/21/64, dis 4/16/64, 6/22/64, age 25, black eyes & hair, dark skin, 6-4, house 446, s 2,4.

LYON, CORBAN. reg 68, co B, enr 4/7/64, 5/21/64, dis 4/16/64, 6/22/64, age 28, blue eyes, light hair, fair skin, 6-0, residence shown on militia list, house n/c, s 2,4,18.

LYON, DAVID. reg 68, co K, enl 5/21/64, dis 6/22/64, age 44, gray eyes, dark hair & skin, 5-6, house 1066, s 2,4.

LYONS, JESSE. reg 5VA, co G, enr 9/2/61 Ceredo, dis 10/3/64 Wheeling WV, age 20, dark hair, hazel eyes, fair skin, 5-4, rem wounded in left thigh at Bull Run VA 8/29/62, house 478, s 1,20.
LYON, LEWIS. reg 68, co A, enl 5/21/64, dis 6/22/64, house 478, s 2,4.
LYON, RANSON. reg 68, co B, enl 5/21/64, dis 6/22/64, age 32, blue eyes, light hair, fair skin, 6-2, house 408 or 614, s 2,4.
LYON, UMBERSON. reg 5VA, co I, enr 9/14/61 Ceredo, enl 9/14/61, age 29, black hair, gray eyes, dark skin, 5-7, rem dis 7/4/62 for disability of left knee & hip pain, house 796, s 1,20.
LYON, WILLIAM L. reg 39, co G, enr 1/26/64, enl 3/29/64 Greenupsburg, dis 9/15/65 Louisville, age 18, dark hair, blue eyes, fair skin, 5-7, house 1066, s 1,2,4.

M

MARCUM, JOHN. reg 39, co I, r musician, enr 9/14/62 Lawrence Co., enl 2/16/63 Peach Orchard, dis 9/15/65 Louisville, age 18, light hair, blue eyes, fair skin, 5-3, residence stated on muster roll, house n/c, s 1,2,4.
MARCUM, THOMAS D. reg 14, co K, enr 11/8/61 Louisa, enl 12/16/61 Lawrence Co., dis 1/31/65 Louisa, age 22, rem prom from 2nd to capt 9/9/64, trans to 14th Vet Inf, co C, r capt, enr 9/9/64, m/in 10/22/64 Galesville AL, m/out Louisville 9/15/65, residence established by List of Officers, house 910, s 1,2.
MARTIN, BENJAMIN. reg 45, co H, enr 7/14/63 Catlettsburg, enl 2/6/64 Mt. Sterling, dis 2/14/65 Catlettsburg, age 21, light hair & skin, gray eyes, 5-6, house 1204, s 2.
MARTIN, B. F. reg 68, co C, enl 5/21/64, dis 6/22/64, age 36, blue eyes, light hair, fair skin, 5-11, residence shown on militia list, house n/c, s 2,4,18.
MARTIN, JOHN P. reg 68, co E, r 1st sgt, enl 4/7/64, 5/21/64, dis 4/16/64, 6/22/64, age 30, light eyes, hair & skin, 6-0, house 786, s 2,4.
MARTIN, MORGAN. reg 14, co G, enr 11/19/61 Louisa, enl 12/10/61 Louisa, dis 1/31/65 Louisa, age 34, black hair & eyes, dark skin, 5-5, rem red from cpl to pvt 5/25/62, house 826, s 1,2,4.
MARTIN, WILLIAM. reg 5 Va., co A, B, enr 7/25/61 Ceredo, enl 8/10/61 Ceredo, dis 9/23/64 Wheeling, age 42, sandy hair, blue eyes, light skin, 5-10, rem enrolled 9th Dist. Of Ky., house 1204, s 1,27.
MATNEY, JACKSON J. reg 45, co D, H, r capt, enr 7/14/63 Catlettsburg, enl 10/17/63 Ashland, dis 2/14/65 Catlettsburg, age 23, light hair, blue eyes, fair skin, rem was 1st lt of co D, prom to capt co H, residence stated on list of officers, house n/c, s 1,2,32.
MAYER, WILLIAM. reg 39, co E, enr 4/12/65 Louisa, enl 5/12/65 Louisa, dis 9/15/65 Louisville, age 18, light hair, blue eyes, fair skin, 5-0, residence shown on CSR, house n/c, s 1,2,4.
MAYNARD, ALVIS. reg 68, co H, enl 5/24/64, age 38, light hair, eyes & skin, 6-2, house 1186, s 4.
MAYNARD, FRANCIS. reg 68, co C, r 2nd lt, enl 4/7/64, 5/21/64, dis 4/16/64, 6/22/64, reg CG, co L, r sgt, enr 6/8/64, enl 7/6/64 Frankfort, dis 3/11/65 Catlettsburg, age 23, fair hair & skin, blue eyes, 5-8, house 919, s 2,4.
MAYNARD, JESSE. reg 14, co H, enr 10/25/61 Catlettsburg, enl 12/10/61 Louisa, dis 1/31/65 Louisa, age 21, dark hair, gray eyes, fair skin, 5-7, house 919, s 1,2,4.
MAYNARD, JOHN B. reg CG, co L, enr 6/8/64, enl 7/6/64 Frankfort, dis 3/11/65 Catlettsburg, age 24, light hair, blue eyes, fair skin, 6-0, residence stated on list of officers, house n/c, s 2,4,32.
MAYNARD, LEWIS. reg 45, co B, enr 7/18/63 Catlettsburg, enl 10/10/63 Catlettsburg, dis 12/24/64 Catlettsburg, age 20, house 919, s 1,2.
MAYS, ELI. reg 68, co F, enl 4/7/64, 5/21/64, dis 4/16/64, 6/22/64, age 25, gray eyes, dark hair, fair skin, 5-3, residence shown on militia list, house n/c, s 2,4,18.

MCCARTY, HENDERSON. reg 68, co E, r lt., enl 4/7/64, dis 4/16/64, age 32, dark eyes, hair & skin, 5-10, house 771, s 4.

MCCLURE, GEORGE. reg 68, co E, enl 4/7/64, 5/21/64, dis 4/16/64, 6/22/64, age 38, dark eyes, hair & skin, 5-4, house 721, s 2,4.

MCCLURE, GEORGE. reg 68, co K, r cpl, enl 4/7/64, 5/21/64, dis 4/16/64, 6/10/64, reg CG, co L, enr 6/8/64, enl 7/6/64 Frankfort, dis 3/11/65 Catlettsburg, age 27, fair hair & skin, blue eyes, 5-8, house 1060, s 2,4.

MCCLURE, SPENCER A. R. reg CG, co L, enr 6/8/64, enl 7/6/64 Frankfort, dis 3/11/65 Catlettsburg, age 22 or 26, black hair, blue eyes, fair skin, 5-6, reg 68, co C, r cpl, enl 4/7/64, 5/21/64, dis 4/16/64, 6/22/64, house 719, s 2,4.

MCCLURE, STROTHER. reg 68, co E, enl 4/7/64, 5/21/64, dis 4/16/64, 6/22/64, age 28, dark eyes, hair & skin, 5-8, house 726, s 2,4.

MCCORMICK, LORENZO D. reg 68, co F, r lt, enl 4/7/64, dis 4/16/64, age 30, blue eyes, dark hair, fair skin, 5-6, house 113, s 4.

MCDOWELL, JOHN. reg 10Cav, co F, enr 1/18/63 Louisa or Mason Co, enl 9/13/62 Maysville, dis 9/17/63 Maysville, age 27, residence stated on muster roll, reg 68, co E, enl 4/7/64, 5/21/64, dis 4/16/64, 6/22/64, age 38, dark eyes, hair & skin, 5-10, house 748, s 1, 2, 4.

MCDOWELL, JOSEPH. reg 39, co G, enr 9/22/62, enl 2/16/63 Peach Orchard, age 44, rem d 3/30/63 Ashland of disease, residence stated on muster roll, house n/c, s 1,2,4.

MCDOWELL, WILLIAM R. reg 68, co A, enl 4/7/64, 5/12/64, dis 4/16/64, 6/22/64, age 38, blue eyes, dark hair & skin, 5-10, house 627, s 2,4.

MCGLOTHLIN, JOHN. reg 14, co H, enr 10/25/61 Louisa, age 20, dark hair, blue eyes, fair skin, 5-8, rem d 2/1/63 Danville of measles & typhoid fever, residence stated on muster roll, house n/c, s 1,2,4.

MCGRANAHAN, L. D. reg 68, co E, enl 4/7/64, 5/21/64, dis 4/16/64, 6/22/64, age 34, light eyes, hair & skin, 5-8, residence stated on muster roll, house n/c, s 2,4,18.

MCGUIRE, JAMES A. reg 39, co E, enr 12/11/63, enl 12/24/63 Catlettsburg, dis 9/15/65 Louisville, age 18, light hair, gray eyes, fair skin, 6-0, house 196, s 1,2,5.

MCGUIRE, LUKE. reg 68, co I, enl 5/21/64, age 20, dark hair & skin, blue eyes, 6-0, house 196, s 4.

MCHENRY, FLEMING. reg 68, co I, enl 5/21/64, dis 6/22/64, age 30, blue eyes, dark hair, fair skin, 5-8, house 1206, s 2,4.

MCHENRY, FREDERICK. reg 68, co I, enl 5/21/64, dis 6/22/64, age 28, blue eyes, dark hair, fair skin, 5-5, house 1206, s 2,4.

MCKINSTER, A. J. reg 68, co G, r sgt, enl 4/7/64, 5/21/64, dis 4/16/64, 6/22/64, age 30, black eyes & hair, dark skin, 5-10, house 282, s 2,4.

MCKINSTER, JESSE. reg 68, co G, enl 5/21/64, dis 6/22/64, age 27, blue eyes, light hair, fair skin, 5-5, residence shown on militia list, house n/c, s 2,4.

MCKINSTER, JOHN. reg 68, co G, r cpl, enl 4/7/64, 5/21/64, dis 4/16/64, 6/22/64, age 35, black eyes & hair, dark skin, 5-6, house 280, s 2,4.

MCKINSTER, SAMUEL. reg 14, co D, enr 10/20/61 Louisa, enl 12/10/61 Louisa, dis 1/31/65 Louisa, age 18, dark hair & skin, black eyes, 5-8, house 281, s 1,2,4.

MCKINSTER, THOMAS. reg 14, co D, r capt, enr 10/20/61 Louisa, enl 12/10/61 Louisa, age 40, rem res 6/8/62, reg 68, r col, enl 4/7/64, 5/21/64, dis 4/16/64, 6/22/64, house 260, s 1,2,4.

MCKINSTER, WILLIAM H. C. reg 14, co D, r sgt, enr 10/20/61 Louisa, enl 12/10/61 Louisa, dis 1/31/65 Louisa, age 18, light hair & skin, blue eyes, 5-9, residence stated on muster roll, house n/c, s 1,4,22.

MCLURE, ALBERT H. reg 68, co C, r 3rd lt, enl 4/7/64, 5/21/64, dis 4/16/64, 6/22/64, reg CG, co L, r sgt, enr 6/9/64, enl 7/6/74 Frankfort, dis 3/11/65 Catlettsburg, age 23, dark hair, blue eyes, fair skin, 5-9, house 719, s 2,4.

MCLURE, MORDECAI. reg 5VA, co I, enr 9/14/61 Ceredo, enl 9/14/61, dis 10/4/64 Wheeling WV, age 25, light hair & skin, blue eyes, 5-9, dis 10/9/62 for disability of spinal irritation, reg 45, co F, r 2nd lt, enr 8/25/63 Peach Orchard, enl 11/2/63 Ashland, dis 12/24/64 Catlettsburg, age 27, dark hair, light eyes & skin, 5-9, house 821, s 1,2,6,20.

MCMILLAN, ARCHIBALD J. reg 14, r chaplain, enr 11/19/61 Louisa, enl 12/10/61 Camp Wallen, age 33, rem res 2/6/63, residence stated on list of officers, house n/c, s 1,2,32.

MCSORLEY, EDMOND. reg 68, co D, enl 5/21/64, dis 6/22/64, age 34, dark hair & skin, blue eyes, 6-0, house 35, s 2.

MEAD, AMBROSE. reg 68, co K, enl 4/7/64, 5/21/64, dis 4/16/64, 6/22/64, age 25, blue eyes, light hair, fair skin, 6-0, house 737, s 2,4.

MEAD, CHARLES. reg 39, co G, enr 12/24/62, enl 2/16/63 Peach Orchard, dis 9/15/65 Louisville, age 18, light hair, blue eyes, fair skin, 5-9, rem wounded & captured 10/2/64 Saltville VA, rel from prison at Richmond VA 2/16/65, house 1026, s 1,2,4.

MEAD, GILBERT. reg 68, co E, enl 5/21/64, dis 6/22/64, age 25, dark eyes, hair & skin, 5-10, house 836, s 2,4.

MEAD, HENRY K. reg 5VA, co I, enr 1/1/62 Parkersburg VA, and 11/1/62, dis 10/4/64 Wheeling WV, age 19, house 735, s 1,20.

MEAD, JACKSON. reg 68, co K, enr 4/7/64, 5/21/64, dis 4/16/64, 6/22/64, age 25, black eyes & hair, dark skin, 5-6, house 735, s 2,4.

MEAD, JOHN. reg 68, co K, enl 4/7/64, 5/21/64, dis 4/16/64, 6/22/64, age 26, black eyes & hair, dark skin, 5-6, house 741, s 2,4.

MEAD, NOAH. reg 68, co E, enl 4/7/64, 5/21/64, dis 4/16/64, 6/22/64, age 28, dark eyes, hair & skin, 6-1, house 809, s 2,4.

MEAD, ROBERT H. reg 14, co D, enr 10/20/61 Louisa, enl 12/10/61 Louisa, dis 1/31/65 Louisa, age 29, light hair, blue eyes, dark skin, 5-7, house 1025, s 1,2,4.

MEADE, SAMPSON. reg 39, co I, r sgt, enr 1/11/63 Peach Orchard, enl 2/16/63 Peach Orchard, dis 9/15/65 Louisville, age 27, dark hair, blue eyes, fair skin, 5-10, residence stated on muster roll, house n/c, s 1,2,4.

MEEK, EDWARD. reg 68, co C, enl 4/7/64, 5/21/64, dis 4/16/64, 6/22/64, age 37, blue eyes, black hair, fair skin, 6-0, house 183, s 2,4.

MEEK, WILLIAM. reg 14, co G, enr 11/19/61 Louisa, enl 12/190/61 Louisa, age 23, rem des 12/15/61 Catlettsburg, house 806, s 1,2,4.

MELLEN, WILLIAM P. reg 9OHCav, co I, enl Zanesville, OH, dis 8/2/65, house 757, s 25.

MICHAELS, HENRY. reg 14, co C, enr 10/10/61 Louisa, enl 12/10/61 Louisa, age 32, dark hair, blue eyes, fair skin, 5-7, rem drowned 4/9/64 near Catlettsburg, house 28, s 1,2,4.

MILLER, ADDISON. reg 5VA, co I, enr 9/14/61 Ceredo, enl 10/1/61, dis 10/4/64 Wheeling WV, age 38, dark hair & skin, gray eyes, 5-10, rem dis 5/22/62 for chronic nephritis, reg 39, co G, r 2nd lt, enr 1/12/63, enl 2/16/63 Peach Orchard, dis 9/15/65 Louisville, age 39, house 752, s 1,2,4,20.

MILLER, ALBERT. reg 68, co E, enl 5/21/64, dis 6/22/64, age 18, dark eyes, hair & skin, 5-6, house 704, s 2,4.

MILLER, ALLEN H. reg 39, co G, r sgt, enr 11/30/62 Peach Orchard, enl 2/16/63 Peach Orchard, dis 9/15/65 Louisville, age 18, light hair, blue eyes, fair skin, 5-8, rem prom from pvt to sgt 9/1/64, house 752, s 1,2,4.

MILLER, EDWARD B. reg 14, co D, r cpl, enr 10/20/61 Catlettsburg, enl 12/10/61 Louisa, dis 9/15/65 Louisville, age 22, dark hair & skin, black eyes, 5-8, rem trans to 14th Vet Inf, co A, enr 2/29/64, m/in 3/15/64 Louisa, cap Lawrence Co. 3/24/63, paroled in eastern KY, house 1059, s 1,2,4.

MILLER, HARRISON. reg 68, co E, enl 4/7/64, 5/21/64, dis 4/16/64, 6/22/64, age 30, dark eyes, hair & skin, 6-4, residence shown on militia list, house n/c, s 2,4,18.

MILLER, JAMES A. reg 14, co E, enr 10/20/61 Catlettsburg, enl 1/10/61 Louisa, dis 9/15/65 Louisville, age 33, black hair, blue eyes, dark skin, 6-0, rem trans to 14th Vet Inf, co A, enr 2/2/64, m/in 3/15/64, house 792, s 1,2,4.

MILLER, JAMES M. reg 14, co H, enr 10/25/61 Catlettsburg, enl 12/10/61 Louisa, dis 1/31/65 Louisa, age 27, dark hair & skin, blue eyes, 5-7, house 699, s 1,2,4.

MILLER, LAFAYETTE. reg 39, co G, enr 12/1/62, enl 2/16/63 Peach Orchard, age 22, rem des 3/1/63 Louisa, house 1065, s 2,4.

MILLER, SAMUEL. reg 14, co D, enr 10/20/61 Louisa, enl 12/10/61 Louisa, age 27, light hair & skin, blue eyes, 5-10, rem d 2/1/62 Louisville accidentally in street fight, house 1018, s 1,2,4.

MILLER, THOMPSON. reg 68, co C, enl 4/7/64, 5/21/64, dis 4/16/64, 6/22/64, age 30, black eyes, dark hair, fair skin, 5-9, house 1017, s 2,4.

MILLER, WILLIAM. reg 14, co E, enr 10/25/61 Louisa, enl 1/10/61 Louisa, dis 1/31/65 Louisa, age 35, brown hair, dark eyes & skin, 5-6, rem trans from co F to co E 8/28/63, back to co F 1/20/65, house 700, s 1,2,4.

MILLER, WILLIAM B. reg 68, co C, r sgt, enl 5/7/64, 5/21/64, dis 4/16/64, 6/22/64, age 35, dark eyes, hair & skin, 5-10, residence shown on militia list, house n/c, s 2,4.

MILLER, WILLIAM B. reg 14, co D, r sgt, enr 10/20/61 Louisa, enl 1/10/61 Louisa, dis 9/15/65 Louisville, age 18, black hair, blue eyes, light skin, 5-11, rem trans to 14th Vet Inf, co A, enr 2/29/64, m/in 3/15/64 Louisa, prom from cpl to sgt 7/14/62, red to pvt 5/1/65, house 1059, s 1,2,4.

MILLS, JESSE. reg 167WV, co Geo. Murray, reg 45, co F, enr 10/4/63 Catlettsburg, enl 11/2/63 Ashland, dis 12/24/64 Catlettsburg, age 18, dark hair & eyes, light skin, 5-4, house 1151, s 1,2,6,23.

MILLS, JOHN. reg 68, co E, enl 4/7/64, 5/21/64, dis 4/16/64, 6/22/64, age 37, light eyes, hair & skin, 6-1, house 1153, s 2,4.

MILLS, JOHN F. reg 5VA, co F, enr 9/2/61 Ceredo, enl 9/14/61, dis 9/23/64 Wheeling WV, age 20, reg 39, co E, rem assigned to 39th Ky Inf by Gen. Palmer, des 1/19/65 Paintsville, house 1151, s 1,2,4,20.

MILLS, THOMAS LAMAR. reg 68, co H, enl 5/21/64, dis 6/22/64, age 21, dark eyes, hair & skin, 5-10, house 1153, s 2,4.

MILLS, WILLIAM. reg 5VA, enr 9/2/61 Ceredo, enl 9/14/62, dis 9/23/64 Wheeling WV, age 27, house 1150, s 1,20.

MILLS, WILLIAM W. reg 45, co F, enr 8/21/63 Peach Orchard, enl 11/2/63 Ashland, dis 12/24/64 Catlettsburg, age 18, dark hair, eyes, & skin, 6-0, rem d 9/11/64 Lexington of typhoid fever, born Lawrence Co., house 1153, s 1,2.

MOLES, JAMES A. reg 14, co K, r cpl, enr 11/8/61 Louisa, enl 12/10/61 Louisa, dis 9/15/65 Louisville, age 20, black hair & eyes, dark skin, 6-0, rem trans to 14th Vet Inf, co A, r cpl, enr 2/29/64, m/in 3/15/64 Louisa, residence stated on muster roll, house n/c, s 1,2,4.

MOODY, DAVID. reg 68, co E, enl 4/7/64, 5/21/64, dis 4/16/64, 6/22/64, age 26, light eyes, hair & skin, 5-8, house 855, s 2,4.

MOODY, FLEMING. reg 68, co E, enl 4/7/64, 5/21/64, dis 4/16/64, 6/22/64, age 27, light eyes, hair & skin, 5-3, residence shown on militia list, house n/c, s 2,4,18.

MOODY, JOHN. reg 5VA, co I, enr 10/1/61 Ceredo, enl 10/1/61, dis 7/12/62, age 35, light hair & skin, blue eyes, 5-8, rem disability on heart condition, house 800, s 1,20.

MOORE, ALEXANDER. reg 14, co D, enr 10/20/61 Louisa, enl 12/10/61 Louisa, dis 1/31/65 Louisa, age 32, light hair & skin, blue eyes, 5-7, residence stated on muster roll, house n/c, s 1,2,4.

MOORE, ANDERSON L. reg 14, co D, enr 10/20/61 Louisa, enl 12/10/61 Louisa, age 22, d 7/3/63 Ashland of dropsy, house 259, s 1,2,4.

MOORE, CORNELIUS B. reg 14, co D, enr 10/20/61 Louisa, enl 12/10/61 Louisa, dis 1/31/65 Louisa, age 29, light hair & skin, blue eyes, 6-0, house 1008, s 1,2,4.

MOORE, DAVID. reg 68, co G, enl 5/21/64, dis 6/22/64, age 40, blue eyes, dark hair, fair skin, 6-2, house 269 or 533, s 2,4.

MOORE, DAVID W. reg 14, co D, enr 10/20/61 Louisa, enl 12/10/61 Louisa, dis 1/31/65 Louisa, age 25, light hair & skin, blue eyes, 5-10, residence stated on muster roll, house n/c, s 1,2,4.

MOORE, ELISHA. reg 68, co G, enl 4/7/64, 5/21/64, dis 4/16/64, 6/22/64, age 35, blue eyes, light hair, fair skin, 6-0, house 994, s 2,4.

MOORE, GARLAND J. reg 68, co G, enl 4/7/64, 5/21/64, dis 4/16/64, 6/22/64, age 25, black eyes & hair, dark skin, 6-3, residence stated on militia list, house n/c, s 2,4,18.

MOORE, GREEN. reg CG, co L, enr 7/6/64, enl 7/6/64 Frankfort, dis 3/11/65 Catlettsburg, age 18, light hair, blue eyes, fair skin, 5-6, house 259, s 2,4.

MOORE, JAMES. reg 39, co I, r cpl, enr 1/11/63 Lawrence Co., enl 2/16/63 Peach Orchard, dis 9/15/65 Louisville, age 27, dark hair, blue eyes, fair skin, 5-10, rem prom to cpl 6/3/65, house 270, s 1,2,4.

MOORE, JAMES H. reg 14, co D, enr 10/20/61 Louisa, enl 12/10/61 Louisa, dis 1/31/65 Louisa, age 34, black hair & eyes, dark skin, 5-11, residence stated on muster roll, house n/c, s 1,2,4.

MOORE, JAMES H. reg 68, co G, r capt, enl 4/7/64, 5/21/64, dis 4/16/64, 6/22/64, age 27, blue eyes, dark hair, fair skin, 5-10, house 532, s 2,4.

MOORE, JOHN B. reg 14, co D, enr 10/20/61 Louisa, enl 12/10/61 Louisa, dis 3/12/64 Louisa, age 35, light hair & skin, blue eyes, 6-6, rem dis for disability of dropsy, reg 68, co I, enl 5/21/64, dis 6/22/64, house 1015, s 1,2,4.

MOORE, JOHN L. C. reg 68, co G, r cpl, enl 4/7/64, 5/21/64, dis 4/16/64, 6/22/64, reg CG, co L, enr 7/18/64, enl 8/30/64 Frankfort, dis 3/11/65 Catlettsburg, age 18, light hair, blue eyes, fair skin, 5-5 or 5-8, house 259, s 2,4.

MOORE, JOHN W. reg 39, co B, enr 3/17/65 Louisa, enl 5/16/65 Greenupsburg, dis 9/15/65 Louisville, age 25, brown hair, hazel eyes, dark skin, 5-7, house 532, s 1,2,4.

MOORE, JOSEPH D. reg 14, co D, r sgt, enr 10/20/61 Louisa, enl 12/10/61 Louisa, dis 1/31/65 Louisa, age 30, dark hair, black eyes, light skin, 6-1, residence stated on muster roll, house n/c, s 1,2,4.

MOORE, LABAN T. reg 14, r col, enr 11/19/61 Louisa, enl 12/10/61 Louisa, dis 1/1/62, age 32, rem res 1/1/62, house 1225, s 1,2,4.

MOORE, MARTIN L. reg 68, co G, r 1st sgt, enl 4/7/64, 5/21/64, dis 4/16/64, 6/22/64, age 18, blue eyes, light hair, fair skin, 5-8, house 246, s 2,4.

MOORE, SAMPSON. reg 14, co H, enr 10/25/61 Catlettsburg, enl 12/10/61 Louisa, dis 1/31/65 Louisa, age 30, dark hair, blue eyes, dark skin, 5-9, residence stated on muster roll, house n/c, s 1,2,4.

MOORE, SAMUEL J. reg 14, co D, r 2nd lt, enr 10/20/61 Louisa, enl 12/10/61 Louisa, age 39, light hair & skin, blue eyes, 5-10, rem res 2/26/62, house 246, s 1,2,4.

MOORE, SAMUEL S. reg 68, co K, enl 4/7/64, 5/21/64, dis 4/16/64, 6/22/64, age 30, blue eyes, light hair, fair skin, 6-0, house 1020, s 2,4.

MOORE, WESLEY. reg 14, co D, r sgt, enr 10/20/61 Catlettsburg, enl 12/10/61 Louisa, dis 1/31/65 Louisa, age 25, dark hair & skin, black eyes, 5-7, rem prom to cpl 3/1/62, to sgt 9/9/64, house 279, s 1,2,4.

MOORE, WILLIAM A. reg 14, co D, enr 10/20/61 Louisa, enl 12/10/61 Louisa, dis 1/31/65 Louisa, age 38, light hair & skin, blue eyes, 5-11, house 732, s 1,2,4.

MOORE, WILLIAM H. reg 167WV, co Ira Copley, enl 8/62 to 2/64, dis 5/2/64, reg 68, co G, r 2nd lt, 4/7/64, enl 5/21/64, dis 4/16/64, 6/22/64, age 29, blue eyes, light hair, fair skin, 6-0, house 1107, s 2,4,23.

MOORE, WILLIAM H. reg 45, co F, enr 10/1/63 Catlettsburg, enl 11/2/63 Ashland, dis 12/24/64 Catlettsburg, age 22, dark hair & eyes, light skin, 6-2, house 143, s 1,2,6.

MORRIS, BENJAMIN B. reg 68, co A, r 1st sgt, enl 4/7/64, 5/21/64, dis 4/16/64, 6/22/64, age 31, blue eyes, light hair, fair skin, 5-8, house 373, s 2,4.

MORRIS, DAVID. reg 14, co G, enr 8/7/63, enl 8/30/63 Louisa, dis 9/15/65, age 30, rem trans to 14th Vet Inf, co D, house 327, s 1,2.

MORRIS, HENRY. reg 14, co B, enr 10/10/61 Louisa, enl 12/10/61 Louisa, dis 4/12/63 Louisa, age 20, black hair & eyes, dark skin, 5-8, rem dis 7/11/62 at Lexington for disability of pulmonalis, residence stated on muster roll, house n/c, s 1,2,4.

MORRIS, RICHARD F. reg 14, co B, r cpl, enr 10/10/61 Louisa, enl 12/10/61 Louisa, dis 9/15/65 Louisville, age 21, dark hair, eyes & skin, 5-6, rem app cpl 6/20/62, cap Lawrence Co. 2/15/63, paroled in eastern Ky., trans 14th Vet Inf, co A, r cpl, enr 2/29/64, m/in 3/15/64, residence stated on muster roll, house n/c, s 1,2,4.

MORRIS, THOMAS C. reg 14, co B, enr 10/10/61 Louisa, enl 12/10/61 Louisa, age 24, light hair & skin, blue eyes, 5-8, rem KIA 7/21/64 near Atlanta, residence stated on muster roll, house n/c, s 1,2,4.

MOSLEY, ALEXANDER. reg 5VA, co F, enr 9/2/61 Ceredo, enl 9/14/61, age 23, light hair, gray eyes, fair skin, 5-8, rem dis 10/20/62 for disability of epilepsy, house 1145, s 1,20.

MUNCY, ARCHIBALD. reg 39, co I, enr 11/20/62 Pike Co., enl 2/16/63 Peach Orchard, dis 9/15/65 Louisville, age 28, dark hair, blue eyes, fair skin, 5-11, residence stated on muster roll, house n/c, s 1,2,4.

MUNCY, DANIEL. reg 14, co H, enr & enl 9/17/62 Louisa, dis 9/15/65 Louisville, age 27, dark hair, eyes & skin, 5-6, rem trans to 14th Vet Inf, co C, enr & m/in 9/17/62 Louisa, residence stated on muster roll, house n/c, s 1,2,4.

MUNCY, D. W. reg 68, co I, enl 5/21/64, age 35, dark hair, eyes & skin, 6-0, house 169, s 4.

MUNCY, JAMES. reg 68, co I, r sgt, enl 4/7/64, 5/21/64, dis 4/16/64, 6/22/64, age 23, blue eyes, light hair, fair skin, 5-6, residence shown on militia list, house n/c, s 2,4.

MUNCY, JAMES. reg 167WV, co Geo. Murray, reg 39, co I, enr 11/63, dis 9/65, house 967, s 5,23,

MUNCY, JAMES. reg 14, co H, enr & enl 9/17/62 Louisa, dis 9/15/65 Louisville, age 25, dark hair, eyes & skin, 5-11, rem trans to 14th Vet Inf, co C, enr & m/in 9/17/62 Louisa, residence stated on muster roll, house n/c, s 1,2,4.

MUNCY, RICHARD. reg 14, co H, enr & enl 9/17/62 Louisa, age 21, dark hair, eyes & skin, 5-1, rem d 1/13/62 Lexington of consumption, residence stated on muster roll, house n/c, s 1,2,4.

MUNCY, SAMUEL K. reg 68, co I, r 1st lt, enl 4/7/64, 5/21/64, dis 4/16/64, 6/22/64, age 38, dark eyes, hair & skin, 5-10, house 159, s 2,4.

MUNCY, THOMAS. reg 68, co C, r cpl, enl 4/7/64, 5/21/64, dis 4/16/64, 6/22/64, age 28, blue eyes, dark hair, fair skin, 5-11, residence shown on militia list, house n/c, s 2,4,18.

MUNCY, THOMAS. reg 39, co I, enr 1/13/63 Peach Orchard, 2/16/63 Peach Orchard, age 45, black hair & eyes, dark skin, 5-6, rem d 5/18/64 Louisa, residence established by descriptive muster roll, house n/c, s 1,2,4.

MUNCY, WILLIAM. reg 39, co I, enr 1/20/63 Lawrence Co., enl 2/16/63 Peach Orchard, dis 9/15/65 Louisville, age 35, black hair & eyes, dark skin, 5-3, rem residence established by descriptive muster roll, house n/c, s 1,2,4.

MUNCY, WILLIAM. reg 14, co H, r sgt, enr 10/25/61 Catlettsburg, enl 12/10/61 Louisa, dis 1/31/65 Louisa, age 39, dark hair, blue eyes, fair skin, 5-8, rem residence established by descriptive muster roll, house n/c, s 1,2,4.

MUNCY, WILLIAM. reg 14, co H, enr & enl 9/17/62 Louisa, dis 2/3/63 Winchester, age 18, dark hair, eyes & skin, 5-11, dis for disability of measles, typhoid & rheumatism, residence established by descriptive muster roll, house n/c, s 1,2,4.
MURRAY, ATTISON W. reg 14, co K, enr 1/8/61, enl 12/10/61 Louisa, dis 1/31/65 Louisa, age 23, residence stated on muster roll, house n/c, s 2,4.
MURRY, GEORGE. reg 68, co C, enl 5/21/64, dis 6/22/64, age 33, blue eyes, light hair, fair skin, 5-11, residence shown on militia list, house n/c, s 2,4,18.

N

NEAL, ABRAHAM. reg 14, co H, enr 10/25/61 Catlettsburg, enl 12/10/61 Louisa, dis 1/31/65 Louisa, age 38, light hair, blue eyes, fair skin, 6-1, house 1219, s 1,2,4.
NEAL, CHRISTOPHER C. reg 68, co E, enl 5/21/64, dis 6/22/64, age 28, blue eyes, light hair & skin, 5-10, house 761, s 2,4.
NEAL, ROBERT. reg 5VA, co I, enr 9/14/61 Ceredo, enl 9/14/61, dis 10/4/64 Wheeling WV, age 22, house 761, s 1,20.
NELSON, GABRIEL. reg 39, co G, enr 2/3/63, enl 2/16/63 Peach Orchard, dis 11/21/64 Ashland, age 44, dark hair & skin, blue eyes, 5-6, house 582, s 1,2,4.
NOLEN, RICHARD. reg 14, co B, enr 10/10/61 Louisa, enl 12/10/61 Louisa, dis 4/10/63 Louisa, age 42, light hair, blue eyes, fair skin, 5-7, rem dis for general disability, house 552, s 1,2,4.

O

O'BRIAN, GEORGE. reg 14, co K, enr 11/8/61, enl 12/10/61 Louisa, age 28, sandy hair, blue eyes, fair skin, 5-8, des 3/27/62 Ashland, shot & killed while trying to escape, residence stated on muster roll, house n/c, s 1,2,4.
O'BRIAN, ISAAC. reg 14, co K, enr 11/8/61, enl 12/10/61 Louisa, dis 1/31/65 Louisa, age 30, sandy hair, blue eyes, fair skin, 5-8, house 247, s 1,2,4.
O'BRIAN, JAMES G. reg 68, co G, enl 5/21/64, dis 6/22/64, age 35, blue eyes, light hair, fair skin, 5-5, house 249, s 2,4.
O'BRIAN, WILLIAM. reg 68, co K, enl 4/7/64, dis 4/16/64, age 41, black eyes & hair, dark skin, 5-6, house 1036, s 4.
O'BRIEN, JAMES H. reg 45, co I, r capt, enr 1/9/64, enl 2/4/64 Mt. Sterling, dis 6/7/65 Louisville, age 26, dark hair, blue eyes, light skin, 6-2, rem residence established by List of Officers, house n/c, s 1,2.
O'BRIEN, OWEN. reg 68, co K, r sgt, enl 4/7/64, 5/21/64, dis 4/16/64, 6/22/64, age 33, blue eyes, light hair, fair skin, 5-8, house 1048, s 2,4.
O'DANIEL, THOMAS. reg 68, co D, enl 4/7/64, 5/21/64, dis 4/16/64, 6/22/64, house 100, s 2,4.
O'ROARK, DAVID C. reg 14, co K, r sgt, enr 11/8/61 Louisa, enl 12/10/61 Louisa, dis 1/31/65 Louisa, age 21, rem cap & paroled on march from Cumberland Gap to Ohio River, house 170, s 1,2,4.
O'ROARK, JAMES. reg 68, co I, enl 4/7/64, 5/21/64, dis 4/16/64, 6/22/64, reg CG, co L, r cpl, enr 6/8/64, enl 7/6/64 Frankfort, dis 3/1/65 Catlettsburg, age 36, dark hair, gray eyes, fair skin, 5-8, house 326, s 2,4.
OSBURN, CHILTON A. reg 14, co B, enr 10/10/61 Louisa, enl 12/10/61 Louisa, age 18, dark hair, blue eyes, fair skin, 5-9, rem app cpl 10/10/61, prom to sgt 1/10/62, 1st lt 6/5/62, cap 2/15/63, KIA near Marietta GA 11/9/64 or d 11/30/64, house 609, s 1,2,4.

OSBURN, EDMUND. reg 14, co B, enr 10/10/61 Louisa, enl 12/10/61 Louisa, dis 6/10/63 Louisa, age 26, dark hair, blue eyes, fair skin, 5-8, rem dis for disability of measles, reg 68, r surgeon, enl 5/21/64, dis 6/21/64, house 625, s 1,2,4.

OSBORNE, THOMAS. reg 5VA, co A, H, enr 9/2/61 Ceredo, VA, enl 8/21/61 Ceredo VA, dis 9/24/64 Wheeling WV, age 37, light hair, blue eyes, fair skin, 5-7, trans to co H 11/24/61, cap Nicholas Co.VA, 11/4/63, d Andersonville prison 6/9/64, house 624, s 20.

P

PACK, DANIEL. reg 5VA, co F, enl 9/14/61, age 20, reg 68, co K, enl 5/21/64, dis 6/22/64, age 25, dark eyes, hair & skin, 5-6, house 1091, s 2,4,20.

PACK, DAVIS. reg 167WV, co Ira Copley, enl 8/62 to 2/64, dis 5/2/64, reg 68, co H, r 1st sgt, enl 4/7/64, 5/21/64, dis 4/16/64, 6/22/64, age 25, dark eyes, hair & skin, 5-10, house 868, s 2,4,23.

PACK, GEORGE. reg 5VA, co F, enl 9/2/61 Ceredo, enl 9/14/61, age 43, gray hair, blue eyes, fair skin, 5-8, rem cap Wayne Co. VA 3/29/62, paroled 4/3/63, dis 5/30/63 for disability of old age, 57 years, house 1116, s 1,20.

PACK, GEORGE W. reg 5VA, co I, enr 10/1/61 Ceredo, enl 10/1/61, dis 10/14/64 Wheeling WV, age 21, house 1046, s 1,20.

PACK, GEORGE W. reg 39, co G, enr 11/30/62 Peach Orchard, enl 2/16/63 Peach Orchard, dis 9/15/65 Louisville, age 18, light hair, blue eyes, fair skin, 5-4, house 1080, s 1,2,4.

PACK, IRA. reg 5VA, co F, enr 9/2/61 Ceredo, enl 9/14/61, dis 9/23/64 Wheeling WV, age 18, rem cap Lawrence Co. 11/29/62, paroled City Point VA 4/3/63, house 868, s 1,20.

PACK, ISAAC. reg 14, co D, enr 6/8/63, enl 10/30/63 Louisa, age 17, dark hair, eyes & skin, 5-10, rem trans to 14th Vet Inf, co B, enr 6/8/63, m/in 8/30/63, Louisa, house 1046, s 2,4.

PACK, JOHN. reg 45, co F, enr 8/25/63 Ashland, enl 12/9/63 Ashland, dis 2/14/65 Catlettsburg, age 25, dark hair, eyes & skin, 6-0, rem trans to co K 5/20/64, house 868, s 2,6.

PACK, JOHN. reg 68, co H, enl 5/21/64, age 38, light hair & skin, blue eyes, 5-10, house 904, s 4.

PACK, JOHN B. reg 39, co G, enr 9/26/62 Peach Orchard, enl 2/16/63 Peach Orchard, dis 9/15/65 Louisville, age 28, dark hair, eyes & skin, 5-10, house 1087, s 1,2,4.

PACK, JOHN W. reg 5VA, co F, r cpl, enr 9/2/61 Ceredo, enl 9/14/61, dis 9/23/64 Wheeling WV, age 28, rem cap Lawrence Co. 3/29/63, paroled 4/3/63, house 1047, s 1,20.

PACK, LEANDER J. reg 14, co D, enr 10/20/61 Louisa, enl 12/10/61 Louisa, dis 1/31/65 Louisa, age 26, light hair & skin, blue eyes, 5-5, residence stated on muster roll, house n/c, s 1,2,4.

PACK, LEANDER JACKSON. reg 39, co I, enr 1/22/63 Lawrence Co., enl 12/28/63 Louisa, dis 9/15/65 Louisville, age 27, dark hair, blue eyes, fair skin, 5-8, house 881, s 1,2,4.

PACK, LEWIS. reg 68, co K, enl 4/7/64, 5/21/64, dis 4/16/64, 6/22/64, age 20, blue eyes, light hair, fair skin, 6-0, house 1046, s 2,4.

PACK, NOAH. reg 68, co H, enl 4/7/64, 5/21/64, dis 4/16/64, 6/22/64, reg CG, co L, enr 6/8/64, enl 7/6/64 Frankfort, dis 3/11/65 Catlettsburg, age 19, dark hair & skin, black eyes, 5-6, house 1116, s 2,4.

PACK, SAMUEL. reg 68, co H, enl 5/21/64, dis 6/22/64, reg CG, co L, enr 6/8/64, enl 7/6/64 Frankfort, dis 3/11/65 Catlettsburg, age 15, light hair, yellow eyes, fair skin, 5-0, house 904, s 2,4.

PACK, THOMAS. reg 14, co G, enr 11/19/61 Louisa, enl 12/10/61 Louisa, dis 1/31/65 Louisa, age 18, black hair & eyes, dark skin, 5-6, house 1116, s 1,2,4.

PACK, WILLIAM. reg 39, co G, enr 9/27/62, enl 2/16/63 Peach Orchard, dis 9/15/65 Louisville, age 19, dark hair, eyes & skin, 5-8, house 1080, s 1,2,4.

PARKER, FRANK. reg 14, co K, enr 11/8/61 Louisa, enl 12/10/61 Louisa, dis 1/31/65 Louisa, age 18, dark hair, gray eyes, fair skin, 5-3, rem wounded between 7/2/64 & 8/1/64 in right forefinger, house 292, s 1,2,4.

PARKER, JAMES. reg 5VA, co I, enr 9/14/61 Ceredo, age 18, rem KIA 6/18/64 Lynchburg VA, house 231, s 1,20.

PARKER, JOHN. reg 14, co K, enr 11/8/612, enl 12/10/61 Louisa, age 30, sandy hair, blue eyes, fair skin, 5-11, rem dis 4/5/63 for disability of abdominal dropsy, house 231, s 1,2,4.

PARKER, SAMUEL. reg 14, co D, enr 10/20/61 Catlettsburg, enl 12/10/61 Louisa, dis 1/31/65 Louisa, age 26, house 237, s 1,2,4.

PARSONS, WILLIAM. reg 39, co K, enr 9/16/62 Lawrence Co., enl 2/16/63 Peach Orchard, age 18, dark hair & skin, blue eyes, 5-3, rem d 4/10/63 of typhoid fever Ashland, residence stated on muster roll, house n/c, s 1,2,4.

PATTON, JOHN. reg 40, co K, enr 10/5/63 Grayson, enl 7/2/64 Lexington, dis 12/30/64 Catlettsburg, age 18, light hair & skin, blue eyes, house 970, s 1,2,4.

PEARY, WILLIAM. reg 68, co D, enr 4/7/64, 5/21/64, dis 4/16/64, 6/22/64, age 26, blue eyes, light hair, fair skin, 5-8, house 349, s 2,4.

PECK, JOHN S. reg 68, co C, r cpl, enl 4/7/64, 5/21/64, dis 4/16/64, 6/22/64, reg CG, co L, enr 6/8/64, enl 7/6/64 Frankfort, dis 3/11/65 Catlettsburg, age 19, dark hair & skin, black eyes, 5-6, house 715, s 2,4.

PECK, JOSEPH. reg 68, co C, enl 4/7/64, 5/21/64, dis 4/16/64, 6/22/64, age 25, black eyes, fair hair & skin, 5-6, house 715, s 2,4.

PELPHREY, WILLIAM R. reg 45, co C, enr 8/3/63 Paintsville, enl 10/10/63 Catlettsburg, dis 12/24/64 Catlettsburg, age 25, house 436, s 1,2.

PENIX, DAVID. reg 68, co E, enl 5/21/64, dis 6/22/64, age 37, dark eyes, hair & skin, 5-8, house 1062, s 2,4.

PENNINGTON, ANDREW J. reg 45, co K, r sgt, enr 9/22/63 Catlettsburg, enl 12/9/63 Louisa, dis 2/14/65 Catlettsburg, age 28, dark hair, eyes & skin, 6-0, house 512, s 1,2.

PENNINGTON, JAMES R. reg 45, co E, enr 10/20/63 Ashland, enl 11/6/63 Ashland, dis 12/24/64 Catlettsburg, age 32, dark hair, blue eyes, fair skin, 5-0, house 509, s 1,2,6.

PENNINGTON, JOHN W. reg 45, co K, r sgt, enr 10/7/63 Ashland, enl 11/9/63 Louisa, dis 2/14/65 Catlettsburg, age 20, black hair & eyes, dark skin, 5-6, rem prom from cpl to sgt 8/3/64, house 515, s 1,2,6.

PENNINGTON, JOHN W. reg 14, co B, enr 10/10/61 Louisa, enl 12/10/61 Louisa, age 24, rem des 1/6/62 Paintsville, house 667, s 1,2,4.

PENNINGTON, JOHN W. reg 68, co F, enl 5/21/64, dis 6/22/64, age 37, blue eyes, dark hair, fair skin, 5-6, house 520, s 2,4.

PENNINGTON, WILLIAM J. reg 14, co B, r sgt, enr 10/10/61 Louisa, enl 12/10/61 Louisa, rem des 1/6/62 Paintsville, house 295, s 1,2,4.

PENNINGTON, WILLIAM NELSON. reg Harlan, co E, enl 10/13/62, dis 1/13/63, house 511, s 2,31.

PERKINS, HENRY C. reg 14, co B, enr 10/10/61 Louisa, enl 12/10/61 Louisa, dis 12/31/63 Lexington, age 19, dark hair, eyes & skin, 5-8, rem wounded in battle of Tazewell TN 8/6/62, right leg amputated, house 649, s 1,2,4.

PERKINS, JOHN H. reg 39, co G, enr 12/8/62 Peach Orchard, enl 8/30/63 Louisa, dis 9/15/65 Louisville, age 22, rem CSR stated at home sick on Georges Creek, Lawrence Co., house n/c, s 1,2.

PERKINS, LEVI. reg 14, co B, enr 10/10/61 Louisa, enl 12/10/61 Louisa, dis 9/15/65 Louisville, age 16, dark hair, eyes & skin, 5-7, rem trans to 14th Vet Inf, co A, enr 2/29/64, m/in 3/15/64, residence stated on muster roll, house n/c, s 1,2,4.

PERKINS, MILTON. reg 14, co B, enr 7/28/63 Louisa, enl 8/10/63 Louisa, dis 9/15/65 Louisville, age 18, dark hair, eyes & skin, 5-5, rem trans to 14th Vet Inf, co B, enr 7/28/63, m/in 8/10/63 Louisa, house 378 or 649, s 1,2,4.

PERRY, HENRY. reg 14, co D, enr 10/8/62 Catlettsburg, enl 10/8/62 Portland OH, dis 9/15/65 Louisville, age 31, dark hair, blue eyes, fair skin, 5-7, rem trans to 14th Vet Inf, app cpl 2/1/65, house 1099, s 1,2,4.

PETERMAN, WILLIAM. reg 14, co C, enr 10/25/61 Louisa, enl 12/10/61 Louisa, dis 1/31/65 Louisa, age 30, dark hair, hazel eyes, fair skin, 5-8, residence stated on muster roll, house n/c, s 1,2,4.

PETERS, JOHN. reg 68, co C, enl 4/7/64, 5/21/64, dis 4/16/64, 6/22/64, age 25, black eyes & hair, dark skin, 5-10, house 944, s 2,4.

PETREY, ANDREW J. reg 68, co D, enl 4/7/64, 5/21/64, dis 4/16/64, 6/22/64, age 31, blue eyes, dark hair & skin, 5-10, house 74, s 2,4.

PHILLIPS, WILLIAM. reg 14, co B, enr 6/8/63 Louisa, enl 6/10/63 Louisa, dis 9/15/65 Louisville, age 18, light hair, blue eyes, fair skin, 5-6, rem trans to 14th Vet Inf, co B, enr 6/8/63, m/in 6/10/63 Louisa, house 596, s 1,2,4.

PIGG, FLEMING. reg 68, co I, enl 4/7/64, 5/21/64, dis 4/16/64, 6/22/64, age 21, dark eyes, hair & skin, 6-0, house 148, s 2,4.

PIGG, GEORGE. reg 68, co I, enl 5/21/64, dis 6/22/64, age 36, dark eyes, hair & skin, 6-4, house 150, s 2,4.

PIGG, THOMAS. reg 14, co K, r cpl, enr 11/8/61 Louisa, enl 12/10/61 Louisa, dis 1/31/65 Louisa, age 21, sandy hair, blue eyes, fair skin, 6-2, rem prom to cpl 9/29/64, house 1208, s 1,2,4.

PIGG, WILLIAM. reg 68, co I, enl 4/7/64, 5/21/64, dis 4/16/64, 6/22/64, age 34, blue eyes, fair hair & skin, 6-2, house 146, s 2,4.

PIGG, WILLIS. reg 68, co E, enl 4/7/64, 5/21/64, dis 4/16/64, 6/22/64, age 30, black eyes & hair, dark hair, 6-0, house 1208, s 2,4.

POE, ISAAC. reg 68, co I, enl 5/21/64, dis 6/22/64, age 25, blue eyes, light hair, fair skin, 6-0, house 130, s 2,4.

POE, JAMES. reg 14, co G, enr 11/19/61 Louisa, enl 12/10/61 Louisa, dis 1/31/65 Louisa, age 18, light hair, blue eyes, fair skin, 5-8, house 134, s 1,2,4.

POOL, LEWIS. reg 68, co I, enl 5/21/64, dis 6/22/64, age 28, blue eyes, light hair, fair skin, 6-0, house 105, s 2,4.

POWERS, JOSEPH D. reg 39, co K, r 1st lt, enr 1/14/63 Catlettsburg, enl 2/16/63 Peach Orchard, dis 9/15/65 Louisville, age 29, dark hair & skin, blue eyes, 5-10, residence stated on muster roll, house n/c, s 1,2,4.

POWERS, WILLIAM P. reg 39, co I, enr & enl 5/1/64 Louisa, age 20, red hair, gray eyes, fair skin, 5-10, rem des 8/10/64 Louisa, residence shown on CSR, house n/c, s 2,4.

PRESTON, ALBERT. reg 68, co E, enl 5/21/64, age 28, light hair, eyes & skin, 5-8, house 816, s 4.

PRESTON, ASBURY. reg 45, co F, enr 8/21/63, Peach Orchard, enl 11/2/63 Ashland, dis 12/24/64 Catlettsburg, age 18, dark hair, light eyes & skin, 5-5, house 751, s 1,2,6.

PRESTON, DAVID. reg 39, co F, enr 2/16/63 Floyd Co., enl 2/16/63 Peach Orchard, age 35, light hair, blue eyes, fair skin, 5-10, house 1115, s 1,2,4.

PRESTON, GEORGE W. reg 167WV, co George W. Murray, reg 68, co H, enl 5/21/64, age 26, dark hair & eyes, light skin, 5-9, house 869, s 4,23.

PRESTON, HAMILTON. reg 5VA, co I, enr 10/1/61 Ceredo, enl 9/14/61, dis 10/4/64 Wheeling WV, age 18, house 751, s 1,20.

PRESTON, JAMES. reg 68, co E, r 1st lt, enl 4/7/64, 5/21/64, dis 4/16/64, 6/22/64, age 31, gray eyes, dark hair, light skin, 5-10, house 859, s 2,4.

PRESTON, JAMES. reg 68, co E, enl 5/21/64, age 25, light hair, eyes, & skin, 5-10, house 815, s 4.
PRESTON, JAMES M. reg 167WV, co George W. Murray, reg 45, co F, r sgt, enr 8/21/63 Peach Orchard, enl 11/2/63 Ashland, dis 12/25/64 Catlettsburg, age 23, dark hair, light eyes & skin, 5-11, house 871, s 1,2,6,23.
PRESTON, JUDGE FRANCIS or FRENCH. reg 5VA, co I, enr 9/14/61 Ceredo, enl 10/1/61, dis 10/4/64 Wheeling WV, age 19, house 798, s 1,9,20.
PRESTON, LEWIS PATRICK ALLEN. reg 167WV, co George W. Murray, reg 45, co F, enr 8/21/63, enl 11/2/63 Ashland, dis 12/24/64 Catlettsburg, age 19, light hair, eyes & skin, 5-10, house 832, s 1,2,6,23.
PRESTON, ROBERT. reg 68, co E, enl 4/7/64, 5/21/64, dis 4/16/64, 6/22/64, age 42, dark eyes, hair & skin, 5-10, house 815, s 2,4.
PRESTON, WILLIAM HARRISON. reg 45, co F, enr 8/25/63 Peach Orchard, enl 11/2/63 Ashland, dis 12/24/64 Catlettsburg, age 18, dark hair, eyes & skin, 5-8, house 825, s 1,2,6.
PRICE, ARCHIBALD. reg 5VA, co G, enr 9/2/61 Ceredo, enl 9/2/61, dis 12/12/64 Wheeling WV, age 24, rem wounded Bull Run VA, 8/29/62, lost two fingers, house 33, s 1,20.
PRICE, DAVID. reg 68, co E, enl 4/7/64, 5/21/64, dis 4/16/64, 6/22/64, age 38, dark eyes, hair & skin, 5-9, house 830, s 2,4.
PRICE, JAMES. reg 68, co E, enl 4/7/64, 5/21/64, dis 4/16/64, 6/22/64, age 43, dark eyes, hair & skin, 5-10, house 856, s 2,4.
PRICE, MAJOR M. reg 68, co E, enl 5/21/64, dis 6/22/64, age 28, dark eyes & hair, light skin, 5-10, house 834, s 2,4.
PRICE, MARTIN. reg 68, co E, enl 5/21/64, dis 6/22/64, age 24, dark eyes & hair, light skin, 5-6, house 833, s 2,4.
PRICE, WILLIAM JASPER. reg 5 Va., co I, r cpl, enr 9/14/61 Ceredo, enl 9/14/61, dis 10/4/64 Wheeling, age 18, dark hair, blue eyes, light skin, 5-8, house 856, rem prom to cpl 4/25/62, born Lawrence Co. Ky., enrolled 9th Dist. Of Ky., wounded left shoulder Bull Run, Va. 8/29/62, house 856, s 1, 27.
PRINCE, ARTHUR. reg 68, co B, r cpl, enl 4/7/64, 5/21/64, dis 4/16/64, 6/22/64, age 18, black eyes & hair, fair skin, 5-0, house 843, s 2,4.
PRINCE, DAVID G. reg 68, co A, r sgt, enl 4/7/64, 5/21/64, dis 4/16/64, 6/22/64, reg CG, co L, enr 6/9/64, enl 7/6/64 Frankfort, dis 3/11/65 Catlettsburg, age 23, fair hair & skin, gray eyes, 6-0, house 534, s 2,4.
PRINCE, JAMES M. reg 14, co B, enr 10/10/61 Louisa, enl 12/10/61 Louisa, dis 9/11/62 Camp Chase OH, age 27, light hair & skin, blue eyes, 5-11, rem dis for accidental wound, injury of testicles, caused by explosion of cartridge, residence stated on muster roll, house n/c, s 1,2,4.
PRINCE, JOHN W. reg 14, co B, enr 10/10/61 Louisa, enl 12/10/61 Louisa, dis 1/31/65 Louisa, age 21, dark hair & skin, blue eyes, 5-10, rem prom from cpl to sgt 4/13/63, red to ranks 8/28/63, house 443, s 1,2,4.
PRINCE, THOMAS. reg 14, co B, enr 8/29/63 Louisa, enl 8/31/63 Louisa, age 40, dark hair, blue eyes, fair skin, 5-6, rem d 7/28/64 Atlanta of fever & disease, house 650, s 1,2,4.
PRINCE, THOMAS. reg 14, co B, enr 10/10/61 Louisa, enl 12/10/61 Louisa, dis 1/31/65 Louisa, age 23, light hair, blue eyes, fair skin, 5-8, house 443, s 1,2,4.
PRINCE, WILLIAM. reg 68, co A, r cpl, enl 4/7/64, 5/21/64, dis 4/16/64, 6/22/64, age 27, blue eyes, light hair, fair skin, 5-9, house 655, s 2,4.
PRINCE, WILSON. reg 68, co A, enl 4/7/64, 5/21/64, dis 4/16/64, 6/22/64, age 40, blue eyes, light hair, fair skin, 5-5, house 651, s 2,4.

PRINCE, ZACHARIAH. reg 68, co F, enl 4/7/64, 5/21/64, dis 4/16/64, 6/22/64, age 39, brown eyes, dark hair & skin, 5-6, house 651, s 2,4.

R

RAMEY, JOHN H. reg 39, co G, enr 12/23/62 Peach Orchard, enl 2/16/63 Peach Orchard, dis 9/15/65 Louisville, age 23, dark hair & skin, black eyes, 5-10, house 584, s 1,2,4.
RAMEY, PERRY. reg 45, co B, enr 8/28/63, enl 10/10/63 Catlettsburg, dis 12/24/64, Catlettsburg, age 19, house 584, s 1,2.
RAMEY, SAMUEL. reg 68, co B, enl 4/7/64, 5/21/64, dis 4/16/64, 6/22/64, age 32, black eyes & hair, fair skin, 5-4, house 585, s 2,4.
RAMEY, WILLIAM. reg 14, co B, enr 10/10/61 Louisa, enl 12/10/61 Louisa, dis 1/31/65 Louisa, age 19, black hair & eyes, dark skin, 5-6, house 584, s 1,2,4.
RAMSEY, ANDREW. reg 14, co H, enr 10/25/61 Catlettsburg, enl 12/10/61 Louisa, dis 1/31/65 Louisa, age 44, light hair, blue eyes, fair skin, 5-7, rem absent one-half month in 1864 digging coal, house 188, s 1,2,4.
RAMSEY, THOMAS. reg 5VA, co I, enr 9/14/61 Ceredo, enl 9/14/61, dis 5/6/62, age 32, dark hair & skin, black eyes, 5-5, rem accidental gunshot wound to tibia, house 766, s 1,20.
RATCLIFF, ISAAC. reg 68, co I, enl 5/21/64, dis 6/22/64, age 23, dark eyes, hair & skin, 5-8, house 129, s 2,4.
RATCLIFF, ROBERT. reg 14, co B, enr 10/10/61 Catlettsburg, enl 12/10/61 Louisa, dis 9/15/65 Louisville, age 21, light hair, blue eyes, fair skin, 5-9, rem trans to 14th Vet Inf, 3/15/64, house 306, s 1,2,4.
REED, EDMUND G. reg 14, co B, enr 10/10/61 Louisa, enl 12/10/61 Louisa, dis 1/31/65 Louisa, age 18, light hair, dark eyes, fair skin, 5-9, house 402, s 1,2,4.
REEVES, JOHN W. reg 14, co D, enr 10/20/61 Louisa, enl 12/10/61, age 19, light hair, blue eyes, fair skin, 5-5, rem d 7/24/62 Barbourville of typhoid fever, residence stated on muster roll, house n/c, s 1,2,4.
REYNOLDS, STEPHEN. reg 39, co K, enr 5/26/64, enl 8/30/64 Louisa, dis 9/15/65 Louisville, age 25, light hair, blue eyes, fair skin, 5-10, residence shown on CSR, house n/c, s 2,4.
RICE, DAVID K. reg 5VA, co E, I, K, enr 9/1/61 Ceredo, dis 10/3/64 Wheeling WV, house 331, s 1,20.
RICE, ELIJAH. reg 68, co D, r sgt, enl 4/7/64, 5/21/64, dis 4/16/64, 6/22/64, age 35, black eyes & hair, dark skin, 5-11, house 95, s 2,4.
RICE, JAKE. reg 68, F&S, enl 4/7/64, dis 4/16/64, co I, enl 5/21/64, dis 6/22/64, age 38, black eyes, dark hair & skin, 5-9, house 1237, s 2,4.
RICE, JAMES H. reg 14, co B, r cpl, enr 10/10/61 Louisa, enl 12/10/61 Louisa, dis 1/31/65 Louisa, age 23, black hair, blue eyes, dark skin, 5-9, rem cap Lawrence Co. 2/15/63, paroled in Eastern KY., wounded in action 6/2/64, house 369 or 609, s 1,2,4.
RICE, JAMES K. reg 68, co I, enl 4/7/64, 5/21/64, dis 4/16/64, 6/22/64, age 30, dark eyes, hair & skin, 5-8, house 337, s 2,4.
RICE, JOHN M. reg 68, F&S, Quartermaster sgt, enl 4/7/64, 5/21/64, dis 4/16/64, 6/22/64, residence shown on militia list, house n/c, may have been Pike Co. resident, s 2,4,18.
RICE, NELSON T. reg 14, co B, r cpl, enr 7/7/63 Louisa, enl 8/10/63 Louisa, dis 9/15/65 Louisville, age 17, dark hair, blue eyes, fair skin, 5-5, rem trans to 14th Vet Inf, co B, enr 7/7/63, m/in 8/10/63 Louisa, app cpl 2/1/65, house 606, s 1,2,4.
RICE, ROBERT. reg 14, co B, enr 10/10/61 Louisa, enl 12/10/61 Louisa, dis 4/12/63 Louisa, age 29, black hair & eyes, dark skin, 5-8, rem dis for disability of dropsy, residence stated on muster roll, house n/c, s 1,2,4.

RICE, WILLIAM. reg 14, co B, enr 10/10/61 Louisa, enl 12/10/61 Louisa, age 24, dark hair & skin, blue eyes, 5-6, rem cap Lawrence Co. 2/15/63, paroled in eastern KY, d 9/22/64 Knoxville TN of wounds received 6/22/64 near Marietta GA, house 640, s 1,2,4.

RICHARDSON, SAMPSON. reg 14, co B, enr 10/10/61 Louisa, age 20, rem des 11/12/61 Paintsville, residence stated on muster roll, house n/c, s 1,4.

RIFE, JOHN P. JR. reg 68, co D, r cpl, enl 4/7/64, 5/21/64, dis 4/16/64, 6/22/64, age 30, black eyes & hair, dark skin, 6-0, house 78, s 2,4.

RIFE, WILLIAM. reg 68, co D, enl 4/7/64, 5/21/64, dis 4/16/64, 6/22/64, age 23, blue eyes, light hair, fair skin, 5-10, house 76, s 2,4.

RIGGSBY, HENRY. reg 68, co B, enl 5/21/64, dis 6/22/64, age 32, black eyes & hair, fair skin, 6-0, house 602, s 2,4.

RIGGSBY, WELBURN. reg 68, co B, enl 5/21/64, dis 6/22/64, age 25, black eyes & hair, fair skin, 6-0, house 600, s 2,4.

RIGGSBY, WILLIS. reg 68, co B, enl 5/21/64, dis 6/22/64, age 36, black eyes & hair, fair skin, 6-0, house 599, s 2,4.

ROBERTS, ALEN T. reg 68, co G, enl 4/7/64, dis 4/16/64, co F, r 3d lt., enl 5/21/64, age 35, dark hair & skin, black eyes, 5-11, house 139, s 4.

ROBERTS, GARNES R. reg 68, co I, r 1st sgt, enl 4/7/64, 5/21/64, dis 4/16/64, 6/22/64, age 25, blue eyes, light hair, fair skin, 5-10, residence stated on muster roll, house n/c, s 2,4,18.

ROBERTS, GEORGE H. reg 14, co G, r 2nd lt, enr 11/19/61 Louisa, enl 12/10/61 Louisa, dis 1/31/65 Louisa, age 27, black hair, blue eyes, fair skin, 5-11, rem prom from sgt to 2nd lt 8/2/62, residence stated on muster roll, house n/c, s 1,2,4.

ROBINSON, HUSTON B. reg 68, co E, enl 5/21/64, dis 6/22/64, age 35, light eyes, hair & skin, 5-10, house 709, s 2,4.

ROBINSON, JAMES W. reg 14, co H, enr 10/25/61 Catlettsburg, enl 12/10/61 Louisa, dis 1/31/65 Louisa, age 45, light hair, blue eyes, fair skin, 5-10, residence stated on muster roll, house n/c, s 1,2,4.

ROMAN, ISAAC. reg 40, co E, enr 9/21/63, enl 9/28/63 Grayson, dis 12/30/64 Catlettsburg, age 18, residence stated on muster roll, house n/c, s 1,2,4.

ROSE, EDWARD. reg 14, co H, enr 10/25/61 Catlettsburg, enl 12/10/61 Louisa, age 24, dark hair & skin, gray eyes, 5-5, rem d 2/9/63 Danville of typhoid fever, house 306, s 1,2,4.

ROSE, GEORGE. reg 39, co G, enr 11/30/62, age 18, rem KIA 12/4/62, residence stated on muster roll, house n/c, s 2,4.

ROSE, JAMES M. reg 14, co B, enr 10/10/61 Louisa, enl 12/10/61 Louisa, age 18, dark hair, blue eyes, light skin, 5-7, rem cap 6/7/64, paroled 5/4/65 in Georgia, house 647, s 1,2,4.

ROSE, JAMES W. reg 14, co B, enr 10/10/61 Louisa, enl 12/10/61 Louisa, age 45, gray hair, blue eyes, fair skin, 5-11, rem d 1/18/62 Paintsville of wounds rec 1/10/62 Battle of Middle Creek, house 647, s 1,2,4.

ROSE, JOHN J. reg 14, co B, enr 10/10/61 Louisa, enl 12/10/61 Louisa, dis 1/31/65 Louisa, age 27, black hair, dark eyes & skin, 6-4, house 648, s 1,2,4.

ROSE, SAMUEL. reg 68, co G, enl 5/21/64, dis 6/22/64, age 35, blue eyes, light hair, fair skin, 6-0, house 647, s 2,4.

ROSE, THOMAS W. reg 39, co K, enl 11/18/62 Lawrence Co., enl 2/16/63 Peach Orchard, dis 9/15/65 Louisville, age 18, dark hair, blue eyes, fair skin, 5-2, residence stated on muster roll, house n/c, s 1,2,4.

ROSE, WILLIAM. reg 40, co E, enr 10/25/63 Grayson, enl 3/10/64 Paris, dis 12/30/64 Catlettsburg, age 20, light hair, blue eyes, fair skin, 5-8, house 416, s 1,2,4.

ROSS, DAVID. reg 14, co B, enr 4/30/63 Louisa, enl 6/10/63 Louisa, dis 9/15/65 Louisville, age 18, dark hair, blue eyes, fair skin, 6-0, rem trans to 14th Vet Inf, co B, house 380 or 481, s 1,2,4.

ROWE, JOHN. reg 68, co C, enl 4/7/64, 5/21/64, dis 4/16/64, 6/22/64, age 25, blue eyes, dark hair, fair skin, 5-10, house 971, s 2,4.
ROWE, WILLIAM. reg 68, co C, enl 4/7/64, 5/21/64, dis 4/16/64, 6/22/64, age 22, blue eyes, dark hair, fair skin, 5-6, house 971, s 2,4.
RUSSELL, ROBERT. reg 68, co C, enl 5/21/64, dis 6/22/64, age 37, dark eyes & hair, fair skin, 5-9, house 186, s 2,4.
RUSSELL, THOMAS. reg 45, co F, r capt, enr 8/21/63 Catlettsburg, enl 11/2/63 Ashland, dis 12/24/64 Catlettsburg, age 37, dark hair, light eyes & skin, 5-7, house 862, s 1,2,6.

S

SALYERS, THOMAS. reg 68, co A, enl 5/21/64, dis 6/22/64, age 32, blue eyes, dark hair & skin, 5-9, house 496 or 821, s 2,4.
SALYERS, ZACHARIAH. reg 68, co E, r sgt, enl 4/7/64, 5/21/64, dis 4/16/64, 6/22/64, age 32, light eyes & skin, dark hair, 5-9, house 802, s 2,4.
SAMMONS, FLOURY. reg 167WV, co Ira Copley, enl 8/62 to 2/64, dis 5/2/64, reg 14, co H, enr 7/2/63, enl 8/29/63 Louisa, dis 9/15/65 Louisville, age 19, rem trans to 14th Vet Inf, co C, house 923, s 1,2,9,23.
SAMMONS, JAMES M. reg 167WV, co Ira Copley, enl 8/62 to 2/64, dis 5/2/64, reg 68, co H, enl 5/21/64, dis 6/22/64, age 23, dark eyes, hair & skin, 6-0, house 1163 or 1168, s 2,4,23.
SAMMONS, JEREMIAH. reg 167WV, co Ira Copley, enl 8/62 to 2/64, dis 5/2/64, house 1168, s 23.
SAMMONS, JOEL. reg 167WV, co Ira Copley, enl 8/62 to 2/64, dis 5/2/64, reg 68, co H, enl 5/21/64, dis 6/22/64, age 21, dark eyes, hair & skin, 5-6, house 1168, s 2,4,23.
SAMMONS, OLIVER. reg 167WV, co Ira Copley, enl 8/62 to 2/64, dis 5/2/64, house 1163, s 23.
SAMMONS, ROLAND. reg 167WV, co Ira Copley, enl 8/62 to 2/64, dis 5/2/64, house 1168, s 23.
SAMMONS, THOMAS. reg 167WV, co Ira Copley, enl 8/62 to 2/64, dis 5/2/64, reg 68, co H, enl 5/21/64, dis 6/22/64, age 40, dark eyes, hair & skin, 5-5, house 1163, s 2,4, 23.
SAMMONS, WILLIAM. reg 167WV, co Ira Copley, enl 8/62 to 2/64, dis 5/2/64, house 1168, s 23.
SANDERS, ALLEN. reg 14, co B, enr 10/10/61 Louisa, enl 12/10/61 Louisa, dis 1/31/65 Louisa, age 25, light hair, blue eyes, fair skin, 5-11, house 548, s 1,2,4.
SANDERS, NATHANIEL P. reg 14, co B, r sgt, enr 10/10/61 Louisa, enl 12/10/61 Louisa, dis 1/31/65 Louisa, age 33, light hair, blue eyes, fair skin, 5-8, rem app sgt 8/28/63, house 548, s 1,2,4.
SANDERS, PETER. reg 68, co B, r sgt, enl 4/7/64, 5/21/64, dis 4/16/64, 6/22/64, age 24, blue eyes, light hair, fair skin, 5-6, house 548, s 2,4.
SEE, GARRED. reg 68, co C, enl 5/12/64, dis 6/22/64, age 27, blue eyes, fair hair & skin, 5-11, residence stated on militia list, house n/c, s 2,4,18.
SEE, WILLIAM. reg 68, co C, enl 5/21/64, dis 6/22/64, age 33, dark eyes & hair, fair skin, 5-8, house 945, s 2,4.
SEGRAVES, WILLIAM. reg 68, co B, enl 5/21/64, dis 6/22/64, age 30, blue eyes, light hair, fair skin, 6-0, house 590, s 2,4.
SERGENT, DAVID F. reg 1WVCav, co G, enl 8/14/61 Ceredo, m/in 9/14/61 Ceredo, age 30 or 31, light skin, brown hair, gray eyes, 5-6, rem residence established by evidence in criminal case, cap Warrenton, VA 8/30/63 & paroled, des 10/18/64, house n/c, s 2, 25.
SHANNON, ANDREW L. reg 5VA, co I, enr 9/14/61 Ceredo, dis 10/4/64 Wheeling WV, age 21, house 706, s 1,9,20.
SHANNON, CORNELIUS. reg 1WVCav, co G, r sgt, enl 9/61, dis 12/64, rem struck by a ball which caused his death, house 707, s 5.

SHANNON, GEORGE. reg 14, co K, enr 11/8/61 Louisa, enl 12/10/61 Louisa, dis 1/31/65 Louisa, age 38, sandy hair, gray eyes, fair skin, 5-6, house 716, s 1,2,4.

SHANNON, JAMES W. reg 14, co K, r 2nd lt, enr 11/8/61 Louisa, enl 12/10/61 Louisa, dis 9/15/65 Louisville, age 19, rem prom from 1st sgt to 2nd lt 9/9/64, trans to 14th Vet Inf, co C, enr 11/8/64, m/in 11/9/64 Johnsonville TN, house 728, s 1,2,4.

SHANNON, JOHN L. reg 45, co E, enr 10/22/63 Ashland, enl 11/6/63 Ashland, dis 12/24/64 Catlettsburg, age 28, house 716, s 1,2.

SHEPARD, ALFRED. reg 68, co D, enl 4/7/64, 5/21/64, dis 4/16/64, 6/22/64, reg CG, co L, enr 6/1/64, enl 7/9/64 Frankfort, dis 3/11/65 Catlettsburg, age 44, yellow hair, blue eyes, fair skin, 5-11, house 59, s 2,4.

SHORT, AARON. reg 14, co G, enr 11/19/61 Louisa, enl 12/10/61 Louisa, dis 1/31/65 Louisa, age 45, dark hair, blue eyes, fair skin, 5-10, rem slightly wounded 6/27/64, house 238, s 1,2,4.

SHORT, GARRED. reg 68, co I, enl 4/7/64, 5/21/64, dis 4/16/64, 6/22/64, age 28, blue eyes, dark hair, fair skin, 5-8, house 1194, s 2,4.

SHORT, JAMES. reg 68, co I, enl 5/21/64, dis 6/22/64, age 27, blue eyes, dark hair, fair skin, 5-8, house 941, s 2,4.

SHORT, JAMES. reg 68, co I, enl 5/21/64, dis 6/22/64, house 239, s 2,4.

SHORT, JAMES. reg 14, co D, G, enr 11/19/61 Louisa, enl 12/10/61 Louisa, dis 1/31/65 Louisa, age 38, dark hair, blue eyes, fair skin, 5-7, rem trans to co D 8/30/63, back to original co 1/20/65, house 942, s 1,2,4.

SHORT, JOHN A. reg 68, co G, enl 4/7/64, 5/21/64, dis 4/16/64, 6/22/64, age 35, black eyes & hair, dark skin, 6-0, house 241, s 2,4.

SHORT, SAMUEL. reg 68, co I, enl 5/21/64, dis 6/22/64, age 22, blue eyes, dark hair, fair skin, 5-8, house 941, s 2,4.

SHORTRIDGE, GEORGE W. reg 68, co D, r sgt, enl 5/21/64, dis 6/22/64, age 30, blue eyes, dark hair, fair skin, 6-0, residence shown on militia list, house n/c, s 2,4,18.

SIMPSON, GEORGE. reg 68, co I, enl 4/7/64, 5/21/64, dis 4/16/64, 6/22/64, age 35, dark eyes, hair & skin, 5-10, house 1197, s 2,4.

SKAGGS, DANIEL. reg 68, co B, enl 5/21/64, age 18, light hair, blue eyes, fair skin, 5-8, house 401, s 4.

SKAGGS, GEORGE W. reg 14, co B, enr 4/4/63 Louisa, enl 6/10/63 Louisa, age 18, light hair, blue eyes, fair skin, 5-5, rem d 8/25/64 Chattanooga TN of chronic diarrhea, residence stated on muster roll, house n/c, s 1,2,4.

SKAGGS, HARVEY. reg 68, co B, enl 4/7/64, 5/21/64, dis 4/16/64, 6/22/64, age 22, black eyes, dark hair, fair skin, 5-8, house 631, s 2,4.

SKAGGS, JAMES. reg 68, co B, enl 5/21/64, dis 6/22/64, age 35, blue eyes, light hair, fair skin, 6-4, house 414 or 434, s 2,4.

SKAGGS, JOHN. reg 68, co B, enl 4/7/64, 5/21/64, dis 4/16/64, 6/22/64, age 24, black eyes & hair, dark skin, 5-8, house 431 or 438, s 2,4.

SKAGGS, LEWIS. reg 68, co B, enl 5/21/64, age 21, light hair, blue eyes, fair skin, 6-0, house 401, s 4.

SKAGGS, MARTIN. reg 68, co B, enl 5/21/64, dis 6/22/64, age 32, black eyes & hair, dark skin, 6-0, house 430, s 2,4.

SKAGGS, MARTIN C. reg 68, co B, enl 4/7/64, 5/21/64, dis 4/16/64, 6/22/64, age 30, blue eyes, light hair, fair skin, 6-0, house 432, s 2,4.

SKAGGS, MILES. reg 68, co B, enl 5/21/64, dis 6/22/64, age 22, black eyes & hair, dark skin, 5-8, house 440, s 2,4.

SKAGGS, PETER. reg 40, co C, enr 12/1/63 Grayson, enl 4/13/64 Lexington, dis 12/30/64 Catlettsburg, age 20, dark hair & eyes, fair skin, 5-9, house 441, s 1,2,4.

SKAGGS, PETER. reg 68, co B, enl 5/21/64, dis 6/22/64, age 28, black eyes & hair, dark skin, 6-0, house 1184, s 2,4.

SKAGGS, RANDOLPH. reg 68, co B, enl 5/21/64, dis 6/22/64, age 24, blue eyes, light hair, fair skin, 5-9, house 401, s 2,4.

SKEENS, JAMES. reg 68, co I, enl 5/21/64, dis 6/22/64, age 30, blue eyes, light hair, fair skin, 6-0, house 992, s 2,4.

SKEENS, JOHN. reg 68, co I, enl 5/21/64, dis 6/22/64, age 23, blue eyes, light hair, fair skin, 6-0, house 940, s 2,4.

SKEENS, PETER. reg 68, co I, enl 5/21/64, dis 6/22/64, age 21, blue eyes, light hair, fair skin, 5-10, house 940, s 2,4.

SKEENS, WILLIAM J. reg 68, co I, enl 5/21/64, age 22, light hair, blue eyes, fair skin, 5-10, house 104, s 4.

SMALL, LEONIDAS. reg 14, co K, enr 11/8/61 Louisa, enl 12/10/61 Louisa, dis 1/31/65, age 18, rem musician red to ranks 3/9/62, house 1229, s 1,2,4.

SMITH, EDMUND. reg 68, co I, enl 5/21/64, dis 6/22/64, age 35, blue eyes, light hair, fair skin, 5-10, house 940, s 2,4.

SMITH, HENRY. reg 68, co I, enl 5/21/64, dis 6/22/64, age 35, blue eyes, light hair, fair skin, 6-0, house 969, s 2,4.

SMITH, JOHN. reg 45, co F, enr 10/15/63 Ashland, enl 11/2/63 Ashland, dis 12/24/64 Catlettsburg, age 44, dark hair, light eyes & skin, 5-6, residence shown on CSR, house n/c, s 1,2,6.

SMITH, JOHN W. reg 14, co H, enr & enl 9/17/62 Louisa, age 34, light hair, blue eyes, fair skin, 5-6, rem trans to 14th Vet Inf, co C, enr 9/17/62, m/in 9/17/62 Louisa, dis 2/21/65 for disability granulated eye lids, residence stated on muster roll, house n/c, s 1,2,4.

SMITH, SAMUEL. reg 45, co K, r cpl, enr 9/22/63 Catlettsburg, enl 12/9/63 Louisa, dis 2/14/05 Catlettsburg, age 33, rem prom to cpl 1/1/64, house 84, s 1,2.

SMITH, THOMAS. reg 39, co A, enr 9/20/62 Peach Orchard, enl 2/16/63 Peach Orchard, dis 9/15/65 Louisville, age 44, black hair & eyes, fair skin, 5-10, house 799, s 1,2,4.

SNOW, DANIEL. reg 10Cav, co F, enr 8/9/62 Boyd Co., enl 9/7/62 Covington, dis 9/17/63 Maysville, age 23, d 1/31/63 or 2/1/63 Danville of typhoid fever, residence stated on muster roll, residence stated on muster roll, house n/c, s 1,2,4.

SNOW, JOHN. reg 14, co C, enr 10/10/61 Louisa, enl 12/10/61 Louisa, dis 9/15/65 Louisville, age 27, light hair, gray eyes, fair skin, 5-2, rem trans to 14th Vet Inf, co A, enr 2/29/64, m/in 3/19/64, house 198, s 1,2,4.

SOWARD, THOMAS H. reg 2KyCav, co L, r 2nd lt, age 20 or 24, enr 5/1/62, m/in 10/1/62 Louisville, rem prom to 1st lt, co B, enr 5/4/64, m/in 5/25/64 Nashville, TN, trans to 2nd Ky Vet Cav, co B, enr 4/1/64 m/in 4/1/64 Louisa, m/out 7/17/65, commissioned by Governor of Kentucky 11/5/61, residence established by List of Officers, house n/c, s 1,2.

SPARKS, DAVID L. reg 14, co B, r cpl, enr 10/10/61 Louisa, enl 12/10/61 Louisa, dis 1/31/65 Louisa, age 18, light hair, blue eyes, fair skin, 6-1, rem prom to cpl 4/15/63, wounded in left shoulder between 7/2/64 & 8/13/64, house 392, s 1,2,4.

SPARKS, HENRY. reg 68, co B, r sgt, enl 4/7/64, 5/21/64, dis 4/16/64, 6/22/64, age 28, black eyes, dark hair & skin, 5-6, house 583, s 2,4.

SPARKS, LEVI J. reg 14, co B, enr 3/4/63 Louisa, enl 6/10/63 Louisa, dis 9/15/65 Louisville, age 32, light hair, blue eyes, fair skin, 6-1, rem recruit to 14th Vet Inf, app hospital steward, enr 3/4/63, m/in 6/10/63 Louisa, house 394, s 1,2,4.

SPARKS, NELSON T. reg 68, co A, enl 4/7/64, dis 4/16/64, age 21, blue eyes, dark hair & skin, 5-9, house 395, s 4.

SPARKS, PETER. reg 14, co G, enr 4/14/63 Louisa, enl 6/10/63 Louisa, dis 9/15/65 Louisville, age 24, light hair, blue eyes, fair skin, 6-0, rem trans to 14th Vet Inf, co D, enr 4/14/63, m/in 6/10/63 Louisa, house 266, s 1,2,4.

SPARKS, REUBEN. reg 39, co A, enr 9/15/62 Peach Orchard, enl 2/16/63 Peach Orchard, age 27 or 37, black hair & eyes, dark skin, 5-11, d 5/4/63 Louisa typhoid fever, house 473, s 1,2,4,8.

SPARKS, REUBEN C. reg 68, co A, enl 5/21/64, dis 6/22/64, age 27, blue eyes, light hair, fair skin, 5-6, residence shown on militia list, house n/c, s 2,4,18,

SPARKS, REUBEN R. reg 68, co A, enl 4/7/64, 5/21/64, dis 4/16/64, 6/22/64, age 38, blue eyes, dark hair & skin, 5-6, house 393, s 2,4.

SPARKS, SAMUEL. reg 68, co B, r capt, enl 4/7/64, 5/21/64, dis 4/7/64, 6/22/64, age 39, black eyes, light hair, fair skin, 6-0, house 366, s 2,4.

SPARKS, THOMAS. reg 68, co K, enl 4/7/64, 5/21/64, dis 4/16/64, 6/22/64, age 28, blue eyes, light hair, fair skin, 5-10, house 1042, s 2,4.

SPARKS, WALTER O. reg 14, co B, r sgt, enr 10/10/61 Louisa, enl 12/10/61 Louisa, dis 4/12/63 Louisa, age 21, light hair, blue eyes, fair skin, 6-2, rem app cpl 10/10/61, prom to sgt 2/5/62, dis for disability of pneumonia, house 392, s 1,2,4.

SPARKS, WASHINGTON. reg 68, co A, enl 5/21/64, dis 6/22/64, age 21, blue eyes, black hair, fair skin, 5-9, house 458, s 2,4.

SPAULDING, JOHN. reg 68, co K, enl 4/7/64, 5/21/64, dis 4/16/64, 6/22/64, age 30, blue eyes, light hair, fair skin, 5-6, house 1027, s 2,4.

SPENCE, GEORGE W. reg 39, co E, enr 12/10/62 Peach Orchard, enl 6/11/63 Louisa, age 20, dark hair, blue eyes, fair skin, 5-10, rem cap 12/18/64 Bristol Co. VA, d 3/6/65 Annapolis MD, a paroled prisoner, house 865, s 1,2,4,8.

SPENCE, HENRY. reg 14, co C, enr 10/25/61 Catlettsburg, enl 12/10/61 Louisa, age 37, light hair, blue eyes, fair skin, 5-11, rem d 5/29/63 Lawrence Co. of disease, house 5, s 1,2,4.

SPENCE, JOHN. reg 68, co H, enl 4/7/64, 5/21/64, dis 4/16/64, 6/22/64, age 34, dark eyes, hair & skin, 5-10, house 866, s 2,4.

SPENCE, JOHNSTON. reg 68, co H, enl 5/24/64, age 31, light hair, eyes & skin, 5-8, house 865, s 4.

SPENCE, MANUEL. reg 68, co H, r cpl, enl 4/7/64, 5/21/64, dis 4/16/64, 6/22/64, age 35, blue eyes, dark hair & skin, 6-1, residence shown on militia list, house n/c, s 2,4.

SPENCER, ANDREW J. reg 39, co I, enr 3/3/65 Louisa, enl 4/15/65 Greenupsburg, dis 9/15/65 Louisville, age 18, light hair, blue eyes, fair skin, 5-10, house 1057, s 1,2,4.

SPENCER, CHARLES. reg 68, co K, enl 4/7/64, 5/21/64, dis 4/16/64, 6/22/64, age 30, blue eyes, light hair, fair skin, 6-0, house 742, s 2,4.

SPENCER, JAMES. reg 5VA, co I, r cpl, enr 9/14/61 Ceredo, enl 9/14/61, dis 10/4/64 Wheeling WV, age 35, house 744, s 1,20.

SPENCER, JOHN. reg 68, co G, enl 4/7/64, 5/21/64, dis 4/16/64, 6/22/64, age 35, blue eyes, light hair, fair skin, 5-10, house 283, s 2,4.

SPENCER, JOHN B. reg 68, co K, r 2nd lt, enl 4/7/64, 5/21/64, dis 4/16/64, 6/22/64, age 25, black eyes & hair, fair skin, 6-0, house 1051, s 2,4.

SPENCER, JOHN H. reg 39, co G, r cpl, enr 9/26/62 Peach Orchard, enl 2/16/63 Peach Orchard, dis 9/15/65 Louisville, age 18, light hair, blue eyes, dark skin, 5-6, house 1058, s 1,2,4.

SPENCER, LEWIS B. reg 68, co K, enl 5/21/64, dis 6/22/64, age 25, blue eyes, light hair, fair skin, 5-8, house 1032, s 2,4.

SPENCER, LEWIS W. reg 14, co D, r 1st sgt, enr 10/20/61 Louisa, enl 12/10/61 Louisa, dis 1/31/65 Louisa, age 18, light hair, blue eyes, fair skin, 5-9, rem prom from pvt to sgt 3/1/62, to 1st sgt 10/18/64, house 1052, s 1,2,4.

SPENCER, THOMAS. reg 14, co D, enr 10/20/61 Louisa, enl 12/10/61 Louisa, dis 1/31/65 Louisa, age 39, dark hair & eyes, light skin, 5-6, house 1058, s 1,2,4.

SPERRY, JOSEPH. reg 14, co F, enr 11/19/61 Louisa, enl 12/10/61 Louisa, age 24, light hair, brown eyes, dark skin, 5-11, rem d 2/14/62 Lawrence Co. of typhoid fever, house 68, s 1,2,4.

SPERRY, MILTON. reg 14, co F, enr 11/19/61 Louisa, enl 12/10/61 Louisa, age 20, light hair, blue eyes, fair skin 5-0, rem d 2/21/62 Lawrence Co. typhoid fever or d 2/12/62 or 2/14/62 Camp Buell, Paintsville, residence stated on muster roll, house n/c, s 1,2,4.

SPERRY, THOMAS R. reg 14, co F, r cpl, enr 9/3/63 Louisa, enl 10/31/63 Louisa, dis 9/15/65 Louisville, age 18, light hair, blue eyes, fair skin, 5-8, rem trans to 14th Vet Inf, co D, enr 9/3/63, m/in 10/31/63 Louisville, app cpl 2/1/65, house 99, 1,2,4.

SPRADLIN, THOMAS. reg 5VA, co I, enr 9/14/61 Ceredo, enl 10/1/61, dis 10/4/64 Wheeling WV, age 23, light hair & skin, blue eyes, 5-7, rem KIA 7/24/64 Winchester VA, house 781, s 1,20.

SPRIGGS, FRANCIS. reg 5VA, co I, enr 10/1/61 Ceredo, enl 10/1/61, age 24, light hair & skin, blue eyes, 5-7, rem wounded 9/19/64 Winchester VA, d of wounds 11/8/64, house 788, s 1,20.

SPROUSE, BERRY. reg 14, co H, age 28, rem des 12/1/62, residence stated on muster roll, house n/c, s 4.

STAFFORD, JOHN. reg 68, co C, enl 4/7/64, 5/21/64, dis 4/16/64, 6/22/64, age 44, blue eyes, fair hair & skin, 5-10, house 185, s 2,4.

STEEL, JOHN P. reg 14, co C, enr 10/25/61 Catlettsburg, enl 12/10/61 Louisa, dis 1/31/65 Louisa, age 19, light hair, blue eyes, fair skin, 5-7, house 13, s 1,2,4.

STEPHENS, ISAAC. reg 68, co A, enl 5/21/64, dis 6/22/64, age 30, blue eyes, black hair, dark skin, 5-4, house 476, s 2,4.

STEPHENS, WILLIAM. reg 40, co K, enr 8/18/63, enl 9/29/63 Grayson, dis 12/30/64 Catlettsburg, age 18, house 482, s 1,2,4.

STEPHENSON, CALVIN. reg 68, co K, enl 5/21/64, dis 6/22/64, age 28, blue eyes, light hair, fair skin, 5-8, house 1078, s 2,4.

STEVENS, DANIEL. reg 68, co A, enl 5/21/64, dis 6/22/64, age 28, black eyes & hair, dark skin, 5-8, residence shown on militia list, house n/c, s 2,4,18.

STEWART, ALVIN. reg 14, co C, enr 10/10/61 Louisa, enl 12/10/61 Louisa, dis 1/31/65 Louisa, age 34, light hair, blue eyes, dark skin, 5-7, house 16, s 1,2,4.

STEWART, DAVID. reg 68, co D, enr 5/21/64, dis 6/22/64, age 30, blue eyes, light hair, fair skin, 6-0, house 17, s 2,4.

STEWART, GEORGE S. reg 68, co I, enl 5/21/64, age 44, dark hair, blue eyes, fair skin, 5-8, house 302, s 4.

STEWART, ISAAC. reg 68, co D, enl 4/7/64, 5/21/64, dis 4/16/64, 6/22/64, reg CG, co L, r cpl, enr 6/9/64, enl 7/6/64 Frankfort, dis 3/11/65 Catlettsburg, age 18, dark hair & skin, black eyes, 5-8, house 58, s 2,4.

STEWART, JAMES H. reg 68, co I, enl 4/7/64, 5/21/64, dis 4/16/64, 6/22/64, age 19, blue eyes, light hair, fair skin, 5-8, house 302, s 2,4.

STEWART, JOHN F. reg 39, r adjutant, enr 2/21/63 Peach Orchard, rem prom from 2nd lt, co B, to adjutant 1/21/63, res 2/26/65 for disability, chronic rheumatism, house 1218, s 1,2,4.

STEWART, MITCHELL. reg 5VA, co G, enr 9/2/61 Ceredo, enl 9/5/61, dis 10/13/64, age 23, rem cap Bull Run VA 9/1/62, paroled Centerville VA 9/30/62, house 29, s 1,20.

STEWART, RALPH. reg 14, co C, enr 10/25/61 Louisa, enl 12/10/61 Louisa, dis 1/31/65 Louisa, age 23, light hair, blue eyes, fair skin, 5-5, house 35, s 1,2,4.

STEWART, ROBERT. reg 68, co D, enl 4/7/64, 5/21/64, dis 4/16/64, 6/22/64, age 35, black eyes & hair, dark skin, 5-10, residence shown on militia list, house n/c, s 2,4,18.

STEWART, WILLIAM. reg 68, co D, enl 4/7/64, 5/21/64, dis 4/16/64, 6/22/64, age 23, blue eyes, light hair, fair skin, 5-10, house 64, s 2,4.

STEWART, WILLIAM. reg 39, co I, enr 1/4/63 Peach Orchard, enl 2/16/63 Peach Orchard, dis 9/15/65 Louisville, age 19, dark hair & skin, blue eyes, 5-3, house, 58, s 1,2,4.

STONE, WILLIAM. reg 10Cav, co F, enr 8/10/62, enl 9/13/63 Maysville, dis 9/17/63 Maysville, age 22, residence stated on muster roll, house n/c, s 1, 2, 4.

STRATTEN, BURILL. reg 68, co C, enl 5/21/64, dis 6/22/64, age 31, blue eyes, fair hair & skin, 5-9, house 191, s 2,4.

STROUD, HARRISON (HARMON). reg 68, co C, enl 4/7/64, 5/21/64, dis 4/16/64, 6/22/64, age 37, blue eyes, fair hair & skin, 5-8, residence shown on militia list, house n/c, s 2,4,18.

STUBBINS, BENJAMIN A. reg 14, r asst. surgeon, enr & enl 8/12/63 Louisville, dis 1/9/65 or 9/15/65 Louisa or Louisville, age 27, rem residence established by List of Officers, house n/c, s 1,2.

STURGEON, DAVID. reg 68, co A, r cpl, enl 4/7/64, 5/12/64, dis 4/16/64, 6/22/64, age 27, blue eyes, light hair, fair skin, 5-7, house 381, s 2,4.

SWAN, LEWIS R. reg 14, co B, enr 10/10/61 Catlettsburg, enl 12/10/61 Louisa, dis 1/31/65 Louisa, age 19, light hair, dark eyes, fair skin, 5-9, rem cap Lawrence Co., paroled in Eastern Kentucky, residence stated on muster roll, house n/c, s 1,2,4.

SWETNAM, MILTON. reg 68, co A, r 2nd lt, enl 4/7/64, 5/21/64, dis 4/16/64, 6/22/64, age 22, blue eyes, light hair, fair skin, 5-7, house 557, s 2,4.

SWORD, WILLIAM J. reg 39, co D, enr 10/22/62 Pike Co., enl 2/16/63 Peach Orchard, dis 9/15/65 Louisville, age 34, dark hair, skin & eyes, 5-11, residence stated on muster roll, house n/c, s 1,2,4.

T

TAYLOR, WILLIAM. reg 68, co D, enl 4/7/64, 5/12/64, dis 4/16/64, 6/22/64, age 35, black eyes, dark hair & skin, 5-11, house 86, s 2,4.

TERRY, BENJAMIN. reg 68, co C, enl 4/7/64, 5/21/64, dis 4/16/64, 6/22/64, age 31, blue eyes, fair hair & skin, 5-11, residence shown on militia lists, house n/c, s 2,4,18.

TERRY, MILES. reg 14, co B, enr 10/10/61 Louisa, enl 12/10/61 Louisa, dis 1/31/65 Louisa, age 18, light hair, blue eyes, fair skin, 5-8, house 437, s 1,2,4.

THOMPSON, ANDREW J. reg 68, co G, enl 4/7/64, 5/21/64, dis 4/16/64, 6/22/64, age 35, blue eyes, light hair, fair skin, 5-10, house 1009, s 2,4.

THOMPSON, ARCHIBALD. reg 68, co K, r cpl, enl 4/7/64, 5/21/64, dis 4/16/64, 6/22/64, age 22, black eyes & hair, dark skin, 5-8, house 1029, s 2,4.

THOMPSON, FLEMING L. reg 45, co K, enr 9/2/63 Catlettsburg, enl 12/9/63 Louisa, age 28, rem des 2/18/64 Mt. Sterling, house 315, s 1,2.

THOMPSON, GEORGE. reg CG, co L, enr 6/10/64, enl 7/6/64 Frankfort, dis 12/8/64 Frankfort, age 23, dark hair & skin, black eyes, 5-10, house 722, s 2,4.

THOMPSON, G. W. reg 68, co C, enl 4/7/64, 5/21/64, dis 4/16/64, 6/22/64, age 23, black eyes & hair, dark skin, 6-0, house 1019, s 2,4.

THOMPSON, GREEN. reg CG, co L, enr 7/30/64, enl 8/30/64 Frankfort, dis 3/11/65 Catlettsburg, age 18, dark hair, blue eyes, fair skin, 5-6, house 1019, s 2,4.

THOMPSON, ISAAC P. reg 68, co G, enr 4/7/64, 5/21/64, dis 4/16/64, 6/22/64, age 24, black eyes & hair, dark skin, 5-8, house 276, s 2,4.

THOMPSON, JAMES. reg 14, co D, age 27, reg 68, co F, enl 4/7/64, 5/21/64, dis 4/16/64, 6/22/64, residence stated on muster roll, house n/c, s 2,4.

THOMPSON, JAMES. reg 39, co G, enr 11/30/62 Peach Orchard, enl 2/16/63 Peach Orchard, dis 9/15/65 Louisville, age 18, dark hair & skin, black eyes, 5-6, rem cap 12/4/62 Floyd Co., paroled City Point VA 4/3/63, house 1024, s 1,2,4.

THOMPSON, JOHN. reg 68, co G, enl 4/7/64, 5/21/64, dis 4/16/64, 6/22/64, age 25, blue eyes, light hair, fair skin, 6-0, house 522, s 2,4.

THOMPSON, JOHN. reg 45, co K, r 2nd lt, enr 11/20/63 Ashland, enl 12/9/63 Louisa, dis 2/14/65 Catlettsburg, age 36, house 1024, s 1,2.

THOMPSON, JOHN S. reg 14, co D, r 2nd lt, enr 10/20/61 Louisa, enl 12/10/61 Louisa, age 27, dark hair, eyes & skin, 5-10, rem prom form 3rd sgt to 1st sgt 1/11/63, to 2nd lt 3/9/64, resigned 9/18/64 rheumatism, house 272, s 1,2,4.

THOMPSON, MAJOR. reg 68, co C, enl 5/21/64, dis 6/22/64, black eyes, dark hair & skin, 5-11, house 195, s 2,4.

THOMPSON, MARTIN. reg 68, co F, r sgt, enl 4/7/64, 5/21/64, dis 4/16/64, 6/22/64, age 21, brown eyes, dark hair & skin, 5-6, house 1019, s 2,4.

THOMPSON, MARTIN V. reg 14, co D, enr 10/20/61 Louisa, enl 12/10/61 Louisa, dis 9/15/65 Louisville, age 18, red hair, blue eyes, fair skin, 5-11, rem trans to co D, 14th Vet Inf, wounded 5/30/64 in fingers, house 313, s 1,2,4.

THOMPSON, MICHAEL. reg 68, co K, r cpl, enl 4/7/64, 5/21/64, dis 4/16/64, 6/22/64, age 27, black eyes & hair, dark skin, 6-0, house 1031, s 2,4.

THOMPSON, RICHARD. reg 68, co C, enl 4/7/64, 5/21/64, dis 4/16/64, 6/22/64, age 19, dark eyes, fair hair & skin, 5-10, house 722, s 2,4.

THOMPSON, ROBERT L. reg 14, co D, age 24, residence stated on muster roll, house n/c, s 4.

THOMPSON, RUSSELL T. reg 14, co D, r 1st lt, enr 10/20/61 Louisa, enl 12/10/61 Louisa, dis 9/15/65 Louisville, age 24, dark hair, eyes & skin, 6-0, rem prom from 1st sgt to 1st lt 9/9/64, trans to 14th Vet Inf, co C, enr 9/9/64, m/in 1/31/65 Louisa, house 275, s 1,2,4.

THOMPSON, SAMUEL. reg 68, co K, enl 4/7/64, 5/21/64, dis 4/16/64, 6/22/64, age 20, blue eyes, light hair, fair skin, 5-6, house 1029, s 2,4.

THOMPSON, SAMUEL. reg 14, co D, enr 10/20/61 Louisa, enl 12/10/61 Louisa, dis 1/31/65 Louisa, age 38, black hair & eyes, dark skin, 6-0, house 1007, s 1,2,4.

THOMPSON, SAMUEL R. reg 68, co G, enl 5/21/64, dis 6/2/64, age 38, black eyes, dark hair, fair skin, 5-5, house 1006, s 2,4.

THOMPSON, SQUIRE. reg 68, co K, enl 5/21/64, dis 6/22/64, age 30, blue eyes, light hair, fair skin, 5-8, house 1030, s 2,4.

THOMPSON, WALLACE. reg 40, co E, enr 8/25/63 Grayson, enl 9/28/63 Grayson, age 18, black hair & eyes, dark skin, 5-5, rem d 5/10/64 Lexington typhoid fever, residence stated on muster roll, house n/c, s 1,2,4.

THOMPSON, WESELY W. reg 14, co E, enr 10/15/61 Ashland, enl 12/10/61 Louisa, dis 1/31/65 Louisa, age 27, red hair, hazel eyes, fair skin, 5-11, residence stated on muster roll, house n/c, s 1,2,4.

THOMPSON, WILLIAM R. reg 68, co G, enl 4/7/64, 5/21/64, dis 4/16/64, 6/22/64, age 30, blue eyes, light hair, fair skin, 5-10, house 272, 1011 or 1029, s 2,4.

THORNHILL, JAMES. reg 39, co G, enr 1/12/63 Peach Orchard, enl 2/16/63 Peach Orchard, age 39, rem des 6/21/64 Louisa, house 908, s 1,2,4.

TILLER, JOHN. reg 68, co D, enl 5/21/64, dis 6/22/64, age 38, blue eyes, light hair, fair skin, 5-10, house 341, s 2,4.

TRAMMELL, WILLIAM H. reg 14, co C, age 22, residence stated on muster roll, house n/c, s 4.

TRAVIS, GREENVILLE. reg 68, co K, enl 4/7/64, 5/21/64, dis 4/16/64, 6/22/64, age 30, blue eyes, light hair, fair skin, 5-8, residence shown on militia list, house n/c, s 2,4,18.

TRAVIS, JOHN SR. reg 14, co G, enr 11/19/61 Louisa, enl 12/10/61 Louisa, dis 2/9/62 Paintsville, age 45, dark hair & skin, blue eyes, 5-8, rem dis for disability, lung disease, 57 years old, residence stated on muster roll, house n/c, s 1,2,4.

TRAVIS, ROBERT. reg 68, co K, enl 4/7/64, 5/21/64, dis 4/16/64, 6/22/64, age 28, blue eyes, light hair, fair skin, 5-8, residence shown on militia list, house n/c, s 2,4,18.

TROY, WILLIAM. reg 68, co C, enl 5/21/64, dis 6/22/64, age 33, dark eyes & hair, fair skin, 5-11, house 1202, s 2,4.

U

ULLAM, ANDREW J. reg 14, co H, enr 10/25/61 Louisa, enl 12/10/61 Louisa, dis 1/31/65 Louisa, age 28, dark hair, blue eyes, fair skin, 5-7, residence stated on muster roll, house n/c, s 1,2,4.

V

VANHOOSE, JOHN. reg 39, co G, r cpl, enr 1/12/63 Peach Orchard, enl 2/16/63 Peach Orchard, dis 9/15/65 Louisville, age 38, light hair & skin, blue eyes, 6-0, rem prom to cpl 2/1/65, house 1049, s 1,2,4.

VANHOOSE, REUBEN N. reg 39, co G, enr 1/29/63 Peach Orchard, enl 2/16/63 Peach Orchard, dis 9/15/65 Louisville, age 22, dark hair & skin, hazel eyes, 5-10, house 830, s 1,2,4.

VANHOOSE, THOMAS. reg 14, co D, enr 9/15/63 Louisa, enl 10/30/63 Louisa, dis 9/15/65 Louisville, age 18, dark hair & eyes, fair skin, 5-6, rem trans to 14th Vet Inf, co B, enr 9/15/63, m/in 10/30/63 Louisa, house 257, s 1,2,4.

VANHOOSE, VALENTINE. reg 39, co G, enr 10/3/62 Peach Orchard, enl 2/16/63 Peach Orchard, dis 9/15/65 Louisville, age 24, light hair, blue eyes, fair skin, 5-11, house 257, s 1,2,4.

VAUGHAN, HARRIS. reg 68, co E, r cpl, enl 4/7/64, 5/21/64, dis 4/16/64, 6/22/64, age 35, dark eyes & hair, light skin, 5-6, house 108, s 2,4.

VAUGHN, JAMES. reg 5VA, co I, enr 9/14/61 Ceredo, enl 9/14/61, dis 10/4/64 Wheeling WV, age 19, house 789, s 1,20.

VINSON, LAZARUS. reg 68, co C, enl 5/21/64, black eyes, fair skin, 6-1, house 934, s 4.

W

WALDECK, WILLIAM. reg 68, co I, r 2nd lt, enl 4/7/64, 5/21/64, dis 4/16/64, 6/22/64, age 21, blue eyes, light hair, fair skin, 6-0, house 1188, s 2,4.

WALDER, JOHN. reg 68, co F, enl 4/7/64, 5/21/64, dis 4/16/64, 6/22/64, house 131, s 2,4.

WALKER, DANIEL H. reg 45, co E, r 1st lt, enr 8/8/63, enl 11/6/63 Ashland, dis 12/24/64 Catlettsburg, age 22, rem residence established by List of Officers, house n/c, s 1,2.

WALKER, JOHN WESLEY. reg 14, co K, enr 11/8/61 Louisa, enl 12/10/61 Louisa, dis 1/31/65 Louisa, age 28, house 1188, s 1,2,4.

WALLACE, AMOS. reg 39, co I, enr 1/28/63, enl 2/16/63 Peach Orchard, dis 9/15/65 Louisville, age 43, dark hair & skin, blue eyes, 5-5, house 1118, s 1,2,4.

WALLACE, SOLOMON. reg 14, co H, enr 10/25/61 Catlettsburg, enl 12/10/61 Louisa, dis 2/3/63 Danville, age 18, dark hair, blue eyes, fair skin, 5-8, rem dis for disability, loss of voice & lung disease, residence stated on muster roll, house n/c, s 1,2,4.
WALLACE, THOMAS. reg 68, r quartermaster, enl 5/21/64, dis 6/22/64, house 1188, s 2,4.
WALLER, ASBURY. reg 14, co D, enr & enl 9/10/63 Louisa, dis 9/15/65 Louisville, age 17, light hair, blue eyes, fair skin, 5-5, rem trans to 14th Vet Inf, co B, enr & m/in 9/10/63 Louisa, house 208, s 1,2,4.
WALLER, HENRY. reg 14, co K, enr 11/8/61 Louisa, enl 12/10/61 Louisa, dis 1/31/65 Louisa, age 42, black hair, blue eyes, fair skin, 5-5, residence stated on muster roll, house n/c, s 1,2,4.
WALLER, JACOB. reg 14, co K, enr 11/8/61 Louisa, enl 12/10/61 Louisa, dis 1/31/65 Louisa, age 19, sandy hair, gray eyes, fair skin, 5-5, rem 6/64 wounded in hospital at Knoxville TN, house 118, s 1,2,4.
WALLER, JAMES. reg 167WV, co Ira Copley, enl 8/62 to 2/64, dis 5/2/64, reg 68, co H, enl 5/21/64, dis 6/22/64, reg CG, co L, enr 6/8/64, enl 7/6/64 Frankfort, 3/11/65 Catlettsburg, age 35, dark hair, blue eyes, fair skin, 5-3, house 987, s 2,4,23.
WALLER, ZACHARIAH. reg 14, co F, enr 11/10/61 Louisa, enl 12/10/61 dis Louisa, dis 1/31/65 Louisa, age 23, brown hair, blue eyes, light skin, 5-5, rem trans to co D 10/30/63, to co F 1/20/65, residence stated on muster roll, house n/c, s 1,2,4.
WALTER, MONROE M. reg 68, co A, enl 5/12/64, dis 6/22/64, age 18, blue eyes, light hair, fair skin, 5-6, house 543, s 2,4.
WARD, JAMES G. reg 14, co K, enr 11/8/61 Louisa, enl 12/10/61 Louisa, dis 1/31/65 Louisa, age 28, dark hair, blue eyes, fair skin, 5-10, house 311, s 1,2,4.
WARD, NATHAN. reg 68, co H, enl 5/21/64, dis 6/22/64, age 40, blue eyes, dark hair & skin, 5-10, house 886, s 2,4.
WARD, NATHANIEL. reg 39, co E, enr 12/6/62 Peach Orchard, enl 2/16/63 Peach Orchard, dis 9/15/65 Louisville, age 18, light hair, blue eyes, fair skin, 5-6, rem trans to co G, 8/63, house 887, s 1,2,4.
WARD, WILLIAM. reg 68, co A, enl 4/7/64, 5/21/64, dis 4/16/64, 6/22/64, age 29, blue eyes, dark hair, fair skin, 5-9, house 637, s 2,4.
WARNICK, WILLIAM. reg 68, co E, enl 4/7/64, 5/21/64, dis 4/16/64, 6/22/64, age 28, dark eyes, hair & skin, 5-8, house 824, s 2,4.
WATSON, ANDREW. reg 68, co F, r cpl, enl 4/7/64, 5/21/64, dis 4/16/64, 6/22/64, age 31, black eyes, dark hair & skin, 5-8, house 5113, s 2,4.
WEBB, ALLEN T. reg 45, co K, enr 10/10/63 Ashland, enl 12/9/63 Louisa, age 18, rem des 12/25/63 Ashland, house 523, s 1,2.
WEBB, ANDREW J. reg 68, co D, enl 5/21/64, dis 6/22/64, age 27, black eyes, dark hair & skin, 6-0, house 87, s 2,4.
WEBB, GEORGE W. reg 68, co F, r sgt, enl 4/7/64, 5/21/64, dis 4/16/64, 6/22/64, age 32, dark eyes, hair & skin, 5-5, house 516, s 2,4.
WEBB, JAMES. reg 45, co K, enr 9/22/63 Catlettsburg, enl 12/9/63 Louisa, dis 2/14/65 Catlettsburg, age 23, light hair, blue eyes, fair skin, 5-9, house 87, s 1,2,6.
WEBB, LEVI. reg 5VA, co H, enr 3/30/62 New Creek VA, enl 8/19/63, dis 9/12/64, Wheeling WV, age 20, house 91, s 1,20.
WELLMAN, CALVIN. reg 14, co H, enr 8/8/63 Louisa, enl 8/29/63 Louisa, dis 9/15/65 Louisville, age 39, light hair, blue eyes, fair skin, 5-10, rem trans to 14th Vet Inf, co C, enr 8/8/63, m/in 8/29/63 Louisa, house 689, s 1,2,4.
WELLMAN, CALVIN. reg 68, co I, enl 5/21/64, dis 6/22/64, age 35, dark eyes, hair & skin, 5-8, house 1203, s 2,4.
WELLMAN, DAVID. reg 68, co I, enl 5/21/64, dis 6/22/64, age 19, blue eyes, light hair, fair skin, 5-6, house 221, s 2,4.

WELLMAN, DELAWARE B. reg 14, co H, enr 9/20/63 Louisa, enl 10/30/63 Louisa, dis 9/15/65 Louisville, age 18, light hair, blue eyes, fair skin, 5-10, rem trans to 14th Vet Inf, co C, enr 9/20/63, m/in 1/30/63 Louisa, house 689, s 1,2,4.
WELLMAN, ELISHA. reg 68, co B, enl 4/7/64, 5/21/64, dis 4/16/64, 6/22/64, reg CG, co E, enr 6/9/64, enl 7/4/64 Frankfort, dis 11/13/64, age 29, black eyes & hair, dark skin, 5-6, house 350, s 2,4.
WELLMAN, ELISHA. reg 68, co I, enl 5/21/64, age 40, light hair, blue eyes, fair skin, 5-10, house 216, s 4.
WELLLMAN, ELISHA D. reg 68, co G, enl 5/21/64, age 35, light hair, blue eyes, fair skin, 5-10, house 164, s 4.
WELLMAN, ELISHA F. reg 14, co G, enr 1/1/62 Johnson Co., enl 1/1/62 Louisa, dis 1/31/65 Louisa, age 18, dark hair & skin, gray eyes, 5-8, house 222, s 1,2,4.
WELLMAN, FLEMING. reg 68, co I, enl 4/7/64, 5/21/64, dis 4/16/64, 6/22/64, age 43, dark eyes, hair & skin, 6-0, house 168, s 2,4.
WELLMAN, JAMES. reg 68, co C, enl 5/12/64, dis 6/22/64, black eyes, dark hair, fair skin, 5-8, house 968, s 2,4.
WELLMAN, JAMES. reg 68, co I, r sgt, enl 4/7/64, 5/21/64, dis 4/16/64, 6/22/64, age 40, blue eyes, light hair, fair skin, 5-7, house 350, s 2,4.
WELLMAN, JAMES JR. reg 68, co I, enl 4/7/64, 5/21/64, dis 4/16/64, 6/22/64, age 28, blue eyes, light hair, fair skin, 5-8, house 1200, s 2,4.
WELLMAN, JOHN D. reg 68, co C, enl 5/21/64, dis 6/22/64, age 33, black eyes, light hair, fair skin, 5-10, b. Wayne Co. VA, rem residence stated on CSR, house n/c, s 1,2,4.
WELLMAN, JOSEPH. reg 14, co H, r cpl, enr 10/25/61 Catlettsburg, enl 12/10/61 Louisa, dis 1/31/65 Louisa, age 22 or 28, house 191, s 1,4.
WELLMAN, LEWIS. reg CG, co E, enl 6/4/64, enl 7/4/64 Frankfort, rem d 9/5/64 Frankfort, house 223, s 2,4.
WELLMAN, LEWIS R. reg 68, co I, r cpl, enl 5/21/64 dis 6/21/64, reg CG, co L, enr 6/8/64, enl 7/6/64 Frankfort, dis 3/11/65 Catlettsburg, age 25, light hair, gray eyes, fair skin, 5-8, house 350, s 2,4.
WELLMAN, NOAH. reg 68, co I, enl 5/21/64, dis 6/21/64, reg CG, co L, enr 6/8/64, enl 7/6/64 Frankfort, age 20, dark hair, blue eyes, fair skin, 5-5, rem d 12/16/64 Frankfort, house 350, s 2,4.
WELLMAN, VAN. reg 68, co C, enl 4/7/64, 5/21/64, dis 4/16/64, 6/22/64, age 20, blue eyes, fair hair & skin, 6-0, house 191, s 2,4.
WELLMAN, WILLIAM. reg 68, co C, enl 5/21/64, dis 6/22/64, age 21, blue eyes, fair hair & skin, 5-6, house 191, s 2,4.
WELLS, LEWIS. reg 68, co A, enl 5/21/64, dis 6/22/64, age 43, blue eyes, light hair, fair skin, 5-9, house 494, s 2,4.
WHEELER, DANIEL. reg 68, co B, enl 4/7/64, 5/21/64, dis 4/16/64, 6/22/64, age 30, black eyes, light hair, fair skin, 5-5, house 558, s 2,4.
WHEELER, HENDERSON. reg 68, co B, enl 4/7/64, 5/21/64, dis 4/16/64, 6/22/64, age 20, black eyes & hair, dark skin, 5-5, house 554, s 2,4.
WHEELER, JAMES L. reg 14, co B, enr 10/10/61 Louisa, enl 12/10/61 Louisa, dis 1/31/65 Louisa, age 19, red hair, blue eyes, fair skin, 5-8, rem 6/64 wounded in hospital in Louisville, residence stated on muster roll, house n/c, s 1,2,4.
WHEELER, JOHN R. reg 68, co B, r sgt, enl 4/7/64, 5/21/64, dis 4/16/64, 6/22/64, age 44, black hair & eyes, fair skin, 6-0, house 562, s 2,4.
WHEELER, STEPHEN M. reg 14, co B, enr 12/16/62 Peach Orchard, enl 6/10/63 Louisa, dis 1/31/65 Louisa, age 28, rem trans from co G, 39th Ky Inf 5/1/63, trans to co G, 39th Ky Inf 1/20/65, trans to Veteran Reserve Corps 5/22/65, house 556, s 1,2,4.

WHEELER, WILLIAM SR. reg 14, co G, enr 11/19/61 Louisa, enl 12/10/61 Louisa, dis 1/24/64 Louisa, age 45, gray hair, blue eyes, fair skin, 5-10, dis for old age & general disability, residence stated on muster roll house n/c, s 1,2,4.
WHITE, JOHN. reg 68, co D, enl 5/21/64, dis 6/22/64, age 30, dark eyes & hair, fair skin, 5-11, house 31 or 171, s 2,4.
WHITE, NELSON T. reg 68, co A, enl 4/7/64, 5/21/64, dis 4/16/64, 6/22/64, age 33, blue eyes, light hair, fair skin, 5-9, house 474, s 2,4.
WHITE, SYLVESTER. reg 14, co H, enr 10/25/61 Catlettsburg, enl 12/10/61 Louisa, age 30, light hair, blue eyes, fair skin, d 8/8/64 of wounds near Marietta GA, residence stated on muster roll, house n/c, s 1,2,4.
WHITLEY, DANIEL J. reg 14, co B, enr 10/10/61 Louisa, enl 12/10/61 Louisa, dis 1/31/65 Louisa, age 18, light hair, blue eyes, fair skin, 5-6, rem wounded between 7/2/64 & 8/13/64, house 217, s 1,2,4.
WHITLEY, WILLIAM J. reg 14, co B, enr 10/10/61 Louisa, enl 1210/61 Louisa, dis 1/31/65 Louisa, age 39, dark hair, eyes & skin, 5-9, house 217, s 1,2,4.
WILEY, MOSES. reg 167WV, co Ira Copley, enl 8/62 to 2/64, dis 5/2/64, reg 68, co H, r cpl, enl 5/21/64, dis 6/22/64, house 912, s 2,4,23.
WILLIAMS, HARDIN B. reg CG, co E, enr 6/9/64, enl 7/4/64 Frankfort, rem des 1/23/65 Paintsville, house 588, s 2,4.
WILLIAMS, JACOB P. reg 68, co A, r 1st lt, enl 4/7/64, 5/21/64, dis 4/16/64, 6/22/64, age 38, black eyes, dark hair & skin, 5-7, house 378, s 2,4.
WILLIAMS, NING. reg 68, co B, r cpl, enl 4/7/64, 5/21/64, dis 4/16/64, 6/22/64, age 33, blue eyes, light hair, fair skin, 6-0, house 595, s 2,4.
WILLIAMS, WASHINGTON. reg 68, co B, enl 4/7/64, 5/21/64, dis 4/16/64, 6/22/64, reg CG, co E, enr 6/9/64, enl 7/4/64 Frankfort, age 21, dark hair, gray eyes, fair skin, 6-6, rem des 1/23/65 Paintsville, house 588, s 2,4.
WILLIAMSON, ALDEN. reg 45, co F, enr 10/1/63 Catlettsburg, enl 11/2/63 Ashland, age 23, light hair, eyes & skin, 6-0, house 1156, s 1,2.
WILLIAMSON, ASA H. reg 167WV, co Geo. Murray, reg 45, co F, enr 8/25/63 Peach Orchard, enl 11/2/63 Ashland, dis 12/24/64 Catlettsburg, age 26, dark hair & skin, light eyes, 5-10, house 1134, s 1,2.
WILLIAMSON, BENJAMIN. reg 39, co D, enr 11/2/62 Pike Co., enl 2/16/63 Peach Orchard, dis 9/15/65 Louisville, age 36, dark hair & skin, blue eyes, 6-1, residence stated on muster roll, house n/c, s 1,2,4.
WILLIAMSON, JACKSON. reg 14, co G, enr 11/19/61 Louisa, enl 12/10/61 Louisa, age 26, light hair, blue eyes, fair skin, 6-0, rem d 2/8/63 Johnson Co., camp fever, CSR lists Lawrence Co. as residence, house 1112, s 1,2,4.
WILLIAMSON, JAMES. reg 39, co A, enr 11/18/62, enl 2/16/63 Peach Orchard, dis 9/15/65 Louisville, age 18, house 1111, s 1,2.
WILLIAMSON, JAMES M. reg 45, co F, enr 8/25/63 Peach Orchard, enl 11/2/63, Ashland, dis 12/24/64 Catlettsburg, age 21, light hair, eyes & skin, 6-0, rem d Flemingsburg 4/27/64, house 873, s 1,2,6.
WILLIAMSON, JASPER. reg 167WV, co Geo. Murray, reg 68, co H, enl 5/21/64, dis 6/22/64, age 22, blue eyes, light hair & skin, 5-10, house 1134, s 2,4,23.
WILLIAMSON, JOHN E. reg 39, co E, r cpl, enr 10/19/63 Peach Orchard, enl 2/16/63 Peach Orchard, dis 9/15/65 Louisville, age 19, house 899 or 1112, s 1,2.
WILLIAMSON, RICHARD. reg 167WV, co Ira Copley, enl 8/62 to 2/64, dis 5/2/64, reg 45, co F, r 1st lt, enr 8/25/63 Peach Orchard, enl 11/2/63 Ashland, dis 12/24/64 Catlettsburg, age 35, dark hair, eyes & skin, 5-6, house 880, s 1,2,6.

WILLIAMSON, SOLOMON. reg 14, co H, r sgt, enr 10/25/61 Louisa, enl 12/10/61 Louisa, dis 1/31/65 Louisa, age 25, dark hair, eyes & skin, 5-8, rem prom to sgt 9/7/64, house 900, s 1,2,4.

WILLIAMSON, STEPHEN. reg 68, co H, enl 4/7/64, 5/21/64, dis 4/16/64, 6/22/64, age 34, light eyes, hair & skin, 5-8, house 1113, s 2,4.

WILLIAMSON, WILLIAM H. reg 14, co C, enr 10/25/61 Louisa, enl 12/10/61 Louisa, dis 9/15/65 Louisville, age 18, dark hair & skin, black eyes, 5-6, rem trans to 14th Vet Inf, co A, enr 2/29/64, m/in 3/19/64 Catlettsburg, house 873, s 1,2,4.

WILSON, CHARLES R. reg 14, co H, enr 10/25/61 Catlettsburg, enl 12/10/61 Louisa, dis 1/31/65 Louisa, age 26, light hair, blue eyes, fair skin, 5-7, residence stated on muster roll, house n/c, s 1,2,4.

WILSON, JOHN. reg 68, co E, enl 4/7/64, 5/21/64, dis 4/16/64, 6/22/64, age 33, light eyes, hair & skin, 5-8, house 743, s 2,4.

WITHEROW, SAMUEL. reg 68, co A, enl 4/7/64, dis 4/16/64, co F, r cpl, enl 5/21/64, dis 6/22/64, age 33, blue eyes, dark hair, fair skin, 5-8, house 236, s 2,4.

WITHROD, SAMUEL. reg 68, co F, r cpl, enl 5/21/64, dis 6/22/64, house 293, s 2,4.

WOODS, EPHRAIM M. reg 68, co F, r cpl, enl 4/7/64, 5/21/64, dis 4/16/64, 6/22/64, age 20, blue eyes, light hair, fair skin, 5-9, house 322, s 2,4.

WOODS, JAMES. reg 68, co F, r cpl, enl 4/7/64, 5/21/64, dis 4/16/64, 6/22/64, age 33, blue eyes, dark hair & skin, 5-10, house 323, s 2,4.

WOODS, JOHN. reg 14, co B, enr 10/10/61 Louisa, enl 12/10/61 Louisa, dis 1/31/65 Louisa, age 18, light hair, blue eyes, fair skin, 5-11, rem cap Lawrence Co. 2/15/63, paroled in eastern KY, residence stated on muster roll, house n/c, s 1,2,4.

WOODS, MEREDITH. reg 14, co B, enr 10/10/61 Louisa, enl 12/10/61 Louisa, age 28, dark hair, blue eyes, fair skin, 5-9, rem d 1/11/62 Louisa of measles, residence stated on muster roll, house n/c, s 1,2,4.

WOODS, ROBERT. reg 68, co A, enl 4/7/64, 5/21/64, dis 4/16/64, 6/22/64, age 28, blue eyes, dark hair & skin, 5-8, residence shown on militia list, house n/c, s 2,4,18.

WOODS, WALTER O. reg 14, co B, enr 10/10/61 Louisa, enl 12/10/61 Louisa, dis 6/5/62, age 40, rem res ill health, house 363, s 1,2,4.

WOODS, WILLIAM. reg 68, co F, enl 5/21/64, dis 6/22/64, age 22, blue eyes, dark hair & skin, 5-10, house 322 or 335, s 2,4.

WOOTEN, CASSELL. reg 39, co B, enr 11/19/62 Peach Orchard, enl 2/16/63 Peach Orchard, dis 9/15/65 Louisville, age 30, dark hair, blue eyes, fair skin, 5-10, house 894, s 1,2,4.

WOOTEN, GEORGE C. reg 5VA, co I, enr 9/14/61 Ceredo, enl 9/14/61, dis 10/4/64 Wheeling WV, age 22, rem cap Bull Run VA 9/1/62, paroled Centerville VA 9/3/62, house 947, s 1,20.

WOOTEN, THOMAS. reg 68, co K, enl 4/7/64, 5/21/64, dis 4/16/64, 6/22/64, age 38, black eyes & hair, dark skin, 5-6, house 1040, s 2,4.

WORKMAN, HARMON. reg 14, co A, enr 5/26/63 Louisa, enl 10/31/63 Louisa, dis 9/15/65 Louisville, age 21, dark hair & eyes, fair skin, 5-9, rem trans to 14th Vet Inf, co D, enr 5/26/63, m/in 10/31/63 Louisa, trans to co F 1/26/65, house 50, s 1,2,4.

WORKMAN, MICHAEL. reg 10Cav, co F, enr 1/18/63 Mason Co., enl 1/25/63 Louisa or 9/13/63 Maysville, dis 9/17/63 Maysville, age 42 or 45, residence stated on muster roll, house n/c, s 1, 2, 4.

WORKMAN, THOMAS. reg 10Cav, co F, r cpl, enr 8/9/62 Boyd Co., enl 9/9/62 Covington, dis 9/17/63 Maysville, age 30, app 8th cpl 8/18/62, residence stated on muster roll, house n/c, s 1, 2, 4.

WRIGHT, ELHANNAN. reg 14, co G, enr 11/19/61 Louisa, enl 12/10/61 Louisa, dis 1/1/65 Louisa, age 20, dark hair & skin, black eyes, 5-10, residence stated on muster roll, house n/c, s 1,2,4.

WRIGHT, JAMES L. reg 14, co B, enr & enl 8/22/63 Louisa, dis 9/15/65 Louisville, age 23, light hair, blue eyes, fair skin, 5-11, rem trans to 14th Vet Inf, co B, enr 8/22/63, m/in 8/31/63 Louisa, residence stated on CSR, house n/c, s 1,2.

Y

YATES, STROTHER J. reg 14, r surgeon, enr 11/19/61 Louisa, enl 12/10/61 Louisa, dis 1/31/65 Louisa, age 45, rem res 2/1/62, reappointed surgeon 5/28/63, house 1226, s 1,2,4.

YATES, WILLIAM. reg 39, co I, enr 11/20/62 Pike Co., enl 2/16/63 Peach Orchard, age 31, rem d on Rockcastle Creek, Lawrence Co., 5/29/63, residence stated on muster roll, house n/c, s 1,2,4.

YOUNG, ABRAHAM. reg 14, co G, enr 4/26/63 Louisa, enl 6/10/63 Louisa, dis 9/15/65 Louisville, age 17, light hair, blue eyes, fair skin, 5-4, rem trans to 14th Vet Inf, co D, enr 4/20/63, m/in 6/10/63 Louisa, cap Atlanta 8/18/64, paroled in North Carolina 2/27/65, residence stated on muster roll, house n/c, s 1,2,4.

YOUNG, AFLRED R. reg 14, co K, enr 11/8/61 Louisa, enl 12/10/61 Louisa, age 24, rem des 9/4/62, house 308, s 1,2,4.

YOUNG, JAMES W. reg 68, co G, enl 5/21/64, dis 6/22/64, age 33, black eyes & hair, dark skin, 5-8, house 294, s 2,4.

YOUNG, JOHN W. reg 68, co G, r 1st lt, enl 4/7/64, 5/21/64, dis 4/16/64, 6/22/64, age 35, blue eyes, light hair, fair skin, 6-0, house 292, s 2,4.

YOUNG, MARION. reg 14, co G, enr 11/19/61 Louisa, enl 12/10/61 Louisa, dis 1/31/65 Louisa, age 18, sandy hair, blue eyes, fair skin, 5-8, rem cap Atlanta 8/18/64, paroled 12/11/64, residence stated on muster roll, house n/c, s 1,2,4.

YOUNG, PERRY. reg 68, co G, enr 4/7/64, 5/21/64, dis 4/16/64, 6/22/64, age 23, black eyes & hair, dark skin, 5-8, house 288, s 2,4,18.

YOUNG, ROBERT (SR.). reg 14, co D, enr 9/15/63 Louisa, enl 10/30/63 Louisa, dis 9/15/65 Louisville, age 23, light hair, blue eyes, fair skin, 6-0, rem trans to 14th Vet Inf, co C, enr 9/15/63, m/in 10/5/63, recruit sick at home in Lawrence Co. and not mustered out, house 632, s 1,2,4.

YOUNG, ROBERT H. reg 14, co G, enr 11/19/61 Louisa, enl 12/10/61 Louisa, dis 1/31/65 Louisa, age 22, dark hair, blue eyes, fair skin, 5-8, rem may have been resident of Johnson Co., house 291, s 1,2,4.

YOUNG, THOMAS. reg 68, co G, enl 4/7/64, 5/21/64, dis 4/16/64, 6/22/64, age 25, blue eyes, light hair, fair skin, 5-8, house 288, s 2,4,18.

YOUNG, WILLIAM. reg 68, co G, enl 4/7/64, 5/21/64, dis 4/16/64, 6/22/64, age 35, black eyes & hair, dark skin, 5-10, house 287, s 2,4.

LETCHER COUNTY UNION SOLDIERS

A

ADAMS, ALEXANDER. reg 19, co D, r capt, enr 12/12/61 Camp Estill Springs, Irvine, enl 1/2/62 Camp Harrod, Harrodsburg, dis 3/9/63 Milliken's Bend LA, age 27, light hair, blue eyes, fair skin, 5-4, b Lee Co. VA, resigned for physical disabilities on surgeon's certificate, house 375, s 1,2.

ADAMS, BENJAMIN F. reg Har, co A, r sgt, enl 10/13/62, dis 1/13/63, house 112, 118, 119, 309 or 334, s 2.

ADAMS, FRAZIER. reg Har, co A, enl 10/13/62, dis 1/13/63, reg 14Cav, co M, enr 1/19/63 Owsley Co., enl 2/13/63 Irvine, dis 3/24/64 Camp Nelson, age 21, house 8, s 1,2.

ADAMS, JESSE. reg 14Cav, co M, enr 1/19/63 Owsley Co., enl 2/13/63 Irvine, dis 3/24/64 Camp Nelson, age 23, house 80, 119, 263, 342, 360, 437, 583, or 263, s 1,2.

ADAMS, JESSE B. reg 39, co K, enr 2/28/64 Louisa, enl 3/29/64 Greenupsburg, age 18, red hair, blue eyes, fair skin, 5-4, b Letcher Co., d 12/13/64 Louisa of smallpox, house 263, s 1,2.

ADAMS, JOHN. reg 14Cav, co M, enr 4/20/63, enl 6/15/63 Irvine, dis 3/24/64 Camp Nelson, house 12, 47, 313, 334, 360, 463, 80 or 263, s 2.

ADAMS, JOHN S. reg Har, co A, enl 10/13/62, dis 1/13/63, house 12, 47, 313, 334, 360 or 463, s 2.

ADAMS, MOSES. reg 39, co F, enr 6/27/63 Floyd Co., enl 8/30/63 Louisa, age 31, dark hair & skin, black eyes, 5-10, b Letcher Co., house 472, s 1,2.

ADAMS, SOLOMON. reg Har, co A, enl 10/13/62, dis 1/13/63, reg 14Cav, co M, enr 4/20/63 Richmond, enl 6/15/63 Lexington, dis 3/24/64 Camp Nelson, age 18 or 20, house 8, s 1,2.

ADAMS, SPENCER. reg Har, co A, enl 10/13/62, dis 1/13/63, reg 14Cav, co M, enr 4/13/63 Richmond, enl 6/15/63 Lexington, dis 3/24/64 Camp Nelson, age 19, house 500, s 1,2.

ADAMS, SPENCER. reg 45, co F, enr 10/2/63, enl 11/2/63 Ashland, age 45, light hair, eyes & skin, 5-7, b Perry Co., trans to 4th Ky. Inf. 4/24/64 Lexington, house 359, s 1,2.

ADAMS, SQUIRE. reg Har, co A, r cpl, enl 10/13/62, dis 1/13/63, reg 14Cav, co L, enr 3/1/63 Irvine, enl 6/15/63 Lexington, dis 3/24/64 Camp Nelson, age 24 or 34, residence stated on muster roll, house 26, s 1,2,4.

ADAMS, STEPHEN. reg Har, co A, enl 10/13/62, dis 2/13/63, house 47, 53, 284 or 605, s 2.

AMBURGEY, JOHN WALKER. reg US Army, enl 10/6/64, enlisted in US Army for frontier service from Camp Chase, house 255, s 31.

B

BAKER, ELIJAH C. reg 19, co D, r 1st lt, enr 11/1/61 Camp Estill Springs, Irvine, enl 1/2/62 Camp Harrod, Harrodsburg, dis 1/26/65 Louisville, age 34, prom from sgt to 1st sgt 2/16/63, to 2nd lt 3/10/63, to 1st lt 4/12/63, cap Sabine Cross Roads LA 4/8/64, taken to Tyler TX, exch 11/2/64, age 27 on census, house 195, s 1,2.

BANKS, HENRY. reg Har, co A, enl 10/13/62, dis 1/13/63, house 10 or 394, s 2.

BANKS, JOHN. reg Har, co A, enl 10/13/62, dis 1/13/63, reg 14Cav, co C, enr 12/25/62 Owsley Co., enl 2/13/63 Irvine, dis 3/24/64 Camp Nelson, age 18, residence stated on muster roll, house 598, s 1,2,4.

BANKS, LUNSFORD. reg Har, co A, enl 10/13/62, dis 1/13/63, reg 14Cav, co L, enr 12/25/62 Owsley Co., enl 2/13/63 Irvine, dis 3/24/64 Camp Nelson, age 20 or 24, residence stated on muster roll, house 598, s 1,2,4.

BENTLEY, JOHN. reg 39, co K, enl 11/16/63 Louisa, dis 9/15/65 Louisville, age 19, dark hair & skin, gray eyes, 6-2, b. Russell Co. VA, credited 6th Cong. Dist., house 144, s 1,2.

BENTLEY, MAY. reg 39, co K, enr 1/15/64 Louisa, enl 3/29/64 Greenupsburg, dis 9/15/65 Louisville, age 24 or 28, light hair, blue eyes, fair skin, 6-1, b Letcher Co., house 150, s 1,2.

BLAIR, ELIHU or ELIJAH. reg 14Cav, co L, r cpl, enr 3/1/63 Irvine, enl 6/15/63 Lexington, dis 3/24/64 Camp Nelson, age 38, prom to cpl 9/1/63, residence stated on muster roll, house 314, s 1,2,4.

BLAIR, ENOCH. reg Har, co B, enl 10/13/62, dis 1/13/63, house 213, s 2.

BLAIR, HIRAM. reg Har, co A, enl 10/13/62, dis 1/13/63, house 314 or 581, s 2.

BLAIR, JOHN. reg Har, co B, enl 10/13/62, dis 1/13/63, house 593, s 2.

BLAIR, SAMUEL. reg Har, co A, enl 10/13/62, dis 1/13/63, house 581, s 2.

BOGGS, ELIHU. reg 19, co D, enr 11/1/61 Camp Estill Springs, enl 1/2/62 Camp Harrod, Harrodsburg, dis 2/13/63 Young's Point LA, age 30, black hair, dark eyes & skin, 5-10, dis on surgeon's certificate of disability, bad cough, house 229, s 1,2.

BOGGS, ELIJAH. reg Har, co F, enl 10/13/62, dis 1/13/63, house 233, s 2.

BOGGS, HENRY. reg Har, co F, enl 10/13/62, dis 1/13/63, house 232, s 2.

BOGGS, ISAAC. reg Har, co F, enl 10/13/62, dis 1/13/63, house 231 or 531, s 2.

BOGGS, JOHN. reg Har, co F, enl 10/13/62, dis 1/13/63, house 531, s 2.

BOGGS, LEVI. reg Har, co F, r cpl, enl 10/13/62, dis 1/13/63, house 230, s 2.

BOHANNON, HADLEY. reg Har, co B, enl 10/13/62, dis 1/13/63, house 109, s 2.

BOLING, JOHN J. reg 45, co H, G, enr 10/22/63 Salyersville, enl 2/6/64 Mt. Sterling, dis 2/14/65 Catlettsburg, age 22, light hair & skin, gray eyes, 5-9, b Tennessee, trans from co H to co G 2/64, back to co H 5/20/64, house 264, s 1,2.

BREEDING, JOHN. reg Har, co A, enl 10/13/62, dis 1/13/63, reg 14Cav, co M, r cpl, enr 2/12/63 Irvine, enl 6/15/63 Lexington, dis 3/24/64 Camp Nelson, age 22, house 322, s 1,2.

BREEDING, JOHN. reg 39, co B, r 1st lt enr 12/15/62 Peach Orchard, enl 2/16/63 Peach Orchard, dis 9/15/65 Louisville, age 19, prom to 4th sgt 8/1/63, to 1st lt 7/7/65, commissioned by Gov. Bramlette, residence stated on List of Officers, house 431, s 1,2,4,32.

BREEDING, PRESTON N. reg 19, co D, enr 11/1/61 Irvine, enl 2/3/62 Harrodsburg, dis 1/26/65 Louisville, age 24, cap Sabine Cross Roads LA 4/8/64, paroled 7/22/64 Red River Landing LA, trans 12/24/64 to 7th Ky. Vet. Inf., age 38 on census, house 431, s 1,2.

BROOKS, ALFRED. reg 14Cav, co M, r cpl, enr 1/1/63 Owsley Co., enl 2/13/63 Irvine, dis 3/24/64 Camp Nelson, age 30 or 38, deserted, house 252, s 1,2.

BROWN, WILLIAM. reg Har, co F, enl 10/13/62, dis 1/13/63, house 35, s 2.

BURGA, ROBERT. reg 14Cav, co L, enr 2/20/63 Irvine, enl 6/15/63 Lexington, dis 3/24/64 Camp Nelson, age 20 or 21, residence stated on muster roll, house n/c, s 1,2,4.

C

CALHOUN, ROBERT. reg 39, co B, enr 4/11/63 Louisa, enl 6/10/63 Louisa, dis 9/15/65 Louisville, age 18 or 19, residence stated on muster roll, house 505, s 1,2,4.

CALHOUN, WILLIAM J. reg 19, co D, enr 11/1/61 Camp Estill Springs, Irvine, enl 1/2/62 Camp Harrod, Harrodsburg, dis 8/6/62 Cumberland Gap, age 19, dark hair & skin, black eyes, 5-9, dis for disability of chronic pleurisy & emphysema, b Letcher Co., CSR: "sick at home in Letcher Co.", house 505, s 1, 2.

CAMPBELL, JOHN. reg Har, co E, enl 10/13/62, dis 1/13/63, reg 14Cav, co M, enr 12/14/62, enl 2/13/63 Irvine, dis 3/24/64 Camp Nelson, house 94, s 2.

CAUDILL, JAMES. reg Har, co C, enl 10/13/62, dis 1/13/63, house 29, 31, 602, 299 or 597, s 2.

CAUDILL, ROBERT G. reg Har, co E, r cpl, enl 10/23/62, dis 1/13/63, house 444, s 2.

CLAY, ELIJAH. reg Har, co F, enl 10/13/62, dis 1/13/63, house 220, s 2.

CLAY, HENRY. reg Har, co B, enl 10/13/62, dis 1/13/63, house 219, s 2.

CLAY, JESSE. reg Har, co F, enl 10/13/62, dis 1/13/63, house 218, s 2.

CLAY, WILLIAM. reg Har, co F, r 1st sgt, enl 10/13/62, dis 1/13/63, house 219, s 2.

COLLIER, DAVID M. reg Har, co F, enl 10/13/62, dis 1/13/63, house 222, s 2.

COLLIER, MARTIN D. reg Har, co B, enl 10/13/62, dis 1/13/63, house 553, s 2.

COLLINS, BENJAMIN T. reg 19, co D, r cpl, enr 11/1/61 Camp Estill Springs, Irvine, enl 1/2/62 Camp Harrod, Harrodsburg, dis 1/28/65 Louisville, age 28, d 3/12/63 on hospital boat Nashville on the Mississippi River of chronic diarrhea, residence stated on muster roll, house n/c, s 1,2.

COLLINS, CALVIN. reg 14Cav, co L, enr 12/15/62 Owsley Co., enl 2/13/63 Irvine, dis 3/24/64 Camp Nelson, age 23 or 24, residence stated on muster roll, house 4, s 1,2,4.

COLLINS, CARTER. reg 14Cav, co L, age 24, not mustered, not on CSR, residence stated on muster roll, house 340, s 4.

COLLINS, COWDEN. reg 14Cav, co L, enr 12/23/62 Owsley Co., enl 6/15/63 Lexington, dis 3/24/63 Camp Nelson, age 23 or 25, residence stated on muster roll, house 316, s 1.

COLLINS, ENOCH. reg 14Cav, co L, enr 12/15/62, enl 2/13/63 Irvine, dis 3/24/64 Camp Nelson, not on CSR, residence stated on muster roll, house n/c, s 2,4.

COLLINS, FIELDING. reg 14Cav, co C, L, r cpl, enr 12/6/62 Owsley Co., enl 2/13/63 Irvine, dis 3/24/64 Camp Nelson, age 18, prom to cpl 12/24/62, residence stated on muster roll, house 318, s 1,2,4.

COLLINS, FINDLEY. reg 14Cav, co C, L, enr 1/15/63, enl 6/15/63 Irvine or Lexington, dis 3/24/64 Camp Nelson, age 25, residence stated on muster roll, house 438, s 1,2,4.

COLLINS, GEORGE N. reg 14Cav, co L, enr 12/15/62 Owsley Co., enl 2/13/63 Irvine, dis 3/24/64 Camp Nelson, age 20, residence stated on muster roll, house 6, s 1,2,4.

COLLINS, HENRY. reg Har, co A, enl 10/13/62, dis 1/13/63, house 6 or 316, s 2.

COLLINS, HENRY. reg 14Cav, co L, enr 12/15/62 Owsley Co., enl 2/13/63 Irvine, dis 3/24/64 Camp Nelson, age 23, residence stated on muster roll, house 6 or 316, s 1,2,4.

COLLINS, JAMES. reg 14Cav, co M, r cpl, enr 3/21/63 Winchester, enl 6/15/63 Lexington, dis 3/24/64 Camp Nelson, age 21, prom to cpl 8/18/63, house 158, s 1,2.

COLLINS, JESSE. reg 14Cav, co L, enr 12/13/62 Owsley Co., enl 2/13/63 Irvine, dis 3/24/63 Camp Nelson, age 20, residence stated on muster roll, house 318, s 1,2,4.

COLLINS, NATHANIEL. reg 39, co B, K, r capt, enr 9/4/63 Peach Orchard, enl 9/22/63 Louisa, dis 9/15/65 Louisville, age 44, prom from pvt co B, to capt co K 9/4/63 by Governor's commission, residence stated on List of Officers, house 574, s 1, 32.

COLLINS, SANDERS. reg Har, co A, enl 10/13/62, dis 1/13/63, reg 14Cav, co C, L, enr 12/21/62 Owsley Co., enl 6/15/63 Irvine, age 25 or 27, trans to co D 19th Ky. Inf 8/1/63, des Booneville 8/15/63, enl Vet. Vol. 2/15/64, m/in 2/29/64 Berwick City LA, cap Sabine Cross Roads LA 4/8/64, paroled Red River Landing LA 7/22/64, trans to 7th Vet. Inf. 12/29/64, dis 1/22/65 Louisville, residence stated on muster roll, house 5, s 1,2,4.

COLLINS, THOMAS. reg 14Cav, co C, L, enr 12/20/62 Owsley Co., enl 2/13/63 Irvine, dis 3/24/64 Camp Nelson, age 40 or 42, residence stated on muster roll, house 6 or 295, s 1,2,4.

COLLINS, WATSON. reg 14Cav, co L, enr 12/15/62 Owsley Co., enl 2/13/63 Irvine, dis 3/24/64 Camp Nelson, age 18 or 19, residence stated on muster roll, house n/c, s 1,2,4.

COMBS, ENOCH. reg 14Cav, co C, L, enr 12/15/62 Owsley Co., enl 2/13/63 Irvine, dis 3/24/64 Camp Nelson, age 24, residence stated on muster roll, house 541, s 1,2,4.

COMBS, JOHN B. reg 19, co D, enr 11/1/61 Camp Estill Springs, Irvine, enl 1/2/62 Camp Harrod, Harrodsburg, d 6/1/63 Vicksburg MS of thigh wound received in battle, residence stated on muster roll, house 7, s 1,2.

COMBS, SHADRACK. reg 14Cav, co D, M, r cpl, enr 1/19/63 Owsley Co., enl 2/13/63 Irvine, dis 3/24/64 Camp Nelson, age 19, prom to cpl 2/14/63, house 7 or 494, s 1,2.

COOK, JOHN H. reg 39, co H, r cpl, enr 12/10/62 Pike Co., enl 6/10/63 Louisa, dis 9/15/65 Louisville, age 21, cap Peter Creek, Pike Co. 12/6/63, confined at Richmond VA 4/1/63, paroled at City Point 4/3/63, house 176, s 1,2.

CORNETT, CLARK. reg 47, co H, enr 8/1/63 Irvine, enl 10/5/63 Irvine, dis 12/26/64 Lexington, age 17, trans to 4th Ky. Vet. Vol. 4/26/64 Paris, residence stated on muster roll, house 413, s 1,2,4.

CORNETT, CLARK S. reg Har, co A, enl 10/13/62, dis 1/13/63, house 398, 405 or 413, s 2.

CORNETT, HIRAM M. reg Har, co A, r sgt, enl 10/13/62, dis 2/13/63, reg 47, co H, enr 9/21/63 Irvine, enl 10/5/63 Irvine, age 31, d 4/19/64 Paris of typhoid fever, house 39, s 1,2,4.

CORNETT, JOSEPH. reg 47, co H, enr 7/21/63 Irvine, enl 10/5/63 Irvine, age 22, des 10/9/63 Irvine, residence stated on muster roll, house 398, s 1,2,4.

CORNETT, SAMUEL. reg Har, co A, enl 10/13/62, dis 1/13/63, house 2, 291, 413 or 415, s 2.

CORNETT, SAMUEL. reg Har, co C, enl 10/13/62, dis 1/13/63, house 2, 291, 413 or 415, s 2.

CORNETT, SAMUEL. reg 47, co H, enr 9/1/63 Irvine, enl 10/5/63 Irvine, dis 12/26/64 Lexington, age 18, residence stated on muster roll, house 413, s 1.

CORNETT, SILAS. reg Har, co A, enl 10/13/62, dis 1/13/63, house 398, s 2.

CORNETT, SIVA. reg 47, co H, enr 7/21/63 Irvine, enl 10/15/63 Irvine, dis 12/26/64 Lexington, age 18, residence stated on muster roll, house 415, s 1,2,4.

CORNETT, WILLIAM. reg 47, co H, enr 8/15/63 Irvine, enl 10/15/63 Irvine, age 21 or 24, des 3/24/64 Booneville, residence stated on muster roll, house 411, s 1,2,4.

CORNETT, WILLIAM H. reg 19, co D, enr 11/1/61 Camp Estill Springs, Irvine, enl 1/2/62 Camp Harrod, Harrodsburg, dis 1/26/65 Louisville, age 18, d 8/20/63 Memphis TN of fever, age 13 on census, house 398, s 1,2.

COX, JAMES. reg 47, co H, enr 8/2/63 Irvine, enl 10/5/63 Irvine, age 19, des 10/8/63 Irvine, house 86, s 1,2,4.

COX, JONATHAN. reg Har, co A, enl 10/13/62, dis 1/13/63, house 86, s 2.

D

DAY, HENRY. reg Har, co F, enl 10/13/62, dis 1/13/63, house 551, s 2.

DAY, JACOB. reg Har, co C, enl 10/13/62, dis 1/13/63, house 548, s 2.

DAY, JOHN B. reg Har, co F, enl 10/13/62, dis 1/13/63, house 524, s 2.

DAY, JOHN B. reg 14Cav, co M, enr 8/13/62, enl 9/9/62 Covington, d 1/12/63 Fleming Co., not on CSR, house 529, s 2.

DAY, WILLIAM. reg Har, co C, enl 10/13/62, dis 1/13/63, house 425 or 445, s 2.

DAY, WILLIAM L. reg Har, co F, enl 10/13/62, dis 1/13/63, house 495, s 2.

DUKE, JAMES M. reg 3rd Ky. Battery, house 473, s 1.

E

EASTRIDGE, WILLIAM. reg 14Cav, co I, G, A, enr 10/20/62 Breathitt Co., enl 2/13/63 Irvine, age 45, died 12/28/63 Perry Co., residence stated on muster roll, house n/c, s 1,2,4.

ENGLAND, ENOCH. reg 14Cav, co I, G, A, enr 12/25/62 Breathitt Co., enl 2/13/63 Irvine, dis 3/24/64 Camp Nelson, age 30, muster roll lists Perry Co. as residence, but he is not on Perry Co. census, house 362, s 1 2.

ESTEP, JONATHAN. reg 45, co C, enr 8/19/63 Paintsville, enl 10/10/63 Catlettsburg, dis 12/24/64 Catlettsburg, age 26, house 184, s 1,2.

F

FIELDS, GEORGE. reg 14Cav, co D, M, enr 12/20/62 Owsley Co., enl 2/13/63 Irvine, dis 3/24/64 Camp Nelson, age 20, age 12 on census, house 268, s 1, 2.
FIELDS, ISAAC. reg Har, co C, enl 10/13/62, dis 1/13/63, house 36, s 2.
FIELDS, JOHN M. reg Har, co A, enl 10/13/62, dis 1/13/63, house 601, s 2.
FIELDS, JOSEPH B. reg Har, co A, enl 10/13/62, dis 1/13/63, reg 47, co H, enr 8/1/63 Irvine, enl 10/5/63 Irvine, dis 12/26/64 Lexington, age 18, residence stated on muster roll, house 36, s 1,2,4.
FIELDS, LARRY B. reg Har, co A, enl 10/13/62, dis 1/13/63, reg 47, co H, enr 8/29/63 Irvine, enl 10/5/63 Irvine, dis 12/26/64 Lexington, age 22 or 24, residence stated on muster roll, house 36, s 1,4.
FIELDS, ROBERT H. reg Har, co A, enl 10/13/62, dis 1/13/63, reg 47, co H, r sgt, enr 8/21/63 Irvine, enl 10/5/63, dis 12/26/64 Lexington, age 25, residence stated on muster roll, house 487, s 1, 2, 4.
FIELDS, STEPHEN. reg Har, co F, r cpl, enl 10/13/62, dis 1/13/63, house 212, s 2.
FRANKLIN, JAMES B. reg Har, co A, r cpl, enl 10/13/62, dis 1/13/63, house 558, s 2.
FRAZIER, DANIEL. reg Har, co A, enl 10/13/62, dis 1/13/63, house 426, s 2.
FRAZIER, JAMES. reg Har, co A, enl 10/13/62, dis 1/13/63, house 389 or 428, s 2.
FRAZIER, SOLOMON. reg Har, co A, enl 10/13/62, dis 1/13/63, house 98, 389, 426 or 428, s 2.

G

GIBSON, ARCHIBALD. reg 19, co D, enr 11/10/61 Camp Estill Springs, enl 1/2/62 Harrodsburg, dis 1/26/65 Louisville, age 23, house 339, s 1,2.
GIBSON, DAVID. reg 14Cav, co L, enr 12/15/62 Owsley Co., enl 2/13/63 Letcher, dis 3/24/64 Camp Nelson, age 18, residence stated on muster roll, house 317, s 1,2,4.
GIBSON, JESSE. reg 14Cav, co L, enr 12/15/62 Owsley Co., enl 2/13/63 Irvine, dis 3/24/64 Camp Nelson, age 23, residence stated on muster roll, house 317, s 1,2,4.
GIBSON, JOHN D. reg 19, co D, r cpl, enr 11/1/61 Camp Estill Springs, Irvine, enl 1/2/62 Camp Harrod, Harrodsburg, age 18, black hair & eyes, dark skin, 5-6, prom to cpl 6/28/62, wounded & cap 4/8/64 Sabine Cross Roads LA, paroled 6/16/64 Red River Landing LA, b Hancock Co., residence stated on muster roll, house n/c, s 1,2.
GILLIAM, ALBERT or ELBERT. reg 47, co H, r cpl, enr 8/24/63 Irvine, enl 10/5/63 Irvine, dis 12/26/64 Lexington, age 22, residence stated on muster roll, house n/c, s 2,4.
GROSS, EDWARD. reg Har, co F, enl 10/13/62, dis 1/13/63, house 368, s 2.

H

HALCOMB, JESSE. reg Har, co A, enl 10/13/62, dis 1/13/63, reg 47, co H, enr 7/4/63 Irvine, enl 10/5/63 Irvine, dis 12/26/64 Lexington, age 19, residence stated on muster roll, house 406, s 1,2,4.
HALCOMB, JOHN. reg 47, co H, enr 8/19/63 Irvine, enl 10/5/63 Irvine, dis 12/26/64 Lexington, age 18, residence stated on muster roll, house 408, s 1, 2,4.
HALCOMB, JOSEPH. reg 47, co H, enr 8/19/63 Irvine, enl 10/5/63 Irvine, dis 12/26/64 Lexington, age 31, residence stated on muster roll, house n/c, s 1, 2,4.
HALCOMB, LINDSEY. reg 47, co H, enr 7/25/63 Irvine, enl 10/5/63 Irvine, dis 12/26/64 Lexington, age 18, residence stated on muster roll, house n/c, s 1, 2, 4.

HALCOMB, MILLARD. reg 47, co H, enr 7/4/63 Irvine, enl 10/5/63 Irvine, dis 12/26/64 Lexington, age 23, residence stated on muster roll, house n/c, s 1, 2, 4.

HALCOMB, MONROE. reg 47, co H, r cpl, enr 7/21/63 Irvine, enl 10/5/63 Irvine, age 22, prom to cpl 3/13/64, residence stated on muster roll, house n/c, s 1,2 4.

HALCOMB, THOMAS. reg 47, co H, enr 8/19/63 Irvine, enl 10/5/63 Irvine, dis 12/26/64 Lexington, age 18, residence stated on muster roll, house 407, s 1, 2,4.

HALCOMB, WILLIAM. reg Har, co A, enl 10/13/62, dis 1/13/63, reg 47, co H, enr 7/4/63 Irvine, enl 10/5/63 Irvine, dis 12/26/64 Lexington, age 21, residence stated on muster roll, house 408, s 1,2,4.

HALE, DRAYTON D. reg 19, co D, enr 11/1/61 Irvine, enl 1/8/62 Harrodsburg, dis 1/26/65 Louisville, age 24, musician, trans to Invalid Corps 12/1/63, residence stated on muster roll, house n/c, s 1,2.

HALE, JOSEPH. reg 19, co D, r cpl, enr 11/1/61 Irvine, enl 1/8/62 Harrodsburg, age 21, died 5/13/62 Cumberland Ford of consumption, house 380, s 1,2.

HALL, AFLRED. reg Har, co A, enl 10/13/63, dis 1/13/63, house 61, s 2.

HALL, BENJAMIN. reg 39, co K, enr 9/27/63 Louisa, enl 10/30/63 Louisa, dis 9/15/65 Louisville, age 19, house 125, s 1,2.

HALL, HIRAM. reg 39, co I, enr 12/12/63 Peach Orchard, enl 12/28/63 Louisa, dis 9/15/65 Louisville, age 21, dark hair, eyes & skin, 5-11, des 8/10/64, returned 5/5/65 under President's Proclamation, b Letcher Co., house 204, 1, 2.

HALL, IRA D. reg 19, co D, enr 11/1/61 Camp Estill Springs, enl 1/2/62 Harrodsburg, dis 1/26/65 Louisville, des 6/20/62 Barboursville, reg Har, co A, enl 10/13/62, dis 1/13/63, reg 47, co H, enr 8/1/63 Irvine, enl 10/5/63 Irvine, age 22, trans to 4th Ky. Vet. Inf., co D 4/30/64, house 61, s 1,2,4.

HALL, JOHN W. reg Har, co A, enl 10/13/62, dis 1/13/63, house 24, 187 or 395, s 2.

HALL, JOHN W. reg 14Cav, co L, r cpl, enr 3/1/63 Stanton, enl 6/15/63 Lexington, dis 2/24/64 Camp Nelson, age 21, wounded and left in Perry Co. 12/24/63, residence stated on muster roll, house 24 or 395, s 1,2,4.

HALL, JOSHUA B. reg Har, co A, r 3rd lt, enl 10/13/62, dis 1/13/63, house 43, s 2.

HALL, PHILIP. reg Har, co A, enl 10/13/62, dis 1/13/63, house 394, s 2.

HALL, THOMAS. reg Har, co A, enl 10/13/62, dis 1/13/63, reg 39, co K, enr 9/27/63, Louisa, enl 10/30/63 Louisa, dis 9/15/65 Louisville, age 22, dark hair, eyes & skin, 6-2, b Letcher Co., house 137, s 1,2.

HENSLEY, JOHN. reg Har, co C, enl 10/13/62, dis 1/13/63, house 577, s 2.

HOGG, JAMES. reg 14Cav, co M, r sgt, enr 1/19/63 Owsley Co., enl 2/13/63 Irvine, dis 3/24/64 Camp Nelson, age 36, prom from pvt to sgt 2/14/63, house 390, s 1,2.

HOGG, RAY. reg 14Cav, co L, r ord sgt, enr 12/15/62 or 12/24/62 Owsley Co., enl 2/18/63 Irvine, age 18, prom to sgt 12/24/62, d 9/24/63 Booneville, residence stated on muster roll, house n/c, s 1,2,4.

HONEYCUTT, ALFRED. reg 45, co C, enr 8/22/63 Paintsville, enl 10/10/63 Catlettsburg, dis 12/24/64 Catlettsburg, age 30, house 522, s 1,2.

HUFF, WILLIAM. reg Har, co C, enl 10/13/62, dis 1/13/63, house 524, s 2.

I

INGRAM, GARRETT. reg Har, co A, enl 10/13/62, dis 1/13/63, reg 47, co H, enr 8/1/63 Irvine, enl 10/5/63 Irvine, dis 12/26/64 Lexington, age 17, residence stated on muster roll, house 412, s 1,2,4.

INGRAM, GOODSON. reg Har, co A, enl 10/13/62, dis 1/13/63, reg 47, co H, enr 8/1/63 Irvine, enl 10/5/63 Irvine, dis 12/26/64 Lexington, age 29 or 35, residence stated on muster roll, house 419, s 1,2,4.

ISON, DOCTOR. reg Har, co A, enl 10/13/62, dis 1/13/63, house 393, s 2.

ISON, GEORGE. reg Har, co A, enl 10/13/62, dis 1/13/63, house 388 or 392, s 2.

ISON, GEORGE. reg 19, co D, enr 11/1/61 Camp Estill Springs, enl 1/2/62 Harrodsburg, dis 1/26/65 Louisville, age 26, house 388 or 392, s 1,2.
ISON, GIDEON. reg Har, co A, enl 10/13/62, dis 1/13/63, house 336 or 393, s 2.
ISON, GIDEON. reg 19, co D, enr 11/1/61 Camp Estill Springs, enl 1/2/62 Harrodsburg, dis 1/26/65 Louisville, age 28, d 1/10/62 Harrodsburg of disease, house 336 or 393, s 1,2.
ISON, JOHN. reg Har, co A, enl 10/13/62, dis 1/13/63, house 429, s 2.
ISON, JONAH. reg Har, co A, enl 10/13/62, dis 1/13/63, house 393, s 2.
ISON, MOSES. reg Har, co A, r 2nd lt, enl 10/13/62, dis 1/13/63, house 393, s 2.

J

JENKINS, ARCHIBALD. reg Har, co B, enl 10/13/62, dis 1/13/63, house 20, s 2.
JENKINS, WILLIAM M. reg Har, co B, r 3rd lt, enl 10/13/62, dis 1/13/63, house 20, s 2.
JOHNSON, FIELDING. reg 14Cav, co C, L, r sgt, enr 12/13/62 Owsley Co., enl 2/13/63 Irvine, dis 3/24/64 Camp Nelson, age 18, residence stated on muster roll, house n/c, s 1,2,4.
JOHNSON, THOMAS. reg 22, co G, r cpl, enr 3/10/62 Pikeville, enl 4/1/62 Cumberland Gap, dis 2/12/63, age 24, app cpl 4/30/62, CSR: "absent sick in Letcher Co. Ky.", reg 14Cav, co C, L, r 1st lt, enr 12/24/62 Owsley Co., enl 2/17/63 Irvine, dis 3/24/64 Camp Nelson, residence stated on muster roll, house 323, s 1,2,4.
JOHNSON, WILLIAM. reg 14Cav, co M, enr 12/11/62, enl 2/13/63 Irvine, dis 3/24/64 Camp Nelson, house 540, s 2.
JONES, GRANVILLE. reg 39, co C, enr 11/10/62 Peach Orchard, enl 2/16/63 Peach Orchard, age 23, des 4/28/63 Louisa, residence stated on muster roll, house n/c, s 1,2,4.

K

KISER, NIMROD. reg 14Cav, co M, enr 12/15/63 Owsley Co., enl 2/13/63 Irvine, dis 3/29/64 Camp Nelson, age 30 or 36, house 319, s 1,2.

L

LEWIS, ABNER. reg Har, co C, enl 10/13/62, dis 1/13/63, may be Harlan Co. resident, house 23, s 2.
LEWIS, JAMES. reg Har, co E, enl 10/13/62, dis 1/13/63, house 208, s 2.
LEWIS, JAMES H. reg 14Cav, co M, enr 5/20/63 Proctor, enl 6/15/63 Lexington, dis 3/24/64 Camp Nelson, age 32, house 25 or 208, s 1,2.
LEWIS, JAMES J. reg Har, co D, enl 10/13/62, dis 1/13/63, house 25 or 208, s 2.
LEWIS, JOHN C. reg 14Cav, co M, enr 5/20/63 Proctor, enl 6/15/63 Lexington, dis 3/29/64 Camp Nelson, house 208, s 1,2.

M

MAGGARD, DAVID W. reg Har, co F, enl 10/13/62, dis 1/13/63, house 224 or 242, s 2.
MAGGARD, JOHN. reg Har, co F, enl 10/13/62, dis 1/13/63, house 561, s 2.
MAY, WESLEY. reg 22EM, co B, enl 5/26/64, dis 6/28/64, house 378, s 2.
MCDANIEL, JOHN. reg 14Cav, co K, enr 5/2/63 Owsley Co., enl 6/15/63 Lexington, dis 3/24/64 Camp Nelson, age 20, house 38, s 1,2.

MCDANIEL, WILLIAM. reg Har, co A, enl 10/13/62, dis 1/13/63, reg 47, co H, enr 7/4/63 Irvine, enl 10/5/63 Irvine, dis 12/26/64 Lexington, age 18, residence stated on muster roll, house 38, s 1,2,4.
MCKNIGHT, JOHN. reg Har, co F, enl 10/13/62, dis 1/13/63, could be Harlan Co. resident, house 217, s 2.
MIDDLETON, DAVID. reg Har, co D, enl 10/13/62, dis 1/13/63, house 62, s 2.
MILES, WILLIAM. reg 47, co H, enr 8/20/63 Irvine, enl 10/5/63 Irvine, dis 5/6/64 Lexington, age 23, trans to 4th Ky. Vet. Inf. 4/30/64, credited to 8th enrollment district, residence stated on muster roll, house n/c, s 1,2,4.
MITCHELL, HIRAM. reg Har, co A, enl 10/13/62, dis 1/13/63, reg 47, co H, enr 8/2/63 Irvine, enl 10/31/63 Camp Nelson, dis 12/26/64 Lexington, age 18, dark hair & eyes, florid skin, 5-11, b Wise Co. VA, des 3/24/64 Booneville, residence stated on muster roll, house 81, s 1,2,4.
MITCHELL, RANSOM. reg 47, co H, 8/1/63 Irvine, 10/31/63 Camp Nelson, age 21, d 8/5/64 Paris of typhoid fever, residence stated on muster roll, house 81, s 1,2,4.
MITCHELL, THOMAS. reg 22EM, co A, enl 5/20/64, dis 6/28/64, house 81, s 2.
MOORE, WILLIAM. reg 22, co G, enr 10/25/61 or 3/10/62, enl 7/10/62 Cumberland Gap, dis 1/20/65 Louisville, age 16, des Camp Virginia 8/2/62, house 321, s 1,2,4.
MOORE, WILLIAM. reg 14Cav, co C, L, enr 12/15/62 Owsley Co., enl 7/3/63 Irvine, dis 3/24/64 Camp Nelson, age 18, residence stated on muster roll, house 321, s 1,2,4.
MORGAN, JOHN. reg 47, co H, enr 8/27/63 Irvine, enl 10/5/63 Irvine, dis 12/26/64 Lexington, age 21 or 22, credited to 8th enrollment district, residence stated on muster roll, house 354, s 1,2,4.
MULLINS, SOLOMON. reg Har, co F, enl 10/13/62, dis 1/13/63, house 247, s 2.

N

NEACE, SAMUEL. reg 39, co B, K, enr 12/15/62 Peach Orchard, enl 2/16/63 Peach Orchard, dis 9/15/65 Louisville, age 44, trans to co K 11/12/63, residence stated on muster roll, house 99, s 1,2,4.

P

PERKINS, JOSHUA C. reg Har, co B, r capt, enl 10/13/62, dis 1/13/63, house 578, s 2.
PHILLIPS, ZACHARIAH. reg 47, co H, enr 8/27/63 Irvine, enl 10/5/63 Irvine, dis 12/26/64 Lexington, age 28, residence stated on muster roll, house n/c, s 1,2,4.
POLLY, CLABOURN. reg Har, co A, enl 10/13/62, dis 1/13/63, reg 47, co H, enr 7/2/63 Irvine, enl 10/5/63 Irvine, age 28 or 38, des 10/8/63 Irvine, residence stated on muster roll, house 414, s 1,2,4.
POLLY, EDWARD, reg 19, co D, r cpl, enr 11/1/61 Camp Estill Springs, enl 1/2/62 Harrodsburg, dis 1/26/65 Louisville, age 19, prom to cpl 8/23/63, cap Sabine Cross Roads LA 4/8/64, exchanged 7/22/64, house 48, s 1,2.
POLLY, HENRY. reg Har, co A, r sgt, enl 10/13/62, dis 1/13/63, house 48, s 2.
POLLY, RANDOLPH. reg Har, co A, enl 10/13/62, dis 1/13/63, house 57, s 2.
POLLY, RICHARD. reg 47, co H, enl 8/2/63 Irvine, enl 10/5/63 Irvine, age 21, trans to 4th Ky. Vet. Inf. 4/30/64, residence stated on muster roll, house n/c, s 1,2,4.

Q

QUILLIN, RICHARD. reg 39, co K, enr 12/15/62 Peach Orchard, enl 2/16/63 Peach Orchard, age 30, dark hair, blue eyes, fair skin, 5-8, d 12/7/64 regimental hospital at Louisa of smallpox, residence stated on muster roll, house 199, s 1,2,4.

QUILLIN, WILLIAM. reg CG, co L, enr 6/8/64 Louisa, enl 7/6/64 Frankfort, dis 3/11/65 Catlettsburg, age 40, dark hair, blue eyes, fair skin, 6-0, b Pike Co., house 192, s 2,4.

R

RALEIGH, WILLIAM. reg Har, co F, enl 10/13/62, dis 1/13/63, house 216, s 2.
REYNOLDS, WILLIAM H. reg 39, co K, enr 5/26/64 Louisa, enl 8/30/64 Louisa, dis 9/15/65 Louisville age 27, light hair, blue eyes, fair skin, 5-8, house 140, s 1,2,4.
ROARK, JESSE. reg Har, co A, enl 10/13/62, dis 1/13/63, reg 14Cav, co M, enr 1/19/63 Owsley Co., enl 2/13/63 Irvine, dis 3/24/64 Camp Nelson, house 98, s 1,2.
ROSS, JAMES P. reg Har, co B, enl 10/13/62, dis 1/13/63, house 113, s 2.

S

SERGENT, ALLEN. reg Har, co C, enl 10/13/62, dis 1/13/63, reg 47, co H, enr 7/5/63 Irvine, enl 10/5/63 Irvine, dis 12/26/64 Lexington, age 26, muster roll lists him as Harlan Co. resident, house 312, s 1,2.
SERGENT, ANDREW. reg 47, co H, r cpl, enr 8/9/63 Irvine, enl 10/5/63 Irvine, dis 12/26/64 Lexington, age 22, prom to cpl 11/30/63, muster roll lists him as Harlan Co. resident, house 312, s 1,2.
SERGENT, DAVID. reg Har, co B, enl 10/13/62, dis 1/13/63, house 312, s 2.
SERGENT, JOHN. reg Har, co B, enl 10/13/62, dis 1/13/63, house 312, s 2.
SEXTON, HENRY W. reg 19, co D, enr 11/1/61 Camp Estill Springs, enl 1/2/62 Camp Harrod, Harrodsburg, dis 1/26/65 Louisville, age 22, cap Sabine Cross Roads LA 4/8/64, exch 7/22/64 Red River Landing LA, residence stated on muster roll, house n/c, s 1,2.
SEXTON, JEFFERSON. reg 19, co D, enr 11/1/61 Camp Estill Springs, enl 1/2/62 Harrodsburg, dis 6/4/64 New Orleans, age 21, black hair, blue eyes, dark skin, 5-11 dis on certificate of disability for chronic diarrhea, house 161, b Carter Co., house 161, s 1,2.
SEXTON, MARION. reg 45, co K, enr 11/24/63, enl 12/9/63 Louisa, dis 2/14/65 Catlettsburg, house 369, s 2.
SEXTON, WILLIAM. reg Har, co A, enl 10/13/62, dis 1/13/63, house 363, 440 or 513, s 2.
SINGLETON, JOSHUA. reg Har, co F, enl 10/13/62, dis 1/13/63, house 557, s 2.
SKEEN, HENRY A. reg 39, co A, enr 9/23/63 Louisa, enl 10/29/63 Louisa, dis 9/15/65 Louisville, age 19, fair hair & skin, blue eyes, 5-11, house 462, s 1,2, 4,31.
SMITH, JAMES. reg 10Cav, co F, r cpl, enr 8/9/62 Boyd Co., enl 9/9/62 Covington, dis 9/17/63 Maysville, age 25, prom to cpl 8/31/63, residence stated on muster roll, house 202, s 1,2,4.
SMITH, JEREMIAH. reg 14Cav, co L, enr 12/28/62 Owsley Co., enl 2/13/63 Irvine, dis 3/29/64 Camp Nelson, age 30, residence stated on muster roll, house 543, s 1,2,4.
SMITH, JOHN. reg Har, co B, enl 10/13/62, dis 1/13/63, may be a Harlan Co. resident, house 307, 399 or 418, s 2.
SMITH, SAMUEL. reg Har, co B, enl 10/13/62, dis 1/13/63, house 418, s. 2.
SMITH, THOMAS. reg 14Cav, co L, r cpl, enr 12/15/62 Owsley Co., enl 2/13/63 Irvine, dis 3/24/64 Camp Nelson, age 25, prom to cpl 12/24/62, residence stated on muster roll, house 542, s 1,2,4.
SMITH, WILLIAM. reg Har, co E, enl 10/13/62, dis 1/13/63, house 307, 402 or 544, s 2.
SMITH, WILLIAM. reg 14Cav, co L, r cpl, enr 12/15/62 Owsley Co., enl 2/13/63 Irvine, dis 3/24/64 Camp Nelson, age 31 or 37, prom to cpl 12/24/62, residence stated on muster roll, house 544, s 1,2,4.
SMITH, WILLIAM R. reg 14Cav, co D, E, M, enr 12/9/62 Owsley Co., enl 12/13/62 Irvine, dis 3/24/64 Camp Nelson, age 21 or 26, trans to co D 2/12/63, to co E 5/1/63, house 307, 402 or 544, s 1,2.

SPARKMAN, RICHARD. reg US Army, frontier service, enl 10/6/64, d Rock Island hospital, residence stated on s. 31, house n/c, s 1,31.

SPARKMAN, URIAH. reg Har, co A, enl 10/13/62, dis 1/13/63, house 401, s 2.

STALLARD, JAMES M. reg Har, co A, r cpl, enl 10/13/62, dis 1/13/63, house 589, s 2.

STAMPER, ALEXANDER. reg Har, co F, r sgt, enl 10/13/62, dis 1/13/63, reg 47, co H, r sgt, enr 8/11/63 Irvine, enl 10/5/63 Lexington, dis 1/26/64 Lexington, age 21, residence stated on muster roll, house 87, s 1, 2, 4.

STAMPER, D. CROCKETT. reg 19, co D, enr 11/1/61 Camp Estill Springs, Irvine, enl Camp Harrod, Harrodsburg, dis 1/26/65 Louisville, age 19, cap Sabine Cross Roads LA 4/8/64, exch 7/22/64 Red River Landing LA 7/22/64, d 2/8/65 Louisville of chronic diarrhea, buried Grave 53, Range 59, residence stated on muster roll, house n/c, s 1, 2.

STAMPER, ENOCH C. reg Har, co A, enl 10/13/62, dis 1/13/63, house 89, s 2.

STAMPER, IRA. reg Har, co B, enl 10/13/62, dis 1/13/63, house 88, s 2.

STAMPER, JOHN W. reg Har, co B, enl 10/13/62, dis 1/13/63, house 18, 87 or 265, s 2.

STAMPER, STEPHEN. reg 14Cav, co L, enr 12/25/62 Owsley Co., enl 2/13/63 Irvine, dis 3/24/64 Camp Nelson, age 18 or 20, residence stated on muster roll, house 442, s 1,2,4.

STAMPER, WILLIAM. reg 14Cav, co L, enr 12/25/62 Owsley Co., enl 2/13/63 Irvine, dis 3/24/64 Camp Nelson, age 18 or 23, residence stated on muster roll, house 442, s 1,2,4.

T

TAYLOR, JOHN R. reg 39, co B, enr 4/29/63, age 24, light hair, blue eyes, fair skin, 5-6, died 6/1/63 Ashland of typhoid fever, residence stated on muster roll, house n/c, s 1,2,4.

TAYLOR, JOSEPHUS S. C. reg 39, co A, enr 9/15/62, enl 2/16/63 Peach Orchard, prom to hospital steward 2/10/63, age 33, d 3/22/63 Louisa, residence stated on muster roll, house 374, s 1,2.

TOLAR, RICHARD M. reg 14Cav, co A, C, I, L, enr 12/5/62 Breathitt Co., enl 2/13/63 Irvine, dis 3/2/464 Camp Nelson, age 40, trans from co C to co A 2/13/63, residence stated on muster roll, house n/c, s 1,2,4.

W

WELLS, EZEKIEL. reg Har, co F, enl 10/13/62, dis 1/13/63, house 546, s 2.

WELLS, JOSEPH. reg Har, co F, r 1st lt, enl 10/13/62, dis 1/31/63, house 214, s 2.

WELLS, WILLIAM. reg Har, co F, enl 10/13/62, dis 1/13/63, house 108, 546, or 552, s 2.

WELLS, WILLIAM. reg 45, co E, F, enr 8/8/63 Catlettsburg, enl 11/6/63 Ashland, dis 12/24/64 Catlettsburg, age 18, trans to co F 5/20/64, house 108, 546 or 552, s 1,2.

WILLIAMS, JOHN. reg Har, co E, enl 1013/62, dis 1/13/63, house 337, s 2.

WILLIAMS, SAMUEL. reg Har, co A, enl 10/13/62, dis 1/13/63, house 77, s 2.

WILSON, ANDREW B. reg Har, co F, enl 10/13/62, dis 1/13/63, house 416, s 2.

WILSON, OSCAR J. reg Har, co A, enl 10/13/62, dis 1/13/63, house 417, s 2.

WRIGHT, JAMES C. reg 39, co B, enr 8/13/63, enl 12/30/63 Louisa, dis 9/1/65 Louisville, age 21 or 25, dark hair, eyes, & skin, 5-7, b Russell Co. VA, house 139, s 1,2.

WRIGHT, JOEL JR. reg 39, co B, enl 8/14/63 Paintsville, age 28, black hair & eyes, dark skin, 5-6, b Letcher Co., des 1/2/64, house 130 or 148, s 1,2.

WRIGHT, JOEL SR. reg 39, co B, enr 8/14/63 Louisa, m/in 8/29/63 Louisa, des 8/11/64, returned 4/16/65, m/out 9/15/65 Louisville, age 28, black hair, dark eyes & skin, 5-6, b Letcher Co., house 130 or 148, s 1,2.

Y

YOUNG, JOBE. reg 39, co K, enr 6/26/63 Pike Co., enl 8/30/63 Louisa, dis 9/15/65 Louisville, age 18, house 341, s 1,2.

YOUNG, REESE D. reg 14Cav, co L, enr 12/20/62 Owsley Co., enl 2/13/63 Irvine, dis 3/24/64 Camp Nelson, age 26 or 34, residence stated on muster roll, house 34, s 1,2,4.

YOUTS, ELIJAH. reg 39, co K, enr 12/25/62 Peach Orchard, enl 2/16/63 Peach Orchard, age 32, light hair, blue eyes, fair skin, 5-6, d 2/26/63 Louisa hospital of lung inflammation, hospital records state he was resident of Letcher Co., house 157, s 1,2,4.

YOUTS, SOLOMON. reg 39, co K, enr 12/27/62 Peach Orchard, enl 2/16/63 Peach Orchard, dis 9/15/65 Louisville, age 25, residence stated on muster roll, house 196, s 1,2,4.

MAGOFFIN COUNTY UNION SOLDIERS

A

ADAMS, BENJAMIN B. reg 45, co D, H, enr 2/17/64 Salyersville, enl 3/14/64 Flemingsburg, dis 2/22/65 Covington, age 22, dark hair, blue eyes, fair skin, 5-10, trans to co H 5/20/64, b Letcher Co., CSR lists Magoffin Co. as residence, house n/c, s 1,2,28.

ADAMS, DANIEL. reg 45, co D, r cpl, enr 9/30/63 Salyersville, enl 10/17/63 Ashland, dis 12/24/64 Catlettsburg, age 22, light hair, blue eyes, fair skin, 5-5, house 426, s 1,2,28.

ADAMS, GREENVILLE. reg 14, co B, I, enr 5/3/63 Louisa, enl 6/10/63 Louisa, dis 9/15/65 Louisville, age 18, trans to 14th Vet. Inf., co B, enr 5/3/63, m/in 6/10/63, CSR: "sick at home in Magoffin Co.", house 402, s 1,2,4,28.

ADAMS, HARVEY M. reg 14, co I, r sgt, enr 11/10/61 Louisa, enl 12/10/61 Louisa, age 31, light hair, blue eyes, fair skin, trans to 14th Vet. Inf. enl 2/29/64, m/in 3/15/64, d 10/7/64 Ashland, residence stated on muster roll, house n/c, s 1,2,4.

ADAMS, JOHNSON. reg 14, co F, enr 9/1/63 Salyersville, enl 10/31/63 Louisa, dis 1/31/65 Louisa, age 35, des 6/25/64 Chattanooga TN, house 27, s 1,2,28.

ADAMS, MOSES. reg 14, co F, enr 6/20/63 Salyersville, enl 8/30/63 Louisa, dis 9/15/65 Louisville, age 18, trans to 14th Vet. Inf., co D, house 402, s 2,28.

ADAMS, PRESTON. reg 14, co B, I, enr 4/2/63 Louisa, enl 6/10/63 Louisa, dis 9/15/65 Louisville, age 33, trans to 14th Vet. Inf., co B, enr 4/12/63, m/in 6/10/63, CSR: "left sick at Salyersville", house 587, s 1,2,4,28.

ADAMS, SIMPSON. reg 14, co I, enr 5/15/63 Louisa, enl 6/10/63 Louisa, age 23, fair hair & skin, blue eyes, 5-10, d 11/19/64 Louisville of typhoid fever, b Letcher Co., residence stated on muster roll, house n/c, s 1,2,4,28.

ADAMS, WILEY. reg 14, co I, enr 11/10/61 Louisa, enl 12/10/61 Louisa, dis 1/31/65 Louisa, age 34, dark hair & skin, black eyes, 5-10, b Floyd Co., house 112, s 1,2,4,28.

ADAMS, WILLIAM RILEY. reg 14, co F, enr 6/20/63 Salyersville, enl 8/30/63 Louisa, age 23, dark hair, eyes & skin, 5-10, wounded in action 6/22/64, b Letcher Co., d 1/5/65 Louisa of smallpox, CSR: "effects to be mailed to parents at Salyersville", age 11 on census, house 27, s 1,2,28.

ADAMS, WILLIAM SMITH. reg 45, co D, r capt, enr 6/2/63 Catlettsburg, enl 10/17/63 Ashland, dis 12/24/64 Catlettsburg, age 27, house 581, s 1,2,28.

ALLEN, SAMUEL D. reg 39, co E, enr 11/7/63 Louisa, enl 12/29/63 Louisa, age 20 or 21, light hair, blue eyes, fair skin, 5-10, des 8/12/64 Louisa, house 87, s 1,2,4.

ALSOP, ROBERT. reg 45, co D, enr 9/27/63 Salyersville, enl 10/17/63 Ashland, dis 12/24/64 Catlettsburg, age 33, dark hair, blue eyes, fair skin, 5-7, b Floyd Co., cap Salyersville 11/30/63, taken to Richmond VA 12/8/63, paroled City Point 4/16/64, returned to duty 6/28/64, house 548, s 1,2,28.

ATKINSON, JOHN MILTON. reg 14, co I, r capt, enr 11/10/61 Louisa, enl 12/10/61 Louisa, dis 9/15/65 Louisville, age 25, prom from sgt to 1st sgt 3/17/62, to 2nd lt 5/5/63, to 1st lt 9/8/63, to capt 6/30/64, trans to 14th Vet. Inf. 6/30/64, residence stated on List of Officers, house n/c, s 1,2,4,28,32.

AUSTIN, GEORGE. reg 14, co I, enr 11/10/61 Louisa, age 19, d 12/12/61 Louisa of pneumonia, residence stated on muster roll, house n/c, s 1,2,4.

B

BACK, SOLOMON. reg 45, co D, H, enr 10/21/63 Salyersville, enl 2/3/64 Mt. Sterling, age 35, light hair, blue eyes, fair skin, 5-7, trans from co H to co D 2/1/64, des 4/3/64 Flemingsburg, b Perry Co., house 386, s 1,2,28.

BAILEY, ALEXANDER L. reg 14, co F, D, enr 6/20/63 Salyersville, enl 8/30/63 Louisa, dis 9/15/65 Louisville, age 16 or 18, trans to 14 Vet. Inf., co D, enl 6/30/63, m/in 8/30/63, house 122, s 1,2,28.

BAILEY, CHARLES P. reg 14, co I, B, enr 9/4/62 Catlettsburg, enl 12/12/62 Richmond, dis 9/15/65 Louisville, age 23, trans to 14 Vet. Inf., co D, house 121, s 1,2,4,28.

BAILEY, HENRY. reg 5th US Volunteers, enl 4/6/65, house 8 or 441, s 1.

BAILEY, JAMES. reg 5th US Volunteers, enl 4/6/65 Camp Douglas, house 8, s 1.

BAILEY, JAMES F. reg 14, co F, r cpl, enr 6/20/63 Salyersville, enl 8/30/63 Louisa, age 25, trans to 14 Vet. Inf., co D, prom to cpl, co D, cap Salyersville 11/29/63, d Andersonville GA prison 5/3/64 of diarrhea, house 122, s 1, 2,28.

BAILEY, LEWIS P. reg 14, co F, D, r sgt, enr 6/20/63 Salyersville, enl 8/30/63 Louisa, dis 9/15/65 Louisville, age 28, trans to 14 Vet. Inf., co D, prom to sgt 2/1/65, house 101, s 1,2.

BAILEY, WALLACE W. reg 16, co C, enr 11/1/61 Camp Guthrie, Johnson Co., enl 12/18/61 or 1/27/62 Camp Lee, dis 1/27/65 Frankfort, age 19, black hair & eyes, fair skin, 6-1, trans to 13 Ky. Inf. 1/16/64, back to 16 Ky. Inf. 6/19/64, b Floyd Co., house 122, s 1,2,28.

BAILEY, WILLIAM. reg 24, co F, enr 11/11/62 Manchester, enl 1/26/63 Frankfort, dis 1/31/65 Covington, age 19, house 179, s 1,2,28.

BAYS, WILLIAM J. reg 14 co I, r cpl, enr 11/10/61 Louisa, enl 12/10/61 Louisa, dis 1/31/65 Louisa, age 25, app cpl 5/5/63, house 340, s 1,2,4,28.

BLANTON, GEORGE W. reg 14, co I, enr 11/10/61 Louisa, enl 12/10/61 Louisa, age 18, d 2/20/63 Ashland of typhoid, residence stated on muster roll, house n/c, s 1,2,4.

BLANTON, JILSON. reg 14, co I, B, enr 2/17/62 Camp Buell, enl 3/15/64 Louisa, dis 9/15/65 Louisville, age 22, light hair, blue eyes, fair skin, 5-10, trans to 14 Vet Inf, co B, enl 2/29/64, m/in 3/15/64, b Johnson Co., residence stated on muster roll, house n/c, s 1,2,4.

BLANTON, JOHN M. reg 16, co C, enr 11/1/61 Camp Guthrie, enl 12/18/61 or 1/27/62 Camp Lee, dis 1/27/65 Frankfort, age 22, trans to 13 Ky. Inf., co C 1/16/64, back to 16 Ky. Inf. 6/19/64, house 92, s 1,2,4,28.

BLANTON, WILLIAM. reg 45, co D, H, enr 10/29/63 Salyersville, enl 2/6/64 Mt. Sterling, dis 12/24/64 Catlettsburg, age 62, red hair & skin, blue eyes, 5-10, b Lee Co. VA, trans from co H to co D 2/1/64, back to co H 5/20/64, house 552, s 1,2,28.

BROWN, DANIEL. reg 39, co E, F, enr 4/25/63 Louisa, enl 6/11/63 Louisa, dis 9/15/65 Louisville, age 44, dark hair, blue eyes, fair skin, 5-8, dis for disability of chronic diarrhea 5/12/65, residence stated on muster roll, house n/c, s 1,2 .

BROWN, HENRY C. reg 45, co H, D, enr 2/1/64 Salyersville, enl 2/6/64 Mt. Sterling, dis 2/14/65 Catlettsburg, age 19, black hair & eyes, 5-10, b Morgan Co., trans from co H to co D 2/1/64, back to co D 5/20/64, house 42, s 1,2, 28.

C

CAUDILL, ABEL. reg 45, co D, enr 9/28/63 Salyersville, enl 10/17/63 Ashland, dis 12/24/64 Catlettsburg, age 26, dark hair & eyes, medium skin, 5-9, b Harlan Co., age 42 on census, house 423, s 1,2,28.

CAUDILL, BENJAMIN L. reg 45, co D, r 1st sgt, enr 10/1/63 Salyersville, enl 10/17/63 Ashland, age 21, light hair, gray eyes, fair skin, 5-8, d 4/21/64 Lexington of pneumonia, b Morgan Co., house 568, s 1,2,28.

COFFEE, ISAAC F. reg 14, co I, B, r sgt, enr 9/17/62 Catlettsburg, enl 12/12/64 Richmond, dis 9/15/65 Louisville, age 19, light hair, blue eyes, fair skin, 5-10, prom to cpl 10/27/64, to sgt 7/1/65, trans to 14th Vet Inf, co B, wounded 5/29/64 in abdomen, b Morgan Co., residence stated on muster roll, house n/c, s 1,2,4,28.

COFFEE, JAMES F. reg 14, co I, enr 9/17/62 Catlettsburg, enl 12/12/62 Richmond, age 22, d 2/12/63 Danville of typhoid fever, house 390, s 1,2,28.

COLE, WILLIAM G. reg 14, co I, F, enr 6/20/63 Salyersville, enl 8/30/63 Louisa, dis 12/6/63, age 29, des 12/6/63 Salyersville, house 149, s 1,2,28.

COLLINSWORTH, EDMOND F. reg 14, co F, D, enr 6/20/63 Salyersville, enl 8/30/63 Louisa, dis 9/15/65 Louisville, age 18, trans to 14th Vet. Inf., co D, house 161, s 1,2,28.

COLLINSWORTH, WILLIAM ATCHISON. reg 14, co I, B, enr 11/10/61 Louisa, enl 12/10/61 Louisa, dis 9/15/65 Louisville, age 28 or 30, light hair, blue eyes, fair skin, 6-3, trans to 14th Vet. Inf., co B, 2/29/64, m/in 3/15/64, b Floyd Co., house 521, s 1,2,4,28.

COLVIN, ABIDE. reg 14, co I, B, r cpl, enr 11/10/61 Louisa, enl 12/10/61 Louisa, dis 9/15/65 Louisville, age 20, light hair, blue eyes, fair skin, 6-0, trans to 14th Vet Inf, enr 2/29/64, m/in 3/15/64, b Floyd Co., house 515, s 1, 2,28.

COLVIN, JEHISA. reg 14, co I, B, enr 10/10/61 Louisa, enl 12/10/61 Louisa, dis 9/15/65 Louisville, age 18 or 20, light hair, blue eyes, fair skin, 5-11, trans to 14th Vet. Inf., co B, enl 2/29/64, m/in 3/15/64, b Floyd Co., house 515, s 1,2,28.

CONARD, MASON. reg 14, co K, C, enr 5/22/63, enl 5/28/63 Louisa, age 27, trans to 14th Vet Inf, co C, trans to Veteran Reserve Corps 3/18/65, residence stated on muster roll, house n/c, s 1,2,4.

CONLEY, CONSTANTINE. reg 45, co D, enr 9/28/63 Salyersville, enl 1/12/63 Ashland, dis 12/24/64 Catlettsburg, age 33, black hair & eyes, fair skin, 5-9, house 109, s 1,2,28.

CONLEY, HOUSTON. reg 14, co I, enr 6/3/63 Louisa, enl 6/20/63 Louisa, age 20, d 9/21/63 Magoffin Co. of typhoid fever, house 424, s 1,4,28.

CONLEY, JAMES. reg 14, co I, enr 11/10/61 Louisa, enl 12/10/61 Louisa, dis 1/31/65 Louisa, age 23 or 24, house 410, s 1,2,4,28.

CONLEY, LEWIS P. reg 14, co I, enr 11/10/61 Louisa, enl 12/10/61 Louisa, dis 1/31/65 Louisa, age 20, house 581, s 1,2,4,28.

CONLEY, WILLIAM. reg 14, co I, enr 11/10/61 Louisa, enl 12/10/61 Louisa, age 22 or 23, dark hair & skin, black eyes, 6-0, b Floyd Co., cap Magoffin Co., confined at Richmond 12/8/63, taken to Andersonville GA 7/14/64, d at Andersonville of diarrhea, house 442, s 1,2,4.

CONLEY, WILLIAM S. reg 45, co D, enr 9/28/63 Salyersville, enl 10/17/63 Ashland, dis 12/24/64 Catlettsburg, age 35, light hair, blue eyes, red skin, 5-11, b Floyd Co., left sick on scout in Magoffin Co, house 103, s 1,2,28.

COOPER, ARCHIBALD P. reg 45, co D, enr 9/27/63 Salyersville, enl10/17/63 Ashland, dis 12/24/64 Catlettsburg, age 36, dark hair, blue eyes, fair skin, 5-9, b Morgan Co., house 421, s 1,2,28.

COOPER, DAVID C. reg 45, co D, enr 9/28/63 Salyersville, enl 10/17/63 Ashland, age 21, cap 10/30/63 Salyersville, d 1/4/64 Richmond VA of varioloid (similar to smallpox), house 528, s 1,2,28.

COOPER, MILTON C. reg 14, co I, B, enr 7/5/63 Salyersville, enl 8/30/63 Louisa, dis 9/15/65 Louisville, age 18, trans to 14th Vet. Inf., co B, hospital document lists Magoffin Co. as residence, house 528, s 1,2,28.

COOPER, SANFORD R. reg 14, co F, enr 6/20/63 Salyersville, enl 8/30/63 Louisa, dis 9/15/65 Louisville, age 16 or 17, trans to 14th Vet. Inf., co D, CSR: "at home sick in Magoffin Co.", house 364, s 1,2,28.

D

DALTON, ALLEN. reg 45, co H, D, enr 10/22/63, enl 2/3/64 Mt. Sterling, age 48, gray hair, blue eyes, fair skin, 6-1, trans from co H to co D 2/1/64, b Grayson Co. VA, d 5/5/64 Ashland, house 176, s 1,2,28.
DAVIS, DAVID. reg 8, co E, enr 10/9/61, enl 1/15/62 Lebanon, age 20, house 221, s 2,4,28.
DYER, DAVID. reg 39, co C, enr 9/10/62 Peach Orchard, enl 2/16/63 Peach Orchard, dis 9/15/65 Louisville, age 20, cap 12/4/62 Floyd Co. and exchanged, paroled at City Point 4/3/63, residence stated on muster roll, house n/c, s 1, 2,4.
DYER, JOSEPH. reg 45, co D, enr 10/29/63 Salyersville, dis 3/24/65 Covington, age 29, black hair & eyes, dark skin, 5-11, b Morgan Co., cap 11/30/63 Salyersville, sent to Andersonville GA 2/11/64, paroled 12/16/64 Charleston SC, house 215, s 1,28.
DYER, WILLIAM. reg 14, co K, enr 11/8/61, enl 12/19/61 Louisa, dis 1/31/65 Louisa, age 21 or 25, dark hair, gray eyes, fair skin, 5-9, muster roll lists Floyd Co. as residence, but he is not on Floyd Co. census, house 50, s 1,2,28
DYKES, JAMES. reg 45, co H, D, enr 10/23/63, enl 2/3/64 Mt. Sterling, dis 12/24/64 Catlettsburg, age 39, dark hair, blue eyes, fair skin, 5-11, b Floyd Co., trans from co H to co D 2/1/64, back to co H 5/1/64, house 209, s 1,2, 28.

E

ELAM, ROBERT P. reg 14, co I, enr 11/10/61 Louisa, enl 12/10/61 Louisa, age 22, d 3/24/62 Camp Buell, shot by accident, residence stated on muster roll, house n/c, s 1,2,4,28.
EVANS, JAMES. reg 14, co F, E, r cpl, enr 10/25/61 or 11/19/61 Louisa, enl 12/10/61 Louisa, dis 1/31/65 Louisa, age 18, trans from co F to co E 8/29/63, prom to cpl 11/25/62, reduced to ranks 8/28/63, trans back to co F 1/20/65, house 104, s 1,2,28.

F

FITCH, ANDREW B. reg 14, co I, r 2nd lt, enr 6/20/64 Louisa, enl 7/16/64 Isom's Ferry GA, dis 1/31/65 Louisa, age 22, prom to sgt 5/1/62, prom to 1st sgt 1/4/64, prom from 1st sgt to 2nd lt 6/30/64, residence stated on muster roll, house n/c, s 1,2,4.
FITCH, JEREMIAH. reg 14, co I, enr 11/10/61 Louisa, enl 12/10/61 Louisa, age 25, d 1/22/62 Paintsville of typhoid fever, house 528, s 1,2,4,28.
FLETCHER, APPERSON. reg 14, co B, I, enr 11/10/61 Louisa, enl 12/10/61 Louisa, dis 9/15/65 Louisville, age 25, dark hair, black eyes, fair skin, 5-10, trans to 14th Vet Inf, co B, enl 2/29/64, m/in 3/25/64, b Floyd Co., house 344, s 1,2,4,28.
FLETCHER, MEREDITH. reg 14, co F, D, enr 6/20/63 Salyersville, enl 8/31/63 Louisa, dis 9/15/65 Louisville, age 25, 27 or 28, trans to 14th Vet. Inf., co D, house 345, s 1,2,28.
FLETCHER, SYLVESTER. reg 39, co G, enr 11/13/62 Peach Orchard, enl 2/16/63 Peach Orchard, dis 9/15/65 Louisville, age 18, light hair, blue eyes, light skin, cap 12/18/64 Bristol TN, released 2/14/65, muster roll lists Johnson Co. as residence but he is not listed on Johnson Co. census, house 506, s 1, 2, 4.

FLETCHER, WALTER. reg 39, co G, enr 9/13/62 Peach Orchard, enl 2/16/63 Peach Orchard, dis 9/15/65 Louisville, age 18, light hair, hazel eyes, light skin, 5-6, muster roll lists Johnson Co. as residence, but he is not listed on Johnson Co. census, house 506, s 1,20,28.

FLETCHER, WINSTON. reg 39, co G, enr 12/24/62 Peach Orchard, enl 2/14/63 Peach Orchard, dis 9/15/65 Louisville, age 18, light hair & skin, hazel eyes, 5-10, muster roll lists Johnson Co. as residence, but he is not listed on Johnson Co. census, house 506, s 1,2,4.

FLINT, HIRAM. reg 45, co H, D, enr 10/23/63 Salyersville, enl 2/3/64 Mt. Sterling, dis 12/24/64 Catlettsburg, age 21, black hair, blue eyes, fair skin, 5-10, trans from co H to co D, 2/1/ 64, back to co H 5/20/64, b Floyd Co., house 111, s 1, 2,28.

FLINT, WILLIAM. reg 14, co I, enr 11/10/61 Louisa, enl 12/10/61 Louisa, age 23 or 24, light hair, blue eyes, fair skin, 5-8, dis 1/1/63 Danville for disability of pulmonalis (tuberculosis), CSR: "at home sick in Magoffin Co.", b. Floyd Co., house 366, s 1,2,4,28.

G

GARDNER, HENRY G. reg 14, co F, r capt, enr 10/10/61 Louisa, enl 12/10/61 Louisa, dis 9/15/65 Louisville, age 19, prom from 2nd lt to 1st lt 5/5/63, prom from 1st lt to capt co I 8/8/63, trans to 14th Vet Inf, co A, wounded in thigh 6/22/64, residence stated on List of Officers, house n/c, s 1,2,28,32.

GULLETT, ALLEN. reg 14, co I, enr 11/10/61 Louisa, enl 12/10/61, age 22, dark hair & skin, blue eyes, b Morgan Co., wounded 2/18/63 in accidental shooting at Louisa rendering left hand useless, dis 3/18/63 Louisa, CSR: "at home in Magoffin Co. on furlough", residence stated on muster roll, house n/c, s 1,2,4,28.

GULLETT, DANIEL. reg 14, co I, enr 11/10/61 Louisa, enl 12/10/61 Louisa, dis 1/31/65 Louisa, age 19, d 2/24/63 Louisa of typhoid fever, house 102, 365 or 584, s 1,2,28.

GULLETT, DIAL. reg 14, co I, B, enr 10/10/61 Louisa, enl 12/10/61 Louisa, dis 9/15/65 Louisville, age 18 or 21, dark hair & skin, blue eyes, 5-8, trans to 14th Vet. Inf., co B, enl 2/29/64, m/in 3/15/64, b Morgan Co., house 555, s 1,2,4,28.

GULLETT, JAMES. reg 45, co G, enr 8/12/63 Mt. Sterling, enl 11030/63 Ashland, dis 2/14/65 Catlettsburg, age 19, black hair, gray eyes, dark skin, 5-7, b Magoffin Co., house 175, s 1,2,28.

GULLETT, LEVI A. reg 40, co E, r sgt, enr 7/7/63, enl 9/28/63 Grayson, dis 12/30/64 Catlettsburg, age 19, prom from cpl to sgt 6/30/64, residence stated on muster roll, house n/c, 1,2, .

GULLETT, LEWIS W. reg 14, co I, r cpl, enr 11/10/61 Louisa, enl 12/10/61 Louisa, dis 1/31/65 Louisa, age 25 or 27, dark hair, blue eyes, fair skin, 5-9, cap Lexington 9/62, paroled at Lexington 9/62, b Knox Co., house 102, s 1, 2,4,28.

GULLETT, MARTIN M. reg 54, co F, enr & enl 9/3/64 Greenupsburg, dis 9/15/65 Louisville, age 30 or 36, light hair, blue eyes, fair skin, 6-2, b Boyd Co., credited to 9th Cong. District, house 373, s 1,2,28.

GULLETT, MATTHEW. reg I, B, enr 4/8/63, enl 6/10/63 Louisa, dis 9/15/65 Louisville, age 25, dark hair & skin, blue eyes, 5-9, b Morgan Co., trans to 14th Vet Inf, co B, wounded 8/3/64 right thigh, residence on muster roll, house 373, s 1,2,28.

GULLETT, WILLIAM S. reg 14, co I, B, enr 3/15/63 Louisa, enl 6/10/63 Louisa, dis 9/15/65 Louisville, age 20, trans to 14th Vet. Inf., co B, house 175, s 1,2,4,28.

H

HACKWORTH, JEREMIAH. reg 14, co I, enr 11/10/61 Louisa, enl 12/10/61 Louisa, dis 1/31/65 Louisa, age 22, hospital card lists Magoffin Co. as residence, house 513, s 1,2,28.

HACKWORTH, JESSE. reg 14, co F, D, enr 6/14/63 Salyersville, enl 8/30/63 Louisa, dis 9/15/65 Louisville, age 16, trans to 14th Vet. Inf., co D, house 513, s 1,2,28.

HALE, JAMES W. reg 39, co K, enr 9/6/63 Louisa, enl 10/3/63 or 10/30/63 Louisa, dis 9/15/65 Louisville, age 29 at discharge, house 67, s 1,2.

HALE, WILLIAM R. reg 68EM, co C, enl 5/21/64 Louisa, age 35, light hair, blue eyes, fair skin 6-1, b Wayne Co. VA, house 317, s 2.

HAMMON, BENJAMIN. reg 14, co I, r 1st sgt, enr 11/10/61 Louisa, enl 12/10/61 Louisa, dis 1/31/65 Louisa, age 25, app cpl 3/1/62, prom to 5th sgt, 1/64, prom to 1st sgt, house 210, s 1,2,28.

HAMMON, HEZEKIAH. reg 14, co I, enr 11/10/61 Louisa, enl 12/10/61 Louisa, dis 1/31/65 Louisa, age 32, cap 11/30/63 Salyersville, confined at Richmond VA 12/8/63, died 4/8/64 Richmond VA of bronchitis, house 212, s 1,2,4,28.

HAMMON, JEPTHA. reg 14, co I, enr 11/10/61 Louisa, enl 12/10/61 Louisa, age 18 or 20, dark hair, black eyes, fair skin, 5-6, b Morgan Co., trans to 14th Vet. Inf., enl 2/29/64, m/in 3/15/64, wounded 6/22/64 Kennesaw Mtn., GA, d 7/1/64 Knoxville TN of wounds, house 204, s 1,2,4,28.

HAMMON, JOHN W. reg 14, co I, B, r cpl, enr 11/10/61 Louisa, enl 12/10/61 Louisa, dis 9/15/65 Louisville, age 20, 21 or 23, dark hair, black eyes, fair skin, 5-6, trans to 14th Vet Inf, co B, enl 2/29/64, m/in 3/15/64, b Morgan Co., prom to cpl 8/2/65, house 204, s 1,2,4,28.

HAMMON, THOMAS. reg 8, co E, B, enr 10/9/61 Camp Estill Springs, enl 1/15/62 Lebanon, age 20 or 30, d 3/11/63 Louisville of disease, house 451, s 1,2,4,28.

HAMMON, WILLIAM PRESTON. reg 14, co I, r 1st sgt, enr 11/10/61 Louisa, enl 12/10/61 Louisa, dis 9/15/65 Louisville, age 21, black hair, dark eyes & skin, 5-6, trans to 14th Vet. Inf., co B, enl 2/29/64, m/in 3/15/64, b Morgan Co., app cpl 6/4/64, prom to sgt 6/30/64, prom to 1st sgt 2/1/65, house 204, s 1,2,4,28.

HARVEY, JOHN T. reg 45, co H, D, enr 10/29/63 Salyersville, enl 2/3/64 Mt. Sterling, dis 2/14/65 Catlettsburg, age 19, light hair, blue eyes, fair skin, 5-4, trans from co H to co D, 2/1/64, back to co H, 5/20/64, b Breathitt Co., age 28 on census, house 284., s 1,2,28.

HELTON, GEORGE. reg 45, co D, enr 9/27/63 Salyersville, 10/17/63 Ashland, dis 12/24/64 Catlettsburg, age 28, house 567, s 1,2,28.

HELTON, JACOB W. reg 45, co D, r 3rd sgt, enr 9/28/63 Salyersville, enl 10/17/63 Ashland, dis 12/24/64 Catlettsburg, age 33, black hair & eyes, dark skin, 6-1, b Patrick Co, VA, prom to 3rd sgt 4/22/64, house 115, s 1,2,28.

HONAKER, ISAIAH D. reg 45, co D, enr 8/22/63 Catlettsburg, enl 10/17/63 Ashland, age 18, light hair & skin, blue eyes, d 3/14/64 Flemingsburg of camp fever, b Russell Co. VA, house 363, s 1,2,28.

HONAKER, MARTIN W. reg 14, co I, B, enr 11/10/61 Louisa, enl 12/19/61 Louisa, dis 3/1/62 Paintsville for epilepsy, age 19, light hair, blue eyes, fair skin, 5-9, b Russell Co. VA, CSR: "at home sick in Magoffin Co.", house 363, s 1,2,4,28.

HOSKINS, JOHN ROBERT. reg 14, co I, enr 11/10/61 Louisa, enl 12/10/61 Louisa, dis 1/31/65 Louisa, age 39, fair hair & skin, blue eyes, b. Breathitt Co., hospital card lists Magoffin Co. as residence, house 350, s 1,2,28.

HOSKINS, MOSES. reg 14, co F, D, enr 8/1/63 Salyersville, enl 8/30/63 Louisa, dis 9/15/65 Louisville, trans to 14th Vet Inf, co D, CSR: "at home sick in Magoffin Co.", house 350, s 1,2,28.

HOWARD, ALLEN L. reg 14, co F, D, enr 6/20/63 Salyersville, enl 8/30/63 Louisa, dis 9/15/65 Louisville, age 26, trans to 14th Vet. Inf., co D, des 3/6/65, house 156, s 1,2,28.

HOWARD, RILEY. reg 45, co H, D, r cpl, enr 10/30/63 Salyersville, enl 2/6/64 Mt. Sterling, dis 4/14/65 Catlettsburg, age 20 or 28, black hair, blue eyes, dark skin, 5-11, b Breathitt Co., trans from co H to co D 2/1/64, back to co H 5/20/64, house 543, s 1,2,28.

HOWARD, SAMUEL. reg 45, co D, enr 9/1/63 Salyersville, enl 10/17/63 Ashland, dis 12/24/64 Catlettsburg, age 22, age 40 on census, house 55, s 1,2,28.
HOWARD, THOMAS S. reg 45, co D, enr 2/17/64 Salyersville, enl 3/14/64 Flemingsburg, dis 1/24/64 Catlettsburg, age 19, dark hair, blue eyes, fair skin, 5-10, b Morgan Co., died 4/8/64 Flemingsburg of typhoid fever, CSR lists Magoffin Co. as residence, house 184 or 414, s 1,2,28.
HOWARD, WILLIAM. reg 45, co D, enr 9/27/63 Salyersville, enl 10/17/63 Ashland, dis 12/14/64 Catlettsburg, age 37, house 416, s 1,2,28.

J

JACKSON, JOHN. reg 45, co D, enr 10/27/63 Salyersville, cap Magoffin Co. 12/4/63, confined at Richmond VA, sent to Andersonville GA 2/14/64, d 4/20/64 of anasarca (extreme swelling), house 152, s 1,28.
JOSEPH, GEORGE. reg 39, co E, F, enr 11/15/62 Peach Orchard, enl 2/16/63 Peach Orchard, age 20, cap 1/1/63 or 1/28/63 Floyd Co., residence stated on muster roll, house n/c, s 1,4,28.

K

KEETON, CATLETT L. reg 8, co B, E, enr 11/1/61 Camp Estill Springs, enl 1/15/62 Lebanon, age 20, wounded Stones River TN 12/30/62-1/3/63, cap Battle of Chickamauga GA 9/19/63 or 9/20/63, confined at Richmond VA 9/29/63, sent to Danville VA 12/12/63, taken to Andersonville GA, believed to have died there about 8/1/64, house 499, s 1,2,4,28.
KEETON, GEORGE W. reg 8, co E, B, enr 11/1/61 Camp Estill Springs, enl 1/15/62 Lebanon, age 18, killed Battle of Stones River TN 1/2/63, buried grave #2423, Section F, Stone's River National Cemetery, house 499, s 1,2, 4,28.
KEETON, HARVEY. reg 8, co B, E, enr 10/9/61 Camp Estill Springs, enl 1/15/62 Lebanon, age 20 or 31, dis 5/5/62 for disability of deafness, house 222, s 1,2,28.
KEETON, JAMES MADISON. reg 14, co I, r cpl, enr 11/10/61 Louisa, enl 12/10/61 Louisa, age 32, d 2/19/63 Louisa of typhoid fever, house 207, s 1,2,4,28.
KENNEDY (CANADY), WILLIS. reg 24, co G, enr 11/5/61, enl 12/31/61 Lexington, age 20, trans to co K, 6th Vet Ky. Cav., residence stated on muster roll, house n/c, s 1,2,4,28.
KIMBERLAIN, JOHN W. reg 45, co H, D, enr 10/27/62 Salyersville, enl 2/3/64 Mt. Sterling, dis 12/24/64 Catlettsburg, age 45, dark hair, eyes & skin, 5-11, trans to co H 5/20/64, back to co D 2/1/64, b Wythe Co. VA, house 123, s 1, 2,28.
KIMBERLAIN, MICHAEL. reg 14, co I, enr 11/10/61 Louisa, enl 12/10/61 Louisa, age 25, dark hair & skin, black eyes, 5-5, b Lee Co. VA, wounded in action 6/2/64 Altoona Mtn. GA, d 6/18/64 Chattanooga TN of wounds, buried grave 217, Section E, N. Cemetery, residence stated on muster roll, house n/c, s 1,2,4.

L

LEMASTER, SAMUEL. reg 45, co D, enr 9/28/63 Salyersville, enl 10/7/63 Ashland, dis 12/24/64 Catlettsburg, age 22, red hair & skin, blue eyes, 5-6, b Morgan Co., house 563, s 1,2,4,6,28.
LITTERAL, MILTON (SHELTON). reg 14, co F, D, r cpl, enr 6/20/63 Salyersville, enl 8/30/63 Louisa, dis 9/15/65 Louisville, age 29, trans to 14th Vet. Inf., wounded 6/22/64, hospital card lists Magoffin Co. as residence, app cpl 2/1/65, house 395, s 1,2,28.

LYKINS, HARRISON. reg 8, co E, enr 10/9/61 Camp Estill Springs, enl 1/15/62 Lebanon, dis 11/17/64 Chattanooga TN, age 18, d 2/15/62 Lebanon of fever, house 382, s 1,2,4,28.

LYKINS, WILLIAM. reg 8, co E, enr 10/9/61 Camp Estill Springs, enl 1/30/62 Lebanon, dis 11/17/64 Chattanooga TN, d 8/4/62 Lebanon, house 382, s 1,2,4,28.

M

MADDOX, HENRY. reg 45, co H, D, enr 10/2/63 Salyersville, enl 2/3/64 Mt. Sterling, dis 12/24/64 Catlettsburg, age 51, dark hair, blue eyes, fair skin, 5-10, b Floyd Co., trans from co H to co D 2/1/64, back to co H 5/20/64, house 171, s 1,2,28.

MADDOX, WILLOUGHBY. reg 45, co H, D, enr 10/29/63 Salyersville, enl 2/3/64 Mt. Sterling, dis 12/24/64 Catlettsburg, age 22, light hair, blue eyes, fair skin, b Pellis Co. MO, trans from co H to co D 2/1/64, back to co H 5/20/64, house 171, s 1,2,28.

MARSHALL, GEORGE W. reg 14, co I, D, enr 2/8/62, enl Paintsville, dis 9/15/65 Louisville, age 18, dark hair, blue eyes, fair skin, 5-7, trans to 14 Vet. Inf., co D, b Floyd Co., CSR lists Magoffin Co. as residence, house 163, s 1, 2,4,28.

MARSHALL, JACKSON. reg 14, co F, D, enr 6/20/63 Salyersville, enl 8/30/63 Louisa, dis 9/15/65 Louisville, age 21, trans to 14th Vet. Inf., co D, wounded in left arm and side 7/19/64 and sent to field hospital, Marietta GA, house 161, s 1,2,28.

MARSHALL, REUBEN. reg 14, co I, B, enr & enl 2/24/64 Paintsville, dis 9/15/65 Louisville, age 24, light hair, blue eyes, fair skin 5-9, trans to 14th Vet. Inf., co B, b Floyd Co., CSR lists Magoffin Co. as residence, age 44 on census, house 355, s 1,2,4,28.

MARSHALL, THOMAS. reg 14, co F, enr 8/3/63 Salyersville, enl 3/30/63 Louisa, dis 12/2/63, age 27, light hair, blue eyes, fair skin, 6-0, b Floyd Co., d 12/2/63 Paintsville of typhoid fever, house 500, s 1,2,28.

MARSHALL, THOMAS J. reg 14, co F, enr 6/20/63 Salyersville, enl 8/30/63 Louisa, age 16, des 1/5/65 Louisa, house 161, s 1,28.

MARSHALL, WILLIAM. reg 14, co F, D, enr 6/20/63 Salyersville, enl 8/30/63 Louisa, dis 9/15/65 Louisville, age 28, hospital card lists Magoffin Co. as residence, house 341, s 1,28.

MARSHALL, WILLIAM C. reg 14, co F, D, enr 6/20/63 Salyersville, enl 8/30/63 Louisa, dis 9/15/65 Louisville, age 19 or 21, light hair, blue eyes, fair skin, 5-8, trans to 14th Vet. Inf., co D, b Floyd Co., house 161, s 1,2,28.

MAY, HENRY HARRISON. reg 14, co I, r cpl, enr 6/20/63 Salyersville, enl 8/30/63 Louisa, age 25, dark hair & skin, blue eyes, 5-11, prom to cpl 11/17/63, b Floyd Co., d 7/22/64 or 7/25/64 Marietta GA of typhoid fever, house 168, s 1,2,28.

MAY, JOHN W. reg 14, co I, enr 11/10/61 Louisa, enl 12/10/61 Louisa, dis 1/31/65 Louisa, age 18, house 134, s 1,2,4,28.

MAY, NOAH. reg 45, co D, enr 2/15/64 Salyersville, enl 3/14/64 Flemingsburg, dis 12/24/64 Catlettsburg, age 35, dark hair, blue eyes, fair skin, 5-4, b Morgan Co., CSR lists Magoffin Co. as residence, d 1/23/64 Lexington of bronchitis, buried grave #579, Lexington National Cemetery, house 560, s 1, 2,28.

MAY, SAMUEL F. reg 45, co D, enr 8/5/63 Salyersville, enl 10/17/63 Ashland, dis 12/24/64 Catlettsburg, age 25, age 45 on census, house 561, s 1,2,28.

MAY, STEPHEN L. reg 14, co F, enr 9/5/63 or 10/5/63 Salyersville, enl 10/31/63 Louisa, age 16, dark hair, blue eyes, fair skin, 5-10, b Floyd Co., d 7/20/64 Chattanooga or Knoxville TN of typhoid fever, house 516, s 1, 2,28.

MAY, THOMAS. reg 45, co D, H, enr 8/5/63 Salyersville, enl 2/3/64 Mt. Sterling, dis 12/24/64 Catlettsburg, age 21, dark hair & eyes, fair skin, b Morgan Co., trans from co H to co D 1/1/64, back to co H 5/20/64, house 527, s 1,2, 28.

MCGUIRE, STEWART N. reg 45, co D, enr & enl 10/24/63 Magoffin Co., dis 4/8/65 Covington, age 25, light hair, blue eyes, red hair, 5-7, b Morgan Co., cap 11/30/63 Salyersville, confined at Richmond VA 12/8/63, sent to Andersonville GA 2/14/64, paroled Charleston SC 12/20/64, house 387, s 1,28.

MCKEE, HENRY. reg 14, co I, enr 9/7/62 or 12/8/62 Catlettsburg, enl 2/18/63 or 3/20/63 Louisa, age 18 or 21, d 8/16/64 Marietta GA of wounds received in action 8/10/64 near Atlanta GA, residence stated on muster roll, house n/c, s 1,2,4.

MEADOWS, THORNTON or THURSTON. reg 24, co G, enr 11/5/61, enl 12/31/64 Lexington, dis 7/14/62 Nashville TN, age 18, brown hair & eyes, dark skin, 5-2, b Magoffin Co., dis for disability of bronchial difficulty, house 358, s 1,2,4,28.

MEADOWS, WILLIAM J. reg 24, co G, enr 11/5/61 Camp Gill, Bath Co., enl 12/31/61 Camp Temple, Lexington, dis 1/31/65 Covington, age 22, house 358, s 1,2,4,28.

MEDLEY, HENDERSON. reg 14, co I, enr 11/10/61 Louisa, enl 12/10/61 Louisa, dis 4/18/63, age 25, black hair, blue eyes, fair skin, 5-8, b Surry Co. NC, dis at Louisa for paralysis of nerves of the ear, residence stated on muster roll, CSR: "at home on furlough in Magoffin Co.", house n/c, s 1,2,4,28.

MINIX, CHARLES W. reg 14, co I, r cpl, enr 11/10/61 Louisa, enl 12/10/61 Louisa, dis 1/31/65 Louisa, age 19, app cpl 8/30/63, house 147, s 1,2,4,28.

MINIX, JAMES. reg 14, co F, D, enr 6/20/63 Salyersville, enl 8/30/63 Louisa, dis 9/15/65 Louisville, age 16, trans to 14th Vet Inf, co D, house 157, s 1,2, 28.

MINIX, LEWIS. reg 14, co F, D, enr 6/10/63 Salyersville, enl 8/30/63 Louisa, dis 9/15/65 Louisville, age 18, trans to 14th Vet Inf, co D, house 157, s 1,2, 28.

MINIX, NOAH. reg 14, co I, enr 11/10/61 Louisa, enl 12/10/61 Louisa, dis 1/31/65 Louisa, age 19, dark hair, blue eyes, fair skin, 5-7, b Floyd Co., house 157, s 1,2,4,28.

MINIX, WILLIAM F. reg 14, co F, D, r cpl, enr 6/10/63 Salyersville, enl 8/30/63 Louisa, dis 9/15/65 Louisville, age 18, trans to 14th Vet. Inf., co D, app cpl 2/1/65, house 147, s 1,2,28.

MONTGOMERY, ISAAC. reg 14, co F, D, enr 6/20/63 Salyersville, enl 8/30/63 Louisa, dis 9/15/65 Louisville, age 17, trans to 14th Vet. Inf., co D, house 144, s 1,2,28.

MONTGOMERY, JOHN. reg 14, co F, D, enr 6/20/63 Salyersville, enl 8/30/63 Louisa, dis 9/15/65 Louisville, age 18, trans to 14th Vet. Inf., co D, house 147, s 1,2,28.

MULLINS, PRESTON. reg 14, co I, enr 11/10/61 Louisa, enl 12/10/61 Louisa, dis 1/31/65 Louisa, age 21, residence stated on muster roll, house n/c, s 1,2, 4.

N

NOE, MARTIN. reg 14, co F, D, enr 6/20/63 Salyersville, enl 8/30/63 Louisa, dis 9/15/65 Louisville, age 35, trans to 14th Vet. Inf., co D, house 158, s 1,2, 28.

P

PACE, JOHN C. reg 14, co I, enr 11/10/61 Louisa, enl 12/10/61 Louisa, dis 1/31/65 Louisa, age 18, 7/63 on detached service in engineer corps at Camp Nelson, house 360, s 1,28.

PATRICK, ALLEN. reg 45, co D, enr 9/27/63 Salyersville, enl 10/17/63 Ashland, dis 12/24/64 Catlettsburg, age 23, house 556, s 1,2,28.

PATRICK, ELIJAH. reg 14, co I, B, enr 12/1/62, enl 12/12/62 Richmond, dis 9/15/65 Louisville, age 26, trans to 14th Vet. Inf., co B, house 549, s 1,2,28.

PATRICK, FRANCIS M. reg 14, co I, B, enr 4/27/63 Louisa, enl 6/10/63 Louisa, dis 9/15/65 Louisville, age 21, dark hair, blue eyes, fair skin, 5-10, trans to 14th Vet. Inf., co B, b Floyd Co., residence stated on muster roll, house n/c, s 1,2,4,28.

PATRICK, JOHN F. reg 14, co I, B, enr 3/3/63 Louisa, enl 6/1/63 Louisa, dis 9/15/65 Louisville, age 21, trans to 14th Vet. Inf., co B, CSR: "left sick in Magoffin Co.", residence stated on muster roll, house n/c, s 1,2,4,28.

PATRICK, JOHN M. reg 45, co D, enr 2/20/64 Salyersville, enl 3/14/64 Flemingsburg, dis 12/24/64 Catlettsburg, age 20, light hair, blue eyes, red skin, 5-10, d 3/8/64 Flemingsburg or 3/28/64 Floyd Co., residence stated as Magoffin Co., house 367, s 1,2.

PATRICK, LEWIS. reg 45, co D, enr 10/27/63 Salyersville, dis 12/24/64 Catlettsburg, age 47, gray hair, blue eyes, fair skin, 5-1, d 5/1/64 Lexington of typhoid fever, b Floyd Co., house 398, s 1,2,28.

PATRICK, REUBEN. reg 39, co D, enr 3/27/65 Louisa, enl 8/15/65 Greenupsburg, dis 9/15/65 Louisville, age 19, light hair, dark eyes, fair skin, 5-10, house 409, s 1,2,4.

PATRICK, SAMUEL. reg 14, co I, B, enr 12/6/62 Richmond, enl 12/12/62 Richmond, dis 9/15/65 Louisville, age 26, trans to 14th Vet Inf, co B, house 286, s 1,2,4,28.

PATRICK, THOMAS C. reg 14, co I, enr 11/10/61 Louisa, enl 12/10/61 Louisa, age 38, dark hair, blue eyes, fair skin 6-0, b Morgan Co., killed in action Kennesaw Mtn. GA 6/22/64, house 409, s 1,2,28.

PATRICK, WILEY. reg 14, co I, r cpl, enr 11/10/61 Louisa, enl 12/10/61 Louisa, dis 1/31/65 Louisa, age 22, hospital record lists Salyersville as address, house 314, s 1,2,4,28.

PATRICK, WILEY C. reg 14, co I, r capt, enr 11/10/61, Louisa, enl 12/10/61 Louisa, age 20 or 26, prom from 1st lt to capt 2/7/63, killed near Altoona Mtn. GA 6/2/64 or 6/22/64, house 201, s 1,2,4,28.

PATRICK, WILLIAM. reg 14, co I, enr 11/10/61 Louisa, enl 12/10/61 Louisa, dis 1/31/65 Louisa, age 23, house 314, s 1,2,4,28.

PATRICK, WILLIAM IRVIN. reg 45, co H, d, enr 10/24/63 Salyersville, enl 2/3/64 Mt. Sterling, dis 12/24/64 Catlettsburg, age 18, light hair, blue eyes, light skin, 5-4, trans from co H to co D 2/1/64, back to co H, house 398, s 1, 2,28.

PERCELL, FLOYD W. reg 24, co G, enr 11/5/61 Camp Gill, enl 12/31/61 Lexington, dis 1/31/65 Covington, age 18, residence stated on muster roll, house n/c, s 1,2,4.

PERKINS, ANDREW. reg 24, co G, enr 11/5/61 Camp Gill, Bath Co., enl 12/31/61 Camp Temple, Lexington, dis 1/31/65 Covington, age 19 or 20, cap 11/11/62 near Lebanon TN or 11/14/62 Nashville, paroled 12/10/62, muster roll lists Morgan Co. as residence, but he is not listed on Morgan Co. census, house 540, s 1,2,4,28.

PERKINS, GEORGE. reg 14, co I, enr 11/10/61 Louisa, enl 12/10/61 Louisa, dis 1/31/65 Louisa, age 22, house 169, s 1,2,4,28.

PERKINS, GEORGE W. reg 24, co G, r cpl, enr 11/5/61 Camp Gill, Bath Co., enl 12/31/61 Camp Temple, Lexington, age 23, prom to cpl and deserted, not on AG, house 540, s 1,4,28.

PERKINS, SPENCER. reg 14, co B, enr 10/10/61 Louisa, enl 12/10/61 Louisa, dis 1/31/65 Louisa, age 21 or 23, muster roll lists Morgan Co. as residence, but he is not on Morgan Co. census, house 540, s 1,2,4.

PERKINS, THOMAS. reg 14, co I, B, enr 11/10/61 Louisa, enl 12/10/61 Louisa, dis 1/321/65 Louisa, age 18, trans to co B 8/31/63, back to co I 1/20/65, age 36 on census, residence stated on muster roll, house n/c, s 1,2,4.

PERRY, RICHARD M. reg 54, co F, enr & enl 9/3/64 Greenupsburg, dis 9/1/65 Louisville, age 21, light hair & skin, hazel eyes, 5-9, b Morgan Co., house 447, s 1,2,28.

PHIPPS, JOHN MARTIN. reg 45, co D, enr 9/2/63 Salyersville, enl 10/17/63 Ashland, dis 12/24/64 Catlettsburg, age 28, black hair & eyes, dark skin, 6-0, b Morgan Co., age 58 on census, house 391, s 1,2,28.

PICKLESIMER, ALFRED. reg 14, co I, enr 11/10/61 Louisa, enl 12/10/61 Louisa, dis 1/31/65 Louisa, age 23, house 282, s 1,2,4,28.

PICKLESIMER, JAMES P. reg 14, co F, enr 8/15/63, enl 8/30/63 Louisa, trans to 14th Vet. Inf., not on CSR, house 97, s 2,28.

PICKLESIMER, JOHN P. reg 14, co F, enr 8/11/63, enl 8/30/63 Louisa, trans to 14th Vet. Inf., not on CSR, house 97, s 2,28.

POE, HUGH. reg 14, co F, D, enr 6/20/63 Salyersville, enl 8/30/63 Louisa, dis 9/15/65 Louisville, age 45, trans to 14th Vet. Inf., co D, age 36 on census, house 289, s 1,2,28.

POE, MEREDITH. reg 14, co F, D, enr 8/3/63 Salyersville, enl 8/30/63 Louisa, dis 9/15/65 Louisville, age 36, trans to 14th Vet. Inf., co D, age 28 on census, house 18, s 1,2,28.

POWER, FLEMING. reg 14, co I, enr 9/17/62 Catlettsburg, enl 2/18/63 Louisa, age 17, d 3/9/63 Louisa of pneumonia, house 291, s 1,2,28.

POWER, HENRY C. reg 14, co F, enr 6/20/63 Salyersville, enl 8/30/63 Louisa, dis 12/11/63 Paintsville, age 19, light hair, blue eyes, fair skin, 5-10, b Floyd Co., d 10/11/63 Paintsville of typhoid fever, house 404, s 1,2,28.

POWER, JAMES. reg 14, co I, enr 11/10/61 Louisa, enl 12/10/61 Louisa, dis 1/31/65 Louisa, age 23 or 33, app cpl 10/10/61, reduced to ranks 5/1/62, CSR: "at home sick in Magoffin Co, Ky.", house 582, s 1,2,4,28.

POWER, JILSON. reg 14, co I, r cpl, enr 11/10/61 Louisa, enl 12/10/61 Louisa, dis 1/31/65 Louisa, age 23, app cpl 3/1/63, severely wounded at Salyersville 11/30/63, house 291, s 1,2,4,28.

POWER, JOHN. reg 14, co I, r capt, enr 11/10/61 Louisa, enl 12/10/61 Louisa, age 45 or 54, black hair & eyes, dark skin, 5-11, b Floyd Co., resigned 2/6/63 Louisa from affliction of foot and leg, house 290, s 1,2,4,28.

POWER, JOHN C. reg 14, co I, enr 11/10/61, enl 12/10/61 Louisa, dis 1/31/65 Louisa, not on CSR, house 291, s 2,28.

POWER, JOHN M. reg 14, co I, F, r cpl, enr 11/10/61 Louisa, enl 12/10/61 Louisa, dis 1/31/65 Louisa, age 22, light hair, blue eyes, fair skin, 5-10, b Floyd Co., prom from 4th cpl to 3rd cpl, trans to co F 8/31/63, back to co I 1/20/65, house 404, s 1,2,4,28.

POWER, MASON H. reg 14, co I, r 2nd lt, enr 10/10/61 Louisa, enl 12/10/61 Louisa, dis 9/15/65 Louisville, age 23, black hair & eyes, dark skin, 5-11, trans to 14th Vet. Inf., prom from sgt to 1st sgt 9/5/65, to 2nd lt 1/4/64, to 1st lt 6/30/64, b Floyd Co., house 290, s 1,2,4,28.

PRATER, JILSON PAYNE. reg 45, co D, enr 9/28/63 Salyersville, enl 10/17/63 Ashland, dis 12/24/64 Catlettsburg, age 40, black hair, blue eyes, fair skin, 6-0, b Floyd Co., d 5/4/64 Irvine, house 362, s 1,2,28.

PRATER, RICHARD MENIFEE. reg 14, co I, enr 11/10/61 Louisa, enl 12/10/61 Louisa, dis 1/31/65 Louisa, age 24, residence stated on muster roll, house n/c, s 1,2,4,28.

PRATER, THOMAS L. reg 14, co F, D, r sgt, enr 10/14/63 Louisa, enl 12/31/63 Louisa, dis 9/15/65 Louisville, age 38, light hair, blue eyes, fair skin, 5-7, trans to 14th Vet. Inf., co D, prom to cpl 8/30/64, prom to sgt 2/1/65, credited to 9th Congressional district, house 352, s 1,2,28.

PRATER, THOMAS W. reg 14, co F, D, enr 12/30/63 Salyersville, enl 12/31/63 Louisa, dis 9/15/65 Louisville, age 26, fair hair & skin, blue eyes, 5-10, trans to 14th Vet. Inf., co D, b Morgan Co., prom from pvt to sgt 2/1/65, credited to 9th Congressional district, house 186, s 1,2,28.

PRATER, WILLIAM W. reg 14, co F, enr 11/10/61 Louisa, enl 12/10/61 Louisa, dis 4/18/63 Louisa, age 33, dark hair, blue eyes, fair skin, 5-7, Floyd Co., app 1st sgt 10/10/61, reduced to 2nd sgt 3/1/62, reduced to ranks 5/1/62, discharged for disability 4/10/63 Louisa, CSR: "at home on furlough in Magoffin Co.", house 126, s 1,2,28.

PUCKETT, BENJAMIN. reg 14, co I, enr 11/10/61 Louisa, enl 12/10/61 Louisa, dis 9/15/65 Louisville, age 18, light hair, blue eyes, fair skin, 5-8, trans to 14th Vet. Inf., co B, enl 2/29/64, m/in 3/15/64, b Morgan Co., house 380, s 1,2,4,28.

PUCKETT, FLEMING. reg 14, co I, C, A, enr 11/10/61 Louisa, enl 12/10/61 Louisa, dis 9/15/65 Louisville, age 19, light hair, blue eyes, dark skin, 5-2, trans to co C 8/1/63, back to co I 1/20/65, trans to 14th Vet. Inf., Co A, enl 2/29/64, m/in 3/15/64, b Magoffin Co., house 380, s 1,2,4,28.

PUCKETT, WILLIAM GREEN. reg 45, co D, r cpl, enr 9/7/63 Salyersville, enl 10/17/63 Ashland, dis 12/24/64 Catlettsburg, age 18, house 380, s 1,2,28.

PUGH, CORNWALLIS. reg 24, co G, enr 11/5/61 Camp Gill, enl 12/31/61 Lexington, dis 1/31/65 Covington, age 23, residence stated on muster roll, house n/c, s 1,2,4,28.

PUGH, WILLIAM. reg 24, co G, enr 11/5/61 Camp Gill, Bath Co., enl 12/31/61 Camp Temple, Lexington, dis 1/31/65 Covington, age 32, brown hair, gray eyes, fair skin, 6-1, b Morgan Co., residence stated on muster roll, house n/c, s 1,2,4.

R

REED, ARONTON. reg 8, co B, E, enr 10/9/61 Camp Estill Springs, enl 12/5/61 Lebanon, dis 11/17/64 Chattanooga TN, age 18, light hair, blue eyes, fair skin, 5-7, enl as veteran volunteer 1/4/64, m/in 2/1/64 Tyner Station TN, cap Saltville VA 4/8/64 confined at Richmond, VA 4/25/64, admitted to hospital with gunshot wound 5/18/64, paroled James River VA 2/12/65, b Tazewell Co. VA, house 392, s 1,2,4,28.

REED, HIRAM H. reg 45, co D, enr 10/27/63 Salyersville, enl 11/5/64 Lexington, dis 12/24/64 Catlettsburg, age 18, dark hair, blue eyes, fair skin, 5-8, cap 11/30/63 Salyersville, confined Richmond VA 1/8/63, paroled City Point 3/6/64, b Tazewell Co. VA, house 392, s 1,2,28.

REED, WILLIAM T. reg 45, co D, H, enr 10/27/63 Salyersville, enl 2/3/64 Mt. Sterling, dis 2/14/65 Catlettsburg, age 18, dark hair, blue eyes, fair skin,5-5, trans from co H to co D 2/1/64, back to co H 5/20/64, b Tazewell Co. VA, age 11 on census, house 392, s 1,2,28.

RICE, DANIEL J. reg 14, co I, r cpl, enr 11/10/61 Louisa, enl 12/10/61 Louisa, age 25, fair hair, blue eyes, dark skin, 5-7, dis 4/18/63 Louisa for disability, b Floyd Co., CSR: at home in Johnson Co. on furlough, but he is not on Johnson Co. census, app cpl 10/10/61, reduced to ranks 3/1/62, house 120, s 1,2, 28.

RICE, MARTIN V. reg 14, co I, enr 11/10/61 Louisa, enl 12/10/61 Louisa, dis 1/31/65 Louisa, age 23, house 375, s 1,2,4,28.

RICE, WILLIAM M. (Jr.). reg 14, co I, B, enr 5/3/63 Louisa, enl 6/10/63 Louisa, dis 9/15/65 Louisville, age 18, light hair, blue eyes, fair skin, 5-7, trans to 14th Vet. Inf., co B, b Floyd Co., residence stated on muster roll, house n/c, s 1,2,4,28.

RILEY, JOHN C. reg 45, co D, enr 8/5/63 Salyersville, enl 10/17/63 Ashland, dis 12/24/64 Catlettsburg, age 20, dark hair, eyes & skin, 5-9, b Illinois, house 475, s 1,2,28.

RISNER, DIAL. reg 14, co F, enr 8/30/63 Salyersville, enl 8/30/63 Louisa, age 25, light hair, blue eyes, fair skin, 5-10, d 8/17/64 Chattanooga TN of typhoid fever, b Floyd Co., house 21, s 1,2,28.

RISNER, FRANCIS M. reg 14, co I, B, enr 2/8/62 Paintsville, enl 2/8/62 Lexington, dis 9/15/65 Louisville, age 20, black hair & eyes, dark skin 5-10, trans to 14th Vet. Inf., co B, b Floyd Co., house 22, s 1,2,4,28.

RISNER, GEORGE. reg 14, co I, B, enr & enl 2/27/62 Louisa, dis 9/15/65 Louisville, age 18, black hair & eyes, dark skin, 5-7, trans to 14th Vet. Inf., co B, enl 2/29/64, m/in 3/15/64, house 22, s 1,2,4,28.

RISNER, KELSEY N. reg 14, co F, D, r cpl, enr 6/20/63 Salyersville, enl 8/30/63 Louisa, dis 9/15/65 Louisville, age 20, light hair, blue eyes, fair skin 5-11, app cpl 2/1/65, trans to 14th Vet Inf, co D, b Floyd Co., house 288, s 1,2,28.

RISNER, MARSHALL. reg 14, co F, enr 6/20/63 Salyersville, enl 8/30/63 Louisa, dis 1/31/65 Louisa, house 19, s 1,2,28.
RISNER, MEREDITH. reg 14, co F, enr 6/20/63 or 8/3/63, Salyersville, enl 8/30/63 Louisa, dis 1/31/65 Louisa, age 33, CSR: "at home sick in Magoffin Co.", house 25, s 1,2,28.
RISNER, MICHAEL. reg 14, co F, enr 6/20/63 enl 8/3/63 Salyersville, enl 8/30/63 Louisa, dis 1/31/65 Louisa, age 22 or 25, CSR: "at home sick in Magoffin Co.", house 22, s 1,2,28.
RISNER, WILSON. reg 14, co I, B, enr 3/15/62 Paintsville, enl Lexington, dis 9/15/65 Louisville, age 22, black hair & eyes, dark skin, 5-9, trans to 14th Vet. Inf., co B, b Floyd Co., credited to Magoffin Co., house 22, s 1,2,28.
ROW, GEORGE. reg 14, co I, enr 11/10/61 Louisa, enl 12/10/61 Louisa, dis 1/31/65 Louisa, age 24, house 275, s 1,2,4.
RUDD, HIRAM HYDEN. reg 45, co D, enr 10/27/63 Salyersville, enl 11/5/64 Lexington, dis 1/24/64 Catlettsburg, age 18, fair hair & skin, blue eyes, 5-10, cap Salyersville 11/30/63, taken to Richmond VA 12/8/63, paroled City Point 4/6/64, b Tazewell Co. VA, credited to Magoffin Co., house 237, s 1,2,28.
RUDD, JOHN FLOYD. reg 8, co B, E, enr 10/9/61 Camp Estill Springs, enl 1/15/62 Lebanon, age 18, light hair, blue eyes, fair skin, 5-8, joined Vet Volunteers 1/4/64, m/in 2/1/64 Tyner Station TN, b Tazewell Co. VA, house 237, s 1,2,4,28.

S

SALYER, WILLIAM. reg 45, co D, H, enr 10/27/63 Salyersville, enl 2/3/64 Mt. Sterling, dis 12/24/64 Catlettsburg, age 18, black hair, blue eyes, fair skin, 5-10, trans from co H to co D 2/1/64, back to co H, b Johnson Co., house 6, 14 or 410, s 1,2,28.
SCOTT, WILLIAM E. reg 14, co I, enr 11/10/61 Louisa, enl 12/10/61 Louisa, dis 1/31/65 Louisa, age 38, cap & paroled Lexington 9/62, house 108, s 1,2, 4,28.
SHEPHERD, JAMES. reg 14, co H, C, enr 5/9/64 Louisa, enl 5/9/64 Marietta GA, dis 9/15/65 Louisville, age 20, dark hair, eyes & skin, 5-6, trans to 14th Vet. Inf., co C, b Lawrence Co., credited to Lawrence Co., but he is not on Lawrence Co. census, house 55, s 1,2,28.
STIDHAM, JOHN W. reg 14, co I, B, enr 5/15/63 Louisa, enl 6/10/63 Louisa, dis 9/15/65 Louisville, age 18 or 19, trans to 14th Vet. Inf., co B, residence stated on muster roll, house n/c, s 1,2,4.
STONE, CUTHBERT. reg 14, co H, enr 10/15/61 Catlettsburg, enl 12/10/61 Louisa, dis 1/31/65, age 35, muster roll lists Floyd Co. as residence, but he is not listed on Floyd Co. census, house 47, s 1,2,28.
STONE, ENOCH. reg 14, co H, enr 10/25/61 Catlettsburg, enl 12/10/61 Louisa, dis 1/31/65 Louisa, age 32, light hair, blue eyes, fair skin, 5-8, b Floyd Co., muster roll lists Floyd Co. as residence, but he is not listed on Floyd Co. census, house 48, s 1,2,28.
STONE, SOLOMON. reg 14, co I, enr 11/10/61 Louisa, enl 12/10/61 Louisa, dis 7/1/62 Cumberland Gap, age 45 or 65, gray hair, blue eyes, dark hair, 5-6, dis for disability relating to age, muster roll lists Floyd Co. as residence, but he is not listed on Floyd Co. census, house 49, s 1,2,4,28.

V

VANDERPOOL, ENOCH. reg 14, co I, enr 11/10/61 Louisa, enl 12/10/61 Louisa, dis 1/31/65 Louisa, age 19, house 142, s 1,2,4,28.
VANDERPOOL, ROBERT. reg 14, co I, enr & enl 6/6/63 Louisa, dis 1/31/65 Louisa, age 19, dark hair, eyes & skin, 5-10, wounded 6/22/64 Kennesaw Mtn. GA, d 7/6/64 of wounds, Knoxville TN, b Floyd Co., house 142 or 143, s 1,2,4,28.

W

WADKINS, (WATKINS) AMBROSE. reg 14 co A, C enr 5/4/64 Louisa, enl 5/7/64 Louisa, dis 9/15/65 Louisa, age 17 or 18, light hair & skin, black eyes, 5-5, trans to 14th Vet. Inf., co C, missing from skirmish line 8/8/64 near Atlanta GA, credited to 9th Congressional district, b Magoffin Co., house 56, s 1,2,28.

WAGES, BENJAMIN. reg 45, co D, H, enr 10/29/63, enl 2/6/64 Mt. Sterling, dis 2/14/65 Catlettsburg, age 37, dark hair, eyes & skin, 5-10, b Morgan Co., trans from co H to co D 2/1/64, back to co H 5/20/64, house 554, s 1,2,28.

WAGES, MARION. reg 45, co K, enr 10/10/63 Ashland, enl 12/9/63 Louisa, dis 2/14/65 Catlettsburg, age 18, light hair, blue eyes, dark skin, 5-0, dis for general disability and typhoid fever, CSR lists Magoffin Co. as residence, house 326, s 1,2,28.

WAGES, THOMAS. reg 45, co I, K, enr 12/10/63 Louisa, enl 2/14/64 Mt. Sterling, dis 2/14/65 Catlettsburg, age 18, light hair & skin, blue eyes, 5-5, trans from co I to co C, 2/1/64, house 326, s 1,2,28.

WARD, ISAAC JEFFERSON. reg 14, co I, r sgt, enr 11/10/61 Louisa, enl 12/10/61 Louisa, dis 1/31/65 Louisa, age 21, prom from cpl to sgt 10/27/64, residence stated on muster roll, house n/c, s 1,2,4,28.

WATSON, JOHN. reg 14, co I, enr 11/10/61 Louisa, enl 12/10/61 Louisa, dis 1/31/65 Louisa, age 22, house 157, s 1,2,4,28.

WHITAKER, DAVID. reg 14, co F, D, enr 8/15/63 Salyersville, enl 8/30/63 Louisa, dis 9/15/65 Louisville, age 27, des 5/12/62 Louisa, returned under President's Proclamation 5/8/65, CSR: "at home sick in Magoffin Co.", house 45, s 1,2,28.

WHITAKER, JOHNSON. reg 14, co F, D, enr 6/19/63 Salyersville, enl 8/30/63 Louisa, dis 9/15/65 Louisville, age 19, trans to 14th Vet. Inf., co D, CSR: "at home sick in Magoffin Co.", house 30, s 1,2,28.

WHITAKER, MORGAN C. reg 14, co F, D, enr 8/15/63 Salyersville, enl 8/30/63 Louisa, dis 9/15/65 Louisville, age 26, light hair, blue eyes, fair skin, 6-0, b Floyd Co., des 5/12/64 Louisa, returned under President's Proclamation 5/8/65, house 44, s 1,2,28.

WHITAKER, ROBERT. reg 14, co F, D, enr 6/20/63 Salyersville, enl 8/30/63 Louisa, dis 9/15/65 Louisville, age 40, trans to 14th Vet Inf, co D, house 162, s 1,2,28.

WHITAKER, SMITH. reg 14, co F, enr 6/20/63 Salyersville, enl 8/30/63 Louisa, age 20, light hair, blue eyes, fair skin, 5-10, des 5/12/64 Louisa, b Floyd Co., CSR: "at home sick in Magoffin Co.", house 43, 1,2,28.

WHITAKER, THOMAS P. reg 14, co F, D, r cpl, enr 8/3/63 Salyersville, enl 8/30/63 Louisa, dis 9/15/65 Louisville, age 32, trans to 14th Vet. Inf., co D, app cpl 2/1/65, house 113, s 1,2,28.

WHITLEY, PLEASANT. reg 24, co G, enr 11/5/61 Camp Gill, Bath Co., enl 12/31/61 Lexington, dis 1/31/65 Covington, reg 47, co I, enl 10/27/63, dis 5/27/64, reg 4, co E, enr 5/26/64, enl 9/9/64 Louisville, m/out 8/17/65, age 18, black hair & eyes, dark skin, 5-7, b Magoffin Co., des 4/19/63 Winchester, house 230, s 1,2,4 28.

WHITLEY, ROBERT. reg 14, co I, enr 11/10/61 Louisa, enl 12/10/61 Louisa, dis 1/31/65 Louisville, age 33, house 268, s 1,2,28.

WHITT, INGRAHAM (INGRAM) B. reg 24, co E, enr 11/5/61 Camp Gill, enl 12/31/61 Lexington, dis 1/31/65 Covington, age 23, light hair, blue eyes, fair skin, 5-8, b Magoffin Co., house 224, s 1,2,4,28.

WHITT, JAMES W. reg 24, co G, enr 11/5/61 Camp Gill, enl 12/31/61 Lexington, dis 1/31/65 Covington, age 19, light hair, blue eyes, fair skin, 5-7, b Magoffin Co., house 235, s 1,2,4,28.

WILLIAMS, SAMUEL. reg 45, co H, D, enr 10/30/63 Salyersville, enl 2/3/64 Mt. Sterling, dis 12/24/64 Catlettsburg, age 23, dark hair, eyes & skin, 5-10, b Letcher Co., trans from co H to co D 2/1/64, back to co H 5/20/64, house 436, s 1,2,28.

WILLIAMS, THOMAS H. reg 14, co I, B, r cpl, enr 11/10/61 Louisa, enl 12/10/61 Louisa, dis 9/15/65 Louisville, age 21, dark hair, black eyes, fair skin, 5-9, trans to 14th Vet. Inf., co B, enl 2/29/64, m/in 3/15/64, b Magoffin Co., app cpl 2/1/65, house 535, s 1,2,4,28.

MORGAN COUNTY UNION SOLDIERS

A

ADAMS, ABSALOM. reg 24, co B, enr 10/3/61 Bath Co., enl 12/31/61 Camp Temple, Lexington, age 28, left sick in Morgan Co., failed to report and was dropped as a deserter 12/31/64, house 1-33, s 1,2,4.

ADAMS, EDWARD. reg 45, co D, enr 8/3/63 Salyersville, enl 2/3/64 Mt. Sterling, dis 2/14/65 Catlettsburg, age 22, black hair, blue eyes, fair skin, 5-8, trans to co H 5/20/64, b Morgan Co., house 1-303, s 1,2.

ADAMS, MATTHEW. reg 45, co G, enr 7/28/63, enl 11/30/63 Ashland, dis 2/14/65 Catlettsburg, age 18, light hair, blue eyes, fair skin, 5-4, b Morgan Co., house 1-303, s 1,2.

ADAMS, RICHMOND. reg 10Cav, co K, enr 8/18/62 Greenupsburg, enl 9/8/62 Covington, dis 9/17/63 Maysville, age 42, house 2-385, s 1,2,4.

ADKINS, CHRISTIAN. reg 40, co E, enr 8/1/63, enl 9/28/63 Grayson, dis 11/30/64 Catlettsburg, age 30, residence stated on muster roll, house n/c, s 2, 4.

ADKINS, SAMUEL PETER. reg US 5th Vol. enl 4/6/65, house 1-402, s 1,31.

ADKINS, WILLIAM R. reg 45, co K, enr 11/24/63 Relief, enl 12/9/63 Louisa, dis 2/14/65 Catlettsburg, age 20, light hair, blue eyes, fair skin, 5-5, des 9/28/64 on march to Saltville VA, house 1-402, s 1,2,35.

AMYX, JAMES M. reg 24, co B, enr 10/8/61 Bath Co., enl 12/31/61 Camp Temple, Lexington, age 20, dark hair, blue eyes, fair skin, 5-10, dis 6/6/62 Louisville or Nashville TN on surgeon's certificate of disability for chronic rheumatism, b Morgan Co., house 1-3, s 1,2,4.

B

BAILEY, ELISHA. reg 24, co B, r 2nd sgt, enr 10/8/61 Bath Co., enl 12/31/61 Camp Temple, Lexington, age 43, dark hair & skin, blue eyes, 5-9, dis 7/3/62 St. Louis, MO, by order of Gen. Davidson, partial paralysis of left hip from rheumatism, house 2-46, s 1,2,4.

BARKER, ANDREW T. reg 24, co B, r 1st cpl, enr 11/9/61 Bath Co., enl 12/31/61 Camp Temple, Lexington, age 19, drowned 3/23/62 Cumberland River, house 1-659, s 1,2,4.

BLAIR, ALVIN. reg 24, co B, enr 10/8/61 Camp Gill, Bath Co., enl 12/31/61 Camp Temple, Lexington, age 19, d 4/5/62 Nashville TN, house 1-334, s 1,2,4.

BLAIR, JAMES. reg 24, co B, enr 11/9/61 Bath Co., enl 12/31/61 Camp Temple, Lexington, age 27, des 11/4/62 Glasgow, house 1-195, s 1,2,4.

BLAIR, WILLIAM. reg 24, co B, enr 10/8/61 Bath Co., enl 12/31/61 Camp Temple, Lexington, age 26, des 11/4/62 Glasgow, residence stated on muster roll, house 1-334, s 1,2,4.

BLANKENSHIP, BENJAMIN P. reg 24, co B, r 4th sgt, enl 10/8/61 Bath Co., enl 12/31/61 Camp Temple, Lexington, dis 1/31/65 Covington, age 37, prom to 4th sgt 4/20/63, house 1-620, s 1,2,4.

BLANKENSHIP, HENRY. reg 24, co B, r 3rd sgt, enr 10/8/61 Bath Co., enl 12/31/61 Camp Temple, Lexington, dis 1/31/65 Covington, age 24, prom to 3rd sgt 7/1/62, house 1-210, s 1,2.

BLANKENSHIP, JOHN. reg 24, co B, enr 11/9/61 Bath Co., enl 12/31/61 Camp Temple, Lexington, age 19, died Nashville TN, date unknown, house 1-559, s 1,2,4.

BLANKENSHIP, WILLIAM. reg 24, co B, enr 11/9/61 Bath Co., enl 12/31/61 Camp Temple, Lexington, age 33, d Nashville TN 11/4/62 of chronic diarrhea, buried grave 1174 City Cemetery, Nashville, house 1-25, s 1,2,4.

BOLLING, ISAAC W. reg 45, co K, G, r 1st sgt, enr 10/10/63 Mt. Sterling, enl 11/30/63 Ashland, dis 2/14/65 Catlettsburg, age 23, black hair, hazel eyes, dark skin, 5-11, trans to co K 2/1/64 as 1st sgt, back to co G 9/20/64, b Morgan Co., house 1-289, s 1,2.
BREWER, WILLIAM. reg US Army, frontier service, enl 10/14/64, house 2-541, s 1.
BROWN, ANDREW J. reg 24, co B, enr 10/8/61 Bath Co., enl 12/31/61 Camp Temple, Lexington, dis 1/31/65 Covington, age 19, trans to 19th Ky. Inf., co C, enl 10/24/63 Glasgow, dis 9/15/65 Louisville, cap Kingston GA 5/24/64, paroled and released 2/26/65 Wilmington NC, house 1-71 or 1-498, s 1,4.
BROWN, EDWARD W. reg 45, co K, r 1st lt, enr 12/1/63 Ashland, enl 12/9/63 Louisa, dis 2/14/65 Catlettsburg, age 19, elected 1st lt 12/1/63, commanded co K from 7/64, List of Officers states Johnson Co. as residence, house 1-341, s 1,2,35.
BROWN, GEORGE W. reg 45, co C, r capt, enr 5/29/63 Paintsville, enl 10/10/63 Catlettsburg, age 27, res 2/6/64, List of Officers states Johnson Co. as residence, house 1-321, s1,2.
BROWN, JAMES H. reg 24, co B, enr 10/8/61 Bath Co., enl 12/31/61 Camp Temple, Lexington, dis 1/31/65 Covington, age 20, residence stated on muster roll, house 1-301, s 1,2,4.
BROWN, JESSE S. reg 40, co E, r sgt, enr 8/26/63 Olive Hill, enl 9/28/63 Grayson, age 21, dark hair & skin, blue eyes, died 12/5/63 Carter Co., residence stated on muster roll, house 1-628, s 1,2,4.
BROWN, NATHAN ASBURY. reg 45, r major, m/in 5/30/63 Lexington 2nd lt, app major 11/30/63 Ashland, dishonorably dismissed 1/23/64, age 35, house 1-320, s 1,2.
BROWN, SAMUEL L. reg 24, co F, enr 10/8/61, never mustered, d 12/15/61 Camp Gill of disease, residence stated on muster roll, house 1-603, s 1,2,4.
BROWN, SOLOMON. reg 24, co B, enr 10/8/61 Bath Co., enl 12/31/61 Camp Temple, Lexington, age 24, d 3/23/64 Knoxville TN, residence stated on muster roll, house 1-71, s 1,2,4.
BROWN, THOMAS D. reg 24, co B, enr 10/8/61 Bath Co., enl 12/31/61 Camp Temple, Lexington, age 19, des 1/12/62 Camp Temple, residence stated on muster roll, house 1-133, s 1,2,4.
BURKE, DAVID T. reg 45, co K, enr 11/24/63 Relief, enl 12/9/63 Louisa, age 20, CSR: "sick at home at Ashland, Ky.", but he is not on Boyd Co. census, d 3/10/64 Flemingsburg or 5/1/64 at home in Morgan Co. of measles, house 1-307, s 1,2,35.
BURKE, LEWIS H. reg 45, co K, enr 11/24/63 Relief, enl 12/9/63 Louisa, dis 2/14/65 Catlettsburg, age 18, light hair, blue eyes, fair skin, 5-6, d 4/9/64 Flemingsburg of measles, b Johnson Co., house 1-307, s 1,2,35.
BURKE, SAMUEL. reg 45, co K, enr 11/24/63 Relief, enl 12/9/63 Louisa, dis 2/14/65 Catlettsburg, age 23, died 4/4/64 Flemingsburg of measles, house 1-307, s 1,2,35.
BYRON, ALEXANDER B. reg 24, co G, r cpl, enr 11/5/61 Camp Gill, Bath Co., enl 12/31/61 Camp Temple, Lexington, age 28, cap 5/24/64 Georgia, d 12/7/64 Charleston SC of chronic diarrhea, residence stated on muster roll, house n/c, s 1,2,4.
BYRON, JASPER. reg 24, co B, age 19, never mustered, not on AG or CSR, residence stated on muster roll, house n/c, s 4.

C

CAMPBELL, JOHN. reg 14Cav, co G, enr 8/15/62 Estill Co., enl 2/13/63 Irvine, dis 3/24/64 Camp Nelson, age 19, house 2-288, s 1,2.
CASKEY, JAMES. reg 40, co E, enr 11/1/63 Grayson, enl 6/28/64 Lexington, dis 12/30/64 Catlettsburg, age 18, light hair, hazel eyes, fair skin, 5-8, b Morgan Co., credited to Morgan Co., house 1-552, s 1,2,4.
CASSITY, ANDREW J. reg 24, co B, enr 11/9/61 Bath Co., enl 12/31/61 Camp Temple, Lexington, dis 1/31/65 Covington, age 25 or 29, residence stated on muster roll, house n/c, s 1,2,4.

CASSITY, DAVID. reg 24, co B, enr 10/8/61 Camp Gill, Bath Co., enl 12/31/61 Camp Temple, Lexington, dis 1/31/65 Covington, age 21, light hair, blue eyes, fair skin, 5-7, b Morgan Co., house 1-618, s 1,2,4.

CASSITY, EDMUND W. reg 24, co B, r sgt, enr 10/8/61 Bath Co., enl 12/31/61 Camp Temple, Lexington, age 24, app cpl 12/6/64, prom to sgt 2/1/65, trans to 6th Vet. Cav., co K, house 1-618, s 1,2,4.

CLEMMONS, WILLIAM. reg 24, co G, enr 11/5/61 Camp Gill, enl 12/31/61 Lexington, age 19, des Camp Temple, Lexington 12/28/61 or 1/28/62, residence stated on muster roll, house n/c, s 1,2,4.

COCK, GEORGE. reg US Army, frontier service, enl Rock Island, house 2-164, s 1.

COFFEE, ISAAC N. reg 14, co I, B, enr 9/17/62 Catlettsburg, enl 12/12/62 Richmond, dis 9/15/65 Louisville, age 18, trans to 14th Vet. Inf., cap 11/30/63 Salyersville, taken to Richmond VA 12/8/63, d Richmond VA 7/19/64, house 1-370, s 1,2,4,28.

CONLEY, ABIDE. reg 45, co K, enr 11/24/63 Relief, enl 12/9/63 Louisa, dis 2/14/64 Catlettsburg, age 24, des 1/18/64 Mt. Sterling, house 1-534, s 1,2,35.

CONLEY, ALLEN. reg 45, co K, enr 11/24/63 Relief, enl 12/9/63 Louisa, dis 2/14/65 Catlettsburg, age 20, black hair, blue eyes, fair skin, 5-8, des 1/28/64 Mt. Sterling, des 9/28/64 on march to Saltville VA, b Morgan Co., house 1-403, s 1,2,35.

CONLEY, EDMOND. reg 45, co K, enr 11/24/63 Relief, enl 12/9/63 Louisa, dis 2/14/65 Catlettsburg, age 21, light hair, blue eyes, fair skin, 5-6, KIA 6/9/64 or 6/10/64 Lexington, b Morgan Co., house 1-332, s 1,2,35.

CONLEY, HENRY. reg 45, co K, enr 11/24/63 Relief, enl 12/9/63 Louisa, dis 2/14/65 Catlettsburg, age 28, house 1-404, s 1,2,35.

CONN, JAMES M. reg 22, co H, enr 10/22/61 Grayson, enl 1/10/62 Camp Buell, Paintsville, age 18, light hair, black eyes, fair skin, 5-9, dis for disability 4/22/62 Gallipolis OH for pulmonary consumption, b Scott Co. VA, residence stated on muster roll, house n/c, s 1,2,4.

CONN, JESSE. reg 22, co H, enr 10/22/61 Grayson, enl 1/10/62 Camp Buell, Paintsville, dis 1/20/65 Louisville, age 21, house 1-485, s 1,2,4.

COOK, MILES. reg 24, co G, r 3rd sgt, enr 11/5/61 Camp Gill, Bath Co., enl 12/31/61 Camp Temple, Lexington, dis 1/31/65 Covington, age 23, 30 or 34, blue eyes, fair skin, 6-0, b Morgan Co., residence stated on muster roll, house n/c, s 1,2,4.

COOPER, ARCHIBALD. reg 14Cav, co D, enr 8/20/62 Mt. Sterling, enl 11/6/62 Mt Sterling, dis 9/16/63 Maysville, age 23, cap & paroled 3/22/63 Mt Sterling by Col. Roy Cluke, house 1-644, s 1,2,4.

COX, JOHN D. reg 24, co B, enr 10/8/61 Bath Co., enl 12/31/61 Camp Temple, Lexington, age 43, dis 6/22/62 St. Louis MO by order Col. Merrell for phthisis pulmonalis (tuberculosis) with aphonia, house 2-612, s 1,2,4.

CRAIG, HENRY. reg 24, co B, enr 11/9/61 Bath Co., enl 12/31/61 Camp Temple, Lexington, dis 1/31/65 Covington, age 19, dark hair, eyes & skin, 5-6, cap & paroled 4/28/63 Rowan Co., failed to report, dropped as deserter 12/31/64, house 1-659, s 1,2,4.

CUNDIFF, STEPHEN. reg 24, co B, enr 10/8/61 Bath Co. enl 12/31/61 Camp Temple, Lexington, dis 1/31/65, age 30, detailed as teamster to 2nd Ohio Inf. 10/20/64, failed to report, dropped as deserter 12/31/64, house 1-129, s 1,2, 4.

D

DAILEY, SILVANIS O. reg 24, co B, enr 11/9/61 Bath Co., enl 12/31/61 Camp Temple, Lexington, age 19, fair hair & skin, blue eyes, 5-4, d 3/24/62 Bardstown General Hospital, b Morgan Co., house 1-53, s 1,2,4.

DAVIS, AMOS. reg 8, co E, B, enr 10/9/61 Camp Estill Springs, enl 11/15/61 Lebanon, age 23, musician, wounded Chickamauga GA in the right leg, re-enlisted 4th Ky. Inf, as Veteran Volunteer, enl 3/28/64, m/in 5/27/64 Chattanooga TN, m/out Macon GA 8/17/65, credited to Morgan Co., house 2-154, s 1,2,4.

DAY, HENRY C. reg 24, co B, enr 11/9/61 Bath Co., enl 12/31/61 Camp Temple, Lexington, age 19, des 1/12/62 Lexington, house 1-56, s 1,2,4.

DAY, JAMES A. reg 40, co E, enr 10/31/63, age 44, not on AG, residence on muster roll, house 1-384, s 1,4.

DAY, WILLIAM S. reg 24, co B, enr 10/8/61 Camp Gill, Bath Co., enl 12/31/61 Camp Temple, Lexington, dis 1/31/65 Covington, age 22, dark hair, blue eyes, fair skin, 5-7, trans to 6th Vet. Cav., b Morgan Co., house 1-56, s 1,2, 4.

DEHART, JAMES. reg 24, co B, enr 10/8/61 or 11/9/61 Bath Co., enl 1/5/62 Camp Temple, dis 1/31/65 Covington, age 22, left sick at Camp Gill 11/28/61, never returned and failed to report, dropped as deserter 12/31/64. Records show he was never mustered and not regarded as being in military service, house 1-34 or 1-508, s 1,2,4.

DELONG, JESSE. reg 22, co I, G, age 20, died 12/30/61, residence stated on muster roll, house n/c, s 1,2,4.

DULIN, BASIL. reg 45, co K, enr 11/24/63 Relief, enl 12/9/63 Louisa, dis 2/14/65 Catlettsburg, age 37, light hair, blue eyes, fair skin, 5-8, des on march 5/28/64, b Morgan Co., house 1-308, s 1,2,35.

DULIN, DAVID. reg 45, co K, enr 11/24/63 Relief, enl 12/9/63 Louisa, dis 2/14/65 Catlettsburg, age 19, d 4/8/64 Flemingsburg of measles, house 1-308, s 1,2,35.

E

EASTERLING, HENRY J. reg 24, co G, r 3rd sgt, enr 11/8/61 Camp Gill, Bath Co., enl 12/31/61 Camp Temple, Lexington, dis 1/31/65 Covington, age 23, des 11/5/62 Glasgow, house 1-300, s 1,2,4.

EASTERLING, JEREMIAH. reg 14Cav, co D, enr 8/20/62 Mt. Sterling, enl 11/6/62 Mt. Sterling, dis 9/16/63 Maysville, age 21, cap Olympian Springs and paroled 6/13/63, house 1-228, s 1,2,4.

EASTERLING, RICHARD. reg 24, co G, r 1st sgt, enr 11/5/61 Camp Gill, Bath Co., enl 12/31/61 Camp Temple, Lexington, dis 1/31/65, Covington, age 24, reduced to ranks and deserted, house 1-300, s 1,2,4.

EASTERLING, WILLIAM H. reg 14, co I, enr 11/10/61 Louisa, enl 12/10/61 Louisa, dis 1/31/65 Louisa, age 23, residence stated on muster roll, house 1-636, s 1,2,4.

ELAM, GILBERT B. reg 8, co E, B, enr 10/15/61 Camp Estill Springs, enl 1/15/62 Lebanon, dis 11/17/64 Chattanooga TN, age 24, left sick at general hospital at Louisville and went home without authority 3/19/62, residence stated on muster roll, house n/c, s 1,2,4.

ELAM, RICHARD M. reg 14, co I, r 2nd lt, enr & enl 12/10/61 Louisa, age 24, prom from 1st sgt to 2nd lt 8/6/63, killed in action 11/30/63 near Salyersville, List of Officers lists Salyersville as residence, but he is not on Magoffin Co. census, house 1-181, s 1,2,4,32.

ELLISTON, DAVID C. reg 24, co B, enr 10/8/61 Bath Co., enl 12/31/61 Camp Temple, Lexington, age 24, d 1/26/62 Camp Martin near Bardstown, residence stated on muster roll, house n/c, s 1,2,4.

ELLINGTON, THOMAS J. reg 24, co B, enr 11/9/61 Camp Gill, enl 12/31/61 Lexington, dis 1/31/65 Covington, age 19, des 1/12/62 Camp Temple, Lexington, house 1-41, s 1,2,4.

ELLIOTT, JAMES A. reg 24, co B, enr 10/8/61 Bath Co., enl 12/31/61 Camp Temple, Lexington, dis 1/31/65 Covington, age 26, cap Kingston NC, paroled NE Ferry NC 2/26/65, d Annapolis MD 3/13/65 of chronic diarrhea & pneumonia, buried grave 1524, Ash Grove cemetery, residence of widow listed as Morgan Co., house 1-68, s 1,2,4.

F

FERGUSON, WILLIAM. reg 14Cav, co C, G, enr 11/26/62 Montgomery Co., enl 2/13/63 Irvine, dis 3/24/64 Camp Nelson, age 18, re-enlisted and trans to 4th Ky. Inf. 3/15/64, house 2-54, s 1,2.

FRALEY, GEORGE W. reg 40, co C, enr 8/20/63 Grayson, enl 9/26/63 Grayson, dis 12/30/64 Catlettsburg, house 1-291, s 1,2,4.

FREEMAN, ANDREW J. reg 14, co D, enr 10/20/61 Louisa or Catlettsburg, enl 12/10/61 Louisa, dis 1/31/65 Louisa, age 28, black hair & eyes, dark skin, 6-1, b Scott Co. VA, house 1-522, s 1,2,4.

FRISBY, WILLIAM JR. reg 24, co B, enr 10/8/61 Bath Co., enl 12/31/61 Camp Temple, Lexington, dis 1/31/65 Covington, age 20, trans to 6th Ky. Vet. Cav, residence stated on muster roll, house n/c, s 1,2,4.

FRISBY, WILLIAM SR. reg 24, co B, enr 11/9/61, enl 12/31/61 Lexington, age 43, des 1/16/62 Glasgow, residence stated on muster roll, house n/c, s 1,2,4.

G

GEORGE, ELIAS. reg 45, co K, r cpl, enr 11/24/63 Relief, enl 12/9/63 Louisa, dis 2/14/65 Catlettsburg, age 21, black hair, blue eyes, fair skin, 5-4, d 4/15/64 Camp Nelson of disease, b Morgan Co., house 1-359, s 1,2.

GILLUM, PLEASANT. reg 14Cav, co B, G, r 2nd lt, enr 8/16/62 Carter Co., enl 11/65/62 Mt. Sterling, age 31 or 38, resigned 4/30/63, prom to 2nd lt 1/14/63, house 1-435, s 1,2.

GOSE, ANDERSON B. reg 24, co B, enr 10/8/61 Bath Co., enl 12/31/61 Camp Temple, Lexington, dis 1/31/65, age 24, des Glasgow 11/4/62, house 1-78, s 1,2,4.

GOSE, HENRY T. reg 24, co B, enr 10/8/61 Bath Co., enl 12/31/61 Camp Temple, Lexington, dis 4/23/64 Cincinnati, age 20, dark hair & eyes, fair skin 5-11, dis because of paralysis of lower extremities, b. Morgan Co., house 2-9, s 1,2,4.

GULLETT, DIAL. reg 45, co G, H, enr 1/26/64, enl 2/6/64 Mt. Sterling, dis 2/14/65 Catlettsburg, age 20, black hair, gray eyes, fair skin, 5-8, trans from co H to co G 2/1/64, wounded in left shoulder 9/8/64 Mt. Sterling, b Morgan Co., house 2-37, s 1,2,35.

H

HALL, ELIJAH. reg 14, co K, enr 11/8/61 Louisa, enl 12/10/61 Louisa, dis 1/31/65 Louisa, age 24, black hair, gray eyes, fair skin, 6-0, b Morgan Co., residence stated on muster roll, stabbed to death by a fellow soldier 12/19/64 or 12/20/64, house n/c, s 1,2,4.

HALL, JOHN H. reg 24, co G, enr 11/5/61 Camp Gill, Bath Co., enl 12/31/61 Camp Temple, Lexington, dis 1/31/65 Covington, age 20, light hair, blue eyes, fair skin, 6-2, trans to 6th Vet. Cav., dis 6/2/65, b Morgan Co., house 1-46, s 1,2,4.

HASTY, WILLIAM. reg 24, co G, enr 11/5/61 Camp Gill, enl 12/31/61 Lexington, age 21 or 24, des 1/10/62 Lexington or 12/24/63 Mt. Sterling, enl 140th Ohio Inf., co I, 5/22/64, under name of George Williams, residence stated on muster roll, house n/c, s 1,2,4.

HAYS, JAMES. reg 14, co B, enr 10/10/61 Louisa, enl 12/10/61 Louisa, dis 1/31/65 Louisa, age 24 or 26, residence on muster roll, house n/c, s 1,2,4.

HAYS, JAMES H. reg 14, co B, enr 10/10/61 Louisa, enl 12/10/61 Camp Wal-lace, Louisa, dis 1/31/65 Louisa, age 24, residence stated on muster roll, house n/c, s 1,2,4,35.

HAZELRIGG, JOHN T. reg 45, co G, r cpl, enr 7/28/63 Mt. Sterling, enl 11/30/63 Ashland, dis 2/14/65 Catlettsburg, age 19, light hair, blue eyes, fair skin, 5-9, b Morgan Co., age 26 on census, house 1-684, s 1,2.

HENRY, DAVID T. reg 24, co B, enl 11/9/61 Camp Gill, Bath Co., enl 12/31/61 Camp Temple, Lexington, dis 1/31/65 Covington, age 33, dark hair & skin, blue eyes, 5-10, des 1/28/63 Frankfort, 5/63, dropped from rolls, b Morgan Co., house 2-490, s 1,2,4.

HENRY, JOHN. reg 24, co B, r 2nd lt, enr 10/8/61 Bath Co., enl Camp Temple, Lexington, age 38, d 1/29/63 or 1/10/62 Lexington of pneumonia, residence stated on muster roll, house 2-730, s 1,2,4,32.

HENRY, PASCHAL. reg 14Cav, co D, enr 8/20/62 Mt. Sterling, enl 8/21/62 Mt. Sterling, dis 9/16/63 Maysville, age 45, house 1-264, s 1,2,4.

HOLBROOK, JOHN H. reg 22, co G, 10/25/61 Grayson, enl 1/10/62 Louisa, dis 1/20/65 Louisville, age 32, residence on muster roll, house n/c, s 1,2,4.

HOLLINSWORTH, DANIEL F. reg 24, co B, r 1st sgt, enr 10/8/61 Bath Co., enl 12/31/61 Camp Temple, Lexington, dis 1/31/65 Covington, age 22, app 1st sgt 12/31/12, house 1-118, s 1,2,4.

HOLLINSWORTH, JAMES M. reg 24, co B, r sgt, enr 10/8/61 Camp Gill, enl 1/22/62 Lexington, dis 1/31/65 Covington, age 19, prom to cpl 2/28/62, app 5th sgt 10/22/64, house 1-118, s 1,2,4.

HUMPHREY, JOHN A. reg 22, co H, r cpl, enr 10/22/61 Grayson, enl 1/10/62 Paintsville, dis 1/20/65 Louisville, age 18, died 7/3/62 Barboursville of fever, house 1-440, s 1,2,4.

HUMPHREY, WILLIAM J. reg 22, co H, enr 10/22/61 Grayson, enl 1/10/62 Paintsville, dis 1/20/65 Louisville, age 22, cap Vicksburg MS 12/29/62, paroled New Orleans LA 3/13/63, house 1-507, s 1,2,4.

HUNT JOHN W. O. reg 24, co B, enr 11/9/61 Bath Co. enl 12/31/61 Camp Temple, Lexington, dis 1/31/65 Covington, age 19, des 11/4/62 Glasgow, house 1-15, s 1,2,4.

HUTCHISON, HENRY M. reg 40, co C, r cpl, enr 9/23/63 Grayson, enl 9/26/63 Grayson, dis 12/30/64 Catlettsburg, age 21, cap Mt. Sterling 6/8/64, house 1-408, s 1,2,4.

J

JACKSON, JAMES. reg 24, co B, enr 11/9/61, enl 12/31/61 Lexington, age 27, d unknown date at St. Louis MO, residence stated on muster roll, house n/c, s 2,4.

JENKINS, FRANCIS. reg 45, co K, enr 11/24/63 Relief, enl 12/9/63 Louisa, dis 2/14/65 Catlettsburg, age 18, brown hair, blue eyes, fair skin, 5-4, des 2/12/64 Mt. Sterling, b Morgan Co., may be Johnson Co. resident, house 1-363, s 1,2,35.

JENKINS, HENRY. reg 45, co K, r cpl, enr 11/24/63 Relief, enl 12/9/63 Louisa, dis 2/14/65 Catlettsburg, age 32, prom to cpl 3/1/64, house 1-353, s 1,2,35.

JOHNSON, BENJAMIN E. reg 24, co G, enr 11/5/61 Camp Gill, Bath Co., enl 12/31/61 Camp Temple, Lexington, dis 1/31/65 Covington, age 18, brown hair, blue eyes, fair skin, 5-2, 11/63 slightly wounded Knoxville TN, b Morgan Co., house 1-31, s 1,2,4.

JOHNSON, HARVEY. reg 14, co I, enr 11/10/61 Louisa, enl 12/10/61 Louisa, age 19, dark hair, eyes & skin, 5-5, d 8/17/64 Knoxville TN of acute diarrhea, CSR: "sick at home in Morgan Co.", b Giles Co. VA, house 1-145, s 1, 2,4.

JOHNSON, JAMES M. reg 45, co K, enr 11/24/63 Relief, enl 12/9/63 Louisa, dis 2/14/65 Catlettsburg, age 45, black hair & eyes, fair skin, 5-8, b Claiborne Co. TN, house 1-49, s 1,2,35.

JOHNSON, JEDEDIAH. reg 24, co G, enr 11/5/61 Camp Gill, Bath Co., enl 12/31/61 Camp Temple, Lexington, dis 2/14/63 Louisville, age 18, brown hair, blue eyes, fair skin, 5-2, dis 2/24/63 Louisville on surgeon's certificate of disability, cardiac disease, b Morgan Co., house 1-31, s 1,2,4.

JOHNSON, SAMUEL S. reg 24, co G, enr 11/5/61, enl 12/31/61 Lexington, age 19, des 9/24/62 Shiloh TN, CSR: "last heard from Morgan Co. Ky.", house 1-23, s 1,2,4.

JONES, ABRAHAM. reg 24, co B, enr 10/8/61 or 11/9/61 Camp Gill, enl 1/31/61 Camp Temple, Lexington, dis 1/31/65 Covington, age 21, des 1/28/63 Frankfort, CSR: "sick Morgan Co. Ky.", residence stated on muster roll, house n/c, s 1,2,4.

JONES, FRANKLIN. reg 22, co E, enr 10/10/61 Carter Co., enl 1/10/62 Paintsville, dis 8/22/64 or 1/20/65 Louisville, age 35, residence stated on muster roll, house n/c, s 1,2,4.

JONES, PINCKNEY M. reg 24, co B, r 7th cpl, enr 10/8/61 Bath Co., enl 12/31/61 Camp Temple, Lexington, dis 10/2/62, age 30, light hair, blue eyes, fair skin, 6-0, dis 10/2/62 Louisville on certificate of disability for partial hemiplegia (paralysis) affecting left side, b Maringo Co. AL, house 2-617, s 1,2,4.

L

LACY, JAMES A. reg 8, co E, B, enr 10/15/61 Camp Estill Springs, enl 1/15/62 Lebanon, age 18, wounded in leg at Battle of Stones River 1/2/63, d 1/9/63, house 1-270 or 2-761, s 1,2,4.

LAWSON, DAVID. reg 24, co G, enr 11/8/61 Camp Gill, Bath Co., enl 12/31/61 Camp Temple, Lexington, dis 1/31/65 Covington, age 18, brown hair, blue eyes, dark skin, 5-7, b Morgan Co., wounded 6/64, house 2-688, s 1,2,4.

LAWSON, JOSEPH JR. reg 24, co G, enr 10/9/61, enl 12/31/61 Lexington, age 25, killed in battle 5/14/64 Resaca GA, house 2-149, s 1,2,4.

LAWSON, JOSEPH SR. reg 24, co G, enr 11/5/61 Camp Gill, enl 12/31/61 Lexington, age 30, d 2/28/62 Louisville of fever, house 2-150, s 1,2,4.

LEMASTER, RICHARD. reg 45, co K, enr 11/24/63 Paintsville, enl 12/9/63 Louisa, dis 2/14/65 Catlettsburg, age 38, red hair, blue eyes, fair skin, 5-8, d 5/15/65 Lexington of erysipelas (skin infection), b Morgan Co., house 1-368, s 1,2,35.

LEWIS, DANIEL P. JR. reg 24, co B, enr 10/8/61 Bath Co., enl 12/31/61 Camp Temple, Lexington, dis 1/31/65 Covington, age 24, house 1-19, s 1,2,4.

LEWIS, DANIEL P. SR. reg 24, co B, r sgt, enr 11/9/61 Bath Co., enl 12/31/61 Camp Temple, Lexington, age 35, died 5/8/62 Savannah TN, house 1-39, s 2,4.

LEWIS, FRANCIS H. reg 24, co B, enr 10/8/61 Camp Gill, enl 12/31/61 Camp Temple, Lexington, age 20, light hair, blue eyes, fair skin, 5-10, des 1/28/63 Frankfort, b Morgan Co., house 1-76, s 1,2,4.

LEWIS, JAMES H. reg, 24, co B, enr 10/8/61 Bath Co., enl 12/31/61 Camp Temple, Lexington, age 25, dark hair & eyes, fair skin, 5-10, dis 7/10/12 on surgeon's certificate, phthisis pulmonalis (tuberculosis), house 1-167, s 1,2, 4.

LEWIS, JOHN T. reg 24, co B, enr 11/9/61 Bath Co., enl 12/31/61 Camp Temple, Lexington, age 19, dis 6/30/62 for disability, house 1-67, s 1,2,4.

LEWIS, JOHNSON. reg 14, co D, enr 10/20/61 Catlettsburg, enl 12/10/61 Louisa, dis 1/31/65 Louisa, age 18, dark hair, blue eyes, light skin, 5-10, b Lawrence Co., CSR: "at home sick Morgan Co.", house 1-172, s 1,2,4.

LEWIS, WILLIAM. reg 24, co B, enr 11/9/61 Bath Co., enl 12/31/61 Camp Temple, Lexington, age 19, dark hair, blue eyes, fair skin, 5-10, dis 6/2/62 St. Louis MO for pneumonia, b Morgan Co., d Bowling Green 9/27/62 of flux, house 1-87, s 1,4.

LINDON, ANDREW. reg 8, co E, r cpl, enr 10/15/61 Camp Estill Springs, enl 1/15/62 Lebanon, dis 11/17/64 Chattanooga TN, age 19, light hair & skin, blue eyes, 5-8, dis 6/3/62 War Trace TN for disability, diseased lungs, b Morgan Co., house 2-88, s 1,2,4.

LINDON, WILLIAM. reg 8, co E, B, enr 10/15/61 Camp Estill Springs, enl 1/15/62 Lebanon, dis 11/17/64 Chattanooga TN, age 21, des 11/8/62 Glasgow, house 2-88, s 1,2,4.

LINK, JOHN. reg 24, co B, enr 10/8/61 Bath Co., enl 12/31/61 Camp Temple, Lexington, age 26, CSR: "sick Morgan Co.", house 1-72, s 1,2,4.

LINK, THOMAS. reg 24, co G, enr 11/5/61 Camp Gill, enl 12/31/61 Lexington, age 19, brown hair, blue eyes, dark skin, 5-8, dis surgeon's certificate of disability, epilepsy, 5/62 Louisville or 6/13/62 Nashville TN, house 1-647, s 1, 2,4.

LITTLE, JAMES S. reg 8, co E, B, enr 11/1/61 Camp Estill Springs, enl 1/15/62 Lebanon, dis 11/17/64 Chattanooga TN, age 19, wounded right thumb 9/19/63 Chickamauga GA, house 2-243, s 1,2,4.

LYKINS, AARON. reg 24, co B, enr 11/9/61 Bath Co., enl 12/31/61 Camp Temple, Lexington, dis 1/31/65 Covington, age 25, CSR: "sick Morgan Co. Ky.", house 1-85, s 1,2,4.

LYKINS, ISAAC W. reg 24, co G, enr 11/5/61 Camp Gill, Bath Co., enl 12/31/61 Camp Temple, Lexington, dis 5/1/65 Covington, age 23, trans to co G, 6th Ky. Vet. Cav., house 2-53, s 1,2,4.

LYKINS, JAMES. reg 14Cav, co G, enr 12/6/62 Montgomery Co., enl 2/13/63 Irvine, dis 3/24/64 Camp Nelson, age 26, paroled 3/15/63, returned to duty 7/1/63, house 2-75, s 1,2.

LYKINS, MILTON. reg 24, co G, r 3rd sgt, enr 11/5/61 Camp Gill, Bath Co., enl 12/31/61 Camp Temple, Lexington, dis 1/31/65 Covington, age 22, prom from pvt 6/29/62, to 3rd sgt 7/5/63, house 2-52, s 1,2,4.

M

MANNIN, AMOS J. reg 24, co G, r 4th sgt, enr 11/5/61 Camp Gill, Bath Co., enl 12/31/61 Camp Temple, Lexington, dis 1/31/65 Covington, age 20, des 5/20/62 Henderson, house 1-45, s 1,2,4.

MANNIN, JAMES F. reg 24, co G, enr 11/5/61, enl 12/31/61 Lexington, age 18, d 2/20/62 Lebanon of pneumonia, house 1-45, s 1,2,4.

MANNIN, ZACHARIAH. reg 24, co G, r cpl, enr 11/5/61 Camp Gill, enl 12/31/61 Lexington, age 20, died 1/7/64 Knoxville TN smallpox, residence stated on muster roll, house, n/c, s 1,2,4.

MARTIN, ANDREW J. reg 24, co B, enr 10/8/61 Bath Co., enl 12/31/61 Camp Temple, Lexington, age 23, fair hair & skin, blue eyes, 6-1, dis 5/10/62 Louisville on certificate of disability, soft place in head from lack of skull bone, b Morgan Co., house 2-137, s 1,2,4.

MARTIN, GEORGE W. reg 24, co B, r cpl, enr 10/8/61 Camp Gill, Bath Co., enl 12/31/61 Camp Temple, Lexington, dis 1/31/65 Covington, age 24, light hair, blue eyes, fair skin, 5-5, musician, prom to cpl 4/25/64, b Morgan Co., house 2-160, s 1,2,4.

MARTIN, JOHN. reg 24, co B, enr 10/8/61 Bath Co., enl 12/31/61 Camp Temple, age 19, d 1/26/62 Lexington of pneumonia, house 2-141, s 1,2,4.

MARTIN, JOHN P. reg 24, co B, enr 10/8/61 Bath Co., enl 12/31/61 Camp Temple, Lexington, dis 1/31/65 Covington, age 27, sick in Morgan Co., failed to report, dropped as deserter 12/31/64, house 2-121, s 1,2,4.

MCGUIRE, JOHN. reg 14Cav, co G, enr 5/20/63 Irvine, enl 6/15/63 Lexington, dis 3/24/64 Camp Nelson, age 35, house 1-281, s 1,2.

MCLAIN, WILLIAM G. reg 24, co E, enr 10/9/61 Camp Gill, Bath Co., enl 12/31/61 Camp Temple, Lexington, age 20, light hair & skin, gray eyes, dis 11/6/62 Nashville TN, imbecility, general disability & chronic diarrhea, b Hazel Green, residence stated on muster roll, house n/c, s 1,2,4.

MEADOWS, ELISHA. reg 45, co K, enr 11/24/63 Paintsville, enl 12/9/63 Louisa, dis 2/14/65 Catlettsburg, age 34, missing Mt. Sterling 6/9/64, house 1-361, s 1,2,35.

MONTGOMERY, WILLIAM. reg 45, co K, enr 11/24/63 Paintsville, enl 2/9/63 Louisa, age 44, dark hair, blue eyes, fair skin, 5-6, died 4/19/64 Ashland or Flemingsburg of measles, b Morgan Co., effects to be sent to wife in Morgan Co., house 1-355, s 1,2.

MOORE, JAMES M. reg 24, co F, enr 10/8/61 Camp Gill, Bath Co., enl 12/31/61 Camp Temple, Lexington, age 24, residence stated on muster roll, house n/c, s 1,2,4.

MORGAN, JAMES H. reg 24, co B, enr 11/9/61 Bath Co., enl 12/31/61 Camp Temple, Lexington, dis 1/31/65 Covington, age 37, dis 3/29/62 Nashville TN physical disability, residence on muster roll, house 1-649, s 1,2,4.

MULLINS, HOUSTON. reg 14Cav, co G, enr 1/1/63 Estill Co., enl 2/13/63 Irvine, dis 3/24/64 Camp Nelson, age 23, house 2-707, s 1,2.
MURPHY, WILLIAM. reg US Navy, enl 7/12/64 Camp Chase, house 2-426, s 1.

N

NICKEL, ALFRED W. reg 24, co B, r sgt, enr 11/9/61 Bath Co., enl 12/31/61 Camp Temple, age 22, des 7/4/62, CSR: "last heard from Morgan Co.", residence stated on muster roll, house n/c, s 1,2,4.
NICKELL, FRANCIS M. reg 24, co B, r 5th cpl, enr 11/9/61 Bath Co., enl 12/31/61 Camp Temple, dis 1/31/65 Covington, age 19, des 1/28/13 Frankfort, house 1-154, s 1,2,4.

O

OAKLEY, BENJAMIN A. reg 22, co G, age 22, des 12/18/61, not on AG or CSR, house 2-450, s 4.
O'HARE, HOUSTON. reg 24, co E, enr 10/9/61 Camp Gill, enl 12/31/61 Camp Temple, Lexington, dis 9/6/65 Covington, age 19, trans to co K, 6th Vet. Cav., house 2-292, s 1,2,4.

P

PATRICK, ROBERT J. reg 14Cav, co D, enr 8/18/62 Mt. Sterling, enl 8/21/62 Mt. Sterling, age 37, cap & paroled Mt. Sterling 3/22/63 by Col. Roy Cluke, d 11/25/63 Camp Dennison OH of pneumonia, b Morgan Co., muster roll states he was resident of Montgomery Co., but he is not on Montgomery Co. census, house 2-596, s 1,2,4.
PENIX, GILBERT. reg 45, co K, r cpl, enr 11/24/63 Paintsville, enl 12/9/63 Louisa, dis 2/14/65 Catlettsburg, age 24, light or black hair, gray or blue eyes, fair or dark skin, 5-7 or 5-10, reduced to ranks 7/4/64, b Morgan Co., CSR: "sick at home in Morgan Co. Ky.", house 1-350, s 1,2,35.
PERKINS, SPENCER. reg 14, co B, enr 10/10/61 Louisa, enl 12/10/61 Camp Wallace, Louisa, dis 1/31/65 Louisa, age 21, residence stated on muster roll, house n/c, s 1,2,35.
PERRY, ALLEN. reg US Army, enl 4/22/65, house 1-619, s 1.
PERRY, CYRUS. reg 24, co B, r cpl, enr 11/9/61 Bath Co., enl 12/31/61 Camp Temple, dis 1/31/65 Covington, age 41, prom to cpl 1/1/64, house 1-84, s 1, 2,4.
PERRY, THOMAS N. reg 24, co B, enr 11/9/61 Camp Gill, Bath Co., enl 12/31/61 Camp Temple, Lexington, age 19, d 1/25/62 Lexington of pneumonia, house 1-84, s 1,2,4.
PEYTON, CHARLES L. reg 24, co B, r 1st sgt, enr 10/8/61 Bath Co., enl 12/31/61 Camp Temple, Lexington, dis 12/31/62 Frankfort because of disability, age 27, house 1-17, s 1,2,4.
PRATER, ELISHA C. reg 24, co G, enr 11/5/61 Camp Gill, enl 12/31/61 Lexington, dis 1/31/65 Covington, age 21, des 11/5/62 Glasgow, house 2-119, s 1,2,4.
PRATER, HENRY C. reg 24, co G, enr 11/5/61 Camp Gill, enl 12/31/61 Lexington, dis 1/31/65 Covington, age 23, des 11/5/62 Glasgow, house 2-15, s 1, 2,4.
PRATER, ROBERT F. reg 24, co B, enr 11/9/61 Bath Co., enl 12/31/61 Camp Temple, Lexington, musician, age 21, left sick at Lexington, des from hospital date unknown, reg 14Cav, co D, enr 8/20/62 Mt. Sterling, enl 8/21/62 Mt. Sterling, dis 9/16/63 Maysville, cap & paroled 3/22/63 Mt. Sterling by Col. Roy Cluke, house 2-29, s 1,2,4.

R

RICE, ALFRED G. reg 22, co G, enr 10/25/63 Grayson, enl 1/19/62 Lexington, dis 1/20/65 Louisville, age 22, des 1/12/__ Louisa, residence stated on muster roll, house n/c, s 1,2,4.

ROBBINS, JAMES. reg 45, co K, r cpl, enr 11/24/63 Paintsville, enl 12/9/63 Louisa, dis 2/14/65 Catlettsburg, age 27, des 5/25/64 near Pound Gap, house 1-380, s 1,2,35.

ROBBINS, NICHOLAS. reg 45, co K, r cpl, enr 11/29/63 Paintsville, enl 12/9/63 Louisa, dis 2/14/65 Catlettsburg, age 19, des 5/25/64 near Pound Gap, house 1-380, s 1,2,35.

ROBBINS, WILLIAM. reg 45, co K, enr 11/24/63 Paintsville or Relief, enl 12/9/63 Louisa, dis 2/14/65 Catlettsburg, age 22, light hair, blue eyes, fair skin, 5-6, des on march 5/28/64, b Morgan Co., house 1-380, s 1,2,35.

ROSS, JOHN. reg US Army, enl 3/24/65 Chicago IL, house 2-428 or 2-568, s 1.

S

SERGEANT, DAVID A. reg 24, co B, r sgt, enr 10/8/61 Bath Co., enl 12/31/61 Camp Temple, Lexington, dis 1/31/65 Covington, age 21, prom to cpl 4/30/62, to sgt 10/31/62, wounded Knoxville TN 11/25/63, detailed to recruit in Morgan Co., house 1-621, s 1,2,4.

SERGEANT, JOHN E. reg 24, co B, enr 10/8/61 Bath Co., enl 12/31/61 Camp Temple, Lexington, age 26, d Nashville TN 4/9/62, house 1-648, s 1,2,4.

SERGEANT, JOSEPH. reg 24, co B, enr 10/8/61 Bath Co., enl 12/31/61 Camp Temple, Lexington, age 38, dark hair & skin, blue eyes, 5-11, dis 5/27/62 Nashville for hydrothorax, CSR: "last heard from Morgan Co.", b Russell Co. VA, house 1-243, s 1,2,4.

SMITH, ELIJAH. reg 45, co K, enr 11/24/63 Relief, enl 12/9/63 Louisa, dis 2/14/65 Catlettsburg, age 26, black hair, blue eyes, fair skin, 6-1, missing Mt. Sterling 6/9/64, b Morgan Co., house 1-536, s 1,2,35.

SMITH, ELISHA. reg 45, co K, enr 11/24/63 Relief, enl 12/9/63 Louisa, dis 2/14/65 Catlettsburg, age 23, black hair, blue eyes, fair skin, 6-0, b Morgan Co., house 1-316, s 1,2,35.

SMITH, HADEN. reg 45, co C, K, enr 8/18/63 Paintsville, enl 10/10/63 Catlettsburg, dis 12/24/64 Catlettsburg, age 18, trans from co C to co K, back to co C 2/1/64, house 1-378, s 1,2.

SMITH, HIRAM. reg 45, co K, enr 11/24/63 Paintsville, enl 12/9/63 Louisa, dis 2/14/65 Catlettsburg, age 22, light hair, blue eyes, dark skin, 5-4, CSR: "at home sick Morgan Co. Ky.", b Morgan Co., house 1-308, s 1,2,35.

STACY, MESHACK. reg 24, co G, enr 11/5/61 Camp Gill, enl 12/31/61 Lexington, dis 1/31/65 Covington, age 32, brown hair, blue eyes, fair skin, 6-1, des 11/2/62 Glasgow, reg 45, co H, enl 2/5/64 Mt. Sterling, dark hair & eyes, light skin, 5-6, or 5-11, m/out 2/14/65 Catlettsburg, trans from co H to co G 2/1/64, back to co H 5/20/64, b Morgan Co., residence stated on muster roll, house n/c, 1,2,4.

STACY, WILLIAM E. reg 24, co G, enr 11/5/61 Camp Gill, enl 12/31/61 Lexington, age 23, d 2/2/62 or 2/3/62 Louisville of pneumonia, house 2-40, s 1,2,4.

STAMPER, JOHN W. reg 24, co G, enr 11/5/61 Camp Gill, enl Camp Temple, Lexington, dis 6/19/65 Camp Chase, age 18, brown hair, gray eyes, fair skin, 5-9, cap 5/24/64 near Kennesaw Mtn. GA, confined at Florence SC 10/5/64, paroled N. E. Ferry, NC 2/26/65, house 1-211, s 1,2,4.

STEELE, JOHN O. reg 45, co G, enr 7/25/63 Mt. Sterling, enl 11/30/63 Ashland, dis 2/14/65 Catlettsburg, age 20, d 12/21/64 Knoxville TN of disease, house 1-639, s 1,2,35.

STEELE, MAHLON R. reg 14, co I, r 2nd sgt, enr 11/10/61 Louisa, enl 12/10/61 Louisa, dis 5/3/65 Covington, age 23, prom from 3rd sgt to 2nd sgt, cap 11/30/63 Salyersville, confined at Richmond VA 12/8/64, sent to Andersonville GA 2/14/64, released at Aiken's Landing VA 3/9/65, house 1-639, s 1, 2,4.

STEGALL, MARTIN. reg 22, co H, enr 10/22/61 Grayson, enl 1/10/62 Paintsville, dis 1/20/65 Louisville, age 23, dark hair & skin, gray eyes, 5-10, d 11/13/62 or 11/15/62 Gallipolis OH of typhoid fever, house 1-504, s 1,2,4.

STEPHENS, SOLOMON. reg 45, co K, enr 11/24/63 Ashland, enl 12/9/63 Louisa, dis 2/14/65 Catlettsburg, age 28, des 3/7/64 Flemingsburg, house 1-460, s 1,2,35.

STEVENS, JAMES. reg 14Cav, co G, enr 12/15/62 Estill Co., enl 2/13/63 Irvine, age 27, died 3/12/63 Irvine of typhoid fever, house 1-427, s 1,2.

STRICKLIN, WILLIAM. reg 24, co G, enr 11/5/61 Camp Gill, Bath Co., enl 12/31/61 Camp Temple, Lexington, dis 1/31/65 Covington, age 18, light hair, gray eyes, fair skin, 5-7, cap Knoxville TN 11/20/63, wounded in right thigh, Battle of Resaca GA 5/14/64, b Morgan Co., may be resident of another county, house 2-158, s 1,2,4.

T

TERRY, JESSE. reg 14, co B, enr & enl 6/2/63 Louisa, dis 1/31/65 Louisa, age 23 or 33, des 8/24/63 Louisa, house 1-253, s 1,2,4.

TURNER, JOSEPH B. reg 24, co B, enr 11/9/61 Bath Co., enl 12/31/61 Camp Temple, d 4/10/63 of malignant variola (smallpox), house 2-743, s 1,4.

U

UTTERBACK, WILLIAM W. reg 40, co E, r cpl, enr 9/30/63 Grayson, enl 9/28/63 Grayson, dis 12/30/64 Catlettsburg, age 21, dark hair, blue eyes, fair skin, 5-10, b Morgan Co., residence stated on muster roll, house 1-55, s 1,2, 4.

W

WALTERS, ELKANA M. reg 8, co B, E, enr 10/15/61 Camp Estill Springs, enl 1/15/62 Lebanon, dis 11/17/64 Chattanooga TN, age 18, des 10/31/62 Corbin, residence stated on muster roll, house n/c, s 1,2,4.

WELCH, JAMES M. reg 24, co B, enr 10/8/61 Bath Co., enl 12/31/61 Camp Temple, Lexington, age 24, d 9/25/62 Bowling Green, residence stated on muster roll, house n/c, s 1,2,4.

WILLIAMS, JACKSON. reg 14, co D, enr 10/20/61 Louisa or Catlettsburg, enl 12/10/61 Louisa, dis 1/31/65 Louisa, age 23, residence stated on muster roll, house n/c, s 1,2,4.

WILLIAMS, LEMUEL. reg 24, co B, r 1st cpl, enr 11/9/61 Bath Co., enl 12/31/61 Camp Temple, Lexington, dis 12/31/62 Frankfort on account of disability, age 28, house 1-649, s 1,2,4.

WYATT, URIAH. reg 14Cav, co G, C, D, enr 8/21/62 Montgomery Co., enl 2/13/63 Irvine, dis 3/24/64 Camp Nelson, age 20, trans to co D 1/13/63, house 1-272, s 1,2,4.

PIKE COUNTY UNION SOLDIERS

A

ABSHER, JOHN B. reg 39, co G, enr 1/14/63, enl 2/16/63 Peach Orchard, age 34, dark hair, eyes & skin, 5-6, rem trans from co H 10/23/63, d 3/10/65 Ashland typhoid fever, house 7-305, s 1,2,4.

ADAMS, ISAAC. reg 14, co C, enr 10/10/61 Louisa, enl 12/10/61 Louisa, dis 9/15/65 Louisville, age 24, light hair, blue eyes, fair skin, 5-4, rem trans to 14th Vet Inf, co A, enr 2/29/64, m/in 3/19/64 Catlettsburg, residence stated on muster roll, house n/c, s 1,2,4.

ADAMS, ROBERT. reg 10cav, co E, enr 8/9/62, m/in 9/9/62 Covington, m/out 9/17/63 Maysville, reg 39, co A, enr 12/25/63 Johnson Co., enl 3/28/64 Greenupsburg, dis 9/15/65 Louisville, age 20, dark hair & skin, gray eyes, 5-7, residence shown on CSR, house n/c, s 1,2.

ADAMS, WILLIAM D. reg 39, co C, r cpl, enr 9/20/62, enl 2/16/63 Peach Orchard, age 21, dark hair, blue eyes, fair skin, 5-3, rem des 8/12/64 Louisa, residence stated on muster roll, house n/c, s 1,2,4.

ADKINS, ANDREW J. reg 39, co B, r 2nd lt, enr 1/21/63, enl 9/9/63 Louisa, age 29, rem prom from sgt to 2nd lt 1/21/63, res 9/3/64, house 1-81, s 2,4.

ADKINS, HENRY. reg 14, co C, enr 10/10/61 Louisa, enl 12/10/61 Louisa, age 25, light hair, blue eyes, fair skin, 5-7, rem d 3/16/62 Paintsville, house 7-42, s 1,2,4.

ADKINS, HENRY. reg 39, co I, enr 9/1/63 Louisa, enl 10/30/63 Louisa, dis 9/15/65 Louisville, age 26, light hair, dark eyes, fair skin, 5-10, house 7-370, s 1,2,4.

ADKINS, HENRY. reg CG, co E, enr 5/26/64, enl 7/4/64 Frankfort, age 18, light hair, blue eyes, fair skin, 6-0, rem des 2/12/65 Paintsville, house 7-41, s 2,4.

ADKINS, JAMES D. reg 39, co D, enr 3/10/65 Louisa, enl 4/15/65 Greenupsburg, dis 9/15/65 Louisville, age 18, light hair, blue eyes, fair skin, 5-6, house 7-76, s 1,2,4.

ADKINS, JESSE. reg 39, co I, enr 11/19/62, enl 2/16/63 Peach Orchard, age 30, dark hair, black eyes, fair skin, 5-8, rem cap 2/1/63 Pike Co., d 4/9/64 Louisa, measles, residence stated on muster roll, house n/c, s 1,2,4.

ADKINS, JOSEPH. reg 39, co E, enr 11/10/62 Piketon, enl 2/16/63 Peach Orchard, age 33, light hair, blue eyes, fair skin, 5-10, rem d 4/8/63 Louisa, residence stated on muster roll, house n/c, s 1,2,4.

ADKINS, LEVI. reg 14, co H, r cpl, enr 10/25/61 Louisa, enl 12/10/61 Louisa, dis 1/31/65 Louisa, age 21, dark hair, blue eyes, fair skin, 5-7, house 7-76, s 1,2,4.

ADKINS, LEWIS. reg 39, co D, r cpl, enr 10/1/62 Pike Co., enl 2/16/63, dis 9/15/65 Louisville, age 19, dark hair & eyes, fair skin, 5-7, rem prom to cpl 12/5/64, residence stated on muster roll, house n/c, s 1,2,4.

ADKINS, OWEN. reg 39, co I, enr 11/14/62 Pike Co., enl 2/16/63 Peach Orchard, dis 9/15/65 Louisville, age 29, dark hair, brown eyes, fair skin, 5-11, rem cap 2/1/63 Pike Co., house 7-42, s 1,2,4.

ADKINS, SAMUEL. reg 39, co B, enr 9/6/62 Louisa, enl 2/16/63 Peach Orchard, dis 9/15/65 Louisville, age 25, dark hair, blue eyes, fair skin, 5-8, house 1-83, s 1,2,4.

ADKINS, SPURLOCK. reg 39, co B, r cpl, enr 11/19/62 Piketon, enl 2/16/63 Peach Orchard, dis 9/15/65 Louisville, age 18, light hair, blue eyes, fair skin, 5-5, rem app cpl 2/1/65, house 1-80, s 1,2,4.

ADKINS, WILLIAM B. reg 14, co H, enl 10/25/61 Louisa, age 32, dark hair, blue eyes, fair skin, 5-8, rem trans to 14th Vet Inf, residence stated on muster roll, house n/c, s 1,2,4.

AKERS, CALEB. reg 39, co B, enr 11/16/62 Piketon, enl 2/16/63 Peach Orchard, dis 9/15/65 Louisville, age 28, black hair, blue eyes, dark skin, 5-7, house 1-99, s 1,2,4.

ALLEN, JEREMIAH. reg 39, co H, enr 5/30/63 Louisa, enl 6/1/63 Louisa, age 22 or 25, black hair, dark eyes & skin, 5-11, rem des 11/28/63, residence stated on muster roll, house n/c, s 1,2,4.

ALLEY, BENJAMIN W. reg 65, co D, enl 5/12/64, dis 6/21/64, age 34, blue eyes, light hair, fair skin, 6-1, house 7-595, s 2,4.
ALLEY, PETER H. reg 65, co D, enl 5/21/64, dis 6/21/64, age 38, gray eyes, dark hair & skin, 6-3, house 7-597, s 2,4.
ALLEY, THOMAS C. reg 65, co D, r cpl, enl 5/21/64, dis 6/21/64, age 25, blue eyes, light hair, fair skin, 6-2, house 7-592, s 2,4.
ANDERSON, DAVID. reg 39, co E, enr 10/6/62, enl 2/16/63 Peach Orchard, dis 9/15/65 Louisville, age 41, house 7-298, s 2,4.
ANDERSON, GEORGE W. reg 39, co C, enr 8/22/63 Pike Co., enl 8/30/63 Peach Orchard, age 25, dark hair & skin, black eyes, 5-7, rem d 2/29/64 Louisa, house 7-299, s 1,2,4.
ANDERSON, JAMES F. reg 39, co C, enr 8/29/63 Pike Co., enl 8/30/63 Louisa, dis 9/15/65 Louisville, age 18, black hair & eyes, dark skin, 5-3, house 7-298, s 1,2,4.
ANDERSON, MILES J. reg 39, co C, enr 9/10/62 Pike Co., enl 2/16/63 Peach Orchard, age 18, black hair & eyes, fair skin, 5-4, rem des 8/12/64 Louisa, house 7-298, s 1,2,4.

B

BAKER, FREELING H. reg 39, co H, enr 12/28/62 Pike Co., enl 2/16/63 Peach Orchard, dis 9/15/65 Louisville, age 20 or 25, fair hair & skin, blue eyes, 5-1, residence stated on muster roll, house n/c, s 1,2,4.
BAKER, HENRY. reg 39, co E, enr 8/24/63, enl 8/31/63 Catlettsburg, age 23, rem des 7/12/64 Louisa, residence stated on muster roll, house n/c, s 1,2,4.
BAKER, JAMES. reg 39, co H, enr 12/27/62 Pike Co., enl 2/16/63 Peach Orchard, dis 9/15/65 Louisville, age 26, dark hair & skin, black eyes, 5-5, residence stated on muster roll, house n/c, s 1,2,4.
BAKER, THOMAS V. reg 39, co D, enr 11/23/62, enl 2/16/63 Peach Orchard, dis 9/15/65 Louisville, age 30, dark hair, blue eyes, fair skin, 5-8, residence stated on muster roll, house n/c, s 1,2,4.
BAKER, WILLIAM. reg 39, co D, enr 11/15/62 Pike Co., enl 2/16/63 Peach Orchard, dis 9/15/65 Louisville, age 28, dark hair, blue eyes, fair skin, 5-7, residence stated on muster roll, house n/c, s 1,2,4.
BARTLEY, JAMES. reg 45, co I, r cpl, enr 12/14/63 Louisa, enl 2/4/64 Mt. Sterling, dis 2/14/65 Catlettsburg, age 21, dark hair & eyes, light skin, 5-9, rem prom to cpl 2/4/64, house 7-105, s 1,2.
BARTLEY, JOHN. reg 39, co K, age 18, residence stated on muster roll, house n/c, s 3,4.
BELCHER, ISAAC. reg CG, co G, r cpl, enr 6/10/64, enl 7/6/64 Frankfort, dis 3/11/65 Catlettsburg, age 26, light hair, gray eyes, fair skin, 5-8, house 7-168, s 2,4.
BEVERLY, WILLIAM. reg 14, co C, enr 10/10/61 Louisa, enl 12/10/61 Louisa, age 25, dark hair & skin, blue eyes, 6-0, rem d 3/4/62 Ashland, house 7-25, s 1,2,4.
BEVINS, GEORGE M. D. reg 39, co E, enr 11/11/62, enl 2/16/63 Peach Orchard, age 19, light hair, blue eyes, fair skin, 5-8, rem dis 6/10/65 Covington for disability, house 7-556, s 1,2,4.
BEVINS, JOHN W. reg 39, co D, enr 9/6/63 Pike Co., enl 10/29/63 Louisa, dis 9/15/65 Louisville, age 18, dark hair, black eyes, fair skin, 5-10, house 7-827, s 1,2,4.
BEVINS, KENAS E. reg 39, co E, enr 11/11/62, age 20, light hair, blue eyes, fair skin, 5-8, rem d 12/15/62 Pike Co. of measles, house 7-556, s 1,2,4.
BILITER, WILLIAM. reg 39, co D, enr 10/5/62 Pike Co., enl 2/16/63 Peach Orchard, dis 9/15/65 Louisville, age 20, light hair, blue eyes, fair skin, 5-7, house 7-961, s 1,2,4.
BLACKBURN, BARNABUS. reg 39, co E, enr 6/25/63, enl 10/31/63 Catlettsburg, dis 9/15/65 Louisville, age 20, light hair, blue eyes, fair skin, 5-6, house 7-466, s 1,2,4.
BLACKBURN, GEORGE. reg 39, co E, enr 11/6/62 Piketon, enl 2/16/63 Peach Orchard, dis 9/15/65 Louisville, age 26, dark hair & skin, blue eyes, 5-7, house 7-254, s 1,2,4.

BLACKBURN, GEORGE W. reg 39, co C, enr 12/5/63 Paintsville, enl 3/29/64 Greenupsburg, age 18, dark hair & skin, black eyes, 5-8, rem d 3/1/64 Louisa of fever, house 7-487, s 1,2,4.

BLACKBURN, GILBERT. reg 39, co E, enr 11/15/62 Piketon, enl 2/16/63 Peach Orchard, age 19, dark hair, blue eyes, fair skin, 5-7, rem cap 2/1/63 Pike Co., des 7/1/63, residence stated on muster roll, house n/c, s 1,2,4.

BLACKBURN, JOHN. reg 39, co D, enr 11/11/62 Pike Co., enl 2/16/63 Peach Orchard, age 31, black hair, blue eyes, fair skin, 5-10, rem d 8/15/63 of knife wound to abdomen inflicted by fellow soldier on 7/31/63, house 7-270, s 1,2,4.

BLACKBURN, NATHANIEL. reg 39, co D, enr 11/11/62, enl 2/16/63 Peach Orchard, dis 9/15/65 Louisville, age 23, house 7-254, s 1,2,4.

BLACKBURN, PEYTON. reg 39, co E, enr 6/25/63, enl 10/31/63 Catlettsburg, dis 9/15/65 Louisville, age 17, light hair, blue eyes, fair skin, 5-6, house 7-466, s 1,2,4.

BLACKBURN, PEYTON SR. reg 39, co E, enr 10/6/62, enl 2/16/63 Peach Orchard, age 40, dark hair & skin, blue eyes, 5-10, rem killed 9/16/64 by bushwhackers at mouth of Brushy Creek, house 7-487, s 1,2,4.

BLACKBURN, THOMAS. reg 39, co E, enr 11/6/62, enl 2/16/63 Peach Orchard, dis 9/15/65 Louisville, age 24, residence stated on muster roll, house n/c, s 2,4.

BLACKBURN, WILLIAM. reg 39, co C, enr 9/10/62 Pike Co., enl 2/16/63 Peach Orchard, dis 9/15/65 Louisville, age 33, black hair, gray eyes, fair skin, 5-8, residence stated on muster roll, house n/c, s 1,2,4.

BLAIR, ISAIAH. reg 39, co B, enr 11/12/62 Piketon, enl 2/16/63 Peach Orchard, dis 9/15/65 Louisville, age 22, dark hair, gray eyes, fair skin, 5-10, house 1-51, s 1,2,4.

BLAIR, JOHN. reg 39, co B, enr 11/12/62 Pike Co., enl 2/16/63 Peach Orchard, dis 9/15/65 Louisville, age 24, light hair, blue eyes, fair skin, 5-8, house 1-51, s 1,2,4.

BLANKENSHIP, BIRD. reg 39, co H, enr 12/10/62, enl 2/16/63 Peach Orchard, dis 9/15/65 Louisville, age 18, dark hair, eyes & skin, 5-5, house 7-725, s 1,2,4.

BLANKENSHIP, FRANCIS MARION. reg 39, co H, enr 12/10/62 Catlettsburg, enl 2/16/63 Peach Orchard, dis 9/15/65 Louisville, age 20, fair hair & skin, blue eyes, 5-9, house 7-717, s 1,2,4.

BLANKENSHIP, GEORGE WASHINGTON. reg 39, co H, enr 1/29/63, enl 2/16/63 Peach Orchard, dis 9/15/65 Louisville, age 27, house 7-725, s 1,2,4.

BLANKENSHIP, ISOM. reg 39, co K, enr 11/20/62 Piketon, enl 2/16/63 Peach Orchard, age 18, black hair & eyes, dark skin, 5-11, rem d 3/21/63 Louisa of lung fever, house 7-716, s 1,2,4.

BLANKENSHIP, OLIVER. reg 39, co H, enr 7/20/63 Pike Co., enl 8/20/63 Louisa, dis 9/15/65 Louisville, age 18 or 24, fair hair, dark eyes & skin, 5-7, house 7-731, s 1,2,4.

BLANKENSHIP, PRESLEY. reg 39, co H, enr 8/27/63, enl 8/29/63 Louisa, dis 9/15/65 Louisville, age 18, rem residence established by descriptive muster roll, house 7-717, s 2,4.

BLANKENSHIP, PRESLEY SR. reg 39, co H, enr 1/28/63 Pike Co., enl 2/16/63 Peach Orchard, age 43, fair hair & skin, blue eyes, 5-9, rem dis 2/26/64 Catlettsburg on surgeon's certificate of general disability, house 7-725, s 1,2,4.

BLANKENSHIP, PRESLEY J. reg 39, co I, enr 11/26/62 Pike Co., enl 2/16/63 Peach Orchard, age 25, light hair, blue eyes, fair skin, 5-10, rem wounded by enemy, residence established by descriptive muster roll, house n/c, s 1,2,4.

BLEVINS, JACKSON P. reg 65, co D, r sgt, enl 5/21/64, dis 6/21/64, age 22, gray eyes, dark hair, fair skin, 5-11, house 7-384, s 2,4.

BLEVINS, JAMES P. reg 39, co E, enr 11/8/62 Piketon, enl 2/16/63 Peach Orchard, dis 9/15/65 Louisville, age 20, light hair, blue eyes, fair skin, 5-5, house 7-375, s 1,2,4.

BOGAR, JOHN G. reg 39, co C, r cpl, enr 9/10/62 Louisa, enl 2/16/63 Peach Orchard, dis 9/15/65 Louisville, age 18, black hair, blue eyes, dark skin, 5-5, rem prom to cpl 5/25/65, house 7-405, s 1,2,4.

BOGAR, MOSES. reg 14, co H, enr 10/25/61 Catlettsburg, enl 12/10/61 Louisa, dis 1/31/65 Louisa, age 37, black hair & eyes, dark skin, 5-8, residence stated on muster roll, house n/c, s 1,2,4.

BOGAR, THOMAS H. reg 14, co H, enr 10/25/61 Catlettsburg, enl 12/10/61 Louisa, dis 3/30/62 Paintsville, age 27, black hair & eyes, dark skin, 5-2, rem dis for disability, residence stated on muster roll, house n/c, s 1,2,4.

BONE, CLELAND. reg 16, co C, enl 7/8/62, dis 7/24/65 Lexington, age 25 or 27, residence stated on muster roll, house n/c, s 1, 4.

BRANHAM, ALFRED. reg 39, co K, enr 2/1/63 Piketon, enl 2/16/63 Peach Orchard, dis 9/15/65 Louisville, age 22, dark hair, black eyes, fair skin, 5-10, house 1-70, s 1,2,4.

BRANHAM, JAMES. reg 39, co K, enr 2/1/63, age 22, black hair & eyes, dark skin, 5-6, rem d 3/21/64 Camp Nelson smallpox, house 1-56, s 1,2,4.

BREEDING, ALBERT J. reg 39, co H, r 1st sgt, enr 11/25/62 Pike Co., enl 2/16/63 Peach Orchard, dis 9/15/65 Louisville, age 30, black hair, blue eyes, fair skin, 5-10, rem prom from pvt to 1st sgt, 1/21/65, residence stated on muster roll, house n/c, s 1,2,4.

BRIANT, JOSEPH. reg 65, co B, enl 5/21/64, dis 6/9/64, age 21, dark eyes, hair & skin, 5-9, house 7-142, s 2,4.

BROWN, JEREMIAH. reg 39, co D, enr 11/15/62 Pike Co., enl 2/16/63 Peach Orchard, age 37, dark hair, blue eyes, fair skin, 5-9, rem dis 7/23/65 Louisa, from wound to right elbow received in action at mouth of Card, Pike Co., house 7-276, s 1,2,4,8.

BROWN, WILLIAM S. reg 39, co D, enr 11/15/62 Pike Co., enl 2/16/63 Peach Orchard, dis 9/15/65 Louisville, age 26, black hair & eyes, dark skin, 5-8, house 7-276, s 1,2,4.

BROWNING, MILES. reg 167WV, co Francis, reg 39, co D, enr 11/10/62 Pike Co., enl 2/16/63 Peach Orchard, dis 9/15/65 Louisville, age 34, black hair & eyes, fair skin, 5-9, house 7-809, s 1,2,4,8,23.

BRUNTEY, JESSE. reg 39, co K, enr 11/16/62, enl 2/16/63 Peach Orchard, age 38, dark hair, blue eyes, fair skin, 6-0, rem des 3/10/63 or 3/22/63 Louisa, house 1-12, s 1,2,4.

BURGETT, MOSES. reg 167WV, co Sampson Kirk, reg 39, co I, enr 7/30/63, enl 8/29/63 Louisa, dis 9/15/65 Louisville, age 20, black hair & eyes, dark skin, 5-10, house 7-565, s 1,2,4.

BURGETT, WILLIAM. reg 167WV, co Sampson Kirk, house 7-596, s 23.

BURK, MOSES. reg 39, co B, enr 9/6/62 Louisa, enl 6/10/63 Louisa, dis 9/15/65 Louisville, age 20, light hair, blue eyes, fair skin, 5-10, house 1-133, s 1,2,4.

BURK, OWEN. reg 39, co B, enr 1/16/63 Louisa, enl 2/16/63 Peach Orchard, dis 9/15/65 Louisville, age 28, light hair, blue eyes, fair skin, 6-1, residence stated on muster roll, house n/c, s 1,2,4.

BURK, STEPHEN. reg 39, co B, enr 9/62, house 1-139, s 5.

BURKE, JAMES. reg 39, co K, enr 11/16/62 Piketon, enl 2/16/63 Peach Orchard, dis 9/15/65 Louisville, age 28, light hair, blue eyes, fair skin, 5-9, house 7-924, s 1,2,4.

BURKE, JARVIS. reg 39, co E, enr 11/21/62, enl 2/16/63 Peach Orchard, age 19, black hair & eyes, dark skin, 5-7, rem des 7/22/63 Camp Beaver, house 1-120, s 1,2,4.

BURRISS, HARRISON. reg 39, co E, enr 1862, dis 9/15/65, house 7-805, s 5.

BURRISS, JAMES. reg 39, co E, enr 11/10/62 Piketon, enl 2/16/63 Peach Orchard, dis 9/15/65 Louisville, age 30, light hair, blue eyes, fair skin, 5-8, house 7-544, s 1,2,4.

BURRISS, WILLIAM H. reg 39, co E, r cpl, enr 11/22/62 Piketon, enl 2/16/63 Peach Orchard, dis 9/15/65 Louisville, age 25, black hair & eyes, dark skin, 5-7, residence stated on muster roll, house n/c, s 1,2,4.

C

CAIN, OLIVER. reg 39, co D, enr 9/10/62 Pike Co., enl 2/16/63 Peach Orchard, dis 9/15/65 Louisville, age 27, dark hair, blue eyes, fair skin, 5-8, rem cap 12/5/62 Floyd Co., house 7-423, s 1,2,4.

CAINS, WILLIAM. reg 14, co C, age 37, rem not on CSR, residence stated on muster roll, house n/c, s 4.

CAMPBELL, DAVID. reg 14, co H, enr 10/25/61 Catlettsburg, enl 12/10/61 Louisa, dis 1/31/65 Louisa, age 29, light hair, blue eyes, fair skin, 5-8, rem trans to co D, 39th Ky 3/13/63, trans back to co H, 14th Ky, 1/20/65, house 7-238, s 1,2,4.

CAMPBELL, JAMES M. reg 39, co D, enr 9/15/62 Pike Co., enl 2/1/6/63 Peach Orchard, age 20, light hair, blue eyes, fair skin, 6-1, rem d 5/9/63 Louisa congestion of bowels, house 7-238, s 1,2,4.

CAMPBELL, RICHARD. reg 68, co E, enl 5/21/64, age 18, dark hair & eyes, light skin, 5-10, house 7-238, s 4.

CARTER, CAMPBELL. reg 39, co H, enr 12/10/62 Pike Co., enl 2/16/63 Peach Orchard, dis 9/15/65 Louisville, age 31, dark hair & skin, blue eyes, 5-9, house 7-750, s 1,2,4.

CARTER, GEORGE W. reg CG, co L, enr 6/9/64, enl 7/6/64 Frankfort, dis 3/1/65 Catlettsburg, age 18, light hair, blue eyes, fair skin, 5-4, house 7-414, s 2,4.

CARTER, HENRY. reg CG, co G, enr 7/16/64, enl 8/8/64 Frankfort, rem des 9/12/64, house 7-529, s 2,4.

CARTER, HENRY S. reg 167WV, co Francis, reg 39, co H, enr 12/10/62, enl 2/16/63 Peach Orchard, dis 9/15/65 Louisville, age 34, black hair, blue eyes, dark skin, 5-10, house 7-779, s 1,2,4,23.

CARTER, QUENTIN. reg 39, co H, enr 12/10/62 Pike Co., enl 2/16/63 Peach Orchard, age 40, dark hair & skin, blue eyes, 5-8, d 4/24/63 Ashland of fever, house 7-529, s 1,2,4.

CASEBOLT, DAVID. reg 39, co K, enr 11/16/62 Pike Co., enl 2/16/63 Peach Orchard, age 24, black hair, dark eyes & skin, 5-9, rem prom to sgt 1/14/63, reduced to ranks for absence 4/5/63, d 11/22/63 Louisa of consumption, house 1-111, s 1,2,4.

CASEBOLT, HIRAM. reg 39, co K, enr 11/16/62 Piketon, enl 2/16/63 Peach Orchard, age 21, dark hair, blue eyes, fair skin, 5-7, rem des 3/24/63 Louisa, house 1-88, s 1,2,4.

CASSADY, ENOCH. reg 39, co I, enr 11/30/62 Piketon, enl 2/16/63 Peach Orchard, dis 9/15/65 Louisville, age 34, dark hair & skin, gray eyes, 5-6, rem cap 12/4/62 Floyd Co., prisoner at Richmond VA five months, residence stated on muster roll, house n/c, s 1,2,4.

CAVINS, WILLIAM. reg 14, co C, enr 10/10/61 Louisa, enl 12/10/61 Louisa, dis 1/31/65 Louisa, age 37, house 7-62, s 1,2,4.

CHANEY, ABNER. reg 39, co I, enr 11/20/62 Pike Co., enl 2/16/63 Peach Orchard, age 27, dark hair, blue eyes, fair skin, 6-0, rem des Camp White, Louisa 3/10/63, residence stated on muster roll, house n/c, s 1,2,4.

CHANEY, JONATHAN. reg 39, co I, enr 11/10/62 Pike Co., age 20, rem cap 2/1/63 Pike Co. or des 2/1/63 Peach Orchard, house 7-255, s 1,2,4.

CHARLES, ANDREW J. reg 39, co E, enr 11/15/62 Piketon, enl 8/31/63 Catlettsburg, dis 9/15/65 Louisville, age 27 or 29, house 7-431, s 1,2,4.

CHARLES, DAVID. reg 39, co E, enr 2/27/63 Piketon, enl 10/31/63 Catlettsburg, age 26, light hair, blue eyes, fair skin, 5-7, rem d in Louisa or Lexington 10/27/64 or 11/15/64 or 11/18/64, house 7-427, s 1,2,4.

CHARLES, GEORGE. reg 167 WV, co Francis, reg 39, co H, enr 7/19/63 Pike Co., enl 10/29/63 Louisa, dis 9/15/65 Louisville, age 20, dark hair & skin, black eyes, 5-7, house 7-767, s 1,2,4,23.

CHARLES, GEORGE W. reg 39, co I, enr 10/20/62 Pike Co., enl 2/16/63 Peach Orchard, age 31, light hair, black eyes, fair skin, 5-10, rem cap 12/4/62 by rebels at Tazewell VA 1/1/63, house 7-436, s 1,2,4,8.

CHARLES, JOHN. reg 167, co Francis, reg 39, co H, enr 7/19/63 Piketon, enl 10/29/63 Louisa, dis 9/15/65 Louisville, age 30, dark hair, eyes, & skin, 5-9, rem cap Peter Creek, Pike Co. 12/16/62, returned 4/30/63, house 7-739, s 1,2,4,23.

CHARLES. JOHN. reg 39, co E, enr 11/14/62 Piketon, enl 8/31/63 Catlettsburg, dis 9/15/65 Louisville, age 30 or 36, light hair, blue eyes, fair skin, 5-9, house 7-422, s 1,2,4.

CHARLES, THOMAS. reg 39, co E, enr 6/25/63 Piketon, enl 8/31/63 Catlettsburg, dis 9/15/65 Louisville, age 34, light hair, blue eyes, fair skin, 5-11, house 7-424, s 1,2,4.

CHILDERS, ALEXANDER. reg 39, co I, enr 3/24/65 Louisa, enl 4/12/65 Covington, dis 9/15/65 Louisville, age 21, light hair, blue eyes, fair skin, 5-7, house 7-73, s 1,2,4.

CHILDERS, DAVID. reg 39, co D, enr 9/15/62 Pike Co., enl 2/16/63 Peach Orchard, dis 9/15/65 Louisville, age 18, black hair, blue eyes, fair skin, 5-6, house 7-73, s 1,2,4.

CHILDERS, FRANCIS MARION. reg 65, co B, enl 5/21/64, age 26, blue eyes, light hair, fair skin, 6-0, house 7-71, s 2,4.

CHILDERS, JACKSON. reg 14, co C, enr 10/10/61 Louisa, enl 12/10/61 Louisa, age 26, rem d 12/23/61 Catlettsburg, house 7-338, s 1,2,4.

CHILDERS, MILES. reg 14, co C, enr 10/10/61, enl 12/10/61 Louisa, dis 1/31/65 Louisa, house 7-72, s 2,4.

CHILDERS, PLEASANT. reg 39, co D, enr 3/31/65 Louisa, enl 4/15/65 Greenupsburg, dis 9/15/65 Louisville, age 18, light hair, blue eyes, fair skin, 5-7, house 7-73, s 1,2,4.

CLARK, ANDREW J. reg 39, co D, enr 10/16/62 Pike Co., enl 2/16/63 Peach Orchard, age 27, sandy hair, hazel eyes, fair skin, 5-6, rem d 7/2/63 Ashland of bronchitis, house 7-459, s 1,2,4.

CLAY, ANDREW. reg 39, co K, enr 12/26/62 Pike Co., enl 2/16/63 Peach Orchard, age 25 or 28, dark hair, blue eyes, fair skin, 5-10, rem cap 2/8/63 Pike Co., house 1-5, s 1,2,4.

CLEVENGER, PINSON. reg 39, co C, enr 11/5/62 Pike Co., enl 2/16/63 Peach Orchard, dis 9/15/65 Louisville, age 36, dark hair, blue eyes, fair skin, 5-8, house 7-916, s 1,2,4.

CLEVENGER, SILAS. reg 39, co D, enr 3/31/65 Pike Co., enl 4/15/64 Greenupsburg, dis 9/15/65 Louisville, age 33, red hair, gray eyes, fair skin, 5-8, house 7-915, s 1,2,4.

CLINE, JACOB. reg 167WV, co Runyon, house 7-759, s 23.

CLINE, PETER. reg 167WV, co Runyon, reg 39, co H, enr 1/15/63 Pike Co., enl 2/16/63 Peach Orchard, age 25, black hair & eyes, dark skin, 6-1, rem dis 11/21/64 Louisa on surgeon's certificate of disability, house 7-760, s 1,2,4,23.

COLE, PARKERSON. reg 39, co C, enr 5/19/63, enl 6/11/63 Louisa, dis 9/15/65 Louisville, age 24, residence stated on muster roll, house n/c, s 2,4.

COLE, THOMPSON. reg 39, co C, enr 9/4/63, enl 10/30/63 Louisa, age 30, dark hair & skin, gray eyes, 5-10, rem d 5/24/64 Louisa, lung inflammation, house 7-164, s 1,2,4.

COLEMAN, CURTIS. reg 39, co D, r sgt, enr 11/10/62, enl 2/16/63 Peach Orchard, dis 9/15/65 Louisville, age 22, light hair, blue eyes, fair skin, 5-7, residence stated on muster roll, house n/c, s 1,2,4.

COLEMAN, DANIEL. reg 39, co D, enr 11/15/62, enl 2/16/63 Peach Orchard, dis 9/15/65 Louisville, age 25 or 28, house 7-218, s 1,2,4.

COLEMAN, DANIEL. reg 167WV, co Francis, reg 39, co H, enr 12/3/62 Lawrence Co., enl 2/16/63 Peach Orchard, dis 9/15/65 Louisville, age 18, fair hair & skin, blue eyes, 5-3, residence stated on muster roll, house n/c, s 1,2,4,23.

COLEMAN, DANIEL B. reg 39, co H, r cpl, enr 11/25/62 Pike Co., enl 2/16/63 Peach Orchard, dis 9/15/65 Louisville, age 24, dark hair & skin, black eyes, 6-0, rem cap 12/4/62 Floyd Co., returned 4/3/63, residence stated on muster roll, house n/c, s 1,2,4.

COLEMAN, DAVID. reg 39, co H, enr 12/31/62, dis 9/15/65 Louisville, house 7-47, s 5.

COLEMAN, ELIXIUS. reg 39, co H, r sgt, enr 12/10/62 Lawrence Co., enl 2/16/63 Peach Orchard, dis 9/15/65 Louisville, age 23, dark hair, blue eyes, fair skin, 6-1, house 7-781, s 1,2,4.

COLEMAN, ISAAC. reg 39, co D, enr 11/10/62 Pike Co., enl 2/16/63 Peach Orchard, age 40, black hair, blue eyes, dark skin, 5-9, rem d 5/24/63 Louisa yellow jaundice, residence stated on muster roll, house n/c, s 1,2,4.

COLEMAN, JOHN B. reg 39, co H, enr 8/17/63, dis 5/29/65, house 7-273, s 5.

COLEMAN, JOSEPH. reg 167WV, co Francis, reg 39, co D, r sgt, enr 11/10/62 Pike Co., enl 2/16/63 Peach Orchard, dis 9/15/65 Louisville, age 22, dark hair, black eyes, fair skin, 6-2, rem trans to co H 2/19/63, prom from cpl to sgt co H 9/15/64, house 7-266, s 1,2,4,23.

COLEMAN, MATTHEW. reg 39, co D, enr 11/27/63 Pike Co., enl 2/16/63 Peach Orchard, age 27, dark hair & skin, blue eyes, 5-4, rem d 6/2/63 Ashland, typhoid fever, house 7-224, s 1,2,4.

COLEMAN, MILES. reg 39, co D, enr 11/13/62, enl 7/24/65 Greenupsburg, dis 9/15/65 Louisville, age 19, light hair, blue eyes, fair skin, 5-10, house 7-218, s 2,4.

COLEMAN, MOSES. reg 167WV, co Francis, reg 39, co D, enr 9/15/62 Pike Co., enl 2/16/63 Peach Orchard, dis 9/15/65 Louisville, age 21, light hair, blue eyes, fair skin, 5-9, house 7-218, s 2,4,23.

COLEMAN, MOSES JR. reg 167WV, co Francis, reg 39, co D, enr 11/15/62 Pike Co., enl 2/16/63 Peach Orchard, dis 9/15/65 Louisville, age 18, light hair, blue eyes, fair skin, 5-4, house 7-55, s 1,2,4,23.

COLEMAN, NATHANIEL. reg 39, co E, enr 11/17/62 Pike Co., enl 2/16/63 Peach Orchard, dis 9/15/65 Louisville, age 20, dark hair, black eyes, fair skin, 5-9, house 7-438, s 1,2,4.

COLEMAN, RILEY. reg 39, co E, r cpl, enr 2/7/63 Pike Co., enl 2/16/63 Peach Orchard, dis 9/15/65 Louisville, age 18, dark hair, black eyes, fair skin, 5-10, house 7-438, s 1,2,4.

COLEMAN, WILLIAM. reg 39, co D, enr 1/20/62 Pike Co., enl 2/16/63 Peach Orchard, dis 9/15/65 Louisville, age 18, light hair, blue eyes, fair skin, 5-4, house 7-227, s 1,2,4.

COLEMAN, WILLIAM F. reg 167WV, co Francis, reg 39, co H, r sgt, enr 12/10/62 Lawrence Co., enl 2/16/63 Peach Orchard, age 26, fair hair & skin, blue eyes, 5-8, rem d 4/17/63 Louisa of erysipelas, house 7-764, s 1,2,4.

COLLINS, HARVEY. reg 39, co D, enr 11/5/62 Pike Co., enl 2/16/63 Peach Orchard, age 33, black hair & eyes, dark skin, 5-10, rem KIA 7/2/63 Mouth of Card, Pike Co., house 7-888, s 1,2,4.

COLLINS, JOHN. reg 39, co I, enr 11/2/62, enl 2/16/63 Peach Orchard, dis 9/15/65 Louisville, age 18, black hair & eyes, dark skin, 6-0, house 7-708, s 1,2,4.

COLLINS, JOHN. reg 39, co B, enr 9/8/63, enl 10/30/63 Louisa, dis 9/15/65 Louisville, age 21, house 7-530, s 2,4.

COLLINS, JOHN. reg 22, co F, enr 12/2/61, enl 1/10/62 Louisa, age 20, rem des 9/1/62 Cumberland Gap, house 7-776, s 2,4.

COLLINS, THOMAS. reg 167WV, co Sampson Kirk, house 7-872, s 23.

COMPTON, JOHN W. reg 39, co B, r sgt, enr 11/14/62 Pike Co., enl 2/16/63 Peach Orchard, dis 9/15/65 Louisville, age 21, light hair, blue eyes, 5-6, house 1-47, s 1,2,4.

COMPTON, WILLIAM. reg 39, co K, B, r cpl, enr 11/16/62 Louisa, enl 2/16/63 Peach Orchard, dis 9/15/65 Louisville, age 28, black hair, blue eyes, red skin, 5-9, rem trans from co K, house 7-932, s 1,2,4,8.

CONAWAY, WILLIAM. reg 39, co E, enr 11/18/62 Pike Co., enl 2/16/63 Peach Orchard, age 23, dark hair & skin, black eyes, 5-8, house 7-437, s 1,2,4.

COOK, JARRED. reg 39, co H, enr 11/25/62 Pike Co., enl 2/16/63 Peach Orchard, dis 9/15/65 Louisville, age 18, fair hair & skin, blue eyes, 5-7, house 7-334, s 1,2,4.

COOK, THOMAS A. reg 39, co G, enr & enl 10/30/63 Louisa, dis 9/15/65 Louisville, age 44, dark hair & eyes, fair skin, 6-0, house 7-334, s 1,2,4.

COOL, JAMES. reg 39, co K, r cpl, enr 12/16/62 Pike Co., enl 2/16/63 Peach Orchard, dis 9/15/65 Louisville, age 33, dark hair, black eyes, fair skin, 5-3, residence stated on muster roll, house n/c, s 1,2,4.
CRABTREE, JOHN. reg 39, co A, enr 9/6/62, enl 2/16/63 Peach Orchard, dis 9/15/65 Louisville, age 30, trans from co B to co A, 1/1/64, house 7-941, s 2,4.
CRABTREE, SOLOMON. reg 39, co H, enr 9/16/62, enl 2/16/63 Peach Orchard, age 26, light hair, blue eyes, fair skin, 5-8, rem d 4/21/63 Ashland of fever, residence stated on muster roll, house n/c, s 1,2,4.
CRABTREE, WILLIAM. reg 14, co C, enr 10/10/61 Louisa, enl 12/10/61 Louisa, age 28, light hair, blue eyes, fair skin, 5-10, rem d 7/21/64 Knoxville TN chronic diarrhea, residence stated on muster roll, house n/c, s 1,2,4.

D

DAMRON, JACKSON. reg 39, co K, enr 2/1/63, enl 2/16/63 Peach Orchard, age 38, light hair, blue eyes, fair skin, 6-0, rem d 9/12/64 Pike Co. consumption, house 1-65, s 1,2,4.
DAMRON, JAMES. reg 39, co B, enr 9/22/63 Pike Co., enl 10/30/63 Louisa, dis 9/15/65 Louisville, age 20, dark hair, blue eyes, fair skin, 5-9, house 1-57, s 1,2,4.
DAMRON, JOHN. reg 39, co K, enr 9/16/62 Pike Co., enl 2/16/63 Peach Orchard, dis 9/15/65 Louisville, age 25, black hair & eyes, dark skin, 5-11, house 1-82, s 1,2,4.
DAMRON, LEWIS P. reg 39, co K, enr 9/26/62 Pike Co., enl 2/16/63 Peach Orchard, age 22, black hair, blue eyes, fair skin, 5-10, rem KIA 8/21/63 Carter Co., house 1-52, s 1,2,4.
DAMRON, MOSES D. reg 39, co B, enr 11/9/62, enl 2/16/63 Peach Orchard, dis 9/15/65 Louisville, age 26, dark hair, blue eyes, fair skin, 6-1, house 1-46, s 1,2,4.
DAMRON, ROBERT. reg 39, co B, enr 11/8/62, enl 2/16/63 Peach Orchard, dis 9/15/65 Louisville, age 24, black hair & eyes, dark skin, 5-6, rem red from cpl 2/1/65, house 1-34, s 1,2,4.
DAMRON, SPURLOCK. reg 39, co K, enr 2/1/63 Piketon, enl 2/16/63 Peach Orchard, dis 9/15/65 Louisville, age 27, light hair, blue eyes, fair skin, 5-7, house 1-64, s 1,2,4.
DAMRON, WILLIAM. reg 39, co B, enr 9/6/62 Louisa, enl 2/16/63 Peach Orchard, dis 9/15/65 Louisville, age 34, dark hair, blue eyes, fair skin, 5-5, house 1-57, s 1,2,4.
DAMRON, WILLIAM. reg 45, co E, enr 8/8/63 Catlettsburg, enl 11/6/63 Ashland, dis 12/24/64 Catlettsburg, age 31, house 1-38, s 1,2.
DAMRON, WRIGHT. reg 39, co B, enr 11/14/62 Piketon, enl 2/16/63 Peach Orchard, dis 9/15/65 Louisville, age 24, black hair, blue eyes, fair skin, 6-2, house 1-46, s 1,2,4.
DANIELS, DAVID. reg 167WV, co Runyon, reg 39, co H, enr 12/28/63 Pike Co., enl 12/30/63 Louisa, age 18, black hair, gray eyes, fair skin, 5-10, rem d 8/7/64 Mt. Sterling of fever, house 7-791, s 1,2,4,23.
DANIELS, LEWIS. reg 167WV, co Runyon, house 7-695, s 23.
DANIELS, RICHARD. reg 167WV, co Runyon, house 7-695, s 23.
DANIELS, WILLIAM. reg 167WV, co Runyon, reg 39, co H, enr 7/19/63, enl 8/29/63 Louisa, dis 9/15/65 Louisville, age 18, dark hair, blue eyes, dark skin, 5-9, house 7-791, s 1,2,4.
DAUGHERTY, DANIEL. J. reg 167WV, co Francis, reg 39, co D, r cpl, enr 7/18/63 Pike Co., enl 8/30/63 Louisa, dis 9/15/65 Louisville, age 25, light hair, blue eyes, fair skin, 5-9, rem prom to cpl 6/7/65, house 7-769, s 1,2,4,23.
DAUGHERTY, FRANCIS M. reg 39, co D, enr 11/11/62, enl 2/16/63 Peach Orchard, dis 9/15/65 Louisville, age 36, light hair, blue eyes, fair skin, 5-11, house 7-746, s 1,2,4.
DAUGHERTY, HIRAM M. reg 167WV, co Francis, reg 39, co H, r sgt, enr 6/10/63, enl 6/10/63 Louisa, dis 9/15/65 Louisville, age 29, fair hair & skin, blue eyes, 6-1, house 7-777, s 1,2,4,23.

DAVIS, GEORGE W. reg 14, co A, enr 7/20/63 Ashland, enl 8/29/63 Louisa, dis 9/15/65 Louisville, age 18, dark hair, blue eyes, light skin, 5-4, rem trans to 14th Vet Inf, co C, enr 7/20/63, m/in 8/29/63 Louisa, house 7-582, s 1,2,4.

DAVIS, JAMES JR. reg 39, co H, enr 12/21/62 Lawrence Co., enl 2/16/63 Peach Orchard, dis 9/15/65 Louisville, age 21, dark hair, blue eyes, fair skin, 5-7, house 7-582, s 1,2,4.

DAVIS, WILLIAM H. reg 39, co E, r cpl, enr 11/16/62 Piketon, enl 2/16/63 Peach Orchard, age 22, light hair, blue eyes, fair skin, 5-10, rem d 4/8/63 Ashland, house 7-539, s 1,2,4.

DESKINS, JOHN. reg 14, co H, enr 10/25/61, enl 12/10/61 Louisa, dis 1/31/65 Louisa, age 41, dark hair & skin, blue eyes, 6-0, residence stated on muster roll, house n/c, s 2,4.

DESKINS, LEWIS. reg 39, co I, enr 11/18/62, enl 10/30/63 Louisa, dis 9/15/65 Louisville, age 32, dark hair, blue eyes, fair skin, 5-11, rem prom to sgt 4/3/63, house 7-388, s 1,2,4.

DIALS, ANDREW P. reg 14, co C, enr 1/4/64 Catlettsburg, age 18, dark hair, blue eyes, fair skin, 5-10, rem d 12/1/64 Ashland, house 7-670, s 1,2,4.

DILS, JOHN JR. reg 39, r col, enr 1/21/63, enl 2/16/63 Peach Orchard, age 43, rem dishonorably dismissed 12/1/63, house 7-969, s 2,4.

DOTSON, ELIJAH. reg 167WV, co Francis, reg 39, co H, enr 2/1/63 Peach Orchard, enl 2/16/63 Peach Orchard, dis 9/15/65 Louisville, age 26, dark hair & skin, blue eyes, 5-10, house 7-775, s 1,2,4,23.

DOTSON, ELIJAH. reg 39, co H, enr 12/27/62, enl 2/16/63 Peach Orchard, age 18, fair hair & skin, blue eyes, 5-8, rem cap 1/9/64 Boyd Co., d 5/21/65 Andersonville GA of scorbutus, residence stated on muster roll, house n/c, s 1,2,4,8.

DOTSON, GEORGE. reg 167WV, co Francis, house 7-736 or 7-761, s 23.

DOTSON, GEORGE W. reg 39, co H, enr 1/19/63, enl 2/16/63 Peach Orchard, dis 9/15/65 Louisville, age 35, dark hair, black eyes, fair skin, 6-2, house 7-761, s 1,2,4.

DOTSON, JOHN. reg 167WV, co Francis, reg 39, co H, enr 7/19/63 enl 10/29/63 Louisa, dis 9/15/65 Louisville, age 31 or 37, dark hair, eyes & skin, 6-0, house 7-737, s 1,2,4,23.

DOTSON, JOHN S. reg 167WV, co Francis, reg 39, co H, r cpl, enr 1/19/63, enl 2/16/63 Peach Orchard, dis 9/15/65 Louisville, age 18, fair hair & skin, black eyes, rem cap Saltville VA 10/2/64, returned 2/2/65, house 7-761, s 1,2,4,23.

DOTSON, JORDAN. reg 39, co H, enr 7/20/63 Pike Co., enl 8/29/63 Louisa, dis 9/15/65 Louisville, age 19, dark hair, eyes & skin, 5-10, house 7-736, s 1,5.

DOTSON, REUBIN. reg 167WV, co Francis, house 7-780, s 23.

DUTY, ISAAC. reg 167WV, co Francis, house 7-768, s 23.

E

ELKINS, ANDREW J. reg 39, co B, enr 12/18/63 Paintsville, enl 3/29/64 Greenupsburg, dis 9/15/65 Louisville, age 27, light hair, blue eyes, fair skin, 5-6, house 1-158, s 1,2,4.

ELSWICK, ISAAC. reg 39, co D, r cpl, enr 9/10/62 Pike Co., enl 2/16/63 Peach Orchard, age 39, light hair, blue eyes, fair skin, 6-1, rem app cpl 3/28/63, cap 7/2/63, in prison at Richmond VA 7/1/763, paroled City Point VA 9/25/63, d 12/6/64 Louisa of smallpox, residence stated on muster roll, house n/c, s 1,2,4.

ELSWICK, JOHN. reg 39, co I, enr 9/12/62 Piketon, enl 2/16/63 Peach Orchard, dis 9/15/65 Louisville, age 24, dark hair & eyes, fair skin, 5-8, residence stated on muster roll, house n/c, s 1,2,4.

ELSWICK, WILLIAM. reg 39, co I, enr 9/12/62 Pike Co., enl 2/16/63 Peach Orchard, dis 9/15/65 Louisville, age 44 or 51, dark hair & skin, black eyes, 5-10, house 1-163, s 1,2,4.

ENDICOTT, SAMUEL. reg 39, co I, enr 2/7/64, enl 3/29/64 Greenuspsburg, dis 9/15/65 Louisville, age 22, rem cap 12/20/64 Wheeler's Ford VA, returned 6/23/65, house 7-821, s 2,4.

ENGLAND, GEORGE W. reg 39, co B, enr 11/16/62, enl 2/16/63 Peach Orchard, dis 9/15/65 Louisville, age 24, house 1-118, s 2,4.
ENGLAND, JAMES. reg 39, co B, enr 11/9/62, enl 2/16/63 Peach Orchard, dis 9/15/65 Louisville, age 18, house 1-118, s 2,4.
ENGLAND, SOLOMON. reg 39, co B, enr 11/10/62, enl 2/16/63 Louisa, dis 9/15/65 Louisville, age 41, black hair, dark eyes & skin, 6-0, residence stated on muster roll, house n/c, s 1,2,4.
EPLING, JAMES H. reg 39, co D, enr 9/21/63 Pike Co., enl 10/29/63, dis 9/15/65 Louisville, age 25, dark hair, black eyes, fair skin, 6-1, house 7-355, s 1,2,4.
EPLING, JOHN B. reg 14, co C, enr 10/25/61 Catlettsburg, enl 12/10/61 Louisa, dis 1/31/65 Louisa, age 20, light hair, dark eyes & skin, 5-10, house 7-341, s 1,2,4.
ESTEP, CHRISLY. reg 39, co H, enr 11/24/62, enl 2/16/63 Peach Orchard, age 44, dark hair, blue eyes, fair skin, 5-9, house 7-785, s 1,2,4.
ESTEP, ELIJAH. reg 39, co H, enr 12/27/62, enl 2/16/63 Peach Orchard, dis 9/15/65 Louisville, age 28, fair hair & skin, blue eyes, 5-10, residence stated on muster roll, house n/c, s 1,2,4.
ESTEP, GEORGE S. reg 39, co H, enr 12/1/62 Pike Co., enl 10/29/63 Louisa, dis 9/15/65 Louisville, age 18, dark hair & skin, black eyes, 5-7, rem cap 12/16/62 Peter Creek, Pike Co., returned 4/30/63, house 7-738, s 1,2,4.
ESTEP, JACKSON. reg 39, co H, enr 11/25/62, enl 2/16/63 Peach Orchard, age 25, fair hair & skin, blue eyes, 5-10, rem d 1/12/65 Louisa consumption, house 7-773, s 1,2,4.
ESTEP, JAMES. reg 167WV, co Francis, reg 39, co H, enr 1/19/63, enl 2/16/63 Peach Orchard, dis 9/15/65 Louisville, age 29, dark hair & skin, black eyes, 5-8, house 7-171, s 1,2,4,23.
ESTEP, JOHN B. reg 39, co H, enr 4/17/63, age 21, dark hair, eyes & skin, 5-8, rem d 8/10/63 Louisa of pneumonia, house 7-738, s 1,2,4.
ESTEP, JOSEPH. reg 39, co H, enr 3/3/63, enl 8/29/63 Peach Orchard, dis 9/15/65 Louisville, age 18, fair hair & skin, blue eyes, 5-5, house 7-751, s 1,2,4.
ESTEP, SAMPSON. reg 39, co H, r musician, enr 12/1/62, enl 2/16/63 Peach Orchard, dis 9/15/65 Louisville, age 41, dark hair, blue eyes, fair skin, 6-0, residence stated on muster roll, house n/c, s 1,2,4.
ESTEP, WILLIAM. reg 39, co H, enr 12/27/62, enl 2/16/63 Peach Orchard, dis 9/15/65 Louisville, age 21, light hair, blue eyes, fair hair, 5-11, residence stated on muster roll, house n/c, s 1,2,4.

F

FARLEY, CLAY. reg 39, co I, enr 8/31/63, enl 10/30/63 Louisa, dis 9/15/65 Louisville, age 42 (at muster out), rem residence established by H. H. Hardesty, house n/c, s 1,2,9.
FARLOR, ALLEN B. reg CG, co E, enr 6/1/64, enl 7/4/64 Frankfort, dis 3/11/65 Catlettsburg, age 19, dark hair, brown eyes, fair skin, 5-7, house 7-544, s 2,4.
FERGUSON, STEPHEN M. reg 39, r lt col, enr 1/21/63, enl 2/16/63, dis 9/15/65 Louisville, age 40, rem prom from surgeon to major 1/21/63, to lt col 12/22/63, house 7-902, s 2,4.
FIELDS, ELIJAH. reg 39, co C, r sgt, enr 9/10/62 Pike Co., enl 2/16/63 Peach Orchard, dis 9/15/65 Louisville, age 22, dark hair, gray eyes, fair skin, 5-9, residence stated on muster roll, house n/c, s 1,2,4.
FIELDS, ELISHA. reg 39, co C, enr 12/2/62, enl 2/16/63 Peach Orchard, age 22, light hair, blue eyes, fair skin, 5-5, residence stated on muster roll, house n/c, s 1,2,4.
FIELDS, HARRISON. reg 39, co D, enr 11/10/62 Pike Co., rem des 12/8/62 Johnson Co., house 7-309, s 1,5.
FIELDS, HIRAM. reg 39, co C, enr 9/30/62, enl 2/16/63 Peach Orchard, age 24, rem d 4/24/64 Louisa, residence stated on muster roll, house n/c, s 2,4.

FIELDS, JOHN. reg 39, co C, enr 9/10/62 Louisa, enl 2/16/63 Peach Orchard, age 25, dark hair, gray eyes, fair skin, 5-8, rem d 4/18/63 Ashland typhoid fever, residence stated on muster roll, house n/c, s 1,2,4.

FIELDS, LEWIS. reg 39, co C, enr 12/12/62 Pike Co., enl 2/16/63 Peach Orchard, dis 9/15/65 Louisville, age 18, dark hair, gray eyes, fair skin, 5-6, residence stated on muster roll, house n/c, s 1,2,4.

FIELDS, WILLIAM W. reg 39, co E, enr 10/17/62 Louisa, enl 10/31/63 Catlettsburg, dis 9/15/65 Louisville, age 30, light hair, black eyes, fair skin, 6-0, rem cap 12/4/62 Floyd Co., house 7-569, s 1,2,4.

FINLEY, SAMUEL. reg 39, co C, enr 9/10/62 Louisa, enl 2/16/63 Peach Orchard, dis 9/15/65 Louisville, age 30, light hair, gray eyes, fair skin, 5-11, house 7-505, s 1,2,4.

FLETCHER, JOSEPH. reg 39, co C, r sgt, enr 9/10/62 Pike Co., enl 2/16/63, dis 5/25/65 Lexington, age 24, black hair & eyes, dark skin, 5-11, house 7-426, s 1,2,4.

FORD, ANDREW J. reg 39, co B, enr 10/10/62 Louisa, enl 2/16/63 Peach Orchard, dis 9/15/65 Louisville, age 34, light hair, blue eyes, fair skin, 6-1, rem red from sgt 8/1/63, house 1-37, s 1,2,4.

FORD, HARRISON. reg 39, co K, r capt, enr 1/14/63 Piketon, enl 2/16/63 Peach Orchard, age 30, dark hair, blue eyes, fair skin, 5-9, rem resigned 8/21/63 because of chronic liver inflammation, house 1-160, s 1,2,4.

FORD, JAMES. reg 39, co B, enr 9/6/62 Louisa, enl 2/16/63 Peach Orchard, age 21, light hair, blue eyes, fair skin, 5-5, rem d 4/26/63 Louisa, house 1-36, s 1,2,4.

FORD, JOHN W. reg 39, co B, r sgt, enr 9/6/62 Louisa, enl 2/16/63 Peach Orchard, dis 9/15/65 Louisville, age 19, light hair, blue eyes, fair skin, 5-9, rem app sgt 9/1/64, house 1-36, s 1,2,4.

FORD, WILLIAM. reg 39, co B, r capt, enr 9/6/62, enl 2/16/63 Peach Orchard, age 41, rem d 11/24/64 Lexington of dysentery, house 1-36, s 2,4,8.

FORRESTER, ANDREW. reg 39, co H, r sgt, enr 11/24/62 Pike Co., enl 2/16/63 Peach Orchard, age 19, fair hair & skin, blue eyes, 5-8, rem d 4/18/83 Ashland of fever, residence stated on muster roll, house n/c, s 1,2,4.

FRANCIS, ANDREW. reg 39, co C, enr 12/22/62, enl 2/16/63, age 37, dark hair, gray eyes, fair skin, 5-10, rem trans from co E 10/29/63, residence stated on muster roll, house n/c, s 1,2,4.

FRANCIS, ANDREW J. reg 39, co H, r cpl, enr 1/28/63, enl 2/16/63 Peach Orchard, dis 9/15/65 Louisville, age 23, fair hair & skin, blue eyes, 5-5, rem cap 10/2/64 Saltville VA, returned 2/2/65, residence stated on muster roll, house n/c, s 1,2,4.

FRANCIS, ELIJAH. reg 39, co C, enr 11/4/62 Pike Co., enl 2/16/63 Peach Orchard, age 35, light hair, blue eyes, fair skin, 5-10, rem des 5/1/64 Louisa, des 5/10/65 Paintsville, house 7-547, s 1,2,4.

FRANCIS, JAMES. reg 39, co C, enr 11/5/62 Pike Co., enl 2/16/63 Peach Orchard, dis 9/15/65 Louisville, age 32, light hair, gray eyes, fair skin, 5-11, house 7-548, s 1,2,4.

FRANCIS, JAMES M. reg 167WV, co Francis, reg 39, co H, r cpl, enr 6/23/63 Pike Co., enl 8/29/63 Louisa, dis 9/15/65 Louisville, age 21, fair hair & skin, blue eyes, 5-7, rem cap Peter Creek KY 12/16/62, returned 4/30/63, house 7-752, s 1,2,4,23.

FRANCIS, MORGAN. reg 39, co C, enr 11/28/62, enl 2/16/63 Peach Orchard, dis 9/15/65 Louisville, age 18, light hair, blue eyes, fair skin, 5-8, house 7-548, s 1,2,4.

FRANCIS, WILLIAM. reg 167WV, co Francis, r capt, rem KIA Pike Co. 1863, house 7-752, s 23.

FULKERSON, MARTIN. reg 39, r quartermaster, enl 10/27/62, enl 2/16/63 Peach Orchard, age 44, rem resigned 6/17/63 for bad health, house 7-21, s 2,4,8.

G

GIBSON, DAVID. reg 68, co D, enl 4/7/64, 5/21/64, dis 4/16/64, 6/22/64, age 27, black hair & eyes, dark skin, 6-1, house 7-199, s 2,4.

GIBSON, WILLIAM. reg 39, co F, enr 6/14/64 Louisa, enl 8/30/64 Lexington, dis 9/15/65 Louisville, age 20, dark hair & skin, blue eyes, 5-8, house 7-742, s 1,2,4.

GILLAM, BERRY C. reg 39, co D, r cpl, enr 9/6/62 Pike Co., enl 2/16/63 Peach Orchard, dis 9/15/65 Louisville, age 22, dark hair, blue eyes, fair skin, 5-11, residence stated on muster roll, house n/c, s 1,2,4.

GILLAM, DEMARCUS L. L. reg 39, co D, enr 12/14/62 Pike Co., enl 2/16/63 Peach Orchard, dis 9/15/65 Louisville, age 23, black hair, yellow eyes, fair skin, 5-9, residence stated on muster roll, house n/c, s 1,2,4.

GILLESPIE, THOMAS R. reg 39, co C, enr 12/10/62 Louisa, enl 2/16/63 Peach Orchard, dis 9/15/65 Louisville, age 18, light hair, gray eyes, fair skin, 5-6, house 7-911, s 1,2,4.

GOFF, MARTIN. reg 39, co E, enr 12/25/62, enl 2/1/63 Peach Orchard, dis 9/15/65 Louisville, age 23, dark hair & skin, blue eyes, 5-7, house 7-429, s 1,2,4.

GOOD, ANDREW M. reg 14, co H, enr 10/25/61 Catlettsburg, enl 12/10/61 Louisa, dis 1/31/65 Louisa, age 21, dark hair, eyes & skin, 5-7, rem cap Lawrence Co. 4/28/63, paroled in eastern KY, house 7-313, s 1,2,4.

GRAY, ISAAC E. reg 39, co D, enr 10/15/61 Ashland, enl Lexington, dis 9/15/65 Louisville, age 23, prom from 2nd lt to 1st lt 3/9/65, to capt 5/6/65, residence shown on List of Officers, house n/c, s 1,2,32.

H

HACKNEY, GEORGE W. reg 14, co C, enr 10/10/61 Louisa, enl 12/10/61 Louisa, dis 9/15/65 Louisville, age 18, dark hair & eyes, fair skin, 5-7, rem trans to 14th Ky Vet Inf, co A, enr 2/29/64, m/in 3/19/64 Catlettsburg, house 7-344, s 1,2,4.

HAILEY, JAMES. reg 14, co H, enr 10/25/61 Catlettsburg, enl 12/10/61 Louisa, dis 9/15/65 Louisville, age 23, dark hair & skin, blue eyes, 5-10, rem trans to 14th Ky Vet Inf 3/29/64, residence stated on muster roll, house n/c, s 1,2,4.

HALL, DAVID. reg 39, co K, enr 11/22/62, enl 2/16/63 Peach Orchard, dis 9/15/65 Louisville, age 22, black hair & eyes, dark skin, 6-1, rem CSR lists Pike Co. as residence, house 1-44, s 1,2,4.

HALL, FLEMING. reg 39, co B, enr 9/6/62, enl 6/10/63 Louisa, dis 9/15/65 Louisville, age 25, light hair, blue eyes, fair skin, 5-5, rem trans from co I, house 7-183, s 1,2,4.

HALL, RICHARD. reg 39, co B, enr 9/6/62 Louisa, enl 2/16/63 Peach Orchard, dis 9/15/65 Louisville, age 20 or 30, black hair & eyes, dark skin, 5-11, house 1-135, s 1,2,4.

HALL, WILLIAM SR. reg 39, co B, enr 9/6/62 Louisa, enl 2/16/63 Peach Orchard, dis 9/15/65 Louisville, age 44, black hair, blue eyes, dark skin, 5-7, house 1-135, s 1,2,4.

HAMILTON, JAMES W. reg 39, co D, enr 11/11/62 Pike Co., enl 2/16/63 Peach Orchard, dis 9/15/65 Louisville, age 37, black hair & eyes, dark skin, 5-8, residence stated on muster roll, house n/c, s 1,2,4.

HARRISON, DANIEL C. reg 39, house 7-533, s 5.

HATFIELD, ANDERSON. reg 39, co E, enr 11/15/62 Piketon, age 33, dark hair, blue eyes, fair skin, 5-10, rem cap 1/15/63 Floyd Co., house 7-665, s 1,2,4.

HATFIELD, EPHRAIM. reg 39, co G, enr 2/3/63 Peach Orchard, enl 2/1/63 Peach Orchard, dis 9/15/65 Louisville, age 23, dark hair, eyes & skin, 5-9, rem trans from co H 10/30/63, house 7-647, s 1,2,4.

HATFIELD, GEORGE. reg 39, co E, enr 11/19/62 Piketon, enl 2/16/63 Peach Orchard, age 23, dark hair & skin, blue eyes, 5-7, rem d 4/8/63 Louisa, house 7-691, s 1,2,4.

HATFIELD, GEORGE. reg 39, co G, enr 2/3/63, enl 2/16/63 Peach Orchard, dis 9/15/65 Louisville, age 19, fair hair & skin, blue eyes, 5-10, rem trans from co H 10/30/63, house 7-626, s 1,2,4.

HATFIELD, JACOB. reg 39, co G, enr 2/3/63 Peach Orchard, enl 2/16/63 Peach Orchard, dis 9/15/65 Louisville, age 18, light hair, blue eyes, fair skin, 5-8, rem trans from co H 10/30/63, house 7-626, s 1,2,4.

HATFIELD, JAMES. reg 39, co H, enr 2/28/63, enl 12/20/63 Louisa, dis 9/15/65 Louisville, age 28, light hair, blue eyes, fair skin, 5-10, house 7-625, s 1,2,4.
HATFIELD, JEREMIAH. reg 39, co G, enr 2/3/63, enl 2/16/63 Peach Orchard, dis 11/3/64 Lexington, age 45, white hair, blue eyes, fair skin, 6-1, rem dis for disability, rheumatism, house 7-626, s 1,2,4.
HATFIELD, JEREMIAH. reg 39, co E, enr 12/25/62 Piketon, enl 2/16/63 Peach Orchard, age 20, dark hair & skin, black eyes, 5-7, rem d 5/10/63 Louisa, house 7-691, s 1,2,4.
HATFIELD, JOHN F. reg 39, co H, enr 2/3/63 Piketon, enl 2/16/63 Peach Orchard, age 19 or 21, dark hair, eyes & skin, 5-8, rem cap 8/14/63 Buchanan Co. VA, cap 1/9/64, paroled City Point VA 4/16/64, house 7-626, s 1,2,4.
HATFIELD, JOHNSON. reg 39, co E, r sgt, enr 11/25/62, enl 2/16/63 Peach Orchard, dis 9/15/65 Louisville, age 25, dark hair & eyes, fair skin, 5-7, rem prom from cpl to sgt 7/1/65, house 7-691, s 1,2,4.
HATFIELD, JOSEPH. reg 167WV, co Francis, house 7-792, s 23.
HATFIELD, THOMPSON. reg 167WV, co Francis, reg 39, co H, enr 7/12/63 Pike Co., enl 12/20/63 Louisa, age 21, black hair & eyes, dark skin, 5-9, house 7-792, s 1,2,4.
HAYNES, JOSEPH W. reg 39, co C, r cpl, enr 10/10/62 Pike Co., enl 2/16/63 Peach Orchard, age 26, light hair, blue eyes, fair skin, 5-11, rem wounded 6/12/64 Cynthiana, d 7/17/64, house 7-899, s 1,2,4.
HAYTON, MOSES. reg 39, co D, enr 9/11/62 Pike Co., enl 2/16/63 Peach Orchard, dis 9/15/65 Louisville, age 33, light hair, blue eyes, fair skin, 5-11, house 7-905, s 1,2,4.
HAYTON, THOMAS. reg 39, co D, r cpl, enr 9/11/62 Pike Co., enl 2/16/63 Peach Orchard, dis 9/15/65 Louisville, age 30, dark hair & skin, hazel eyes, 6-0, rem cap 7/2/63, paroled City Point VA 7/14/63, residence stated on muster roll, house n/c, s 1,2,4.
HELTON, CHARLES. reg 39, co I, r 2nd lt, enr 1/15/63, enl 2/16/63 Peach Orchard, age 30, rem dropped from rolls by general court martial 10/20/64, house 7-111, s 2,4.
HELTON, HIRAM. reg 39, co I, enr 10/27/62, enl 2/16/63 Peach Orchard, age 31, rem des 8/11/64 on the march, residence stated on muster roll, house n/c, s 2,4.
HELTON, ROBERT. reg 39, co B, enr 10/5/63, enl 12/28/63 or 3/29/64 Paintsville or Greenupsburg, age 35, dark hair & skin, black eyes, 5-7 or 5-10, rem d 9/8/65 on steamer Mason of accidental gunshot wounds, house 7-138, s 1,2,4,8.
HELVEY, JACOB. reg 39, co C, r 2nd lt, enr 11/18/62, enl 2/16/63, dis 9/15/65 Louisville, age 21, house 7-860, s 2,4.
HELVEY, WILLIAM M. reg 39, co C, r cpl, enr 11/5/62 Pike Co., enl 2/16/63 Peach Orchard, age 25, black hair, gray eyes, fair skin, 5-5, rem prom to cpl 9/1/64, dis 4/3/65 for disability, residence stated on muster roll, house n/c, s 1,2,4.
HENSON, PAUL. reg 3 US Vol Inf, enl 10/13/64, house 7-153, s 31.
HOGSTON, WILLIAM J. reg 39, co D, r cpl, enr 10/1/63 Pike Co., enl 10/29/63 Louisa, dis 9/15/65 Louisville, age 19, light hair, blue eyes, fair skin, 5-9, house 7-78. s 1,2,4.
HOPKINS, COLUMBUS C. reg 39, co C, enr 9/10/62 Louisa, enl 10/30/63 Louisa, dis 9/15/65 Louisville, age 30, black hair & eyes, dark skin, 5-8, house 7-4, s 1,2,4.
HOPKINS, GEORGE W. reg 39, co E, enr 11/8/62 Piketon, enl 8/31/63 Catlettsburg, age 21, dark hair, eyes & skin, 5-7, house 7-31, s 1,2,4.
HOPKINS, JAMES C. reg 39, co D, enr 12/18/62 Pike Co., enl 2/16/63 Peach Orchard, dis 9/15/65 Louisville, age 19, black hair, gray eyes, fair skin, 5-11, residence stated on muster roll, house n/c, s 1,2,4.
HOWELL, THOMAS W. reg 39, co C, enr 10/10/62 Pike Co., enl 2/16/63 Peach Orchard, age 31, dark hair & skin, gray eyes, 5-8, rem des 9/22/63 Louisa, house 1-80, s 1,2,4.
HUNT, JOHN. reg 39, co E, enr 11/15/62 Piketon, age 22, light hair, blue eyes, fair skin, 5-6, rem des 12/4/62 Floyd Co., cap 1/15/63 Floyd Co., house 7-312 or 7-651, s 1,2,4.

HURLEY, HIRAM. reg 39, co H, enr 11/25/62 Pike Co., enl 2/16/63 Peach Orchard, age 22, dark hair, black eyes, fair skin, 5-7, rem dis 11/21/64 Louisa on surgeon's certificate of disability, house 7-712, s 1,2,4.

HURLEY, JOHN. reg 39, co H, enr 12/10/62, enl 2/16/63 Peach Orchard, dis 9/15/65 Louisville, age 44, dark hair, eyes & skin, 5-6, house 7-712, s 1,2,4.

HURLEY, JOHN B. reg 39, co I, r cpl, enr 12/12/63 Peach Orchard, enl 12/28/63 Louisa, dis 9/15/65 Louisville, age 22, dark hair, blue eyes, fair skin, 5-5, rem prom to cpl 9/1/64, house 7-713, s 1,2,4.

HURLEY, JOHN R. reg 39, co H, enr 11/25/62, enl 2/16/63 Peach Orchard, dis 9/15/65 Louisville, age 18, dark hair, black eyes, fair skin, 5-5, rem cap 1/9/64 Boyd Co., confined at Richmond VA 1/25/64, paroled 5/8/64, house 7-712, s 1,2,4.

HURLEY, JOHN W. reg 39, co H, enr 11/25/62, enl 2/16/63 Peach Orchard, dis 9/15/65 Louisville, age 18, fair hair, eyes & skin, 5-5, house 7-723, s 1,2,4.

HURLEY, JOSIAH. reg 39, co H, enr 11/25/62, enl 2/16/63, dis 9/15/65 Louisville, age 20, dark hair, blue eyes, fair skin, 5-6, house 7-712, s 1,2,4.

HURLEY, SAMUEL. reg 39, co H, enr 11/25/62, enl 2/16/63 Peach Orchard, age 23, black hair & eyes, fair skin, 5-8, rem d 10/24/63 Mt. Sterling of erysipelas, house 7-712, s 1,2,4.

HURLEY, WILLIAM. reg 39, co H, enr 11/25/62, enl 2/16/63 Peach Orchard, dis 9/15/65 Louisville, age 39, fair hair & skin, blue eyes, 5-9, rem cap Turman's Ferry 1/9/64, returned 5/8/64, house 7-723, s 1,2,4.

HYLTON, JAMES W. reg 14, co F, enr 10/25/61 Louisa, enl 12/10/61 Louisa, age 37, light hair, blue eyes, fair skin, 5-10, rem d 10/4/64 Chattanooga TN of typhoid & chronic diarrhea, house 7-326, s 1,2,4.

J

JAMES, ABNER. reg 39, co C, enr 9/12/62 Pike Co., enl 2/16/63 Peach Orchard, age 45, white hair, blue eyes, fair skin, 5-8, rem dis 12/64 for disability, rheumatism, residence stated on muster roll, house n/c, s 1,2,4.

JEWELL, JAMES. reg 39, co H, enr 9/14/62 Peach Orchard, enl 2/16/63 Peach Orchard, dis 9/15/65 Louisville, age 23, dark hair & skin, blue eyes, 5-4, rem trans to co G 10/23/63, residence stated on muster roll, house, n/c, s 1,2,4.

JOHNSON, CORNELIUS. reg 39, co C, r sgt, enr 11/4/62, enl 2/16/63 Peach Orchard, dis 9/15/65 Louisville, age 27, dark hair, blue eyes, fair skin, 5-9, rem prom to sgt 4/5/63, house 7-889, s 1,2,4.

JOHNSON, JOHN. reg 39, co D, enr 11/19/62 Pike Co., enl 2/16/63 Peach Orchard, age 22, light hair, gray eyes, fair skin, 5-9, rem d 1/5/64 Ashland, house 7-212, s 1,2,4.

JOHNSON, JOHN. reg 39, co E, enr 11/9/62 Piketon, enl 2/16/63 Peach Orchard, dis 9/15/65 Louisville, age 35, dark hair, blue eyes, fair skin, 6-0, house 7-959, s 1,2,4.

JOHNSON, JOSEPH. reg 39, co C, enr 9/10/62 Louisa, enl 2/16/63 Peach Orchard, dis 9/15/65 Louisville, age 29, light hair, blue eyes, fair skin, 5-9, house 7-472, s 1,2,4.

JOHNSON, PEYTON. reg 167WV, co Runyon, reg 39, co D, enr 11/29/62 Pike Co., enl 2/16/63 Peach Orchard, dis 9/15/65 Louisville, age 24, light hair, blue eyes, fair skin, 6-1, house 7-702, s 1,2,4,23.

JOHNSON, RICHARD. reg 39, co E, enr 11/14/62 Piketon, enl 2/16/63 Peach Orchard, age 20, light hair, blue eyes, fair skin, 5-10, rem d 4/3/63 Ashland, house 1-142, s 1,2,4.

JOHNSON, SOLOMON. reg 39, co C, r sgt, enr 10/5/62 Pike Co., enl 2/16/63 Peach Orchard, dis 9/15/65 Louisville, age 22, dark hair & skin, gray eyes, 6-3, residence stated on muster roll, house n/c, s 1,2,4.

JOHNSON, WILLIAM H. reg 39, co C, enr 11/4/63, enl 1/15/62 Pike Co., age 24, light hair, brown eyes, fair skin, 6-0, rem trans for co H, 14th Ky Inf, reg CG, co E, enr 5/14/64, enl 7/4/64 Frankfort, dis 3/11/65 Catlettsburg, age 24, house 7-193, s 1,2,4.
JOHNSON, W. P. reg 167WV, co Runyon, reg 39, co D, enr 11/29/62 Pike Co., enl 2/16/63 Peach Orchard, dis 9/15/65 Louisville, age 29, black hair, gray eyes, fair skin, 6-2, residence stated on muster roll, house n/c, s 1,2,4,23.
JONES, JESSE. reg 39, co H, enr 8/29/63 Pike Co., enl 8/29/63 Louisa, dis 9/15/65 Louisville, age 35, dark hair, blue eyes, fair skin, 6-0, house 7-333, s 1,2,4.
JONES, JOHN. reg 39, co C, enr 11/5/62 Pike Co., enl 2/16/63 Peach Orchard, dis 9/15/65 Louisville, age 35, dark hair & skin, blue eyes, 5-4, house 7-531, s 1,2,4.
JUSTICE, ALEXANDER. reg 39, co D, enr 11/16/62 Pike Co., enl 2/16/63 Peach Orchard, dis 9/15/65 Louisville, age 18, dark hair & eyes, fair skin, 5-7, house 7-245, s 1,2,4.
JUSTICE, BAZEL. reg 39, co H, enr & enl 8/29/63 Lawrence Co., dis 9/15/65 Louisville, age 40, dark hair, eyes & skin, 6-2, residence stated on muster roll, house n/c, s 1,2,4.
JUSTICE, GILMORE. reg 39, co I, enr 11/10/62 Peach Orchard, enl 2/16/63, age 30, rem cap 2/1/63 Floyd or Pike Co., des place & date unknown, house 7-262, s 1,2,4.
JUSTICE, HIRAM. reg CG, enr 6/17/64, enl 7/6/74 Frankfort, rem des 8/28/64, house 7-297, s 2,4.
JUSTICE, JAMES C. reg 39, co D, enr 11/16/62 Pike Co., enl 2/16/63 Peach Orchard, age 24, black hair & eyes, fair skin, 5-9, rem dis 2/15/64 Louisa for consumption, house 7-949, s 1,2,4.
JUSTICE, JOHN. reg 39, co D, enr 11/13/62 Pike Co., enl 2/16/63 Peach Orchard, dis 9/15/65 Louisville, age 22, brown hair, dark eyes, fair skin, 5-6, house 7-302, s 1,2,4.
JUSTICE, PEYTON C. reg 39, co B, enr 10/17/62 Catlettsburg, enl 2/16/63 Peach Orchard, dis 9/15/65 Louisville, age 21, black hair, blue eyes, fair skin, 6-0, rem red from sgt 8/1/63, house 7-18, s 1,2,4
JUSTICE, WILLIAM. reg 39, co C, enr 9/10/62 Louisa, enl 2/16/63 Peach Orchard, dis 9/15/65 Louisville, age 37, dark hair & skin, gray eyes, 5-8, house 7-481, s 1,2,4.
JUSTICE, WILLIAM C. reg 39, co D, enr 11/16/62 Pike Co., enl 2/16/63 Peach Orchard, dis 9/15/65 Louisville, age 29, black hair & eyes, fair skin, 5-10, house 7-949, s 1,2,4.

K

KEATHLEY, CHRISTOPHER C. reg 39, co B, enr 9/6/62 Louisa, enl 2/16/63 Peach Orchard, dis 9/15/65 Louisville, age 22, dark hair, blue eyes, fair skin, 5-5, house 7-940, s 1,2,4.
KEATHLEY, JAMES A. reg CG, co G, enr 6/9/64, enl 7/6/64 Frankfort, dis 3/11/65 Catlettsburg, age 26, light hair & skin, blue eyes, 5-7, house 7-940, s 2,4.
KEATHLEY, SIMPKINS. reg 39, co B, enr 9/6/62 Louisa, enl 2/16/63 Peach Orchard, dis 9/15/65 Louisville, age 21, light hair, blue eyes, fair skin, 5-9, house 7-925, s 1,2,4.
KEATHLEY, WILLIAM. reg 39, co B, enr 11/15/62, enl 2/16/63 Peach Orchard, dis 9/15/65 Louisville, age 19, dark hair, blue eyes, fair skin, 5-5, house 7-928, s 1,2,4.
KEEL, SAMUEL. reg 39, co K, r 2nd lt, enr 11/15/62 Piketon, enl 2/16/63 Peach Orchard, dis 9/15/65 Louisville, age 36, dark hair, blue eyes, fair skin, 6-2, house 1-111, s 1,2,4.
KEEN, JAMES. reg 39, co H, enr 12/15/62 Pike Co., enl 2/16/63 Peach Orchard, age 18, dark hair & skin, black eyes, rem cap 1/9/64 Turman's Ferry, Boyd Co., d 2/15/65 Richmond VA of fever, residence stated on muster roll, house n/c, s 1,2,4.
KEEN, JOHN. reg 14, co F, enr 11/19/61 Louisa, enl 12/10/61 Louisa, age 33, light hair, blue eyes, fair skin, 5-8, rem d 2/10/62 Camp Buell, Paintsville, typhoid fever, house 7-336, s 1,2,4.

KENDRICK, GEORGE M. reg 39, co G, enr 11/10/62 Peach Orchard, enl 2/16/63 Peach Orchard, dis 9/15/65 Louisville, age 20, light hair, blue eyes, fair skin, 5-9, rem cap 12/4/62 Floyd Co., residence stated on muster roll, house n/c, s 1,2,4.
KENDRICK, THOMAS J. reg 39, co I, enr 11/10/62 Peach Orchard, enl 2/16/63 Peach Orchard, age 18 or 28, rem cap 2/1/63 Floyd Co., des by 2/1/63 place unknown, house 7-257, s 1,2,4.
KENDRICK, WILLIAM. reg 39, co G, enr 11/10/62 Peach Orchard, enl 2/16/63 Peach Orchard, dis 9/15/65 Louisville, age 26, dark hair & skin, blue eyes, 5-8, rem trans from co I, cap 12/4/62 or 2/1/63 Floyd Co., house 7-257, s 1,2,4.
KING, FRANKLIN. reg 39, co H, enr 4/18/63 Louisa, enl 6/10/63 Louisa, dis 9/15/65 Louisville, age 18, black hair, dark eyes & skin, 5-9, house 7-401, s 1,2,4.
KING, HARRISON. reg 65, co D, enl 5/21/64, dis 6/21/64, age 34, blue eyes, dark hair, fair skin, 5-8, house 7-408, s 2,4.
KING, JOHN. reg 39, co E, enr 10/6/62, enl 6/11/63 Louisville, dis 9/15/65 Louisville, age 27, dark hair & skin, blue eyes, 5-8, house 7-455, s 1,2,4.
KING, LEWIS. reg 39, co H, enr 1/15/63, enl 2/16/63 Peach Orchard, age 44, dark hair, blue eyes, fair skin, 5-10, rem dis 11/21/64 Louisa for rheumatism, residence stated on muster roll, house n/c, s 1,2,4.
KING, SAMUEL M. reg 39, co E, enr 12/3/62 Piketon, enl 2/16/63 Peach Orchard, dis 9/15/65 Louisville, age 18, dark hair & skin, gray eyes, 5-6, house 7-401, s 1,2,4.
KING, WILLIAM. reg 39, co H, r capt, enr 1/15/63, enl 2/16/63 Peach Orchard, dis 9/15/65 Louisville, age 32, house 7-314, s 2,4.
KINNEY, HENRY. reg 39, co B, enr 11/7/62 Piketon, enl 2/16/63 Peach Orchard, dis 9/15/65 Louisville, age 25, black hair, dark eyes & skin, 5-6, house 1-105, s 1,2,4.
KINNEY, JOHN W. reg 39, co B, enr 11/7/62 Piketon, enl 2/16/63 Peach Orchard, dis 9/15/65 Louisville, age 21, black hair, dark eyes & skin, 6-1, house 1-104, s 1,2,4.
KINNEY, WILLIAM. reg 39, co B, enr 11/7/62, enl 2/16/63 Peach Orchard, dis 9/15/65 Louisville, age 19, dark hair & skin, blue eyes, 6-0, house 1-104, s 1,2,4.

L

LAMBERT, JOSEPH. reg 39, co K, enr 2/1/63 Piketon, enl 2/16/63 Peach Orchard, dis 9/15/65 Louisville, age 20, red hair, blue eyes, fair skin, 5-10, residence stated on muster roll, house n/c, s 1,2,6.
LAYNE, DAVID. reg 167WV, co Francis, reg 39, co H, enr 12/10/62 Pike Co., enl 2/16/63 Peach Orchard, dis 9/15/65 Louisville, age 24 or 34, dark hair, eyes & skin, 5-9, house 7-707, s 1,2,4.
LAYNE, JOHN. reg 167WV, co Francis, reg 39, co H, enr 2/23/63 Pike Co., enl 2/16/63 Peach Orchard, dis 9/15/65 Louisville, age 36, black hair & eyes, dark skin, 5-9, house 7-752, s 1,2,4.
LAYNE, JOHN NATHANIEL. reg 39, co C, enr 9/10/62 Louisa, enl 2/16/63 Peach Orchard, dis 9/15/65 Louisville, age 18, dark hair & skin, black eyes, 5-10, house 7-463, s 1,2,4.
LEEDY, ABRAHAM. reg 39, co C, enr 9/7/62 Pike Co., enl 2/16/63 Peach Orchard, dis 9/15/65 Louisville, age 27, dark hair & skin, black eyes, 5-8, residence stated on muster roll, house n/c, s 1,2,4.
LITTLE, FRANCIS M. reg 14Cav, co B, enr 8/16/62 Maysville, enl 11/6/62 Mt. Sterling, age 32, m/out 9/16/63 Maysville, house 1-59, s 2.
LITTLE, REUBEN. reg 39, co K, enr 12/26/62, enl 2/16/63 Peach Orchard, dis 9/15/65 Louisville, age 20, black hair, dark eyes & skin, 5-10, house 1-77, s 1,2,4.
LOWE, ARRISON. reg 39, co E, enr 11/10/62, enl 2/16/63 Peach Orchard, dis 9/15/65 Louisville, age 43, light hair, blue eyes, fair skin, 5-7, house 7-563, s 1,2,4.
LOWE, GEORGE W. reg 39, co E, enr 11/10/62 Piketon, enl 2/16/63 Peach Orchard, dis 9/15/65 Louisville, age 19, dark hair, blue eyes, fair skin, 5-7, house 7-813, s 1,2,4.

LOWE, ORRISON B. M. reg 65, co D, r sgt, enl 5/21/64, dis 6/21/64, age 24, blue eyes, light hair, fair skin, 5-5, house 7-564, s 2,4.

LUSTER, CALVIN. reg 39, co H, enr 12/10/62, enl 2/16/63 Peach Orchard, dis 9/15/65 Louisville, age 18, fair hair & skin, blue eyes, 5-8, house 7-772, s 1,2,4.

LUSTER, RAINEY. reg 39, co H, enr 2/3/63 Lawrence Co., enl 2/16/63 Louisa, age 22, fair hair & skin, blue eyes, 6-0, rem cap 1/9/64 Boyd Co., confined at Richmond VA 1/25/64, sent to Andersonville 3/4/64, d 4/7/64 Andersonville GA of chronic diarrhea, residence stated on muster roll, house n/c, s 1,2,4.

LYKINS, MOSES. reg 39, co C, enr 11/5/62 Pike Co., enl 2/16/63 Peach Orchard, dis 9/15/65 Louisville, age 30, black hair, blue eyes, dark skin, 6-1, residence stated on muster roll, house n/c, s 1,2,4.

M

MARTIN, JACOB. reg 22, co F, enr 12/2/61, enl 1/10/62 Louisa, age 18, house 522, rem d 3/26/62 Ashland, s 2,4.

MARTIN, JOHN. reg 22, co F, enr 12/2/61, enl 1/10/62 Louisa, age 20, house 522, rem d 2/25/63 Memphis, TN, s 2,4.

MASTERS, NATHANIEL. reg 39, co C, enr 10/19/62, enl 2/16/63 Peach Orchard, age 22, dark hair, blue eyes, fair skin, 6-2, rem des 8/12/64 Louisa, residence stated on muster roll, house n/c, s 1,2,4.

MAY, CHARLES. reg 39, co I, enr 12/2/62 Piketon, enl 2/16/63 Peach Orchard, dis 9/15/65 Louisville, age 22, light hair, blue eyes, fair skin, 5-9, house 7-943, s 1,2,4.

MAY, DANIEL. reg 39, co E, enr 11/15/62 Piketon, enl 2/16/63 Peach Orchard, dis 9/15/65 Louisville, age 38, dark hair & skin, blue eyes, 5-8, house 7-686, s 1,2,4.

MAY, DAVID C. reg 39, co I, enr 12/21/62 Piketon, enl 2/16/63 Peach Orchard, dis 9/15/65 Louisville, age 19, dark hair, blue eyes, fair skin, 5-7, house 7-943, s 1,2,4.

MAY, HARVEY. reg 39, co E, enr 11/15/62 Piketon, age 30, light hair, blue eyes, fair skin, 5-6, rem cap 1/15/63 Floyd Co., des 12/10/62 Peach Orchard, house 7-649, s 1,2,4.

MAY, HENDERSON. reg 39, co I, enr 12/2/62, enl 2/16/63 Peach Orchard, dis 9/15/65 Louisville, age 21, light hair, hazel eyes, fair skin, 5-8, house 7-943, s 1,2,4.

MAY, JOHN H. reg 39, co E, enr 11/24/62, enl 2/16/63 Peach Orchard, dis 9/15/65 Louisville, age 30, dark hair & skin, blue eyes, 5-10, house 7-684, s 1,2,4.

MAY, JOSEPH. reg 39, co E, enr 11/10/62 Piketon, enl 2/16/63 Peach Orchard, age 35, light hair, blue eyes, fair skin, 5-4, rem d 5/17/63 Ashland typhoid, residence stated on muster roll, house n/c, s 1,2,4.

MAY, SOLOMON R. reg 39, co B, enr 12/18/63 Paintsville, enl 3/29/64 Greenupsburg, dis 9/15/65 Louisville, age 18, light hair, dark eyes, fair skin, 5-6, house 1-45, s 1,2,4.

MAY, WILLIAM JR. reg 39, co E, enr 11/18/62, age 28, light hair, blue eyes, fair skin, 5-7, rem des 12/10/62 Peach Orchard, cap 1/15/63 Floyd Co., residence stated on muster roll, house n/c, s 1,2,4.

MAYNARD, AMOS. reg 39, co C, enr 11/12/62, enl 2/16/63 Peach Orchard, dis 9/15/65 Louisville, age18, light hair, gray eyes, fair skin, 5-7, house 7-512, s 1,2,4.

MAYNARD, BENJAMIN. reg 39, co C, r cpl, enr 9/10/62 Pike Co., enl 2/16/63 Peach Orchard, dis 9/15/65 Louisville, age 45, dark hair, blue eyes, fair skin, 6-0, rem severely wounded Cynthiana 6/11/64, prom to cpl 1/1/65, house 7-812, s 1,2,4,8.

MAYNARD, DECATUR. reg 39, co C, r cpl, enr 9/10/62 Pike Co., enl 2/16/63 Peach Orchard, dis 9/15/65 Louisville, age 18, light hair, blue eyes, fair skin, 5-9, house 7-857, s 1,2,4.

MAYNARD, JACKSON. reg 167WV, co Sampson Kirk, reg 39, enr 11/63, dis 9/65, house 7-579, s 5,23.

MAYNARD, JAMES. reg 39, co K, enr 2/1/63 Pike Co., enl 2/16/63 Peach Orchard, age 27, dark hair, gray eyes, fair skin, 6-1, rem des 7/22/63 Floyd Co., residence stated on muster roll, house n/c, s 1,2,4.

MAYNARD, JAMES E. reg 2ndOhioCav, co M, enl 2/14/65, dis 9/28/65, house 7-474, s 5.
MAYNARD, JOHN. reg 45, co K, enr 12/8/63 Grayson, enl 12/9/63 Louisa, dis 11/17/64, age 21, rem dis for disability, consumption, house 7-512, s 1,2.
MAYNARD, JOHN H. reg 39, co H, enr 2/3/63 Pike Co., enl 2/16/63 Peach Orchard, dis 9/15/65 Louisville, age 27, fair hair & skin, blue eyes, 5-10, house 7-722, s 1,2,4.
MAYNARD, JONATHAN. reg 39, co E, enr 11/5/62, enl 2/16/63 Peach Orchard, dis 9/15/65 Louisville, age 32, light hair, blue eyes, fair skin, 5-10, house 7-416, s 1,2,4.
MAYNARD, STEPHEN. reg 39, co E, enr 11/22/62 Piketon, enl 2/16/63 Peach Orchard, age 22, light hair, blue eyes fair skin, 5-11, rem d 4/23/63 Ashland of pneumonia, house 7-419, s 1,2,4.
MCCOWN, JAMES. reg 39, co K, enr 11/16/62, enl 2/16/63 Peach Orchard, dis 9/15/65 Louisville, age 18, black hair, blue eyes, fair skin, 5-9, house 1-194, s 1,2,4.
MCCOWN, THOMAS. reg 39, co D, r sgt, enr 12/14/62 Pike Co., enl 2/16/63 Peach Orchard, dis 9/15/65 Louisville, age 25, light hair, gray eyes, fair skin, 5-10, rem prom to cpl 12/1/64, to sgt 6/7/65, house 7-911, s 1,2,4.
MCCOY, ASA HARMON. reg 167WV, co Runyon, rem cap 12/6/62 Pike Co., reg 45, co E, enr 10/20/63 Ashland, enl 11/6/63 Louisa, dis 12/24/64 Ashland, age 24, house 7-765, s 1,2,23.
MCCOY, ELIJAH. reg 39, co D, enr 11/5/62 Pike Co., enl 2/16/63 Peach Orchard, age 26, light hair, gray hair, fair skin, 6-0, rem d 5/8/3 Ashland of disease, house 7-479, s 1,2,4.
MCCOY, HENDERSON. reg 65, co D, enr 5/21/64, dis 6/21/64, age 27, gray eyes, light hair, fair skin, 5-11, house 7-803, s 2,4.
MCCOY, JOHN. reg 167WV, co Runyon, rem cap 12/6/62 Pike Co., d 4/25/63 U.S. Military Hospital, house 7-676, s 23.
MCCOY, JOHN. reg 39, co H, enr 1/25/63, enl 2/16/63 Peach Orchard, dis 9/15/65 Louisville, age 22, dark hair, blue eyes, fair skin, 5-9, rem residence established by descriptive muster roll, house n/c, s 1,2,4.
MCCOY, JOHN R. reg 39, co H, enr 2/3/63 Pike Co., enl 2/16/63 Peach Orchard, dis 9/15/65 Louisville, age 22, fair hair & skin, blue eyes, 5-6, rem residence established by descriptive muster roll, house n/c, s 1,2,4.
MCCOY, PLEASANT. reg 167WV, co Runyon, house 7-636, s 23.
MCCOY, ULYSSES. reg 39, co H, enr 12/10/62 Pike Co., enl 2/16/63 Peach Orchard, dis 9/15/65 Louisville, age 18, fair hair & skin, blue eyes, 5-4, residence stated on muster roll, house n/c, s 1,2,4.
MCGUIRE, WILLIAM. reg 39, co C, r cpl, enr 9/27/62 Pikeville, enl 2/16/63 Peach Orchard, dis 9/15/65 Louisville, age 32, black hair, blue eyes, dark skin, 5-11, rem cap 12/4/62 Pike Co., confined at Richmond VA, returned 5/19/63, prom to cpl 9/1/64, house 7-252, s 1,2,4.
MCKENZIE, BALLARD P. reg 39, co K, r cpl, enr 11/16/62 Pike Co., enl 2/16/63 Peach Orchard, age 19, light hair, blue eyes, fair skin, 5-6, rem d 9/5/65 Lexington, chronic diarrhea, house 1-23, s 1,2,4.
MEADE, JAMES M. OR W. reg 39, co C, enr 11/8/62, enl 2/16/63 Peach Orchard, dis 9/15/65 Louisville, age 18, dark hair, gray eyes, fair skin, 5-10, residence stated on muster roll, house, n/c, s 1,2,4.
MILLER, JACOB P. reg 39, co B, enr 11/5/62 Pike Co., enl 2/16/63 Peach Orchard, dis 9/15/65 Louisville, age 20, dark hair, blue eyes, fair skin, 5-7, house 7-443, s 1,2,4.
MILLER, SAMUEL. reg 39, co K, enr 11/16/62 Piketon, enl 2/16/63 Peach Orchard, age 19, dark hair, blue eyes, fair skin, 5-9, rem cap 12/4/62 Floyd Co., des 6/30/63 Louisa, house 1-165, s 1,2,4.
MIMS, KENAS F. reg 39, co C, enr 11/5/62 Pike Co., enl 2/16/63 Peach Orchard, dis 9/15/65 Louisville, age 19, light hair, black eyes, fair skin, 5-6, house 7-863, s 1,2,4.
MITCHELL, JOHN D. G. reg 16, co C, enr 11/10/61 Camp Hopeless Chase, enl 12/18/61 Camp Lee, dis 7/24/65 Lexington, des 2/19/63 Lebanon, reg 39, co D, enr 3/16/63 Pike Co., enl 6/10/63 Louisa, dis 9/15/65 Louisville, age 19, light hair, blue eyes, fair skin, 5-10, residence stated on muster roll, house 7-491, s 1, 2, 4.

MORGAN, WILLIAM. reg 39, co B, enr 11/9/62 Piketon, enl 2/16/63 Peach Orchard, age 37, light hair, blue eyes, fair skin, 6-0, rem d 7/19/63 Ashland fever, house 7-301, s 1,2,4.

MOUNTS, ASBURY. reg 167WV, co Runyon, reg 39, co G, enr 1/29/63 Pike Co., enl 2/16/63 Peach Orchard, dis 9/15/65 Louisville, age 19, light hair, blue eyes, fair skin, 5-6, rem trans from co H 10/30/63, house 7-700, s 1,2,4,23.

MOUNTS, CHARLES W. reg 39, co H, enr 1/20/63, enl 2/16/63 Peach Orchard, dis 9/15/65 Louisville, age 26, fair hair & skin, blue eyes, 5-9, residence stated on muster roll, house n/c, s 1,2,4.

MOUNTS, DAVID. reg 167WV, co Runyon, reg 39, co I, enr 11/27/62 Piketon, enl 2/16/63 Peach Orchard, dis 9/15/65 Louisville, age 33 or 37, light hair, blue eyes, fair skin, 5-10, house 7-699, s 2,4,23.

MOUNTS, ELIJAH. reg 167WV, co Runyon, reg 39, co I, enr 11/28/62 Pike Co., enl 2/16/63 Peach Orchard, age 44, dark hair & skin, blue eyes, 5-6, house 7-790, s 1,2,4.

MOUNTS, HARRISON. reg 167WV, co Runyon, reg 39, co I, r cpl, enr 10/8/63 Louisa, enl 3/29/64 Greenupsburg, age 21, dark hair, blue eyes, fair skin, 5-9, rem prom to cpl 6/1/64, des 8/11/64 on the march, house 7-703, s 1,2,4.

MOUNTS, JACKSON. reg 39, co H, enr 2/3/63 Pike Co., enl 2/16/63 Peach Orchard, dis 9/15/65 Louisville, age 38, dark hair, eyes & skin, 5-5, residence stated on muster roll, house n/c, s 1,2,4.

MOUNTS, JAMES. reg 39, co I, enr 1/5/63 Louisa, enl 2/16/63 Peach Orchard, age 18, dark hair, blue eyes, fair skin, 5-2, rem d date & place unknown, house 7-703, s 1,2,4.

MOUNTS, MITCHEL. reg 167WV, co Runyon, reg 39, co C, enr 1/4/64, enl 3/29/64 Greenupsburg, age 44, dark hair & skin, blue eyes, 5-3, rem des 6/10/64, house 7-703, s 1,2,4.

MULLINS, JEFFERSON. reg 39, co C, enr 10/18/62, enl 2/16/63 Peach Orchard, age 22, light hair, blue eyes, fair skin, 5-8, rem des 8/12/64 Louisa, house 7-192, s 1,2,4.

MULLINS, JOHN V. reg 39, co H, enr 4/2/64 Catlettsburg, enl 5/15/64 Catlettsburg, dis 9/15/65 Louisville, age 27, dark hair, blue eyes, fair skin, 5-8, house 1-149, s 1,2,4.

MULLINS, SOLOMON. reg 39, co C, enr 11/14/62 Pike Co., enl 2/16/63 Peach Orchard, age 32, light hair, gray eyes, fair skin, 6-0, rem d 1/28/64 Paintsville, house 7-190, s 1,2,4.

MULLINS, WILLIAM S. reg 39, co H, enr 4/3/64, enl 5/15/64 Catlettsburg, age 35, dark hair, blue eyes, fair skin, 5-9, rem d 2/28/65 Louisa of smallpox, house 7-156, s 2,4.

MURPHY, ALEXANDER. reg CG, co E, enr 1/31/65, enl Catlettsburg, age 18, black hair & eyes, fair skin, 5-5, house 7-68, s 4.

MURPHY, ANDREW J. reg 14, co K, enr 11/8/61, enl 12/10/61 Louisa, dis 1/31/65 Louisa, age 23, sandy hair, blue eyes, fair skin, 6-1, house 7-634, s 1,2,4.

MURPHY, WILLIAM. reg 14, co C, enr 10/10/61 Louisa, enl 12/10/61 Louisa, dis 12/31/62 Lexington, age 22 or 25, rem dis for disability, reg 39, co D, enr 8/10/63 Pike Co., enl 8/30/63 Louisa, dis 9/15/65 Louisville, age 24, dark hair, blue eyes, fair skin, 5-11, house 7-57, s 1,2,4.

N

NEW, DAVID. reg 167WV, co Runyon, house 7-771, s 23.

NEW, ISAAC. reg 167WV, co Runyon, house 7-697, s 23.

NEWSOME, DAVENPORT. reg 39, co B, enr 11/7/62 Peach Orchard, enl 2/16/63 Peach Orchard, dis 9/15/65 Louisville, age 26, dark hair, eyes & skin, 6-0, rem trans to co K, house 1-103, s 1,2,4.

NEWSOME, DAVID. reg 39, co K, enr 2/1/63 Peach Orchard, enl 2/16/63 Peach Orchard, dis 9/15/65 Louisville, age 24, black hair & eyes, dark skin, 6-0, house 1-72, s 1,2,4.

NEWSOME, FREDERICK. reg 39, co C, enr 9/10/62 Pike Co., enl 2/16/63 Peach Orchard, dis 9/15/65 Louisville, age 22, black hair & eyes, dark skin, 5-10, house 1-103, s 1,2,4.

NEWSOME, HARRISON. reg 39, co K, enr 2/1/63 Peach Orchard, enl 8/30/63 Louisa, dis 9/15/65 Louisville, age 24, black hair, blue eyes, fair skin, 6-2, house 1-79, s 1,2,4.
NEWSOME, HENRY. reg 39, co C, enr 11/4/62, enl 2/16/63 Peach Orchard, dis 9/15/65 Louisville, age 25, dark hair, blue eyes, fair skin, 6-2, house 1-72, s 1,2,4.
NEWSOME, JARVEY. reg 39, co K, enr 11/16/62 Piketon, enl 2/16/63 Peach Orchard, dis 9/15/65 Louisville, age 22, black hair & eyes, dark skin, 5-10, residence stated on muster roll, house n/c, s 1,2,4.
NEWSOME, LACKEY G. reg 39, co B, enr 11/7/62 Piketon, enl 6/10/63 Louisa, age 25, dark hair, eyes & skin, 5-10, rem trans to co K, KIA 2/15/65 Piketon, house 1-100, s 1,2,4.
NEWSOME, ROBERT. reg 39, co K, enr 11/16/62 Pike Co., enl 2/1/63 Peach Orchard, dis 9/15/65 Louisville, age 24, black hair & eyes, dark skin, 5-10, house 1-102, s 1,2,4.
NEWSOME, SAMUEL. reg 39, co K, enr 11/16/62 Piketon, enl 2/16/63 Peach Orchard, dis 9/15/65 Louisville, age 21, dark hair & eyes, fair skin, 5-8, house 1-79, s 1,2,4.
NEWSOME, WILLIAM P. reg 39, co C, enr 11/4/62, enl 6/11/63 Louisa, age 19, black hair & eyes, dark skin, 5-7, rem d 2/24/64 Louisa, house 1-156, s 1,2,4.
NICHOLS, JAMES. reg 14, co C, enr 10/25/61 Louisa, enl 12/10/61 Louisa, dis 9/15/65 Louisville, age 18, dark hair, eyes & skin, 5-8, rem trans to 14th Vet Inf, co A, enr 2/29/64, m/in 3/19/64 Catlettsburg, 6/64 in Knoxville TN hospital for wound, residence stated on muster roll, house n/c, s 1,2,4.
NORMAN, WILLIAM. reg 167WV, co Francis, reg 39, co H, enr 12/28/62 Lawrence Co., enl 2/16/63 Peach Orchard, dis 9/15/65 Louisville, age 44, fair hair & skin, blue eyes, 5-8, house 7-690, s 1,2,4,23.
NORMAN, WILLIAM R. reg 167WV, co Francis, reg 39, co H, enr 11/25/62 Pike Co., enl 2/16/63 Peach Orchard, dis 9/15/65 Louisville, age 19, fair hair & skin, blue eyes, 5-11, house 7-690, s 1,2,4,23.
NUNNERY, THOMAS. reg 39, co D, enr 11/18/62 or 12/22/62 Pike Co., enl 2/16/63 Peach Orchard, dis 9/15/65 Louisville, age 21, light hair, blue eyes, fair skin, 6-1, house 7-452, s 1,2,4.

O

OSBORNE, SHERWOOD. reg 39, co K, enr 9/22/63, enl 10/30/63 Louisa, dis 9/15/65 Louisville, age 18, light hair, blue eyes, fair skin, 6-1, house 7-189, s 1,2,4.

P

PARSONS, DILLARD. reg 39, co E, r 1st lt, enr 9/13/62, enl 2/16/63 Peach Orchard, age 41, rem res 3/11/63 for ill health, house 7-830, s 1,2,4.
PARSONS, HIRAM B. reg 39, co E, r cpl, enr 9/2/62, enl 2/16/63 Peach Orchard, dis 9/15/65 Louisville, age 20, light hair, blue eyes, fair skin, 5-7, house 7-830, s 1,2,4.
PAULEY, JOHN S. reg 39, co C, enr 9/10/62 Louisa, enl 2/16/63 Peach Orchard, age 23, light hair, black eyes, fair skin, 5-5, rem d 4/8/63 Ashland, house 7-555, s 1,2,4.
PAULEY, JONATHAN. reg 39, co C, enr 11/10/62 Louisa, enl 2/16/63 Peach Orchard, age 44, dark hair & skin, black eyes, 5-5, rem d 4/8/63 Ashland of pneumonia, measles & typhoid fever, house 7-555, s 1,2,4.
PAULEY, JOSEPH S. reg 39, co C, enr 4/1/63 Pike Co. enl 8/3/63 Peach Orchard, age 20, black hair & eyes, dark skin, 5-7, rem trans to co E 10/29/63, residence stated on muster roll, house n/c, s 1,2,4.
PAULEY, SHADLE R. reg 39, co C, r 2nd lt, enr 9/10/62 Piketon, enl 2/16/63 Peach Orchard, dis 9/15/65 Louisville, age 21, red hair, blue eyes, fair skin, 5-5, rem trans to co E, prom from pvt to sgt 1/1/65, prom from sgt to 2nd lt 6/1/65, house 7-555, s 1,2,4.

PHILLIPS, FRANCIS. reg 14, co H, enr 7/12/63 Louisa, enl 8/29/63 Louisa, age 22, dark hair, eyes & skin, 5-9, rem trans to 14th Vet Inf, co C, enr 7/12/63, m/in 8/29/63 Louisa, d 1/19/65 Louisville of chronic diarrhea, residence shown on CSR, house n/c, s 1,2,4.

PHILLIPS, WILLIAM. reg 39, co H, enr 9/1/63 Pike Co., enl 10/29/63 Louisa, age 28, dark hair, eyes & skin, 5-10, rem cap Turman's Ferry 1/9/64, d Richmond VA 2/21/64 of scorbutus (scurvy), house 7-379, s 1,2,4,8.

PINSON, HARRISON. reg 45, co E, enr 8/29/63 Catlettsburg, enl 11/6/63 Ashland, age 18, dark hair, eyes & skin, 5-0, rem des 11/8/63 Ashland, born Pike Co., house 7-409, s 1,2,6.

PINSON, HENRY CLAY. reg 39, co E, enr 9/20/62, enl 2/16/63 Peach Orchard, age 20, light hair, blue eyes, fair skin, 5-7, rem d 3/8/63 or 3/14/63 Louisa of disease, house 7-410, s 1,2,4.

PINSON, MOSES. reg 39, co E, r cpl, enr 11/13/62, enl 2/16/63 Peach Orchard, dis 9/15/63 Louisville, age 22, rem prom to cpl 7/1/65, residence stated on muster roll, house n/c, s 2,4.

PINSON, THOMAS. reg 39, co E, r sgt, enr 11/4/62, enl 2/16/63 Peach Orchard, dis 9/15/65 Louisville, age 24, black hair, dark eyes, fair skin, 6-1, rem cap 12/4/62 Floyd Co, trans from co H 8/10/63, prom to sgt 6/7/65, house 7-416, s 1,2,4.

PINSON, WILLIAM R. reg 39, co E, enr 12/30/62, enl 2/16/63 Peach Orchard, dis 9/15/65 Louisville, age 18, rem d unknown date, house 7-448, s 1,2,4.

PLYMALE, HUGHY. reg 39, co D, r 1st lt, enr 11/16/62 Pike Co., enl 2/16/63 Peach Orchard, dis 9/15/65 Louisville, age 31, dark hair, blue eyes, fair skin, 5-6, rem prom from sgt to 2nd lt 3/9/65, to 1st lt 5/6/65, house 7-58, s 1,2,4.

PLYMALE, JAMES. reg 14, co C, enr 8/27/63 Catlettsburg, enl 10/31/63 Catlettsburg, age 18, light hair, blue eyes, fair skin, 5-6, rem wounded between 7/2/64 & 8/13/64, d 8/7/64 Marietta GA, of wounds & disease, house 7-59, s 1,2,4.

PLYMALE, JOHN. reg 14, co C, r cpl, enr 10/25/61 Catlettsburg, enl 12/10/61 Catlettsburg, dis 9/15/65 Louisville, age 22, dark hair & skin, blue eyes, 5-8, rem prom to cpl 8/14/63, trans to 14th Vet Inf co A, enr 2/29/64, m/in 3/19/64 Catlettsburg, house 7-59, s 1,2,4.

PLYMALE, WILLIAM H. reg 39, co D, enr 10/15/62 Pike Co., enl 2/16/63 Peach Orchard, age 18, light hair, blue eyes, fair skin, 5-7, rem cap on scout 8/24/63, d 7/29/64 Andersonville GA of chronic diarrhea, house 7-59, s 1,2,4.

POLLEY, JAMES. reg 14, co H, r cpl, enr 10/25/61 Catlettsburg, enl 12/10/61 Louisa, dis 1/31/65 Louisa, age 45, dark hair & skin, blue eyes, 5-9, rem app cpl 6/63, residence stated on muster roll, house n/c, s 1,2,4.

POLLY, JOHN. reg 14, co H, enr 10/25/61 Catlettsburg, enl 12/10/61 Louisa, age 28, dark hair & skin, black eyes, 5-10, rem d 5/28/62 Flat Lick KY of typhoid fever, house 7-324, s 1,2,4.

PORTER, ANDREW. reg 39, co E, enr 9/5/62 Piketon, enl 2/16/63 Peach Orchard, age 34, dark hair, blue eyes, light skin, 6-1, rem trans from co D 7/1/63, d 12/29/63 Ashland of pneumonia, house 7-475, s 1,2,4.

PORTER, ELIJAH. reg 39, co C, enr 9/14/62, enl 2/16/63 Peach Orchard, dis 9/15/65 Louisville, age 19, black hair & eyes, dark skin, 5-6, house 7-471, s 1,2,4.

PORTER, JAMES R. reg 16, co I, enr 3/29/62 Piketon, enl 9/23/63 Loudon TN, dis 4/24/65 Lexington, age 36, 40 or 42, des 3/14/64 Maysville, residence stated on muster roll, house n/c, s,1, 4.

PRATER, DANIEL. reg 39, co E, enr 12/10/62 Lawrence Co., enl 2/16/63 Peach Orchard, dis 9/15/65, age 36, black hair & eyes, dark skin, 5-10, house 7-734, s 1,2,4,8.

PRATER, DANIEL. reg 39, co H, enr 2/3/63 Lawrence Co., enl 2/16/63 Peach Orchard, age 19, black hair, dark eyes & skin, 5-8, rem cap 1/9/64, d 2/17/64 Richmond VA of scorbutus (scurvy), residence stated on muster roll, house n/c, s 1,2,4.

PRATER, EZEKIEL. reg 39, co F, enr 12/26/62 Floyd Co., enl 2/16/63 Peach Orchard, dis 9/15/65 Louisville, age 41, black hair & eyes, dark skin, 5-10, house 7-934, s 1,2,4.

PRATER, PLEASANT M. reg 39, co E, r cpl, enr 2/3/63 Peach Orchard, enl 2/16/63 Peach Orchard, dis 9/15/65 Louisville, age 21, light hair, blue eyes, fair skin, 6-0, residence stated on muster roll, house n/c, s 1,2,4.

PREECE, JOHN. reg 39, co D, enr 11/16/62 Pike Co., enl 2/16/63 Peach Orchard, age 37, dark hair, blue eyes, fair skin, 5-7, rem dis 6/25/64 Ashland, deformity of spinal column, residence stated on muster roll, house n/c, s 1,2,4.

PRICE, JOHN W. reg 39, co D, r cpl, enr 11/10/62 Pike Co., enl 2/16/63 Peach Orchard, age 32, light hair, blue eyes, fair skin, 6-2, rem app cpl 3/28/63, cap 7/2/63, d 1/12/64 in prison at Richmond VA, house 7-896, s 1,2,4,8.

PRICE, WILLIAM C. reg 39, co D, enr 11/18/62 or 12/14/62 Pike Co., enl 2/16/63 Peach Orchard, age 42, light hair, blue eyes, fair skin, 6-0, rem d 4/10/63 Louisa of disease, house 7-896, s 1,2,4.

PRIEST, WILLIAM. reg 39, co C, enr 9/10/62 Louisa, enl 2/16/63 Peach Orchard, dis 9/15/65 Louisville, age 33, black hair, gray eyes, fair skin, 5-10, house 7-456, s 1,2,4.

R

RAINES, JOHN. reg 39, co H, enr 11/15/62, enl 2/16/63 Peach Orchard, age 33, rem des 2/28/63 or 3/13/63 from Camp White, Louisa, house 7-273, s 1,2,4.

RAMEY, MILES. reg 39, co D, enr 9/19/62, enl 2/16/63 Peach Orchard, dis 9/15/65 Louisville, age 18, rem reduced to ranks from cpl 12/1/64, house 7-97, s 1,2,4.

RAMSEY, GEORGE W. reg 39, co B, enr 11/9/62 Pike Co., enl 2/16/63 Peach Orchard, dis 9/15/65 Louisville, age 23, light hair, blue eyes, fair skin, 5-7, house 1-38, s 1,2,4.

RAMSEY, JAMES W. reg 39, co B, r cpl, enr 11/8/62 Pike Co., enl 2/16/63 Peach Orchard, dis 9/15/65 Louisville, age 26, dark hair & eyes, fair skin, 5-8, residence stated on muster roll, house n/c, s 1,2,4.

RAMSEY, JOHN F. reg 39, co B, enr 9/6/62 Louisa, enl 2/16/63 Peach Orchard, age 36, dark hair, blue eyes, fair skin, 5-8 or 5-11, rem d 3/25/63 or 3/27/63 Louisa of disease, house 1-39, s 1,2,4.

RATLIFF, ANDREW J. reg 39, co C, r cpl, enr 9/6/62, enl 2/16/63 Peach Orchard, dis 9/15/65 Louisville, age 22, light hair, gray eyes, fair skin, 5-8, rem cap 12/4/62 Pike Co., returned 5/19/63, house 7-858, s 1,2,4.

RATLIFF, COLBERT. reg 39, co D, enr 11/19/62, enl 2/16/63 Peach Orchard, dis 9/15/65 Louisville, age 19, light hair, blue eyes, fair skin, 5-5, house 7-209, s 1,2,4.

RATLIFF, HARRISON. reg 39, co D, enr 11/19/62 Pike Co., enl 6/10/63 Louisa, age 23 or 34, light hair, blue eyes, fair skin, 5-11, house 7-210, s 1,2,4.

RATLIFF, JAMES. reg 39, co I, enr 12/7/62 Peach Orchard, enl 2/16/63 Peach Orchard, age 18, rem cap 2/1/63 Pike Co., residence stated on muster roll, house n/c, s 1,4.

RATLIFF, JOEL. reg 39, co D, enr 11/19/62 Pike Co., enl 2/16/63 Peach Orchard, dis 9/15/65 Louisville, age 19, black hair, blue eyes, dark skin, 5-11, house 7-222, s 1,2,4.

RATLIFF, JOHN (SR.). reg 39, co D, enr 12/27/63 Pike Co., enl 12/27/63 Louisa, age 30 or 36, light hair, blue eyes, fair skin, 6-0, rem d 7/27/63 Louisa of consumption, house 7-266 or 7-910, s 1,2,4.

RATLIFF, JOHN (JR.). reg 39, co D, enr 11/15/62 Pike Co., enl 2/16/63 Peach Orchard, dis 9/15/65 Louisville, age 19, dark hair, eyes & skin, 5-7, rem residence established by descriptive muster roll, house 7-283, s 1,2,4.

RATLIFF, JOHN. reg 45, co K, enr 9/29/63 Catlettsburg, enl 12/9/63 Louisa, dis 2/14/65 Catlettsburg, age 18, light hair, blue eyes, fair skin, 5-4, house 7-913, s 1,2.

RATLIFF, MARION. reg 45, co K, enr 9/29/63, enl 12/9/63 Louisa, dis 2/14/65 Catlettsburg, age 18, dark hair, blue eyes, fair skin, 5-5, house 7-119, s 2,6.

RATLIFF, NOAH. reg 45, co K, enr 9/29/63 Catlettsburg, enl 12/9/63 Louisa, dis 2/14/65 Catlettsburg, age 18, dark hair, blue eyes, fair skin, 5-4, house 7-430 or 7-954, s 1,2.

RATLIFF, SQUIRE. reg 39, co E, enr 11/10/62 Piketon, enl 2/16/63 Peach Orchard, age 38, dark hair & skin, blue eyes, 5-8, rem d 4/14/63 Louisa, house 7-858, s 1,2,4.

RATLIFF, THOMAS. reg 39, co C, enr 9/10/62 Pike Co., enl 2/16/63 Peach Orchard, age 18, dark hair & skin, black eyes, 5-6, rem d 4/8/63 or 4/13/63 Ashland of pneumonia, house 7-858, s 1,2,4.

RATLIFF, VINSON D. reg 39, co C, enr 11/14/62 Pikeville, enl 2/16/63 Peach Orchard, dis 9/15/65 Louisville, age 18, light hair, blue eyes, fair skin, 5-7, house 7-913, s 1,2,4.

RAY, JACKSON. reg 39, co K, enr 11/20/62, enl 2/16/63 Peach Orchard, dis 9/15/65 Louisville, age 18, dark hair, yellow eyes, fair skin, 5-6, house 1-109, s 1,2,4.

RAY, JAMES L. reg 39, co K, enr 11/18/62 Piketon, enl 2/16/63 Peach Orchard, age 18, dark hair, blue eyes, fair skin, 5-11, rem des 4/16/63 Pike Co., house 1-6, s 1,2,4.

RAY, JOSEPH. reg 39, co C, enr 2/1/63, enl 2/16/63 Peach Orchard, dis 9/15/65 Louisville, age 18, light hair, black eyes, dark skin, 5-8, rem, residence established by descriptive muster roll, residence stated on muster roll, house n/c, s 1,2,4.

RAY, REUBEN. reg 39, co K, enr 11/20/62 Piketon, enl 2/16/63 Peach Orchard, dis 9/15/65 Louisville, age 24, dark hair, black hair, fair skin, 5-10, rem residence established by descriptive muster roll, house n/c, s 1,2,4.

REED, AMOS. reg 39, co E, enr 3/7/64 Peach Orchard, enl 5/7/64 Louisa, age 19, dark hair, blue eyes, fair skin, 5-7, rem d 6/2/64 Louisa or 11/18/64 Lexington, house 7-559, s 1,2,4.

RICE, JAMES M. reg 39, co B, G, r 1st lt, enr 10/30/62 Catlettsburg, enl 2/16/63 Peach Orchard, dis 9/15/65 Louisville, age 28, dark hair, blue eyes, fair skin, 5-6, rem residence established by List of Officers, prom to 1st lt 5/30/63, house n/c, s 1,2,4.

RILEY, DANIEL. reg 39, co C, enr 9/10/62 Peach Orchard, enl 2/16/63 Peach Orchard, dis 9/15/65 Louisville, age 26, house 7-5, s 1,2,4.

ROBERTS, BENJAMIN L. reg 39, co A, enr 5/3 or 30/63 Johnson Co., enl 6/11/63 Louisa, dis 9/15/65 Louisville, age 18, rem des 4/17/65 Ashland, residence stated on muster roll, house n/c, s 1,2,4.

ROBERTS, PRESTON. reg 39, co C, enr 11/22/62, enl 2/16/63 Peach Orchard, dis 9/15/65 Louisville, age 23, rem trans from co I 8/31/63, residence stated on muster roll, house n/c, s 1,2,4.

ROBERTS, RICELY. reg 39, co I, r cpl, enr 11/15/62, enl 2/16/63 Peach Orchard, dis 9/15/65 Louisville, age 31, dark hair, gray eyes, fair skin, 6-0, rem cap Floyd Co. 12/4/62, paroled 4/3/63 City Point VA, residence stated on muster roll, house n/c, s 1,2,4.

ROBINETT, HIRAM. reg 39, co C, enr 9/10/62, enl 2/16/63 Peach Orchard, age 22, black hair, gray eyes, dark skin, 5-11, rem d 3/10/63 Louisa of disease, house 7-454, s 1,2,4.

ROBINETT, WILLIAM. reg 167WV, co Runyon, reg 39, co H, enr 8/1/63 Pike Co., age 31, dark hair, eyes & skin, 5-9, rem cap Buchanan Co. VA 8/15/63, d 1/19/64 Richmond VA or 6/11/65 Andersonville GA, house 7-710, s 1,2,4,8,23.

ROBINSON, DANIEL M. reg 39, co C, enr 4/18/63 Pike Co., dis 9/15/65 Louisville, age 21, dark hair, blue eyes, fair skin, 6-0, residence stated on muster roll, house n/c, s 1,2,4.

ROBINSON, HARVEY. reg 39, co B, enr 11/9/62 Piketon, enl 2/16/63 Peach Orchard, dis 9/15/65 Louisville, age 25, dark hair, blue eyes, fair skin, 5-5, house 7-69, s 1,2,4.

ROBINSON, RICHARD P. reg 39, co B, enr 10/30/62 Piketon, enl 2/16/63 Peach Orchard, dis 9/15/65 Louisville, age 24, light hair, blue eyes, fair skin, 6-0, house 7-1, s 1,2,4.

ROBINSON, SAMUEL. reg 39, co B, enr 9/6/62 Louisa, enl 2/16/63 Peach Orchard, dis 9/15/65 Louisville, age 44, black hair, gray eyes, fair skin, 5-7, house 7-515, s 1,2,4.

ROBNET, STEPHEN. reg 65, co D, r cpl, enl 5/21/64, dis 6/21/64, age 37, gray eyes, dark hair & skin, 5-8, house 7-503, s 2,4.
ROMANS, WILLIAM A. reg 39, co E, enr 11/24/64 Piketon, age 19, light hair, blue eyes, fair skin, 5-10, rem cap 2/1/63 Floyd Co., des 1/18/63 Peach Orchard, residence stated on muster roll, house n/c, s 1,2,4.
ROSS, JAMES. reg 39, co C, enr 9/10/62 Louisa, enl 2/16/63 Peach Orchard, dis 8/11/64, age 18, dark hair, gray eyes, fair skin, 5-8, residence stated on muster roll, house n/c, s 1,2,4.
ROWE, APPERSON. reg 14, co C, enr 10/25/61 Catlettsburg, enl 12/10/61 Louisa, age 22, light hair, blue eyes, fair skin, 5-9, rem d 11/28/62 Winchester of disease, residence stated on muster roll, house n/c, s 1,2,4.
ROWE, ARQUILLIS. reg 39, co I, enr 7/15/63 Pike Co., enl 8/29/63 Louisa, dis 9/15/65 Louisville, age 18, light hair, brown hair, fair skin, 5-9, house 7-83, s 1,2,4.
ROWE, BORILIUS. reg 39, co I, enr 5/14/63 Louisa, enl 8/29/63 Louisa, dis 9/15/65 Louisville, age 18, dark hair, gray eyes, fair skin, 5-5, house 7-83, s 1,2,4.
ROWE, HUFFMAN. reg 39, co D, enr 11/15/62 Pike Co., enl 2/16/63 Peach Orchard, age 33, dark hair & eyes, fair skin, 5-10, rem d 11/9/63 in rebel prison at Richmond VA, house 7-214, s 1,2,4.
ROWE, JACOB. reg 39, co D, enr 7/29/63, enl 8/30/63 Louisa, dis 9/15/65 Louisville, age 31, light hair, blue eyes, fair skin, 5-7, house 7-81, s 1,2,4.
ROWE, JOHN A. OR W. reg 14, co C, enr 10/25/61 Catlettsburg, enl 12/15/61 Catlettsburg, age 26, light hair, blue eyes, fair skin, 5-6, rem KIA 8/3/64 near Atlanta, house 7-56, s 1,2,4.
ROWE, LLOYD. reg 39, co D, enr 9/11/62 Pike Co., enl 2/16/63 Peach Orchard, dis 9/15/65 Louisville, age 34, light hair, blue eyes, fair skin, 5-9, house 7-93, s 1,2,4.
ROWE, REUBEN. reg 14, co C, enr 11/15/61, enl 12/15/61 Catlettsburg, dis 12/31/62 Lexington, age 21, light hair, blue eyes, fair skin, 5-7, rem dis for disability, back pain, heart fluttering & rheumatism, residence stated on muster roll, house n/c, s 1,2,4.
ROWE, REUBEN H. JR. reg 39, co D, enr 12/1/63 Pike Co., enl 12/27/63 Louisa, dis 9/15/65 Louisville, age 18, light hair, blue eyes, fair skin, 5-6, house 7-213, s 1,2,4,
ROWE, SOLOMON. reg 39, co D, r wagoner, enr 11/26/62, enl 2/16/63 Peach Orchard, dis 9/15/65 Louisville, age 40, residence stated on muster roll, house n/c, s 2,4.
ROWE, STEPHEN. reg 39, co D, enr 10/1/62 Pike Co., enl 2/16/63 Peach Orchard, age 34, dark hair, black eyes, fair skin, 5-8, rem dis 8/18/65 Louisa because of wounds received in action, house 7-80, s 1,2,4.
ROWE, STEPHEN W. reg 39, co D, enr 9/6/62, enl 2/16/63 Peach Orchard, age 29, dark hair, blue eyes, fair skin, 5-9, rem d 4/2/63 Louisa, house 7-91, s 1,2,4.
RUNYON, ALEXANDER. reg 39, co H, enr 1/28/63, enl 2/18/63 Peach Orchard, age 18, rem trans to co I, 3/1/63, residence stated on muster roll, house n/c, s 2,4.
RUNYON, THOMAS. reg 39, co E, r cpl, enr 11/13/62 Piketon, enl 2/16/63 Peach Orchard, dis 9/15/65 Louisville, age 30 or 32, light hair, blue eyes, fair skin, 6-1, house 7-258, s 1,2,4.

S

SANDERS, JACOB. reg 39, co D, enr 9/29/62, enl 2/16/63 Peach Orchard, dis 9/15/65 Louisville, age 25, light hair, blue eyes, fair skin, 5-7, house 7-197, s 1,2,4.
SCARBERRY, JACOB. reg 167WV, co Wm. Francis, reg 39, co H, enr 12/10/62, enl 2/16/63 Peach Orchard, dis 9/15/65 Louisville, age 23, dark hair, blue eyes, fair skin, 5-6, house 7-705, s 1,2,4,23.
SCARBERRY, JOHN. reg 167WV, co Wm. Francis, reg 39, co H, enr 12/10/62 Pike Co., enl 2/16/63 Peach Orchard, dis 9/15/65 Louisville, age 27, dark hair, eyes & skin, 5-5, house 7-705, s 1,2,4,23.

SCARBERRY, THOMAS. reg 39, co H, enr 12/10/62 Pike Co. or Peach Orchard, enl 2/16/63 Peach Orchard, dis 9/15/65 Louisville, age 30, dark hair & skin, black eyes, 5-4, rem residence established by descriptive muster roll, house n/c, s 1,2,4.

SCARBERRY, WILLIAM. reg 167WV, co Wm. Francis, reg 39, co H, enr 12/10/62, enl 2/16/63 Peach Orchard, dis 9/15/65 Louisville, age 28, dark hair, eyes & skin, 5-9, house 7-706, s 1,2,4,23.

SCOTT, HENDERSON. reg 39, co E, enr 7/2/63 Piketon, enl 10/31/63 Catlettsburg, dis 9/15/65 Louisville, age 20, light hair, blue eyes, fair skin, 5-6, house 7-450, s 1,2,4.

SCOTT, THOMAS. reg CG, co E, enr 6/9/64, enl 7/4/64 Frankfort, rem des 12/29/64 Paintsville, house 7-642, s 2,4.

SCOTT, WILLIAM M. reg 39, co E, r 1st sgt, enr 11/15/62 Piketon, enl 2/16/63 Peach Orchard, age 25, red hair, yellow eyes, fair skin, 5-7, rem dis 10/31/64 Lexington for disability, house 7-475, s 1,2,4.

SHORTRIDGE, ANDREW. reg 14, co H, enr 10/25/61 Catlettsburg, enl 12/10/61 Louisa, age 22, fair hair & skin, blue eyes, 6-0, rem des 5/4/62, residence stated on muster roll, house n/c, s 1,2,4.

SHORTRIDGE, JEFF. reg 14, 39, co D, enr 9/20/62 Piketon, enl 2/16/63 Peach Orchard, dis 9/15/65 Louisville, age 18, light hair, blue eyes, fair skin, 5-8, rem originally enlisted in co H, 14th Ky. Inf, trans from 39th to 14th 3/21/63, trans to co D, 39th 1/20/65, house 7-345, s 1,2,4.

SHORTRIDGE, JOSEPH. reg 14, co H, enr 10/25/61 Louisa, enl 3/14/64 Louisa, dis 9/15/65 Louisville, age 20, fair hair & skin, blue eyes, 5-7, rem trans to 14th Vet Inf, co A, enr 2/29/64, m/in 3/14/64 Louisa, house 7-345, s 1,2,4.

SIPPLE, JOHN S. reg 39, co C, r cpl, enr 10/11/62 Pike Co., enl 2/16/63 Peach Orchard, age 20, dark hair & skin, gray eyes, 5-5, rem d 2/7/63 Peach Orchard, house 7-868, s 1,2,4.

SIPPLE, LEROY B. reg 39, co I, enr 9/15/62 Peach Orchard, enl 2/16/63 Peach Orchard, age 30, light hair, blue eyes, fair skin, 6-0, rem d 5/11/63 Ashland of disease, house 7-10, s 1,2,4.

SLATER, NAPOLEON. reg 39, co I, enr 9/1/63 Peach Orchard, enl 10/30/63 Louisa, dis 9/15/65 Louisville, age 27, dark hair & skin, gray eyes, 6-0, house 7-599, s 1,2,4.

SLONE, JARRETT. reg 39, co D, enr 11/15/62 Pike Co., enl 2/16/63 Peach Orchard, age 22, black hair, gray eyes, fair skin, 6-0, rem d 4/10/63 Ashland of typhoid fever, house 7-526, s 1,2,4.

SLONE, MORGAN. reg 39, co I, enr 11/12/62 Peach Orchard, enl 2/16/63 Peach Orchard, age 26, rem cap 2/1/63 Pike Co., des time & place unknown, house 7-275, s 1,2,4.

SLONE, SIMEON. reg 39, co I, enr 11/10/62 Peach Orchard, enl 2/16/63 Peach Orchard, dis 9/15/65 Louisville, age 18, auburn hair, hazel eyes, fair skin, 5-11, cap 2/1/63 Pike Co., house 7-529, s 1,2,4.

SMALLWOOD, ELIJAH R. reg 39, co D, enr 9/6/62 Pike Co., enl 2/16/63 Peach Orchard, age 43, dark hair, eyes, & skin, 6-2, rem dis 2/15/64 Louisa for chronic bronchitis, house 1-14, s 1,2,4.

SMALLWOOD, JOHN. reg 39, co D, enr 9/6/62 Pike Co., enl 2/16/63 Peach Orchard, dis 9/15/65 Louisville, age 20, light hair, gray eyes, fair skin, 5-9, house 1-14, s 1,2,4.

SMALLWOOD, WILLIAM H. reg 39, co D, enr 9/6/62 Pike Co., enl 2/16/63 Peach Orchard, dis 9/15/65 Louisville, age 18, light hair, blue eyes, fair skin, 5-11, house 1-14, s 1,2,4.

SMITH, ALI. reg CG, co G, enr 7/16/64, enl 8/8/64 Frankfort, dis 3/11/65 Catlettsburg, age 53, house 7-606, s 2,4.

SMITH, CURTIS. reg 167WV, co Wm. Francis, reg 39, co D, enr 11/10/62 Pike Co., enl 2/16/63 Peach Orchard, age 21, black hair, blue eyes, fair skin, 5-6, rem d 4/8/63 Ashland typhoid fever, house 7-774, s 1,2,4,23.

SMITH, JEREMIAH. reg 39, co C, enr 11/15/62 Peach Orchard, enl 2/16/63 Peach Orchard, dis 9/15/65 Louisville, age 18, dark hair, gray eyes, fair skin, 5-11, house 7-413, s 1,2,4.

SMITH, JONATHAN. reg 39, co H, enr 8/5/63 Pike Co., enl 8/29/63 Louisa, dis 9/15/65 Louisville, age 35 or 37, dark hair, eyes & skin, 5-10, house 7-749, s 1,2,4.

SMITH, MILTON. reg 39, co C, enr 11/15/62 Peach Orchard, enl 2/16/63 Peach Orchard, dis 9/15/65 Louisville, age 18, dark hair & skin, gray eyes, 5-7, house 7-413, s 1,2,4.

SMITH, ROBERT. reg 39, co C, enr 11/8/62 Peach Orchard, enl 2/16/63 Peach Orchard, dis 9/15/65 Louisville, age 26, dark hair & skin, blue eyes, 5-9, house 7-442, s 1,2,4.

SMITH, WILLIAM. reg 39, co C, enr 9/10/62 Peach Orchard, enl 2/16/63 Peach Orchard, age 20 or 26, light hair, gray eyes, fair skin, 5-10, rem d 8/3/63 Ashland of pneumonia, typhoid fever & diarrhea, house 7-972, s 1,2,4.

SMITH, WILLIAM. reg 167WV, co Wm. Francis, house 7-782, s 23.

SOUTHARDS, BLUFORD. reg 39, co K, enr 12/25/62 Peach Orchard, enl 2/16/63 Peach Orchard, age 32, light hair, blue eyes, fair skin, 5-11, rem des 3/24/63 Louisa, residence stated on muster roll, house n/c, s 1,2,4.

SOWARDS, ANDREW J. reg 39, co C, enr 11/18/62 Peach Orchard, enl 2/16/63 Peach Orchard, age 23, rem d 3/31/63 Louisa of pneumonia, house 7-180, s 1,2,4.

SOWARDS, GEORGE W. reg 65, co B, E, enl 5/21/64, dis 6/21/64, age 19, light hair, blue eyes, fair skin, 5-7, reg 45, co H, enr 7/14/63, enl 2/6/64 Mt. Sterling, dis 2/14/65 Catlettsburg, rem assigned to 39th Ky Inf to make up four months lost by desertion, house 7-167, s 1,2,4.

SOWARDS, HARMON. reg 65, co B, enl 5/21/64, rem des 5/30/64, house 7-167, s 4.

SOWARDS, HENRY C. reg 14, co H, enr 10/25/61 Catlettsburg, enl 12/10/61 Louisa, dis 1/31/65 Louisa, age 19, dark hair & eyes, fair skin, reg 39, co E, r 1st sgt, enr 9/26/62 Peach Orchard, enl 2/16/63 Peach Orchard, age 19, light hair, gray eyes, fair skin, 5-7, rem trans to co E, 39th Ky Inf, back to co H, 14th Ky Inf 1/20/65, prom to 1st sgt 3/1/63, house 1-28, s 1,2,4.

SOWARDS, JAMES M. reg 39, co E, r 1st lt, enr & enl 3/12/63 Louisa, age 26, rem prom from 2nd lt to 1st lt 3/12/63, res 2/21/65, house 1-27, s 2,4.

SOWARDS, LEWIS. reg 14, co H, enr 10/25/61 Catlettsburg, enl 12/10/61 Louisa, age 45 or 50 or 54, reg 39, co E, r capt, enr 9/13/62 Peach Orchard, enl 2/16/63 Peach Orchard, age 44, rem resigned 11/17/64 on surgeon's certificate of disability, chronic diarrhea, house 1-28, s 1,2,4.

SOWARDS, MARTIN B. reg 39, co C, enr 11/8/62 Louisa, enl 2/16/63 Peach Orchard, age 23, light hair, gray eyes, fair skin, 5-8, rem d 3/30/63 Louisa of typhoid & pneumonia, house 7-181, s 1,2,4.

SOWARDS, MORGAN C. W. reg 14, co H, enr 10/25/61 Catlettsburg, enl 12/10/61, age 27 or 35, reg 68, co E, enl 5/21/64, dark hair & skin, gray eyes, 5-7, rem des, house 1-28, s 1,2,4.

SOWARDS, THOMAS JEFFERSON. reg 14, co H, enr 10/25/61 Catlettsburg, enl 12/10/61 Louisa, dis 1/31/65 Louisa, age 20 or 29, reg 39, co C, r capt, enr 11/18/62 Peach Orchard, enl 2/16/63 Peach Orchard, age 26, rem resigned 3/27/65 because of deafness, house 7-27, s 1,2,4,8.

SOWARDS, WILLIAM H. reg 39, co E, r 5th sgt, enr 9/10/62 Peach Orchard, enl 2/16/63 Peach Orchard, dis 9/15/65 Louisville, age 18, dark hair, yellow eyes, fair skin, 5-4, house 1-28, s 1,2,4.

SPEARS, ARNETT C. reg 39, co D, enr 7/20/63 Pike Co., enl 8/30/63 Louisa, dis 9/15/65 Louisa, age 18, light hair, blue eyes, fair skin, 5-5, house 7-88, s 1,2,4.

SPEARS, GEORGE W. reg 39, co D, enr 9/3/63 Louisa, enl 10/29/63 Louisa, dis 9/15/65 Louisa, age 39, dark hair, blue eyes, fair skin, 5-11, house 7-88, s 1,2,4.

STACY, WILLIAM. reg 39, co C, enr 11/4/62 Pikeville, enl 2/16/63 Peach Or-chard, dis 9/15/65 Louisville, age 18, light hair, gray eyes, fair skin, 5-6, rem residence established by descriptive muster roll, house 7-527, s 1,2,3.

STAFFORD, ELEXIUS. reg 39, co I, enr 11/24/62 Peach Orchard, enl 2/16/63, age 21, dark hair, fair skin, blue eyes, 5-10, rem cap 2/1/63 Pike Co., taken to Richmond, Va., 4/1/63, paroled City Point, Md., 4/3/63, d 3/19/65 Ashland, typhoid fever, house 7-793, s 1,2.

STAFFORD, FLEMMON. reg 167WV, co U. Runyon, reg 39, co H, enr 12/18/62 Pike Co., enl 2/16/63 Peach Orchard, age 38, fair hair & skin, blue eyes, 5-9, rem dis 2/26/64 Catlettsburg on surgeon's certificate of disability, chronic rheumatism, house 7-793, s 1,2,4,23.

STAFFORD, JOHN F. reg 39, co H, enr 1/28/63 Lawrence Co., enl 2/16/63 Peach Orchard, dis 9/15/65 Louisville, age 19, house 7-793, s 1,2,4.

STAIR, LEVI. reg 39, co C, enr 11/2/62 Peach Orchard, enl 2/16/63 Peach Orchard, dis 9/15/65 Louisville, age 35, house 7-581, s 1,2,4.

STAIR, MADISON. reg 167WV, co Sampson Kirk, house 7-580, s 23.

STEEL, PARIS. reg 14, co C, enr 10/25/61 Louisa, enl 1/10/61 Louisa, dis 9/15/65 Louisville, age 18, light hair, blue eyes, fair skin, 5-8, rem trans to 14th Vet Inf., co A, enr 2/29/64, m/in 3/19/64 Catlettsburg, prom to cpl 10/10/62, to sgt 8/12/65, house 7-884, s 1,2 4.

STEPP, JOHN. reg 167WV, co Sampson Kirk, house 7-558, s 23.

STEPP, THOMAS. reg 167WV, co Sampson Kirk, house 7-558, s 23.

STEWART, ABRAHAM. reg 68, co B, enl 4/7/64, 5/21/64, dis 4/16/64, 6/21/64, age 25, black eyes & hair, dark skin, 5-8, house 7-150, s 2,4.

STILTNER, CLAIBORNE W. reg 39, co H, enr 11/25/62 Peach Orchard, enl 2/16/63 Peach Orchard, dis 9/15/65 Louisville, age 18, dark hair, blue eyes, fair skin, 5-4, residence stated on muster roll, house n/c, s 1,2,4.

STILTNER, FREDERICK. reg 39, co I, enr 11/20/62 Peach Orchard, enl 2/16/63 Peach Orchard, dis 9/15/65 Louisville, age 37, black hair, hazel eyes, fair skin, 5-10, rem prom to sgt 2/16/64, reduced to ranks 5/12/65, residence stated on muster roll, house n/c, s 1,2,4.

STRATTON, ALEXANDER W. reg 39, co C, enr 9/10/62 Peach Orchard, enl 2/16/63 Peach Orchard, dis 9/15/65 Louisville, age 23, dark hair, gray eyes, fair skin, 6-0, house 7-464, s 1,2,4.

STRATTON, HARVEY. reg 39, co C, enr 9/10/62 Peach Orchard, enl 2/16/63 Peach Orchard, dis 9/15/65 Louisville, age 23, dark hair, blue eyes, fair skin, 5-11, house 7-466, s 1,2,4.

STRATTON, HENRY. reg 39, co C, enr 9/10/62 Peach Orchard, enl 2/16/63 Peach Orchard, dis 9/15/65 Louisville, age 19, light hair, blue eyes, fair skin, 5-9, house 7-458, s,1,2,4.

STRATTON, HIRAM W. reg 39, co C, enr 9/10/62 Peach Orchard, enl 2/16/63 Peach Orchard, dis 9/15/65 Louisville, age 28, light hair, blue eyes, fair skin, 5-11, residence stated on muster roll, house n/c, s 1,2,4.

STRATTON, RICHARD. reg 39, co D, enr 9/10/62 Pike Co., enl 2/16/63 Peach Orchard, dis 9/15/65 Louisville, age 30, light hair, blue eyes, fair skin, 6-0, house 7-457, s 1,2,4.

STRATTON, TANDY. reg 39, co C, enr 9/10/62 Peach Orchard, enl 2/16/63 Peach Orchard, dis 9/15/65 Louisville, age 21, dark hair, blue eyes, fair skin, 5-10, house 7-458, s 1,2,4.

STRATTON, WILLIAM H. reg 39, co C, enr 9/10/62 Louisa, enl 6/11/63 Louisa, dis 9/15/65 Louisville, age 26, dark hair, blue eyes, fair skin, 5-9, house 7-460, s 1,2,4.

STUMP, ANDREW J. reg 39, co H, enr 7/19/63 Pike Co., dis 9/64, age 24, dark hair & skin, blue eyes, 5-11, house 7-376, s 1,5.

STUMP, GEORGE. reg 167WV, co Wm. Francis, house 7-377, s 23.

STUMP. HENRY. reg 39, co I, enr 11/18/62 Peach Orchard, enl 2/16/63 Peach Orchard, age 23, dark hair, blue eyes, fair skin, 5-11, rem d 3/28/64 Ashland typhoid fever, house 7-381, s 1,2,4.

STUMP, JAMES. reg 167WV, co Wm. Francis, reg 39, co H, r 2nd lt, enr 12/30/62 Peach Orchard, enl 2/16/63 Peach Orchard, dis 9/15/65 Louisville, age 21, dark hair, blue eyes, fair skin, 6-0, rem prom from 1st sgt to 2nd lt 1/13/64, house 7-306, s 1,2,4.

STUMP, LORENZO D. reg 167WV, co Wm. Francis, reg 39, co E, enr 7/20/63 Pike Co., enl 8/29/63 Louisa, age 18, fair hair & skin, blue eyes, 5-8, house 7-376, s 1,2,4.

SWINDAL, JOHN W. reg 39, co K, r 1st sgt, enr 11/18/62 Peach Orchard, enl 2/16/63 Peach Orchard, dis 9/15/65 Louisville, age 36, black hair, blue eyes, fair skin, 5-9, residence stated on muster roll, house n/c, s 1,2,4.

SWINEY, SPENCER. reg 39, co D, enr 12/18/63 Pike Co., enl 12/27/63 Louisa, dis 9/15/65 Louisville, age 29, light hair, blue eyes, fair skin, 5-7, house 7-110, s 1,2,4.

SWORD, JOHN W. reg 39, co K, r cpl, enr 11/18/62 Piketon, enl 2/16/63 Peach Orchard, age 21, black hair & eyes, dark skin, 5-8, rem d 21/21/64 Ashland smallpox, house 1-10, s 1,2,4.

SWORD, WILLIAM. reg 39, co K, r sgt, enr 10/18/62 Pike Co. or Peach Or-chard, enl 2/16/63 Peach Orchard, dis 9/15/65 Louisville, age 43, dark hair, blue eyes, fair skin, 5-9, rem cap Pike Co. 8/25/63, confined at Richmond VA, paroled City Point VA 3/7/64, house 1-10, s 1,2,4,8.

SWORD, WILLIAM H. reg 39, co K, r cpl, enr 10/26/62 Peach Orchard, enl 2/16/63 Peach Orchard, dis 9/15/65 Louisville, age 23, dark hair, blue eyes, fair skin, 5-8, rem residence established by descriptive muster roll, house n/c, s 1,2,4,8.

SYCK, DANIEL W. reg 39, co D, enr 10/6/62 Pike Co., enl 2/16/63 Peach Or-chard, dis 9/15/65 Louisville, age 21, dark hair, gray eyes, fair skin, 5-4, house 7-958, s 1,2,4.

SYCK, GEORGE W. reg 39, co D, enr 10/6/62 Pike Co., enl 2/16/63 Peach Or-chard, dis 9/15/65 Louisville, age 23, light hair, blue eyes, fair skin, 5-9, house 7-958, s 1,2,4.

T

TACKETT, BENJAMIN. reg 39, co B, enr 9/6/62 Peach Orchard, enl 2/16/63 Peach Orchard, dis 9/15/65 Louisville, age 24, dark hair, blue eyes, fair skin, 5-9, house 1-82, s 1,2,4.

TACKETT, GEORGE. reg 39, co B, enr 11/16/62 Peach Orchard, enl 2/16/63 Peach Orchard, dis 9/15/65 Louisville, age 19, light hair, blue eyes, fair skin, 5-7, house 1-115, s 1,2,4.

TACKETT, HARVEY. reg 39, co B, enr 11/7/62 Peach Orchard, enl 2/16/63 Peach Orchard, dis 9/15/65 Louisville, age 23, dark hair, blue eyes, fair skin, 5-7, house 1-114, s 1,2,4.

TACKETT, ROBERT. reg 39, co K, enr 11/24/62 Peach Orchard, enl 2/16/63 Peach Orchard, dis 9/15/65 Louisville, age 22, dark hair, blue eyes, fair skin, 5-10, house 1-110, s 1,2,4.

TACKETT, WILLIAM. reg 39, co B, enr 11/7/62 Pike Co. or Peach Orchard, enl 2/16/63 Peach Orchard, dis 9/15/65 Louisville, age 32, light hair, blue eyes, fair skin, 5-6, house 1-121, s 1,2,4.

TAYLOR, ALVIS. reg 39, co E, enr 11/9/62 Peach Orchard, enl 2/16/63 Peach Orchard, age 26, light hair, gray eyes, fair skin, 5-10, rem cap 2/1/63 Pike Co., des 9/19/63 Louisa, residence stated on muster roll, house n/c, s 1,2,4.

TAYLOR, ANDREW C. reg 14, co H, enr 10/25/61 Catlettsburg, enl 12/10/61 Louisa, age 27, dark hair, eyes & skin, 5-4, residence stated on muster roll, house n/c, s 1,2,4.

TAYLOR, JOHN. reg 14, co H, enr 10/25/61 Catlettsburg, enl 12/10/61 Louisa, age 24, dark hair, eyes & skin, 5-6, rem d 2/15/62 Paintsville camp fever, house 7-812, s 1,2,4.

TAYLOR, WILLIAM A. reg 39, co E, enr Pike Co. or Peach Orchard, enl 2/16/63 Peach Orchard, dis 9/15/65 Louisville, age 41, light hair, blue eyes, fair skin, 5-9, house 7-668, s 1,2,4.

THACKER, THOMAS. reg 39, co I, enr 11/10/62 Peach Orchard, enl 2/16/63 Peach Orchard, age 38, rem cap 2/1/63 Pike Co., des date & place unknown, residence established by descriptive muster roll, house n/c, s 1,2,4.

THOMPSON, ALBERT. reg 39, co D, r cpl, enr 11/15/62 Pike Co., enl 2/16/63 Peach Orchard, dis 9/15/65 Louisville, age 28, light hair, blue eyes, fair skin, 5-7, house 7-852, s 1,2,4.

THOMPSON, SAMUEL. reg 39, co D, enr 10/6/62 Pike Co., enl 2/16/63 Peach Orchard, dis 9/15/65 Louisville, age 36, light hair, blue eyes, fair skin, 5-11, house 7-944, s 1,2,4.

THORNSBERRY, LEVI. reg 14, co H, enr 10/25/61 Catlettsburg, enl 12/10/61 Louisa, dis 1/31/65 Louisa, age 40, dark hair & skin, blue eyes, 5-10, rem dis for disability, dropsy 2/15/64, reg 39, co D, rem trans from 39th Ky Inf 3/21/63, house 1-24, s 1,2,4.

THORNSBURY, JAMES M. reg 14, co H, enr 10/25/61 Louisa, enl 12/10/61 Louisa, dis 1/31/65 Louisa, age 25 or 35, dark hair, blue eyes, fair skin, 5-7, reg 39, enr 11/25/62 Peach Orchard, enl 2/16/63 Peach Orchard, dis 9/15/65 Louisville, age 24, rem des from 14th Ky Inf 1/11/62 Prestonsburg, cap Turman's ferry 1/9/64, escaped from prison 12/1/64, prom from 2nd lt to 1st lt 1/13/64, house 7-316, s 1,2,4.

THORNBURY, MARTIN. reg 39, co D, r major, enr 9/6/62 Pike Co., enl 2/16/63 Peach Orchard, dis 9/15/65 Louisville, age 34, dark hair, blue eyes, fair skin, 5-11, rem prom from capt to major 3/31/65, house 7-339, s 1,2,4.

THORNBURY, WALTER. reg 14, co H, enr 10/21/61 Catlettsburg, enl 12/10/61 Lawrence Co., age 34, reg 39, co D, r 2nd lt, enr 9/6/62 Pike Co., enl 2/16/63 Peach Orchard, age 36, light hair, blue eyes, fair skin, 5-7, rem des 14th Ky Inf, KIA 9/22/63 by bushwhackers mouth of Marrowbone Creek, Pike Co., house 7-338, s 1,2,4.

TRIVETTE, NATHANIEL C. reg 39, co E, enr 11/22/62 Piketon or Peach Orchard, age 25, dark hair, black eyes, fair skin, 5-9, rem d 5/27/63 Ashland of pneumonia, house 7-185, s 1,2,4.

V

VANOVER, DAVID. reg 39, co B, enr 8/13/63 Louisa, enl 8/29/63 Louisa, dis 9/15/65 Louisville, age 24, dark hair, blue eyes, fair skin, 6-5, house 7-177, s 1,2,4.

VANOVER, ELIJAH. reg 65, co A, enl 5/21/64, dis 6/21/64, house 7-178, s 2,4.

VANOVER, HENRY. reg 39, co B, enr 6/3/63 Louisa, enl 6/10/63 Louisa, dis 9/15/65 Louisville, age 28, dark hair, blue eyes, fair skin, 6-2, house 7-178, s 1,2,4.

VARNEY, ALEXANDER. reg 39, co E, enr 11/10/62 Piketon, enl 11/10/62, dis 9/15/65 Louisville, age 26, light hair, blue eyes, fair skin, 5-10, house 7-668, s 2,4.

W

WAGGONER, TOBIAS. reg 39, co D, r 1st sgt, enr 11/6/62 Pike Co., enl 2/16/63 Peach Orchard, dis 9/15/65 Louisville, age 37, brown hair, gray eyes, fair skin, 6-0, rem prom to sgt 7/1/65, house 7-896, s 1,2,4.

WALLACE, AMOS. reg 39, co H, enr 1/28/63 Peach Orchard, enl 2/16/63 Peach Orchard, age 43, dark hair & skin, blue eyes, 5-5, rem cap Pike Co. 3/10/63, confined at Richmond VA, paroled City Point VA 4/13/63, trans to co G or I 8/15/63, residence stated on muster roll, house n/c, s 1,2,4.

WALLACE, SOLOMON. reg 39, co G, enr 10/24/63 Louisa, enl 10/29/63 Louisa, age 44, light hair, blue eyes, fair skin, 5-9, rem d 6/9/64 Louisa of consumption, house 7-698, s 1,2,4.

WALTERS, JOHN E. reg 39, co C, r 1st sgt, enr 9/10/62 Peach Orchard, enl 2/16/63 Peach Orchard, age 19, dark hair & skin, black eyes, 5-5, rem dis 4/22/65 to accept commission in 6th Colored Cavalry, prom to 2nd lt, U.S. Colored Cavalry, house 7-899, s 1,2,4.

WALTERS, WILLIAM (WILBURN). reg 39, co C, r cpl, enr 9/10/62 Louisa, enl 2/16/63 Peach Orchard, dis 9/15/65 Louisville, age 36, dark hair & skin, black eyes, 5-10, rem prom to cpl 1/1/65, house 7-896, s 1,2,4.

WEAVER, PLEASANT. reg 39, co E, enr 11/29/62 Peach Orchard, enl 2/16/63 Peach Orchard, dis 9/15/65 Louisville, age 29, fair hair & skin, blue eyes, 5-10, rem cap 2/10/63 Pike Co., trans to co H 12/20/63, house 1-137, s 1,2,4.

WEDDINGTON, HENRY. reg 39, co D, enr 9/6/62 Pike Co., enl 2/16/63 Peach Orchard, dis 9/15/65 Louisville, age 26, dark hair, blue eyes, fair skin, 5-5, rem cap 7/2/63, paroled City Point VA 7/14/63, house 7-887, s 1,2,4.

WEDDINGTON, JACOB. reg 39, co A, enr 9/12/62 Louisa, enl 2/16/63 Peach Orchard, age 44, dark hair & skin, black eyes, 5-8, rem d 2/5/65 Ashland chronic diarrhea, house 7-468, s 1,2,4.

WEDDINGTON, WILLIAM. reg 39, co D, r 2nd lt, enr 9/6/62 Pike Co., enl 2/16/63 Peach Orchard, dis 9/15/65 Louisville, age 22, dark hair, black eyes, fair skin, 5-9, rem prom from sgt to 2nd lt 6/1/65, house 7-468, s 1,2,4.

WEDDINGTON, WILLIAM. reg 40, co E, enr 10/25/63 Grayson, enl 3/10/64 Paris, dis 12/20/64 Catlettsburg, age 18, light hair, hazel eyes, fair skin, 5-7, house 7-891, s 1,2,4.

WEDDINGTON, W. M. reg 68, co C, enl 5/21/64, dis 6/22/64, light hair, blue eyes, fair skin, 6-2, house 7-887, s 2,4.

WHERLEY, HARVEY. reg 39, co K, r wagoner, enr 11/20/62 Peach Orchard, enl 2/16/63 Peach Orchard, dis 9/15/65 Louisville, age 20 or 40, residence stated on muster roll, house n/c, s 1,2,4.

WHITE, DAVID. reg 39, co I, enr 11/24/62 Pike Co., enl 2/16/63 Peach Orchard, dis 9/15/65 Louisville, age 18, dark hair, gray eyes, fair skin, 5-5, residence stated on muster roll, house n/c, s 1,2,4.

WHITE, EDWARD. reg 39, co I, enr 11/24/62 Pike Co., enl 2/16/63 Peach Orchard, age 20, dark hair & skin, blue eyes, 5-4, rem d 1/9/65 Louisa, smallpox, residence stated on muster roll, house n/c, s 1,2,4.

WHITE, HARRISON. reg 14, co C, enr 1/25/61 Louisa, enl 12/10/61 Catlettsburg, dis 9/15/65 Louisville, age 22, dark hair, black eyes, fair skin, 5-7, rem trans to 14th Vet Inf, co A, enr 2/29/64, m/in 3/19/64 Catlettsburg, house 7-25, s 1,2,4.

WHITE, HENLEY. reg 14, co C, enr 11/15/61 Catlettsburg, enl 12/15/61 Catlettsburg, dis 9/15/65 Louisville, age 21, light hair, dark eyes, fair skin, 6-0, rem trans to 14th Vet Inf, co A, enr 2/29/64, m/in 3/19/64 Catlettsburg, house 7-69, s 1,2,4.

WHITE, JAMES. reg 167WV, co U. Runyon, reg 39, co I, enr 11/24/62 Pike Co., age 22, dark hair, gray eyes, fair skin, 5-7, rem d 1/1/63 Peach Orchard, inflammation of the brain, residence stated on muster roll, house n/c, s 1,2,4,23.

WHITE, LEWIS. reg 39, co D, enr 10/8/63 Pike Co., enl 10/29/63 Louisa, age 18, light hair, blue eyes, fair skin, 5-7, rem d 3/4/64 Louisa typhoid fever, house 7-64, s 1,2,4.

WHITE, PYRUS. reg 39, co I, enr 11/30/62 Pike Co., age 36, dark hair, gray eyes, fair skin, 5-8, rem d 12/25/62 Peach Orchard inflammation of liver, residence stated on muster roll, house n/c, s 1,2,4.

WHITE, SYLVESTER. reg 39, co I, enr 11/30/62 Piketon, enl 2/16/63 Peach Orchard, dis 9/15/65 Louisville, age 34, light hair, blue eyes, fair skin, 5-5, residence stated on muster roll, house n/c, s 1,2,4.

WHITT, WILLIAM. reg 39, co E, enr/10/62 Piketon, enl 2/16/63 Peach Orchard, age 30, dark hair, blue eyes, fair skin, 5-8, rem cap 1/1/63 Pike Co, des 3/7/63 Louisa, house 7-840, s 1,2,4.

WILLIAMS, ACHILLAS M. reg 39, co H, enr 2/28/63 Louisa, enl 6/10/63, dis 9/15/65 Louisville, age 20, dark hair & skin, blue eyes, 5-5, house 7-399, s 1,2,4.

WILLIAMS, ELIJAH. reg 39, co C, enr 11/18/62, enl 2/16/63 Peach Orchard, age 18, rem trans to co E, 39th Ky Inf, residence stated on muster roll, house n/c, s 2,4.

WILLIAMS, JOHN W. reg 68, co E, enl 5/21/64, age 42, dark hair & skin, light eyes, 5-10, house 7-391, s 4.

WILLIAMS, WILLIAM. reg CG, co E, enr 5/17/64, enl 7/4/64 Frankfort, dis 3/11/65 Catlettsburg, house 7-390, s 2,4.

WILLIAMS, WILLIAM H. reg 39, co H, r sgt, enr 1/14/63 Peach Orchard, enl 2/16/63 Peach Orchard, dis 9/15/65 Louisville, age 22, dark hair & skin, black eyes, 5-6, rem prom to sgt 4/9/63, house 7-399, s 1,2,4.

WILLIAMSON, BENJAMIN. reg 39, co E, r 1st sgt, enr 10/6/62 Piketon, enl 2/16/63 Peach Orchard, age 44, light hair, blue eyes, fair skin, 5-10, rem d 4/18/63 Louisa, house 7-845, s 1,2,4.

WILLIAMSON, ELIJAH. reg 39, co E, enr 9/10/62 Pike Co., enl 2/16/63 Peach Orchard, dis 9/15/65 Louisville, age 18, dark hair, blue eyes, fair skin, 5-8, rem trans to co C, 10/29/63, wounded at Cynthiana, 6/11/64, house 7-828, s 1,2,4.

WILLIAMSON, JAMES. reg 39, co A, enr 10/27/62 Johnson Co., enl 2/16/63 Peach Orchard, dis 9/15/65 Louisville, age 18, light hair, blue eyes, fair skin, 5-5, house 7-845, s 1,2,4.

WILLIAMSON, JOHN B. reg 39, co E, enr 10/6/62 Piketon, enl 2/16/63 Peach Orchard, age 21, light hair, blue eyes, fair skin, 5-10, rem d 6/7/64 Ashland, house 7-845, s 1,2,4.

WILSON, ASA. reg 167WV, co U. Runyon, reg 39, co D, enr 11/15/62 Pike Co., enl 2/16/63 Peach Orchard, dis 9/15/65 Louisville, age 30, red hair, black eyes, fair skin, 5-10, rem cap in battle 7/2/63 mouth of Card, Pike Co., held at Richmond VA until 7/12/63, paroled at City Point VA, wounded Cynthiana 6/11/64, house 7-693, s 1,2,4,23.

WILSON, HENRY. reg 167WV, co Wm. Francis, house 7-694, s 23.

WOLFORD, ANDREW. reg 167WV, co Wm. Francis, house 7-754, s 23.

WOLFORD, DANIEL JR. reg 167WV, co Wm. Francis, reg 39, co D, enr 1/28/63 Pike Co., enl 2/16/63 Peach Orchard, dis 9/15/65 Louisville, age 23, dark hair & skin, blue eyes, 5-9, rem trans from co H to co D 3/1/63, wounded mouth of Card 7/2/63 Pike Co., house 7-762, s 1,2,4,23.

WOLFORD, DANIEL SR. reg 167WV, co Wm. Francis, house 7-753, s 23.

WOLFORD, FREDERICK. reg 167WV, co Wm. Francis, reg 39, co I, enr 2/25/65, enl 4/12/65 Covington, dis 9/15/65 Louisville, age 19, dark hair, blue eyes, fair skin, 5-8, house 7-758, s 1,2,23.

WOLFORD, GEORGE. reg 167WV, co U. Runyon, reg 39, co D, enr 11/20/62 Pike Co., enl 6/10/63 Louisa, dis 9/15/65 Louisville, age 21, black hair, blue eyes, fair skin, 6-1, rem cap 12/6/62 Pike Co., paroled City Point VA 4/3/63, house 7-757, s 1,2,4,23.

WORKMAN, DANIEL (DAVID). reg 39, co I, r cpl, enr 6/7/63 Pike Co., enl 8/29/63 Peach Orchard, dis 9/15/65 Louisville, age 30, house 7-872, s 1,2,4.

Y

YATES, HOWARD. reg 39, co D, enr 11/11/62 Pike Co., enl 2/16/63 Peach Orchard, dis 9/15/65 Louisville, age 19, light hair, yellow eyes, fair skin, 5-7, rem cap 7/2/63, confined at Richmond VA, paroled City Point VA 7/14/63, house 7-351, s 1,2,4.

YATES, JOHN. reg 39, co I, enr 11/20/62 Pike Co., enl 2/16/63 Peach Orchard, dis 9/15/65 Louisville, age 23, light hair, blue eyes, fair skin, 5-8, residence stated on muster roll, house n/c, s 1,2,4.

YOST, LORENZO D. reg 39, co B, enr 9/6/62 Peach Orchard, enl 2/16/63 Peach Orchard, dis 9/15/65 Louisville, age 30, dark hair & skin, blue eyes, 5-11, house 7-968, s 1,2,4.

YOUNG, GEORGE. reg 167WV, co Sampson Kirk, house 7-563, s 23.

SOLDIERS WHO SERVED IN BOTH ARMIES

The following is a list of soldiers who served on both sides during the war. Unit designations include regiment and company.

Name	Confederate Unit	Union Unit	County
Jesse B. Adams	13D	39K	Letcher
Moses Adams	13A	39F	Letcher
Spencer Adams	5F	45F	Letcher
Samuel Adkins	5B	39B	Pike
Samuel Peter Adkins	13C	5USVol	Morgan
Amburgey, John W.	5F,13A	USArmy	Letcher
James K. P. Auxier	5E	65C	Johnson
Henry Bailey	13C	5USVol	Magoffin
James Bailey	13C	5USVol	Magoffin
William Baldridge	5F	65C	Johnson
Alexander Baldwin	5G	39B	Floyd
Jarvy Baldwin	5G	39B	Floyd
James Bartley	10K, 21VA, VSL5	45I	Pike
Isaac Belcher	5C	CGG	Pike
May Bentley	13D	39K	Letcher
William Bentley	13D	39K	Floyd
Willoughby Biggs	13F	39F	Floyd
John Blankenship	5Riffe	45F	Lawrence
Presley Blankenship	10H, 2VSL	39H	Pike
Daniel Blevins	5B,K, FR	65D	Johnson
Lewis Blevins	5B,E	65E	Johnson
Elijah Boggs	13D	HarF	Letcher
Henry Boggs	13D	HarF	Letcher
Hugh Boggs	5D	14B	Lawrence

James Boggs	5D	40D	Lawrence
Levi Boggs	13D	HarF	Letcher
Isaac Bowling	FR	45K	Morgan
William Brewer	5C, 10E	US Army	Morgan
Edward W. Brown	FR	45K	Morgan
William Brown	5C	65B	Johnson
Jesse Brunty	10D	39K	Pike
Moses Burgett	2VSL	39K	Pike
James Burke	5G	39K	Pike
Robert Calhoun	13H	39B	Letcher
John Campbell	13B	HarE, 14CavM	Letcher
George W. Carter	5G	68I	Lawrence
John W. Carter	FR	68I	Lawrence
David Casebolt	5G	39K	Pike
Hiram Casebolt	5G, 7Conf Cav	39K	Pike
Henry Cassady	5H	39D	Johnson
Abel Caudill	5F,C	45D	Magoffin
Jackson Caudill	13B	39K	Floyd
Thomas Chandler	5Riffe	65F	Johnson
Ryburn Chapman	7Conf Cav	68K	Lawrence
John E. Clark	5G	39E	Floyd
Andrew J. Clay	5G, 10K	39K	Pike
George Coburn	13	39K	Floyd
George Cock	5B	US Army	Morgan
Thompson Cole	13H	39C	Pike
Carter Collins	13H	14CavL	Letcher
William W. Collins	10H	14G	Johnson
John W. Compton	5G, 10I	39B	Pike
William F. Compton	5G	39B	Pike
David H. Conley	FR	65E	Johnson

Levi Conley	FR	14F	Johnson
Bailey Crisp	10A	14H	Floyd
Wright Damron	5G	39B	Pike
James H. Davis	1Bat Cav	45G	Johnson
William L. Day	13A	HarF	Letcher
James M. Duke	13B	US 3rd Ky. Battery	Letcher
James Dyer	5F,K	68D	Lawrence
Harry Easterling	5A	24G	Morgan
Garbiel Endicott	5E	68H	Lawrence
Enoch England	13H	14CavI	Letcher
James England	5G	39B	Pike
James Estep	2VSL	39H	Pike
Joel Estep	5E	45G	Floyd
Jonathan Estep	13E	45C	Letcher
Joseph Estep	2VSL	39H	Pike
Lilburn Estep	5K	45C	Johnson
Stephen Fields	13h	HarF	Letcher
Joseph Fletcher	5G	39C	Pike
George Fraley	5K	40C	Morgan
George W. Frasher	16VaCav	USArmy	Lawrence
Henry H. Gamble	5C	14B	Lawrence
John Gamble	5C	68B	Lawrence
Peter Gillum	5F	68B	Lawrence
Elias George	5F	45K	Morgan
Jesse Gibson	13D	14CavL	Letcher
Francis M. Green	FR	45D	Johnson
C. J. Grim	5K	65F	Johnson
James Hale	13F	39K	Magoffin
Benjamin Hall	13D	39K	Letcher
Elisha Hall	5D	68K	Lawrence

Fleming Hall	5F	39B	Pike
Hiram Hall	13D	39I	Letcher
Riley Hall	13E	39K	Floyd
Samuel Hall	5G	39K	Floyd
Thomas Hall	13D	HarA,39K	Letcher
William Hall	5A	39G	Johnson
John Hamilton	5G	CG F	Floyd
Samuel Hamilton	5G	39K	Floyd
Adam Handshoe	5E, 13F	39F	Floyd
James W. Harmon	5E	39G	Floyd
Henry C. Haywood	5E	CG E	Floyd
Paul Henson	3USVolInf	13D	Pike
James H. Hereford (Sr.)	13K	39 F&S	Floyd
James H. Hereford (Jr.)	5E,13K	68E	Floyd
John Hinkle	5	39H	Lawrence
Thomas Hill	7ConfCav	45E	Johnson
William J. Hogston	10C	39D	Pike
John H. Holbrook	5D	68B	Lawrence
William H. Holbrook	5K	40I	Lawrence
Alfred Honeycutt	5F	45C	Letcher
Walter Hughes	13F	39F	Floyd
John B. Hurley	2VSL E, 10H	39I	Pike
W. J. Hutton	5E, 10K	US Army	Floyd
James Jackson	5G	40K	Lawrence
Henry Jenkins	FR	45K	Morgan
Andrew Justice	10H	45F	Pike
Gilmore Justice	10C	39I	Pike
Hiram Justice	10H, VSL	CG	Pike
George W. Kelly	5D	CG D	Lawrence
Thomas J. Kendrick	10C	39I	Pike

William H. Kendrick	10C	39G	Pike
Robert Kile	13F	39G	Floyd
Henry Kinney	5G	39B	Pike
John W. Kinney	5G	39B	Pike
William Kinney	5G, 4VSLF, 10L	39B	Pike
James Laferty	10A	65A	Floyd
Eleazer Lemaster	5K	39E	Johnson
James Lemaster	5K	14K or 45C	Johnson
Richard Lemaster	FR	45K	Morgan
James L. Litton	5E	Reg Army	Floyd
James Lykins	5A	14CavG	Morgan
Henry Marshall	5E	65A	Floyd
John Marshall	5E	39K, or 45C	Johnson
George Martin	13F	39F	Floyd
William J. Martin	5G, 13F	39F	Floyd
Solomon May	VSL	39B	Pike
Thomas McCown	5E	39D	Pike
John McDaniel	5A,B	14CavK	Letcher
William McDaniel	13H	47H, HarA	Letcher
David McGuire	5E, 10A	45K	Floyd
John McIntyre	5E	39D	Johnson
Andrew J. McKenzie	FR	CGK, 65F	Johnson
Ballard P. McKenzie	5G, 10L	39K	Pike
Henry McKenzie	FR, 5F,K	14D	Johnson
Hiram E. McKenzie	10L, 5F	39B	Johnson
Elisha Meadows	5F	45K	Morgan
William Miles	13H	47H	Letcher
Samuel H. Miller	5G, 2VSL, 10L	39K	Pike
Levi Mollett	10D	14G	Johnson
John Morgan	13H	47H	Letcher

Name			
Ezekiel Morris	13F	US	Floyd
William Mosley	5E, 10A	39G	Floyd
Harrison Mounts	1VSLI	167WV, 39I	Pike
Andrew J. Mullins	5E	CG K	Floyd
Solomon Mullins	13E	45C	Letcher
James C. Murphy	10G	39A	Johnson
Robert Murphy	10G	65C	Johnson
William Murphy	2MRD,7ConfCav	USNavy	Morgan
John C. Oney	13F	US Army	Floyd
David Osborn	13F	39F	Floyd
Repts Osborn	13F	39F	Floyd
Sherwood Osborn	10C	39K	Pike
Thomas Osborn	13F	39F	Floyd
Robert Patrick	5B	14CavD	Morgan
Samuel Patton	5G	39F	Floyd
Stephen Patton	13F	39F	Floyd
Daniel Pelphrey	5D	65E	Johnson
David Pelphrey	FR, 5F	45C	Johnson
Andrew J. Pennington	2BattMR	45K	Lawrence
John W. Pennington	2BattMR	45K	Lawrence
Milton Pennington	5K	14K	Johnson
Allen Perry	2MRA	US Army	Morgan
John Prater	5C, 13F	39D	Floyd
Newman Prater	13F	39F	Floyd
William W. Prater	5C, 13F	39F	Floyd
Henry Preston	FR	65A	Johnson
Richard Quillin	13D	39K	Letcher
Samuel Ramey	5C	65A	Johnson
Jackson Ray	5G	39K	Pike
James L. Ray	5G, 10H	39K	Pike

William H. Reynolds	13D	39K	Letcher
James Robbins	5B	45K	Morgan
William Robbins	5B	45K	Morgan
William Robinett	1VSLI	167WV, 39H	Pike
Harrison Robinson	10A	45K	Floyd
William A. Romans	10C	39E	Pike
William Rose	5D	40E	Lawrence
John Ross	10B	US Army	Morgan
John Rowland	5E	45E	Johnson
Riley Salyer	5F,10B	US	Johnson
William L. Seagraves	FR	68B	Lawrence
Drury Sellards	5E	US Army	Floyd
William R. Shepherd	13F	14H	Floyd
Thomas J. Sherman	5E	14D	Johnson
Joshua Singleton	13D	HarF	Letcher
Thomas Skeans	5C	39F	Floyd
Henry Skeen	13I	39A	Letcher
George W. Slone	13B	45H	Floyd
John P. Slone	13E	39F	Floyd
Simeon Slone	10C	39I	Pike
Tandy Slone	13F	39F	Floyd
Haden Smith	5F	45K	Morgan
Jeremiah Smith	13D	14CavL	Letcher
Samuel Smith	13I	HarB	Letcher
Richard Sparkman	13B	US Army	Letcher
Henry W. Sparks	5G	68B	Lawrence
Nathan Sparks	5K	14D	Johnson
Reuben Sparks	FR	68A	Lawrence
Thomas W. Spears	10D	65C	Johnson
James H. Spradlin	5E	65A	Johnson

William Stacy	2VSLE	39C	Pike
James Stafford	5D	65A	Johnson
William Stapleton	5C	45E	Johnson
John O. Steele	1VSLI	167WV, 45G	Pike
Isaac Stephens	5B	68A	Lawrence
William J. Sword	5G	39D	Pike
Harvey Tackett	5G	39B	Pike
William Tackett	5K,F	CG E or 14I	Johnson
Jesse Terry	5B	14B	Morgan
William Thomas	5A	14D	Lawrence
Fleming Thompson	2Batt MR	45D	Lawrence
Samuel Thompson	5B	39D	Pike
William Trimble	5A	65E	Johnson
William Troy	5C	68C	Lawrence
John Vaughn	10A,C	45K	Floyd
Ambrose Watkins	10B	14A	Magoffin
James W. Wells	5E	65C	Johnson
Marcus L. K. Wells	10D	45C	Johnson
Lewis White	10C	39D	Pike
James P. Whitt	3MRA	39F	Floyd
John Bunyan Whitt	5E, 10A	39F	Floyd
Ning Williams	5K	68B	Lawrence
James Wright	13D	39B	Letcher
Uriah Wyatt	5A	14CavG	Morgan
Alexander Yates	5B	39A	Floyd
Elijah Younts	13D	39K	Letcher
Solomon Younts	13D	39K	Letcher

www.ingramcontent.com/pod-product-compliance
Lightning Source LLC
Chambersburg PA
CBHW060508300426
44112CB00017B/2589